"Suzanne Marrs has written an admirable, engrossing and gently gripping biography fully worthy of its remarkable subject."
—*Los Angeles Times Book Review*

"By the end, honored for both her literary output and her generous spirit, Eudora Welty was probably the best loved writer in America. To read this biography is to understand why."
—*The Plain Dealer* (Cleveland)

"Ms. Marrs' gentle, and conscientious telling is an excellent resource."
—*The Washington Times*

"It's a relief to see this daring and imaginative writer finally set free from traditional perceptions." —*The San Diego Union-Tribune*

"In Suzanne Marrs, Eudora Welty has a responsible and thorough biographer who looked back, with a smile to be sure, but with a steady understanding as well." —*The Times Picayune* (New Orleans)

"*Eudora Welty* is an engaging, informative and valuable book."
—*The News & Observer* (Raleigh, NC)

"Happily, *Eudora Welty: A Biography* pushes no reductive thesis. Ms. Marrs embraces Welty's own largely joyous take on her life even while probing its difficulties and disappointments."
—*The Wall Street Journal*

"Likely to become the touchstone for all scholarly discussion of Welty's work and life." —*America*

"Provides more facts and a much more intimate view of Welty's love life. For Weltyians this biography is indispensable." —*The New York Sun*

"An engaging, well-researched and—to my way of thinking— necessary read for any self-respecting Americanist and Welty scholar." —BookReporter.com

"Marrs's strength is in literary analysis, evidenced in her insightful exegesis of Welty's major works and her tracing of Welty's writing career." —*The Boston Globe*

"Captures the humorous and unconventional spirit of one of the South's greatest writers." —*The Dallas Morning News*

"It is useful to have Suzanne Marrs's calmer and vastly more detailed account of this side of Welty's life." —*The Washington Post Book World*

"Debunks the myths and quotes enough of the writing to make you hunger for the novels and stories. Marrs takes pains to refute the image of Eudora as a perfect 'Southern Lady,' ... The rest of us get to love her as a writer, and with this biography—the whole of her extraordinary world." —*Publishers Weekly* (starred)

"Few distinguished American writers have been as honestly yet sympathetically understood as Eudora Welty is in Suzanne Marrs's scrupulous book." —Reynolds Price

SUZANNE MARRS

Eudora Welty

A BIOGRAPHY
· · · · · · · · · · ·

A HARVEST BOOK
HARCOURT, INC.
Orlando   Austin   New York   San Diego   Toronto   London

www.HarcourtBooks.com

Permissions acknowledgments begin on page 634 and
constitute a continuation of the copyright page.

The Library of Congress has cataloged the hardcover edition as follows:
Marrs, Suzanne.
Eudora Welty: a biography/Suzanne Marrs.—1st ed.
p.   cm.
Includes bibliographical references and index.
I. Welty, Eudora, 1909–2001   2. Authors, American—20th century—Biography.
I. Title.
PS3545.E6Z7728   2005
813'.52—dc22   2004030490
ISBN-13: 978-0-15-100914-5   ISBN-10: 0-15-100914-7
ISBN-13: 978-0-15-603063-2 (pbk.)   ISBN-10: 0-15-603063-2 (pbk.)

Text set in Centaur MT
Designed by Linda Lockowitz

Printed in the United States of America
First Harvest edition 2006
A C E G I K J H F D B

To Wanda and Alton Marrs

CONTENTS

• • • • • • • • • • •

A wide-ranging cast of characters comes to us through the pages of Eudora Welty's fiction: An aged African American woman walks miles through woods, over hills, across log bridges to obtain medicine for her grandson; a small-town postmistress proclaims that she is not "one-sided. Bigger on one side than the other"; a tenant-farming couple burn their few bits of furniture in an effort to stay warm; a nineteenth-century outlaw plans a slave rebellion in the American Southwest; a young woman commits suicide after a love affair fails; the sorceress Circe declares that "it takes phenomenal neatness of housekeeping to put it through the heads of men that they are swine"; a Depression-era prison inmate escapes a day before his scheduled release so that he may be on time for his family reunion. From the mouths of these characters or from the pen of Welty as narrator emerge dialogue and descriptions that are hilarious—"Edna Earle could sit and ponder all day on how the little tail of the 'C' got through the 'L' in a Coca-Cola sign"; or hauntingly enigmatic—"Cutting off the Medusa's head was the heroic act, perhaps, that made visible a horror in life, that was at once the horror in love"; or tragically consoling—"any life . . . was nothing but the continuity of its love." Widely considered a master of the short-story form, Welty wrote in many modes, creating the comic terror of a small-town beauty parlor, the 1807 "season of dreams" that arrived in Mississippi with Aaron Burr, the tortured interior monologue of a husband who imagines beating his wife's lover with a croquet mallet, and a ghost story of sorts in "No Place for You, My Love."[1] Her novels—*Delta Wedding, Losing Battles, The Optimist's Daughter*— and her novellas— *The Robber Bridegroom* and *The Ponder Heart*— show a determination to experiment and to approach head-on issues of love and death, oppression and transcendence. Her collected essays and reviews delve into the writing process and offer appreciations of authors ranging from Jane Austen ("The sheer velocity of the novels, scene to scene, conversation to conversation, tears to laughter, concert to picnic to dance, is something equivalent to a pulsebeat") to Virginia Woolf ("Hers was a sensitivity beside which a Geiger counter is a child's toy made of a couple of tin cans and a rather common piece of string"), from Anton Chekhov ("The realist Chekhov, speaking simply and never otherwise than as an artist and a humane man, showed us in fullness and plenitude the mystery of our lives") to Patrick White ("The common barriers of sex, age, class, nationality *can*, in uncommon hands, operate as gates . . . Passing us through these barriers is what Mr. White is doing in his writing").[2] And her photographs, taken in the 1930s and first collected in 1971, put a human face on the Great Depression as they evince empathy for and from her subjects, black and white, old and young, male and female.

Eudora Welty's achievements were widely recognized during her lifetime: She received a Pulitzer Prize, the French Legion of Honor, the Howells' Medal for Fiction, the Gold Medal for Fiction from the National Institute of Arts and Letters, the National Book Foundation Medal for Distinguished Contribution to American Letters, the Presidential Medal of Freedom, and the National Medal of the Arts. She was elected to membership in the National Institute of Arts and Letters and then elevated to the American Academy of Arts and Letters. And she received honorary degrees from at least thirty-nine colleges and universities, Harvard, Yale, Columbia, and Princeton among them. She was surely one of the most "honoraried" writers in the history of American letters.

Clearly, Eudora Welty was a major force in twentieth-century literature, but over the course of her nearly century-long life, she also became a cultural icon. Her awards came to seem tributes as much to her person as to her work. As she told *New Yorker* fiction editor William Maxwell, "I've just had too much awarded me."[3] Her legion of readers—and a legion of admirers who never read her work—remember Eudora Welty as someone they would like to have known, indeed as a person they felt they did know. In a world where writers have often proven imperfect public figures—indulgent and self-destructive or ardent recluses or intellectual snobs—Welty was not. She had a self-deprecating sense of humor and a genuine interest in people. She loved her parents and was unashamed to say so. She loved the natural beauty of her native Mississippi, the scale and pace of life, the close friends she had there. She granted interviews to reviewers and scholars, she spoke at colleges and universities, she allowed herself to be the featured attraction at fund-raising benefits for good causes, she appeared on national television, she even invited into her home strangers who knocked on her door. From her late sixties onward, Welty was a celebrity. But though she made herself accessible, she maintained a firm sense of decorum and a clear distinction between what she deemed her public and her private life. Her most deeply felt emotions—loves and fears, hostilities and insecurities—were not the subjects for interviews or speeches, but for fiction. Fiction, she wrote in her essay "Must the Novelist Crusade," "has, and must keep, a private address. For life is *lived* in a private place; where it means anything is inside the mind and heart."[4]

Not surprisingly, therefore, Welty looked askance at being the subject for biography. In a 1979 interview, for instance, she said, "I've always been tenacious in my feeling that we don't need to know a writer's life in order to understand his work and I have really felt very opposed to a lot of biographies that have been written these days, of which the reviewers say they're not any good unless they reveal all sorts of other things about the writer . . . It's brought out my inherent feeling that it's good to know something about a writer's background, but only what pertains."[5] In 1984, at age seventy-five, Welty hoped to preempt future attempts at a biography of her life by publishing an auto-biographical work that focused only on those elements of her life she deemed *pertinent.* In *One Writer's Beginnings,* which had begun as a series of lectures at Harvard, she followed her hosts' sugges-tion that she describe the ways in which her family, her commu-nity, her early reading, her youthful travels, her education, had shaped her career as a writer. These lectures-turned-essays spoke of family love and the tensions inherent in loving, the power of time and the urgency it imposes, the writer's passion for her art, and her desire to give it until there is no more left to give. The most memorable events recounted in this book are tragic and emotional in nature: Welty's mother, at the age of fifteen, taking her own father by raft and train to the Baltimore hospital where he died of appendicitis; Eudora, as a young child, discovering with delight two gleaming nickels in her mother's bureau, only to learn that they had covered the eyes of a dead brother she had not known or been told about; and the aspiring writer witness-ing, at age twenty-two, her father's death during a blood transfu-sion. Painful memories, but she faced them and shared them. She also shared, in an understated fashion, the devotion and the dis-cord, the admiration and the guilt, that characterized her rela-tionship with her mother.

What she avoided were expansive accounts of her adult life. She made scant mention of her long sojourns far from home, or of her loves and her loneliness, or of her intense and enduring interest in politics. In its concentration upon childhood and her

Mississippi roots, *One Writer's Beginnings* helped to create an image of Welty as shy and retiring, though perceptive, provincial, and most reviews stressed this image. In the *Washington Post,* Jonathan Yardley wrote, "A life spent . . . in the quiet of a house in a quiet Mississippi town will seem, to many readers, cramped and isolated. Welty argues to the contrary, and she is absolutely correct. She closes this lovely little book by saying: 'As you have seen, I am a writer who came of a sheltered life. A sheltered life can be a daring one as well. For all serious daring starts from within.'" C. Vann Woodward in the *New York Times,* though he observed that in Welty's fiction "distinctions between love and hate, joy and sorrow, innocence and guilt, success and failure, victory and defeat are often left vague," described her life as less complex: "In 'One Writer's Beginnings,' we find that in a turbulent period when authors commonly wrote in anger, protest and political involvement and many of them had reason to do so, one of them led a sheltered, relatively uneventful life, never married and always made her home in a provincial community. The same could have been said of Jane Austen." And Edmund Fuller, in the *Wall Street Journal,* concluded his review by stating that "all her work shines with . . . lovingness, none more than the present lovely book." In his 1990 convocation address at Dartmouth College, President James O. Freedman echoed the focus of such reviews. He spoke perceptively about Welty's fictional portraits of individuals who encounter life's terrors, but he depicted her life as cloistered indeed: "With grace and energy, Eudora Welty has taught us that we have worlds to learn from a woman who has never married, who has rarely traveled, and who still lives in the home in which she spent her childhood."[6]

The writer whose beginnings included profound experiences of grief and guilt is not the woman reviewers portrayed. The adult who in 1937 would travel with friends by car to Mexico, or who in 1947 would spend several months in San Francisco in order to be near the man she loved, or make three long unaccompanied visits to Europe, England, and Ireland in the early 1950s, or enjoy a whirlwind of drinks, dinners, and plays during frequent trips to New York, or struggle with writer's block for more than two decades, or spend more time on the road than at her typewriter during her later years, or write her local newspaper, denouncing racist demagogues—this is not the woman reviewers saw. And to the general public, who thought of Welty only as the happy child in scenes from *One Writer's Beginnings* or as the witty, elderly lady being interviewed by Diane Sawyer or Dick Cavett, she came to seem, as her dear friend the writer Reynolds Price put it, not the worldly woman her friends cherished, but "the Benign and Beamish Maiden Aunt of American Letters."[7]

Some accused Welty of failing to write a "truthful autobiography." In her book *Writing a Woman's Life*, the late scholar and writer Carolyn Heilbrun asserted, "I do not believe in the bittersweet quality of *One Writer's Beginnings*, nor do I suppose that the Eudora Welty there evoked could have written the stories and novels we have learned to celebrate." Heilbrun argued that Welty must have been masking "unrecognized anger," and she went on to suggest that women reared before the onset of the "current women's movement, before, let us say, 1970," at some level, conscious or unconscious, inevitably resented their mothers and dreamed of lives "without the intrusion of a mother's patriarchal wishes for her daughter, without the danger of injuring the much loved and pitied mother."[8] She did not entertain the possibility that Welty's mother might have encouraged her to reject "patriarchal wishes," or that Welty might have accepted, comprehended, and transcended aspects of the past without feeling great residual anger, or that *One Writer's Beginnings* was perhaps as "truthful" as her own account of experience, or indeed that "truth" resists categorical statements. Heilbrun accepted reviewers' interpretations of *One Writer's Beginnings* but offered a rather different assessment of the book's veracity.

One Writer's Beginnings thus left a vast territory for prospective biographers to explore, and it simultaneously helped to create a myth they might seek to debunk. A number of distinguished scholars began to consider undertaking a full-scale biography but were eventually deterred by Welty's refusal to participate in the project. Then in the mid-1990s Ann Waldron, the biographer of Caroline Gordon and Hodding Carter, decided to make Welty her next subject and to press ahead without the writer's cooperation. In *Eudora*, published by Doubleday in 1998, Waldron attempted to humanize the mythic "Miss Eudora" but instead created an equally reductive image: the charming and successful ugly duckling. In response to the biography, Claudia Roth Pierpont, writing in the *New Yorker*, offered a third condescending stereotype, depicting Welty as "a perfect lady—a nearly Petrified Woman."[9]

I had been a Eudora Welty reader for twenty-three years and her friend for fifteen when these works appeared. I first encountered Welty's fiction in 1975 when I read *Losing Battles*. I was hooked by the way she walked a tightrope between humor and tragedy, by the way she could structure a four-hundred-page novel so that it had the intricacy of a lyric poem, by the humanity of her characters, by the range of styles she incorporated into a single work. I immediately set about reading all of Welty's works and incorporating some of them into my classes at the State University of New York at Oswego. In 1980 when I took my first sabbatical leave, I decided to write about Welty's fiction. Having done so and published two or three short essays, I was eager to meet the author herself and to discuss *Losing Battles*.

In the summer of 1983, I drove from upstate New York, where I was still teaching, to Jackson, Mississippi. I had written to Miss Welty, as I then called her, asking for an appointment but had received no reply. I came ahead anyway, knowing that the riches of the Mississippi Archives would be in themselves worth the trip. I settled into a work routine at the Archives, looking closely at drafts of *Losing Battles*, and I asked the staff there about the possibility of interviewing Welty. A curator working closely with the Welty papers approached Charlotte Capers, Welty's old friend and former director of the Archives, and Charlotte interceded on behalf of me and my friend Mary Hughes Brookhart, another Welty scholar. An interview was scheduled.

Mary Hughes and I arrived at the Welty house late on a hot July morning and took Miss Welty to lunch. We had a grand time. I asked about her ties to Robert Penn Warren, Allen Tate, and John Crowe Ransom, three of the Nashville Agrarians who in the 1930 book *I'll Take My Stand* had so ardently preferred the agricultural South to the industrialized North. She spoke fondly and admiringly of them as individuals and writers but asked me not to label her as a member of their group. A discussion of her debt to Proust, to his concepts of time and memory, ensued, but I only vaguely remember her response to that line of inquiry. What I do vividly remember is feeling a sense of connection, of ease, of the common sensibility that typifies friendship. At that first meeting, I, like so many of her visitors, felt that Eudora, as I soon came to call her, was my friend; she probably enjoyed our conversation but little expected that she and I would become close. Amazingly we did. In 1985–1986, I was the Eudora Welty Scholar-in-Residence at the Mississippi Archives and depended heavily on Eudora's input as I cataloged her manuscripts, photographs, and correspondence. Then, in 1988, I joined the faculty of Millsaps College in Jackson, Mississippi, and began to visit with Eudora on a regular basis. We met several times a week to discuss her fiction, or to watch the evening news and comment upon it, or to have drinks and dinner along with wide-ranging conversations, or simply to share stories we found amusing.

In 1998, though Eudora had often told me that she did not want her biography written and that she did not want a biographer to impose upon her friends, I asked permission to write my own account of her life, a request she promptly granted. (Unbeknownst to me, she had by this point already begun to retreat from her opposition to biography: She had given Reynolds Price permission to talk, as she had done, with the biographer of Kenneth Millar [aka detective novelist Ross Macdonald] and to reveal the love she and Ken had for each other.) She offered me only one caution: "You may be getting into deeper water than you imagine."

Given Eudora's past opposition to any biography of her, I was surprised to learn of the massive collection of additional correspondence, manuscripts, date books, and photographs that she planned to bequeath to the Mississippi Department of Archives and History, and which she and her nieces made immediately available to me. Reynolds Price and Ken Millar had both urged Eudora not only to save her correspondence but also to make it public. Her reading of the published letters of Virginia Woolf, Anton Chekhov, H. L. Mencken, and others had further discouraged any plan she'd had to destroy her letters. So the day I began research for a biography, I encountered a wealth of unpublished material that had yet to be seen by scholars. John Robinson, the man with whom Eudora was romantically involved from 1937 until 1952, had returned her letters from the period of their courtship. Both sides of Eudora's extensive correspondences with Millar, with her agent Diarmuid Russell, with *Harper's Bazaar* fiction editor Mary Lou Aswell, and with lifelong friend Frank Lyell were in her possession. Letters from William Maxwell, Reynolds Price, Katherine Anne Porter, Elizabeth Bowen, E. M. Forster, Robert Penn Warren, and many others were carefully stored in Eudora's house. Family letters, however, were not available to me. In her will, Eudora provided that they be sealed for a period of twenty years from the date of her death. Though she did not seek to protect herself or those who had given their blessing to the preservation of the correspondence, she did wish to protect the privacy of her parents, her brothers, and her brothers' families.

The letters Eudora wrote after 1984 are generally less revealing than earlier missives, largely because she had outlived most of her closest friends and confidantes. But other papers to which she and her nieces gave me access helped provide a comprehensive view of her entire life. Manuscripts of early stories, a novella, and three late unfinished novels, date books outlining her social and business engagements between 1976 and 1995, photographs of places she visited, of her friends, and of herself (belying the "ugly duckling" theory), as well as her mother's travel journal and scrapbooks, provided a wealth of information. And Eudora's blessing encouraged her friends and family to talk about her with me: The poet William Jay Smith, Reynolds Price, Diarmuid Russell's daughter Pamela, and the publisher and book dealer Ralph Sipper, all of whom had been very close to Eudora, granted me long and informative interviews; her nieces and her sisters-in-law spoke with me, as did a number of old Jackson friends. And, of course, from 1983 until her death in 2001, Eudora and I had many conversations about her work and her life. Together we traveled to conferences, celebrated holidays and birthdays, and entertained visitors.

Never did I see the mythic Eudora. She was not prim or sheltered: She told me of admiring Orson Welles's 1936 all-black production of *Macbeth,* with its nude, male Hecate, and of being impressed by the French film noir *Diabolique.* She was far from apolitical: Often she enlisted me to take her to the polls, and her long-term, enduring commitment to liberal causes and Democratic Party presidential candidates was well known in conservative Mississippi. And she was not provincial. She traveled widely, frequently, and for extended periods, being entertained by such notables as Bernard Berenson and David Rockefeller but also enjoying third-class shipboard accommodations, Parisian left-bank cafés, and the company of bohemian sorts.

This is but to say that a tremendous amount of new information is now available, information that should demonstrate what misleading public images of Eudora have emerged since the publication of her autobiography and subsequent portraits. In the biography that follows, I do not attempt to provide detailed analyses of Eudora's work—my book *One Writer's Imagination: The Fiction of Eudora Welty* is devoted to that task—but I use her work to illuminate, as best I can, her inner life, the "private place" where fiction is born. I focus on Eudora the woman, describing her routines and her travels, her friendships and enmities, her encounters with love and death, her responses to war and social change. I attempt to show the people and events that helped to make her a writer, to deal with the cultural and personal contradictions—the "polarities and oppositional elements"— that psychologists believe are a spark to the imagination, even as I acknowledge the mystery that lies at the heart of creativity. Recognizing that, as Hermione Lee, Virginia Woolf's acclaimed biographer, has asserted, "there is no such thing as an objective biography," I attempt to present Eudora Welty's life as fully as possible by allowing many voices to guide me—the voices in her fiction; the voices in her letters to friends, editors, colleagues; the voices of individuals who knew her not as a marble statue, but as a living, breathing, changing, developing, witty, sensitive, and complicated personality. Over the course of her ninety-two years, Eudora engaged the world with all her powers and never retreated into a single, narrowly defined role. Openness to experience complemented her creative genius and helped her to produce some of the most memorable fiction of the twentieth century. She was not the contentedly cloistered "Miss Eudora" in whom so many believed or wanted to believe, but was someone far more passionate and compelling: a woman and a writer with a "triumphant vulnerability . . . to this mortal world."[10]

ONE

Shelter and Beyond
1909–1931

On April 13, 1909, Eudora Alice Welty was born to Christian Webb and Chestina Andrews Welty. The young couple had been living in Jackson, Mississippi, since their marriage five years earlier. He had come from Ohio, she from West Virginia; they had met when Chris, as he was known, worked one summer at a logging camp near her home. Courtship had led to love, and they had chosen to begin their married life in Mississippi's rapidly growing capital city; Jackson's population had been slightly less than eight thousand in 1900, but by 1910 it would have more than tripled. In this booming town, the Weltys prospered: In 1906 Chris joined the newly established Lamar Life Insurance Company as its cashier, becoming the assistant secretary by year's end, and in 1908 the couple built their first house, on North Congress Street. Though Chestina, or Chessie as her husband called her, kept a cow and chickens in the backyard, the Weltys lived within six blocks of Chris's office and of the downtown theaters, department stores, and grocers; within two blocks of the state capitol; and within three blocks of Galloway Methodist Church, to which they belonged. They also lived across the street from a grammar school and within sight of a cemetery. Their first child, a son born in 1906, lay in that cemetery, having died at the age of fifteen months. This loss had been devastating, but now the birth of a daughter was cause for both great rejoicing and great resolve. Chris and Chessie would be protective parents indeed.

An ardent amateur photographer as well as an excited new father, Chris constantly snapped pictures of his daughter—as a babe in her mother's arms; in a specially ordered bonnet; on her first Christmas; on a trip to West Virginia and Ohio the summer after her birth; at home, attempting her first steps; with a miniature baby carriage and doll; in the yard with her mother's chickens; in a fine dress for her three-year-old birthday party. Chestina gathered these pictures and many others into an album and wrote captions for the photos; below a picture of Chris and Eudora she wrote "a proud Daddy," and below one of herself with the baby, she added "and mother too." From the first, Eudora Welty was reared in an atmosphere of abundant parental love.[1]

She was also reared in a book-filled environment. By the time she was two or three years old, Eudora knew, as she wrote in her autobiography, that "any room in our house, at any time of day, was there to read in, or to be read to. My mother read to me. She'd read to me in the big bedroom in the mornings, when we were in her rocker together, which ticked in rhythm as we rocked, as though we had a cricket accompanying the story. She'd read to me in the diningroom on winter afternoons in front of the coal fire, with our cuckoo clock ending the story with 'Cuckoo,' and at night when I'd got in my own bed. I must have given her no peace. Sometimes she read to me in the kitchen while she sat churning, and the churning sobbed along with *any* story."[2] From the start, Eudora loved the written word, and her keen ear for language and inflection began to develop long before she could read for herself. After she became a reader on her own, Eudora followed a pattern set by her mother and would often have several books underway, one for each of the various rooms in her house.

Having spent three years as an only child, Eudora might have felt displaced when her brothers, Edward Jefferson Welty and

Walter Andrews Welty, were born in 1912 and 1915. But though Chris took a photo of Eudora pouting behind Chessie and the newly arrived Edward, Chessie's photo caption noted that her daughter was "not as sorry as she looks." Indeed, she was not. She and Edward proved kindred spirts from the start: "I can't think I had much of a sense of humor as long as I remained the only child. When my brother Edward came along after I was three, we both became comics, making each other laugh. We set each other off, as we did for life, from the minute he learned to talk. A sense of the absurd was communicated between us probably before that." Though Walter even as an infant proved more serious than his older siblings, his sister doted on him and sought to entertain him: Once, she reported, "I snatched up his baby bathtub and got behind it and danced for him, to hear him really crow. On the pink bottom of his tub I'd drawn a face with crayons, and all he could see of anybody's being there was my legs prancing under it." And of course Eudora's parents were proud of the new additions to their family. When the city of Jackson held a baby parade in 1916, the *Jackson Clarion-Ledger* reported that Christian Welty participated with three-and-a-half-year-old Edward, who was on a velocipede—or tricycle, as we know it today—and that Chestina Welty strolled with six-month-old Walter in his baby carriage decorated with roses.[3]

The closeness of family life was something Eudora treasured. In *One Writer's Beginnings*, she recalled hearing her parents perform their own version of Franz Lehar's "The Merry Widow Waltz" as she buttoned her shoes in the morning: "They would begin whistling back and forth to each other up and down the stairwell. My father would whistle his phrase, my mother would try to whistle, then hum hers back. It was their duet. I drew my buttonhook in and out and listened to it—I knew it was 'The Merry Widow.' The difference was, their song almost floated with laughter: how different from the record, which growled from the beginning, as if the Victrola were only slowly being wound up." And she loved to lie in bed listening to her parents across the room talk or read to each other: "I don't remember that any secrets were revealed to me, nor do I remember any avid curiosity on my part to learn something I wasn't supposed to—perhaps I was too young to know what to listen for. But I was present in the room with the chief secret there was—the two of them, father and mother, sitting there as one."[4] The strength of her parents' union betokened a larger union of parents and children. Family activities for the Weltys were constant. They went for early-morning swims, they attended lectures, concerts, and plays brought by the Circuit Chautauqua to Poindexter Park, they looked at the stars through Chris's telescope, they flew homemade kites in pastures outside of town, they consulted the dictionary to determine the meaning of words that had baffled one of them during dinner conversation, and they journeyed to Ohio and West Virginia to visit grandparents, uncles, and cousins. Each summer mother and children also journeyed about fifteen miles from Jackson and spent several weeks trying to escape the city heat. Their destination was a small resort called Hubbard's Wells, a place where healthful waters could be drunk, where paper lanterns hung from the trees, and where local pianist Eddie Stiles provided live entertainment some evenings. Chris joined his family on weekends.

Back home in Jackson, the Welty children were part of a lively neighborhood. They joined other children in riding velocipedes, and eventually, bicycles (Eudora was proud to own a "Princess" bicycle). With friends they played hopscotch and jacks, jumped rope, and roller-skated. At twilight they pulled their "choo-choo boats" made from shoe boxes, with holes cut out in the shape of the moon and stars and with lighted candles inside. And they shared rides in pony carts.

Eudora and her friends loved strolling to the movies.

Setting out in the early summer afternoon on foot, by way of Smith Park to Capitol Street and down it, passing the

Pythian Castle with its hot stone breath, through the one
spot of shade beneath Mrs. Black's awning, crossing Town
Creek—then visible and uncontained—we went carrying
parasols over our heads and little crocheted bags over our
wrists containing the ten or fifteen cents for the ticket (with
a nickel or dime further for McIntyre's Drug Store after the
show), and we had our choice—the Majestic or the Istrione. At the Majestic we could sit in a box—always empty,
because airless as a bureau drawer; at the Istrione, which was
said to occupy the site of an old livery stable, we might see
Alice Brady in "Drums of Jeopardy" and at the same time
have a rat run over our feet. As far as I recall, there was no
movie we were not allowed to see, until we got old enough
not to see "The Sheik."

The little girls, Eudora also recalled, spent entire summer days
making "batteries" of paper dolls and having them perform "exciting scenes we thought up."[5] The future story writer was at an
early age actively engaging her imagination.

Other activities were for children and adults alike. In Smith
Park, neighborhood families picnicked or attended evening band
concerts together. And parents, Chris and Chessie included, often
organized more far-flung expeditions for the children, traveling
to the clay banks on the Terry road or to the military park in
Vicksburg. When a family whom Chessie saw as disreputable established residence on Congress Street, she sought to deny her
children their company, but her daughter was eager to transcend
class boundaries. In an early and never-published novella, Courtney, a character clearly based upon Eudora, longs to play with the
Hockin children, whose family has rented an apartment across
the street. Her mother discourages this practice: "I can't understand how those Hockins could have gotten into this neighborhood. They are as common as they can be. Courtney, I would
rather you didn't play with them so much, dear." The Hockins in

this story are deemed objectionable not because of lineage or poverty but because they are loud, indecorous, impolite, even unbathed. The mother in Eudora's 1942 story "The Winds" makes class distinctions based on similar criteria, even as her daughter Josie looks up to the disreputable Cornella. Such aspects of this story, Eudora told her agent Diarmuid Russell, "were little fragments out of my own life and what I sent you is the first story I've tried directly attempting to remember exact real sensations."[6]

Despite Chessie's attempt to shelter her children, young Eudora was always listening for stories, typically from her elders. There was the lady who, Eudora recalled, "invited me to catch her doodlebug; under the trees in her backyard were dozens of their holes. When you stuck a broom straw down one and called, 'Doodlebug, doodlebug, your house is on fire and all your children are burning up,' she believed this is why the doodlebug came running out of the hole. This was why I loved to call up her doodlebugs instead of ours. My mother could never have told me her stories, and I think I knew why even then: my mother didn't believe them. But I could listen to this murmuring lady all day. She believed everything she heard, like the doodlebug. And so did I." Then there was the seamstress who came to the Weltys' house and, "along with her speed and dexterity, brought along a great provision of up-to-the-minute news." As exciting as the storytellers were the out-of-towners who appeared mysteriously: The acrobats who picnicked in Smith Park while they were in Jackson with the circus; the Mexican hot-tamale man who sold his delicacies on the street corner, and the blackberry lady and the watermelon man who sold door-to-door; the farmer who drove his wagon down residential streets as he sang, "Milk, milk, / Buttermilk, / Snap beans—butterbeans— / Tender okra—fresh greens . . . / And buttermilk"; the gypsies who descended upon Jackson each fall; the organ grinder who, with his monkey, appeared at unexpected moments.[7] To Eudora, all seemed to have emerged from the pages of fiction.

Not so exotic, perhaps, was an old African American man who ran the elevator at Mississippi's state capitol and whom Eudora would later try to place in her early novella about a fictional alter ego.

> He was an old servant of a family up the street from Court-
> ney and still occupied the old servant's house in their back
> yard. Every morning about nine o'clock Uncle Lewis, bent
> and mumbling (though not to himself, the children argued,
> because he was deaf) would hobble down the street. It was
> his manner of walking which most impressed the children.
> His feet, in long soft black shoes, slapped out in almost a
> straight angle, like a clown's. Uncle Lewis would lean on his
> yellow cane with one hand and rest the other behind his
> back and proceed slowly on his way. The children would see
> him far up the street, run to meet him and call out "Hey,
> Uncle Lewis? How come you walk that-a-way? Look! This
> is the way you walk!" And they would all show him. He
> would pat their heads and give them licorice. One day
> Courtney and Sam and Martha and Edward all played fol-
> low the leader down the street, with Uncle Lewis, in front,
> as the unconscious leader. It was painfully funny to all the
> children. They made a practice of walking behind Uncle
> Lewis every morning, mocking him. One day he turned
> around and saw them. He did not understand the sight of
> four little children with contorted legs and thought nothing
> of it, but gave them licorice. "I aint goin' to do that agin,"
> vowed Courtney. "Fraidy-cat," said Sam. "I am not," said
> Courtney. "Fraidy-cat," said Martha. "Sticks and stones
> may break my bones but words will never hurt me," said
> Courtney, running into the house.[8]

Like Courtney, young Eudora, her brother, and friends, it seems, had mocked an arthritic old black man, as they would not have dared to mock a white man of their own social circle. But clearly

Courtney, aka Eudora, felt tremendous guilt when Uncle Lewis saw what the children had been doing; at a young age, she learned to respect the dignity of this most vulnerable man, whatever other children might say.

By the age of five Eudora was able to read as well as be read to, and her mother felt the time had arrived for a more formal education than home and neighborhood could offer. Like the fictional Courtney of her unpublished novella, Eudora may have been so active that her parents needed some respite: "When Courtney was five years old, her mother and father decided to send her to public school, although the term was well under way. Courtney seemed to them too exuberant to retain for another year in the home which was without, it seemed, sufficient outlet for her over-abundance of energy." Eudora did indeed begin grammar school at midterm. Chessie spoke to Miss Lorena Duling, the principal of Davis School, who agreed that after Christmas vacation Eudora should enter the first grade. There she would encounter some exceptional teachers and would make fast friends. Miss Duling set high standards, and a competent corps of classroom teachers enforced them. There were also a singing teacher, a physical-training teacher, and an art teacher. Each appeared for an hour once a week. From the start, Eudora relished learning. And she also relished the company of her classmates. Among her closest friends were Elizabeth Heidelberg, whose father ran a furniture store; Emily White Stevens, whose father was a lawyer and a judge; and Willanna Buck, whose father served as clerk to the Supreme Court. Willanna recalls that Eudora was at once shy and outgoing, someone who loved to be with people, to talk, and hear others talk, but someone who was never a show-off. She did command special attention from her classmates, however, for she owned a basketball and, during recess, could retrieve it from her house, just across the street.[9]

Outside of school there were other educational opportunities: art instruction under the tutelage of Marie Hull, whose works had been exhibited across the nation; piano and dance lessons under more provincial instructors; and the public library, a mere three blocks from Eudora's house. There she encountered Miss Annie Parker, the librarian whose rules could not be violated. Girls had to wear as many petticoats as were required to keep Miss Parker from "seeing right through them." And no one could check out more than two books a day—returning books on the same day they had been checked out was strictly forbidden. Eudora chafed under this restriction, for she was an avid reader. *The Five Little Peppers, The Wizard of Oz, The Little Colonel, The Green Fairy Book, V. V.'s Eyes, Randy's Spring, Randy's Summer, Randy's Fall, Randy's Winter,* were among the many books that captured her imagination. Though the library could not supply books quickly enough, there were other, and often more interesting, books at home. At the age of nine or ten, Eudora received the ten-volume set of *Our Wonder World* and found herself especially entranced by volume five: *Every Child's Story Book.* In its pages she found fairy tales like "The Goose Girl," "The Fisherman and his Wife," and "Snow White." Here she also discovered nonsense songs by Edward Lear. And in the travel narratives contained in *Our Wonder World,* she encountered a cultural diversity not to be seen in Jackson, Mississippi. In a section entitled "Child Life in Many Lands," were descriptions of China, Spain, Turkey, India, Russia, Japan, Italy, Sweden, Norway, Persia, and the islands of the South Pacific. But even *Our Wonder World* could not long satisfy Eudora. Happily, there was her parents' collection of Mark Twain, a collection she began to read before she had left grade school.

Not content with reading the works of others, Eudora herself was a youthful author. Before she even entered school, Eudora had composed in her imagination plays for her dolls: she did not want to mother baby dolls, but to own larger dolls that she could use in her theatricals. Before long, impromptu dramas gave way to written work. In 1921 twelve-year-old Eudora won the Jackie Mackie Jingles contest and received twenty-five dollars along with a citation expressing the hope that she would "improve in poetry to such an extent as to win fame." Evidently in that same year, she became her own publisher, creating a "book" to entertain her brother Edward. In *The Glorious Apology*, Eudora set forth the preposterous and hilarious adventures of Fitzhugh Green (the son of the "whispering saxophonist" Artimus H. Green) and his wife, Lallie. She illustrated this text with clippings from newspapers and magazines, and she also began the book with blurbs selectively cut from magazines and pasted on construction paper: "HEAR WHAT THE CRITICS SAY ABOUT IT! ANDREW VOLSTEAD—'Never heard of it.' WAYNE B. WHEELER—'I haven't read it.' JOHN ROACH STRATTON—'I know nothing about it.'"[10]

In September of 1921 Eudora entered the eighth grade at Jackson High School. This brought about an important widening of her world, and she granted such expanding vistas to her fictional counterpart, Courtney: "Until she was sent to high school, Courtney's life centered almost wholly on her neighborhood. Experience for her was bounded on one end of the street by the state capitol, where kidnappers were believed by all the children to lie in wait, and on the other end by the blind institute, from whence at intervals of once a month two white-headed young men came down Allen street with large black spectacles and armfuls of brooms which they carried gun-like over their shoulders."[11] There were neither kidnappers nor white-headed broom carriers threatening Eudora's access to Jackson High, and there she met students from other parts of the city and from the local Baptist and Methodist orphanages. She did not, of course, attend class with any African American students, for schools were racially segregated. Black schools were woefully underfunded and included no grade above the ninth. Richard Wright, who was seven months older than Eudora but whose formal schooling had been sporadic, entered the fifth grade at Jackson's all-black

Jim Hill School as Eudora entered the eighth at Jackson High. Wright knew a Jackson from which Eudora had largely been sheltered, one where because of race he was barred from libraries, denied opportunity for advancement, subjected to violence. An outstanding student nevertheless, he moved through his classes on an accelerated basis and graduated as valedictorian of Smith-Robertson School in 1925. He and Eudora never met, though both would eventually be numbered among America's finest writers.

Instead of racial diversity, Eudora encountered another sort of diversity at Jackson High. John Robinson and Lehman Engel, for instance, came from different grammar schools and rather different backgrounds from Eudora's. John, who lived near Jackson's Millsaps College, came from a pioneering Mississippi Delta family with large landholdings; his stepgrandfather was a former governor and senator, J. K. Vardaman, the ardent racist who had been hung in effigy for his opposition to World War I and defeated in his senate-reelection bid for the same reason. Lehman Engel, on the other hand, was Jewish, the grandchild of immigrants, the son of a traveling salesman with a penchant for gambling, and the nephew of a prominent businessman and civic leader. Not only did Jackson High students come from such divergent backgrounds, many also went on to lead notably accomplished lives. Among Eudora's friends who graduated between 1923 and 1928 were an artist (Helen Jay Lotterhos), a composer and conductor (Engel), two college professors (Frank Lyell and Bill Hamilton), a journalist (Ralph Hilton), a lawyer (Joe Skinner), an Episcopal priest (George Stephenson), and a *New York Times Book Review* editor (Nash Burger). Amid this talented group of students, Eudora thrived academically, compiling a ninety-five percentile scoring average for her four years of class work and continuing to think of herself as a writer-to-be. In 1924, when Jackson High School officials decided to add grade twelve to their program, the eleventh graders were divided: Those with the top grade averages were named the senior class; the others would become seniors the following year. Eudora, who had begun her schooling at age five, was chosen for the senior class and would graduate from high school at the tender age of sixteen.

Her life was active outside the classroom, as a story she penned for the 1924 school yearbook, *Quadruplane*, reveals. "The Conference Condemns Caroline" describes a teenage girl studying late into the night only to find that from her textbooks living figures begin to emerge, seemingly arriving for a committee meeting: Cicero, Archimedes, Shakespeare's Touchstone, and a contemporary legislator greet Caroline and begin to criticize the hour of their meeting. Cicero, in particular, bitterly complains: "[W]ho of us do you suppose does not know the reason of this outrage? It is Caroline of the Junior class, Caroline of the Basket Ball Team, Caroline of the Picture-Show Club! It is Caroline, I say, who does everything else before she studies her lessons, and then falls asleep over a masterpiece like my oration against Catiline!" The legislator then moves that they adopt a series of resolutions condemning Caroline, but before the resolutions can be enacted, the clock strikes eleven thirty and wakes the young woman, who realizes she "must have dreamed it all" and who declares, "Tomorrow I'm going to study in the afternoon." Surely Eudora was writing comically about herself, for in 1924, she was almost as busy as Caroline: She was a substitute forward on the girls' basketball team, worked on the yearbook staff, drew four illustrations for the *Quadruplane*, and wrote a "Toast to the Class of '25."[12]

In 1925 Eudora published a second poem in *St. Nicholas*—the first had appeared in a 1923 issue of this national publication for young people—and this time around, she won a silver badge. "In the Twilight" is a poem indebted to both Thomas Gray's "Elegy Written in a Country Churchyard" and Edgar Allan Poe's anapestic "Ulalume."

The daylight in glory is dying away;
The last faded colors are fast growing gray;
The sun nears the beckoning portals of night,
And leave [*sic*] to the skies his long, ling'ring light.

The sunbeams had hid 'neath a sad, misty veil,
And softened to shadows—dim, silvery, pale.
The Queen of the Night shyly peeps o'er the hill
And reigns in her radiance—soft, cold and still.
A lone cyprus-tree, with its feathery grace,
Casts delicate shadows, like old Spanish lace,
On the cool, trembling waters that meet the gray sky,
And the moon rules supreme in her palace on high.[13]

The young poet had not found her own voice; she must have known as much. Though she had won national attention, Eudora's head was not turned. She continued to work hard on the JHS yearbook, supplying in 1925 fourteen illustrations, writing "Youth and Age" (a conversation between the new Jackson High building and the old), and contributing another witty story called "The Origin of Shorthand." During her senior year, she was secretary to the Dramatic Club, appeared in a play called *Three Live Ghosts*, and served as literary editor of the *Jackson Hi Life*. She and several girlfriends also formed a study group, whose members met over lunch to prepare for their Virgil class: The Girgil Club's motto was "Listen, cram, and be careful / For eighth period you may read," its colors were black and blue, and its club book was *The Aeneid*.

Active as she was, Eudora was not the typical Jackson High student. She was absolutely uninterested, for instance, in being a cheerleader or being the girlfriend of a sports hero, two goals of the JHS southern belle. Though she lacked the appearance and flirtatious manner of a belle, she did not crave them. And though she was not a siren, neither was she the ugly duckling biographer Ann Waldron suggests she was. She was a tall, pleasant-looking young woman (as pictures reveal), with brilliant blue eyes and a bit of a toothy smile, in love with language and ideas, and smitten by male classmates who shared those loves. Her intelligence, geniality, sense of humor, and reliability made her popular, and classmates named Eudora "Demeter (Most Dependable)" and "Irene (Best All 'Round)." But neither of these was the title she most desired. When an article called "What They Intend to Do" appeared in the 30 April 1925 issue of *Jackson Hi Life*, a single word was listed opposite Eudora's name: "Author."

One popular high school group Eudora belonged to despite grave reservations—the Hi-Y Club. In this club, Eudora recalled, "You won points for doing good, specific points for specific good. You had ceremonies by candlelight and your first achievement was a thin wire ring, the Golden Circle. You were supposed (I think you were asked to swear) that you would never take it off even when you were married and after you were old and gray you were supposed to hang onto it still—not die until you had asked to be buried in it. It had to do with purity." The teacher who sponsored this club was obsessed with puritanical notions and often told the girls cautionary tales: "They were awful stories. One was of a girl who let herself be kissed, and wherever those lips had touched her, a great black mark came out on her skin and no soap or water would ever wash it off. It was like some befuddled version of *The Scarlet Letter* . . . I thought then of the corollary, everybody would know it too if you hadn't been kissed."[14] A narrow-minded and moralistic mind-set did not then, or ever, appeal to Eudora. Perhaps she was even able to move the club away from this mind-set when she appeared in the suggestively titled (though quite innocent) burlesque "Wild Nell: The Pet of the Plains" at her senior Hi-Y banquet.

In 1923 the Welty family had temporarily moved to rental property in Belhaven, Jackson's first suburb, where they would build a house. Edward and Walter enjoyed skinny-dipping in a nearby lake. Eudora had fun enlisting her brothers and other young people to perform in neighborhood theatricals. But all the Weltys were eager for their own house on nearby Pinehurst Place to be completed. Chris had steadily progressed in the Lamar Life hierarchy— becoming a member of the board of directors, then general manager and vice president. Under his direction, Jackson's first skyscraper was being erected, and the architect for that building had also designed the Pinehurst Place house for the Welty family. Chessie and Chris expected to bring a new baby to their new house. Then, on the evening of January 26, 1924, a very premature daughter was stillborn in a local hospital and the next morning was buried. Just as a few years earlier they had kept Chessie's surgery for breast cancer a secret from their children, and just as they tried not to mention the 1907 death of a son, Chessie and Chris never discussed this new loss with Eudora, Edward, and Walter. In silence they sought to anesthetize themselves and shield their children.

Chestina's grief at the loss of an infant daughter further strengthened an already intense devotion to her surviving daughter. Such devotion seems likely to have prompted an act of self-sacrifice that summer and to have resulted in a double-edged response from Eudora. Eudora had in recent years enjoyed traveling with her father to New York and Chicago. Now Chestina resolved that her daughter would see the West Coast. As Eudora recalled, "When I was 15 she suddenly decided, the day before she & my father were to take the train to California on a 'company trip' for my father's best insurance agents, that she would stay at home and I should go. They already had the family friend arranged . . . to be with the children at home. She had all her clothes. I had no clothes for traveling on a fine trip. My father said he would take me shopping in New Orleans [the city from which the westbound train departed]—The first thing, in the hotel room in Los Angeles, I washed my hair and sat brushing it out of the window to blow in the day, smelling and breathing the Pacific air, transported with the strangeness and the distance from home. As I sat drying my hair at this high window, I was aching with guilt for all my mother had given up and all that was ahead of me."[15] For Eudora, the transporting pleasures of travel seemed sadly, as they would again and again, to have been purchased by her mother's deprivation.

In May 1925 the Pinehurst house was still not ready for the family, but Chessie, who was already engaged in landscaping the property, organized a graduation party for Eudora to be held in the garden. Perhaps dreading the day their daughter would leave home for college, her parents took the family on a long car trip that summer. On July 19 they headed for Trout Lake, Wisconsin, spent a week there, then visited Chicago, where they purchased clothes for Eudora and toured the city with Grandpa Welty, who had journeyed up from southern Ohio. Chris's mother had died when he was a child, but his father remained hale, hearty, and able to travel in his later years. The Mississippi Weltys drove Grandpa back to his home, before heading to West Virginia and a reunion with Chessie's family.[16] When they returned to Jackson, it was time for Eudora to prepare for life as a college student in Columbus, Mississippi. Her parents had wanted sixteen-year-old Eudora to remain in Jackson, at Millsaps College, while she had longed to go farther afield. Visits to major cities with her father, the wanderlust instilled by *Our Wonder World*, and her need for independence made going away to college seem imperative. The Mississippi State College for Women, more commonly known as MSCW, was the compromise parents and daughter reached.

At MSCW Eudora discovered the very environment her parents had hoped she would—an academic community focused upon shelter. The college was also in many ways the epitome of provinciality: Its marching drills, which students performed in costumes modeled on those of French colonial Zouave troops, must have seemed exceedingly strange and amusing to a girl who had hoped for more contemporary sophistication. So, too, must have seemed her elevation to "fire chief of Hastings Hall." And as she told Jackson friend Dorothy Simmons, daily prayer meetings in the post office lobby drove her to distraction: "The way it makes me feel is what I call hell." Nevertheless Eudora warmly embraced many aspects of college life. She wrote plays and performed in them, composed articles for the student paper, and penned her own stories and poems. Her skit "The Gnat," a takeoff of a Broadway hit called "The Bat," poked fun at the college faculty and staff in a rather Perelmanesque fashion; Eudora had read the young S. J. Perelman and was smitten. Her fiction of the time was clearly in the Perelman vein, and in two stories Eudora looked ironically at her own literary ambitions. In "The Great Pinning-ton Solves the Mystery," the narrator asserts, "I am going to write a book. All my friends say that they are confident I can write some-thing big and different, and this is it." In a second story, titled "'I' for Iris—Irma, Imogene," the narrator begins, "It was while I was sitting helplessly at the table during one of those inevitable Ohio Sunday dinners, wherein meat, bread, potatoes and kinfolks make a prim struggle for supremacy, that one of the last named made the fatal suggestion. Wouldn't it be nice if I should go to see the new neighbor! She was an artist, they said significantly, and paused. It is generally believed among my relatives that I have an artistic temperament, although they go by only the first two syllables." Eudora's poetry, on the other hand, tended away from the satiric or ironic. A stanza from the poem "Autumn's Here," for example, shows her debt to the English romantics, for it offers, despite a wry glance at James Whitcomb Riley, a sort of seasonal variation on William Wordsworth's "Written in March."

> Oh, the autumn of the year has come
> — there's color everywhere!
> There's a dusky, husky, musky,
>   smoky smelling in the air!
> And the leaves are dancing gaily—
>   they don't give the world a care,
>   Autumn's here![17]

Perhaps this poem also shows Eudora's debt to Mr. Lawrence Painter and his English-literature survey, but her interest in verse was not merely backward-looking. At MSCW she discovered the power of contemporary poetry, reading the work of William Alexander Percy, the Mississippian who in the years since 1915 had had three books of poems published by Yale University Press.

She also discovered that she could escape the shelter of MSCW's walls. Though unchaperoned students were forbidden to leave campus for such places as the Gilmer Hotel dining room—doing so was a so-called shipping offense that could result in dismissal—Eudora found ways to dine downtown without college officials discovering her crimes. Presumably the Princess Theatre was not off-limits, and it was there that Eudora, always a good dancer, won a Charleston contest. So, too, did she, along with friends, occasionally manage to leave campus and walk fifteen miles, cross a railroad bridge, and picnic at the abandoned antebellum mansion called Waverley. The house, vacant for over a decade, had never been vandalized; its massive chandelier, piano with mother-of-pearl keys, and double stairway ascending to the top of the octagon-shaped foyer would twenty years later provide Eudora with the appointments for the house Marmion in *Delta Wedding*. However useful these excursions would prove to the future writer, they may have been ill-advised: On one of their country adventures, the girls were greeted by a woman from Memphis who sold them cigarettes, invited them to come to her home, and made vaguely lesbian propositions to some of them. No takers. Their rebellion took other routes. Eudora wrote to the Hershey company in Pennsylvania, complaining that poverty in Mississippi left her and her pals hungry at day's end. Could the company provide them with chocolate nourishment? It did. Then on April Fools' Day 1927, Eudora placed a note in the society column of the student paper: "Misses Frances Davis, Lois Prophet, Katie Davidson, Frances Motlow, Thomasine Josephine Burnadetta Kathleen Cady, Dana Davis, Eudora Welty, May Risher, and Earline Agatha Robinson were drowned Thursday evening while boating on the Tombigbee. Everyone expresses regret that these promising young women should meet so untimely a death. Miss Frances Davis had been Editor of *The Spectator* and Miss Lois Prophet had been Editor of *Meh Lady,* while the remaining girls were all very popular with faculty and students." Here Eudora laughed at the formulaic prose of columnists who so often made the significant seem trivial and the trivial significant. She would adopt a similarly subversive irony years later when she actually covered Jackson social events for the Memphis *Commercial-Appeal,* and even now she feared and resisted being pulled into that world, which seemed to be her birthright. In a 1927 poem called "Prophecy," she anticipates turning thirty (she was eighteen) and speculates that she will have become conventional, given up believing in fairies, and begun praying. But she also asserts that she will have "a house of my own" and will retain an inner self that is a "deep black hiding-place." In this deepest part of herself, she proclaims, she will keep her "opals made of dreams and pagan prayers," occasionally revealing them to others. But not to be revealed, she declares, are her

> Pearls like stars when all their shooting lights
> Have died, and left calm loveliness
> And hopelessness. And when the moon has set
> I watch them all alone—all through the night.[18]

Eudora was in two details mistaken—she would not be conventional nor would she literally have a home of her own at age thirty. But she was amazingly self-aware and far seeing in this prophesy of an independent life characterized by the enduring light of imagination, the presence of melancholy intertwined with joy, and the heartfelt need for privacy. Most immediately, the poem, prompted by her reaction to life in Mississippi, predicted her response to the midwestern university where she would transfer and become much more introspective than she had ever been.

After two years at MSCW, Eudora wanted to move on. She had traveled about the country with her father, taking particular pleasure in attending the theater wherever they went. In the fall of 1926, with her entire family, she had again visited New Orleans, where her mother relished being immersed "in the strange babel of tongues and in the sight of the foreign looking people" at the farmers' market and where Eudora had bought "an old dilapidated copy of Burns" and "an old book containing Napoleon's confidential correspondence." She was eager to expand her travels. And her parents felt that their eighteen-year-old daughter was now ready for more independence. Accepted by both Randolph-Macon Woman's College and the University of Wisconsin, Eudora opted first for the southern school. She took the train to Lynchburg, Virginia, and prepared to enroll. Only then did she discover that Randolph-Macon would not accept all of her credits from MSCW. Eudora phoned home, consulted with her parents, and her father suggested that she take the train to Madison, Wisconsin, and enroll there instead. On arrival, Eudora wrote Nash Burger that she was delighted about the change, and Nash responded: "You have become quite a will-o'-the-wisp. I read in the paper where you are off for Randolph Macon, Ward Belmont, or some such place and then comes a post from Wisconsin in gleeful vein narrating how you are an art-student in the beer-drinking country."[19]

At Wisconsin Eudora roomed for a time with Dana Davis, a friend from MSCW, but when Davis left after a semester, Eudora was on her own in a new, somewhat foreign, but also stimulating, world. Her drawing class used live models, and this was far different from the more conservative lessons of her youth. Though she languished in her math, education, and psychology courses, she flourished in her comparative literature and English classes. Her young English professor Ricardo Quintana found her a "brilliant" student with "an unusually acute literary sense," and Quintana proved to be a powerful teacher, introducing Eudora to the passion that animated the works of John Donne and

Jonathan Swift. Eudora made friends in Madison, many of them Jewish girls who felt as displaced in the Midwest as she did. Migs Schermerhorn, a fellow English major from Oak Park, Illinois, and Felicia White, a sociology major from New York City, were especially good chums. Both Migs and Felicia would later visit Eudora in Jackson, and during the thirties Eudora would see a good bit of Felicia in New York City. Helen Iglauer, Oenia Payne, and Jeanne Meyer were also part of Eudora's social circle, and in that circle affectionate nicknames abounded. Helen was predictably known as "Igi," Eudora, unpredictably, as "Hunky." For a time Eudora dated a boy named Pete Dorsett, but no serious relationship developed. At Eudora's rooming house, the landlady's daughter introduced her to bathtub gin that "tasted like 3 in 1 or Fitch's Dandruff remover shampoo"; the Mississippi girl preferred "needle beer," a corked bottle of nonalcoholic beer into which raw alcohol had been inserted with a syringe. The boardinghouse seems also to have introduced Eudora to a tale about a builder of privies who often made the crucial holes too large; the punch line was an expression Eudora would use for the rest of her life: "There you are, jack-knifed." During the 1928 Christmas vacation, Eudora traveled to Lewistown, Montana, to work for the newspaper run by a classmate's father—a vast improvement from a previous and briefly held job washing dinner trays at the Madison Y. In Lewistown Eudora was surprised one evening when a woman snowshoed into town to inform her that the newspaper had printed an erroneous story: Her husband had *not* shot her. Years later Eudora would turn this experience into the story "A Piece of News," but she was not yet ready or able to use this material. She was writing fiction, however, though she did not publish it as she had at MSCW. In 1927 Nash Burger had asked her to contribute a long piece to *Hoi-Polloi*, a college magazine he and Jackson pal George Stephenson hoped to make viable, but Eudora contributed merely a drawing for a cover. "Shadows," an eight-line Welty poem, not story, appeared in the

April 1928 *Wisconsin Literary Magazine.* Still this poem dealt with a theme that would eventually pervade her fiction—the inexorable power of time. Then in 1928 and 1929, she composed and submitted a novella, now lost, as her thesis requirement. Surprisingly, "All Available Brocade" commanded only a grade of B. One is tempted to suppose that a block-headed academic simply refused to recognize genius. Nash, who himself hoped for a writing career, certainly must have thought so. He was impressed with Eudora's work and felt that she had a promising future: "You will be famous with your novel some day, while I will clip my coupons, and wonder who did right," he lamented.[20] But it is possible that Eudora's grade of B was deserved, that the work's dialogue and plot were as unconvincing and contrived as were those elements in the early unpublished stories she later gave to the Mississippi Department of Archives and History.

Despite her classes, her writing, and her friends, Eudora never felt at ease in Madison. When she came home for Christmas 1927, her mother found her looking thin and wan, and shortly after Eudora returned to campus, Chestina mailed her daughter a care package including food supplements. Ironically amused, Eudora found this motherly effort at protection misdirected; during her time in Wisconsin, she would need a different sort of nourishment. In a 1941 letter to her literary agent, Diarmuid Russell, she looked back wistfully on these years, recalling her alienation and the comfort she drew from discovering the works of Yeats and of Russell's father, the Irish mystic A.E.

> I don't know what I apprehended from them when I read them first—it was not what I understand now or what I may understand later—but I suppose it was what I needed. It was the first crisis of a certain kind in my life, and I was frightened—it was when I was sent to the Middle West to school. I was very timid and shy, younger than the rest and those people up there seemed to me like sticks of flint, that

lived in the icy world. I am afraid of flintiness—I had to penetrate that, but not through *their* hearts. I used to be in a kind of wandering daze, I would wander down to Chicago and through the stores, I could feel such a heavy heart inside me. It was more than the pangs of growing up, more more [*sic*], I knew it then, it was some kind of desire to be shown that the human spirit was not like that shivery winter in Wisconsin, that the opposite to all this existed in full. It was just by chance, wandering in the stacks of the library, that I saw one of these books open on one of the little tables under a light. I can't tell you and it is not needed to, what it was like to me to read A.E. but it was a little like first waiting on a shore and then being enveloped in a sea, not being struck violently by a wave, never a shock—and it was the same every day, a tender and firm and passionate experience that I felt in all my ignorance but with a kind of understanding. I would read every afternoon, hurry to read, it was the thing the day led to, and at night what I had read would stay as my secret heart, for I did not let anybody there really know me. What you look for in the world is not simply for what you want to know, but for more than you want to know, and more than you can know, better than you had wished for, and sometimes something draws you to a discovery and there is no other happiness quite the same.[21]

Welty's own A.E.-like mystic experiences would years later come into her story "A Still Moment," and her fascination with Yeats would inform *The Golden Apples*, but from 1927 to 1929 her reading of Irish literature was an end in itself, a compensation for the alienation she felt in Madison, a jewel to be stored in the "deep, black hiding place" of self she had described in the poem "Prophecy."

In 1929 Eudora received her BA in English and decided to return to Mississippi. Back in Jackson, she lived at her parents' home on Pinehurst Place and presumably worked at a part-time job. Nash Burger was now in school at Sewanee and urged her to submit some pen-and-ink drawings to *Mountain Goat,* the University of the South student magazine he was editing. She did, but within a year, Eudora had abandoned college publications. During the spring and early summer of 1930, she wrote witty essays for the *Jackson Daily News.* In "Postoffices Shifted Many Times in City," Eudora provided a bemused history of the U.S. mail in Jackson: "The first postoffice was on the site of the Tucker Printing House on North State. This is according to the undated memory of one of Jackson's fine old ladies who can recollect that an immense amount of whittling went on at this location. Little girls, of course, could not go in postoffices and it was indiscreet to look in the door, but this old lady is firmly certain that the postoffice was there." In "Weekly Baby Clinic Is Becoming Popular," Eudora extolled the cause of the Junior Auxiliary's baby clinic, but she also subtly mocked the condescending label "underprivileged" that the Auxiliary had pinned on children in attendance: "One child hangs ingratiatingly over the bannister of his crib, looking like Bertrand Russell at the lecture stand. Another golden-haired baby looks about the room, her gaze lifted unconcernedly above the heads of her companions, a soft smile on her face, as if to say patiently and indulgently, 'You others may be underfed, all right, but I, after all, am under-privileged.' But it would take A. A. Milne to fully give you the force of this scene in the clinic." And in yet another of her articles, Eudora wrote a sort of tongue-in-cheek sketch about vacations: "In the days of the cave man, the vacation was extremely simple. Only the men went on them. No man is going to drag a woman 40 miles. Of course the simple cave man could not say a complicated word like 'vacation.' He called it 'Koko' or 'Phew-phew' instead of 'Boop poop pah doop,' but all the same he managed to get away from the grind. Jerking a few of his wife's bangs, he would say, along about June, 'Well, pet, I'm off tomorrow on my Koko. You

can fix that towel rack in the bathroom while I'm away. Don't follow me. And have some sandwiches ready when I get back.' And
that was that."[22] Clearly Eudora was not destined for mainstream
journalism. She needed a medium that would encourage, not
merely accept, flights of fancy.

While back in Jackson, Eudora was reunited with friends who
made her feel more readily at ease than she had felt in Wisconsin,
and several of these friends were planning to enter Columbia
University's graduate schools in the fall of 1930. Aimee Shands,
Mary Frances Horne, Joe Skinner, and Frank Lyell had secured
parental blessings for this venture and had made successful applications for admission. Leone Shotwell, who had also been admit-
ted, was encountering resistance from her aunt Mary, who felt
New York might be too dangerous an environment for her ward.
At some point late in 1929 or early in 1930, Leone countered by
asking Eudora to come along and by telling her aunt that anyone
would be safe in the company of Eudora. Eudora agreed to apply,
sent the university all of its required forms, and, like her friends,
was accepted. She was ready to reenter the halls of academe,
thinking that in the company of kindred spirits a second voyage
into the North would be less alienating.

At Columbia Eudora enrolled in an advertising/secretarial
program—her father had counseled that an English major would
never bring her a job and had been apprehensive about the move
to Manhattan. Only her willingness to enroll in a practical course
of study convinced him that the time in New York would prove
beneficial. Along with Leone, Mary Frances, and Aimee, Eudora
set up housekeeping in Johnson Hall, Columbia's graduate dormitory for women. Protecting young women was a concern even
at a major university in New York City, and the Jackson girls, all
under age twenty-one except for Eudora, were not allowed to
share the off-campus apartment they so much wanted. Instead
they lived under the watchful eye of Miss Eliza Rhees Butler, the
sister of Nicholas Murray Butler, Columbia's president. Still, Miss

Butler's tyranny was a source of entertainment to Eudora. Miss Butler warned her female charges against the white-slave traffic—never accept an aspirin from a stranger, or you may wake up in Buenos Aires in a house of prostitution. Amused, Eudora sent off for buttons that read "WST," which she and her friends proceeded to wear; Miss Butler never realized that the acronym stood for "white-slave traffic." When she was not being paranoid, Miss Butler was often being condescending to southerners. For instance, she denied southern girls free opera tickets—they were not sophisticated enough to enjoy the opera, she reasoned. But those very southern girls attended the opera nevertheless and were pleased one evening to hear a familiar voice boom out just before the curtain went up: "I am Eliza Rhees Butler, and I have been seated behind a post." What satisfaction. And what satisfaction to turn Miss Butler into the subject of doggerel: "Where'er she goes forever more, / The Butler bosom goes before. / But still in all, I think you'll find / That most of Butler goes behind."

Bemused by her living arrangements, Eudora was simply indifferent to the business curriculum. She paid scant attention to her own classes, save perhaps the comparative literature class she audited; she made As in advertising, a C in marketing, Bs in typing and stenography.[23] She paid more attention to the classes her friends took, and she managed to attend them rather frequently. She and Frank attended a lecture on abnormal psychology delivered by the renowned Professor H. L. Hollingworth—renowned or not, Hollingworth elicited rather irreverent, illustrated notes from Eudora.[24] On the other hand, she found herself fascinated by one of Alfred Adler's courses; she would never forget a class during which he staged a robbery, had the students write their descriptions of the event under the misapprehension that they were doing so to help when the police arrived, and then showed the class how erroneous their eyewitness reports had been. Engaged as she was by this Adler course, Eudora was annoyed by the research project—a study of fatigue—that Aimee Shands had begun under Adler's direction. Hoping for interviews with exhausted individuals, Aimee would lie in wait for tired compatriots returning from late nights on the town, then make them stay up and become research subjects.

The threat of interviews with Aimee notwithstanding, Eudora spent more time on the town than in the classroom or library. Museums and galleries, nightclubs in Harlem or Greenwich Village, movies at the Little Carnegie, night court, Broadway theaters—these were the places that drew Eudora and her friends. The Metropolitan Museum was a regular stop for Eudora, just as the Art Institute in Chicago had been during her Wisconsin years, but she also loved the small New York galleries. Music, too, entranced Eudora, especially jazz. A Jackson boyfriend named George Greenway was a musician who had taken Eudora on drives into the countryside around Jackson so that he might serenade her on his trumpet, and during Eudora's year at Columbia, he took a brief break from his graduate studies in North Carolina and drove up so that together they might visit the Cotton Club and Small's Paradise, two Harlem nightspots that, according to the African American editor, novelist, and playwright Wallace Thurman, were often frequented by "theatrical performers and well-to-do folks about town" or by "smart white patrons, the type that reads the ultrasophisticated *New Yorker*." There the young couple might have heard Duke Ellington or stride pianists like Willie "the Lion" Smith and James Johnson.[25]

As the Jacksonian least absorbed with class work, Eudora often went to Times Square to buy theater tickets for the group—the New York theater scene was vibrant and inexpensive if you were willing to sit in the cheap seats. After the first act of most plays, Frank loved to move down from the balcony to unoccupied orchestra seats he had spotted; Eudora was more hesitant. So, too, was Eudora reluctant to follow Frank's practice of going ticketless to shows: With Eudora in tow, he would mingle with an intermission crowd in a lobby, follow the crowd back into the theater, and then see the second act at no charge. A particularly interesting experience—with tickets—must have been seeing Ethel Barrymore in a dramatization of Julia Peterkin's Pulitzer Prize–winning *Scarlet Sister Mary*. This play about African Americans living off the coast of South Carolina typified, as Langston Hughes later noted, an era in which whites were simultaneously fascinated with and patronizing toward black culture: "It was a period in which white writers wrote about Negroes more successfully (commercially speaking) than Negroes did about themselves. It was the period (God help us!) when Ethel Barrymore appeared in blackface in *Scarlet Sister Mary*." Like Hughes, Frank and Eudora found Barrymore's use of blackface and the Gullah dialect wholly unconvincing. At MSCW Eudora had acted in a campus minstrel show, but now she recoiled from a serious, nonmusical counterpart to that genre. What Peterkin thought of the 1930 Barrymore performance is unknown, but she attended the same matinee that Frank and Eudora saw. During the intermission, they were able to talk with Peterkin, thanks to Frank's having met her at the apartment of Norma and Herschel Brickell.[26]

Norma and Herschel Brickell were Mississippi friends of Jackson's Columbia student contingent. Norma, née Long, had grown up in Jackson; Herschel had been editor of the *Jackson Daily News*. The couple married in 1918 and now were successfully ensconced in New York where Herschel, who had first been book editor for the *New York Post*, became General Editor at Henry Holt. At the Brickells' apartment on the Upper East Side, the young Jacksonians would happily gather for card games or would mingle with the literati at cocktail parties. Norma and Herschel had created a sense of Jackson-in-New York.

Lehman Engel lived less lavishly than the Brickells—he was still a student at Juilliard—but his apartment in Greenwich Village was also a home away from home for Eudora and the gang. One notable evening, Eudora and Frank dropped by Lehman's, found a group of friends there, and had a good time eating and drinking, after which they stopped by a Greenwich Village restaurant and looked in on the festivities. Romany Marie's was celebrating its seventeenth anniversary; every table had been reserved by bohemian sorts, and Romany Marie was herself in attendance, stomping out cigarette butts with her bare feet. Marie's partner, Ariel Durant, or Marie's loyal customers, like the architect and inventor Buckminster Fuller; the sculptor, designer, and architect Isamu Noguchi; and the philosopher Will Durant may have been among those Eudora and Frank observed.[27]

Eudora had arrived in New York with friends from home and had discovered the city in the company of those friends, but in New York she had clearly moved beyond her sheltered beginnings. Moreover, her circle of friends extended beyond the Jackson contingent. Fellow Columbia student Nettie St. Helens, a native of Rochester, took Eudora to the Finger Lakes region of New York State. Nettie later found employment in nearby New Jersey, where Eudora would also visit her. Wilma Gallagher was a boon companion in Johnson Hall, with plans for a career in the city. And Eudora's University of Wisconsin friend Felicia White lived in an elegant apartment at Riverside and Eighty-fourth, where she entertained Eudora and her friends. Eudora sensed that her own future lay in New York. So, in the midst of the 1931 spring term, she resolved to find a job that would help pay for her student expenses and allow her to remain in Manhattan when the term was finished. Her parents had been stretched financially in supporting Eudora as well as Edward, who was in the architecture school at Georgia Tech. Both her mother and father were delighted, however, with Eudora's good experience in the city and were happy to know that she might find a way to extend it. With the assistance of the Columbia University placement office, Eudora did find an advertising job, evidently on a trial basis, but was dismissed two weeks later as part of a ruse by which the employer regularly avoided paying wages. Eudora reported this bit of "skullduggery" to Columbia and began to look anew for work. But at semester's end she was called home. Her father had developed leukemia and would not live through the autumn.[28]

In *One Writer's Beginnings* Eudora focused on the years from her birth through her graduate education as the ones crucial to her development as a writer, and clearly they were. Eudora had had a happy childhood and adolescence and a happy entrance into adulthood—a prosperous and loving family, good friends, a community that captured her imagination, the opportunity to exercise her talent, a variety of rich educational opportunities. But even happy children, adolescents, and young adults experience the sort of oppositions, polarities, paradoxes, that eventually can fire the imaginations of creative individuals. As a child, for instance, Eudora was aware that her parents' ardent love for each other was subject to tension. She indicated as much in a youthful memory she later deleted from her 1983 Harvard lectures.

> Mother sent me often to look through her sewing machine drawers for her thimble. Once I came upon one of her "correspondence cards" tucked in there with her spools, the kind she kept in her writing desk; there was "CAW" on them, her monogram which I supposed to be a word mysteriously chosen to head her messages. "Caw," I read, "I had believed the clock you gave me at Christmas would chime only happy hours—" My mother wrote this correspondence card to my father: he had given her the clock. Was he meant to find it in her sewing machine drawer with the spools of thread? Or should I tell him where to look? But this turned out to be one of the days when he walked home from the office bringing her a box of her favorite Elmers Chocolate Creams, the finest to be had in Jackson, made in New Orleans, with a card stuck under the ribbon on which *he'd* written to *her,* in

his most legible hand. I read that too: "To My Sweetheart." He had beaten her to it. [29]

Just as there were occasional misunderstandings between her parents, there were strains in Eudora's own relationships with Chestina and Chris. Her parents' efforts to protect their children at times forced Eudora to feel guilty about her need for independence. In the autobiographical Courtney story, Eudora describes Courtney imagining her mother's response to a recent adventure: "'Well, you have done things away from Mother, I can see now . . . And I'm glad of it!' This last thought gave Courtney an expected feeling of excitement, for it was a daring one. Her mother glad of it? That was a little too much." It was also too much for the protective Weltys to talk willingly with their children about tragedy; Chris never did, and Chessie quite reluctantly. When a very young Eudora, for instance, came upon "a small white cardboard box" containing "two polished buffalo nickels, embedded in white cotton," she innocently asked permission to spend them. In *One Writer's Beginnings* Eudora recalled that her mother's response was an immediate and passionate *no:* "Then she sat down, drew me to her, and told me that I had had a little brother who had come before I did, and who had died as a baby before I was born. And these two nickels that I'd wanted to claim as my find were his. They had lain on his eyelids, for a purpose untold and unimaginable." Immediately for the child Eudora, there arose new questions, which would torment her and for which there were no adequate and protecting answers: "[Mother] hadn't died. And when I came, I hadn't died either. Would she ever? Would I ever? I couldn't face *ever.* I must have rushed into her lap, demanding her like a baby."[30] All these tormenting questions arose as a consequence of avoidance, self-protection, attempted protection of the children, and as a consequence of love.

Other paradoxes centered around regional culture more than family experience. Eudora must have recognized at some level and at some point that her privileged world was different from the world of African Americans in Jackson. The separate and unequal shopping districts and neighborhoods; the separate entrances for blacks and whites at the movies and the fact that blacks had to sit in the balcony; the presumption of deference on the part of blacks for whites; the absence of black children at Davis School and Jackson High School—all of these differences must have impinged upon Eudora's consciousness, even if she never openly questioned them. Her reading in *Our Wonder World* must also have seemed problematic to her. The very book that encouraged cultural relativism in its portrait of most societies was distinctly patronizing in describing children of color: For instance, it depicts a "Negrito" child of the Philippines, who is called "little Blackie" and who "is most amusing when he climbs a tree or anything else that invites him, as he can hang on with his toes quite as well as with his hands. It is a funny sight to see his little tattooed black body clambering among the branches of his favorite cocoanut tree. He can also stick on to the great back of the water-buffalo and disdains the help one is inclined to offer him in mounting." The diametrically opposed attitudes implicit in *Our Wonder World* were also part of Eudora's family heritage. Chris was one of only three white Republicans in Jackson, and in the South of this era white Republican attitudes toward African Americans, though at times opportunistic, tended to be more progressive than Democratic ones. Chessie came from a family that had freed its slaves and rejected the myth of the Lost Cause. Yet, though Eudora's parents were atypical in their views of race, they accepted in many ways the South's racial hierarchy. On the family's 1925 auto trip, for instance, Chestina was offended when this hierarchy broke down: She noted that when she entered a service station restroom in Gary, Indiana, "I had to wait while a big fat negro woman washed her child's face and hands at the lavatory. At least I thought she was a negro until I heard a stream of some foreign language. Anyway she wasn't white."[31] But even here, in a private log of her journey, Chessie used the word *negro* rather than the commonly used pejorative *nigger*, and she acknowledged at least some ambiguity of racial categories. Moreover, though she objected to an absence of deference for whites, she did not object to an integrated facility per se. Eudora, a most perceptive teenager, must have noted in conversations with her mother attitudes that at once endorsed and undermined the prevalent southern racial standards. Her own youthful imitation of "Uncle Lewis" and her decision not to mock him again suggests an early attempt not to follow in this pattern. And eventually Eudora's visits to Harlem would enlarge her sense of African American culture, its richness and vitality, and would help Eudora, as Toni Morrison has noted, to "write about black people in a way that few white men have ever been able to write. It's not patronizing, not romanticizing—it's the way they should be written about."[32]

A sense that society's conventions could be both meaningful and irrelevant or even ridiculous was an additional legacy to Eudora from her parents. First Chessie, and then Chris, joined the First Methodist Episcopal Church, South, in 1905, but neither was a regular church goer. Chris refused to participate in a revival led by the nationally known evangelist Gypsy Smith, Chessie preferred reading her Bible at home to attending Sunday school, and when missionary societies solicited funds from Chessie, she declared that people in other countries should not be told what to believe. In fact, Chessie was more direct and outspoken than most Jackson women, and she encouraged her daughter to excel in academics when other Jackson ladies might speak dismissively of girls who were "brains." But it was Chessie who evidently found nothing amusing or endearing in her seven-year-old daughter's naked and joyful run around her grandmother's West Virginia mountain home, and it was Chessie who organized a very conventional bridge party for Eudora the summer before she left for Columbia University: On June 22, 1930, the Jackson *Daily*

Clarion-Ledger reported that "the handsome home of Mr. and Mrs. C. W. Welty, Pinehurst Place, was on Thursday afternoon at three-thirty o'clock the scene of beautiful entertaining when Mrs. Welty was hostess at eight tables of bridge honoring her attractive daughter Miss Eudora Welty." Like Courtney of her unpublished story, Eudora was likely uncomfortable with this sort of event. Courtney feels distinctly out of her element at a Thursday bridge gathering: "Her throat was dry, and she seemed to be continually laughing politely. She found herself calling out gay things to people without consciously making herself do it. She wondered repeatedly about the refreshments. She felt that the others were feeling she was high-hat. She spoke of herself deprecatingly but at the wrong times, she was afraid."[33] At Columbia, however, no such gatherings were required, and feeling out of place must have become a thing of the past. There Eudora would reject outright the narrow-minded conventionality of Eliza Rhees Butler and embrace the diverse world of New York, though in some senses Eudora would remain more an observer than an insider of the city—an onlooker at Romany Marie's or the Cotton Club.

As Eudora in her twenties and early thirties recalled her youth, she would realize that her childhood had been a complex one indeed. The loving family had at times proved oppressive in its protectiveness, the cohesive white community destructive in its insistence upon a racial divide and upon conventionality, her own parents models both of social standards and of rebellion from them. Her college years away from home—first in Columbus, Mississippi, then in Madison and New York—would give her the distance from which to assess a sheltered past and the courage to move beyond the self-consciously clever or openly derivative poems and stories of her youth. A writing life lay before her. A Mississippi world beyond the one she had known and a job that took her out into it would spark her imagination, and Eudora would find her own distinctive voice in story after story.

Self-Discovery
1931–1941

On April 13, 1931, as she enjoyed her twenty-second birthday, Eudora Welty was still in the process of discovering her voice, her vocation, her identity, but during the next decade, she would experience a number of defining moments that would set the course of her professional and personal life. One of those moments occurred before six months were out. Though she had hoped to find work, continue her education, and remain in New York after the 1931 spring term at Columbia University, she had come home because her father, only fifty-two, was seriously ill. Then, late in September, she witnessed his death. More than half a century later, she described this horrific experience in *One Writer's Beginnings:*

When my father was dying in the hospital, there was a desperate last decision to try a blood transfusion. How much was known about the compatibility of blood types then, or about the procedure itself, I'm unable to say. All I know is that there was no question in my mother's mind as to who the donor was to be.

I was present when it was done; my two brothers were in school. Both my parents were lying on cots, my father had been brought in on one and my mother lay on the other. Then a tube was simply run from her arm to his.

My father, I believe, was unconscious. My mother was looking at him. I could see her fervent face: there was no doubt as to what she was thinking. This time, *she* would save *his* life . . .

All at once his face turned dusky red all over. The doctor made a disparaging sound with his lips, the kind a woman knitting makes when she drops a stitch. What the doctor meant by it was that my father had died.

My mother never recovered emotionally. Though she lived for over thirty years more, and suffered other bitter losses, she never stopped blaming herself. She saw this as her failure to save his life.[1]

Eudora would be haunted by the loss of her dearly loved father and by the plight of her equally loved mother, who was racked with grief and guilt. From childhood, she had longed to be an author, but that desire now took on new shape and direction and intensity. She needed to transfuse her life's blood into fiction, to create new life in the face of death, to write stories conveying the ephemeral nature of human experience and the consequent urgency "to do, to understand, to love." For a time, this desire would exceed her ability, but in the coming years, she would hone her skills. She would eventually and powerfully depict the failure of love to overcome separateness or protect individuals from harm, and in the process, Eudora would, paradoxically, find connection. "I never doubted . . . ," she wrote almost fifty years later, "that imagining yourself into other people's lives is exactly what writing fiction is." In the pages of stories, she further realized, writer and reader met, jointly bringing their imaginations to bear upon a narrative and upon characters (be they bootleggers, tenant farmers, or itinerant musicians) who can transcend isolation, if only momentarily, in shared acts of imagination, in shared visions of the future or recreations of the past. As Eudora noted in retrospect, "The emotions, in which all of us are alike involved for life, differ more in degree than in kind."[2]

In late 1931, however, Eudora was unable to translate her deepest concerns into fiction. Though she worked at stories, she published none, and the prospects of earning a living as a writer were dim. Supporting herself and her writing via other avenues seemed more realistic. She accepted a job at radio station WJDX, established by her father, where she applied her writing talents producing the station's newsletter. She also began to take a great many photographs, with the hope that doing so might lead to creatively satisfying employment. Her father had loved photography, had helped to establish Jackson's first camera store, and had used his camera to document his travels, to capture images of his wife, and to record the lives of his children. His passion for photography was an important legacy to Eudora, who took her own and rather different sort of snapshots. At first she and her friends photographed each other in amusing poses, with Eudora often the photographed rather than the photographer, wearing a fright wig and mustache, or lying atop a tomb, or playing the ukelele in a pasture full of wildflowers. Then in the 1930s Eudora more and more began to think of photography as an artistic endeavor. Using a Kodak camera with a bellows, she photographed Mississippi and Mississippians, developing her pictures in a jerry-rigged darkroom and hoping to publish them.

Still she was melancholy and ambitious for more than she felt Mississippi could offer. Reunited with Frank Lyell during his Thanksgiving vacation, Eudora discussed the sense of ennui that had been broken only by her reading of Virginia Woolf's *To the Lighthouse*. The two Jacksonians agreed that *The Waves*, Woolf's most recent novel, was far less successful, and both resolved separately to register their views with Woolf. Eudora's letter to the English novelist began in an effusive, self-consciously Woolfian but nonetheless heartfelt fashion.

First let me say that I am yours humbly. To me "To the Lighthouse" is perfect and life-giving and yours the only inspired writing today. It was better to have read "To the Lighthouse" than to have written any other book, or, almost, to have lived any given life. It dissolved all the sediment of loneliness of my dull days into a perfect amorphous stream of motion and intensity that flows clear and penetrative over the mosaic of my imagination, or perhaps yours. It was light under a door I shall never open. It was alchemy, insinuating into my veins a drop of all too golden blood and into my ghost-like world (for nothing may ever happen) an integration of the elements of loneliness that clings through stretches of pointless time with a significance that could easily be the only beautiful thing about my life. One could become enslaved by the wonder of one's own impenetrable aloneness, since you have given aloneness its wonder, did not you yourself enter it by perfect recognition and prove such enslavement an insensitive act.

But despite this lavishly self-effacing opening to her letter, Eudora did not hesitate to offer Woolf criticism and advice about her newest novel. In advance of any substantial publication of her own, Eudora was thinking seriously about character and voice.

Feeling your power as I do, with perhaps more rhapsody than accuracy, I bought "The Waves" with a high heart, anticipating that its conception would be a development more intensely centerward toward the core of "To the Lighthouse," a development which your superb imaginative insight had further directed. Oh well, of course "The Waves" is beautiful; there are places in it where, one feels, only you would not fear to tread; but the sections of the book about Bernard close over the divine footprints and almost make one doubt what is now obscured and roughened away by lesser surges of inspiration. The flaw, one feels, is not in the fitness of Bernard's existence in "The Waves," or in his portrayal, certainly, but in your use of such an unworthy medium as Bernard's personality for your writing. It seems wrong for you to shine there within Bernard; the spirit has descended to inhabit at those times an object we cannot worship. And Mrs. Woolf, to end the book from his lips is cruel.

Having offered these reservations about Woolf's narrative strategy, Eudora backed away from criticism. "Forgive the impertinence of even the praise. It seems, already, an offensive attempt at precarious intimacy with austerity and greatness. But I probably have quite a long life ahead of me, and the fact that you will be writing other books which, like 'To the Lighthouse,' will stun me speechless is only too heavenly to contemplate."[3]

This epistle to Virginia Woolf, with its ostensible focus on *The Waves*, perhaps offers more insight into the letter writer than into Woolf's novel. Eudora was dissatisfied with home, here proclaiming her Mississippi world "ghost-like . . . (for nothing may ever happen)." She longed for a vital cultural life and would continue to do so. But above all, she longed to become a writer; "to have read 'To the Lighthouse,'" she told Woolf, was almost better than "to have lived any given life." Only the writing life, Eudora felt, could provide her existence with "motion and intensity."

As 1933 began, feeling that her mother was now coping with grief and loss, Eudora traveled to New York. After a month of pounding the pavement and interviewing for positions, she had not found work. Still she managed to stay in New York past her birthday, living in an apartment with friends, looking for a job, perhaps finding temporary positions, taking in concerts, plays, and art exhibitions. The city was a tonic for her. Her equanimity returned, and her sense of humor was at times irrepressible. Years before she had read S. J. Perelman in *College Humor*, and she remained under his spell, laughing out loud while perusing his regular contributions to the *New Yorker*. Even her own application for a position at the *New Yorker* had a Perelmanesque flair: "How I would like to work for you! A little paragraph each morning—a little paragraph each night." After penning these lines, she turned punny. If she couldn't work at the *New Yorker*, she said, she could dance in Vachel Lindsay's *Congo*: "I congo on. I rest my case."[4] Other applications drew a more restrained performance from Eudora. Ever the lover of travel, she applied to *National Geographic* magazine, and ever the realist, she sought secretarial work. Nothing suitable materialized, but Eudora's time in New York was not wasted.

From the start, the diversity of life there had had a powerful impact upon Eudora, and it continued to do so. She was not to be a stereotypical white girl from Mississippi, for her openness to experience brought her in contact with cultures vastly different from her own. She had already come to appreciate the world of jazz and the African American jazz artists she had heard at the Cotton Club and Small's Paradise. In 1933 she would feel the pull of Hindu culture as she twice saw Uday Shan-Kar dance. Even the *New York Times* was under his spell. As John Martin wrote on January 1, 1933:

> Because Uday Shan-Kar, the Hindu dancer, is an artist in the universal sense, he is able to illuminate for the Western mind the dancing of his people—an art so delicate and with so many ramifications. The performances of his company of dancers and musicians at the New Yorker Theatre are revelations of a culture in many ways antipodal to our own and one which is not to be understood in any real sense by the perusal of books. When we are led through the sensitive agencies of kinesthetic response to a sympathetic reaction to Hindu dancing, the door is thrown open for us to a genuine and trustworthy, if not an intellectual or rational, experience of Hindu culture.

Such was Eudora's experience. Immediately after seeing Shan-Kar, she wrote to Frank Lyell: "you must see Shan-Kar—i dont know of anything you would like more—he is marvelous—very beautiful—he is continuously divine—really his dances are like the humours of the gods—(just as john martin to john martin i tell you this)— he has the most enchanting body i have ever seen, he uses it like a voice—i dont know anything about the hindu cosmos but the appeal of all he does is very direct and you are instantly enchanted."[5] Shan-Kar was not the only source of enchantment for Eudora in New York at this time. During the first week in February, she saw Martha Graham dance. And in April she saw Alla Nazimova, the Russian actress, perform in *The Cherry Orchard*. Life in Manhattan remained compelling and cosmopolitan, but Eudora found no way to earn a living there. Instead she returned to Jackson.

At home Eudora was still in quest of a way to be self-supporting. Her father, an insurance executive, had left her a hundred shares of Lamar Life Insurance stock and had made her the beneficiary of a life insurance policy with the face amount of five thousand dollars; for the remainder of her life, the policy would pay slightly less than twenty dollars a month, far less than a monthly wage in the 1930s for even a clerical job but the equivalent of approximately 250 to 280 twenty-first-century dollars. Edward and Walter had received identical bequests. And to Chestina, Chris Welty had willed the family home, the benefits of a larger policy, and more stock. Family members had been provided for, but they were understandably cautious with funds. The country was in the midst of the Great Depression. Banks had failed, insurance had become a luxury most people could not afford, stocks were devalued. Not long after Chris's death, Chessie had taken in roomers and begun to give bridge lessons. Now Eudora sought to find a fulfilling and remunerative career. For the time being, she simultaneously held a number of part-time jobs: She resumed her position at WJDX, worked for five months on her friend Ralph Hilton's *Jackson State Tribune,* and began an almost two-year stint writing weekly, and subtly tongue-in-cheek, Jackson society columns as a stringer for the Memphis *Commercial-Appeal.* Eudora undertook occasional days of substitute teaching, filling in for English, psychology, and even Spanish teachers (Spanish by mistake—she didn't speak the language) during 1934 and 1935, and coaching a May Day pageant in 1934. In addition, photography seemed for a time to promise a creative outlet as well as a steady income. Late in 1933 Eudora and Hubert Creekmore worked for the Jackson Junior Auxiliary, taking pictures for the organization's *Clarion-Ledger* exhibition; and in August of 1934, Eudora applied for admission to a New School for Social Research photography class taught by Berenice Abbott, who had established her reputation in Paris by photographing artists like Jean Cocteau, André Gide, and James Joyce, and whose documentary photographs of New York City were part of exhibitions in the United States. Eudora hoped that the New School course would provide her with "entree into the business world of photography." In her letter of application, she told Abbott that she had "a contract with a dress shop for fashion photographs, which have been reproduced by the local paper." She also said that she had "photographed everything within reason or unreason around here, having lately made particular studies of negroes, with an idea of making a book, since I do not like Doris Ulman's [*sic*] pictures." Doris Ulmann's photographs of African American tenant farmers illustrated Julia Peterkin's recently published book about the Gullah culture of the South Carolina Sea Islands. Like Ulmann, Eudora had long been interested in black culture, but unlike Ulmann, Eudora eschewed sentimental, softly focused, carefully staged images. She snapped most of her photographs, as she later reported, "without the awareness of the subjects or with only their peripheral awareness." "The snapshots made with people's awareness," Eudora also recalled, "are, for the most part, just as unposed: I simply asked people if they would mind going on with what they were doing and letting me take a picture. I can't remember ever being met with a demurrer stronger than amusement." Without doubt her privileged status as a white person made it almost impossible for her African American subjects to decline. Still, the most remarkable quality of the Welty photos is the affinity photographer and subject so often seem to feel toward each other. Never are the pictures patronizing; never do they deny the subject's dignity. Eudora thought that her pictures of African American life might attract publishers, and when admission to Abbott's class was not forthcoming, she contacted publishers directly. In October and November of 1934, having given up her position at WJDX, she journeyed to New York to attempt to sell her photographs but had no success. Early in 1935 she planned to return and try the publishing houses again. As she told Frank Lyell, Hubert "thinks I ought to wait until I can take a baptising [sic] and a ball game, but I can't wait. I am afraid somebody else will get out something like it or the publishers or the public will become saturated with photography books. I want to get some money for it and then go somewhere else to make another book, like Mexico or Alaska." Matters became more urgent when in May 1935 Eudora lost her *Commercial-Appeal* job to a Jacksonian claiming greater financial need for the position. Though Eudora had hopes that a career in photography would replace her newspaper post, she concealed them behind self-deprecatingly humorous remarks. On July 29, 1935, she told her friend Robert Daniel, a Sewanee student to whom Frank had introduced her, that she had "been to NY twice and NC once, shooting whatever I see, click . . . I made a speech on my photos at an exhibit in Chapel Hill, after which everyone got drunk— the cart before the horse."[6]

Despite attempts to establish herself as a photographer, Eudora's first love was fiction, and fiction she continued to write. In 1934 or so she finished a story, which would not be published for forty-three years. "Acrobats in a Park" describes a multigener-ational Italian family of acrobats on their stop in Jackson; infi-delity, brother betraying brother, attempts to find reconciliation, are set against the backdrop of Eudora's hometown. The human pyramid formed by the troupe and broken a bit obviously and ar-tificially by one member's weakness represents the family and its troubles. This symbol lacks the subtlety that would characterize those in Eudora's stories to come. Years later Eudora looked back on the story with some amusement: "I recognize in 'Acrobats in a Park' some risky things about my writing self as a beginner. It can hardly have occurred to me to ask myself first what I knew about acrobats; the answer would have been, as little as I knew about incest, Europeans, or the Catholic Church, also elements in the story." But though Eudora was somewhat dismissive of her early work, she also came to see it as prophetic of work to come: "What strikes me now, and what I was unaware of then, was that these acrobats were prophesying for the subject that would con-cern me most in all my work lying ahead . . . : the solid unity of the family thinking itself unassailable, and the outsiders who would give much to enter it—most often out of love and with the effect, sometimes, of liberation."[7] A variation on this subject was evident in what seems to be another 1934 story, "The Chil-dren." A failed youthful romance, a protective mother who will call her daughter back from a despairing love, a rose-garden setting, help to convey the constraints and strengths of family life, constraints and strengths that Eudora herself was perhaps feeling upon her return to Jackson. Though plot, character, and locale never seem part of a cohesive whole in this work, Eudora was beginning to find her voice. She would eventually incorporate parts of "The Children" into the powerful 1942 story "At the Landing."

Living at home and on a relatively tight budget, working part-time jobs, making many photographs and developing them in a makeshift darkroom, writing poems and stories, Eudora also managed to find time for inexpensive frivolity. She never sought, as Claudia Roth Pierpont's *New Yorker* profile suggested she did, social acceptance. Though she would join the Junior League in deference to her friends who were already members, Eudora's interests were rather different and her circle of friends more wide-ranging. Four young men were particularly important to her, and all were iconoclastic sorts. Nash Burger had returned to Jackson from the University of the South and had become a teacher at Central High School, Lehman Engel summered in Jackson while he was studying at Juilliard, Hubert Creekmore was back in residence after attending the Yale School of Drama, and Frank Lyell visited during his summer vacations from Princeton. During summers of the early thirties, the group gathered frequently at the Welty house to drink and talk and laugh and listen to music—literature and the theater and the New York scene filled their conversations, and they loved hearing both classical music and jazz. They also engaged in activities that Lehman eventually labeled "camp." When Jackson ladies, for instance, advertised that their night-blooming cereuses would be in flower on a given night and invited one and all to witness the annual bloomings, Eudora and her friends attended. They went on to name themselves the Night-Blooming Cereus Club and took as their motto a slightly altered line from a Rudy Vallee song: "Don't take it cereus, Life's too mysterious." Years later, in *The Golden Apples,* Eudora would use the "naked, luminous, complicated flower" as an emblem of life's beauty and its fragility, and she would have a character repeat what one Jackson lady had said about the cereus blossom, "Tomorrow it'll look like a wrung chicken's neck." But at the time, none of the Night-Blooming Cereus Club members anticipated such symbolic implications of their activities. For them the cereus was and remained an emblem of good fellowship, of the pleasure imaginative individuals could share if they embraced the world around them. In 1956, recalling the happy past and hoping that a dramatization of *The Ponder Heart* would meet with success, Lehman sent to Eudora on opening night the closest thing he could find to a cereus bloom, and when Eudora later used the cereus as an image in *Losing Battles*, she informed Lehman she had done so for him.[8]

These friends lived up to their motto; they did not take their society too seriously. They mocked an emphasis on beauty and cosmetics when Frank Lyell photographed Eudora posed like a Helena Rubinstein or Elizabeth Arden model, ready to apply pea soup, shoe polish, even a household cleanser to her face, instead of cosmetics. And they mocked the stock elements of literary romance when Lehman photographed an aloof Eudora in a Mexican shawl scorning the advances of Frank in a sombrero. Word games fascinated the Night-Blooming Cereus Club; they played them frequently, among themselves and with others. With Frank's English acquaintance Shaun Wylie, they "played a game called Who were you with, Where were you, and WHAT were you doing, and he said, 'I'm in Lake Louise with Hitler, and—we're being married.'" With Robert Daniel, they played similar games, which he then introduced to Sewanee, where he was an undergraduate. In February of 1934 he informed Eudora that he and Jacksonian George Stephenson, also at Sewanee, had "even gone so far as to revive the Movie and Wine Test, Dullest Remarks, and Cliches, to relieve the monotony." And the next year, Daniel told Eudora that he had mentioned the movie test to a fellow student, who responded, "What movie actress, if the first letter of her last name were changed to B, would remind you of a donkey?" The answer was Fay Wray.[9]

The Night-Blooming Cereus Club members shared many other Jackson friends, of course. One was Bill Hamilton, then teaching at Central High, but eventually to become a Duke University professor. It was Hamilton who recommended that they all read Robert Coates's *The Outlaw Years*, a legendary history of a frontier trail called the Natchez Trace, along which traders and settlers found themselves attacked by thieves and murderers. Eudora would draw upon this book when she wrote *The Robber Bride-*

groom. Eudora had occasional dates, seeing her old flame George Greenway when he returned to Jackson, going out with Marshall and then his brother Charles Hurt at different points. And she enjoyed the company of artists Helen Jay Lotterhos, Karl Wolfe, and William Hollingsworth and of her old friends Willia Wright, Dolly Wells, Dorothy Simmons, Joe and Mary Frances Skinner, Barron Ricketts, Leone Shotwell, and Margaret Harmon. Eudora and Seta Alexander, the daughter of a Supreme Court judge and a friend Eudora had met through her brother Walter, spent a good bit of time together, joined by Hubert and Jimmie Wooldridge, a Jackson insurance man like Walter. The four loved a game Eudora had invented: Old Magazines. Eudora saved magazines, located amusing photographs of individuals posed together, and drew dialogue balloons coming from the mouths of those pictured. Then the four friends each chose a separate balloon, secretly wrote imagined comments in it, and read aloud the resulting, often hilarious conversations. In addition to game playing, there were evenings spent listening to George Burns and Gracie Allen or to Guy Lombardo on the radio, or going to the movies to see Katharine Hepburn, Charles Laughton, Fred Astaire, Ed Wynn, the Marx brothers. A particular pleasure was attending concerts by African American artists: In October 1934 Eudora joined Hubert Creekmore and Margaret Harmon for a concert by Mamie Smith, a nationally prominent blues and jazz recording artist, at the Alamo Theatre in Jackson's black business district. The only white people present, they sat in the balcony and relished the event.

Eudora's most important times, of course, were spent in solitude as she wrote. In her upstairs bedroom at the Pinehurst Street house, when she had no eight-to-five job, she established a pattern that would typify her writing career, devoting most mornings and early afternoons to composing, taking time off for reading and gardening, perhaps, but often not changing from her nightgown until she had reached a stopping point in a story. She had positioned her typing table so that she did not directly face the windows overlooking the large front yard, but so that she might look over her shoulder when she needed a glimpse of the outside world. From the first she typed drafts of her stories—she would give up her manual typewriter only when, many years later, arthritis in her hands made first an electric machine and then longhand composition necessary. In her early writing years, Eudora produced stories rather quickly and devoted little time to revision. Drawing upon bits of conversations she had heard, gestures she had observed or photographed, notes she had jotted down on the back of an envelope or on whatever scrap of paper came to hand, she happily, excitedly, and intensely wrote. By the time she was at work on *Delta Wedding* in 1945, Eudora had become an ardent revisor, using a method she would ever afterward follow—typing a draft chapter, spreading it out on the bed, or on the dining room table downstairs, cutting paragraphs, or even sentences, out of a page and attaching them with straight pins in new locations, before preparing a new typescript and starting the process again. But in the 1930s, with the audacity of youth, Eudora had not discovered the need for elaborate revisions. As she wrote, she was filled with exhilaration, beginning to realize more and more fully the power of her imagination to transform the actual into a new and very different reality. She was embracing the writer's double vision, the ability to see "two pictures at once in his frame, his and the world's," and was also honing her ability "to make the reader see only one of the pictures—the author's—under the pleasing illusion that it is the world's."[10]

By 1935 Eudora felt that she might be writing something worthy of her ambitions. She told Lyell that "having nothing else to do all day I read The Golden Bough, the Decline of the West, and all kinds of folk tales and fairy tales and take notes. Not that I'll ever have any practical use for them—but it has always been a pleasant sensation to feel any kind of knowledge mounting up. Have also written some stories and poetry which are much better than I ever thought I'd do."[11] Her reading, of course, did have a very practical use; it was crucial in stoking Eudora's imagination and inspiring her writing. In the early thirties, she read a wide range of fiction: Thomas Mann's novels, Gustave Flaubert's *Salammbô*, and Thames Williamson's *The Woods Colt, A Novel of the Ozark Hills,* for example. She also found her imagination sparked by Sir Arthur Eddington's *The Nature of the Physical World,* a treatise on the philosophic import of modern science.

Solitary time spent reading as well as writing was clearly essential to Eudora's happiness, but her productive use of that time did not keep her from missing bright lights and big cities. Visits to New Orleans provided essential compensation for her absence from Manhattan. One such visit in February of 1935, with her Wisconsin classmate Migs Schermerhorn, was particularly noteworthy for its high spirits, for their decision to pick up two flirtatious men who proved to be flat broke, and for what Eudora called a "peculiar experience in the Monteleone after changing to cheaper room with privilege of using ladies room down hall." As she reported to Frank Lyell, "A team with a coach lived next door and when we would take a bath they would look over the partition and comment. We reported them in huffy manner and house dick was sent up to sit down hall with grey fedora over knee and black cigar, nodding to us every trip. But team got in and wrote on one door Ladies and on the other Gents and on bath Both Sex. We fetched house dick who clutched towel and rubbed it off blushing like fire." But however much fun such trips were, they did not provide enough variety for Eudora. In March she set out for New York, planning to look for a job. No job materialized, but while she was in the city, Eudora took many photographs with her new Recomar plate camera. Some of them present the beautiful patterns of light and dark that play about stairways to the city's elevated trains; others depict rather ordinary looking people who during conventional business hours sit on Union Square park benches or gather for protests because they have no jobs to occupy their days and provide them with purpose and sustenance. The plight of unemployed New Yorkers would eventually be the subject of Eudora's story "Flowers for Marjorie," but not for more than a year. Back in Jackson before month's end, Eudora was again discontent, and by the summer of 1935, she told Frank Lyell that she was "sick of Jackson."[12] Eager to see new territory, she planned a bus trip to Charleston, South Carolina, and then on to North Carolina to visit transplanted Jacksonian Emily White (née Stevens) and her husband John Maclachlan. Throughout the late spring and early summer, Eudora had diligently typed chapters of Lyell's Princeton thesis, which he sporadically posted to her, but a vacation in the Carolinas took precedence over typing his final, much delayed, installment. Her need for change was that strong.

Periodic escapes from home, however, were not the sort of change that Eudora most needed; recognition and self-confidence were, and they arrived in 1936. Sometime early that year, Eudora went to New York in hopes of selling her photographs. A spontaneous decision to stop by the galleries of Lugene Opticians, Inc., proved fortuitous. Samuel Robbins was impressed by her pictures and offered Eudora a one-woman show. In March Eudora's success was doubled. Editor John Rood enthusiastically accepted the two stories she had submitted to *Manuscript* magazine: "Without any hesitation," he wrote, "we can say that DEATH OF A TRAVELING SALESMAN is one of the best stories that has come to our attention—and one of the best stories we have ever read. It is superbly done. And MAGIC is only slightly short of it in quality." The exhibition at Lugene Galleries ran from March 31 to April 15. Then, in May, "Death of a Traveling Salesman" was published. For Eudora, merely having this story accepted had been thrilling: "That was a great day in my life because for the first time something was being looked at critically. This was from afar, an objective point of view, and they liked it and were going to print it. I didn't care a hoot that they couldn't, they didn't pay me anything. If they had paid me a million dollars it wouldn't have made any difference. I wanted acceptance and publication." Her desire had been realized in the form of a story about R. J. Bowman, an unmarried salesman who has just recovered from a long bout with influenza. He becomes lost in sparsely settled, rural Mississippi, drives absentmindedly to the literal end of a road, abandons the car just before it plunges over a precipice, and takes refuge with a farm couple. To him, these people seem to hold "some ancient promise of food and warmth and light," but he later realizes that they represent only "a marriage, a fruitful marriage." "That simple thing," he thinks. "Anyone could have had that." The family, as it had been in "The Children" and in "Acrobats in a Park," was Eudora's subject, but this time she had written about the sort of Mississippians she knew well, had created a complex protagonist who flees even as he seeks human connection, and had used both plot and setting to develop her character's spiritual dislocation. Eudora was proud of the story and bristled a bit when Frank Lyell ventured to be slightly critical of the way she had presented Bowman. "I agree that more facts in the gent's past would have lent clearer perspective and pointed the present more," she told Frank. "But I did have all sympathy with him. Perhaps I took him for granted. It's funny how people do, a publisher (at Covici-Friede) wrote me how sympathetically and vividly I made the same character! (Also asked me for a novel, but you know I ain't got one.)" Like Frank, Robert Daniel expressed a minor reservation about the story: "Am I permitted to offer a critique? I liked it much because of the feeling of discomfort which the salesman had in the presence of Domestic Ties, no matter how squalid the surroundings. That was well put across—and I trust it was what you intended. The only thing adverse I can say is that you overdid the similes somewhat. One or two were almost incomprehensible, and there were so many that it was tiring. You could remedy it with a twist of the wrist by converting some of them into metaphors . . . Do you find my remarks quite, quite valueless? I suppose so." Hubert Creekmore did not share such compunctions about "Death of a Traveling Salesman." As Lehman Engel told Eudora, "I saw Hubert yesterday and he tells me it is very swell indeed and he also told me about the letters from the publishers which only bears out what I have been murmuring on the beaches of Livingston [Lake in Jackson] for the last several summers; now see that you get to work."[13]

Eudora continued to pursue both photography and fiction as the year advanced. In June "The Doll," a contrived story about an engaged couple discovering their essential separateness, appeared in a Grinnell College magazine called *The Tanager*; in July she applied for a position at the Resettlement Administration, a New Deal program that employed photographers to document living and working conditions in America, only to be rejected at month's end; in the fall she saw "Magic," a sexual initiation story set in a Jackson cemetery, printed by *Manuscript*. In October she sent four stories to *Literary America*, which in due course rejected them all— "Flowers for Marjorie" and "Petrified Man" would eventually be published elsewhere, but "Responsibility"and "Shape in Air" would not find their way into print and seem not to be extant. Then, in November, very encouraging word arrived: Samuel Robbins wrote to confirm that his new business, The Camera House, would mount an exhibition of Eudora's photographs in the coming year and to say that Eudora should be able to "make better photographs than ever" with the Rolleiflex camera she had recently purchased.[14]

The excitement accompanying Eudora's literary and photographic efforts notwithstanding, her creative work brought no income. Eudora applied to the Works Progress Administration for a position, and in the summer of 1936 she was hired by this relief agency, which sought to provide jobs for the unemployed. Working as a junior publicity agent, Eudora began to see Mississippi in new ways. "I was so ignorant to begin with about my native state," she later recalled. "I was in my early twenties. I had gone to MSCW for two years, and that should have taught me, because I met girls from all over the state. But I didn't really get an idea of the diversity and all the different regions of the state, or of the great poverty of the state, until I traveled and until I had talked to people. I don't mean schoolgirls like myself that were at college with me, but *people*, you know, in the street."[15] Eudora's WPA duties were far less interesting than the terrain and people she observed. To Frank Lyell, she complained, "There are seven working here doing the job of ½. I write publicity, get it, paste it in books, retype it for files, retype it for mimeographs to the state dailies, retype it for the weeklies, and finally eat it. Last week 200 women came to town for a conference of WPA women and they all contacted me for various things like photographing a trailer from Tupelo, making bus reservations, driving a tour through the city, etc. You know how even one bridge-table of middle aged females can enervate me. Multiply the exhaustion by 50 and you get a high temperature and bad dreams. Last night I dreamed Jack Benny was put in charge of this office. It ran along about the same." And a month later, she urged Frank, "Let me know when you expect to come to Jackson so I can plan not to be in Noxapater photographing a cold storage plant." Whatever the job's frustrations, the WPA sparked at least one piece of fiction. During her travels for the agency, she heard "about a little Negro man in a carnival who was made to eat live chickens," and she came to understand more deeply the grotesque nature of racism. The little man who had been so cruelly treated became the title character of "Keela, the Outcast Indian Maiden." Though her WPA photographic responsibilities tended to be uninspiring, Eudora used her off-duty hours to photograph black and white Mississippians she had met in the course of her job assignments, recording their resilience in the face of extreme poverty. In the process, she learned that "trouble, even to the point of disaster, has its pale" and that "joy the same as courage" can endure great suffering.[16] What Eudora the photographer recorded on film, Eudora the writer recorded in memory. She did not, as she later told interviewers, consult her photographs when writing, but the memories of those photographic occasions stood her in good stead and would frequently appear in her fiction. Unfortunately, Eudora's time at the WPA was short-lived; she received a termination notice in November when the national office chose to close its Mississippi branch.

After 1936 Eudora Welty was a different person—more confident, surer of the direction her life would take. Her family and friends had provided an environment in which her imagination could flourish, could transcend convention and conventional beliefs, and could take its own course. Her sojourns in New York had widened her vision of experience and given her a new perspective of home. The Mississippi world in which she lived, and a job that took her out into it, had provided her with better and better material for stories. And the time spent at her typewriter had honed her craftsmanship.

January of 1937 began, however, with frustration. "Petrified Man," which had been submitted unsuccessfully to *Literary America*, also came back from the *Southern Review*. Robert Penn Warren had reservations about the structure of this comic story set in a small-town beauty parlor, and Eudora now felt it was doomed. She burned it in the kitchen woodstove at home. Her photography was languishing, as well—*Life* magazine returned her "valentine collection," though it wanted time to further consider her "tombstone prints" and expressed interest in her "Negro Holiness Church story." These frustrations, happily, did not long continue. Warren wrote Eudora to regret his decision about "Petrified Man," many of Eudora's prints went on exhibition at the Camera House (March 6–31), *River* magazine published the story "Retreat," and in May the *Southern Review* accepted "A Piece of News." Though "Retreat" was rather unconvincing in its portrait of a clinically depressed escaped convict who returns to Vicksburg, Mississippi, and his mother, "A Piece of News" was a triumph. In this story, Mississippian Ruby Fisher, hale, hearty, and unwounded, reads in a newspaper that "Mrs. Ruby Fisher had the misfortune to be shot in the leg by her husband this week" and fails to realize that the paper has been brought from Tennessee by a traveling salesman and that the newspaper's Ruby Fisher merely shares her name. Instead she thinks, "That's me," and becomes angry with her husband. Though she soon realizes that "it was unlike Clyde to take up a gun and shoot her," she pushes that knowledge from her mind and goes on to imagine her own death: "She lay silently for a moment, composing her face into a look which would be beautiful, desirable, and dead."[17] The scene is more than merely comic. Because of the written word, this simpleminded character, living a routine and barren existence, senses that something dramatic can happen even to her. The power of the imagination, the power that was Eudora's lifeblood, had become the subject of a story.

The power of Eudora's imagination and her subversive sense of fun were also evident when she, Frank Lyell, and Robert Daniel compiled their own anthology of parodies, complete with pseudonyms and fake biographies of the authors. They chose the title suggested by Daniel, "Lilies That Fester," playing on the line from Shakespeare's ninety-fourth sonnet: "Lilies that fester smell far worse than weeds." Their poems were all festerings of, or take-offs on, poems that they identified as lilies. Eudora's talent for parody here proved keen, and it came in handy elsewhere. In previous years she had worked backstage at Jackson's Little Theatre, as had Hubert Creekmore, and like Hubert, though less successfully, she had even submitted a script for consideration. Now she took to the boards, playing the comic role of a housekeeper in a June 3–4 production of *Gold in the Hills,* a melodrama in which rural innocents encounter evil in the New York Bowery of the 1890s.

In 1937 Eudora's camaraderie with bright young men continued to be as strong as ever, but it took a different direction when she became better acquainted with John F. Robinson, whom she had known since their days at Jackson High School. He was now a man so handsome that one of Eudora's New York friends would call him an "Adonis." Tall, slender, and rather debonair, Robinson was working as an insurance adjuster out of New Orleans, but he was often home for visits and often called upon Eudora. At age twenty-eight, Eudora perhaps felt ready for "a marriage, a fruitful marriage," such as the one that had taken on a mystical dimension for the forlorn bachelor protagonist in "Death of a Traveling Salesman." Certainly, by the time Robinson was serving in World War II, Eudora's letters show that she was deeply in love with him, and she may well have been in love as early as 1937. On July 4 of that year, in the face of opposition from her mother, she joined Robinson, his sister Anna Belle and brother Will, on a car trip to Mexico. Chestina opposed not the unconventional travel arrangements, but the danger of a journey over primitive roads to a foreign country. Still Eudora issued her own minor declaration of independence, and the first day of the journey boded well. The four Jacksonians began with "a mighty breakfast," then, "a long long time" later shared a watermelon on three beaches, lunched "where people going by talked in French," and, late in the evening, "met a boy [who] was selling ice cream while we waited for the ferry." In Mexico they saw beautiful villages and they met fellow southerners, most notably North Carolinian Vincent Rousseau, an engaging college student from Charlotte who for many years would correspond with Eudora. Eudora took photographs at every opportunity. Writing from Mexico, she told Robert Daniel, "This is the best trip in the world, bar none."[18] Not all of the Jacksonians' experiences, however, were idyllic. On their return journey, an Indian child dashed out in front of their car; they stopped to assist the child, who had been struck, and were then detained by the local police. The scenario had evidently been staged for the purposes of extortion. Eudora phoned her mother for the funds needed to assuage the authorities, officials at an American consulate advised immediate departure, and the four left Mexico posthaste.

Safely at home, Eudora saw "Flowers for Marjorie" and "Lily Daw and the Three Ladies" published respectively in the summer and winter issues of *Prairie Schooner.* "A Memory," the story of an artistic young girl who finds that the world cannot be as carefully framed or as decorous as she would like, appeared in the autumn *Southern Review.* Eudora had published five stories in a single year, and the year's accomplishments extended beyond fiction. In November *Life* magazine asked her to provide photographs for an article describing a tragedy in Mount Olive, Mississippi. A doctor in the small town had, in treating bacterial infections, prescribed the drug sulfanilamide in its new liquid form only to discover that the drug in this form was deadly. Six of his patients died in spite of his courageous efforts to warn them. Elsewhere in the country the drug took thirty-five more lives. Eudora and Seta Alexander drove to Mount Olive, where a man with the unlikely name of Coot Chain showed them the town. Eudora provided *Life* with six photographs and urged the magazine not to vilify the doctor who, she felt, was himself a victim.

The year 1938 began with personal pleasures and professional triumphs. Eudora seems to have attended Benny Goodman's historic January 16 concert in New York's Carnegie Hall—at least she sent Frank a program from the concert. As she returned home from New York, she visited Frank in Raleigh, where he was teaching at North Carolina State, and then back in Jackson, she saw John Robinson, whose work brought him in and out of town. The couple spent two late January evenings together, once waking their friends Joe and Mary Frances Skinner at 1:00 A.M., delivering congratulations on a bridge tournament victory, and touring the Skinners' new house. During this same month, "Lily Daw and the Three Ladies" had been selected to be in *The Best American Short Stories 1938,* and in February the *Southern Review* accepted "Old Mr. Grenada," the story of a man leading a double life, shuttling back and forth between his aristocratic and lower-middle-class families. Eventually this satire of social class would be retitled "Mr. Marblehall" and be set in Natchez, Mississippi.

In March Robert Penn Warren encouraged Eudora to apply for a Houghton Mifflin Fellowship and promised that he, Cleanth Brooks, and Katherine Anne Porter would support her application. He also asked to see "Petrified Man" again. Eudora, who a year ago had burned her only copy, was slow to respond to this request. She did, however, work on a novella and submit it to Robert N. Linscott at Houghton Mifflin. The work is strange indeed: It centers upon a female artist who has rented a tenant-farming house in the rural Mississippi woods; onto this plot, Eudora attempted to graft characters drawn from "A Piece of News" and "Lily Daw," along with material she would eventually publish in "The Key."[19] Not surprisingly, as Linscott noted, the novella's architecture was weak, and Eudora failed to win the prize. But she had won Linscott's attention and interest.

Eudora was in flow. Everything she undertook or experienced seemed to enrich her writing. In the early spring of 1938, Eudora had driven to Utica, Mississippi, to visit her friend Dorothy Simmons. Spending the night in the Simmonses' fine home, Eudora was awakened by the sound of a shrill whistle echoing through the town. Rushing out into the hall, she encountered Dorothy, who told her not to be alarmed. The whistle merely signaled a freeze, and the local tenant farmers would now cover their plants. The next morning Eudora looked out over fields covered with sheets and quilts, with clothes and bedclothes. A new insight into the meaning of poverty was hers, and her story "The Whistle" was the result. In August *Prairie Schooner* accepted the story of Jason and Sara Morton and their desperate but ineffectual efforts to protect their crop and themselves from the cold. In September Warren again asked to see "Petrified Man," and this time Eudora sought to resurrect the story she had burned in

January 1937. Relying solely on memory of the earlier version, she typed another "Petrified Man." This hilarious tale depicts a small-town southern beauty parlor as a sort of torture chamber in which women, who are being tormented into "beauty," brag about their power over men. The story would appear in the *Southern Review* in the spring of 1939 and would become one of Eudora's most anthologized pieces.

Since 1931 Eudora had attempted to help her mother cope with the loss of her husband, and in 1938 she finally felt able to translate her mother's sense of loss into fiction and to transform her mother's garden into an evocative symbol. After Chris's death, Chestina Welty had discovered solace in gardening. With Eudora as her interested and committed "yard man," she spent long hours, year after year, planting, weeding, and shaping a garden, which was "satisfying, though never perfect." In fact, the garden was satisfying to Chessie *because* it was never perfect, because it was alive and evolving. Perhaps as a result, it brought her a sense of harmony not to be experienced elsewhere. As she noted in "The Perfect Garden," a small (and never published) essay, "The loved garden . . . flaunts its colors joyously when we are glad, its peace and fragrance are soothing to frayed nerves when we are weary from contact or perhaps conflict with the everyday world, and its recurrent beauty whispers a message of comfort and hope when our hearts are lonely or sorrowful." Bringing such a haven into existence was an artistic endeavor, and Chestina took pleasure in that thought. "Creating a garden," she observed, "is much like painting a picture or writing a poem, and artists and poets often make lovely gardens. But sometimes we less articulate folks, who can neither paint pictures nor write poems, yet feel the need of expressing ourselves, find a garden a very happy medium." What might be seen as a conventional domestic activity was far more for Chestina. Her work in the garden was not unlike her daughter's work in fiction.[20]

In "A Curtain of Green," Eudora looked more deeply and

more ominously at the link between gardening and fiction. This story's gardener, like the writer, confronts the dark irrationality of human experience and attempts to deal with that irrationality. Mrs. Larkin has seen her husband killed by a falling chinaberry tree and has realized that her love could not protect him. In the depths of her grief, she then ventures deeper and deeper into gardening, becoming "over-vigorous, disreputable, and heedless" in the eyes of her neighbors. Mrs. Larkin seeks not Chestina's "well designed [garden] plot," but seeks "to allow an over-flowering"; in the process, she finds that the garden provides not solace but immersion in a hostile force. She finds herself on the brink of killing Jamey, the young black man who, as he works in the garden with her, seems to be caught up in "a teasing, innocent, flickering and beautiful vision." She seeks to penetrate and participate in the mystery of nature, which has killed her husband and destroyed both her faith in the power of love and her ability to partake of visions like Jamey's. But at day's end, she drops the hoe she had contemplated using as a weapon, and she finds release in the afternoon rain and in the garden's "quiet arcade of identity." Momentarily, at least, she accepts both nature's mystery and its beauty. Surely, Mrs. Larkin's isolation from her community, her grief, her venturing into the garden, and her discovery of some consolation there draw in oblique ways upon Chestina's own experience. Mrs. Larkin's love, which like Chestina's seeks to but cannot protect her beloved, sprang in part from a key source of tension between Eudora and her mother—their efforts to protect each other— but the story ultimately seems to find its roots in the depth of Chessie's love for her husband, in her abiding grief at his loss (a grief that loomed over a concerned daughter), in her intellectual and creative toughness, and in her refusal to retreat into a mindlessly conventional consolation.[21]

When she had finished the story, Eudora sent "A Curtain of Green" to the *Southern Review*, which quickly published it. Both "Petrified Man" and "A Curtain of Green" would subsequently be honored—"Petrified Man" in the *O. Henry Memorial Award Prize Stories of 1939* and "A Curtain of Green" in *The Best American Short Stories 1939*. Still in circulation were "Keela, the Outcast Indian Maiden" and "Why I Live at the P.O.," both rejected by *Story* magazine and both destined to become classics of the short-story genre. Eudora had hit her stride. All of her early publications reveal just how far beyond her sheltered childhood Eudora had traveled and how accomplished a writer she had become. She was not, as Reynolds Price astutely comments, "the mild, sonorous, 'affirmative' kind of artist whom America loves to clasp to its bosom," but was instead a writer with "a granite core in every tale: as complete and unassailable an image of human relations as any in our art, tragic of necessity but also comic." Certainly that description fits "Lily Daw and the Three Ladies." The story is funny, very funny, but it is tragic as well. The story's three ladies have protected the retarded Lily Daw from an abusive father and provided her with housing, but they also rule her life. Though the town band plays the "Independence March" at the story's close, Lily has no freedom, and her hope chest, a gift from the three ladies, leaves on a train from which Lily has been snatched. She and a xylophone player, who may or may not have seduced her, are soon to be victims of social proprieties and a shotgun wedding. "The Whistle" has a similar granite core, depicting the despair that poverty can inflict. In this story, tenant farmers Jason and Sara Morton have battled the natural elements for so long and to such little effect that they are exhausted and incommunicative, going days, even weeks, without speaking. In the face of freezing weather, Jason and Sara, year after year, rise in the night to cover their plants, using even the clothes off their backs. Then one night, after they retreat into their cabin, Jason burns their last log and then their few bits of furniture in an effort to provide momentary warmth. But however short-lived the effect, "the fire the kitchen table had made seemed wonderful to them—as if what they had never said, and what could not be, had its life, too, after all." Their common past, their desperate present, do not bind Jason and Sara together, but the fire helps them jointly to imagine the relationship they have missed, a relationship that momentarily seems to live, but that will not endure. In "Keela, the Outcast Indian Maiden," the destructive power of racism as it affects both blacks and whites is portrayed in an equally unflinching manner. The story describes a crippled black man who was once kidnapped into carnival work as a geek called Keela, the Outcast Indian Maiden, and further deals with a carnival barker named Steve, who recognizes that by acquiescing to this evil, he has become part of it. In these and her other early stories, Eudora created a fictional world that denied readers any comforting formulas and instead offered visions of human vulnerability and cosmic mystery. Though she had not reached her thirtieth birthday, she had established herself as a powerful writer, and writing about life's terrors, transforming them into works of art, was paradoxically a source of contentment, even joy. As she later wrote to John Robinson, "When a story is going on, then you feel things highly and even more than you knew you might, and they reveal themselves to you in a way that gives some pain too, but in the work something is resolved, and let go."[22]

Eudora's tremendous productivity in 1937 and 1938 led to her first major literary connection. On October 25, 1938, Katherine Anne Porter wrote to Eudora: "Ford Madox Ford has been given control of the fiction department of the Dial Press, and asked me to help him look about for Candidates for publication. I thought of you first, with your admirable short stories. It seems to me that if you have no other plans, and have a book length collection of stories, it would be an excellent idea to write to Ford, giving him some notion of your manuscript. He will then no doubt ask to see it." Porter went on to say she would gladly recommend Eudora for a Guggenheim Fellowship, adding, "I take this liberty because of my admiration for your very fine work."[23]

This was recognition of the first order from a master of the short story, and Eudora felt sustained in her choice of a career.

Ford Madox Ford followed Porter's suggestion that he read stories by Eudora, and he did indeed like them. On January 7, 1939, he wrote to tell Eudora that he would be delighted to recommend a book of her stories to publishers, and on January 19, he asked her to send a copy of her stories to Stanley Unwin in London. For his part, Ford promised to try to place the stories with a New York publishing house. Neither of these efforts on Eudora's behalf would be successful—no one wanted short stories; everyone wanted a novel.

Eudora continued to write short stories nevertheless. On August 11, 1939, the *Southern Review* accepted "The Hitch-Hikers." Drawing upon trips she had made with John Robinson across the Mississippi Delta in the two years since their return from Mexico, Eudora had created a new version of the traveling salesman depicted in her first published story. This purveyor of office supplies seems remarkably like John Robinson, who traveled not as a commercial agent but as an insurance adjuster. Attractive, intelligent, affable, always welcome in small Delta towns, always avoiding emotional commitments, the character Tom Harris perhaps embodies in some ways Eudora's sense of the man with whom she was probably now in love and suggests why she seems to have been restrained in expressing that love. Late in the story, a young woman named Carol, who remembers Tom from his days playing piano on the Gulf Coast, tells him that she was "crazy about" him then and that she still is.[24] She offers Harris her love, but he merely buys her a cup of coffee and sends her home in a taxi. Unhappy as its autobiographical implications were, this story was one with which Eudora must have been aesthetically pleased. It would be included in *The Best American Short Stories 1940,* but "The Death of Miss Belle," a story that prefigures "Asphodel," would be rejected by the *Southern Review.*

In June 1939 Ford Madox Ford died, and Katherine Anne Porter suggested that her husband, Albert Erskine of the *Southern Review*, might be able to pick up where Ford had left off in his efforts to help Eudora. Eudora, however, felt that publication seemed less important in view of Ford's loss and in the wake of Germany's invasion of Poland. In September she told Porter, "The news about Mr. Ford was so distressing—I keep thinking about it even when everything is swallowed up in the war. . . . All along I'm thinking about a novel. But with everything on an international scale and a world scale, it is hard to think in a small straight line."[25] Though Eudora did not produce a novel, though Erskine did not place her stories, and though a fall 1939 job at the Mississippi Advertising Commission was a bit dreary, there were bright days ahead. In November, Walter Welty married his high school sweetheart, Mittie Creekmore, Hubert's sister. Eudora was a bridesmaid. And that same month, Eudora and her stories attracted the interest of a perceptive New York editor, John Woodburn, who came through Jackson on a talent-scouting expedition for Doubleday, Doran. He phoned Eudora; she picked him up at his hotel and brought him home to meet her mother and have breakfast. There he looked over her stories and asked to take them with him to New York. Not long after Woodburn's visit, Eudora placed "Keela" with *New Directions* and was offered a fellowship at the Bread Loaf Writers' Conference. There were also disappointments: She was informed that she would not receive a Guggenheim, and she met rejection from Harcourt Brace and from Putnam's, both of which wanted a novel, not stories. But the best of luck lay ahead.

On May 28, 1940, Diarmuid Russell wrote to Eudora on behalf of his new literary agency:

> John Woodburn of Doubledays [*sic*] has suggested that I write to you to see if you might need the services of an agent. I suppose you know the parasitic way an agent works

taking 10% of the author's takings. He is rather a benevo-
lent parasite because authors as a rule make more when they
have an agent than they do without one. We ourselves are
quite new but we have the good wishes of many of the publishers who have offered to send to us all their authors without agents. Their feeling is that there are few good agents in
New York and that these few are too large to be able to extend any editorial assistance; we hope to be able to do this.

I myself have been in literature for a long time being
the son of an Irish Author (A.E.). I have been sub-editor on
journals, worked in book stores and for a couple of years
was editor in a New York publishing house.

If you should need the services of an agent we would
be glad to help. If you are ever in New York I hope you will
call to see us.

Eudora was quick to respond, "Yes—be my agent," and on June
3, Russell cautioned her about such precipitous actions: "Such
promptness is not to be expected in this world. When one hangs
out a shingle one has to sit down and wait—that is the tradition
and business shouldn't come rushing to one. How do you know
that we are honest or competent? We think we are but we never
expected to be taken at our own word. I must say it gives us a
warm feeling." Russell himself was quick to act on his warm feelings. He expressed reservations about "Clytie" and an unfinished
story set in Rodney's Landing;[26] he praised both "The Key," the
portrait of a deaf couple who hope that a visit to Niagara Falls
will bring them closer together, and "Powerhouse," the recently
composed story of a black jazz musician performing in the segregated South; and he further agreed to market a short-story collection rather than insisting that Eudora write a novel.

In August, on her way to Bread Loaf, Eudora stopped in New
York to meet Russell and his colleagues. John Slocum of the
agency took Eudora out for a night on the town, and she spent

the weekend with Russell and his wife at their Westchester County home, where she introduced Russell to a legendary history of Mississippi, Robert Coates's *The Outlaw Years.* Author and agent discovered that they shared an interest not only in folklore but in gardening as well and that they were both avid readers of murder mysteries. They also had an intuitive, and, as it turned out, well-placed faith in the other's integrity. The affinity between them was strong. Eudora wrote Frank Lyell that "Diarmuid Russell is a wonderful Irishman indeed." On her way home from Bread Loaf, Eudora again saw Russell. The two visits were the beginning of one of the closest friendships of Eudora's life. The time between the two visits, however, proved less than satisfactory.

Eudora was discontent at Bread Loaf. Though the location was beautiful, she found the conference itself a bit strange: "rare, literary, talky when you wish it were quiet." To Frank she noted, "A lot of old ladies are here, they change hats for every meal," and she commented on the presence of Carson McCullers, "who is an odd little 22-year-old with long hair, bangs, cigarette cough, boy's clothes, & a new pal of Louis Untermeyer the *wit.*" During the course of her Bread Loaf tenure, Eudora's distaste for Mc-Cullers intensified. More congenial was Edna Frederikson, who had yet to publish but in whom Eudora saw promise. Eudora also liked Kentucky poet James Still, and she especially enjoyed Katherine Anne Porter's visit to the conference; that visit gave Eudora a chance to become better acquainted with her champion, whom she had met only once before. Porter's support notwithstanding, Eudora's story "Powerhouse" was unsympathetically received at Bread Loaf. Sometime before coming to the conference, she had shown Diarmuid Russell this innovative story based on a Fats Waller concert she and Seta Alexander had heard on May 8 in Jackson's city auditorium. At intermission, the two friends had left their seats in order to stand by the edge of the stage for the second set. Eudora had gone home that night and immediately transformed her impressions of Waller into fiction. The story's point of view, as Eudora later noted, "is floating around some-where in the concert hall—it belongs to the 'we' of the audi-ence." The white audience dismisses the character Powerhouse as one of *"them*—Negroes—band leaders—they would play the same way, giving all they've got, for an audience of one." But for Eu-dora, a writer driven "by the love of her art and the love of giv-ing it, the desire to give it until there is no more left," Powerhouse was a sort of alter ego, an emblem of artistic alienation. Ironi-cally, after Frank mailed a new Fats Waller recording to her at Bread Loaf, she learned that her transformation of Waller into the fictional Powerhouse had baffled the conference participants. It was the last straw. She left the conference without regret. She and Edna Frederikson dropped Carson McCullers off at the Boston railway station, happy to see the last of her, and then drove to Yaddo, the famous artists' colony near Saratoga Springs, New York, where they visited Katherine Anne Porter and James Still, staying out until "3 or 4 in the morning when we quit our observations of the race track peoples in one of the bars. Amaz-ing sights. We thought Yaddo itself was pretty scarey."[27]

Back in Jackson, Eudora was eager to resume writing. Dissat-isfied with the Bread Loaf artsy atmosphere, she turned to the unpretentiously complex world of Mississippi. She had encour-aged Russell to read Coates's *Outlaw Years,* and now she began to think of writing fiction drawing upon Coates and the Natchez Trace. She soon wrote to Russell about the possibilities of a "Mississippi book."

> There are some things about a state that nobody could even know about who has not lived there a long time, and those things should determine the whole approach, don't you think? . . . and I believe I could find stories, old ones & new ones, and beliefs and songs and violent events all over the place to show what the life here is, to my belief. . . . Think of all the people who would be in my book—wonderful

Indians to start with, and the Indian tales are beautiful and dramatic and very touching some of them—and Aaron Burr & Blennerhassett, and Lafayette, and Audubon, and Jefferson Davis, and the bandits (you keep "The Outlaw Years," there is one around Jackson), and Lafitte the pirate, and all kinds of remarkable people.

When the first of these tales, *The Robber Bridegroom*, was complete, Eudora sent it to Russell, who replied that "The mad blending of bandits, Indians, the rich planter, the beautiful daughter is wonderful. It is as if you had spent many dreamy afternoons meditating on the romantic history of the South and on the fairy and folk tales of your youth." But Russell worried that such a story might not sell: "Publishers, as a rule, are conservative, and anything that seems out of the way fills them with deep suspicion. They are as cautious as kittens approaching an unknown object. At the moment the general war hysteria has made them even more cautious; they seem dubious of everything that does not seem too familiar and shrink with panic from the original." Russell nevertheless wrote Woodburn about his suggestion that Eudora string "a series of stories on the necklace of the Natchez Trace." Woodburn agreed that the idea was a good one. Having read *The Robber Bridegroom*, he wrote Eudora to endorse the idea of "an entire book of Mississippi stories."[28]

That fall Russell was frustrated by his inability to place Eudora's completed stories at any of the major national magazines—such placement, he felt, was crucial if he were to convince a publisher to accept a book of Welty stories. Eudora surely shared Russell's frustration, but she never doubted him, and she never stopped writing. By October Eudora had a new Natchez Trace story, "A Worn Path," which depicts the courage of an old African American woman who periodically makes a long journey on foot, braving hostility and condescension, in order to obtain medicine for her grandson. She subsequently wrote to tell Russell how much his responses had come to mean to her work.

> I am one of those who believe that to communicate is the hope and purpose and the impulse and the result and the test & value of all that is written and done at all, and if that little spark does not come, and with a little sheltering, flash back & forth, then it's the same as being left confined within ourselves just when we wished most to reach out and touch the surrounding life that seemed so wonderful in some way. You can see that I have been burning to say this. If you keep telling me when what I write is clear and unobscured and when it is not, as it appears to you, then I will have something so new to me and of such value, a way to know a few bearings. Is this what was in our contract? I didn't understand it would be so much.

Because of Diarmuid, Eudora had truly found her bearings. Her stories had captured his imagination, and his responses to them captured her, helping her to refocus or reconceive problematic passages and plots. In early December both "Powerhouse" and "A Worn Path," the latter destined for O. Henry recognition, were accepted by the *Atlantic Monthly*. As 1940 drew to a close, Woodburn indicated that Doubleday would like to bring out a book of Eudora's early stories. When the formal offer for her book of stories arrived in Russell's office, however, the agent deemed it unsatisfactory. Woodburn then convinced his publisher to meet Russell's terms, and a deal was struck on January 21, 1941. Woodburn and Russell both advised Eudora to include "A Worn Path" in her book but to save *The Robber Bridegroom* for separate publication, and Russell further advised Eudora to omit "Acrobats in a Park," which he felt was far weaker than her other work. For her part, Eudora was delighted with the contract and delighted, after some indecision, to accept this advice. She felt Russell had accomplished wonders and lauded Woodburn as well. Russell modestly downplayed his own efforts and agreed that John's role had been crucial, but the most important factor, he insisted to Eudora, was the quality of her stories, which "no one but a nitwit could fail to recognize."[29]

Now under contract, Eudora labored to fine-tune the stories that were to constitute her first book publication while Russell worked diligently to place in periodicals all of the stories to be collected in book form. In January Russell sent "Why I Live at the P.O." to the *Atlantic*, which accepted it. Narrated by the post-mistress of the "next to smallest P.O. in the entire state of Mississippi," this comic masterpiece begins with the postmistress's declaration that her sister has stolen the affections of Mr. Whitaker. "Of course I went with Mr. Whitaker first, when he first appeared here in China Grove, taking 'Pose Yourself' photos, and Stella-Rondo broke us up. Told him I was one sided. Bigger on one side than the other, which is a deliberate, calculated falsehood: I'm the same."[30] In February Diarmuid sent "The Key" to Mary Lou Aswell, the fiction editor at *Harper's Bazaar*, who made this melancholy tale the first of nine Welty stories she would take over the years. In March Russell placed "Clytie," the portrait of a character driven to madness by her isolation, with the *Southern Review*, and "A Visit of Charity," the story of a Camp Fire girl's obligatory visit to a nursing home, with *Decision*. All of the stories in *A Curtain of Green* were now guaranteed both periodical and book publication.

Even as Russell and Eudora worked on *A Curtain of Green*, they turned their attention to new books. In November 1940, when Eudora had written Russell about the possibilities for a "Mississippi book," she asked, "Do you think I dare to have honest-to-God people walking around in the stories? The thing about this part of the country in the great days is that people like Aaron Burr, J. J. Audubon, [the fanatical nineteenth-century evangelist] Lorenzo Dow, and goodness knows who, were as thick as blackbirds in the pie, and once the pie is opened, they are going to begin to sing." In the same letter, despite her question, Eudora reported that "the story on Lorenzo is begun." In January, however, Eudora had sent Russell the draft of a different historical story, one about Aaron Burr and about a character she had invented, a young deaf boy named Joel Mayes. Russell found the story of Burr interesting but thought it needed substantial revision.

> This conception you are trying to work out here is a terribly difficult one. The idea of trying to make a deaf boy give an impression of Burr has an element of subtlety and nobility that I like very much. But what must have impressed Joel were things difficult to make come through in writing—the expression of Burr's face, a sudden noble gesture, an aura of fate and personal magnetism. Henry [Volkening, Russell's partner] was a little baffled by the emphasis on the winter scene but I suspect what you were trying to do was in some manner to link up the unusual winter with Burr, much as the old Romans would link the appearance of a comet with unusual happenings.
>
> But the whole concept, though magnificent, demands tightrope walking, and though you do this sort of writing superbly you sometimes fall off and I think you have taken a tumble here and as in the first "Clytie" there is too much obscurity and the full vision does not come through.

Here Russell expanded his role as an editor of sorts, reacting, defining areas of weakness, suggesting lines for revision, but never intervening in the writing itself. It was exactly the sort of guidance for which Eudora had longed and which she would value throughout her long association with Russell. She agreed with his reservations and addressed his question about her focus on the winter season: "Yes, I was using the extreme winter as a sign in the sky, and for contrast to the fiery meetings, and for the way it drove people to an inner intensity, and for its visual worth as a horizon &

perspective, all the outward coldness. Maybe that was the trouble with the story, everything (for me) carried the burden of being so many things at once. But that trouble, and I hope you will think that I am right, I take as a sign that there is a good story possible, when there seem to be numbers of other stories being written in writing that, when every word that is put down will be carrying along with it all these things that are floating around it."[31] Eudora concluded that she needed distance in time from the story in order to revise it adequately, and she set it aside for five months.

After tabling "First Love," Eudora moved on to other stories, writing "The Purple Hat," a ghost story set in a New Orleans casino, and "Asphodel," the tale of a woman obsessed by the need for power and control. She also wrote "The Winds," a female initiation story based upon her own youthful experience during a Jackson tornado. This latter story both intrigued and baffled Russell, and he advised reducing the number of flashbacks in it. Still he sent the story, along with "The Purple Hat" and "Asphodel," out to the rounds of magazines—all would ultimately win acceptance, and "Asphodel" would be included in *The Best American Short Stories 1943.* In the meantime, John Woodburn suggested that Henry Miller visit Eudora as he toured the United States, under contract to write *The Air-Conditioned Nightmare,* a collection of critical essays about America. By way of introduction, Miller wrote to Eudora and offered to put her in touch with a pornographic publisher who could increase her earning power. Eudora declined, but she welcomed Miller to Jackson. For three days she, Nash Burger, and Hubert Creekmore drove Miller about the countryside and took him out to dinner, but he was not invited to the Welty house. Chestina was offended by his ill-conceived offer to help Eudora enter the world of blue fiction. Miller, however, proved anything but lewd during his visit. He was instead conventional and humorless. And when he expressed surprise that a small town like Jackson would have three good restaurants, Eudora knew he was also unobservant. He had been to only one, the Rotisserie, located at the aptly named Five Points and therefore possessing several entrances.

In March, shortly after Miller left town, Eudora revised and sent Russell an essay she had written in the thirties. Titled "Cindy," it described a late-nineteenth-century African American religious leader in Grenada, Mississippi. Cindy had led a group of people known as Cindy's Band, who believed the end of the world was coming, and who marched through the streets exhorting people to repent and reform. Cindy was not above using deception to win converts: She let it be known that she could walk on water, and indeed she did walk on water, courtesy of a platform built beneath a local lake. Eudora had met two former members of Cindy's Band when she visited the home of Mary Moore Mitchell, her roommate from the Mississippi State College for Women, and she recalled that these African Americans were part of an attempt to gain power and independence in a segregated environment. Russell liked the essay but was unsure where he might be able to place it. Within the month, Eudora sent him another essay written in the 1930s—"A Pageant of Birds" described her visit to a black church pageant where parishioners had made themselves bird costumes and performed in the character of their respective birds. Eudora clearly admired the cleverness of the conception and the effort of the congregation to make money not for a new piano, but for a better one. And in recounting the birds' song, "And I want Two wings / To veil my face / And I want Two wings / To fly away / And I want Two wings / To veil my face / And the world can't do me no harm," she focused on the need for masking and the desire for freedom that African Americans felt in a Jim Crow society.[32] Perhaps as a gesture of protest, she resurrected both essays as Hitler extended his power over Europe while proclaiming and acting upon a racist agenda.

Despite the ominous international scene, March 1941 offered professional and personal promise to Eudora: Katherine Anne Porter informed her that an invitation to Yaddo would be forthcoming. Eudora wrote of her excitement to Russell, who was also delighted. However, when by late April no formal invitation had been sent, Russell wrote "a gentle inquiring letter" to Porter on Eudora's behalf.[33] By early May the invitation was confirmed, and in June Eudora visited Russell on her way to Saratoga Springs.

Yaddo proved an enlarging and happy and awkward experience. Eudora wrote at length about the community in a letter to John Robinson.

> This is a crazy way to live. I don't know how long I'll last, and they keep saying the invitation is to be extended, and extended . . . It's a terrible gloomy mansion with indoor fountains that sound like the worst thing you can imagine, just a little trickle in the hush that envelopes the place, and hundreds of marble cupids and some little gilded Norwegian sleighs, and bishop's chairs, and other bric-a-brac. I just sat there, though—I live out at the farm, which is just big enough for 4 writers. It is a simple unpretentious place—I have the silver and gold room with bamboo trimmings, known to the cleaning woman as the 'the baboo room' and to others as the opium den. The lamp—of the lamp—it is 3 feet high, flesh colored marble, and it is Cupid and a dolphin, meeting. I lie up in bed and turn the lamp on, then off, or just look at it. Then I have a private stairway, which seems sinister somehow, and my studio is a kitchen, complete with mouse trap. On the kitchen table where my typewriter goes is a large gold lamp with lion legs, to light me as I create.

Having described the setting for Robinson, Eudora next described her fellow residents.

> The Armenian was the first one I saw here—he had on a snow white rubber cape which reached to the ground (it was

raining), and oh how beautiful he was, really, flashing eyes, black hair—I thought he might have on tights underneath and would any minute bite a rope and ascend as a living butterfly. He laughs all the time, is in a constant state of exhilaration, I guess because he is an Armenian. His name is Karnag Nalbanion [Karnig Nalbandian] and he etches, and I think I'll send you one of his things. He rushes off and goes fishing, and has a case knife ten inches long, a Ford of the T-model type tied together with clothesline, and a dollar violin and a flute. Then also in our house is Katherine Anne Porter, of whom I am deeply fond as you know, and a composer named Colin McFee [McPhee], who has been in Bali and plays Balinese music and listens to Balinese records and wears Balinese ties—he took off our gate with his car and said, 'It's a boah.' But up at the mansion is—don't look now, but it's Carson McCullers. The little devil, there she is, as horrible as ever, but thank God not in the same house with me or Katherine Anne, who hates her insides. There is the usual set of N.Y. Jews writing novels about the Harlem Negroes, and a little set of refugees, all nice, with intense reading of mail usually going on, and sad little funny stories, and the funniest Spanish sculptor you ever saw. He is quite old, wears [B]oy [S]cout shorts and no one knows what language he really speaks (he has a Dutch name, de Creef [Creeft], Jose)—but always uses the words "mais" and "qui" etc., and none of the French speaking people can understand his French or the Spanish people his Spanish. He speaks in a sort of mixture, and seems to be at his best in broken English. He is obsessed with what is happening to his cat in N.Y., who is undergoing a cesarian operation at the price of $22. "My cat, he have kits" (he hasn't even got sex straight) "and fine big ambulance come, qui take him to hospital, mais they tell me, 'You got $22?' I say, 'Am I a millionaire?'" Then he looks crosseyed, to show you how he stared at them. He says he went to N.O. and brought home some Spanish moss, which he put all around his studio in N.Y. "He live four months!" I told him that it was a parasite and was probably living off the furniture, at which he blanched and the next morning was gone to N.Y. on an errand of emergency—whether it was the kits or the moss I don't know yet.

Eudora found herself largely unable to write at Yaddo. She missed, as she told Russell, "my own easy-going lighthearted people . . . and my garden, and the interruptions, and all that is domestic." But simply being at Yaddo was a formative experience. Her artistic community was becoming national, even international—Armenians, Dutchmen, travelers to Bali, refugees from the war in Europe. The young Mississippian perhaps saw "New York Jews writing about Harlem Negroes" as a project doomed to fail in understanding, but later that summer she attempted to dissuade Katherine Anne from stereotyping Jews of any origin. Shortly after Eudora left Yaddo, Katherine Anne wrote to complain about troubles with her vision and about "A beastly fellow . . . , the very kind of one anti-semites mean when they say Jew." And Katherine Anne added, "To cap all, he is . . . climbing to 'success' with cleated shoes over the faces of any one who gets in his way. It is a sad fact that race produces too many too regularly of his kind. Jews should recognize him as their real enemy, he brings their disasters upon them. I have been suffering an acute attack of Jew-phobia ever since he got in the house." Eudora's return letter gently suggested that Katherine Anne's eye ailment had perhaps distorted more than her physical vision: "When you can see better through the glasses, the Jew-phobia won't be so acute maybe."[34]

During her two months in residence at Yaddo, Eudora never suffered from such "distortions of vision," and she clearly recognized opportunities for good times. She enjoyed the companionship of Nalbandian and de Creeft, with whom she often went to the races in Saratoga Springs. She became better acquainted with Edna Frederikson, whose company she had enjoyed at Bread Loaf. She entertained John Woodburn and Frank Lyell when they visited her. She posed for a portrait José de Creeft made of her. She spent time with Porter, trying to teach Katherine Anne to drive, going with her to view the renovation of South Hill, the nearby farm that Katherine Anne had purchased. And while at Yaddo Eudora did manage to revise "First Love." She came to fear, however, that the story might be seen as sympathetic to fascism and wrote Russell about her fears.

> I'm working on "First Love" but even though it is better now it would not do for you to send out—Do you realize that it might be interpreted as pro-fascist, poor Aaron Burr's unexplained little dream, that I meant to be only a symbol of what everyone has—some marvelous sway and magnetism that it can give— It is stupid and wild, but that is the way people seem to be thinking, everything is dynamite, suspicious. Even KAP, who wants us to enter the war instantly, sees fascism in everything she doesn't like, and while it may be a very intricate insight into deep relationships, I still hate that fever to creep into what we think of books or music, because eventually it will leave nothing to be itself.[35]

Here is the argument that Eudora would make famous in her 1965 essay "Must the Novelist Crusade?" which decries the effect that ideological blinders can have upon readers of fiction. It asks that a work of literature be appreciated for its literary qualities—its language, structure, character development—and it calls for literature to be as complex and ambiguous as the world that it depicts. But even in her letter to Russell, Eudora suggested that there is some merit in ideological or political readings.

Viewed from a political perspective, "First Love" seems not pro-fascist, but antifascist. Seeing the relationship between Burr

and the young deaf and mute Joel Mayes as that between a charismatic leader and a devotee may, in fact, provide what Eudora herself
calls "a very intricate insight into deep relationships" even as it
suggests that this particular relationship is essentially warped.
Joel feels committed to Burr not because Burr has proven himself
to be a worthy guide, but because Burr provides some sense of
direction or purpose for him. Burr, on the other hand, feels nothing for Joel or for any of the people who support him after his
arrest, and Burr's plan is to become an absolute dictator. Joel does
not fully recognize Burr, but we as readers surely do. The story
thus conveys the "magnetism" and the dangerous power fascist
leaders have over needy individuals such as Joel Mayes.[36]

Whatever the import of Eudora's story, Russell was pleased
with it and immediately submitted it to the *Atlantic Monthly*. Russell was not pleased, however, with Katherine Anne's delay in writing a promised introduction to Eudora's first book of stories,
which had now been titled *A Curtain of Green*. Neither was John
Woodburn pleased. But Eudora felt that broaching the subject
with Katherine Anne would be a violation of friendship. Woodburn had no such compunctions and urged Porter to move ahead.
She did, but at her own pace, and Woodburn postponed the publication date from September 5 to November 7.

As Eudora's two months at Yaddo drew to an end, Russell
wrote in a bemused fashion to report that the Junior League had
requested permission to print something by her; he wondered if
she were a member of the League. She sheepishly acknowledged
the fact—her old friends were members of the organization and
the group had exempted Eudora from many duties she might deem
onerous, though she found its social climate alien. She told Russell she would like to accommodate the League and allow them to
publish free of charge an essay she had at home, one previously rejected by the *New Yorker*.[37] Russell obliged, and "Women!! Make
Turban in Own Home" went to the *Junior League Magazine*. Eudora
now looked forward to seeing Russell and talking with him, and

he was similarly eager to see his first and best client. They soon met in New York and at the Russells' Westchester County home, in Katonah, even though a visit from Rosie's mother precluded Eudora's staying there. Instead she spent her nights in nearby Mount Kisco with Eileen McGrath, who along with her sister and brother-in-law, Peggy and David Rockefeller, were friends of the Russells and would become Eudora's friends as well.

Once back in Jackson, Eudora was delighted to be able to work in her garden again. In writing to Russell about the experience, she moved toward a mood and style that would soon enter her fiction.

> Every evening when the sun is going down and it is cool enough to water the garden, and it is all quiet except for the locusts in great waves of sound, and I stand still in one place for a long time putting water on the plants, I feel something new—that is all I can say—as if my will went out of me, as if I had a stubbornness and it was melting. I had not meant to shut out any feeling that wanted to enter. It is a real shock, because I had no idea that there had been in my life any rigidity or refusal of anything so profound, but the sensation is one of letting in for the first time what I believed I had already felt—in fact suffered from—a sensitivity to all that was near or around. But this is different and frightening—no, not really frightening—because for instance when I feel without ceasing every change in the garden itself, the changes of light as the atmosphere grows darker, and the springing up of a wind, and the rhythm of the locusts, and the colors of certain flowers that become very moving— they all seem to be a part of some happiness or unhappiness, an unhappiness that something is lost or left unknown or undone perhaps—and no longer simple in their beautiful but *outward* way. And the identity of the garden itself is lost. This probably sounds confused and I am, but *it* is not.

The intensity is very great, it is too much not to regard seriously, and to try to understand and even be glad for, but I
can't remember it clearly enough to write it down here, although the feeling I could not forget.

To Russell alone could Eudora write such letters. The two shared,
as Russell noted, an Emersonian sense of the mystical union between man and nature, a sense that would emerge some months
later in Eudora's story "A Still Moment." This powerful sense of
oneness with the natural world, however, was disrupted in September 1941 by "great waves of sound" that came not from locusts,
but from military planes. Eudora asked Russell, "Are big bombers
flying all over New York and do they fly low, in under your desk?
They do here, they fly under my bed at night, all those in the
Louisiana maneuvers go over Jackson when they make a curve,
and really one went under the Vicksburg bridge over the Mississippi River the other day, too lazy to clear it. I feel as if my bones
are being ground to pieces but I suppose I will get used to it if I
stay here for Jackson is filled with air bases, air schools, air fields,
and barracks and tents, a changed little place, loud and crazy."[38]
Despite her preoccupation with the garden and the distraction of low-flying bombers, Eudora quickly finished "The Wide
Net," inspired by anecdotes John Robinson had told her. She
dedicated it to him, a mark, perhaps, of their growing closer to
commitment. Russell then sent the story on its round of magazines. Eudora also completed her application for a Guggenheim
Fellowship and told Russell that Herschel Brickell, Cleanth
Brooks, and Katherine Anne Porter had agreed to recommend
her. Her devouring of fiction by others continued apace; she
reread To the Lighthouse, read several novels by M. P. Shiel that Russell had recommended, and again read The Candle of Vision, by A.E.,
Russell's father. As a Wisconsin student, she had first experienced
the power of A.E.'s work, and now as Diarmuid Russell's close
friend, she relished reading it once more—renewing her acquain-

tance with A.E.'s mysticism would henceforth strengthen a note of mystery in her stories.

At home she was also glad to be reunited with old friends. Seta Alexander and her fiancé, Tom Sancton, a writer Russell was interested in signing as a client, visited one weekend early in September, and Robinson came to Jackson the next weekend. In dry Mississippi, as Eudora told Frank Lyell, these visits were a boon to the local bootleggers, who were located along the Pearl River and close to the town of Pocahontas: "We have sat around on various porches drinking beer, etc. John Robinson was up last weekend and we did the same with Old something (Taylor?) which has gone up to the sky out on the Pocahontas road—Mister Beasle's has *been* closed, didn't you-all know? I had been tired of swallowing things from Yaddo and hadn't done a bit of it since."[39]

The porch parties at home soon gave way to a series of parties in New York. Publication day for *A Curtain of Green* was November 7, and Eudora enjoyed her publication party and the subsequent activities during her time in New York. She waxed eloquent in a letter to Frank.

> The New York trip was swell, and the party was a nice one, at the Murray Hill Hotel, I was surrounded by a little cordon of friends so the rest did not scare me. Lehman came, de Creeft, Nalbandian, Dolly, and of course John, Diarmuid and Henry [Volkening]. The only glamorous (I protect myself with a *sic*) personage there was Viki Baum, who looked like Grand Hotel with a lot of velvet makeup, tasselled eyelashes, and plush bosom. Everybody just sat around or stood around and talked and there was a bar in another room and two soldiers came, thinking it was one of those hospitality stations, and went with us all evening, if I remember even to the Village to eat. We went to Café Society afterwards, a few of us, so the party lasted into the morning. The next day I went to Henry's for dinner and

then home with Diarmuid for the weekend. The Aswells
(she of H. Bazaar, he of Harper's) were at Henry's, also
Joseph Kesselring and Peter Monro Jack (that I always
thought was 3 people trying desperately hard to make a living
by reviewing every book published, but he is a little tiny ar-
gumentative Scotsman) and their wives. Mrs. Aswell wore a
leopard jacket (real) and a leopard top to her evening gown
(unreal) and was gay and invited me to lunch and couldn't
remember whether she had and asked Diarmuid on the
phone and he said she certainly had. So I went to lunch,
after numerous phone calls from her secretary to the Bristol
(getting Dolly, and asking: "Is this Miss Welty's maid?" I
told Dolly she should have replied, "No, Miss Welty is my
maid") and changing times, and finally we went to the Passy
where you have probably been and Kay Boyle came also wearing unreal leopard. They were nice to me at the office and
showed me all over and I got to see George Grosz's original
drawings for my story last month, which I hope you loved in
reproduction. Let me see. All this time I have been waiting
till I had free time to write all, and now it has left me. I got
interviewed by Robert van Gelder but it was not scarey, just
like a date—he took me to a place to eat down on the wa-
terfront, some ancient & noted place which I have forgotten
the name of, and then out driving up the Hudson, and was
very nice. I don't know whether [the interview] has ever been
written up or not, but I did not mind it as feared. Lehman
gave me such a nice cocktail party, with all the good foods
& drinks well known. We missed you there as everywhere."[40]

When she returned to Jackson, Eudora began to read good,
but what she must have felt were somewhat distorted, reviews of
her book. Kay Boyle, writing in the *New Republic*, called Eudora
"one of the most gifted and interesting short-story writers of
our time" and then compared Eudora to Emily Dickinson: "They

are both American women writers of exceptional distinction who, each in her own century and in her own conditions, instinctively mistrusted the outer paraphernalia of literary contacts and activity and who, each in her own way, sought and found in silence an inner and almost mystical tongue." To be labeled "gifted and interesting" surely was pleasing, but the suggestion that Eudora was a silent and withdrawn spinster must have seemed ridiculous to her. Louise Bogan, in the *Nation*, described Eudora and her book in a quite different light. She distinguished the gothic quality of Faulkner's fiction from that quality in Eudora's work, noting that Eudora Welty "proceeds with the utmost simplicity and observes with the most delicate terseness. She does not try mystically to transform or anonymously to interpret. The parallel forced upon us, particularly by those of Miss Welty's stories which are based on an oblique humor, is her likeness to Gogol." These reviews and many others pleased Chestina. She pasted them, along with ads for the book and newspaper pictures of Eudora, in a scrapbook, in which she also included some limericks of tribute by an anonymous bard.

> There is a pen-pusher Eudora,
> As a writer she is a top-scorer.
> > Her "Curtain of Green"
> > Is a beauty I ween
> And surpasses a Northern Aurora.
>
> -x-
>
> This girlie is surnamed Miss Welty,
> So tall and so lissome and svelt—e!
> > For her stories so good,
> > Such a la carte food,
> All critics have praise and no pelty.[41]

Despite all "praise and no pelty," Eudora was not content to rest upon her laurels. She quickly returned to writing. This time she worked on an essay about Ida M'Toy, a black Jackson midwife who had become a used-clothing dealer. As she neared completion of the essay, Eudora wrote to Russell about the novel Katherine Anne Porter was struggling to complete: "She starts with people embarking on a long voyage, and then they are whole, real people, strangers and to be explored, and their relationships are to grow, and that part is written really superbly, a wonderful thread of feeling that follows from person to person and yet remains taut and true. But she wishes to show the superiority of some *races* and the inferiority of others, and I cannot think this is worthy of the work—the characters will have to contract and shrink in size in order to fit into a prejudice that should have nothing to do with them."[42] The juxtaposition of Eudora's comments on Katherine Anne and her work on "Ida M'Toy" is suggestive. In "Ida" Eudora sought to deny classifications based on race, and surely she saw the irony of Katherine Anne's maligning her German characters in the same way Germany's leader was denouncing all non-Aryans. Eudora would brook neither claim.

Eudora completed the essay and sent it to Russell, who in turn shipped it to *Harper's Bazaar* on December 1. A day or two later, Eudora drove to New Orleans to meet John Robinson, who was returning from Florida, and along with Robinson and his friends Charles and Emily Bein, she took in the culinary wonders of the city. Then Eudora and Robinson drove to Jackson for his sister Anna Belle's December 7 wedding to Paul Davis. Only when the wedding festivities had ended did Eudora learn of the attack that day on Pearl Harbor. Life would be transformed; worry about her brothers, about Robinson, and about other friends would be at the center of her existence for the next four years.

THREE

"Being Apart from What Matters"
World War II and the Home Front, 1941–1945

From the moment World War II began, Eudora Welty was overwhelmed by what was at stake and by an excruciating apprehension about the toll war would exact. "All the opposites on earth," she sensed, "were close together, love close to hate, living to dying; but of them all, hope and despair were the closest blood—unrecognizable one from the other sometimes, making moments double upon themselves, and in the doubling double again, amending but never taking back."[1] It would be seven years before Eudora wrote those words in her story "The Wanderers," but her life during the war embodied their truth. Eudora hated the destructiveness and self-destructiveness of war, but she revered the heroism of those who fought against fascism and for an open society. She counted on the safe return of her brothers and friends who entered military service, but she feared for their lives. And when John Robinson, the man she loved, was sent into combat, she experienced most intensely the doubling and redoubling nature of hope and despair. By autumn 1942, writing fiction, which had brought Eudora so much fulfillment, came to seem more and more apart from what mattered. Love and war, war and love, were wound inextricably together at the center of her life, and she would struggle to make that tangled knot a part of her fictional world.

Even before America entered the war, Eudora's reaction to the international conflict had been profound and complex. At the end of August 1941, she had told Katherine Anne Porter of the double emotions war aroused in her.

I felt worse about the war lately than I ever have since last summer—I don't know why—I was saying goodnight to my mother as she sat by the little radio in her room and she said, "The Russians just blew up one of their biggest dams—" and she looked so—I can't describe it—but the whole feeling of utter destruction & self-destruction came over me— it was the particular & the human reaction to it, which you instinctively keep down from day to day in order to endure your thoughts. The same day, a small thing—but the same feeling—came when the Little Theatre here was found broken into and everything in it smashed with a thoroughness which you couldn't believe—I used to be with sets & properties, so I felt a personal hurt—scenery had been slashed and lights had been methodically broken, furniture had been thrown down through the trap door and paint poured in on top of it, the curtain had been painted all over with obscene words, every seat in the house was coated with white paint, and tools had all been stolen except for the saw, which was neatly covered with paint and left on the floor—"snowballs" of paint had been hurled at the framed paintings and photographs in the green room—a job which had taken not one night but a number of nights to do—in other words not impulse, but plain undigressing malice. I think you are right when you say it is loose in the world, and that it is all part of the same thing. And it strikes what is tender and "amateur," I think that was somehow symbolic ... Somehow the good people never seem to be very accomplished. Goodness is really too profound a thing to take to tricks, I guess. But if it has a chair pulled out from under it it can get up.[2]

Thinking about the war, trying to understand it in terms of personal experiences, brought Eudora both despair and hope, a sense of "undigressing malice" loose in the world and of the goodness that would endure its blows and rise again.

On 7 December 1941, however, the Japanese struck a blow more staggering than anyone, save the attackers, could have imagined. In the wake of the assault on Pearl Harbor, Diarmuid Russell and Eudora exchanged letters about the war. Russell's spirits were low indeed, and he observed that "this great war has come about because people and even governments all over the world have refused to see and have even denied the existence of a world spirit." Eudora agreed.

> I know, and just as the world is one place, so is the whole war one organism, like one of the nebulae, which is not divided into two sides, but must be seen as a system of structure and motion that is going its way until it is itself condensed into its stars. I would rather look at it as an organism in distant space but it has to be remembered that even in looking at the stars a person is changed and has made his little change in the universe, for the star's light has affected his retina and the tiny reflection from his eye has begun a long travel back through space and years toward the star, and they say it is literally true that the stars' motions weigh upon our motions and that a person cannot move his little finger, so absolute is the force of gravity, without the stars being affected. What the war has done to the people this time I believe will be more powerful than what the people can do in making the war, if that could be a physical fact. But it is true, it must be, that it is the outrage to the world spirit you mention that we feel above the viciousness of each single thing, and all seems to be in the solemn shadow of this violation—no, in the shadow of this spirit to which the violation is done, which is still as

powerful as ever and in being denied is the more irrevocably defined.

The darkness of war now affected Eudora more intensely than it had before. Though she had anticipated writing about Johnny Appleseed, her first story of the new year was "A Still Moment," with its portrait of the nineteenth-century Mississippi outlaw John Murrell, a man who hoped his so-called Mystic Rebellion would make him the leader of a pirate kingdom. When Eudora's Murrell imagines himself "proudly in a moment of prophecy going down rank after rank of successively bowing slaves to unroll and flaunt an awesome picture of the Devil colored on a banner," the story evokes images like those of Hitler in Leni Riefenstahl's "Triumph of the Will."[3]

Shortly after completing "A Still Moment," Eudora learned that Mary Lou Aswell and *Harper's Bazaar* were interested in "The Winds," a story she had completed a year earlier. Aswell, however, felt the story needed substantial revisions. Eudora set about making them, and "The Winds" was soon accepted. So, too, was "The Wide Net," though taken by *Harper's*, rather than *Harper's Bazaar*. With these stories successfully placed and with no new work underway, Eudora welcomed Eileen McGrath, her friend from Mount Kisco, New York, to Jackson and then drove her to New Orleans. Eileen, on a crusade to improve public health, had appointments with New Orleans officials to discuss the treatment and prevention of syphilis. One appointment, she told Eudora, was in the "Paramount Cat Building." Luckily, John Robinson was able to deduce that Eileen really should go to the Père Marquette Building.

In March Eudora received a Guggenheim Fellowship. There could, obviously, be no trip to Europe, which she had wished for when applying the previous fall. She would spend her fellowship money at home. And at home, Eudora produced another story, one that would be selected for an O. Henry Award. "Livvie" depicts the plight of a young black woman trapped in a passionless marriage to Solomon, an old man who owns his land and has striven all his life for the security and respect typically denied African Americans. Diarmuid was pleased with the story and promptly sent it to the *Atlantic Monthly,* which rushed it into print. *The Robber Bridegroom,* however, had languished at Doubleday for more than a year. Frank Lyell, growing resentful on Eudora's behalf, stopped by the publishing house during a visit to New York and berated editor Donald Elder. Whether or not Lyell's tirade had any effect, Doubleday shortly thereafter announced plans to publish the novella separately rather than in a book of stories.

Late in May, Eudora traveled to New York, spending a weekend with Diarmuid and Rosie, and then came home by way of North Carolina, where she saw Frank. She remained fearful that John Robinson might be drafted and concerned about friends already in the military: Vincent Rousseau, Jimmie Wooldridge, and John Bennett, her old friend Willia's husband. During the summer months, she finally began work on another story, but her progress was slow. When Edna Frederikson, her novelist friend from Bread Loaf and Yaddo, came to Jackson in July and remained as a houseguest well into August, Eudora found it difficult to concentrate on fiction or even be polite. Especially disconcerting must have been Edna's presence when John Robinson came home on furlough shortly after enlisting in the Army Air Corps. Eudora told Frank Lyell that she "was glad to see [Edna] and yet glad when she left—I guess the strain of the past weeks, the army and all, kept me from being *quite* the perfect hostess I really *am,* but it was just the wrong time for me to think of anybody's novels in any minute degree." Indeed it was. By August 1942 Eudora was both deeply in love and deeply concerned about the future. "My friend John Robinson, of New Orleans," she told Russell, "is in the Air Force now and what can I do but think about his life, which is dear to me & close to mine. I know it is the same story everywhere."[4] She also worried about Hubert

Creekmore, recently sent to Corpus Christi by the Navy, and she was apprehensive about what sort of military duties lay ahead for her brothers, Edward and Walter. Nevertheless, somehow Eudora managed to complete her new story, "At the Landing," and send it to Diarmuid. In this story, sheltered and protected Jenny Lockhart falls in love with the river man Billy Floyd, who "violates" her. And when, despite his act, she hopes for a life with him and seeks to find him at a fishing camp on the Mississippi River, Jenny is gang-raped by the men of the camp. "At the Landing" on a personal scale may well suggest the self-absorption, misuse of power, and violation of individual sanctity that Eudora associated with fascism and even at times with politicians more generally. Still she was unsatisfied with the story and on August 8 told Diarmuid that he might want to throw it away. Unsatisfactory or not, it was the twelfth piece of fiction Eudora had sent to Russell in the course of two years. She had been incredibly productive and surely expected her writing difficulties to pass away in short order.

Throughout her career Eudora passionately sought to transform experience into fiction; doing so was a way of understanding, coping with, even redeeming what seemed irredeemable. As she told Ken Millar in 1976, "We somehow do learn to write our stories out of us, however disguised and given other players [i.e., characters in the stories] who can move and act where possibly we can't."[5] But between August 1942 and December 1944, Eudora would write very little out of her experience. Worry, omnipresent worry, left her unable to write. The war had become a major force in her emotional life, but it now resisted transformation into fiction. How could she incorporate her sense of war as a more and more overwhelming force—"a system of structure and motion" vast in extent— into the very specific, personal, domestic events about which she typically wrote? How could writing about her personal response to war assuage fear rather than intensify it? And how could she find the concentration that writing required? There seemed to be no answers.

For now, in the face of anxiety and frustration, Eudora sought distractions. She told Lyell, "John sent me a beautiful Bach aria one day that I keep playing, and I play records all the time now and work in the yard and read poetry and make rugs—have to." Clearly she *had* to do these things to keep herself from thinking only of the war and of the danger those she loved would inevitably face. Bach, Beethoven, Mozart, Rachmaninoff, Chopin, Tchaikovsky, Mendelssohn, Schubert, provided for her what such music would provide for Eugene MacLain in "Music from Spain." He feels, as he listens to a classical guitarist play, "a lapse of all knowledge of Emma as his wife, and of comprehending the future, in some visit to a vast present time. The lapse must have endured for a solid minute or two, and afterwards he could recollect it. It was as positively there and as defined at the edges as a spot or stain, and it affected him like a secret." Eudora had experienced similar moments in her garden, and gardening further allowed her to create order and beauty rather than dwelling on war. For similar reasons, painting interested her; her friend Helen Jay Lotterhos was an accomplished artist, and Russell a rather good amateur. Eudora herself returned to watercolors, which she had loved doing as a child, and wrote Russell about her efforts: "What are your sketches like? Mine might be too squigly and impatient looking for you to approve of them, I can hardly do it fast enough. Water color appeals much more to me than oil, to look at, but I've never tried oils or had much interest in trying for they seem to say, Go over this again and again—just as a medium they invite sluggishness and repetition—and water colors demand that you think quick and keep one step ahead of them and make fresh sketches always instead of working over one old one, so they're always new. I am not any good but I like to paint something on the spot and then go home and paint it from memory and then paint again out of the idea that came out of that memory—and if I were good I would keep going and see where that led me."[6] She might well have been anticipating the process of revision that would be hers when she came to write *Delta Wedding*: drafting the chapter of a novel, cutting the manuscript apart, pinning it together in a new order, and retyping a story. But for now, writer's block persisted and watercolors occupied her creative time.

Though she was not satisfied with her painting, Eudora continued to dabble in it and to find other ways of diverting her thoughts from the war and of reaffirming values that were threatened by the war. She had always been accepting of and fascinated by cultures different from her own, and in 1942 she was particularly engaged, as she had been in the thirties, by African American culture in Mississippi. Sometime that summer, Eudora wrote to Robinson about a visit to a rural black church:

> I went to a colored church that had a sign out front, "Fruit & Vine Service, Everybody Welcome See Hundreds of Ladies as Trees and Vines." Inside were little signs tacked up, all the way round the room, all different. "Grow Fruit." "Send Fruit." "Give Fruit." "Love Fruit." "Eat Fruit." "Bring Fruit." The window shades all had something hanging on the string, a cucumber, tomato, peanuts strung like beads, snapbeans, bell pepper, squash, etc. On the altar table was a watermelon surrounded by little fruits and leaves. The text was from St. John, "I am the true vine, etc." "Welcome to sit under our tree," said the preacher, "and have spiritual and financial benefit." It turned out that different ladies had been appointed trees and vines, and "these trees have been asked to produce a certain amount of fruit." It was a gyp that way though, because I waited and waited and in the end they all went out of the room to do it, and when they came in the results were announced in dollars and cents. I thought

it was a little cryptic. But the sermon was good. It was a little pagan. How we grow out of the earth, and he said "If
we want to be spiritually alive, stay in the ground! I want to
be a fruit bearing vine. I want to be a good tree." I really felt
delight, he said more than he knew.

Eudora had felt similar delight in September when she, Frank
Lyell, and Joe and Mary Frances Skinner went to an outdoor
dance on Jackson's Farish Street. The dance took place, she wrote
Robinson,

> in front of the Alamo with 3 bands, colored, the best being
> the Piney Woods Girls—the whole street that night looked
> like a dark ocean with even waves all over it, they all danced
> the same way and you know what way and with such cease-
> less energy and now and then a really good jitterbug would
> take a leap clear out of it all like a fish. The men all danced
> in their big wide hats with the feathers, and some were puff-
> ing strong cigars. The best man of them all, just like a cock
> in a cockfight, in a snow white shirt, had a little frowny
> complaining partner with a screwed up face that complained
> to him all the time they were dancing, doing acrobatic an-
> swers to his stalkings but just fussing and nagging. A lot of
> their feet were moving in double time, if we could only have
> seen better, just the ripples would rise up and go off at their
> shoulders, like. Some in caps and overalls with cotton stick-
> ing to them. Two little tiny black girls in hair ribbons were
> jitterbugging with each other right in the center of all,
> solemn as monkeys.[7]

Her description of the dance reveals that Eudora felt at some remove from the dancers, and it may momentarily suggest the era's
stereotypical white response to African Americans. But Eudora
was not given to stereotyping. She had deplored Katherine Anne
Porter's attempts "to show the superiority of some *races* and the

inferiority of others," and Welty stories, as Toni Morrison has observed, neither patronize nor romanticize, but depict African Americans as distinct individuals. In the massive correspondence available for research, Eudora used the word *nigger* four times as a descriptor: In letters to John Robinson written between 1946 and 1948, the word characterized three African American youths and a male actor playing the female role of Hecate ("a nigger man too, in the Negro Macbeth"). Subsequently, in a 1949 and a 1950 letter to Robinson, Eudora quoted and condemned the word's usage, and in a 1950 conversation with William Jay Smith, both Eudora and Robinson asserted that the title of Ronald Firbank's *Prancing Nigger* was offensive. The word, which was pervasively used by southern whites and which was an element of realism typifying assorted voices in her 1940s stories, was not used by Eudora herself except in these few instances. Beyond the issue of terminology, of course, lay Eudora's openness to cultural diversity. In the early 1940s when the African American novelist Ralph Ellison welcomed Eudora to dinner at his New York City apartment, he was struck by that openness, and he later commented on it in a conversation with Reynolds Price.[8] At the end of World War II and again during the Civil Rights Movement, Eudora would publicly oppose racism and support egalitarian change. And at the Farish Street dance in 1942, Eudora's appreciation of the "ceaseless energy" of the African American dancers, of men in zoot suits and men still in the overalls they had worn to pick cotton, of old and young, ecstatic and complaining, was not stereotypical, but individualized, vivid, and admiring. She was one of the few whites who attended such an event and who embraced it. Though she was unable wholly to bridge the gap between black and white, Eudora appreciated in an exuberant street dance what could have been, but was not, the subject for a wartime story: the freedom and diversity that were at the heart of America's ideals and were the goals of its war effort.

Early in October Eudora's brother Edward left Jackson for military training. Walter was due to depart a month later, and during the interim, Eudora sought out far-flung loved ones. She took the train to New York City in order to visit Russell and his family in nearby Katonah. She and Diarmuid painted side by side in the woods near the Russells' house. Then, on her way home, Eudora visited John in St. Petersburg, Florida, where he was stationed. For two days they enjoyed "going swimming and seeing fine sunsets over the Gulf, one bright day and one stormy. Little sandpipers, mother and young, were always running along the shore like tiny waves, all moving as a unit and instantaneously. We could just stay until dark, on account of the Coast Guard, but late enough to stir phosphorous when we swam."[9]

Back in Jackson, Eudora saw Walter off for his Navy service, painted watercolors of the Mississippi countryside, played records on her top-of-the-line Ansley Dynaphone (purchased with the second-place O. Henry Prize money for "The Wide Net") and took fleeting satisfaction in the publication of her long-since completed novella *The Robber Bridegroom*. The reviews of the book were quite good, but they failed to note that issues of power and race, so relevant to the international scene, were important elements in the novella. Nathan Rothman in the *Saturday Review*, for instance, praised *The Robber Bridegroom* as "a miracle of imagination, done with a prose forged especially, it seems, for this, in simple, singing sentences like struck notes of music." But Rothman cautioned, "Perhaps you will not like it, since it really means nothing, tells nothing, is only an experience."[10] On the contrary, *The Robber Bridegroom* deals with rape—Jamie Lockhart's rape of Rosamond, who would have given what he insists upon taking, and Little Harp's rape of the Indian maiden; both are assertions of power that deny the freedom and value of another person. Hero and villain are both culpable. The novella also deals with white settlers' displacement of Native Americans, annihilation of entire Indian tribes, and self-serving rationalizations for this course of action. Writing this novella in 1940, Eudora could not have known about the German death camps, but she would have known a good deal about Hitler's systematic misuse of power to disenfranchise and discriminate against Jews. From the time Hitler became German Chancellor in 1933 until the war commenced, the *New York Times,* Eudora's favorite newspaper, was filled with stories of German anti-Semitism, and the *Jackson Daily Clarion-Ledger,* her hometown newspaper, ran similar though less-extensive stories. In March 1933, for example, both papers covered the Nazi dismissal of Jewish doctors, judges, and attorneys from their positions; both covered the abuse of Jewish citizens and tourists; and both covered the 55,000-person Madison Square Garden interfaith demonstration against Nazi policy. In 1935 both the *Times* and the *Daily Clarion-Ledger* reported on the promulgation of the Nuremberg Laws that banned marriage or sexual relations between Jews and non-Jews and denied other civil rights to Jews. And in 1938 the *Times* and the local paper covered and denounced the deadly violence of Kristallnacht. Because of extensive press coverage, Eudora was aware of the human rights violations in Europe, and *The Robber Bridegroom* deals with similar violations that had taken place in late eighteenth-century Mississippi and that in different incarnations persisted. In 1940 she had been able, through the metaphor of plot, to suggest the need for change both abroad and at home. Not now.

In November, as she went about her Jackson routines, Eudora's loneliness was keen. "This is an empty house and an empty town," she wrote to Katherine Anne Porter. In the past Eudora's stories had described characters with just this sense of desolation—Joel Mayes in "First Love" and Jenny Lockhart in "At the Landing," for instance. But now the sense of emptiness was Eudora's own. And at times her hometown seemed worse than empty. She volunteered to work at the Red Cross and learned how blind her fellow volunteers could be to the horror of war:

"When I go to the Red Cross," she told Robinson, "those scatter-brained ladies have domesticated the war and talk all cosily and I feel anger in my whole heart against them—just at people—gossips and gluttons for whatever is at hand—poor *ignorant* things—it is the stupid people who have the true dream life—it takes some imagination to know the realest things, don't you think that— But I hate it and it terrifies me when little scatter-brained women are blood-thirsty—I guess they have just been bewitched—they don't know what they are wishing for."[11]

At the end of the month, Eudora's focus on the war was disrupted by a minor professional crisis. John Woodburn, her editor at Doubleday, wrote to tell her that he was moving to Harcourt, Brace and asked that she come with him. Appreciative of the role Woodburn had played in publishing her first two books and of his friendship, Eudora agreed. But by Christmas 1942 Eudora was again oppressed by the wartime situation at home and abroad: "The holidays seemed," she told Porter, "nightmarish with all the ones I love off at war." And anxieties continued to block any attempts at fiction. As the new year began, Eudora resisted Russell's suggestion that she expand "At the Landing" into a novel, and instead sought employment at the Office of War Information, where her talents might contribute to the war effort. No job was forthcoming and with time on her hands, Eudora wrote to S. J. Perelman, sending along an item that she thought he might use in a *New Yorker* article. He was delighted and wrote back: "I hope you won't think I'm being unduly familiar when I ask for permission to kiss the hem of your expensive garment, but I'm an obscure member of the Welty Fan Club, whose other name, I understand, is Legion. Another paid-up member, he asks me to inform you, is Ogden Nash. None of this will pay your grocer's bill, I admit, but it may stave off boredom." Even praise from the comic genius, however, did not prompt new stories from Eudora. During the spring of 1943, she merely readied stories, written months earlier, for publication in *The Wide Net*. She devoted the bulk of her remaining time to reading, to long (five- to ten-mile) walks in the countryside with friends like Lotterhos, Willie Spann, and Dorothy Simmons, to work in her garden, and to war-bond drives, bandage rolling, and USO (United Service Organizations) duties rather than focusing on her career. William Faulkner, nevertheless, did for a moment offer support for that career. On April 27 he wrote to her from Hollywood: "Dear Welty," he began, "You are doing fine. You are doing all right. I read THE GILDED SIX BITS, a friend loaned me THE ROBBER BRIDEGROOM, I have just bought the collection named GREEN something, haven't read it yet, expect nothing from it because I expect from you [sic]. You are doing very fine. Is there any way that I can help you?" Although he confused Eudora with Zora Neale Hurston and although Eudora found the letter "strange stuff," praise from Faulkner must have been heartening.[12]

Not so heartening was the plight of so many friends. Lehman Engel and Frank Lyell were, like Creekmore, Wooldridge, Robinson, and her brothers, now in the service. Though all were at this time still stateside, they were far from home. When she met soldiers stationed in the Jackson area, Eudora treated these men as she hoped her friends, family, and the man she loved were being treated. She once drew a librarian's wrath for attempting to check out a book on behalf of a Dutch flier who was training in Jackson, and she became friends with four other Dutch airmen stationed in her hometown. On May 11, 1943, she wrote to tell Robinson about one memorable gathering with these new friends. The young officers, quartered in a Jackson house, had formed their own string quartet and invited some of the neighbors, including Frank Lyell's parents, over to hear them play. Eudora joined the group for an evening of Scotch, sandwiches, bonbons, and then Beethoven; the evening, she told Robinson, "was charming, wonderful, and ironic, and so moving—a kind of interplay of all kinds of strings, and outside the rain falling through the trees and wet leaves brushing the window."[13]

But such meetings provided no enduring consolation. At the end of May or the beginning of June, having returned from a visit to New York, where Robinson joined her for a weekend at the Russells, Eudora was feeling melancholy indeed. "I've felt very lonely since I got back," she wrote Porter. "I also feel that I may have seen my friend John Robinson, in the army, for the last time till the war is ended, and Diarmuid for the last time in a long time too."[14] Her comments were prophetic in one case—the thirty-four-year-old Robinson, who had enlisted as a private in the Air Corps, then gone through officer training and become a second lieutenant, was sent to North Africa.

That summer there was happy family news for Eudora. Her brother Walter and his wife, Mittie, announced that they were to have a baby, and Edward married Elinor Saul. But professionally, Eudora did not prosper. With difficulty, she completed an essay, "Some Notes on River Country," for *Harper's Bazaar* but was unable to do more. Although she wrote to Russell about the possibility of a story, she soon abandoned this attempt. Worry about John Robinson intervened. For some time after the July 10 Allied invasion of Sicily, Eudora knew only what newspapers reported about the battle, though she felt sure that Robinson had been involved. By early August, Robinson had sent word of his participation in the landing and of his safety, but it provided scant comfort. On August 8 Eudora wrote to him, "I feel very scared. What can they be thinking of to have you in a foxhole—when your work demands so much else—I know you will be careful— Please be careful where you sleep—I hope it will be over soon." After the battle was finally over, Eudora received a long letter from Robinson, her only wartime letter from him known to be extant:

I think we were all terribly afraid those first two awful days. None of us knew war, and, I, knowing least of all, took my que [sic] from the rest and was probably doubly afraid. The first two times we were strafed by planes I was terrified. The first time we were riding over a hill in the jeep on a road the engineers had just dragged thru a vineyard. We were with our battalion, or near them, those first two days being somewhat disconnected. I had my field glasses in my hands looking at planes, or had been, when somebody yelled watch out German plane. I turned the glasses and looked behind and beheld the most enormous Messerschmitt I ever saw in my life. We leaped from the jeep on both sides and fell into a cactus hedge. Bullets pounded all about us but nobody, not even the jeep was touched. A little later another came at us—it was beginning to seem quite personal. I got under the jeep, which was a very bad idea, but I had no time to get anywhere else. No casualties again, and I got so I could lie on my back and look up as they strafed. Now it just seems a nuisance when we have to leave the radio right in the middle of a message and take to cover, usually a stone wall or behind a well, or something.

Following this harrowing account, Robinson's description of the Italian people and their response to the Allies offered contrasting images of harmony and goodwill: "They have given us some of the olives all along, you know the kind that Italian delicatessen in N.O. has in the antipasto—sort of chewed looking with lots of garlic, and some small branches for seasoning. Good. They are forbidden to sell soldiers wine, and refuse. But we simply hold out a very small bottle and inquire 'Avete vino?' And always get enough to have with our rations. Giving a few cigarettes in return or a can of hash. They don't ask for anything, and are most generous." Stories of wine and olives, however, did not deter Robinson from returning to the subject of war:

When I think of war I think of an odor, a burn smell of flesh, powder, vegetation, intermingled. Of corpses lying around under trees in the moonlight, killed by artillery fire, everything burned, of bodies by the roadside, and I wonder what they were doing when they were killed. Wrecked vehicles along the mountain roads, tanks, trucks, piles of unused ammunition, and in places canteens, clothes, blankets left behind in hurried retreat. Deaths of people I know. I ask about people I like with fearful misgivings. Today I learned that a captain I liked a lot on the boat coming over—we used to hang over the bow every night and watch the water—stepped on an S mine, very badly injured. The boy who won all the money at poker coming over, he was very obstreperous and over-talkative in a way, and childish and I think I thought of him as silly—he was among the first killed, jumped up to throw a hand grenade and was killed by machinegun fire. The paratroopers have been very brave. They have dropped down and taken up with various units and fought like demons in the first part of the war. That is, most of them. But they too are human and some seemed always moving about behind, riding in carts, on donkeys. One I knew talked an awful lot about the battle and knew all, but I think he never saw it. Others are very silent, they visit a day or two, say little, and are off again. Even a Lt. Col. was the same, just dropped in one day, stayed two days and dropped out again. They are wanderers in a way. They look like wanderers when you meet them in the road and talk to them. They are usually alone, and have everything about them, no destination, no plans. I can tell a wanderer I think. And the stragglers. Not really intentionally so, probably, but the war just moves too fast for them.

On August 26 Eudora answered this long letter that had taken almost three weeks to reach her: "Nothing has meant quite this to me. I should have written before now to thank you for sending it. There was no doubt in my heart that you had been on some great crest, or the crest of the truth of the whole event rose up in you—because it could in you, and you stopped and wrote this when you could still see all. I will keep this— I have kept everything. I haven't even told Mother of these things—you did make me see them, as well I could when you told me so carefully and clearly, but they went to that part of my life where all things stay secret—somehow like the tenderest things." Though she could not confide the depth of her anxiety or of her relief to any friends or family, her relief was tremendous, and only when she was sure that Robinson had indeed escaped unharmed and was not part of the September invasion of the Italian mainland did she admit to him how distraught she had been. On September 24 she wrote, "I don't see how I lived through Sicily."[15]

For a time, Eudora could abandon worry for loneliness. She knew that Robinson had been assigned to the British in Northern Africa and that no longer was he literally under fire. For his part, Robinson "felt guilty about leaving the battalion for a headquarters job in Algiers."[16] Eudora felt no such compunctions; she was simply glad Robinson had left the front, and she was eager to be in closer touch with him. During her long period of uncertainty, she had knitted a sweater for him and was now able to send it as a token of love. She would go on to immerse herself in reading de Joinville's medieval memoir of the Seventh Crusade and André Gide's North African works—literature over the vast expanse of time attracted her because it told her of the place where Robinson was now based. And when Robinson wrote home to describe the thousands of amaryllis belladonna he had seen growing in Sicily, Eudora promptly ordered a dozen of the bulbs, noting that John's friend Charlie Bein had said they were tricky to plant. By mid-November 1943 Eudora could proudly report that the belladonna bulbs had sprouted their winter leaves. New life would emerge from the season of death.

Just as she sought to bring Robinson's world to Mississippi, Eudora also sought to send Robinson a piece of home. In August she had mailed him the jacket of her upcoming book *The*

Wide Net with a letter on the back, and she promised to send this book about Mississippi's Natchez Trace when it came out in September. Later she would also send *Time Magazine*'s very negative review of her stories, but negative reviews seemed insignificant to Eudora during wartime. "I saw the Time review but they say those things just because I happen to live in the South—but nobody else had better say I am unhuman," Eudora wryly told Diarmuid Russell. No other review echoed *Time*'s conclusion that the new Welty stories were "about as human as a fish," but there were few raves. The *New York Times* offered qualified praise, while Diana Trilling and Isaac Rosenfeld complained of aestheticism. Trilling, failing to see the oblique references to fascism in "First Love" and "A Still Moment," argued that Eudora presented not the "day to day horror of actual life" but "only the horror of dreams."[17]

Even as these reviews were appearing, Eudora began a new story, one for Robinson, one that she hoped would capture his imagination and brighten his days. Thinking of John as her audience, thinking of the story as a way of communicating more fully with him and of making his situation more bearable, freed her to write. It was her first story in more than a year, and she turned to the Mississippi Delta, which Robinson's ancestors had helped to settle, where he had taken her to visit, and about which he had told her so much. By early November she had completed "The Delta Cousins" and had mailed it not only to him, but also to her agent. Despite its very personal origins, Eudora felt the story might speak to a national audience. Robinson liked the story; Diarmuid Russell and his colleague Henry Volkening were more conflicted. Diarmuid told Eudora, "Both Henry and I have read the story, have talked about it and are more or less in agreement—every individual section seems good and yet as a whole it doesn't quite have the effect it ought to have. I wish we could say why this is but this is the feeling we have and so we mention it to you."[18] At *Harper's Bazaar*, where Russell first sought to place the story, Mary Lou Aswell shared the agents' reservations. She thought the story should be substantially cut and suggested that digressive episodes could be eliminated. Eudora was not persuaded and refused to make cuts.

The story opens with nine-year-old Laura Kimball making a train journey like ones Robinson had often made, a journey from Jackson to see her Shelton cousins who live in the Delta, cousins much like Robinson's own. The story goes on to detail Laura's love for Uncle Raymond, the visit she and cousins Cindy and India make to the cabin of a black servant, the experience Laura has making mayonnaise with Aunt Mim, and the Sheltons' picnic on the banks of the Sunflower River. Set in the 1920s, these scenes seem far removed from any contemporary relevance. But in developing two events for the story, Eudora was perhaps beginning to address her wartime concerns while still keeping the private focus that prompted the story in the first place and that she believed to be the essence of fiction. The malice a retarded cousin named Maurine inexplicably demonstrates toward Laura and a bee man who exposes himself to Laura and her cousin India, momentarily seeming to threaten sexual assault—these dangers come both from within and from outside the family circle and represent on a small stage the malice and violation that dominated "the huge fateful stage of the outside world."[19] When more than a year later Eudora expanded upon "The Delta Cousins," transforming it into the novel *Delta Wedding*, she added other ominous elements—death and the threat of death, the relation of the family to its African American servants, the class issues involved in the upcoming marriage of cousin Dabney to the plantation overseer Troy, and the trials faced by the Fairchilds' (previously called Sheltons) frontier ancestors. Without these additions, however, the story lacked narrative power.

"The Delta Cousins," nevertheless, served an important function: It cheered John Robinson up. Safe in North Africa and the recipient of Eudora's story, Robinson seems to have been moved by Eudora's devotion, and he in turn sent her tokens of his love. His Christmas presents to her arrived on November 26, and she immediately wrote to say that she was wearing the rosary he had sent, that the leather portfolio was the "softest, most magnificent thing—so beautiful," and that the cocktail napkins and handkerchief were also wonderful. On December 5 she was still writing her thanks and her longing: "I love the presents so, I miss you so much." And in a December 15 letter, she described her love as a beacon: "When you get this, it might be the New Year. All I feel about it can turn into only one thing, hope, but if it starts out of my love now, maybe so much energy of the heart can make it shine as bright as if it could stay its first way and you will know it is a daily kind of hope, not ever idle."[20]

Her completed story and Robinson's safety were not the only sources of pleasure for Eudora in late 1943 when otherwise the war news was grim: In November her brother Edward managed to come home. "It was grand," Eudora wrote to John, "we played our old duets on the piano—Jingle Bells— We have odd strange beer now—names like Silver Fox—a wartime Jax on dit [i.e., "one says"]. Whiskey is $6 a pint and takes all the gas to get it—out where it's buried—just a lady in a feather boa to car-hop. It makes it sort of special."[21] At Christmas, Edward was gone again, but Walter unexpectedly returned and a Christmas tree was put up in his honor. One may presume that a trip to the feather-boa-ed bootlegger further enhanced the festivities and that there ensued many a toast to those absent friends who were blessedly safe: Hubert Creekmore was in New Caledonia but uninvolved in combat, and other close friends were still scattered about the United States.

The new year seemed, however, to bring danger to Robinson. On January 22, 1944, he was stationed in Naples when the Anglo-American attack on the beaches of Anzio began. As part of the intelligence staff for the American Sixty-second Fighter Wing, Robinson might well have been involved with the amphibious landing, and Eudora began to fear as much after she read newspaper reports of the battle. By February 8 she expressed her concern and urged that he take care: "I tell you this so much because of no way to have you safe by sending love—though it is new each day as if it would next time know how to make you safe." On February 10, knowing that American troops had not moved beyond the beachhead, she wrote to ask if he were giving her the whole picture of his situation and told him that, for her, knowing the truth, even if frightening, was better than living in suspense. Eudora continued to write to Robinson throughout the month, reciting funny stories, reporting on her reading and her garden, but such letters masked her worry. Finally, on February 28, she could express relief at his distance from the front. He had written about living in relative comfort back in Naples with a self-made stove. Not until April, however, was Robinson free to tell Eudora the details of his experience at Anzio as a "guest" of British General Harold Alexander. John had not been in combat but had observed it. Eudora responded immediately: "It must have been something to see the calm unfolding of a thing you had worked over with paper & maps—on such scale—with men—with the time element & the rest— And now you have the General's eye view (& he has yours)."[22]

A desire to know more about the Anzio landing and subsequent fighting prompted Eudora to suggest that John write a book. American newspapers, she felt, were not presenting an accurate picture of the war. On March 3 she told Robinson, "I have meditated about a book by you and I start like this, that the truth of the event will come from the man greater than the event—because the understanding is more vision than it is watchfulness, and as much wisdom about people, and courage and fear, and hope, as it is about the deed that goes with them or begins with them." And then she added that most reporters write "with the war's passion and it is not enough . . . I think the human feeling came first, a feeling for the life that war is obliterating for its time. The whole is overwhelming— You have done so many things and

I thought it must be, among other things, to see the common truth." When Robinson evidently resisted her suggestion and inquired whether Eudora felt it necessary for him to become a writer, she replied she did not, but encouraged him to do so nevertheless: "It's a thing I think of as a secondary thing in my life which gives me intense pleasure (I mean secondary in that it is work—definition)—it is not quite like gardening. If I feel something and try to say it truly then the easiest way to do it is writing a story, for me. Since there is so much wrong being said about the war, by all agreements, I knew you would say what is true and what it is *like*." Eudora thought that Robinson, who had seen the war as she had not, could write about it with authority and a focus on its human dimension. On March 26 Eudora mailed Robinson several reviews of books about the war, surely an implicit call for another, more credible tome. And on April 17 she wrote, "The Stars & Stripes came day before yesterday and I was glad to have it—leaned in the door and read it all through and later times again—had Mother read it too, so we should not miss anything. It was good to read straight news—a great deal in 4 pages—ours is a kind of fantasy—is it ignorance mixed with a kind of shoulder-clapping I hate so—it's bad anyway and like belittling something too vast for anything but a few true facts if they would just give them to us. I was glad to know a little of your idea of [Ernie] Pyle—had wondered. He seems honest here and as if he is close to the men and likes them but of course we could not tell about his facts. Of course he has that lure about him that maybe today, tomorrow, he will tell us something—it might slip out like a nugget in the gossip, like an overheard remark that supplies a precious piece of news."[23] Eudora, it seemed, would have to be content with journalist Ernie Pyle. Robinson was not free to write a book; he was trapped into writing what he hated—public-relations pieces for the U. S. Army Air Corps.

This disappointment notwithstanding, in the spring of 1944 Eudora felt less anxious: Edward was at least off the combat list, though doctors had discovered he had a condition akin to hemophilia; Walter was still stationed in the United States; and Robinson's work in intelligence now kept him in relatively secure locations. Eudora also had the great joy of informing a local couple that their son was no longer missing in action but was alive and well—at Eudora's request, Robinson had made inquiries about and located C. D. Jones. And her niece Elizabeth had been born, a powerful sign of hope. Buoyed by good news, Eudora now felt able to write again, and she produced a story set at Hubbard's Wells, where she had gone as a child, and in a house that had belonged to someone in Robinson's family. In late April she mailed "A Sketching Trip" to Russell. The story would eventually claim an O. Henry Award, but writing fiction now failed to satisfy Eudora. She wanted to see Robinson, to view the conditions under which he lived and fought, to know more than the carefully controlled press reports and censored mail conveyed. Robinson had evidently expressed the thought that she might come abroad and write about the war, and she embraced the idea. When she learned that she had won a thousand-dollar prize from the American Academy of Arts and Letters and was expected to accept in person, she saw her trip to New York as the first leg of a transatlantic journey. Although she was concerned that her venture into the European theater of war would be another nagging worry for her mother, who was already tormented by war news, she pursued the idea energetically.

After her May 1944 arrival in New York, however, Eudora learned that she could travel overseas only as a designated foreign correspondent and that these positions were few in number. Still her hopes were not dashed. She anticipated that Robert Van Gelder might offer her a position on the *New York Times Book Review*, and she thought this job might lead to the one she really wanted. Van Gelder did indeed offer Eudora an internship, and in June she began working as a copyeditor and reviewer at the *Times*, though not everyone shared Van Gelder's enthusiasm for Eudora.

On June 1 Eudora wrote to Robinson, "After they begged me daily to take this job then I had to go see some high-up who yelled 'Sit down! So you've been trying to make a living writing book reviews, eh?' & then put me through a questionnaire on the basis of *my* having applied to the *NY Times* on the justification of my newspaper experience— I just walked around the streets afterwards with tears in the eyes, he was so *rude*." Then on June 5 she noted that Orville Prescott, "an un-admirer in print of my books, who is daily book ed., refuses to be in the same office and so it is now being torn up by three men with implements, even parts of walls carted off, which makes me feel rather haughty as I sit typing this in the middle of the banging."[24] Sexism was alive and well.

Despite this inauspicious beginning, Eudora came to enjoy the *Times* and most of her coworkers. At the desk next to hers sat seventy-four-year-old Isaac Anderson, the detective-story editor, who was silent all day, whom she alone greeted each morning, and from whom she alone received a good-bye at day's end. Another reviewer, William DuBois, sat at a desk behind Anderson; he was, she reported to Robinson, "a power plant of a man who grabs the phone and hollers into it and is so busy that in his spare time he is writing a play—he never stops—I watch the expressions on his face which I think he assumes for the characters—snarls, gritted teeth, and fond, pursed lips at successive intervals." Also in the office, Eudora reported, was "a very young little Turkish hunchback girl—her face is one of the truly beautiful faces you see in this town." This girl was, in fact, of Armenian descent. Nona Balakian would become a very good friend. Van Gelder himself Eudora liked tremendously, though early in her tenure she came into some conflict with her boss: In copyediting Agnes Meyer's review of Thomas Mann's *Joseph the Provider*, Eudora had made substantial cuts. Meyer, an old friend of Van Gelder's, objected, and Eudora wondered whom Van Gelder would support. He was, she then felt, a man "unsure of his literary judgments," but Eudora acquiesced gracefully when Van Gelder reinstated material she had deleted.[25] And as the summer progressed, she became very fond of Van Gelder and his wife.

Early in the summer, Eudora was not fond of New York itself. New Yorkers, she felt, failed to appreciate the sacrifices American troops were making for them and failed to embrace the values for which the war was being fought. On May 31, she wrote to Robinson, "the people here make me sick—all they think of is themselves & their precious money & business— I lost my temper at a party & practically wished the eruption of Vesuvius on NYC—did no good." And on June 19, she was still resentful: "The Old Guard [are always] talking about the money. (I've gotten so I hate the rich, which is strange when you consider I don't care at all how much money they have.) The many Jewish refugees are a kind of rich, ripe, fruity, complaining background to most restaurant scenes or hotel lobbies. '*Why* are the best tables all taken—a pity, a pity.'" The materialistic and self-indulgent preoccupations of wealthy, white, Protestant, "Old Guard" New Yorkers, she felt, extended even to those Jewish refugees, who, unlike their compatriots she had known at Yaddo, seemed to have lost touch with the world of suffering they had escaped and which Jews who remained in Europe had to face. The underlying principle of any viable society, Eudora felt, was concern for others, a regard for each individual as an individual, overseas and at home: "If you treat everybody *first* as a human being—people you love best, & people you hate most—& people you have yet to understand—isn't that the only way, the only basis."[26]

Eudora continued to hope that she might travel to Europe and write about the war. The Allied capture of Rome, June 5, and the D-day landings in Normandy, June 6, made the prospect seem more likely. Late in June she reassured Robinson that however grim the realities of the Italian theater of war, she would take great joy in seeing him: "I would like to come, & have the chance of seeing you, & if I could, do you see, to know a little better how you were getting along would be a glamorous thing to me & life would be all right." But Eudora would not have the chance "to know a little better how" Robinson was "getting along." On July 10 she told him that being in New York was not helping her efforts to join him in Italy: "It is not true that it is any easier to find a way to get on a boat, and only the hopeful look of the war keeps me at all placated." When Robinson suggested that she read Martha Gellhorn's reports from abroad, she replied: "That phony can get over there and 'use material' for a mag. like Collier's when an honest person (like me) can't be authorized by a decent paper, even, to do even a report." But Eudora's disdain for Gellhorn was balanced by her admiration for the wartime drawings and diary that George Biddle published that summer and that Eudora reviewed on July 16, writing under a pseudonym Diarmuid had created for her—Michael Ravenna. Biddle had in fact done exactly what Eudora might have hoped to do—see and report on the 1943 battles in Italy, including the battle of Sicily in which Robinson had participated. And Biddle's book responded to many of Eudora's concerns about wartime reporting. Eudora's opposition to censorship was Biddle's as well. "The artist makes his book a case against censorship and the deleting of the evils and horrors of war. He asks how, as long as the people are ignorant of what our men really do and endure, they can contribute that essential support which is so needed both at home and at the front." Though Biddle was prone to stereotyping, sometimes rather crudely, almost every nationality whose citizens he encountered, Eudora felt that he saw beyond generalizations: "No matter where he goes," she wrote, "Mr. Biddle sees the human being."[27] Eudora did feel that Biddle, in his efforts to create a permanent record of the war, at times failed to appreciate the fighting man's focus upon the present moment and his impatience with the artist's purpose, but Biddle's account would be Eudora's closest approach to Italy for many years.

Though discontented with her inability to become a foreign correspondent and occasionally discontented with life in New York, Eudora took comfort in the post–D-day wartime developments and increasingly enjoyed city life. She wrote John to describe a massive concert at Lewisohn Stadium. Seeing conductor Sir Thomas Beecham, the sixty-five-year-old Englishman, and hearing pianist Arthur Rubinstein, a Polish Jew who with his family had blessedly escaped from Paris ahead of the Nazi occupation, was an indelible experience for Eudora and eighteen thousand others. Both men displayed, in words Eudora would forty years later use to describe herself, the love of their "art and the love of giving it, the desire to give it until there is no more left":

> Rubinstein played with great passion & vigor—that beautiful Rachmaninoff concerto, no. 2— That was last, & the audience—did I tell you there are 18000 people in it— would not let it be last—again & again they called him & a great *roar* would go up from them when he sat down again at the piano— He played all alone then without the orchestra—Chopin, so clear, single notes out in the night that was absolutely still— Again—he played Liebestraum—again, & the Ritual Fire Dance (I think) of de Falla— Each time he gave an encore he would first sit down & run his hands up & down the keys striking chords thinking what he would play— The night was starry— Once during a Tchaikovsky waltz a great moth flew under the arch & circled & dipped under Sir T.'s baton— Sir T. was carried away tonight too & once during Scheherazade he gave a *groan* of anticipation as he drew a sound from the strings.

Performers and audience alike seemed carried away, and to Eudora, the concert suggested that many, many New Yorkers shared her concern for the Allied forces and for the Europeans they sought to liberate. As she explained to Robinson, "For the first

time I was *sure* about the city & you would have felt their responsiveness, as if they could suddenly open their minds & hearts, it
was a real feeling of *opening*—once there was something great
given to them— I don't think any smallness of politicians can
stifle them or stop them & I think the greatness of what men are
doing can reach them— Besides, each one of them must have
someone overseas that he puts ahead of the evil everywhere &
even in his own heart if it is there—& so each one must have
learned for himself, we understand by our own— I think it is all,
really, individual, all unique for each one, but at the concert it
was (through release) suddenly general & you would have been
certain that the feeling for great things is everywhere deep & positive— And I can't tell you how *definite* it was—not vague in the
least. Do you see at all."[28]

The Rubinstein concert seems to have been a watershed for
Eudora, leaving her more open to and enthusiastic about city life
despite one or two moments of recurring doubt. She and Dolly
Wells, a longtime friend from Jackson, together sublet an apartment in the Greenwich Village building where Nancy and Alice
Farley, Robinson's friends from Oxford, Mississippi, lived. Delighted to be free of hotel life, Eudora was surprised and amused
by Dolly's attitude toward housekeeping: "Dolly tickles me—she
never wonders *what* scours the tub, boils the dishrag, defrosts the
refrigerator, changes the sheets, etc—she doesn't think it's
anybody—Fairies like at home." No matter who took care of
household duties, Eudora, Dolly, and the Farleys had many good
times together. They traveled to the country, spending a weekend
at the Katonah home of Diarmuid and Rosie Russell while Russell and his family were vacationing in Maine. They shared meals
in their apartments and in local restaurants. And they enjoyed life
in Greenwich Village. Eudora, in particular, relished the Village
atmosphere, the church bells on Sunday morning, the Italian
organ-grinder who played Neapolitan songs in the street outside

their house, and the busker who "sang to our windows the other night and we hung out, a tenor, Irish, My Wild Irish Rose, and did a little dance with hands to stomach and back—a fling."[29]

Well might these southerners have congregated in New York, for they at times faced a reverse sort of prejudice, as Eudora explained to Robinson.

> I worry & wish there were less ignorance & more knowledge involved (as it's to be wished there were in everything—there in Europe & here—) Is it always the wrong people, who do not hesitate to "solve" things? Who do not understand anything but have statistics & quotations—The trouble is (& the reason you get so mad probably, being put on the stand every day for the South) is there is just enough truth in the actual situation, just enough badness to mislead "intellectuals" (how I hate them)— I think the reason I'm so tired at night is I'm given body blows & have gotten mad to no avail on behalf of Mississippi— Every Southerner I know here is the same . . . The other day going down on an elevator someone introduced a girl "from PM" & me "from Miss." & when I said How do you do, *she* said "Oh you're from *Mississippi* where they persecute the Negro & have the highest percentage of illiteracy in the union." "Ground floor" said the elevator boy—& that time I was speechless & only in a dumb fury at the unfairness & rudeness & smugness of these people.[30]

Eudora acknowledged the truth of Mississippi's apartheid character, but she also loved her home and felt defensive when it was attacked. And she resented being stereotyped.

Occasional hostility toward southerners notwithstanding, New York had become a community to Eudora, and not just a community of Mississippians in the city. Eudora spent time with a diverse group of friends, with coworkers at the *Times,* with Maggie Cousins, the Texan who was then assistant editor at *Good*

Housekeeping, with John Woodburn, her editor at Harcourt, and with her friend Eileen McGrath, who had now decided to pursue a medical degree. During the summer before her studies began, Eileen had time on her hands and introduced her Jackson friend to some interesting spots. One evening she took Eudora first to the Harvard Club, which Eileen had been instrumental in convincing to admit women, and afterward to a new, small, family-operated Italian restaurant in a basement apartment on Thirty-first Street near the East River. Eileen was frustrated by the restaurant's slow service, but Eudora, ever the observer of human nature, was fascinated by its clientele: "At another table were 3 girls who, if they worked, were models & very innocent looking & fed their men ½ the radish, then they pulled it back & ate the other ½ etc. etc. They got tight and all told dirty jokes, still starry eyed. One of the men asked a girl at another table to throw him a roll, & when she did, his date I was sure was going to bite him (literally)— It was interesting to watch them for 3 hours straight."[31] The evening seemed to be a story-in-the-making, but nothing came of it.

One of the greatest pleasures of Eudora's New York stay was the opportunity to spend more time with Diarmuid Russell. The two met often. Once, Diarmuid took her to Alfred Stieglitz's gallery, and they had the good fortune to encounter the famous photographer. In a letter to Robinson, Eudora described the event.

> I'll try to tell you as exactly as I can remember a conversation with Stieglitz that Diarmuid and I just had, as we ran up to see some Marin watercolor at lunchtime. You know he is an old man, 82 he said,—with snow white hair, white mustache, deep brown eyes, rather fitfully dressed in an old open shirt with undershirt showing—it had a yellow colored band up it—and old vest hanging open, and worn old pants. Very contemplative voice. When others talk in his pauses he holds up one hand and says "Wait, wait." You know he only loves or believes in one man painter in the

world, John Marin, and one woman Georgia O'Keeffe, who is his wife—all of them are in their 70s or 80s now and still painting canvas after canvas, which they seem to just bring automatically up to Stieglitz's office and gallery.

In addition to showing art galleries to Eudora, Diarmuid occasionally joined her for dinner, once meeting Eudora and her housemates at a Brazilian restaurant and another time enjoying after-dinner conversation until three in the morning. This was not the only late night Eudora and Russell shared. She wrote Frank Lyell in August, "I feel bad today after a good party last night—I gave it myself, but the van Gelders insisted it be at their house—which was very nice. It was from 6 to 4 (instead of vice versa). Planters Punches. The van G.s are both swell to me and about 8 people came—Dolly and the Farleys, Diarmuid and Henry, Margaret Cousins, and John W., who got very very drunk and insulted all, mostly Dotty van Gelder whom he told how beautiful she was but dumb. (not true) O me."[32]

Eudora's most cherished weekends during her five months in New York were spent at the Russells' Katonah home, with Diarmuid and his wife, Rosie, and their two children. In Katonah there were often small dinner parties in Eudora's honor. Typically the men in the room all gravitated toward Eudora, and Rosie often commented on Eudora's striking ability to charm the opposite sex. Diarmuid had a similar ability, but Eudora appreciated him for more than this. He had become one of her closest friends, and she told Robinson, "When I think of him my heart sort of overflows— He is one of the real people—one of the good people— I can never quite understand what he's doing in that city— running a business—& not just sitting on a hill in Ireland, which is his heart. I hope he gets back some day."[33]

Eudora shared her growing enthusiasm for New York with visitors from home and with her fellow writers. Frank Lyell came to New York several times while on leave and took Eudora to swank restaurants, notably the St. Regis Roof and 21. Her brother Edward and his wife, Elinor, visited in July, and Eudora took them to the Rainbow Room, to the Cloisters, and to *Carmen Jones*, an African American version of the Bizet opera. Eudora was pleased by a visit from Mary Frances and Joe Skinner, friends she and Robinson shared. And she delighted in a chance meeting with Katherine Anne Porter in a Swedish rathskeller in Lower Manhattan. For Eudora, New York City had become a second home, one in which she knew people as individuals, one in which she felt connected to friends rather than alienated from self-centered strangers. Perhaps as a result, Eudora interceded on behalf of her lifelong Jackson friend Nash Burger, helping him to secure a position at the *New York Times Book Review.* She felt reconciled to the city, which early in the summer had seemed indifferent to wartime sacrifices. It now seemed the sort of place for which the war was rightly being fought and in which her friends could lead happy lives.

Still, Eudora was not writing fiction. Denied the opportunity to write about the war as a journalist, she continued to have great difficulty translating her wartime emotions into fiction; she had been able to write only two short stories in the past two years. But New York continued to distract Eudora from the frustration she inevitably felt. She heard the Philharmonic play Mendelssohn, going afterward to a jive session in the company of Ed Holmes and Rex Brown from Jackson. She saw a Greek and Egyptian exhibit at the Metropolitan. And the theater proved, as it always had, a source of great pleasure. She and Dolly saw Mae West in *Catherine Was Great,* and Eudora reported that Mae was "just the same—the old walk and the old jawroll still there. Very lavish— very lavish bed, and she wore trains that went halfway across the stage. Her opening line—she entered through a lane of guards in white tunics, fur hats, crossed swords, and switched her train around, and sank to the throne, then flung a glance at one guard and said, 'Are you new here?' It was full of knocks at the door

and her saying throatily, 'En-ta!' At the curtain call she rolled out
demurely and said 'Thank you very much ladies and gentlemen. I
understand Catherine had 400 lovahs in thuhteen years, of course
I did what I could in a couple of hours!'" Two months later, Eudora and Dolly went to see *Oklahoma.* They loved the play, but
found the audience itself as entertaining: "It's fun & any time I
would like to be in the chorus, barn dances (with banjos) & reels
all the time—Dolly & I patted, up in the peanut roost—a contingent surely from Oklahoma was there, in 3 sections, hollering,
all real fat, all women but one (he was a card, put on all their hats
& hung out his tongue) & greeting each other & hollering 'Aren't
you hot? I'm dripping!' across the audience, & the grey haired
women thumbing their noses & passing binoculars down long
rows of strangers."[34] New York gave Eudora the opportunity to
pat her feet in time to the music of *Oklahoma,* to laugh at the an-
tics of Mae West, and to know some respite from worry about
the war and about the writer's block that had plagued her.

When Eudora left New York in October 1944, her internship at an end, she did so with regret. As her train for home
pulled out of Penn Station, Eudora wrote to Robinson about the
experience: "It will seem strange no longer going to work—
through clouds of caramel popcorn & fish, constantly invited to
send my name on a live turtle, let a Gypsy read my future, develop my muscles or dance with 50 queens upstairs—or to go to
Chinatown (that man practically whispers) & finally turning the
corner & fighting my last half block to the office through the
line going to the morning show at the Paramount— And all the
time the sidewalk opening up under my feet for a plumber to
come up on an elevator with a little bell ringing that sounds silver & something—what is it, soot or fine rain, that falls there?"
The street life was captivating and Eudora was sorry to leave it,
even as she longed for her garden and for a quieter existence. For
his part, Diarmuid Russell felt that a return to Jackson was essential if Eudora were to write again: "It's probably not a bad

thing that you went for you'd never do any work up here and you write too well for us to accept that very happily."[35]

As she traveled toward home, it seemed that the war was headed toward conclusion and that friends and family members were as safe as possible. In July Jimmie Wooldridge had been sent to France, but his duties were behind the front lines and his letters about the liberation of French villages quite cheering. Soon after she returned to Jackson, however, Eudora learned that John Robinson was participating in night-fighter missions. With southern Italy secured, U.S. Army Air Corps fliers were being deployed on missions directed at the northern part of the country. Robinson, feeling guilty about scheduling young men for these missions, chose to accompany them. When Eudora realized that he had willfully put his life at risk, she was distraught: "Are you all right? This nearly kills me—I didn't know you didn't need to go— What is it? Tell me or whatever you want—only don't go . . . This is with all my heart. I wish I could think of a way to ask you that would prevail, but do ask you so hard, not to go & be in all the worst danger & it not needed—O God I feel shaky & may be am stupid in my head but it sounds wild & crazy & overworked to me & I want you to come out of it—quick— Do you remember we love you so." Five days later she sought to apologize for questioning his decisions: "I could never hate anything you do— of course it's part of you—I see—I see for ever I think. Just let me know how you are. I hold those flights inside me too, tenderly, no difference. But tell me all the time how you are—you will, won't you? I hope fine tonight and that the whole night goes safely." Her fears eased somewhat when Robinson was allowed a furlough. From peaceful Egypt, he sent Eudora a picture of himself upon a camel, some Egyptian seeds and plants for her garden, gardening gloves, a pair of yellow shoes, some wine glasses, and a little painting on bone with her name in Arabic.[36]

This anxiety-free interlude did not last long. Mittie's brother Hubert Creekmore had returned from the Pacific but was ill in a

New Orleans hospital. Eudora and her family were intensely worried about Walter, speculating that he might be involved in minesweeping operations that preceded the Battle of Ormoc Bay, and Eudora further worried when her mother, who suffered from high blood pressure, compulsively listened to the radio war news all night long. Coupled with fear for Walter and her mother was Eudora's sense that Robinson was back in danger. On November 14 Eudora again wrote to urge that he cease his post-furlough nightflying, and on November 16 she told him, "Mother went out to lunch a while ago & I thought now I can just cry, in peace by myself, for you. I haven't heard since a letter you wrote 4 weeks ago—and just as I ran upstairs the phone rang & it was Frank—leave, had just flown in— So I had to rejoice with him." A month later, at last, she could relax somewhat. Walter was safe and so was Robinson: "I'm glad to know about the nightflying being in the past— *They* know you wouldn't send them to do a thing you wouldn't do— You were doing so much—it sort of hurts—You're still up all night, I guess— I had wanted to know what it was like in the plane & now that I do, I'm twice as glad you don't go any more."[37]

In the midst of—and perhaps because of—her renewed concern for Robinson and her sense of his heroism, Eudora returned to fiction and the characters she had created for him in "The Delta Cousins." In "A Little Triumph," she developed episodes that she would eventually revise and incorporate into her novel *Delta Wedding*. Shortly before Christmas, she sent the new story to both Russell and Robinson. Russell liked the story, but he failed to see any contemporary relevance in it: "I think it just confirms me that somehow or other you must get your mind in the right kind of mood and expectation to work on the DELTA COUSINS for here as there is the same kind of wonderful atmosphere—the South just as I imagine it must have been, may still be for all I know." Robinson, however, sensed that "A Little Triumph" contained more than a portrait of the South, and Eudora expressed pleasure with his reaction, even as she belittled her achievement: "If you like my new story I do feel glad—it means a lot to try to write now—harder than it used to be and somehow it ought to be better work than it naturally would be, or why did I do it. Yet that doesn't *enable* me to write better. It means so much if you don't have a feeling of it's being apart from what matters. Maybe if you weren't kind you would have it, because from where you are I feel that everything must look too small for the eye to see that is not of a certain worth and perhaps of a certain use. I know that I cherish much that is not—life being so personal to me, more than ever now if anything—but it is personal to you too and so I feel proud and in delight if a story pleases you, that's in proportion. You know what I try, which is so comforting—you see how far I can get and where I have to stop and just where that is—a little spot on the wayside—and it's as restful & sleepy as a picnic when you read it & get there too, and know just where & when & all."[38]

Eudora was especially pleased that Robinson did not see the story as "being apart from what matters." And indeed it confronts, much more explicitly than "The Delta Cousins" had, issues relevant to the Second World War. It speaks in opposition to the racial categories on which Hitler insisted, which had so long characterized southern culture, and which denied the importance of the individual. But it also offers a positive vision. In this story, Dabney recalls seeing Uncle Raymond (to be called George in *Delta Wedding*) emerging stark naked from a swim in the river and then stopping a knife fight between two young black boys.

Uncle Raymond grabbed the little Negro that wanted to run, and pinned down the little Negro that was hollering. Somehow he held one, said "Hand me that," and tied up the other, tearing up his own shirt. He used his teeth and used the Negroes' knife and cussed. It was a big knife—she was sure it was as big as the one Ben carried now. There was blood on the sunny ground. Uncle Raymond cussed the little Negro for being cut like that. The other little Negro got all quiet and leaned over and looked at all Uncle Raymond was doing, and in the middle of it his face crumpled—with a loud squall he went with arms straight out to Uncle Raymond, who stopped and let him dry a minute. And then the other little Negro sat up off the ground, the small black pole of his chest striped with bandages, and climbed up to him too and began to holler, and he crouched there holding to him two little black boys who cried together melodiously like singers, and saying "Damn you! Damn you both." Then what did he do to them? He asked them their names and let them go.

Raymond embraces the two black children, takes them to his bare body with no sense of separation, and grants them their individuality by asking their names. Dabney recalls being shocked by this behavior, but also remembers that Raymond "hugged her tight against his chest, where sweat and water pressed her mouth, and tickled her neck a minute, and said 'Damn you too.' All the Shelton in her had screamed at his interfering—at his taking part—*caring* about anything in the world but them. And poor boy, he had done it all naked."[39] Raymond cares about black and white children alike, he embraces both, he chastises both, he literally and figuratively exposes himself to both. Raymond lives by values that Nazi Germany abominated and that are shocking to his family members as well. Eudora's opposition to the Nazi value system and recognition of a parallel between those values and southern cultural taboos are both implicit in the scene. So, too, is her faith—despite a war that had torn the world apart—in the indestructible capacity of the single, separate person to renounce self-glorification and care about more than himself, his family or race or nation.

The china night-light of the story furnishes a less dramatic but equally relevant domestic dramatization of issues with international import. Aunt Jim Allen and Aunt Primrose insist that Dabney accept a china night-light as their wedding present to her. The night-light had belonged to their mother during the Civil War and now it will be Dabney's. It is "a tiny porcelain lamp with a cylinder chimney decorated with a fine brush, and an amazing little tea-pot, perfect spout and all, resting on its top." Primrose takes a match and lights the candle inside the chimney, which has a picture of London painted upon it. "Next, in the translucence, over the little town with trees, towers, people, and a bridge, over the clouds and stars and moon and sun, you saw a redness glow and the little town was all on fire, even to the motion of fire, which came from the candleflame drawing."[40] The old aunts and their young nieces are delighted; here is a magical family treasure that has for generations provided children with the security of light in the midst of night's terrors. Ironically, however, the night-light depicts the Great Fire of London. When Dabney later rushes to rejoin her fiancé, she drops and breaks the night-light, oblivious to the fact that she has done so. Metaphorically, she breaks with the past and embraces life in the present. But that present, she fails to realize, may prove as destructive as the fire that destroyed London in 1666 or as the fires that were devastating Europe in 1944 when Eudora wrote the story.

Having returned to fiction and been freed, if only temporarily, from worry about her brother and Robinson, Eudora seized Christmas Day 1944 as "a little spot on the wayside" of time, joining with friends and family in a sort of all-day picnic. She described the day to John.

We got up about 9 o'clock and had a little eggnog and our breakfast. Our tree looked gay—we put it on your wooden box from Italy covered with tissuepaper and snow and presents. We had red candles in the candlesticks. Nash called while we were at breakfast—of course he'd started at 5 AM with 2 little boys and was ready to settle down & drink by somebody's fire. In a minute, in burst Frank—you aren't surprised, are you. Flew home from ORD since his boat not quite ready and the CO turned out to be a brother of one of Judge's old school debating society team or something. He went over Jackson on a foggy night and they put him down in Texas—the Adolphus Hotel—but he was here for Christmas morn—it was fine to see him. Mittie and the baby came over—we had our tree—the baby likes eggnog and tissuepaper . . . Walter had sent one of their friends little cards all written out and the money and she had come put under the tree boxes for all—of course we almost couldn't stand that either. In Edward's box was some *bacon.* And a doll for the baby which she took and rubbed noses with and put her forehead to its forehead and whispered to. Mother was enchanted—the baby loved Christmas, never went to sleep the whole day, wore Walter's pink cap with the frill around it. Our eggnog turned out all right—made it two or three times—Hubert ate the most. Mother *made* me a bathrobe out of a pink blanket—trimmed with the blanket ribbon—really a masterpiece, and so warm and soft—I trailed it like princess robes through the morning, with my Algerian slippers. Shining on the wall was AE's painting [a gift from Diarmuid]. We had a turkey and all, just Mother and me for dinner but it was all nice. In the afternoon I went over to Willie Spann's—she is down in the bed for Christmas—I took her and Miss Pearl a glass of eggnog and visited on the bed a while. Helen came out and we drank some whiskey and water and Frank and Hubert and Nash and Marjorie and Seta and Tom began coming in and we had a good time—ate what we could for supper and had some drinks and sat talking—about "Life on the Mississippi," one thing, and what happened to Frank's Pole (investigated for relations with a strange lady—a spy?) and

every now and then we would suddenly say "Oh I wish——"
It began to rain about 10:30 and people have gone home
early. Now it is lightning and thundering loudly——like a
spring storm——shaking the house. I hope your day was full
and good like this.[41]

As the new year commenced, few days seemed good to John
Robinson. He was disillusioned with the war. He wrote his old
Jackson friend Bill Hamilton to ask, "What do you think of the
state of things, or the shape of things to come? Any more hopeful than I am? It wouldn't take much. From where I stand I see no
real vision in anything proposed for the future——I'm only hoping
this children's game will be over soon and I'll be too old for the
next one." Surely Robinson addressed similar remarks to Eudora,
who had been skeptical of the course the war had taken since that
moment in 1942 when the English had demanded an Italian campaign. Now her attention to wartime goals and strategies focused
even more sharply on the country in which John was stationed. In
January she sent Robinson a Bell Syndicate newspaper clipping
speculating on English motives toward Italy. "One factor which
has complicated the situation," the clipping read, "has been evidenced [*sic*] that England intends to move in on Italy commercially and politically after the war. Some of the finest Italian
textile machinery has been moved out of Italian factories by the
British." Three weeks later, sensing that Italy had been betrayed
and Americans unnecessarily sacrificed, she told Robinson, "It is
still Italy that breaks my heart with its little paragraph of news
each day that is just a weather report and how I wish the Russian
business [a 1945 major offensive moving southward] would be a
help there soon to you." Then on February 9, she again expressed
concern about Italy and doubt about international policy con-
cerning it: "The war news is good about the [Russian] fighting,
though what the Big 3 meeting now going on will perpetrate is a
different thing——there's something Machiavellian about it. And

what can be done about Italy by now—can they atone for what's
been done and not done? At least we can hope they will try."[42]
Eudora realized that the battle for Italy had involved ill-advised
attacks, a campaign waged in the most difficult terrain, Allied
losses and Allied suffering through a difficult winter, and tremendous civilian suffering in a war-torn zone. She seemed to suspect
Churchill's motives in pushing for an invasion of Europe through
Italy; she hoped Stalin and Russia would help to shorten the war,
but she didn't place any faith in Stalin; only Roosevelt did Eudora regard highly, not realizing that his capitulation to Churchill
in the matter of Italy was a rejection of the advice of his military
leaders.

But Eudora's focus upon the war did not merely concern issues of policy; in 1945 she continued working for the Red Cross
and for the local USO. Robinson had written to express his admiration of enlisted men and his disdain for many officers, and
Eudora shared these views and was also impatient with bureau-
cratic red tape. On January 8 she wrote to Robinson that she had
tried to get a "sick marine a ticket to Chicago hospital where his
folks could come to see him" but the "Red Cross wouldn't accept
his little pieces of paper as proof and his hands trembling to go
through his paper suitcase of clothes—looking for what would
convince them." A week later she wrote Robinson about another
young man she had met at the USO. He had been in Africa, Sicily,
Italy (theaters where Robinson served) and in France. Back in the
States with a bomb fragment in his foot, the young man possessed a Bronze Star and a Purple Heart, and he was now on his
way home to Kentucky. Eudora couldn't convince him to take a
Pullman—he felt the cost was prohibitive. She described him for
Robinson: "Flower-blue eyes, black hair, very courteous and could
wait so—something dignified & almost worldly."[43] For Eudora
this young man possessed the sort of dignity that "slick" reports
from the front had denied to enlisted men though those same reports extolled the men's war efforts.

Even as she speculated about the politics of war and as she sought to help individual soldiers who were returning home, Eudora returned to writing fiction in an intense and consistent fashion. She had discovered that centering her fiction on the private lives of individuals involved not an escape from contemporary terrors, but a call for values she believed the nature of war threatened—respect for each individual's sacred worth, faith that personal courage and concern for others were as real as the malice and hatred that underlay fascist regimes. Having written two interrelated stories about a Mississippi Delta family, Eudora set about doing even more with the subject, and a visit to John Robinson's cousins in the Mississippi Delta provided the spark she needed. When Eudora traveled to the Delta early in February 1945, she was able to read the diaries of Nancy McDougall Robinson, John's great-grandmother, and those diaries helped her to incorporate the two short stories into a novel. In mid-February Eudora wrote to Robinson, describing her reaction to the diaries.

There was a kind of greatness about her that seemed to make everything else fall in place—I can't tell you how all she said and did in those diaries moved me—it was a stirring and beautiful kind of experience, that kept me reading without stopping a day, most of a night, all the next day, and when I did fall asleep I seemed not to be forgetting her—not dreaming anything about her, but *thinking* of her through the night. I still do. All she went through, yes, but the simplicity that was really a tragic and poetic approach to life, a higher dignity than mere fortitude—of course the love she grew to have for her husband (and his very real & warning presence is as real in the pages as a fire on the hearth, isn't it?) was the real fire in which she was so formed and her suffering purified, I thought, not the hurtful fires of her troubles—I mean there was a point where she might have been formed by things or destroyed by them, and she was very heroic in trouble but she was also very tender and malleable in devotion to him, and so did not break. Did you feel this? I wonder, if it's true, if she did consciously—of course she knew it, if it's true, deep inside, and was quite introspective. I kept thinking as I read, what a strange thing to do—to receive in two days and a night by reading, a whole, other, intimate life—it seemed wrong and beautifully revealing—things that could never be seen the slow way, living from day to day, evident in startling clearness and in a serious and inevitable way, a beautiful way, from this unnatural speed and from this distance and time. Her wisdom seemed so very deep inside her, so innate, not raw or freshly learned, but instinctive or profoundly given to her by love and friendship, things she would not question or need to. She knew all she needed to—how little people can do besides give of themselves—she knew anxiety and trouble were real. The dangers of the world she knew about. And pleasure she knew from knowing dangers more than from memories of those flighty days in Port Gibson, I think. She knew it from wishing her world to be a good place, now in that moment, present joy for people she loved. But you see she has me under some spell.[44]

Eudora recognized Nancy McDougall Robinson as a woman who could face anxiety, trouble, danger, with courage, who wished "her world to be a good place," and who sought "present joy for people she loved." Eudora's tremendous anxiety for John Robinson, her fear for his safety, had their nineteenth-century parallel in John's great-grandmother, and Eudora sensed the sort of courage and serenity in his ancestor that she sought in her own life.

Nancy Robinson had come to the Delta as a young bride, in 1832, and her journals reveal just how much a frontier region nineteenth-century Mississippi was. Her first Delta home, Nancy writes, was a house made of "sticks and mud like a dove's nest" where she lived "more than 150 miles from any near relative in the wild woods of an indian nation, a stranger and unknown sitting in a low roofed cabbin [sic] by a little fire, nothing to be heard (that is cheerful) save the shrill note of the skylark the loud shriek of the night owl or the tinkling of a distant bell."[45] Nancy goes on to describe the bears her husband and, later, sons killed in the wilderness, the visits from plantation to plantation that family members made or received, the yellow fever epidemics that threatened the Delta population, her efforts to nurse both blacks and whites afflicted by fever, the devastating effects of the Civil War, the arrival of a Federal steamboat on the bayou, and the 1869 conflict between her son and a business associate, a conflict that resulted in the associate shooting at her son Douglas and in Douglas returning fire and killing his assailant.[46]

In "The Delta Cousins" and "A Little Triumph," Eudora made little attempt to create a sense of the Delta past, but in *Delta Wedding*, the novel Eudora began to build in February 1945, the diaries provide a history for the fictional Fairchild family, as it gathers in 1923 for a wedding. Two characters in the novel, George and Dabney, grant the family past its meaning, a meaning that embraces rather than denies mystery. These individuals recognize the courage with which their ancestors confronted isolation, death, the unknown, the courage with which they faced those realities rather than retreating from them. Writing in 1945 to readers of the forties, Eudora clearly relied upon dramatic irony. She and her readers knew that neither George nor Dabney, nor any of the Fairchilds would be able to remain in the relatively secure world of 1923. They would have to face a severe economic depression and a world war; the courage of their ancestors would have to become their own if they were to lead meaningful lives.

Writing about the prewar Mississippi Delta thus complemented Eudora's concern with wartime dangers. That concern intensified when President Roosevelt died and when Walter's ship saw action in the Pacific. Like most Americans, she took FDR's death hard. On April 14 Eudora wrote to Robinson, "I felt that in Roosevelt we had something that would save some suffering and time and would be a force against the powers and big shots and military— I did have faith in him for that, didn't you? Just in his magnitude as a man if nothing else— I felt he had ambition to some extent, but that it was kept subservient, and would be kept subservient." In the same letter she worried about Walter, noting that since the Battle of Okinawa had begun, eighteen days ago, the family had received no letter from him. By the time victory in Europe was proclaimed, at least Eudora's political doubts were assuaged. Churchill and Truman now seemed as statesman-like to Eudora as she had previously thought FDR. "It's V-E Day—& I am wondering what you might be doing—and thinking how it would be to see you," she wrote to Robinson. "I woke up when it was day, not to miss the broadcasts— You must have heard them & how simply & with dignity Truman spoke—& Churchill— 'The evil-doers now prostrate at our feet'—iambic pentameter— & the way he concluded. I could hear it in the air yet, out taking a walk just at dark to the hill over State Street, Advance Britannia! Long live the cause of Freedom! God Save the King!—All very Empire throughout, wasn't it—but mightily stirring & eloquent & the loathing in his *voice* when he swiftly named Jodl, gave his rank—he was calling him every foul thing without a word— One of the great moments to me was that note from the horns, just afterwards— I could hardly bear it."[47] A week later, Eudora waxed philosophical about the rise and fall of Axis nations. She saw fascist dictators as the product of the people they had ruled, and she hoped that from the people would come a new and more life-enhancing vision of leadership. "I think as you do," she told Robinson, "about the terrible demand of the people producing Hitler and Mussolini—just as I feel that it is in the people now that hope must lie and the vision spring up, like the evil which was also a vision and transcended them. I had that same feeling of the littleness of those men once they

were dead—they were of no consequence instantly—all the vitu-
peration seemed to take the dignity from the vituperators."[48]

Despite the high spirits of V-E Day and the sense that European dictators were now "of no consequence," there was the horror of the concentration camps to confront. None of Eudora's
letters speak directly about the camps—as she had told Robinson after he graphically described his experience in battle, reports
of such violence and malevolence "went to that part of my life
where all things stay secret"; they had to be translated into other
terms. But her attitude toward Germany had hardened over the
course of the war. In a 1944 letter to John Robinson, she had
suggested the defeat of Germany should not lead to its partition.

> Don't you think a question like the peace, too, must be met
> as human being to human being, by the nations? It seems
> the only clue, as to how to begin, the only practical key—
> the use of judgment of character— That is why I'm against
> partition of Germany—as unhealthy & breeding ills—&
> for a subjection of the integrated nation by establishing
> public cooperatives (for one thing) with all the European
> interests concerned represented—you would not dismem-
> ber a person to keep his character in control—that would at
> the outset destroy the hope of your work & the chance of
> its evolution to any good— Suppression & tearing apart
> never do any good, & make a rigid, inflexible system that
> when broken, is as if it had never been— We should have
> to fight revolt forever—& would anybody trust anybody, or
> even breathe easy— Let Germany use her industries & her
> achievement of a single organized nation, but *for others,* for a
> while—I still feel that to destroy Germany would destroy
> something in us too— But to *use* her, to benefit all the ones
> she has hurt, would show all.

Then Eudora asked, "Do you think this at all— I am far from
everything & mostly just think to myself—& I am no problem

solver in my thoughts—instead I mostly have feelings & they are that the life, whatever it is for all of us, will in the end be the little, personal, everyday things—a personal matter, individual— I cherish that still & always— *Moments* will count, still, then—& be magical & colored, good & bad, as some little thing makes it— War & peace do not change that, do they? Not any sheltered thing will seem to have been lost—that is my hope—that days will still be beautiful & nothing between you & the sky like Naples now." Three months later Eudora's views of Germany were harsher. Worried about land mines in Europe, she wrote Robinson that "the Germans really think so carefully into other people's carefree ways—it's so technical besides so mean—the poor Italians, at their hands." On February 2, 1945, she was distressed by German bombing raids. Then on May 1, after the Buchenwald concentration camp had been liberated and newspaper accounts of its terrors had been published, she implored Robinson not to "be relating yourselves, requisitioning, to any Germans—to cruel men— It makes me want to cry out. I do cry out."[49] She desired to "cry out" against German war crimes and cry out she did, ultimately using her hometown newspaper as a forum for lambasting anti-Semitic political candidates and movements at home.

Even as she faced the reports of mass murder coming from Europe, Eudora continued to be plagued by personal worries. On May 25 Eudora told Diarmuid, "My brother is in the fleet off Okinawa so we have been anxious and still are, because they keep on bombing it, but we had a letter yesterday, and just hope maybe the little minesweepers though they shoot at planes won't be counted as targets."[50] Eudora also worried that Robinson might be sent to the Pacific. Both worries proved unfounded. Walter emerged from the war unscathed and was decorated for his service; Robinson remained posted in Europe. But another great horror lay ahead: the atomic bomb.

Long distressed about the civilian casualties and dislocations occasioned by the politics of war, Eudora reiterated that feeling to Robinson early in 1945: "I wish it would all be over and hope it but it is hard to see how it can be soon either in the fighting or inside people, just now— I hate it for what you all think over there, of nations and politics and schemes. The belief has never left me that in the people themselves is what's in me, bound to be, a tremendous hate of that, and so schemes can't break that greater power, but the wrong ones suffer. Did you get my letter wondering if you could seize time to write a 'Letter from Italy' from your recent tour that would tell the real things about it— as well as permitted—you could convey something essential without telling, I feel it is needed." But these concerns paled in August 1945 when atomic bombs were dropped on Japan, bombs that inflicted untold suffering and seemed to threaten the future. After both Hiroshima and Nagasaki had been devastated, Eudora closed a letter to Russell in a spirit of profound sorrow. "I hope this ends before we have to do any more—before we drop another one. I am one of those that tremble about the universe— only you can't really tremble for a whole universe. In an H. G. Wells story, the scientists could have the bombs accidentally fall on their own heads and somebody would say, better that their secret died with them."[51]

This is not to say that Eudora had become a pacifist. She had not. She believed that the United States' military actions constituted a tragic necessity. She deeply regretted but did not decry President Truman's use of the atom bomb, hoping its use would bring victory in the Pacific "before we have to do any more—before we drop another one." That hope was immediately realized. The war at last had ended. Eudora could rejoice in the safety of her brothers, of her friends, and of John Robinson. With other Jacksonians, Eudora took a moment for celebration. "We went downtown and stayed a minute, I saw a lady walking down Capitol St. holding a flag with 5 stars on it right over her stomach—where the sons all came from in the first place. People sitting all over the mansion and church grounds, like the Fair. Nash sent me some Confetti from Times Square."[52]

Less than two weeks after this celebration, Mississippi Senator Theodore Bilbo, for whom anti-Semitism and prejudice against African Americans went hand in hand, announced that he would seek reelection on a platform opposing the Fair Employment Practices Committee and anti-poll tax laws. Eudora had long opposed politicians like Bilbo, and his new declaration intensified her opposition: The announced platform built upon Bilbo's virulent and outspoken racism, and his popularity in Mississippi made Eudora feel that the state was unworthy of its returning soldiers, who had bravely fought against racist regimes. Immediately she expressed her concern to Robinson and voiced a desire to crusade against such politicians and policies.

> Mississippi is as bad as those things make you believe and a little worse for the lack of even regret among the people here who could have minded or could start now. Yes, a trance—that is what it must be—if trances are that stubborn. What will happen if we let it keep us—want it to keep us—from seeing things as they really are in Mississippi. I think "when the men come back" many times a day and it gives me both hope and dread—thinking then a little hard-headed sense will be brought to bear, and then aching to think what the men will find if we don't come to. I realize of course, and more from what you just said, that all they've seen too is dependent on the individual—I know not to look for them in numbers to have seen at all what you would see and know anyway, but I can't help but think that regardless and regardless, the *hope* is there—and God knows it ought to be *here*, cherished at home and fed some. I've never been a crusader, being a more shy and private per-

son, but I may be now—the way I speak out, and can't sleep from indignation.

The next day, Eudora sent similar comments to Russell. "I started reading *A Passage to India* again—the politics in Mississippi make me so sick I have to get some release and there really isn't any against the rage that comes over me—what is going to happen, with things like this and people like that Bilbo— It's too much for me."[53]

Just as reading E. M. Forster's novel about British racism in colonial India brought Eudora a cathartic experience, so, too, did her own writing. In September 1945 she was finally able to complete work on her first novel, *Delta Wedding*. Building upon revised versions of her two unpublished short stories about the Mississippi Delta and upon her reading of Nancy Robinson's diaries, Eudora had honed a narrative that implicitly endorsed values antithetical to Bilbo's. And in incidents she had added over the spring and summer and now at last put in final form, she spoke cogently about her wartime fears. In 1980, thinking back on her work of the war years, Eudora noted, "That was a terrible time to live through. I couldn't write about it, not at the time—it was too personal. I *could* write or translate things into domestic or other dimensions in my writing, with the same things in mind."[54] It is true that Eudora could not write autobiographically about her wartime concerns and for periods of time could not write at all. It is also true that the fiction she produced between 1943 and 1945 was not merely a translation of the personal "into domestic or other dimensions," but the elevation of the personal into a political principle. Believing that "life is lived in a private place, where it means anything is inside the mind and heart," Eudora could not countenance fascist insistence on goose-stepping conformity, and she saw the survival of "private places" as a goal of the Allied war effort. Nevertheless, she feared that the demands of waging war would cause even the Allies to dismiss the personal as inconsequential. In *Delta Wedding* she incorporated this double-edged concern into the story of the Yellow Dog, a local train that threatens the lives of the Fairchilds as they walk across a railroad bridge on their way home from a picnic. As the Dog unexpectedly approaches, family members begin to jump in panic from the bridge, but the retarded child Maureen catches her foot and cannot do so. Uncle George's attempts to help her are unavailing, but he will not leave her side as the train pulls upon them. It stops at the last minute, and all are safe. But George's wife Robbie is infuriated with him. He has put his life at risk for Maureen, not thinking how his death would have devastated his surviving family. Robbie's objections are like those Eudora raised when John voluntarily participated in night-flying missions, but by the time she completed her novel, Eudora had come to see such objections in a more complex light. In the face of death, George acts to save his enigmatic, unsympathetic, unpredictable niece. To abandon her would be to abandon the essence of his being, the principle that makes him so precious to Robbie and others in his family. Here a personal family crisis is an emblem of the sort of crises that occurred regularly during the war, and here the protection of the single, separate person seems a worthy ideal by which to live, even though that ideal could involve tremendous cost.

For long periods between 1941 and 1945, Eudora Welty found herself unable to do what she loved most—write fiction. War occupied her attention. She read analyses of wartime politics and military strategies, she reviewed books about the war, she speculated about the far-reaching consequences of dropping the atomic bomb. But above all, Eudora experienced the war on a personal level, thinking about John Robinson, her brothers, and her friends in the military, writing them letters, sending them care packages, agonizing about their situations. Such activities for a time made it impossible for her to concentrate on writing fiction, and when she did think of doing so, the war seemed too large for her fictional canvas. Ultimately, however, Eudora came to believe that a focus upon the personal was crucially important to the international scene. Two paradoxes of the United States' war effort—an attempt to protect the sanctity of nations and individuals from arbitrary assertions of power, even as it employed tremendous power itself, the criticism of reductive stereotypes abroad, even as such stereotypes persisted among its own citizens and institutions—these paradoxes, Eudora believed, must be confronted in the private place where life is lived. And for Eudora that private place was the subject for fiction, and it was to fiction that she finally returned. As she wrote "The Delta Cousins," then "A Little Triumph," and ultimately *Delta Wedding*, Eudora dramatized more and more fully her deepest and most personal response to war, her sense that love and hate, life and death, hope and despair "were the closest blood—unrecognizable one from the other sometimes, making moments double upon themselves, and in the doubling double again, amending but never taking back."

• • • • • • • • • • • •

"Love First and then Separateness"
1945–1951

The postwar world was one of great promise, and in late 1945 Eudora felt this keenly. Those she loved had returned home, and her career as a writer was well established. She had published three books and had another forthcoming. National literary and artistic circles were now her own. Her time at Yaddo in 1941 had led to close relationships with artists Karnig Nalbandian and José de Creeft, with composer Colin McPhee, and with fellow writers Katherine Anne Porter and Edna Frederikson, and her 1944 summer in New York City had deepened her friendship with agent Diarmuid Russell and brought her new friendships with Robert Van Gelder and Nona Balakian of the *New York Times Book Review*. Her world was growing wider and wider, and her place in it was becoming more and more distinguished. But at the center of her life was still John Robinson. Between 1945 and 1951 their romance would ebb and flow. During 1946 and 1947 Eudora would twice journey to San Francisco and spend several months living there near John. In 1950 John would follow Eudora to Europe, where they would share good times on the Côte d'Azur and in Florence. But there were long periods of separation between these meetings, and by the end of 1951 their relationship seemed doomed. Like Lorenzo Dow in "A Still Moment," though her concerns were earthly rather than divine, Eudora would know "Love first and then Separateness," not the reverse.

As 1945 drew to a close, Eudora was ready to chart a new course as a fiction writer, to embrace new places and new people, to share her life with John Robinson, and to move beyond the provincialities of her native state even as she held tight to her Mississippi connections. She finished writing *Delta Wedding* and a bit later treated herself to almost three weeks in New York City (although she had to sleep on a cot in Dolly Wells's room at the Albany—there were few rooms available in the postwar boom). By early November her brother Edward and his wife, Elinor, were back in Jackson, Hubert Creekmore had sold his first novel, and Walter had hopes of being home by Christmas. On Armistice Day Eudora wrote to Frank Lyell in high spirits indeed, reporting that she and John Robinson's sister Anna Belle were going to bring John home the next day: "That will be wonderful. He got in last Wednesday and called me from NY and is getting discharged at Shelby. It has been a long time."[1]

Eudora was thrilled by Robinson's safe return. This keenly intelligent, well-read, handsome man, with a sense of humor akin to Eudora's own, could now be part of her life. Robinson's friends—Ella Somerville of Oxford, Mississippi; University of Mississippi law professor Bob Farley and his sisters; Jacksonians Joe and Mary Frances Skinner—were similarly devoted to him and delighted at the prospect of a reunion. Robinson's homecoming did not, however, end worries about him. He seemed anxious and unsettled. Why? Answering that question is a bit complicated. Though John may well have discussed his emotional state in postwar letters to friends, few of these letters are extant. Those he sent to Eudora—perhaps more than two hundred written between 1946 and 1951—she destroyed sometime in the 1970s so as to protect his privacy.[2] But in 1983, John's nephew discovered a hoard of Eudora's letters to John stored under the old family home, and John quickly decided they should be returned to her. By giving them back, he gave his blessing to their preservation. The surviving correspondence, though one-sided, clearly indicates that John was in turmoil about his future—he did not want to resume his career as an insurance adjuster, he thought longingly of permanent residence in Italy, he was moody and often depressed.

Eudora's own discontent with Mississippi was different from Robinson's but was more powerful in some ways. She increasingly felt that politics in her own state betrayed the values for which the war had been fought. On December 20, 1945, she wrote the *Jackson Clarion-Ledger* to complain about the paper's coverage of Gerald L. K. Smith's recent visit. While in Jackson, Smith, who according to Walter Goodman was "the country's noisiest anti-Semite," proclaimed himself opposed not only to "Stalinism" but also to "Internationalism and other forms of alienism" and sought to expand his Nationalist movement in the South. Knowing that Smith both blamed Jews for the Great Depression and World War II and denied the reality of the Holocaust, Eudora was offended by the *Clarion-Ledger's* neutral coverage of his speech. Recognizing the legacy of Nazism and the spirit that would eventually fuel McCarthyism, Eudora asked the editor, "Isn't there anybody ready with words for telling Smith that that smells to heaven to us, that we don't want him, won't let him try organizing any of his fascistic doings in our borders, and to get out and stay out of Mississippi?" She went on to ask, "Is there still nothing we can do to atone for our apathy and our blindness or our closed minds, by maintaining some kind of vigilance in keeping Gerald Smith away?" Eudora concluded her letter by denouncing Smith's ideological pals: "We will get Bilbo and Rankin out when their time, election time, comes, God willing."[3] In her hometown newspaper, the usually circumspect Eudora thus made a forceful and impassioned political statement, a statement for openness, tolerance, freedom of speech and of belief, the very values she had championed in her wartime fiction and would continue to champion. Eudora denounced the isolationism, anti-Semitism, and racism that were the staples of Senator Theodore Bilbo and U.S. Representative John Rankin, recognized that the defeat of Nazism had not destroyed the hatreds it represented, and called for change. Eudora sought to "atone for our closed minds" and hoped that Mississippi might prove a more open society than it had in the past.[4]

The Jackson response to Eudora's letter was mixed. "Got some phone calls of approval," she wrote Diarmuid Russell, "and 1 anonymous letter saying I was known as a dirty Communist and to keep my mouth shut." Russell told Eudora that her expression of disgust would "probably . . . have the Klan out for your blood," but she seemed unworried by that prospect. Her worries were focused on Robinson. John, she told Russell early in 1946, had "been a little low in his mind," and as a consequence Eudora felt low, too. "I feel nervous and bad, really not like any way I ever felt before—don't know what I can do about it," she wrote Russell. She turned to work, revising the character of overseer and bridegroom Troy Flavin and sharpening her portrait of class conflict in Mississippi for the book publication of *Delta Wedding*. And when John's spirits seemed to rise, so did hers. In late March she told Frank Lyell that in the face of unlikely weather she had organized "a picnic last night, John, Anna Belle & her husband who is back & out—big fire, & fried chickens— Cold but nice." And at the end of April, she reported on a party given by her longtime pal Jimmie Wooldridge at the Robert E. Lee Hotel. It was, she wryly observed, a "freeflowing party, John made old fashions, and we missed you."[5]

Delta Wedding was released in mid-April, and the reviews of her first novel were alternately distressing and pleasing to Eudora. Orville Prescott, her old nemesis, was harshly critical in the daily *New York Times*, calling the book "pallid, over-refined, painted for admirers of a particular school of esthetics, not for the general public," but in the Sunday *Book Review,* Charles Poore praised the novel highly. *Time Magazine* branded it a "Cloud-Cuckoo Symphony," far removed from reality, but Hamilton Basso, in the *New Yorker,* called it "as fine a novel as any contemporary American author has turned up with in recent years." Diana Trilling, Eudora told Frank Lyell, had accused her of "xenophobia and narcissism," and Eudora took exception to a number of other reviews because "they say why didn't the author write a different book from this?" Harnett Kane, in the *New York Herald Tribune,* for instance, regretted that the novel displayed "less than a passing interest in the cancers within an economic system than can produce . . . Mississippi's Bilbos and Rankins," but even he rejoiced that "Mississippi has given the nation something to compensate, at least in part, for such 'contributions' as its savage clowns in Congress. The work of a Eudora Welty comes like a clean breath after the miasmic outpourings of the state's ill-tempered Claghorns." A year would pass before Elizabeth Bowen reviewed the British edition of *Delta Wedding;* she called it "a beauty" and went on to assert, "I don't imagine that anyone who is on the look-out for anything new and great in writing can by now have overlooked the work of this young American, or that anybody susceptible to the magic of writing can have forgotten hers, once met."[6]

The emotional highs and lows brought by her *Delta Wedding* reviews, however, could not match the highs and lows in Eudora's relationship with John Robinson. At the end of May, Robinson visited law professor Bob Farley and his wife, Alice, in Oxford, Mississippi, where he was literally as well as figuratively distant from Eudora. As a result, she was troubled. "How could I be all right in my heart or my mind," she wrote him, "while not knowing how you felt or doing anything or being anything that would count. It seems a preposterous life to me. Sometimes I feel part of something I don't know all of—or its destinations—sometimes left, no part. It is all right the not knowing, but not the not being."[7] Clearly, Eudora longed for commitment and Robinson felt unable to give it. The end of the war had not truly brought them together.

Instead of languishing in Jackson in "a preposterous life" of uncertainty about her relationship with Robinson, Eudora decided to spend much of the summer in New York City even as Robinson traveled westward. New York provided just the tonic Eudora needed. During her eight weeks or so in the city, she visited with Dolly Wells, Lehman Engel, Nash and Marjorie Burger, saw a good bit of poet Allen Tate and his wife, the novelist Caroline Gordon, went to Mount Kisco with Eileen McGrath, took a long drive by the Palisades with the Robert Van Gelders, and spent two long weekends with Rosie and Diarmuid Russell in Katonah. At the end of June, Eudora made a short trip to Washington, DC, where Frank Lyell was now stationed. Lyell and the artist Marcella Comes arranged a party for Eudora, and it was a rather enticing affair. Eudora was self-effacing, but the distinguished guests were delighted to meet her. According to Comes, Eudora's

> attitude was one of regret that the party was not for a "glamour girl," and trepidation at meeting such people as Alexis Leger [the French poet and former diplomat] and the State Department (as represented by the Macys, Coxes and John Vincents). She was so obviously a creative person who would never be spoiled by success that she stood out for what she is—the real thing . . . They all loved her. I had a rum punch in the garden and it was a lovely day. Everyone feeling very informal and happy. Mrs. Landon, who wrote ANNA AND THE KING OF SIAM, was there though not sharing honors. She was attractive, looking-like a suburban house-wife . . . Betty Vincent asked where in the world I got so many attractive men. They outnumbered the ladies 3 to 1! About 30 people.

Afterward, Marcella painted Eudora's portrait. When Marcella "told me I had an eyelid-fold like G. Garbo I thought it was fine from the start," Eudora wrote to Robinson.[8] And indeed she did like the portrait. She was not prepared, however, for Comes's assumption that she would buy it at the price Comes assured her was a bargain. Though Eudora returned to New York without the painting—it was still not quite dry—she was unwilling to offend and would soon purchase it.

On July 19, having spent a satisfying month in the city, Eudora suggested that Robinson might also like living in New York. She wrote to tell him that "out of a clear sky I had an apt. offered me for 3 months, Oct. on. Shouldn't I take it, for you or for me or both? It has a back gallery on quiet court." Robinson demurred. He traveled on from Jackson, Wyoming, to San Francisco, still uncertain where he wanted to settle. Norma Brickell urged that he join her and her husband, Herschel, when they traveled to Spain. Reluctant to make a precipitous decision, John sought Eudora's advice, and she suggested he follow his heart and not the Brickells.

You should have peace when you want it, & where—and privacy—& a view—I don't believe you would ever be happy working for anything that wasn't more or less idealistic—& that didn't make sense to you personally—& didn't ask something real—& I think that one day before long you might be working for yourself entirely if you found the thing you liked—which I hope—Maybe now it is Italy & the Italians—then you should do it—I don't see anything good in the Spain idea. Norma would drive you mad before the boat was an hour at sea—you know that—And Spain is a compromise, it's not Italy—so why take it—I don't think it's right for you to feel forced to decide anything before you're ready—I don't have the feeling it's wanting to get away from here that makes you want to go, so it isn't that urgent—it would mean things were really desperate for you to change them for a life with Norma—*not her* care—so if it's wanting to go *to* a place & that is possibly Italy, don't rush to Spain—I think it's terribly important what you do about this & that the only thing for you to do is the thing you really want— If it seems to change still, won't something in good time say, this is really it? I hope so, so you can be rested of this—Don't worry, my dear, please don't suffer about it. Nothing can really press & rush you, & tell Norma to go to hell before you let her do it.[9]

In opposing his trip to Spain, Eudora was surely concerned about her own proximity to Robinson, but she was more concerned about Robinson's welfare. Norma Brickell was a notoriously dominating personality, and travel with her promised to be problematic. Robinson found Eudora's reasoning to be sound, did not join the Brickells, and did not give up on Italy.

Before she left New York, Eudora was able to help Robinson in a very practical way. He hoped to be a writer and was working at fiction, posting his stories to Eudora for editorial advice. She found his story "A Room in Algiers" quite good and promptly sent it to the *New Yorker* without waiting to ask his permission. Eudora, now a seasoned veteran of publishing, knew what daring it took to submit a story and expose oneself to rejection; Robinson was self-deprecating and hesitant, but in this case he needn't have worried. The story, based on his 1943 encounter with an eccentric Algerian landlady, was accepted and published two months later. When Robinson expressed concern that the *New Yorker* had taken his story as a favor to her, Eudora quickly replied that the *New Yorker* had not yet accepted one of her own stories. Still, she felt that Robinson could write even better stories if he would draw upon the trauma of war, and she believed that doing so was crucial to his regaining emotional equilibrium. "All this *must* come out somehow," she wrote to John, "before you will feel really better. What more natural cause and effect than for it to hurt you and then keep hurting you, all of it inside? I think of trying to tell you what happens when you write to any extent—it will change for you as you go, like from going around the block to going around a city, maybe at some moment the world—I don't mean 'progress' but just that it's as sensitive & variable a thing as the mind could need perhaps. When a story is going on, then you feel things highly and even more than you knew you might, and they reveal themselves to you in a way that gives some pain too, but in the work something is resolved, and let go." She went on to say that writing "purifies experience, in a way, and what hurts most about experience may not be its pain, which is pertinent but (I think this) its dross, its alloy, residue. You make something. Its truth is somehow related to your honesty and torment. It's a little like loving someone in that, you can't let anything false go from you, it has to be true from a certain moment. Then you know the lovely ease this makes happen." She urged him to write about his most haunting experience and added that "I will be the one you can send it to and I can stand anything (I think)—terrible or hateful or beautiful, whatever you have a desire to make of it. You didn't let very much out in this story, it was that kind of story and just right that way."[10]

Eudora herself was coming to terms with personal experiences by writing fiction about them. In September Diarmuid Russell read "The Whole World Knows," the first story Eudora had completed in almost a year. He was impressed but found the story "filled with an almost intolerable anguish of spirit."[11] That anguish was surely a more dramatic version of Eudora's own. The story describes a marriage on the rocks and a husband's longing for reunion with his wife even as he feels suffocated in a southern small-town environment. Eudora's sense of the constricted nature of Mississippi life and her fear that an alternatingly warm and distant relationship with Robinson might never break from that cycle are implicit in the narrative.

At the same time she was writing "The Whole World Knows," Eudora was also working on two other stories. She seems to have destroyed one—a story centered upon the characters Aunt Studney and Dabney from *Delta Wedding*; the other she would first call "The Golden Apples of the Sun" and eventually "June Recital." She wrote to Robinson, asking his advice about German phrases that the story's music teacher might use and about recital pieces to have her characters play on the piano. He then asked her advice about the writing process. Eudora's response discouraged John from excessively revising his stories, citing Katherine Anne Porter as a case in point.

> About keeping things and changing them forever—that was always a bone of contention between K. A. Porter and me—she suffered, really suffered, from not wanting to let any story go. She has things she had kept 7 years, or 14 I believe, still taking out words or maybe just reading over, and not writing the last paragraph. She is a perfectionist—which horrifies me some deep way. I think it might be another term for a toiler in either fear or vanity—is it the same thing? for after 7 years of working on maybe a single moment of life or a single incident, the vitality will have gone and only the spectacular casing she provided for it remains—a beautiful casket, if she doesn't watch out. Maybe I am hard on her, and it's not that I don't know her writing is fine, but a story is a story, no more and no less, and not something too precious for this world. The best story we can write is not as precious as what it strives to contain—that is part of the emotion of writing. You can never write well enough—no, you never can.

A week later Eudora reassured Robinson, who evidently felt his writing might be somewhat old-fashioned, that it was not. "I have a feeling," she told him, "that people have tried to get complexity in their writing by the wrong methods sometimes—by fussy embroidering and obscurities. It's not in fancy applique but in design itself, new line and form, that the new things come that open our eyes—the conception itself, which is the goodness of the mind it came from—I feel this anyway. Most 'experimental' writing makes me feel impatient and sort of ashamed to read it— and the old and fine writers of all time seem constantly to be experimenting and to renew themselves, the stories, the more you read. I never air my views like this—something has unloosed me. What you do excites and pleases me—because I believe you do what you mean to do." And almost a month after offering this passionately phrased encouragement, Eudora wrote to counsel patience. "One of my theories (I just have a few, maybe just this one) about stories is that time itself is one of the ingredients— just as much as talent & work—It takes a certain *amount* of time plus the rest."[12]

Even as Eudora sought to encourage Robinson to have the drive and the stamina needed for a publishing career, she longed to see him. "Often I ache to see you with my eyesight but I can get along fine providing you are all right there—Just keep me sure—I care so bad." She need not worry, his reply must have indicated. Not only was he all right, but he had also written a new story, which he asked her to read. "Sure," she in turn responded, "send it to me. I will do my best to tell you what occurs to me if that would be useful." A story seemed to bode well for the future, and Eudora went on to express confidence in John's talent and prospects for publication. His creative endeavors, she felt, were like hers—sustained by faith in their desire for and devotion to each other. "Sometimes I have a notion we are like phoenixes. Each story is the nest going up in flames and the fire. Then again. —Except that a phoenix is so alone and I have you and you me." In Eudora's metaphor, fiction was a nest in which she and John lived as phoenixes. Her love of writing and love of John were inextricably connected, a single burning passion, but such was not the case for him.[13]

In October, Eudora experienced a period of intense anxiety, fearing that Diarmuid Russell had cancer. Great was her relief when doctors declared he did not. Not long afterward Eudora sent Russell what he most liked to receive from her—a new story. "The Golden Apples of the Sun" pleased Russell, but he worried that the story's length (seventy-three typed pages) would make it difficult to sell. Eudora responded almost immediately. "I'm glad you liked the story. Do you think the title is too fine? I thought maybe I should call it 'The Window and the Door,' but yielded in the end to the more beautiful one. I expect it needs more work—did you feel it? I knew the form, length, would be the devil for you, and am sorry for such untoward length—but it kept getting longer the more I worked to get it shorter." Still she was less concerned with her story's fate than with Robinson's on-going quest for publication. She asked Russell to write to John. "He would be cheered to hear from you thinking so highly of you—if you had a moment to send him a note to Box 706, San Francisco. He is absorbed in it & it would mean such a lot if he had luck now."[14]

While seeking to provide encouragement to Robinson, Eudora also conceived of a project that would bring them together, and she wrote to suggest that they publish a magazine. She had saved $5,000, which she was willing to invest, and also wanted to seek funding from other sources. John welcomed the idea, and in mid-November Eudora traveled to New York with this project as a high priority. She spoke with Allen Tate and Harcourt editor Lambert Davis, who had run magazines on their own, asking about the feasibility and cost. Tate thought that $3,000 would do for a start, but Joseph Henry Jackson of the *San Francisco Chronicle* told John that $150,000 was a more realistic figure. At one point the funding issue seemed to have been solved. Editors at two Hearst publications—Eudora's friend Maggie Cousins of *Good Housekeeping* and Arthur Gordon of *Cosmopolitan*—took her out for drinks and promptly proposed using the resources of their magazines to subsidize the effort. "Hearst $$ to finance us," Eudora excitedly reported to John "&, the revolution, to nationally advertize our little magazine in their big regular magazines, inviting new, good writers to contribute, paying them, & putting it down to their own advertizing fund as the great laboratory-or-workshop magazine made possible by Good House, Cosmo, et al—How do you like it? . . . Of course we're not to breathe about it—I doubt if old Hearst himself would ever even be told. But Maggie & Gordon (a Savannah boy) will see what can be done."[15] Ultimately nothing could be done, and Eudora's high hopes for the project were dashed.

This disappointment not withstanding, Eudora was elated when Robinson suggested that she come to San Francisco for Christmas. On December 18, 1946, she was aboard a train called the Challenger, and she would find that her stay in San Francisco offered personal and artistic challenges, as well as many good times. By Christmas Day she was ensconced at the Hotel Whitcomb, and she wrote to thank Diarmuid and Rosie Russell for a gift. "This morning in the hotel room I have, John & a friend of his & I had our own Christmas tree—a real one, with some stuff on it, & some very small presents under the tree as we were poor, & the clock dressed up things & *went off,* the alarm, as I took it out of the box. If it had *sung,* & said 'Merry Christmas' I wouldn't have been more surprised."[16]

On New Year's Eve, Eudora joined John and his friends Art and Antoinette Foff, themselves struggling writers, for a small but enthusiastic celebration, and a day or so later reported on the event to Russell. "The Foffs are terribly nice—he is young, Jewish I think but don't know, bright, full of enthusiasm & energy—friendly & *so* curious about you . . . His wife, just a child, is brighter than he is, pretty, French I think, (Antoinette) writes detective novels—'in defense.' They had John & me out to a spaghetti supper New Years Eve, & we sent you a postcard. All the evening we had been talking about Faulkner, Foff had lent me 'As I Lay Dying'—'My mother is a fish' is out of a Faulkner mouth, have you ever read it? I think I'll send it to you—Mod.

Library seems to have got out 'As I Lay' & 'The Sound & the Fury' in one volume—It is a magnificent story—well, both are."[17] Eudora also reported that John had suggested that she stay on the West Coast and try out the city for a month or so.

John's original request that Eudora visit him in San Francisco and his subsequent proposal that she remain there marked an increasing ardor on his part. Though that ardor would persist—in 1950 he would tell the poet William Jay Smith of his love for Eudora—John was reluctant to equate love and marriage. Between 1947 and 1951 he was by turns encouraging and withdrawn, retreating from commitment after suggesting it might be forthcoming. The stories he worked on during this time clearly show his pattern of vacillation. In ". . . All This Juice and All This Joy," he depicted, as Harriet Pollack has noted, a "recently discharged young soldier and a more hesitant young woman who are heading toward their first intimacy." They walk along a California beach, then up into the shelter of some trees, where an ardent Tom kisses her, overcomes her reluctance, and makes love to her. Afterward he draws back from the young woman. "'So that's that,' he thought. It seemed to be the end of a long journey and why he had set out on it was not so clear to him."[18] Whether John and Eudora ever became lovers is unclear; it is clear, however, that like his character Tom, John both desired and retreated from Eudora.

As 1947 began, John was in pursuit, not retreat. He had declared his wish to have Eudora near him, and she responded by looking for a San Francisco apartment. On January 4 she wrote Diarmuid to say that "an apartment burst upon me, to be sub-let by the week, so I took it—big room, bed in a door, big kitchen, quiet, $14.50 per week—I'm moving in it today—probably the only person in San Francisco who found an apartment today. It's a good chance to stay on a little while, the woman will want it back in a few weeks *if* she leaves her husband—she told me all— an Italian lady married to a German. She may want it back sooner than I think. I hope to write a story in such a nice quiet place."[19]

By the end of the month, Eudora felt more secure financially and more able to remain on the West Coast—"The Whole World Knows," after causing a row at the *New Yorker* between its champion William Maxwell and the magazine's kingpin Harold Ross, had been wisely bought for the sizeable sum of $750 at *Harper's Bazaar* (the story would go on to win an O. Henry Award).

Settled in the city, regularly cooking dinner for herself and Robinson, taking long walks, going to see Pierre Monteux at the symphony, hearing Andrés Segovia play the classical guitar, taking in art exhibitions at local museums, spending time with Robinson and his friends, enlisting Russell's aid for Art Foff, and working at stories, Eudora nevertheless began to be ill at ease. John was not in the best of spirits. "I get worried at times," Eudora wrote Russell in early February. "I'm under no illusion I help him any because that has to come from himself, but it seems hard not to be able. My hope is a story will sell and he will get interested or confident enough to throw himself into writing. The way he feels now, he might just leave S.F. one day, it wouldn't surprise me." On Valentine's Day, she wrote to Lyell about her concerns. "John has written some but is not very settled or happy at all it seems to me—he is still more or less nervous—on edge— I hope he'll get to feeling better."[20] Robinson's inability to place another story depressed him as did a sense that Eudora was his more accomplished benefactor. As a result Eudora sought to provide aid in a sub-rosa fashion. She asked Russell to help John locate writing commissions. "I knew if John were in NY and available," she explained to Russell, "you might be having things come up you could put him onto, so this is just to hope you might think of something for him out here, not mentioning I wrote you, and your notes mean a lot to him, so if you could just mention something that might be possible that would be a help."[21]

While she was still in San Francisco, Eudora and Russell exchanged letters about a possible operetta of *The Robber Bridegroom*.

John Bauer, who had helped to establish the Ojai Music Festival, in California, had asked to write the libretto and indicated that Bernard Rogers, who taught at the Eastman School of Music, would compose the score. Before long, Rogers demurred, and Bauer had second thoughts about his own involvement as a writer. Still hoping to be the producer, Bauer suggested two other possible librettists—Paul Horgan, the novelist and historian who had studied at the Eastman School, and Langston Hughes, the distinguished poet and dramatist who had played such a central role in the Harlem Renaissance. Eudora approved of both writers but was not interested in being personally involved with the operetta. "If I had my wish," she wrote Russell,

> I wouldn't have anything to do at all with any libretto, and hope I won't have to. As to the problem of working on it with Mr. Hughes, that couldn't be solved practically if it had to be done in Mississippi, and he probably knows better than I the difficulties. There wouldn't be a place he could stay, or where we could sit together. He sounds like a fine person to write the libretto though, if he wants to set about it on his own. Mr. Horgan too sounds good—but my opinion is a lay one on the whole subject. I don't want to go way back to the Robber Bridegroom and start worrying again on that old piece of work—and hope I won't be asked to—and don't imagine Mr. B. [Bauer] and I would take much of a shine to each other, to make that part go very smoothly. If a person like Langston Hughes or Paul Horgan takes over a libretto job it should be a good one and not need my meddling. Don't you think so?[22]

Eudora clearly admired Langston Hughes's poetry and was willing to entrust him with her story. She was unwilling, however, to expose him to the insult or debasement he as an African American might encounter in Mississippi, and she would also have been loath to bring social opprobrium or worse upon her mother by entertaining Hughes in Jackson. In the early 1940s John Woodburn had taken her to dinner at Ralph and Fanny Ellison's apartment; going to the home of this distinguished writer and his wife had been her first social contact with African Americans, and she and the Ellisons became fast friends. But the Ellisons lived in New York. Jackson presented a more complex problem for black and white interaction.

A highlight of Eudora's stay in San Francisco came when Bennett Cerf visited the city, inviting her to dinner and taking her on stage and back to meet Danny Kaye, a particular favorite of Eudora's. Kaye was performing at a local movie theater between showings, and Eudora repeatedly went to see his performances. Eudora told Russell that Kaye had "a real demonaic gift. When he gets the audience to giving him back the Hi-de-Ho it's not so different from the old times of Dionysus and those other frenzies, I bet." By mid-March Eudora felt better about Robinson, who had had the flu and been unhappy. She wrote Russell that "John seemed to be so much better when he was over Sunday that I was very heartened—his look and all seemed different, maybe this makes me feel changed in spirits, for it's bad to see a friend suffer and know you can't really help. I hope he keeps on feeling improved until all is well with him again." As for herself, Eudora had almost completed a new story, begun in January and set in San Francisco. At the end of March, when she decided it was time to leave California and return home, she sent the story to Russell. "My story will probably get to you in the week," she wrote. "John's read a version of it, I've done it over a few times, and thinks it's depressing, so I warn you. It is, too, but I hadn't realized anything but the work part of it, until I got to typing it up and can hardly drag through it—sounds worse every minute, doesn't it? I'll be anxious to know what you think of it, for I did a lot of hard work on this baby."[23] This story she titled "Music from Spain," and in it she depicted Francis Dowdie, a man trapped in an unhappy marriage and drawn toward Bartolome Montalbano, a Spanish guitarist whose playing was based upon Andrés Segovia's. The ambivalent sexuality of her protagonist Dowdie may have suggested what Eudora had begun to fear was troubling Robinson. Or perhaps, as Pollack contends, Dowdie's courting of the guitarist is a version of John's courting of Eudora, of his longing to be the creative artist or at least be connected to one. But at day's end, Dowdie abandons the Spaniard, and Eudora may have sensed a similar abandonment in her future.

Back in Jackson, Eudora learned that the *Atlantic Monthly* would publish "Hello and Good-Bye," a satiric story about beauty contestants that Russell had for some months been trying to place. Enjoying spring at home, she relaxed by tending her garden and worked diligently to revise the San Francisco story, which had already been rejected by the *New Yorker.* In mid-April, she mailed a new version of "Music from Spain" to Russell and turned seriously to revising "The Golden Apples of the Sun," which had been declined by both *Good Housekeeping* and the *Atlantic.* She also encouraged Robinson in his writing, suggesting that he try to accumulate enough stories for a book. Robinson sensed that Eudora's faith in his writing was misplaced, and he contemplated abandoning his hopes for a literary career and moving to Wyoming. When Eudora seemed not to take these plans seriously, he chided her. Her response was prickly. "Yes, I tend to believe your letters & think this is a reliable practice— Good luck—if you're going the other way—& so long." In the same letter, however, she quickly abandoned an injured tone and moved to a discussion of fiction, a place where injury could be transfigured and transformed. "I feel a little differently from you about form—I think that too comes through the *work* of writing—is almost one with it—that maybe each piece of work has implicit in it its own form, & the writing keeps at it & discovers & best brings out this form— But we each & all write a different way—being different human beings."[24] And Robinson, for his part, remained actively engaged in such discussions of writing; he decided to forgo a move to the northern plains and instead to move across San Francisco Bay to Berkeley. Nevertheless, this choice could hardly put to rest Eudora's concerns about her future with Robinson. His alternating roles as a suitor and as a man fleeing commitment were profoundly disturbing. A week after expressing concern about his literally "going the other way," Eudora wrote to describe her interest in Freud's biography of Leonardo da Vinci, a biography investigating the sexuality of a great artist. Had Eudora consciously thought Robinson to be homosexual, she probably would not have recommended the book. But her suggestion that he read this volume indicates that Eudora at some level understood the deeply submerged conflicts in Robinson's life, which he would eventually resolve by entering into a long-term and devoted relationship with a man.

In May Eudora received a letter from E. M. Forster. "Finding myself in your country," Forster wrote, "I feel I should like to give myself the pleasure of writing you a line and telling you how much I enjoy your work. *The Wide Net*, with the wild and lovely things it brings up, have often been with me and delighted me. I am afraid that I am unlikely to have the good fortune of meeting you while I am over here, since my itinerary keeps to the North and the West. Still, there are meetings which are not precisely personal, and I have had the advantage of one of these through reading you, and I would like to thank you for it. With kind regards and good wishes."[25] This tribute from a writer she greatly admired must have buoyed Eudora's confidence as she headed in new fictional directions. Ironically, of course, this support came from a man who, like Robinson, refused openly to acknowledge his homosexuality. Unbeknownst to her, the letter was an emblem of the central difficulty in her personal life.

By the first of June Eudora had completed "The Golden Apples of the Sun," shortening the title to "Golden Apples" but lengthening this already long story. This story, ultimately to be called "June Recital," depicts a "passionate and strange" piano teacher and her variously talented small-town pupils. Although the story's Miss Eckhart is like Eudora in the passion she feels for her art, Eudora never shared Miss Eckhart's love of teaching. Not surprisingly, then, even as she finished work on this story, Eudora declined a renewed invitation to teach at the Iowa Writers' Workshop. She did, however, accept an offer to deliver a single lecture in August at the 1947 Northwest Pacific Writers' Conference in Seattle, and she went on to devote most of the summer to preparing that lecture, "Some Views on the Reading and Writing of Short Stories."

Eudora departed Jackson for Seattle on July 25, 1947. There she saw old friends Robert and Dotty Van Gelder, visited with Robinson's army buddy Sol Katz and his wife, delivered her lecture to an enthusiastic reception, and then left on August 12 for another stay in San Francisco, near Robinson. Her ten weeks or so in San Francisco, however, were not all spent in close proximity to him. By mid-September, having sublet an apartment in the city, Eudora found herself responding to letters from John. From Laytonville, California, on his way to a vacation at Lake Louise, John had written twice in rapid succession, mentioning his plans for a new story. Sensing that upon his return John would need privacy in which to work, Eudora asked, "Do I conflict with [your privacy], or could I help you keep it—can you tell?" John's response to this inquiry evidently convinced Eudora to remain in San Francisco so that they might have more time together, but his temporary absence must have prompted Eudora to think ruefully of a story he had written during the summer and to which she had offered an equivocal response. Titled "The House of Mirth," this story depicts a young man named Mack who has an affair with and then marries Susie; afterward he feels that others have forced him into the marriage and that the marriage is a trap. When this story reached her in Jackson and she read it, Eudora believed that John had not fully come to terms with his material and told him so. "The wedding, respectability, conformity are really just the things a character like Mack would seek—why in the world would he be bitter except that he really knows inside his real reasons." And then Eudora added a word about the unfortunate Susie. "The real scapegoat is the wife of course, whom Mack married not to love." To Eudora it seemed that Mack had placed himself in fetters, then "searched" for "the object of his blame" and "ruthlessly" forced his wife to become that object.[26] Now, in San Francisco on her own, Eudora must have feared that John, though he was not seeking respectability and conformity, was feeling similarly trapped, as he failed to find success in the writing career, for which he had sought her assistance and which she had encouraged. Perhaps in beginning a vacation trip three weeks or so after Eudora arrived in San Francisco, John was fleeing the trap and placing blame. Unlike the character Susie, however, Eudora had no intention of allowing herself to become a scapegoat.

With and without Robinson, she used her time in California to complete "Moon Lake," a story set in the 1930s at a rural Mississippi summer camp for girls, and "Shower of Gold," a story of the virile, unfaithful King MacLain and his long-suffering wife, Snowdie. While still in San Francisco she realized that these two stories as well as "The Whole World Knows" and "Golden Apples" could involve a common cast of characters: Virgie Rainey, the young piano student who betrays her talent; Loch Morrison, the lifeguard at Moon Lake; Easter, the orphan girl he saves from drowning; Ran and Eugene MacLain, the twin sons of King and Snowdie; Jinny Love Stark, the daughter of the town matriarch; and a host of others. This realization sent Eudora's mind spinning; she told Lyell of episode after episode that began to occur to her. "My new plan is to go ahead with the stories and have a book of inter-related stories. What do you think of it? Not to bother with plot-threads and all that, but just to take up these people whenever and wherever in their lives that might interest me. For instance, I see Virgie in New York living with a gangster! I'd like to deal with Loch later, Easter later, Virgie, and have done so with Jinny, of course, and I don't know what all." Though Virgie never would make it to New York and though Loch and Easter would not appear as adult characters, Eudora did connect her stories, not into a novel, but into a book focusing upon the fictional town of Morgana, Mississippi, as it and its residents evolve over an almost fifty-year period. In creating these interlocking stories to be collected in *The Golden Apples*, Eudora experimented with form in the very way she had recommended to Robinson. "It's not in fancy applique but in design itself, new line and form, that the new things come that open our eyes."[27]

The birth of Mittie and Walter's second daughter (Mary Alice), Robinson's return to Berkeley in late September or early October of 1947, and Eudora's ongoing friendship with Art and Antoinette Foff provided personal rewards to balance her professional satisfactions, and her resolve to support the careers of John and the Foffs remained strong. She continued to encourage Robinson's writing efforts, and she recommended Art Foff for a Guggenheim Fellowship. But when Eudora felt the time had come for her to return to Mississippi, she was worried that Robinson's lingering cold might be pneumonia and that the "damn solitude" he desired might keep them always apart. The journey home provided a respite from such concerns. Traveling to Mississippi via the Grand Canyon, Eudora responded to the Arizona landscape and to the natural wonder at its northern edge. Wanting to see more, she changed her train ticket to stay an extra day. She wrote Russell that "nothing is like that Arizona air though and that fine, fine cold, and the yellow aspen trees. The whole state is amazing and beautiful, and I'm trying to track down some books about it—such old country." And in a letter to Robinson, she described two long walks along the canyon rim and a riveting lecture by a geologist. She was disturbed, however, by the plight of the Native Americans she saw. To Robinson she reported, "The sad thing is the *Indians*"; and to Russell she wrote, "The Indians there though are starving, truly, it is said. People seem to be investigating, but not doing anything about it yet." After reaching Jackson, Eudora continued to be concerned; she wrote to Robinson about the ominous situation that threatened an ancient culture: "You can see ruins—from the train window—of villages, I could hardly believe it—but looked up in a book since coming back and they were ruins when the Spaniards found them in the sixteenth century. And cliff dwellers. It was terrible to see the little huts with Indians living in them now, for in Arizona I read in the local papers how the Navahos are starving and the government will not help. They seem really to be ending now before people's eyes, the race."[28]

Back at home Eudora turned her attention to the garden, to drives in the Mississippi countryside, and to reading the works of Elizabeth Bowen and Peter Taylor, both of whom she admired greatly. She found Bowen's work particularly compelling. On the first of December, she wrote to Robinson about the novel *Friends and Relations.*

> The Bowen—was so curious to know what you'd think of it. When I was reading it, I would come to places where I thought you might admire—then to places, "John would hate that."—and always it was somewhere where I myself thought quite a different way, for instance I didn't hate anything in it (except the story—that of-so-inept, stretched out and don't wake me quality, too too attenuated, just like that movie we didn't like the Noel Coward one—Brief Encounter—I kept thinking maybe she herself was being harsh with that as well, that she too was mad at her plot. After all, *she's Irish*, remember—am I at the end of this parenthesis) I hadn't spotted about the slapstick quality of the action—of course—I like that. I loved Theodora when she was young, too—Bowen herself always seems so worth reading to me,

though I didn't think this novel was up to her stories, or to the other novels of hers I've read (Death of the Heart is one, and The House in Paris)—suppose it's an early one, as it's Penguin. I notice in stories now she leaves out, where she used to put in. I *see* the torture in the style, but I don't *feel* it. It doesn't bother me, it interests me— But I had the feeling about her before and most of all in this book, men and women are bound to see her from two different sides—she is so good about women, and I feel so much more sympathetic to them than to any men, but then her men are all Englishmen, and maybe they *are* like her characters, and maybe Englishmen like the men in her books—are in rapport. I thought Edward eminently not worth a tear. It's interesting, a book of her stories I'm reading now has people in them like sketches round and about and in and out of that novel—square ladies who love their husbands only insofar as Janet loved hers, one of them here takes up with a ghost of some other wife of somebody, having no one to talk to really. There is another story that could be Theodora and Denise beginning their life together, at the school. The reason I don't mind any thing about her style that you feel as discomfort is just that I like several things being managed at once per se.[29]

Eudora's affinity for Bowen's work was matched by Bowen's affinity for Eudora's. On the first of December, Russell mailed Bowen's laudatory review of *Delta Wedding* to his client. Small wonder the two writers would become close friends once they met in 1950.

However far from Robinson Eudora was literally and emotionally after her fall 1947 stay in San Francisco, she continued to hope that marriage to Robinson was part of her future. The possibility seemed to improve when Robinson, after returning home for Christmas and staying almost two months, moved to De Lisle, Mississippi. In March and April 1948 Eudora would

visit him there. And she also sought to arrange for a private printing of his story "Rite of Spring," eventually to be titled "... All
This Juice and All This Joy," complete with a photograph of
Winged Victory. Her attempts with a variety of printers proved fruit-
less. Her own career, on the other hand, continued to prosper. In
the spring she completed another of her interrelated stories. This
one was titled "Sir Rabbit," and like "Golden Apples," it made
use of a Yeats poem—this time "Leda and the Swan" was her
focus as "The Song of Wandering Aengus" had been before. "Sir
Rabbit" would not be accepted by a magazine for several months,
but the by-now-much-traveled "Music from Spain" had been accepted by the Levee Press, in Greenville, Mississippi. That February, in the process of revising her San Francisco story, Eudora
decided that it, too, had Mississippi roots and should be connected to others she had written since the war. Just before her
typescript went to the Levee Press to be printed, she renamed her
protagonist: Francis Dowdie became Eugene MacLain, the displaced native of Morgana, Mississippi.

Though in 1948 Eudora continued to find the home place a
congenial spot for writing, her dissatisfaction with social progress
in Mississippi had not abated. She deemed the state legislature
a congregation of morons, and she thought the state's major
newspaper, the *Jackson Clarion-Ledger,* equally benighted. In mid-
February, she wrote to Robinson in De Lisle: "I feel like burning
the Clarion Ledger every morning. Well, I just won't go into it.
And the Legislature a disgrace every day, and altogether Mississippi seems to get more hopeless all the time. Jeeze! The other
day a bill was proposed wherebody (whereby anybody) who did-
n't like Mississippi could get a free ticket out of it, the state to
provide the RR fare and a ten dollar bill to spend when you've
got out. Hooray! I'll be the first one—I'll go somewhere nice and
be a twenty-minute queen." And less than a month later she objected to the inane treatment the *Clarion-Ledger* had given to a Klan
event. "A fiery cross was burned in Jackson the other night by

'hoodlums' and Bob Hederman wrote, 'The main question developing out of the incident was, How do they burn a fiery cross? (Paragraph) The answer is simple: Just the way you burn any other two pieces of wood.'"[30]

Eudora's resolve to spend more time out of state was a result of such incidents, and she hoped that Robinson might accompany her. Three times in the spring Eudora wrote to suggest the joint venture. "I love you and think of our lives in a real and prideful way," she told John. But Robinson seems to have been unmoved. By the end of April, Eudora had relinquished her hope that they might travel together. "My little idea was to go up to Vermont in my red Ford & find a studio of sorts & try to do a story or so—& pay rent by book reviews, class, or whatever offered & see the country round about—I'd just thought if you'd like coming too, it was fine. I think of going in May. The lady gave me such short time but think now I'll tell her no on her cottage & drop by her inn one day & look around for myself."[31] No trip to Vermont was in store for Eudora and John. Instead, early in May they went to Oxford, Mississippi, where John had many good friends. Dr. John Culley and his wife, Nina, hosted a dinner for them. Bill (William) and Estelle Faulkner, Bob and Alice Farley, and Nina's sister Ella Somerville were the only other guests, and the evening included an irreverent round of hymn singing. The next day Eudora, Nina, and John Robinson visited the Faulkners at their home called Rowan Oak. The Faulkners, Eudora excitedly wrote to Frank Lyell, "showed us over the place—the house is same age as Nina's, built by same architect in fact, but is less 'restored'—has old wallpaper, soft old wood, a lovely patina—& I felt that *cool* you always said was in such houses in the country— Faulkner has three oil paintings stuck over his mantel, of himself & a lady & man, ancestors—all of whom look like Robert E. Lee—his mother painted them, I understood—and there is a bronze owl on his bookcase— He (F., not owl) had on shorts & a blue shirt, had come in from seeing about his race horse—which daughter Jill rides." Faulkner himself, Eudora wrote, "is besides being the greatest writer to me, an attractive, darling person—quiet, listening to all kinds of stuff, amusing when he speaks."[32]

At the close of May, despite the good times offered by such Mississippi outings, Eudora left on her own for New York City and would remain there until the end of August. The summer seems to have been a glorious one for her, and she seems to have made peace, temporarily at least, with her separation from Robinson. The city certainly offered many attractions. Eileen McGrath and her sister Peggy Rockefeller welcomed Eudora with a party in her honor, held at Peggy and David Rockefeller's apartment. Eudora was able to see a Pierre Bonnard show, to meet artist Maurice Sterne, to see (and dislike) *A Streetcar Named Desire*, to attend a Lewisohn Stadium concert conducted by her San Francisco favorite Pierre Monteux. In July she and Dolly Wells spent a vacation on Martha's Vineyard, and Eudora painted the natural beauty of the setting. Back in New York, Eudora began a long stint of house-sitting for the Eddie Merrills in Westchester County. There she and Hildegard Dolson, another client of Diarmuid's, worked on a theatrical revue, and there Eudora entertained friends from the city and the Russells, who lived nearby. The large house was not as inviting as Eudora had hoped—considerable construction was underway and workmen were underfoot—but she managed to master the Aga stove, which she was required to keep burning twenty-four hours a day, and she loved nighttime skinny-dipping in the Merrills' pool—nude swimming would be part of her next story. During the summer, Eudora's thoughts often turned to Robinson—she was a faithful correspondent, she showed enthusiastic interest in the course work he had now begun at the University of California in Berkeley, and she sent his story "... All This Juice and All This Joy'" to *Horizon*, where it was eventually published. But the attractions of New York and Westchester County offset her loneliness for Robinson.

In September, when she returned to Mississippi, Eudora immediately began a new story and completed it before the month's end. A clearer understanding of her relationship with Robinson was implicit in this story, and she sounded the keynote of the story in a September 2 letter to John. "I think in us all there are Perseus & the Medusa—must keep on being— Only in a breathtaking piece of art or in myth or poetry is the separation ever bearably consummated—& then only as far as the very moment—too unexplorable beyond—even for heroes, much less for human beings— And then I feel too that the Medusa *is.* Haven't I felt it all too! Sometimes love & friendship & the Medusa were the same to you—I knew that— Maybe always will be a little— It's all right— There's something there— Anyway all right." The Perseus and Medusa imagery of the story to be first titled "The Humming-Birds" and later "The Wanderers" is here in Eudora's letter to Robinson. In the letter, Eudora depicted herself as the Medusa in Robinson's eyes, as one whose love and assistance had at times, or so it seemed to him, threatened to set his course in stone and deny his need for independence and solitude. But in the same letter Eudora also recognized the Medusa as a victim of Perseus, as a living being who had been mortally wounded by the legendary hero. She suggested that the hero and the monster, the murderer and the victim, were part of "us all." That is the very realization that comes to Virgie Rainey as "The Wanderers" draws to a close. Forty-something Virgie, in the wake of her mother's death, the lone surviving member of her family, single and at the end of a meaningless love affair, has long since squandered her talent as a pianist, but she nevertheless takes comfort in the power of great music to convey the truths of myth and to transfigure life's terrors: "Cutting off the Medusa's head was the heroic act, perhaps, that made visible a horror in life, that

was at once the horror in love, Virgie thought—the separateness . . . In Virgie's reach of memory a melody softly lifted, lifted
of itself. Every time Perseus struck off the Medusa's head, there
was the beat of time, and the melody. Endless the Medusa, and
Perseus endless." Of course, Eudora continued to feel keenly "the
horror in love . . . the separateness." As she wrote to John on September 23, "I love you, you know it. When I do wrong in it it
nearly kills me. Part of me too slow, part too fast, maybe. Wish I
could be transformed and made even and bright."[33] Perhaps Eudora had been "too fast" in seeking to help Robinson establish a
writing career, perhaps she had been "too slow" in recognizing
his need for space from her. More likely, she had been unjust in
blaming only herself. Robinson had consistently sent Eudora
mixed messages, urging her to spend extended time in San Francisco, then shying away from commitments; asking her to read
his stories, then insisting he was unworthy of her praise. His own
conflicted sexuality—his love for Eudora, but his secret need for
a male companion—must have tormented him and prompted his
inconsistent behavior with her. Fortunately, during her summer
in New York, Eudora had found personal ways to cope with lingering grief about the state of their romance, and on her return
to Mississippi she discovered artistic release and wrote one of
her finest stories.

In her story she also found a way to cope with the strain her
extended stays in San Francisco must have occasioned between
herself and Chestina. Eudora's unconventional decision to join
John in California surely caused talk in Jackson, and Chestina
must have also sensed that the relationship would never develop
as her daughter wished. For her part, Eudora must have regretted
the worry she had brought to her mother. Unfortunately, correspondence that might support these assumptions is not yet available; letters between the two Welty women are sealed until 2021.
But in "The Wanderers," Eudora seems to approach her own
mother/daughter tensions in an oblique fashion. Katie Rainey, so

different from Chestina in terms of class and intellectual interests, is like Chestina in her devotion to her daughter, Virgie, and
perhaps in her regret that Virgie's love affairs have prompted
unchivalrous gossip. And Virgie is like Eudora in loving her
mother deeply, but also perhaps in feeling a need to be free of
her mother's opinions or judgments, expressed or unexpressed.
The night after Katie dies, Virgie goes to the banks of the Big
Black River, removes all her clothes, and swims in the nude. As
she moves through the water, all her senses are engaged, and she
feels herself becoming one with the natural world. Part of that
mystic oneness is feeling released from "a bondage that might
have been dear." Surely Eudora longed for freedom from a
mother she cherished, a freedom that involved not a literal death,
but the metaphorical death of guilt, and that allowed for the kind
of sensual experience that is Virgie's. That longing is implicit in
"The Wanderers."

Having written this new story, Eudora still had a theatrical
revue to complete, and she worked on it sporadically and unen-
thusiastically. Even now Robinson's desire to establish a writing
career claimed considerable attention. After contemplating a joint
effort at dramatizing Faulkner's *Sanctuary,* Eudora and Robinson
began long-distance work on a screenplay of *The Robber Bridegroom.*
Less than two years earlier, she had resisted such a project, but
with Robinson's welfare in mind, she did no longer. After the presidential race between Republican Thomas Dewey and Democrat
Harry Truman, the man she supported as "the nearest to liberal"
candidate, had come to a close, Eudora and Robinson mailed each
other drafts of their separately assigned scenes. Eudora's efforts
were clearly the better contributions, though she complimented
Robinson on his. Work on the script, however, was far from en-
compassing. Eudora took time, for example, to entertain the Oxford artist John McCready and his wife on their visit to Jackson
and to write the *New Yorker* about Edmund Wilson's review of *In-
truder in the Dust.* The review, she felt, denigrated William Faulkner

simply because he was a southerner who had chosen not to immi-
grate to the urban Northeast. "It's hard to listen to anyone being
condescended to, and to a great man being condescended to pre-
tentiously," Eudora wrote. "Nearly all writers in the world live,
or in their day lived, out of the U.S. North and the U.S. South
alike, taking them by and large and over random centuries . . .
And it does seem that in criticizing a novel there could be more
logic and purity of judgment than Mr. Wilson shows in pulling
out a map." Shortly after she defended Faulkner in this letter, she
found herself disturbed by a legal case in Mississippi's Jones
County, one involving incest and miscegenation: "What an Eliz-
abethan [story], and what a Jones County one too—the double
incest didn't cause the lift of a brow, just the miscegenation—
and the poor man will have to go to jail for five years, to correct
things."[34] Eudora was appalled by the racist law and by the community's concept of morality, but the Jones County tragedy
seemed to transcend time and place and may have eventually influenced Eudora when she wrote what is perhaps her most
Faulknerian story. In "The Burning," a black slave woman bears
the son of her white master, provides that child with a devotion
his white, plantation-owning family will not permit itself, and
sees him go up in flames when Yankees torch the plantation
house. Subsequently, she assists in the double suicide of the boy's
white aunts but continues her own life with a stoic fortitude. This
sort of gothic South, however, is not typically Eudora's. More
often her stories center upon the rituals of southern small-town
life—its piano recitals, weddings, funerals, ladies' teas, political
speakings—even as they transcend a regional focus. They confront questions of love and death, passion and repression, tolerance and bigotry, just as fully as do stories with more lurid plots,
but in the use of the mundane, they suggest that life's terrors lie
close at hand, not in a distant past or an exceptional event.

As 1949 began, Eudora was still struggling with her contributions to the theatrical revue she and Hildy Dolson had begun

during the summer; New York producers, on the other hand, were interested not in the revue, but in dramatizing "Music from Spain." Both Maurice Evans and Eddie Dowling wrote Eudora about the prospect. Eudora had no script for this story, but she did have *The Robber Bridegroom* screenplay. Lehman Engel cautioned against her approaching Dowling with it. "Eddie is apt to get very excited about something and go so far," Lehman confided, "then upon encountering obstacles, large or small, might simply relax and forget about it."[35] Eudora was undeterred by this advice, Dowling was intrigued by the possibilities, but Lehman proved prophetic. Negotiations about the Welty/Robinson script eventually came to a dead end. By contrast, seven stories Eudora had written since 1946 were getting launched. Harcourt had accepted Eudora's collection of interrelated stories, and Eudora spent spring 1949 in Jackson, readying them for book publication as *The Golden Apples.*

That spring Jackson itself offered particularly interesting and surprising diversions. Early in March Eudora saw Martha Graham and her troupe dance in Jackson, and afterward she was exhilarated by conversations with Graham and with her young dancers. To Robinson, Eudora wrote, "Last night had a wonderful time—went out and ate with the young Martha Graham dancers—to my surprise. Went to the performance—pitifully small audience, rattling around in the auditorium but appreciative—the Wolfes, other painters, & music faculty at [Millsaps]—and she had sent message to come speak to her and was a gracious person besides such a fine dancer I think. We talked, she said she felt in reading my stories I could do something for the stage—hooray! Then the kids—6 of them, about 18 or 20—3 boys and 3 girls—took me along to eat at Primos, and so alive, intelligent, attractive, wide-awake—you would have enjoyed so—interested in the whole world. And what a performance—nothing 'arty' or sissy anywhere of course, but very new and if anything too intellectual for my taste."[36] Later that month more intellectual stimulation came Eudora's way—she traveled to Memphis for a visit with the writers Allen and Caroline Tate and with their daughter and son-in-law.

In April Eudora learned that her application for a second Guggenheim had met with success, but before making any plans about using it, she turned her thoughts to proofing *The Golden Apples* and to attempting yet again to place the movie script of *The Robber Bridegroom*. Eddie Albert, she learned, was to be in New York in May. Albert might, Harcourt editor Ted Amussen had indicated, be interested in the Welty/Robinson script. When she left on April 28 for New York, Eudora took the script with her and was still thinking of additions and revisions to it. Shortly after she arrived in the city, Robinson wrote to suggest that she come to California, but he must have in some turn of phrase betrayed a lack of faith in their future. In January while studying at Berkeley, he had longed to be near her in Mississippi, telling Nancy and Alice Farley that "Eudora makes me yearn for that part of the country," but then had backed away from his professed yearning with the qualifying phrase "has been so wretchedly cold here." His new invitation must have conveyed a similarly mixed message, and Eudora was hesitant about making a return trip to the West Coast. Instead she suggested that Robinson travel eastward. She said she would come to him "if you thought that place good," but quickly added that the Bay Area "hasn't done you well enough, the way I think." As for herself, she noted, "I don't honestly like to go back to a place that hasn't been too good, and think a place can influence things too much, help or hurt, to go against it unless it really must be done. But place comes second, and I would like meeting."[37]

In fact, the East Coast had many attractions that held Eudora in the summer of 1949. She met writer Jean Stafford and had the opportunity to hear E. M. Forster speak at the American Academy of Arts and Letters. She occasionally dined with *New*

Yorker fiction editor William Maxwell and his wife, Emmy, and joined them for a weekend at their country house. She and Dolly were amused to meet the English aristocrat and aesthete/author Stephen Tennant. He had written to Eudora in Jackson proposing that she visit him in Florida or that he stop by for tea in Jackson. Made aware of the vast distances involved, he did not act on either idea. But one afternoon in New York, he knocked on Dolly Wells's door, inquiring after "Miss Welty" and telling Dolly that her apartment was "delightfully bare."

Early in June, Eudora and Dolly took off for a Boston vacation—Eudora fell in love with this city she had never before visited and was entranced by a Matisse show at the Fogg Museum. "How beautiful and alive. Not a wasted or useless or unspontaneous-looking line or space. It's a kind of hyperspontaneity he finally achieves, I think. We should understand, grasp such, I think we do a bit. In all he does you feel how he is finding such joy in life." But soon she was back in New York, resolved to spend the summer. She stayed first at the Gramercy Park Hotel and then managed to sublet an apartment. Eudora made a lunch date with Eddie Dowling, only to be stood up, and seems never to have established contact. She and Dolly one night went dancing "with two boys that liked those German-American and Swiss dance halls—more fun. Picnic like. A good summer night thing to do and cheap." She saw a good bit of Herschel Brickell, helping him with some typing chores and learning that he had voted against her Guggenheim because, as he put it, "them as has gits." Learning that Herschel thought she was being rewarded for past successes rather than new promise was disheartening. These comments, Eudora told Robinson, "Rather sunk me." But she was sunk only momentarily. Movies, art galleries, theaters, and concerts claimed her attention. She saw celebrities like Greta Garbo on the street and saw her friend Jean Stafford off on a ship for Europe. And she began to plan her own European trip. John, who earlier in the summer had asked Eudora to come to San Francisco but who had been unwilling to visit her in New York, was now in the process of seeking a Bender or Fulbright Fellowship for study in Italy. "Hope Italy looks sure," Eudora wrote to John. "Did you know I counted on seeing you there, is it all right with you?"[38]

Eudora returned to Mississippi early in August, and so did John. *The Golden Apples* appeared shortly afterward. Maxwell, who had long wanted to publish Eudora's stories in the *New Yorker* and who had by this time become a good friend, immediately wrote Eudora to praise the book and to offer accolades from his wife as well.

I had finished reading (while the lawn mower stood idle on the lawn) the first section of The Golden Apples, and was three pages along in June Recital, when Emmy came out on the porch to get away from the cereal worms she had been pursuing through the kitchen cupboard, and I went back and read her the three pages and she smiled and said "It couldn't be nicer." She is dreadfully critical and so I was as pleased for you as I would be for myself that she was pleased. She went back into the house and I went on reading, stopping once to take the folding chair out into the yard, lay a fire, and get the stepladder and take some things to the attic, at her polite request, and then, having done all these things without my mind, rushed back to your book. At one point I was aware that I was holding my breath, a thing I don't ever remember doing before, while reading, and what I was holding my breath for is lest I might disturb something in nature, a leaf that was about to move, a bird, a wasp, a blade of grass caught between other blades of grass and about to set itself free. And then farther on I said to myself, this writing is corrective, meaning of course for myself and all other writers, and almost at the end I said reverently This is how one feels in the presence of a work of art, and finally, in the last paragraph, when the face came through, there was nothing to say. You had gone as far as there is to go and then taken one step farther.[39]

Published reviews by such notables as Hamilton Basso, Herschel Brickell, Malcolm Cowley, and Francis Steegmuller echoed this private one from Maxwell.

Mythological allusions had reverberated throughout the pages of *The Golden Apples,* but in her next story, Eudora approached myth head-on rather than allusively. Having reread the *Odyssey* on her train ride home from New York, she immediately wrote a short story about Circe and titled it "Put Me in the Sky!" In this story Circe describes the torment of loving Odysseus, who chooses his crew and the onward journey rather than staying with her. Perhaps Eudora was feeling a similar sense of rejection, but ultimately she, in advance of Robinson, would embark on an adventurous journey.

For several weeks, however, the two were together in their home state. Late in August, Robinson and Eudora drove to Oxford, Mississippi, where once again they saw William Faulkner. Eudora wrote to Jean Stafford about this second encounter.

William Faulkner took us sailing on his sailboat on a big inland lake they've cut out of the woods there—waves and everything, big. We were late getting there—got lost and went to Blackjack, Miss.—and when we found the lake there was Faulkner cruising around, and headed right for us, through the dead cypresses and stumps and all, pulled down his sail and took the oar, and hollered, "You all better take your shoes off and get ready to wade," which we did snakey—got pulled on board and then we sailed all around, all quiet and nice—what a wonderful person he is, the most profound face, something that nearly breaks your heart though, just in the clasp of his hand—a strange kind of life he leads in Oxford, two lives really. We never, either time

I've been with him, talked about anything bookish of
course—it's his life, not his opinions, that seems to be with
you all the time. He can do or make anything, and can sail
beautifully. We got in his 20 year old Ford touring car which
he hunts and fishes and goes over the farm in, with holes in
the floor ("well, I know where the holes are") and when we
couldn't open a back door he said, "There's a cupboard latch
on it," you ought to see that car.[40]

Sharing a private meeting with Faulkner must have been
tremendously exciting for Eudora and John, but they came to the
meeting from radically different perspectives. Eudora met the
master as herself a mature writer whose career was well established, Robinson as a novice attempting to find his way in the literary world. Eudora and John's love for each other could not
bridge this gap in achievement, and the gap between them literally widened in October when Eudora sailed for Europe, and
Robinson, still without a fellowship or grant to finance transatlantic travel, left for Mexico. The two planned to collaborate on
a fiction anthology, using Eudora's Seattle lecture as an introduction. But for a time, at least, that work would have to be done by
mail at a very long distance.

When Eudora sailed for Europe on October 14, 1949, the
very day Russell sent "Put Me in the Sky!" to *Accent*, where it
would be published, she did so as a woman of forty, an accomplished writer who was confident of her literary stature. Confident but not arrogant and certainly not blasé, Eudora would revel
in the freedom of traveling alone and would greet the experience
of Europe with both the enthusiasm of a child and the appreciation of an artist. Her experience abroad would prove extraordinary. Eudora was already far, far from a sheltered provincial, but
she did not relinquish a sense of wonder at all she had encountered. Neither an innocent nor a cosmopolitan exactly, she was an
independent woman and an artist on whom nothing was lost.

Eudora's 1949 voyage to Italy itself was an exhilarating experience, one she would later incorporate very directly into the story "Going to Naples." She loved traveling *turistica*, and even before reaching Italy, wrote Robinson to describe her time on shipboard.

You'd have lots of practice in different Italian dialects if you'd been on this boat, I think—at my table is a gentleman from Palermo, a gentleman from Naples—really Bari—and across from me a Corsican, a Roman, and the old man with the 10-cent whistle—I don't know what he is! A real devil flint in his eyes—wears an old green sweater and dirty pants, has grizzly gray hair, drinks all the wine up every meal, causing high words with the Corsican (dangerous, looks like) and at any moment he sees fit during the meal he takes out the whistle and blasts it. It's in particular for another old man, some way up the dining room—this old man has moles over his eyebrows like a second, finer set—like real moles—and makes him start right up and shout. The steward—a just-so type, without a part in his hair—came over once right at first and spoke to the old man, asking why, and brought out a story about once on boat with little boy (gesture just above floor) might get lost, and when he blew this (TWEET!!):—*Papa*. The steward gave up and he still blows it—not enough to make you listen for it, a real comic sense of timing. The ladies—I'm with the shawl crowd. Several mothers with daughters taking over to marry them in Italy. Within five minutes after the boat sailed I found myself talking to a Palermo lady who had just been voted Most Typical Italian Mother and whose picture is going to be on all the posters for Holy Year, you can watch for it. A really placid, gentle, sensitive nice lady but her daughter! The Sicilian Patsy Kelley [an American film actress and comedienne]. She speaks frequently of her money, house, car, and prospects, but has to play pingpong [*sic*] with the 12-year old boy, but she yells at each ping. I avoid them since the first, unless I can see Mama alone, but of course these mothers are right behind their daughters every minute, watching and listening. Some of the old ladies are mean as the devil—send back all their food, get other dishes, send that back, and spill everything—having to eat through shawls, head shawls, scarfs and all that they wrap up in, and then never having been professionally waited on—treat the waiters just like home. And the waiters all so polite and nice to them—mamas are really like the V.M. [Virgin Mary] aren't they? What they expect. The men are much more interesting. Of course we will lose a good many Portuguese in the morning. (One invited me to spend a week with him in Lisbon. Now he cuts me.) We also have Spanish, and a number of Sicilians. I look at them and think of all that behind their faces, Greek, Saracen, Roman, Ostrogoth!—or whatever. My Sicilian lost his tie pin immediately. It could have been, he said, waiving to those on shore—"Goodbye! Goodbye!"—he showed me at the table. On the bulletin board since that day has been a notice in Italian and English, Lost, a golden brooch for the tie, initials D.L. The Neapolitan beside him has showed how the tiepin can be made more secure—by including both ends of the tie and the shirt in its grip. His is a cameo. He wears a green suit and tweed cap, has nice hands and small feet, very nice person. He leaves off all the last syllables of what few words I recognize and all proper names, Palerm, Napol, etc. He also says "Natch." Natch. He can't read or write—the young bridegroom who is the 4th at our table asked him to read "Bari" on an envelope and the Neapolitan made an abrupt final gesture with his hand. It had been he though who was so very pleased to be given the passenger list. "Can keep this," he beamed, putting his in his pocket. Everybody was pleased with the passenger list, much comparing of names in print. Part of the excitement of the first night—all dampened when forms were passed around next, to fill out. Depressed everybody. Now that bridegroom—he too came up to me in the first five minutes out, and showed me a poem. Apologizing because the paper was dirty, it was written on a train. "Waterfall" rhymed with "animal." He'd been looking out the window from Chicago, where he lives on Division St. in the Polish neighborhood, he is half Russian and half Pole and is going to Bari to marry an Italian girl he's courted by correspondence, never seen. He is unbelievably uninformed, not misinformed, just un-. Looks like Gene Autry. In fact, he likes Gene Autry I found out last night at the ship's dance where he entered swinging an imaginary lariat, only he called "Hi-ho-*Sliver.*" Works in a machine shop. Ran the needle through his finger once, of course, it won't bend up. I am surprised he has not done worse—he is appealing, too, has a voice just full of anticipation and excitement, tenor— rather like the musical comedy hero entering. He is unworried by any questions about this marriage. Her picture—he passed it around while they were changing the reel at the movie one night, started it down the row of the audience— shows a pretty, lively girl. All the Italian boys say no question she could marry in Italy. The Neapolitan one day asking "You ever seen this girl you marry?" and being told no, made the same gesture he made about reading and writing. I helped the Polish bridegroom fill out some paper and he said "I can tell, you're an office girl—so patient." He tells all to all. At first he was the laughingstock of the Italians, now they sort of look up to him—he does just what they expect, and now shows off all the time, and they applaud him when he jumps up at the table to repeat to the whole room some remark he's just made that went over with us. The Italian girls can hug and nudge him and carry on, since he is marked goods and it doesn't count.

Only one passenger in tourist class did Eudora find objectionable—an American lady who suspected all the passengers of Italian descent of being thieves and who used the word *nigger* and did
so within the hearing of the "two colored gentlemen" on the ship.
Other passengers proved more congenial than the bigoted lady.
Especially appealing to Eudora was an Italian American actor
named Jimmy Festa. Festa had been appearing on Broadway in
Annie Get Your Gun, and he taught Eudora some of the songs from
that musical so that together they might perform them on board.
Festa and Eudora also made the acquaintance of a very literate
machinist mate who took them out to dinner in Palermo. The arrival in Palermo itself was one of the trip's most spectacular
events. "You would have been delighted at the welcome to
Palermo," she wrote Russell, "boatloads of family connections
rowed out into the harbor to meet us, and such cries and such
wavings—'Umberto!'—'Pepiiiiita!' One rowboat had 13 big fat
Sicilians in it rowed by one poor man, the rest wildly waving and
almost upsetting. It was dramatic." Also dramatic for Eudora was
visualizing the dangerous landing that Robinson had made in
Sicily during the World War II invasion of the island. "My lord,
the approach to Sicily—how was any landing ever even tried
there, I looked and looked at those great stone mountains rising
out of mist—caves, embattlements, all kinds of places where
Guilliano and who else could forever hide and look out. We didn't
go by way of Gela of course but up around the little knob where
Palermo fits down."[41] Here was the place where John had seen
dangerous action in 1943, the place where she had hoped to work
as a foreign correspondent in 1944, the place that had been the
center of her emotional life throughout the war. She had finally
reached Sicily, but John was as far from her as he had been in
those terror-filled years.

After Palermo, Eudora's arrival in Genoa was somewhat anti-
climactic. She found Genoa and northern Italy "brisk and busi-
nesslike," so different from the southern region. Her hotel was

grand indeed but rather impersonal. Unable to book a train to Paris until November 11, Eudora set about seeing the country-side outside of Genoa—Rapallo, San Remo, and Portofino all pleased her. And ultimately she found herself, as she wrote to Robinson, very amused by a tour of Genoa itself.

> The "tour de ville" has a wonderful guide, so enthusiastic and with friends everywhere. Took us to the big cemetery in Genoa that's full of 19th Cent. full-sized marble figures in costumes of the day, big family scenes in stone, kissing of portraits by baby on tiptoe, angels, lady with poppy in mor-phia dream, etc. "*Don'* you think this soul looks like coming out the tomb, eh?" (Sure enough, the soul's hem was on the other side of simulated door-ajar.) "Ladies & gentleman (only 1 gent.) will you please pass to the next tomb, this artist was a special for angels. Look, *this way please*, this sister die young, look how she come to enjoin the other sister she die before her wedding day. Don' you think it's sad, hmmm? See that tear on this widow's cheek, get beneath and take the perspective up, what you think of that?" Lady from Tex. with stilletto [*sic*] in hat (undrawn) said "This was worth the whole trip to Italy to me"—full response to the guide—point of tears. He bought us all some Cinzano and took us to see a house on fire free.[42]

By mid-November Eudora had traveled north to Paris and set up residence at the Hotel des Saints Pères, a small and somewhat shabby left-bank establishment, but one more to Eudora's liking than the stately Genoa hotel had been. At the Saints Pères, she worked on a story about her voyage, then abandoned it. (She would return to the story, eventually titled "Going to Naples," and complete it three years later.) While still in Paris, she also devoted considerable thought to the anthology she and Robinson hoped to bring out. But Eudora was not focused upon literary endeavors in late 1949—coping with the weather, making friends, seeing the art and architecture of the city were her main interests. For a Mississippian, Paris in November seemed very cold. Eudora bought après-ski boots to wear and was lucky to have a hotwater pipe behind one of her walls. The water pipe kept the room relatively warm, and a warm room attracted the hotel's less fortunate residents. American soldiers at the hotel would ask if they could sit against her wall in order to relieve the chill. Of course, Eudora soon discovered another and even better source of relief—the warmth of Parisian nightlife. She particularly liked, as she told Robinson, "a little spot where they sing ballads at midnight in French, English, Spanish—negro and white man alternate—as each request is sung, the candle at that table is snuffed out, leaving him finally in the dark—the landlady above objects to clapping, so there is only a gentle concerted snapping of fingers for applause—nice."[43] More important than such clubs was the circle of literary and artistic friends Eudora quickly found in Paris. Most notably, Mary Mian, a New Englander and a client and friend of Russell's, lived in nearby Meudon with her husband, the French sculptor Aristide Mian. Through Mary and Aristide, Eudora would come to know an interesting assortment of Americans and Parisians. On November 16, Mary took Eudora to lunch with Kay Boyle—*New Yorker* European correspondent and author of novels, short fiction, poetry, children's books, and essays. A dynamic and outspoken woman, Boyle would eventually run afoul of an unfounded McCarthy-like attack and be blacklisted. But that attack lay in the future, and her conversation with Mary and Eudora probably did not center on political issues. Other gatherings with Mary and Aristide Mian, however, were distinctly political in tone. Though Aristide would gallantly present a rose from his garden to all female guests to his home, his gallantry did not rule out political debate with women. When Janet Flanner, the *New Yorker's* Paris correspondent whom Eudora had met during her first week in Paris, called on the Mians, as she did at least once when Eudora was present, discussion was likely to be lively, and at some point Aristide would command one of his children, "Bring me my papers!" He relied on his writing to explain and buttress his conservative political position, and Eudora relished such debates.

Visits with the Mians were also just plain good fun. With the Mians, for instance, Eudora saw a French circus, in which a magician turned water into Pernod. One of the Mians' daughters tried to do the same at home but failed—to the amusement of her parents and their Mississippi friend. On another outing, Eudora and the adult Mians saw Yves Montand perform. Janet Flanner had seen him as well. In her December 8, 1949, "Letter from Paris," she told readers of the *New Yorker* that "Yves Montand, who was trained by Edith Piaf, has now retrained himself and has been delighting adult crowds at the old vaudeville house L'Etoile, where he follows the acrobats and constitutes the entire last half of the bill. A former factory hand, he wears a kind of overalls on the stage. He has learned to make, in the best sense, a perfect show of himself—of his virile, suburban personality, his gift for miming and deftly timed gestures, his carefully clumsy dancing, and his happy hedonist's voice. His songs are short stories of sentiment and character. The favorites are 'Clementine,' which is about a best girl; 'Paris,' about a lonely country boy newly arrived in the city; and 'Les Feuilles Mortes,' about lovers whose spring has changed to dead leaves."[44] Eudora was totally charmed by Montand's performance, but she was also thoroughly amused by something that happened when she, the Mians, and two other friends left the music hall. Aristide hailed a Paris taxi for the group only to have the driver proclaim a four-passenger limit. In a triumph of French logic, Aristide convinced him that the five were really four—perhaps he based his argument on the size of the passengers, perhaps on their nationalities, Eudora could not understand French well enough to know. Whatever the line of reasoning, everyone got a ride home.

In addition to seeing the Mians, Eudora had two memorable

encounters with Stephen Tennant, who had once called upon her in New York. Early in December, Tennant again sought out Eudora, inquiring whether she would join him and Lady Harvey, the British ambassador's wife, at a performance of the Folies-Bergère. More than the show, Eudora remembered Tennant's response to it: "Darling, I'd forgotten how ravishing blue ostrich can be." Eudora saw Tennant in Paris at least once more. He invited her for a meal at the fabulous—and fabulously expensive—Tour d'Argent, and when the bill came, he asked Eudora, who was traveling on a rather tight budget, "Darling, shall we share?"

The Parisian art world captivated Eudora during her stay in France. She became the friend of art dealer Pierre Durand-Ruel, who took her and the Hungarian writer Eva Boros to the villages of Sens and Moret outside of Paris and who probably arranged for Eudora to be invited to what developed into a particularly exciting dinner party. At this dinner, Eudora was startled when her host told his guests that barrels of artwork were in his basement, unopened since they had been stored during the war. Whether the Nazis had disdained these works because they were "decadent" and deemed unfit for the Aryan plundering or whether they had miraculously escaped discovery or whether they had been recovered from Nazi looting is unclear. What is clear is that Eudora's host chose that particular evening to take his guests to the basement and to open the casks. From them, as she recalled, he drew forth plates that had been painted by Claude Monet and other impressionists, and he drew forth canvases by a number of artists including Picasso. The presence of an unassuming, keenly intelligent Mississippi writer, a woman alive to the wonder of Paris, had perhaps prompted this revelation. And, for her part, Eudora was overwhelmed by the excitement of the revelation and by the proximity of masterpieces she expected to see only in museums.

The Mians, Boyle and Flanner, Tennant and Lady Harvey, Durand-Ruel and Boros, were not Eudora's only companions in Paris. One day, as she told Robinson, Truman Capote appeared in her hotel lobby, asking for her. "When I went down, he had: blue jeans, black clinging turtleneck sweater, red knitted shawl, fringed, around neck hanging to waist, overcoat and moccasins. Said (in key of F# [sharp]) Tangier was the place—more kinds of depravity there than anywhere else in the world—cobras being sold in the street, too—he stayed 5 months. I had to take a drink off him—but not like breaking bread, was it?" If Capote's company was somewhat unnerving, the company of Mary Lou Aswell, the *Harper's Bazaar* fiction editor and Eudora's longtime friend, and her new husband Fritz Peters, himself a novelist, was wholly welcome. Eudora and the Peters met frequently at the Mians and on their own. On one occasion, the two women spent a moment in front of Monet's *Femme a l'ombrelle.* Years later Eudora would send Mary Lou a postcard of the painting and ask, "Do you remember seeing this waiting at the head of the stairs on a cold dark winter's day in Paris & how it shone down on us." On another occasion, Eudora and the Peters heard a trio of southern African American women sing at the ABC Music Hall. Coincidentally named the Peters Sisters, these women were especially delighted to meet a fellow southerner and invited Eudora and her friends to a Christmas party. Eudora accepted, though she dined first at the Mians in Meudon and then "dashed in on the last train" to join the Peters Sisters. She described the event in a letter to Frank Lyell.

(This I didn't tell before, thinking wouldn't be so good for Jackson Xmas reports!—you would like this part though.) They are vast black ladies who do a wonderful show—there are 3 in the act, and 2 others and Mama, a California Unity Church member. She had made eggnog and potato salad and chicken salad—and they expected to throw a huge party, the tree all decorated, mistletoe hung, then had to go fill an engagement at a club at 2 AM, which is just when I arrived—and all put on baby blue velvet gowns and rushed

out, I imagine the party began with most of the same guests
when they returned at 6 . . . [They] have an apt. overlooking
the Arch of Triumph, 3 bathrooms, etc. An old Lincoln,
with French chauffeur. Having a wonderful time in Paris.
[The elderly French cabaret singer] Mistinguette is in the
same show—and oh lord, how I wish she'd quit it—as the
Peters's sisters said (Mattaye really was the one who said it)
(the fattest), "She don't need the money and she don't know
none of her lines—has to be prompted every one—don't
know why she keep on. The French they say it's *lamen-table*."

Having violated Mississippi social protocol by attending a party
given by African Americans, Eudora violated it again when she
stopped by a rather bohemian establishment after leaving the Peters's apartment in the wee hours of the morning. She and the
writer Ira Morris had a 3:00 A.M. glass of champagne at the only
open café they could find, "a brasserie on St. Germaine called
Royal-St. Germaine." As Eudora told Frank, "All tables had been
reserved—by what looked like lots of people who had come on
motorcycles—boys with fur collars on leather jackets, girls in
striped suits and hornrims, etc., etc., all in paper hats too, and
throwing darts with burrs in them at Ira and me . . . That was a
third kind of Reveillon, and fun too. Looked like the setting for
a [Georges] Simenon murder to me, that last place."[45] Ardent
reader of murder mysteries that she was, Eudora felt her imagination sparked by this "third kind of Reveillon," but no real-life
Inspector Maigret arrived to investigate the scene.

In January 1950, despite her richly varied and fascinating experience in and around Paris—being moved to tears by early Italian paintings, hearing the Strasbourg choir sing at Notre Dame,
visiting music halls and cafés, conversing with writers and artists,
touring the Chartres cathedral—Eudora was ready to see new
territory. She went south, first to Nice and then to nearby
Beaulieu, where John Robinson, who had at last received a Ful-

bright scholarship to study Italian and had just established residence in Florence, sought her out; next came the Fritz Peters, and
later Mary Mian and Hildy Dolson. John spent about ten days
with Eudora, but he had the flu during this time. And in letters
to friends Eudora expressed more interest in her surroundings
than in her relationship with John. After he left, she traveled to
Antibes for a Picasso show and to Cagnes for a Renoir exhibition. Mary Mian took her on a day trip to La Turbie, where they
visited friends who were restoring a "beautiful old house" and
had a working farm—almonds, olives, vegetables, flowers, cows,
rabbits, chickens. To Eudora it seemed "a day picked out—and
the sound of those church bells coming from the town as we
walked down the hill to leave." Another notable day, she joined
Lady Harvey for lunch in Monte Carlo. In a letter to Frank, Eudora described the luncheon conversation: "Heard a story you'd
love—she said they'd noticed old Rothschild there at their hotel,
(Hotel de Paris) constantly with a girl typist since he doesn't need
one—what was the relationship? Then a mutual friend remarked,
'I say, have you seen old Maurice Rothschild and his *blood donor?*'"
But the highlight of Eudora's Mediterranean stay was carnival in
Nice and its Battle of the Confetti. "It was tres apache the Battle
of the Confetti, so we forewent the Battle of the Plaster! But the
high spirits were so genuine and *so* high, it was wonderful to see.
Those little old children were the worst, and only Beatrice Lillie
can get away with hitting children really hard, especially the ones
wearing glasses. The principle of the Confetti is to push it into
the mouth of the other party, first bending the party back-
wards—you grab from behind. And little children throw it
straight up from under you—repeatedly! The fireworks were marvelous—they turned out all the lights in the city, and shot straight
at the Moon—the most beautiful and elaborate I've ever seen."[46]

Late in February, Eudora left Beaulieu, headed for Florence, while Mary and Hildy returned to Paris. In Florence, Eudora took a room with a view at the Berchielli and was reunited

with Robinson, who had invited her to visit. From the start, Eudora luxuriated in the wonders of the place. "Florence," she wrote Diarmuid Russell, "is at present smiting me in the eye with so much that I just don't look except for a little a day." Eudora appreciated the efforts of a new acquaintance, American Margaret Ferguson, to introduce her to Florence, but she told Mary Lou that unfortunately Ferguson "brought the consul down on our heads." This man, Eudora reported about the consul, was "Confederate Alabama, complete with Mama, 92, and maiden sister who makes fudge for the consulate parties." The Confederate atmosphere was, thankfully, limited. As poet Willliam Jay (Bill) Smith has noted, the city itself provided the sort of environment Paris had offered following World War I. Intellectuals, writers, and artists from Europe and America gathered there, enjoying the glories of the city, their contact with one another, and the opportunity to live well on very little money. The artist Oskar Kokoschka, poets Stephen Spender, W. H. Auden, and Edith Sitwell, historians Harold Acton and Kenneth Clark, novelists Ralph Ellison, John Steinbeck, and Sinclair Lewis—all frequented Florence in the early 1950s. It was a mecca, and into this lively intellectual milieu Robinson introduced Eudora. She met the Italian writer Eugenio Vaquer, who would later visit her in Jackson, the French publisher Maurice Dumoncel, the Florentine aristocrat Francesco Guicciardini (descendant of the noted medieval diplomat of the same name), and she particularly relished the companionship of Bill Smith and his wife, poet Barbara Howes. Robinson, Eudora, and the Smiths got along famously, shared a particularly glorious trip to Siena, attended parties, and danced together, Eudora and Smith performing a memorable tango. Barbara had become a particular favorite of art critic Bernard Berenson. She occasionally served as a hostess for him and kept him informed about American writers in Florence. As a result, he invited Eudora, along with Robinson and the Smiths, to lunch at his villa I Tatti, an honor granted to a select but diverse company. The magnificent art collection and the beautiful gardens were legendary, but according to Sylvia Sprigge, Berenson could be an intimidating host: "He was very ruthless with . . . three categories. To a beautiful but dull young woman at lunch he would suddenly say, 'Tell me, my dear, what do you do that is useful?' To a solemn professor who had talked much he would say when at last the conversation flagged, 'Academic life is full of a lot of humbug, don't you think?' To anyone who seemed to receive their inspiration through alcohol or drugs, he could be devastating." Not falling into any of these three groups, Eudora herself was treated warmly, though Berenson seemed most interested in what she could tell him about William Faulkner's fiction. She wrote to Mary Lou Aswell Peters to describe the visit. "He is so lively, and so scheduled—all organized it is in that household, goes clicking by, people of the proper categories on hand for lunch or tea or dinner or going through the library or whatever, and Mr. B. with the busiest wits and most impeccable service— whisked in and whisked out just right, and I suppose extracting just a bit of nourishment, some way or other vaguely, from each guest as they pass through—actually keenly interested—and I should guess he could be killing about some of it that goes on. Afterwards, too, you hear how you did at Berenson's— 'you went over big,' or I suppose, 'you flunked it.'" Eudora, it seems, went over big. After she had returned to the United States and mailed Berenson a copy of her essay "Short Stories," he wrote back to commend her efforts as a literary critic. He felt she had written an original work, free from the scholasticism that doomed so much critical thinking. Still later he recalled the good conversations in which Eudora had participated: "How naughty of you & the Bill Smiths— to whom my love—to be so far away! Think of all the talks if you were here."[47] And when in 1954 Eudora sent him a copy of her novella *The Ponder Heart*, his comments were full of praise.

During all of these good times in Florence, Eudora felt closer to Robinson than she had for several years. Their time together in France had been merely cordial, but in Florence the old affinity was rekindled. Upon her arrival, Robinson had taken Eudora to see the infant David Smith, who was in the care of a nanny while his parents were briefly away in England. When Bill and Barbara Smith returned and met Eudora, they sensed that the attention John and Eudora had devoted to young David was a sign of regret for missed opportunities and of a move toward marriage. During the month Eudora spent in Italy, the Smiths came to feel that Eudora and Robinson were ideal for each other, that their gentleness, their humor, their intellects, their talents were perfectly harmonious. Weeks before Eudora's arrival in Florence, they had heard John sing her praises and long for her arrival; now they understood why. At this time Smith did not suspect that Robinson was gay—in fact, Robinson was particularly vehement in criticizing men in Florence who were flamboyantly homosexual. Barbara and Bill Smith both felt that marriage was in the offing for Eudora and John, and Bill went so far as to ask John why they hadn't yet married. Robinson's reply was ominous: "Oh, we love each other too much for that."[48] Once again Robinson seemed inclined to draw back from commitment, and by the end of March, Eudora was looking forward to a trip on her own to England and Ireland before returning for another month in Italy.

Eudora arrived in London in early April and found herself much relieved to be hearing, after eight months, the sound of English echoing through the streets and in the shops. She hadn't realized what a strain it had been to struggle with Italian and French. Her arrival in London was at first disconcerting and then reassuring. A stranger who had asked to share her cab from the train station left her, though she had little British currency, with the entire fare, but the cabbie absolutely refused to take Eudora's last shilling. Moreover, he insisted on waiting until she had safely checked into the Chelsea hotel that Pamela Travers had recommended. In London she hoped to see Cyril Connolly and V. S. Pritchett, but evidently did not. She did see her London agents

C. H. Brooks and Patience Ross, her London publisher Hamish Hamilton, and Travers.

By her birthday in 1950, Eudora had left London and was at the Hotel Russell in Dublin. Eudora loved Dublin and the surrounding countryside, riding city buses beyond the city limits so that she could wander down country lanes and observe infinite shades of green in the landscape. Mary Lavin was ill during Eudora's time in Dublin, but the two writers did finally manage a good visit at the Lavins' new, and still uncompleted, house on the River Boyne. While she was in Dublin, Eudora received a telephone call from Elizabeth Bowen inviting her to Bowen's Court—British literary critic Raymond Mortimer, who had made Eudora's acquaintance in Italy, had written Bowen to say that Eudora was in Ireland. Eudora wrote Robinson from Bowen's Court to describe the glories of the place, waxing eloquent about the house, grounds, and environs. She said less about Bowen than about Bowen's Court. Perhaps this is the reason Bowen would say that she and Eudora preferred places to people. Bowen's conclusion was certainly overstated, for this meeting signaled the start of one of Eudora's close friendships. From Bowen's Court, Eudora returned to Dublin, this time finding Mary Lavin hale and hearty. The two women climbed Tara, "a kingly & magnificent place—from which you can see 20 of the 32 counties if I remember aright."[49]

When she returned to England, Eudora met novelist Henry Green at a literary cocktail party, and the two were immediately smitten. As editor John Lehmann noted in his diary, "Henry and Eudora flung themselves at one another, & I have never seen Henry work so hard, be so reckless, madly ebullient . . . E. drank more & more & was completely swept off her feet." The next morning Green phoned to invite Eudora to his house, and that evening they discussed, to use her words, "heaven knows—everything, I think. I cannot remember. I was captivated."[50] However captivating this evening, which was topped off by a pub crawl, Eudora was soon on her way back to Florence, pausing briefly in Paris to bid the Mians and the Fritz Peters farewell. In Italy Eudora was joined by her lifelong friend Dolly Wells. The two traveled with John Robinson to Capri, Pompei, Amalfi, and Rome, then Dolly left for Lake Como and Eudora for Assisi before they regrouped at Robinson's villa outside of Florence. At this villa Robinson felt thoroughly at home. He easily adopted the role of country gentleman that he associated with his Mississippi ancestors. Perhaps partially in response to Robinson's contentment there, Eudora found herself entranced by the setting and what grew on it. She loved its peaches and berries and grapes, and she was interested in Robinson's wine-making; she criticized only the unkempt maid Robinson found so unsuitable and inescapable. But Eudora's future was not in Italy. Robinson gave her and Wells a farewell dance party, and the two women joined Bill and Barbara Smith for one last Italian excursion, this time to Venice. Then, in early June 1950, Eudora and Dolly sailed for New York on the *Saturnia*.

Back in Jackson, Eudora's thoughts frequently turned to Italy. From Florence John wrote that his story to be published in *Harper's Magazine* was dedicated to her—was this merely an expression of gratitude or was it a declaration of love? Eudora must have wondered. But by now she was rather cautious in responding to Robinson. During the summer her letters to him were newsy, not ardent. She expressed worry about John's safety in driving his Lambretta motor scooter, and she sent a large box of clothes for the Italians she had encountered at his villa—for the vile maid, La Tosca, and for Raoli, Mario, Julia, and Luciano, servants who had worked on the house and garden. That same summer, Eudora also wrote a story far removed from her European experiences—she turned to Mississippi and the Civil War. Late in August, she mailed the story to Russell, but she was unsatisfied with it and spent the fall reworking it. Ultimately, "The Burning" was taken by Mary Lou Aswell Peters at *Harper's Bazaar* and would win second prize in the 1951 O. Henry Awards.

The dissatisfaction Eudora felt for her new story was matched by her dissatisfaction at home. She and her mother had lived companionably together, but mothers rarely give up mothering. Now Eudora wanted the sort of independence that had typified her time in Europe, and she sought a room of her own. In late September she wrote to Robinson, "I found a piece of land yesterday, tiny, 3 acres, that I'm hoping I can get for little & build a cabin on & get place to work— Woods now, highest point in Hinds Co., it looks like, Zion Hill, on road between Utica & Vicksburg, with old gravel pit adjoining, & one side hanging over Natchez Trace—oaks, sweet gums, pines, big dogwood, & gullies & vines every which way—no good for farming, said a store keeper I asked about it (LeGrand Yates, of Cayuga). So may be cheap—keep your fingers crossed. Opposition emotional in home quarters— Wish I had it now." The prospect of an unpleasant neighbor, not her mother's opposition, ultimately derailed this purchase, but Eudora found another attractive prospect: "A quieter road, toward Learned, Miss., and an old house on it, looks 1840, in ruins and abandoned, with hay stored in the breezeway and a scarecrow in a back room, making me knock on the door, but if I could have it and afford, I'd work at it with my own hammer and nails. A view like W. Hollingsworth landscapes—sedge, cedars, low hills, and little ponds from the front porch. It makes me ache to come out and speak of it."[51] This possibility too proved unattainable—the owner did not want to sell to an unmarried woman.

In mid-November 1950 Eudora was in New York. She and Nash heard Elizabeth Bowen speak at the Young Men's Hebrew Association Poetry Center (eventually to be known as the Ninety-second Street Y), and then at Thanksgiving, Elizabeth visited Eudora in Jackson. There the two had a grand time. They drove down to Rodney and then Natchez, crossed the Mississippi River by ferry four times, seeing St. Francisville, Louisiana, along the way. They may even have met a ghost at Longwood House outside of

Natchez. In an interview with Peggy Prenshaw and Albert Devlin, Eudora recalled that event.

> I took her to see Longwood because I thought that would amuse her. We got out of the car on a Sunday morning and walked up through the woods. I knew she loved strange houses, I knew she'd be fascinated by it. We were walking around it and this man came out of the woods from beyond and said, "Would you like to see the house? I can take you over it if you'd like to," and Elizabeth said, "Very much." So we went in the house and he said, "Would you care for a drink?" [laughter] It was about ten o'clock Sunday morning and we said, "Thanks, no, not now." So he took us all over the house—a very garrulous old man. He explained that the reason he knew the house so well was that he lived in it as a caretaker for all these years. After I got back to Jackson, I was talking to a friend about seeing Longwood and I said, "The caretaker took us over." She said, "Oh, he couldn't have, he was killed in an automobile accident about three months ago."[52]

Bowen was ultimately to be disconcerted by this information, but at the time Eudora was more disconcerted by the shortness of Bowen's trip south. She hated to see Bowen leave Jackson and was delighted to be invited to come back to Bowen's Court in the spring.

At some point during the Christmas and New Year's holiday season, Eudora managed briefly to see John Robinson, whose Mexico-bound ship had stopped in New Orleans. Then, early in 1951, tragedy threatened the Welty family. Eudora's younger brother was stricken by respiratory difficulties and faced an operation on his lungs. With her sister-in-law Mittie, Eudora kept vigil for Walter in a New Orleans hospital. She wrote to Russell, describing the experience.

We were in a sort of fantastic place in a fantastic time, the Ochsner Foundation Hospital is at present in an old Army barracks out under (or anyway right by) the Miss. River bridge, and you know, just boards nailed together—the cold wave that was everywhere reached New Orleans too of course and it was 17 there, with most of the hospital without heat or water—thank heaven they kept the patients warm. While Walter was being operated on it was snowing—and in the room where the family wait for the doctor to come out, no heat and they wrapped us in blankets and fed us coffee, and when the doctors came out blankets were thrown around them. I thought maybe some kind of retribution was being made you there for your hard time in India. There was a patient from Bombay who was taken sick off a ship in port there, and I suppose operated on, and there he lay, young, dignified, bearded, with his hands clasped behind his head staring out into a point in space, unvisited and so black.[53]

The nightmarish evening, however, led to Walter's recuperation, and by the end of February, Eudora felt comfortable in leaving home for another extended stay abroad.

On March 14, 1951, Eudora sailed for England. Eudora was glad to be onboard the *Liberté*, though she objected to the largely German population on the boat—she still felt antagonisms roused by the war. At her table in the dining room were more congenial companions: "A nice young English couple, she a horticulturalist, he a psychologist (born in Germany but nice somehow), and Mrs. Abdullah, a colored girl very attractive and nice, looking like a Polynesian—I think West Indies origin—sensational looks and I liked her too, going to join her husband Carlos Abdullah (??) a G.I. studying Fine Arts in Milano. The food was French and delicious."[54] In London Eudora settled into the

Montague Hotel. She sent John Robinson a long letter upon arriving, and then on March 31, she wrote Russell describing a visit in Sussex with her English agent Patience Ross, a trip to Brighton, and a visit with Pamela Travers. She had been using Bowen's Regent's Park house as a place to work, but on April 1 she left to join Bowen in Ireland at Bowen's Court.

The journey from London to Ireland proved a memorable one. Eudora recounted it in detail to Robinson and would later use almost all those details in her story "The Bride of the Innisfallen."

The train journey was *grand*—you're in Ireland the minute you get on the car in Paddington Station—I was in a compartment with 6 Irish, & 1 Welshman who got on in Cardiff & rode almost to Fishguard— The Irish always think it's *their* train, & the Welsh naturally think it's *theirs*— He [Welshman] cross-examined them every one:—a man going home to Creath [?] on holiday, now raising canaries in Somerset—cross-examined him on raising canaries— He (Welshman) got after them on the Catholic Church—etc. etc. One real comedian of a woman—Hair like Geo. Washington, hat *down*—with beat-up old flowers & veil—a rain coat buttoned over her coat from neck to floor—Dead pan—The others called her "the bride"— She went in the diner & ate & came back & said "Oh 'twas a lovely dinner: chicken." But a man stood up in the aisle & claimed "Tis rabbit" & they had to calm him, & another man left & came back telling how during the course of the meal they had shifted the carriages around & his was *not in the place he left it*— I felt a certain pity for the man. He left & came back again, saying it was not in place he left it & the porter requested another gentleman to please go along with the poor man & find his carriage for him & he *refused*—etc. etc.— Can't make it sound as it did, but her story convulsed the rest of us, we were all dying laughing. The man from Creath

saying "*Oh* my god!"— He said: 3 miles out on the boat we
could get whisky, because out of the law of countries "then
it's only the sea & glory"— Terrific storm in the night but I
slept through all. They couldn't get the boat turned around
to dock it (or something)— They also sang—exhibited
their passports— Elizabeth says there is usually somebody
walking their greyhounds up & down the corridor, but I
missed that.

As memorable as the boat-train journey was the arrival in Cork,
an arrival that Eudora also incorporated into "The Bride of the
Innisfallen." "It was so lovely coming. Just right for coming *anywhere* you love—the boat enters Cork by a 3-hour journey up the
River Lea in early morning—passing by little towns of pink &
buff & gray houses in lines up the green hills & old houses in
parks & old forts in ruins with the seagulls flying over the river,
& the usual hundred watchers— I was met by car in Cork, then
drove 30 miles or so up and over the hills here— I think Elizabeth must be right when she says there is a real thing to feel in
the south-ness of South, (only she said it better)—you do feel it
as a geographical sensation."⁵⁵
  Having returned to Elizabeth's home, Eudora settled into a
routine of writing in the mornings and joining her hostess for
drives about the countryside in the late afternoons. Eudora liked
Bowen's husband and guests, and she loved the rituals of Bowen's
Court: The dressing drink served to guests as they donned their
evening wear; the fine meals served in the dining room (though
not the bats that emerged from the room's curtains and darted
for the ladies' hair); the after-dinner card games and fine conversation; playing Happy Families (the British variation on the game
Authors) with Bowen and Eddy Sackville-West. Eudora found
that the stories told by artist Norah McGuinness and Bowen reminded her of Mississippi. During this visit, John Robinson was
in Eudora's thoughts, and she told Bowen about him. Elizabeth

ventured a bit of advice, which Eudora conveyed to John: "Last night Elizabeth was asking more about your writing & finally said maybe you hadn't discovered your subject perhaps? The one that *would have* you at work writing on it. She has instinct. Most gently & tentatively she was offering it & I pass it on for that."[56]

When Eudora left Bowen's Court, she proceeded to the Shelbourne Hotel in Dublin, for Bowen had been at work on a book about this fine old hotel and McGuinness had been at Bowen's Court to illustrate the book. Back in Dublin, Eudora missed connections with Mary Lavin, but upon return to England she would meet with Lavin's patron, Lord Dunsany, a now elderly novelist and dramatist. Invited to his home near Shoreham, Eudora arrived in her Sunday best, including stockings and heels, to be met by Dunsany himself at the train station. Dunsany then proceeded to lead his inappropriately shod guest through pastures and across streams to his house, Dunstall Priory. There his spaniels, their tails undocked and flying like flags, greeted the two writers. Dogs, Dunsany told Eudora, deserved the dignity of their tails. Once inside, Lord Dunsany and his wife served tea to Eudora, and Dunsany read to her from his works.

Living in London, Eudora was happy to have a friend she had met in Paris, Eva Boros, also in residence; Eva and her new husband, noted photographer Bill Brandt, took Eudora to a memorable performance of *The Three Sisters,* starring Ralph Richardson, and then on to a meal at the Piccadilly Hotel, where Brandt enjoyed watching his American guest watch suburban Londoners who had come to town for the theater. Also while in London Eudora was pleased by a visit from Mary Mian. The two women took themselves to Glyndebourne for the opera, only to discover that the atmosphere was as engaging as the music. Both were richly amused when a gentleman, prompted by his very unladylike companion of the evening, ordered "a bottle of your cheapest hock." Glyndebourne offered more than high culture; it offered great people-viewing opportunities.

Eudora saw a good bit of the English countryside as well. She visited Frank Lyell's friend Pamela Redmayne in the Cotswolds. And then she again journeyed to Brighton, where she loved all things about the city, from the Prince Regent's Palace to the pleasure piers, though she told Robinson she missed seeing Bowen, who would be in America until the first of June. Eudora managed to do some work in the seaside city; she wrote Robinson that she had finished the Irish story based on her boat-train journey from London to Cork and had roughed out one set in Brighton. Only "The Bride of the Innisfallen," the story of a young American wife who journeys alone to Ireland, would be published. Early in June, Bill Maxwell wrote to express his enthusiasm for it. "I love your train story beyond all possibility of telling you. I loved it so much, while I was reading it, that I could hardly bear to pass it on to the next reader."[57] By the time Eudora returned to the United States, the *New Yorker* would have accepted Maxwell's recommendation and, at very long last, its first Welty story.

That happy and lucrative news lay ahead. Eudora spent another month in the British Isles before sailing home. She stayed for a time in Hythe, at the White Hart, a seventeenth-century coaching inn, then moved to a London apartment. In London, Eudora was delighted to see Bowen, and Bowen gave a dinner party in honor of her American friend. Eudora would long remember the evening's dramatic conversation about Guy Burgess, the first secretary at the British Embassy in Washington and one of five highly placed Cambridge University graduates who had just been exposed as long-term spies for the Soviet Union. To Frank Lyell she wrote, "I must have told you of being at Elizabeth Bowen's for dinner in London & John Lehmann arriving waving a paper and in a fury at [poet Stephen] Spender, who had suggested, in a letter to the Express! that he, J.L., might know Burgess's whereabouts, and also suggested the investigation of [poet W. H.] Auden's house . . . They said it was exactly like a

reformed Communist to conscientiously report on his friends, &
not to friends, to the newspaper! They were all furious at Spender
then." On June 7, before Burgess surfaced in Moscow, now a de-
fector, Eudora was on her way for a second happy sojourn in Ireland. She visited Mary Lavin for a weekend in County Meath and
was somewhat unsettled by Mary's "underlying antagonism" for
the Anglo-Irish, even though Mary adored the fiction of Anglo-
Irish writer Elizabeth Bowen. Eudora was also unsettled by news
from home, news that Fritz Peters had become abusive to Mary
Lou. To Robinson she wrote, "I don't really know why people
marry at all."[58] But no worries would mar Eudora's pleasure when
she went on to Bowen's Court for two and a half fine weeks before returning to England. At some point Elizabeth, too, returned, and together she and Eudora went to visit writer
Elizabeth Taylor at her home in Buckinghamshire. Finally, on
July 11, 1951, Eudora sailed home on the *Ile de France,* writing to
thank Bowen for her hospitality and to express her deep regret
at leaving.

The developing relationship with Bowen was tremendously
meaningful to Eudora and occurred at a propitious moment in
Eudora's life. When she met Bowen, both were established writers; Bowen greeted her as an equal, and to be accepted on such a
basis was quite heady stuff for Eudora. (In contrast, Eudora's relationship with Katherine Anne Porter would always be affected
by its acolyte/mentor beginnings and by the mentor's expectation
of deference.)[59] In the course of her 1950 and 1951 meetings
with Bowen, Eudora became increasingly admiring. She came to
see Bowen in idealized terms, and for Eudora the ideal life had
always involved writing fiction. In an April 1951 letter, Eudora
was effusive in thanking Bowen for her good times in Ireland, and
in the letter, she declared, "I wish we had been born related."
Then Eudora added, "Oh Elizabeth I didn't mean to sound as if
I didn't love it all exactly the way it was—nothing ought to in-
trude on such lovely visits, not a wish that runs back in time for

40 years— It's just that I miss and will miss & have missed you, but knowing that doesn't take away, it adds to. But it's so strange, isn't it, the crisscross of where & when we are with all we love & must love." At age forty-two she was overwhelmed to discover in an enchanting foreign land a sort of spiritual older sister, a writer to whom she had metaphorically "been born related." She and Bowen were of common blood, were related in the ways they viewed the world and in the values that defined them, in ways that overcame the separateness about which Eudora had so often written. Bowen was a distinguished writer who was absolutely devoted to the writing life; she felt, according to Victoria Glendinning, "on occasion at least, that she was a writer before she was a woman," and Eudora, too, loved the writing life. Bowen led a cosmopolitan existence that Eudora found fascinating. Eudora was infatuated with Bowen's Court, with the Anglo-Irish and Irish traditions of the locale, and with the life of a writer who lived in the midst of all of this. But even the seemingly exotic was similar to home; Eudora valued Bowen's rootedness, the same sort of rootedness that Eudora herself felt in Mississippi and had shared with Bowen during their 1950 Thanksgiving visit. In *Bowen's Court* (1942), Bowen had written of the power of place:

> What runs on most through a family living in one place is a continuous, semi-physical dream. Above this dream-level successive lives show their tips, their little conscious formations of will and thought. With the end of each generation, the lives that submerged here were absorbed again. With each death, the air of the place had thickened: it had been added to. The dead do not need to visit Bowen's Court rooms—as I said we had no ghosts in that house—because they already permeate them ... The land outside Bowen's Court windows left prints on my ancestors' eyes that looked out: perhaps their eyes left, also, prints on the scene. If so, those prints are part of the scene for me.

This passage seemed to anticipate Eudora's 1944 essay "Some Notes on River Country," in which she stated, "Perhaps it is the sense of place that gives us the belief that passionate things, in some essence, endure. Whatever is significant and whatever is tragic in its story live as long as the place does, though they are unseen, and the new life will be built upon these things—regardless of commerce and the way of rivers and roads, and other vagrancies."[60]

Beyond expressing attitudes that Eudora revered and shared, Bowen was a model of independence, moving freely in Europe and America, setting her own course as Eudora had found herself able to do from 1949 to 1951. Moreover, Eudora liked Bowen tremendously well. Theirs was an immediate meeting of the minds, especially as their minds turned to fiction: Both believed a story should reveal rather than resolve mystery. And they were deeply alike in their responsiveness to other people. In this way, perhaps, both writers differed from Katherine Anne Porter. Eudora's distinction between Porter and Bowen might be a distinction between Porter and herself: "Katherine Anne might enjoy having a circle around her, but there she really remained within herself. Elizabeth was just the opposite; she was an in-taker. She just took everything in. She was curious and fascinated by most people she met, and she really wanted to know."[61]

Small wonder that Eudora would be starstruck, would wish that she and Bowen "had been born related." Small wonder that she would write Bowen, from the *Ile de France* as she sailed from England in 1951, "You were sweet—you are beyond any saying, all you thought & did & knew & brought about—you did *so much*—but I let you, loved it & took my pleasure, I let you as I love you—and I could imagine how I would like doing so much for you." In language that to the contemporary ear might sound sexually charged, Eudora bid farewell to the convergence of two writing lives, and characteristically, she found a writer's consolation: "For myself I have that whole world to think of—I loved it—every moment so and I can get back so quickly to it in imagination."[62]

Ardent as these two letters to Bowen are, neither of them, nor any of Eudora's other letters to Bowen, suggest real intimacy. In addition to expressing gratitude for hospitality and companionship and expressing affection for Bowen's husband, Alan Cameron, they are filled primarily with anecdotes and descriptions entertainingly recounted. From 1949 to 1951 in letters to her old friend Diarmuid Russell, Eudora would write in detail of her brother Walter's operation, of her worries about Mary Lou Aswell at *Harper's Bazaar* or about Aswell's marriage, of her concerns about her brother Edward's health. Though Eudora and Bowen may have occasionally talked of such things—a letter from Eudora to Robinson mentions Bowen's assessment of Fritz Peters's stability—no such concerns enter Eudora's letters to Bowen. Bowen herself acknowledged that distance was crucial to her good relationship with the younger writer. She recalled Eudora's first visit to Bowen's Court, saying "She's reserved (in itself, I think, a good point these days) so although we have chatted away a good deal, I really know little about her life, nor she about mine." And after Eudora's spring 1951 visit, Bowen told Blanche Knopf that Eudora proved a good houseguest because she was a working writer, not "an ordinary 'social' guest." Distance, for Bowen, was often the key ingredient of lasting friendships. As Victoria Glendinning has written, Bowen could encourage self-revelation and devotion, but "when the boundaries were becoming dangerously low, Elizabeth could instinctively avert danger by some prosaic practical remark, which earthed the current, put a stop to the flow. This facility for cutting short a mood—or occasionally a relationship—could be disconcerting; chiefly it was self-protective."[63] Boundaries in the Welty/Bowen relationship never became "dangerously low," even letter writing largely ceased, and as a result, perhaps, the relationship became a less intense but a fond and lasting one after 1951. The curious blend of intensity and distance, the blend that tormented Eudora in her relationship with Robinson, was a welcome element in her friendship with Bowen.

Though in 1951 Eudora left England and Bowen with regret, her voyage to the United States was a pleasant one. She met an old friend on the ship, Cary Richardson, whose son had been playing in the Wimbledon tennis tournament, and John Robinson was on hand to meet her ship in New York. When Robinson had written to suggest this plan, Eudora at first declined, but a great desire to see him at the earliest possible moment was irresistible. "Oh do meet me!" she had eventually written. Soon she was reunited with Diarmuid Russell and Mary Lou Aswell as well as John, but what she found after her return proved disturbing. Mary Lou's marriage was falling apart, and John seemed set on a course that would exclude her from his life. When the previous winter, at age forty-one, John had left Italy for Mexico, a twenty-year-old man named Enzo Rocchigiani was with him. Eudora seems to have assumed that John was merely trying in his good-natured way to be of assistance to a young friend; she seems not to have assumed that the two men would remain together once Rocchigiani attained an American visa. They did, however. In May she had written Robinson to express pleasure that Enzo had received the visa and to ask, "Now what?"[64] She suggested that Robinson, who had decided to move to New York, meet her friends William Maxwell, Hildy Dolson, and Jean Stafford but did not suggest such meetings for Enzo. Then, in New York, after John had settled into a clerical job for the *New York Times*, Eudora saw the two men together. In late July, when she entertained Dolly, John, and Enzo with a cold supper, Eudora sensed that the two men were a couple.

Though she was and would remain accepting of gay friends, showing them affection and loyalty, Eudora's attitude toward ostentatious public displays of homosexuality, as toward any ostentation, could be dismissive. In 1941 at Yaddo, she and Porter had found Carson McCullers's whining advances toward Katherine Anne unbearable. In spring 1949 she praised the male dancers in Martha Graham's troupe because they were not "sissy." In a letter to Mary Lou Aswell early in 1950, Eudora had ironically reported on "two hefty Lesbians" who "had a ghastly quarrel" at the Hotel des Saints Pères in Paris. And in letters to Robinson himself, Eudora had felt free to make the sort of casual denigrating comments about homosexuals that he, too, had occasionally made. In May of 1949 she complained about the way "fairies" on the staff of the *New York Times Book Review* were treating Nash, and in November she mocked Truman Capote's high-pitched voice. As late as May of 1951, Eudora was still unguarded in her comments to Robinson. In a letter discussing Fritz Peters's cruel treatment of Mary Lou, for instance, Eudora told Robinson, "What chance the boy ever had I don't know—brought up out of the Middle West with Lesbians, Gurdjief[f], the army & war of course, homosexuals, South of Frances beaches of nudist colonies Truman [Capote]—what others have done to him! So now he's paying us all back through the dear and loving ML."[65] But within two months, Eudora must have become more circumspect about such matters. As she later told Bill Smith, seeing Robinson and Enzo together in the summer of 1951 brought her suspicions about Robinson's sexuality to the fore.

In August, finally at home, Eudora was eager to see Edward, who during her absence had suffered a nervous breakdown but who, under a doctor's "friendly care," now seemed to be improving. Reassured, Eudora soon began work on a new story about "a girl in a claustrophobic predicament: she was caught fast in the over-familiar, monotonous life of her small town, and immobilized further by a prolonged and hopeless love affair; she could see no way out." But Eudora could not complete the story. Perhaps she was too close to this material, having just returned to her relatively small town and having sensed that her own on-again/

off-again romance with Robinson was unlikely to be rekindled. Hoping that some time in an air-conditioned New Orleans hotel room might jump-start the story, she bought a ticket on a train called the Rebel and took herself south. Lunching at Galatoire's a day or so later, she met Carvel Collins, a young Harvard University English professor and accepted an invitation to accompany him on a drive "south of South" to Venice, Louisiana. The trip excited and entranced her, and she wrote to Elizabeth Bowen, describing the adventure:

> We . . . crossed the river on a good ferry at Pointe a la Hatche, full of Cajuns combing their hair and giving each other baskets of shrimp (what coals to Newcastle!)—we went into a remarkable cemetery that (but you must see it *just like this*) was two rows of elevated graves, like bureau drawers, with the fronts newly whitewashed, the cartracks [*sic*] paved between—car almost touched as we drove— straight down this alley to the church, green and white frame with poinsettias planted around it—and beyond the church was the priest's house with his cassock hung out on the clothesline to air—all in an enormous red sunset light—the white and the black and the vivid green, and the raging sound of all those crickets and locusts and what-all in the jungle around it. Crawfish scuttled across the road in front of us— Big okra patches high as your head and white as snow from dust—lots of little fishing boats right at any break in the forest—the water. The towns began with Arabi—and there was Port Sulphur, Jesuit Bend, Naomi, Alliance, Junior, Diamond, Socola, Happy Jack, Empire (a bad smell there, burning old fish?), Buros, Triumph, Concession, Phoenix, Nero, Ostrica and Venice. I don't mean we found all those—where were they? But they were on the map—maybe taking in both sides of the river. I wished for

you. Except the mosquitoes were so thick, everybody on the road carried a branch of a palm to keep flailing around ... Huge sky, and the biggest moon came up—and after dark, the dust was like lakes all around us, with fires burning in their centers, and around the fires, cows—all untended—standing in a ring—in the heat and the night, to keep off mosquitoes—away off in the marshes, you could see their horns standing up black against that lonely glow. Life is very gay in the villages—movies ("Rocket-Ship X-M"), Booga Red's Place, Te-Ta's Place, Paradise—cards and you could tell it was a dance floor too—slot machines. Juke boxes lit up. Full of children. They were going to have a Shrimp Dance the next night—I longed to return. Huge catfishes were lying on people's front porches. The whole place was amphibious— The people were dark, merry, with white teeth, teasing—one old man in the Paradise where we were having a bottle of beer at the bar came over and apologised to Carvel in a low voice for having just come in with a rib-ald remark—we didn't hear it, but his pals told him a lady was present. Everybody had on wonderful bright shirts—lavender, and such colors—I didn't see any women, I was possibly in the wrong place in the Paradise, it was for men and little children—holding each other up to play the slot machine—which *never once* paid off.[66]

These descriptions, with changes in place-names, would eventually become part of "No Place for You, My Love," the story that kept the feeling but revised everything else in the draft Eudora had brought to New Orleans. Interestingly, Collins's account of the trip included one detail Eudora omitted from her letter to Bowen; in a conversation with Albert Devlin, Collins recalled that on the return journey to New Orleans he stopped the car and kissed Eudora. Surely this is the source of the kiss that Eudora put into her story, and just as surely the Welty/Collins relationship was as fleeting as the one in her story, a story she would not finish revising for another year.

The New Orleans respite now over, Eudora worked in her Jackson garden, visited with friends, and wrote page after page of a long, unruly story with a large cast of characters that she listed in a letter to John: "Mr. Jep Wilder, Hallie Wilder, Venetia Wilder (young girl), Miss Lu Livingstone, Mr. Beau (Beauregard) Livingstone (dead), Rush Livingstone (dead), Rose Livingstone, Thad Longstreet, Miss Vashti Longstreet, Miss Marion Longstreet, Miss Nannie Longstreet, Georgine Darden, Alma Darden, Duchess Stovall, Katie Lee Stovall, Curly Stovall, Joe Martin, Gladys Martin, Gloria Martin (little girl), Berry Young (Gypsy), Madame X (?), Horace Green (young man from the North), and the following Negroes, Hilliard, Viola, Belle, Dove (stabs Viola offstage), and Ernest. So many, but I deal with them in clusters. (This is just from memory, there may be even more.) There was a politician named Alonzo Sizer also."[67] She would return to this story in the 1960s and 1970s, but never would she bring it under control. She totally abandoned other projects: No longer was she intent on collaborating with Robinson on a story anthology, and she had much earlier ceased work on a screenplay of *The Robber Bridegroom.* Baldwin Bergersen and William Archibald had signed a contract in February 1951 to transform the novella into a stage musical, and in September they exercised their option to extend the contract. But though Eudora's professional collaboration with Robinson was at an end, she was still very much concerned about him.

By October 1951 Dolly Wells, who had years earlier discouraged Eudora from following John to San Francisco, was now even more seriously distressed on Eudora's behalf. She felt that Enzo Rocchigiani posed a threat to John's and therefore Eudora's happiness. From her New York apartment, Dolly wrote to her old friend: "I haven't seen John since he got back from Washington.

As he may have written you, he took Enzo down there to try to get him in the army, or something. I am really anxious for a report. I am hoping that it is to be the army or the homeward trip for that child. As long as he is here John is going to be spending most of his time nursing him and is not going to settle down even halfway to doing any writing or anything else for himself. I don't know how you feel about this, but I feel *strongly*. I will admit, however, that it is certainly none of my business." Less than a week after receiving this letter from Dolly, Eudora learned that Enzo would likely return to Italy. "It is cheering a little," she wrote to a seemingly undismayed John, "to think Enzo may be going his own way soon, a release of a kind for you though you may miss him and worry—whatever happens I hope turns out good for your end of it. I've been wishing you a little time and peace to write in all along." By Thanksgiving, because of visa difficulties, Enzo had left the United States, on his way to serve in the Italian army, and John was miserable. In response to his expression of misery, Eudora's sympathy waned, and she responded somewhat tartly: "In honesty and love what answer is there to 'I can't bear to suffer.' There isn't any of course. I hate to suffer too, my dear—somehow though to me that just isn't the point." The point for Eudora was a desire for John to turn his suffering into fiction, for "in the work something is resolved, and let go."[68] And surely Eudora hoped that John would also let Enzo go and would resolve his sexual ambivalence in favor of heterosexuality.

Of course, Eudora had many close and enduring friendships with homosexual men. Among her youthful friends in Jackson, a number were or were considered gay (Hubert Creekmore, Lehman Engel, Frank Lyell), and beyond Jackson, Walter Clemons, a reviewer for the *New York Times* and, later, *Newsweek*, and novelist Reynolds Price would eventually be among those she held close. Clemons she would ask to be her literary executor, and Price she would regard as almost a son. On the periphery were homosexual men she knew less well but whose company she enjoyed. Was she drawn to these friends and to John, *because* of their sexuality? That seems highly unlikely given Eudora's at times bemused distance from, at times discomfort with, men and women who self-consciously flaunted their homosexuality. She was typically drawn to her friends, gay or not, men or women, because they were lively, engaging, intelligent *individuals* who shared her passion for literature and language and who pursued careers related to the arts. Eudora consistently valued the individual over the category. As she had written to John during World War II, "If you treat everybody *first* as a human being—people you love best, & people you hate most—& people you have yet to understand—isn't that the only way, the only basis."[69] With John, however, Eudora hoped for more, much more, than this. Like Rosamond Musgrove in *The Robber Bridegroom*, Eudora longed to give herself in spirit and in flesh, not to escape physical intimacy but embrace it. But in the novella, Jamie Lockhart takes what Rosamond would have given freely: He rapes her. Jamie cannot yet accept a woman who is his equal in strength and resourcefulness. In turning this novella into a screenplay, Eudora and John perhaps recognized the issue of artistic power, which ultimately, along with his sexual orientation, would separate them. After John returned from World War II and began to write, he knew that his own stories were inferior to Eudora's, and he felt indebted to her for their publication. She had given him what he really wanted to take for himself but could not. To marry Eudora, he must have felt, would be to live a double lie, both artistic and sexual in nature. Unlike Jamie Lockhart, John could have accepted a life of equality, but he did not want a career he would always owe to his wife, nor did he want a marriage to which he was not sexually committed. As he had told Bill Smith, he loved Eudora too much for that. Instead, John allied himself with a man more than twenty years his junior who was absolutely uninterested in literature, a man who was his devoted companion and who made issues of power irrelevant. Although, as 1951 drew to a close, John was separated from Enzo, that separation would be short-lived.

Her troubled relationship with John notwithstanding, Eudora must have taken considerable satisfaction in the course she had charted between fall 1945 and fall 1951. Though she cherished her family and friends in Jackson, she had relished the discovery of a widening circle of friends who shared her own passion and commitment to artistic lives. She also relished being free from the familiar world of home, from the town where she and her family were so well known, from familial duties and responsibilities and restraints. During extended stays in San Francisco and New York, she had lived independently, spending a great deal of time with friends but also treasuring her solitude. Eudora's voyages to and from Europe, save one, were made without a companion, and in Europe she typically had a room of her own in a hotel not shared with family or friends. In 1949 in Paris, though she cherished her friends old and new, she spent much time learning the city by herself. When she left Paris, she went on her own to Nice and then Beaulieu before being joined by her American compatriots. Robinson was her guide in Florence, but her journey to England and through England and Ireland was a solitary undertaking—she didn't even pause to phone friends when her London-bound train stopped for several hours in Paris. In 1951 Eudora again went to Europe alone, spending time in London and Brighton and Hythe, with occasional visits to and from friends.

This independence was, of course, a mixed blessing. Independence for Eudora would eventually mean a life without John Robinson by her side. But ultimately, Eudora knew that she possessed the resources to lead a full life with or without the man she loved. For her, as for Elizabeth Bowen, the independent life of a writer was a profoundly satisfying one. And in her fiction of the late forties and early fifties, Eudora repeatedly suggests the importance of independence for women. Of course, Eudora never directly depicted her time at Robinson's villa or at Bowen's Court—to have done so would have been a violation of privacy and hospitality as surely as it would have been to make Berenson's I Tatti or the Mian household a locale in her stories. Perhaps she also sensed that the world of Europe was not a world she knew intimately and therefore was a world about which she must write from the perspective of an outsider. Indeed, she published only two stories drawing upon her European experiences, but both of those stories are about travelers to Europe. A voyage from New York to Naples and a boat-train journey from London to Cork became her subjects; in both stories Eudora's central characters are strangers to the European experience. More importantly, perhaps, in both stories her female protagonists find fulfillment not in relationships but in discovering their independence and self-sufficiency. Though Mrs. Serto in "Going to Naples" hopes that her daughter's shipboard romance may lead to marriage, Gabriella instead learns that an unmarried girl has the power "to be happy all by herself." And the American woman in "The Bride of the Innisfallen," a story Eudora wrote while in residence at Bowen's Court, knows great joy when, after leaving her husband, she comes alone to Ireland and walks into a "lovely room full of strangers."[70] These characters are like the solitary Virgie Rainey, who breaks away from Morgana, Mississippi, at the end of *The Golden Apples.* Similarly, in her American and European travels from 1946 through 1951, Eudora found herself free to move about on her own, cherishing close friendships but always acting independently, knowing she could be happy all by herself. She was a cosmopolitan woman still expecting to encounter and savor something new and unusual, still filled with the joy of seeing and hearing and writing.

FIVE

Finding a Way Out
1951–1956

In August 1951 Eudora had begun work on a story about a young woman caught in "a prolonged and hopeless love affair" from which she could find "no way out." For a number of years, of course, this had been Eudora's own plight. From the time she visited John Robinson in San Francisco in the fall of 1947, their breakup had seemed inevitable, but the relationship had endured a roller-coaster ride for four more years. Now that ride was in the process of ending. Eudora needed to find a way out of the relationship and away from her focus on John. In the early 1930s she had anticipated living in New York City, frequenting its theaters, galleries, and concert halls even as she pursued a writing career. When she abandoned hope for union with John, Eudora sporadically returned to this youthful ideal. She began to spend extended periods in Manhattan, subletting apartments, seeking a more profound sense of fulfillment than she had yet known. She was restless, moving back and forth between her native state and the city that had become a second home, but she was neither isolated nor alienated. She enjoyed the companionship of her close-knit family, of many good friends in Jackson and New York, and of an agent who was her soul mate; and between 1951 and 1956, her friendships with writers who, to use Eudora's words, were "true to their talent" deepened and expanded. Elizabeth Bowen, who had established herself as a major literary force; William Jay Smith, who was now building a reputation as a poet; and Reynolds Price, a talented Duke University student at the very outset of his career—these writers and others would be tremendously important to her. Marriage was not to be hers, but the love of writing continued to be a source of strength, a way of transforming and overcoming disappointments, however severe. More and more significant awards and recognition came her way, and such external validation, in turn, enabled Eudora to provide assistance to young writers and to other literary friends. City life and home ties, writing and rewriting, the continuity of old friendships and the development of new ones, gradually provided Eudora with a way out of her relationship with John and, at the same time, opened new paths for her, paths into rich and rewarding experiences.

In October 1951 Elizabeth Bowen arrived in the United States for an extended lecture tour and with plans to visit Eudora late in November. Eudora was delighted to have Bowen's long-anticipated return to Mississippi firmly on the docket, and she hoped that John Robinson would add his name to her guest list for the Thanksgiving holidays. Unfortunately, though he was without Enzo, who had returned to Italy, John was not free to join the celebration. His absence, however, did not put a damper on the high spirits of Eudora or Elizabeth. On November 18, Bowen wired Eudora from Missoula, Montana. "WILDLY HAPPY AT PROSPECT OF SEEING YOU SOON NOW HOPE ALL STILL WELL IF I ARRIVE JACKSON BY AIR 8:55 P.M. WEDNESDAY NEXT 21ST AM NOW AT FLORENCE HOTEL MISSOULA MONTANA TILL TUESDAY MIDDAY LOVE ELIZABETH." Bowen in fact arrived a day later due to weather complications. Then the two women drove to the Mississippi Gulf Coast to visit Elizabeth Spencer. Years earlier, when Spencer was a student at Belhaven College, located directly across the street from the Welty house, she had asked Eudora to come to a gathering of student writers, and a story Spencer wrote for the session had impressed Eudora. Eudora had since followed Spencer's career, put her in contact with Diarmuid Russell, and provided publicity quotes for her two books. Now she sought to introduce Spencer to a greatly admired writer and friend. In her autobiography Spencer vividly recalled the meeting.

> The two of them came by to see me before proceeding to New Orleans, where Miss Bowen was to lecture. We planned to meet for lunch at Friendship House, an attractive sprawled-out restaurant on the beach drive between Gulfport and Biloxi. The day was mild and the broad windows looked out on the sound and on the beach drive lined with oaks. The water lay placid and blue beyond.
>
> I was charmed by the delightful sound of Miss Bowen's very English voice, not exactly marred by stuttering, but made a little comical when she came to speak of our wonderful b-b-buh-bourbon whiskey. Or related coming into the airport of some Western city (she had been lecturing throughout the United States), and how she admired those numerous neon s-s-suh-signs. I wondered at her courage to undertake lectures at all, but am told that her certainly imposing looks—she was tall, strongly built, with red hair swept back—more than made up for the flaw . . .
>
> The two ladies were late in appearing that day, not having started early enough from Jackson. I had been seated in the restaurant foyer waiting for a good while when two young officers from the nearby air base came out of the bar and started to talk. Was I waiting for someone? Yes, two women friends from Jackson. Both from Mississippi? No, one was from Ireland. "Ah, a Jackson doll and an Irish babe!" When the imposing pair actually came through the door, regal in their tweeds, the Air Force wilted away.[1]

After visiting Spencer and then spending an evening with Emily and Roy Turner, John's friends in Pass Christian, Mississippi, Eudora and Bowen drove to New Orleans for Bowen's

lecture and later went to Shreveport for another Bowen performance. There the friends parted but were reunited early in December when Eudora joined Bowen at the Drake Hotel in Chicago
and attended Bowen's University of Chicago presentation. Bowen
then left to meet her longtime lover, Charles Ritchie, in Montreal. By mid-month, at home in London, Bowen wrote to tell
Eudora of the happy reunion with Ritchie and to say how much
she had enjoyed her time in Chicago, New Orleans, and Jackson.
"That time of ours was the most lovely time—the curious cosi-
ness of Chicago (*our* Chicago, other than the melting pot) on top
of the lovely beauty of those days in your car, and in New Orleans. And of course I did so love the day in Jackson—I will not
recuperate everything in cold words, but *you* know how things
which have been perfect are imprinted for always in one's heart
and one's senses as well as in the literal clear sharp memories of
one's mind."[2]

Back in Jackson Eudora missed Elizabeth but had high expectations for John's career as a writer. He had been invited to Yaddo,
based on her recommendation and a recommendation from John
Malcolm Brinnin, his friend from Berkeley, who was now director of the Poetry Center at the Young Men's Hebrew Association
(YMHA) in New York. She hoped John would find Saratoga
Springs more livable than he had found New York City, and she
anticipated that uninterrupted time for writing would help him
to hit his stride. Eudora herself began to work on new stories
and settled into a lively social life. She and seven other friends
gathered almost weekly for dinner, conversation, and parlor
games; they called themselves the Basic Eight. Charlotte Capers,
then assistant director of the Mississippi Department of Archives
and History, which she would eventually head, was a central figure in the group. One of the world's great raconteurs, even if the
world beyond Mississippi did not know it, Charlotte also wrote a
regular column for the *Jackson Daily News* under the pseudonym of
Miss Quote. Charlotte's young assistant Ann Morrison and Ann's

architect husband, Bill, were also members of the Basic Eight as were Jacksonians Jimmie Wooldridge and Major White. The seventh and eighth places were filled variously by friends who returned to Jackson on regular visits—Frank Lyell and Hubert Creekmore most frequently. A different group member would entertain each week—once at the Morrisons' the guests saw their hosts climb into a bathtub in order to wrap a large roast in layers of wet, salted newspapers, emerging to place the wrapped meat in a barbeque of hot coals. Another time the group painted a mural in the stairway that led from the Morrisons' basement apartment to Charlotte's house above. One evening they met to see a moonflower bloom at the home of Major White. At anyone's home they might play word games: each person writing one line in the set pattern of a story, folding a piece of paper to conceal what he or she had written on it, then passing the paper to another, who would complete a second part of the pattern and so on. Eventually all eight or more lines would be revealed to the assembled group. The results could be hilarious. One exchange led to this sentence:

> The beauteous
> Marlon Brando
> jocosely
> accosted
> the lu[s]cious but naughty
> Greta Garbo
> by the sea
> He said, "I *want* you."
> She said: "It couldn't matter to me less, one way or the other."
> They rode off on a bicycle built for two.[3]

The Basic Eight never themselves rode bicycles built for two, but they did make excursions together. A favorite overnight stop was twenty miles north of Jackson at Allison's Wells, a notably eccentric spa. There one evening soap bubbles began to waft from the laundry up through the dining room, and the proprietor, Hosford Fontaine, made the best of a bad situation: "Aren't they beautiful, aren't they lovely?" she rhetorically inquired. Like Hosford, the Basic Eight knew how to find amusement and pleasure wherever they gathered.

Members of the group entertained, together or separately, notable writers, editors, agents, and photographers who came through Jackson to see Eudora. In February 1952 Robert Penn Warren delivered a lecture at Belhaven College and then spent an evening with Eudora and Charlotte. "Not a serious word was spoken," Warren later recalled with pleasure. For Eudora this meeting was especially sweet. She had never before met Warren, who had done so much to launch her career, and she was delighted to have that opportunity and to find him so simpatico. After their meeting, she wrote to Diarmuid, saying that Warren was "a darling man—with lots of tales." Red Warren was also pleased to meet Eudora and wrote to tell her, "You did noble about giving me likker and feeding me and getting me on planes. And I am eternally grateful to you on all counts. Besides, I just had a fine time without any gratitude thrown in."[4]

During the good times in Jackson, Eudora continued to think about John Robinson. Since January she had read and commented on his writing, worried about his short stint in the Saratoga Springs hospital, and contemplated seeing him again. For his part, John had worked hard at Yaddo, and shortly before March 22, when he was due to leave, he sent Eudora the story that had claimed most of his time. This tale, narrated by a nineteen-year-old man and focused on an older artist named Tom, frustrated and angered Eudora. Responding much more critically than she ever had to his work, Eudora wrote that the story's mode of narration was problematic. The narrator, she noted, "isn't involved, but he isn't detached either, except physically being crippled—he doesn't particularly see or care, only somewhat." Eudora particularly objected to the narrator's inability to convey the nature of Tom's relationships with his landlord, Nick, and with Carl, a young man who had been a nude model for one of his paintings. "You limit the point of view on purpose, and through this the story emerges confused and hectic and part of the scenery, as it were, the atmosphere and the tension altogether that of a love affair, but never translatable to the narrator into the other things that most surely are there . . . It is (if I see it at all) eventually a story of self-delusion—Tom in this lush and strange and brutal world thinking to seize and hold to youth, beauty, what-you-will, painting and one way & another, & failing but through all enveloped in the *place*, this hysterical place." Eudora's letter about the story is suggestive. Perhaps it was not so much the story's execution as its subject matter that prompted her frosty tone. Perhaps she saw John and Enzo lurking in the shadows of the story, in a love affair between an older, talented artist and a young man, who finds art beyond his scope. Such a relationship, Eudora must have felt, would bring only heartache for all concerned. Or perhaps she had simply grown impatient with John's reluctance to view his own situation clearly. She certainly resented the story's hostile view of women and its seemingly implicit criticism of her. To Tom, at one point in the text, a scolding female blue jay has come to seem "almost like another person and it got on his nerves—he and the bird were like two old maids who had lived too much alone, getting on each other's nerves, that sometimes he could have gladly wrung that bird's neck."[5] Whatever her frustrations with the story, Eudora retreated from criticism as she brought her letter to a close. In her next letter Eudora again apologized for the harshness of her comments, but the intimate and expansive nature of her letters to Robinson ended, not to be renewed for many years. She had reached the breaking point in her relationship with him.

In March Katherine Anne Porter arrived in Jackson, and she and Eudora promptly left for the Gulf Coast, where they visited

Elizabeth Spencer. Eudora sought for the second time in less than
a year to introduce Spencer to an established woman writer—
first Elizabeth Bowen and now Katherine Anne. Shortly after this
good time on the coast, however, Eudora became put out with
Katherine Anne, who, having committed herself to speak in April
at the Mississippi State College for Women, in typical Porter
fashion had reneged on the commitment; Eudora was asked to
fill this slot and felt duty-bound to do so. Though she enjoyed
working with Randall Jarrell at the "W," she for some time remained miffed with her old friend.

Serving as Katherine Anne's substitute briefly delayed Eudora's return to an intensive schedule of writing, but return she
did. By May 1952 she had finished her story "Kin" and was
pleased with the result. Now she planned a trip to New York.
She was excited about her induction into the National Institute
of Arts and Letters; she was eager to see Diarmuid and to visit
the Russells, especially her godson, Will Russell, in Katonah; and
she was delighted that Elizabeth Spencer had been selected to receive a thousand-dollar prize from the Institute. This trip to New
York, moreover, proved the occasion for an important development in Eudora's professional and personal life: The *New Yorker*
had accepted "Kin," and Eudora worked closely with William
Maxwell in editing the story about twenty-one-year-old Dicey,
who like the aged Uncle Felix, longs for a wider, more cosmopolitan life than rural Mississippi can offer. Though Eudora had for
many years liked Maxwell, their relationship now became closer.
Maxwell proved an ideal editor to work with her—respectful of
her wishes, astute in his suggestions. Beyond that, he and Eudora
were kindred spirits, and he, along with his wife, Emmy, would
soon be numbered among Eudora's closest friends.

During her month in New York, Eudora also saw John
Robinson and learned that he would soon be sailing for Italy,
where he would look for work, establish residence, and be reunited with Enzo. Though John escorted Eudora to her Jackson-

bound train when she left New York, and though she wrote him a warm thank-you note for doing so, they had relinquished any lingering hopes for a life together. During the next five years, they would write to each other fondly, but scarcely more than once per annum. The Atlantic Ocean would now lie between Eudora and John, but metaphoric oceans had already irreparably separated them. It is tempting to think that John's unpublished story drawing on his 1935 correspondence with the writer Martha Dodd was written in 1952 and depicted the end of the romantic attachment he and Eudora had shared. In that story, the narrator writes to a woman from whom he has finally separated: "On the boat I wrote a letter to her, I framed it ever so carefully. Somewhere we'll meet along that glittering, devious path that touches along the thin outer edges of this life. Would she care enough to be angry. Would it justify me some. You can come down to earth again and then come around to see me. We had said rather mean things at times. We had delved rather deeply and incoherently at times until our gauntlets were quite threadbare. The letter was the end, I said, the thin sharp edges of finality."[6]

When John wrote these lines is unclear. It is quite clear, however, that shortly after his departure for Italy, Eudora returned to the story "No Place for You, My Love" and by the end of July had completed it. In this story two strangers meet over lunch in a New Orleans restaurant and then spend the afternoon and evening together, driving south of the city to land's end. Both the man from Syracuse and the woman from Toledo are unhappy in love. He has delayed his trip home so that his wife may entertain some old college friends; his marriage seems a passionless one. The woman from Toledo seems to be involved with a married man, and the bruise above her temple suggests that her love affair has taken a violent turn. The suffering that love has brought to both these individuals leaves them in quest of "imperviousness"; they want to avoid thinking about their situations, and they want to avoid exposing their situations to others. The man will not discuss his wife with the woman from Toledo, and the woman resents his intuitive recognition of her plight: "How did it leave us—the old, safe, slow way people used to know of learning how one another feels," she wonders. But as much as they may desire to shield themselves, a relationship springs up between them, and they know that "even those immune from the world, for the time being, need the touch of one another, or all is lost." Like the woman from Toledo, Eudora had sought imperviousness in the face of a failing relationship—her fun-filled evenings with the Basic Eight perhaps served that purpose—but she ultimately found a source of comfort not available to her character. "When a story is going on," she had once told Robinson, "then you feel things highly and even more than you knew you might, and they reveal themselves to you in a way that gives some pain too, but in the work something is resolved, and let go."[7] In writing this story, Eudora was beginning to let go of the past. As soon as she completed "No Place for You, My Love," it was accepted by the *New Yorker*, the third of her stories to be published in that magazine. Now the *New Yorker* wanted more work by Welty. At the end of August, Maxwell asked Eudora to sign a "First Reading Agreement" with the magazine, but Eudora found herself unwilling to be so bound, however fond she was of Maxwell.

In the late summer of 1952, Eudora turned her attention to two long stories. One called "Never Mind, Uncle Daniel" ultimately became the novella titled *The Ponder Heart.* The name "Daniel," she joked with Frank Lyell, had come to her in the midst of a Billy Graham revival. The other story seems to have been one Eudora eventually deemed an abject failure; it may well have been the story of the Wilders, Livingstones, Longstreets, and Dardens about which she had told Robinson and to which she would return in the 1960s and 1970s. On the personal front, Eudora continued to enjoy the company of her Jackson friends, though she worried about one friend who had had a nervous breakdown and was temporarily in the State Mental Hospital at nearby Whitfield. She visited her friend two or three times a week, but told Frank, "Listen: if I ever end up out there in White Female Receiving, I don't want *anybody* to come to see me there. Just send me detective stories (English country house) and then English Literature if I'm moved to Convalescent, there's a bench by the lake. Send me War & Peace then."[8]

In September, Eudora returned to New York for a lengthy stay. Bill and Barbara Smith had sublet a furnished apartment at 16 West Tenth that they would not be able to use for some time and had offered it to Eudora. The apartment proved rather mysterious. It had, as Eudora told Jean Stafford, "Spanish Inquisition period furniture, with IHS over the carved headboard, heavy hangings, oil paintings of great big martyrs & wrought iron everywhere & no bed light . . . Come see it: It's scarey & I can't tell sex of occupant." The "scarey" nature of the apartment included what Nona Balakian, Eudora's friend from the *New York Times Book Review,* called a poltergeist experience—startling noises, falling objects, and the inexplicable laddering of her freshly washed stockings.[9] Diarmuid counseled Eudora to leave immediately, but she stayed until the Smiths' arrival, moving to the Hotel Irving in mid-October.

Eudora's time in New York seemed to promise a way of refocusing her life. She had found her way out of the relationship with John and now wanted to be, on a daily basis, part of an artistic community. And in New York she was. She saw a new exhibition of work by her Yaddo pal Karnig Nalbandian, longing to buy some of the beautiful pieces, then dined with him at Nona Balakian's. She spent one weekend with the Russells and another visiting the Robert Penn Warrens and the Cleanth Brooks in New Haven. She attended the opening of Lehman Engel's *Mikado* and went to a party at his apartment. She recorded three stories for Caedmon Records. She visited with Hubert Creekmore and worked on further revisions of "Kin" with Bill Maxwell. She heard Katherine Anne Porter read at the Young Men's Hebrew Association and later, as she reported to Frank Lyell, "had a nice evening of talk in which [Katherine Anne] said nothing but nice things about all our mutual friends, and me, and was full of good feeling toward the world it seemed, instead of bad. I hope this has really happened to her. At any rate, relations between her and me are now easy again, thank God. I hate feeling that there is animosity somewhere at work between me and an old friend."[10] Eudora also managed to see comedienne Bea Lillie's new show one evening and later took thirteen-year-old Pamela Russell, who loved Lillie's song "There are Fairies at the Bottom of Our Garden," to a matinee. In the midst of this performance, just before singing Pam's favorite song, Lillie dedicated it to Pamela and asked her to stand and be recognized. Pam could not believe that Lillie was calling to her, and she refused to stand despite Eudora's urging. She realized only years later that Eudora had arranged for this magical moment.

Eventually, however, neither magical moments in the theater nor the world of art and literature was enough for Eudora. Forsaking her position on the sidelines of political campaigns, she canvassed for Adlai Stevenson and attended a Stevenson rally: "He came into a little room where I and 100 ladies were stuck, stood on a chair, and said 'Ladies, I understand you are an overflow,' and made us a little private speech. Like having the parade come by your house when you were sick in bed and prepared to miss it."[11] Stevenson, Eudora felt, brought to the public stage the very values that animated her fiction. She admired his forthright nature, his acceptance of diversity, his keen intellect and complexity of thought, and his use of the English language. Stevenson's eventual defeat was devastating for Eudora. Before the election, she had told Frank Lyell, "I feel if Stevenson is not elected we had all just better get out of the country. I feel so strongly moved by that man, think him so great. I've been mailing his speeches home, as of course none of them get printed down there." Whether his speeches were printed there or not, Stevenson carried Mississippi but lost nationally. After the election,

Eudora publicly expressed her dismay in a letter written for publication in the *New Republic*. In this letter, she praised Stevenson for having "intelligence ... charged to communicate, ... shaped in responsibility and impelled with learning and curiosity, [and] ... alight with imagination."[12] In no other leader did she see these talents. To Eudora, progressive political policies now seemed unobtainable.

The fall of 1952 was marked by personal as well as political losses. In late August Elizabeth Bowen's husband had died; Eudora was fond of Alan Cameron, saddened by his death, and concerned for Elizabeth. Then, in early November, Eudora learned that John Woodburn, her first editor, had died. "It seems he simply dropped dead while shaving, at home in the country," she wrote Frank Lyell, expressing her great distress and horror. And Eudora worried about Woodburn's wife. "I have never met his present wife, but everyone says she is extremely nice, a lovely person—and she must be so terribly shocked by the way it happened."[13] Woodburn, who had been Eudora's champion in 1940 at Doubleday, was now gone, and Eudora's sense of time's power was confirmed and intensified.

Late in November Eudora went home. In December she had company—an Englishman named P. H. Newby, who was on a State Department tour of the United States. Eudora wrote to Jean Stafford to describe this visit.

> Did I tell you about Mr. Newby visiting me—or did I think you were strong enough. We were strangers, he was just on a tour around US as guest of State Dep't, you know, and I was on his route. He was so reserved. All I could get was that the South was a lot like Egypt—so many blacks, though too many trees—and he would like to be shown crocodiles. And (on a ride to Vicksburg) "Hello! Fancy seeing Hereford cows so far from their home." And "Hello! English names on the mailboxes there, along such an alien

road." It was homesickness. He said he'd gone into a bar in Albuquerque and asked for "Bour-bon"—giving it its proper French pronunciation—and got *beer.* That's how lucky he was everywhere, but it was so sad somehow. He said he had not one drop of anything but pure English York- shire blood, no Welsh, no Irish, and no Scotch—wouldn't you know it? Mother kept calling him "Mr. Pamby"—thank heaven it didn't happen to his face. He will be safely back home by now, seeing the right cows in the right places.[14]

Freed from company, Eudora spent Christmas and New Year's with family and friends, but by mid-January 1953 she had returned for another stay in New York. For two weeks she resided at the Hotel Grosvenor at Fifth Avenue and Tenth Street, then moved into an apartment for the month of February. Her time in New York was again rich and pleasing. In January she read at the YMHA to a receptive audience; she took the Smiths (Bill and Barbara) and Mary Lou to see Bea Lillie, noting that Lillie "was in top form & had added on many little touches & lines since I saw her last"; and she managed to see Elizabeth Bowen several times. She took Elizabeth to a party where Anne Lindbergh, Robert Penn Warren, and Warren's wife, the novelist Eleanor Clark, were in attendance, and Bowen took Eudora to PEN cock- tail parties and Knopf events. In February, settled in a sublet, Eu- dora began to feel as if New York were home. She attended many more Broadway shows than short trips permitted. She saw Danny Kaye four or five times, loved *Misalliance* and Lehman's *Wonderful Town,* but advised Frank Lyell to avoid *The Crucible.* And Eudora enjoyed the domestic routines of apartment life in Manhattan. As she told Frank, "My apartment worked out fine—wished you'd been up there so you could have come to eat with me— twice I cooked dinner, for Dolly and Mary Lou once, and for the Russells and Charles & Mary Poore once—it had two bedrooms, so Elizabeth was able to stay with me too a few nights—I saw her off at Idlewild the Tuesday before I left Friday—she flew back."[15]

Eudora managed to work as well as play during her time in the city. In February, as a favor to Mary Lou, she read at the Cosmopolitan Club. But mostly she revised the Uncle Daniel story she had begun the previous summer, eventually reading *The Ponder Heart*, as it was now titled, aloud to Bill and Emmy Maxwell. This story of the innocent Daniel Ponder, who, to his grandfather's dismay, would willingly give away the family fortune and who literally tickles his young wife to death, captivated the Maxwells. In 1988 Bill recalled Welty's 1953 visit to their Murray Hill brownstone: "I see Eudora standing by the window with the manuscript in her hands. It went on all morning and all afternoon, as I remember, with time out for lunch. As a reader Eudora is better than a whole company of actors and when I am moved to laughter, it is often accompanied by tears of amusement. I shed them all through the first half of the book but was dry-eyed during the second half, not because it wasn't funny, but because the tear glands gave up."[16] The Maxwells' response confirmed Eudora's sense that the story was now in final form, though she later would return to the manuscript and make more revisions before it saw publication. For his part, Maxwell wanted the story for the *New Yorker* and asked Diarmuid Russell to let him have first crack at it. Maxwell also had personal reasons for being fascinated with Eudora's novella. The narrator Edna Earle's frequent references to roses intrigued him, for he was himself a rose grower. Eudora promised to send him a Cherokee rose rooted by her mother, the first in a line of roses she would send as gifts.

In March Eudora was back in Jackson, where she enjoyed a visit from an Italian writer she had met in Florence in 1950. Eugenio Vaquer spent five days in Jackson, and when he left to continue his tour of the United States, Eudora recommended that he visit Frank Lyell in Austin. Once Vaquer had departed, Eudora returned to writing, this time on a long story "taking place in Brighton and Romney Marsh." "Where Angels Fear," with its Forster-like title, has not survived. Even as she worked on this "mad English pursuit," Eudora began a new story, one set in Mississippi. At the end of April Diarmuid Russell wrote that her story "Spring" was "delightful." A week later he offered more specific praise. "It pleased me because it was visible every minute—as you thought too."[17] In this story a young boy is unable to understand a romantic triangle that has developed in his small town: His father's clumsy efforts to end an affair, his mother's angry response to infidelity, the "other" woman's desperate attempts to express her love, all lie beyond his comprehension. Eudora knew that the lovers in her story needed to discover just what she and John had been seeking—a way out of their relationship.

In May, Mary Lou Aswell arrived for a visit in Jackson, and the two old friends drove to New Orleans and toured the city. Then Eudora and Basic Eight member Jimmie Wooldridge took Mary Lou to the Mississippi Delta. In Jackson the entire Basic Eight fell in love with Eudora's most recent visitor and entertained her royally. At some point Eudora showed Mary Lou *The Ponder Heart* typescript. Mary Lou had recently left her job at *Harper's Bazaar* and was struggling to establish herself at Ballantine Books. She greatly admired Eudora's novella, and immediately wrote to Diarmuid, asking if Ballantine might become the publisher. Eudora longed to help Mary Lou, but Diarmuid was adamantly opposed to such an arrangement. He did not like paperback editions, he had hopes of placing the novella with both Harcourt and a major magazine, and he felt that Eudora would suffer financially if she went with Ballantine. Eudora had long left all business decisions in Diarmuid's hands, and when informed of his position, Mary Lou endorsed Diarmuid's advice.

Eudora herself was not finished with *The Ponder Heart*. Late in May she began to worry that "Uncle Daniel ought not to have finished Bonnie Dee off" but ultimately decided that there was no turning back on that. Still she tinkered with the story, in June writing Diarmuid that she had "fixed" it. "Spring" posed other problems for revision. The *New Yorker* did not want the story, and *Harper's Bazaar* wanted it only with substantial cuts. Eudora was unwilling to make the cuts and felt that Alice Morris of the *Bazaar* had failed to understand her story. Eudora wondered if Mary Lou's friend Margaret Caetani might be allowed to run the story in *Botteghe Oscure,* an Italian periodical, but Diarmuid worried about international copyright issues raised by that possibility. In the meantime Eudora continued to work on her English story and on another story, which was based on her 1949 journey by ship from New York to Naples.

During the summer of 1953, Diarmuid and Eudora conferred by mail about her publishing options. Ultimately they decided that *The Ponder Heart* should be published before a collection of stories. That agreed upon, they turned their attention to the composition of her story collection. The English story, both felt, might not be worthy of the book. Eudora proposed that "The Burning," "Kin," "No Place for You, My Love," "Spring," and "The Bride of the Innisfallen" should be included along with her new boat story ("Going to Naples"). And she wondered if "Circe" might not be part of the collection, though she told Russell she had revised the story since its periodical publication four years earlier.

In mid-July Diarmuid wrote to tell Eudora that he had come to terms with Harcourt about publishing *The Ponder Heart,* and then a few days later he reported that the *New Yorker* would also publish the entire novella in a single issue. Once again Eudora felt that Russell had worked miracles on her behalf. "It really is just marvelous news and dazzles my head when I try to think about it till I'm not sure I've taken it in. It was a feat you did—for sure— I'm more pleased than anything that it worked out exactly as it came to you it might."[18]

In August Eudora returned to New York this time bringing her nine-year-old niece Elizabeth with her. Eudora enjoyed the company of imaginative children and was a particularly doting aunt. In New York she took her niece to the typical tourist attractions, to the theater, and to visit the Russells in Katonah and the Maxwells at their country home. Eudora sought to introduce Elizabeth to a world larger than Mississippi, and the young Welty won the affection of her New York hosts. But looming over the trip were the preliminary *New Yorker* galleys of *The Ponder Heart*. Eudora proofed and revised the galleys immediately upon return home, and Maxwell praised the changes she had made.

Once work on the galleys had been completed, Eudora turned her attention to the "boat story," finally sending it to Russell in late October. Then she celebrated by throwing a Halloween party for the Basic Eight. As she reported to Frank Lyell, "Charlotte, Ann and Bill arrived in identical costumes—covering sheets, padded inside, witch masks, and tall witch hats, and as they stood on the doorstep each carried a placard and they read across, 'Witch Is Witch?'" Shortly after Halloween, Mary Lou Aswell and Bill and Emmy Maxwell planned their own party to toast *The Ponder Heart*, which was to be dedicated to them. Mary Lou expressed her joy and gratitude in a letter to Eudora. "It's such a wonderful gift it makes me shy about acknowledgment. I called Bill at once and he and Emmy are coming here next week to celebrate, but I don't know how I can say what I feel to *you*—I feel so unworthy and that will exasperate you because you *won't* see your friends in their light only in yours." The Maxwells shared Mary Lou's sentiments, writing, "We are both so happy to be identified in your mind with that story, and the story with that afternoon, and so touched, and if you think it really would be Uncle Daniel's wish—but who would know better than you what his wish would be, and on Tuesday we are going to Mary Lou's for supper in honor of everything. Make no other engagements, so you can be with us in spirit, and if that is too far, where would half-way

be—Cincinnati, Memphis, Pittsburgh? Shall we meet and con-
gregate in Marietta, Ohio?"[19] Eudora's own high spirits about the
dedication and her forthcoming publications were soon daunted
when the *New Yorker* rejected "Going to Naples," but they lifted
for a time when *Harper's Bazaar* took the story and when "The
Ponder Heart" actually appeared in the *New Yorker.*

No sooner had "The Ponder Heart" made its December periodical debut than theatrical producers began to express interest
in bringing it to the stage. The well-known producer Herman
Levin was very interested, but Lehman Engel counseled against
signing with a producer before a writer. Lehman felt that Jerome
Chodorov and Joseph Fields, authors of *Wonderful Town*, for which
he had directed the orchestra, might be a good choice. Eudora informed Diarmuid of Lehman's advice. Nevertheless, it was Levin
upon whom Diarmuid decided, and Eudora signed the option
agreement early in January.

Despite the prospect of a Broadway show, Eudora was once
again blue. She was on the same sort of emotional roller coaster
that her relationship with Robinson had occasioned, but now the
source of her distress was harder to identify. Although, at the insistence of Hubert Creekmore, she began 1954 with a party, she
did so without elation. To Mary Lou she wrote, "I've felt sort of
low & weak in the health—nerves, I'm sure, the wretched
wretches! Maybe after the book comes out & all is irrevocable I'll
get over it." She did not. The book itself sold well and received
high marks from the daily *New York Times,* where Charles Poore labeled her the Mozart of southern literature (Faulkner he saw as
its Wagner), and from the *Saturday Review,* where William Peden
found the novella "as successfully contrived as is the mouth-
melting peach pie with which Miss Edna regales Old Judge Waite
during a recess of Uncle Daniel's trial." But the reviews failed to
satisfy Bill Maxwell, who was concerned about Eudora's spirits.
In January he told her, "The reviews, the ones I have seen, are so
excruciatingly stupid that I cannot bring myself to send them

along to you. Especially Pritchett's. Though all are praising, no-body happened to have any talent for that kind of writing. So few reviewers do know how to do it intelligently. You and Francis [Steegmuller] and Brendan Gill and Miss Porter, about exhausts the list. Anyway, I winced my way through them, and wished somebody would have had the sense—somebody with his head on his shoulders—to say that *The Ponder Heart* is a comic master-piece and let it go at that." Though the Pritchett review to which Maxwell took particular exception had actually commended Eu-dora, Pritchett devoted most of his attention in the *New York Times Book Review* not to the novella itself, but to the traditions of re-gional writing, saying, "They are a protest by old communities, enriched by wounds, against the success of mass, or polyglot cul-ture. They make a pawky local bid against the strong hand of the centralized society we live in." And this failure to focus upon Eudora's achievement irritated Maxwell in his role as devoted friend.[20]

Eudora, as usual, wasted little time worrying about the re-views of her new book, but she did worry about Dolly, whose parents were old and ailing, and about Mary Lou, who was in a financial bind and quite depressed. And Eudora's own spirits con-tinued to be low. At the end of February Bill Maxwell gently sought to provide advice and support. "I said to Emmy that your letters had a sad overtone ever since the publication of *The Ponder Heart*, and she said, with her much greater perspicacity, that they have had a sad sound ever since you went home, having just dis-covered that you could be happy living in New York. Perhaps we are both imagining."[21] Completing both *The Ponder Heart* and the seven stories that would constitute *The Bride of the Innisfallen* may simply have left Eudora at loose ends and anxious. Or, as Emmy suspected, Eudora's living arrangements may have been a source of dissatisfaction. In 1954 apartments were just beginning to be widely available in Jackson, and single adult daughters remain-ing in their hometown generally resided with family members—

Eudora's friends Charlotte Capers, Willie Spann, and Dorothy Simmons certainly did, as did Eudora. For Eudora, this arrangement occasionally led to friction. Chestina did not approve of violating prohibition laws and buying alcoholic beverages; Eudora did. Chestina at times disapproved of Eudora's visitors—she had not allowed Henry Miller in the house, and she had felt inconvenienced by having Art and Toni Foff, Eudora's San Francisco friends, as houseguests. Even Frank Lyell, whom Chessie valued highly, could irritate her by standing on the porch and calling up to Eudora's bedroom window, "Eudora, are you decent?" Chestina was more comfortable with distinctions of class and race than was her daughter. And a strong sense of independence not only provided a strong bond, but also prompted tension between the Welty women. More importantly, Jackson, despite Eudora's close ties there, was not a place with which she was content. She was still disgusted with Mississippi politics, she knew her prospects for love and romance were dim in Jackson, she longed for a more vibrant cultural life, and her most intimate, confiding friendships were not with people in Jackson but in New York and environs: Diarmuid, Bill Maxwell, Bill Smith, Mary Lou, and Dolly Wells. Why then didn't she move? Her mother might have resisted the notion, but Chestina had accepted Eudora's lengthy absences with equanimity and in 1931 had even encouraged Eudora's plans to establish a career in New York. She would have eventually accepted and adapted to her daughter's move. It seems clear that Eudora was conflicted, that she simultaneously wanted to leave Mississippi and remain there. Working with her mother in the garden they both loved, living in the house her father had built, being near to lifelong friends and to her brothers' families, escaping the aggressiveness and fast pace of New York all appealed to Eudora. And despite the inevitable strains that arise between any mother and daughter, Eudora and Chestina were devoted to each other and had many common interests. Chestina was exceedingly proud of Eudora's achievements and kept scrapbooks about her daughter's various publications; Eudora admired her mother's vast knowledge of gardening, talent for garden design, and community service. Both women were great readers, avid bridge players, followers of the national news. They were both prone to challenge many southern social conventions. And, apart from occasional sparring, they granted each other the space to follow separate lives within the same household—Chestina meeting with her bridge club, penning a history of the Jackson Garden Club or a newspaper article about the Little Theatre; Eudora writing away in the privacy of her upstairs room or socializing with the Basic Eight. Mother and daughter were friends, who, as longtime housekeeper Eddie Mae Polk recalled, kept to their own, very distinct spheres within the household. So, a simple desire to live in New York was not the only source of Eudora's discontent; she could not be wholly satisfied by either Manhattan or Jackson. Perhaps Eudora also recognized that producing works like *The Ponder Heart*, though she might tinker with them on trips to the city, depended upon her Mississippi base, on the complex and contradictory society that she knew so well, that was so powerful a spark to her imagination, and that was a congenial environment in which to write. As Diarmuid had recognized long ago, New York with its many distractions was a place where Eudora might happily live but not one where she could work consistently and effectively.

As winter 1953–1954 drew to a close, Jackson visits by far-flung friends and acquaintances helped to meliorate, though not end, Eudora's discontent. In February the French sculptor Aristide Mian and his New England wife, Mary, came to Jackson and renewed the friendship established in 1949 in France. Then, in March, Elizabeth Bowen paid a third visit to Mississippi. Eudora drove her to the Delta, then to Oxford to meet Miss Ella Somerville, the cosmopolitan friend of John Robinson and William Faulkner. With Charlotte Capers, Eudora also took Bowen to Allison's Wells, the popular resort just north of Jackson. Bowen was charmed by Charlotte, Miss Ella, and Allison's and wrote to express her gratitude to Eudora for making these introductions. Shortly after Bowen's departure, John Malcolm Brinnin, and Rollie McKenna, who had photographed many writers for Brinnin's Poetry Center at the YMHA, were in Jackson. McKenna, who had grown up in Mississippi and who was a Manhattan neighbor of Mary Lou Aswell, photographed Eudora in Jackson and at Windsor, the ruins of an antebellum mansion that lay fifty or sixty miles to the southwest, and the Basic Eight held a dinner party in honor of the two out-of-town guests. Eudora's response to the visitors was ambivalent. She wrote to Mary Lou, saying, "It was fun to have Rollie & John Brinnin—never was quite sure what they came to get, or knew what they aimed to do with it. I was glad to show them (as well as I could, but it wasn't easy) any scenes they could photograph typical of my stories. But I was uneasy when Rollie, without warning, began photographing *me*— in the grocery etc. I told her I wanted none of that,—but don't know if she understood my complete *aversion* to publicity-like stuff. (Being her hostess I may have not expressed myself as violently as I feel.) *You'*ll help explain if it ever comes up, won't you? Whole thing may have been simply on speculation."[22] In April, Eileen McGrath, whom Eudora had long ago met through the Russells, whom she often saw in New York, and who was now a medical doctor, came for a visit. Frank and Hubert were also in town, and the Jacksonians took Eileen to Windsor for a picnic.

In the midst of all this entertaining, Eudora worked to prepare a typescript of her new story collection for Harcourt. The need to complete this undertaking became more urgent when she was invited to deliver a series of lectures in July at Cambridge University's American Studies Conference. The invitation marked international recognition of her stature as a writer. She had proven herself a master of comedy in stories like "Why I Live at the P.O." and of tragedy in stories like "At the Landing." She had written historical fiction in "First Love" and "A Still Moment" and a fairy tale in *The Robber Bridegroom*. She had composed a novel and then had written a story cycle, in which she resisted the novel's demand for resolution even as she used recurring characters and a common locale to tie her stories together. She had successfully imagined herself into lives far different from her own as she created traveling salesmen, a Delta bride on the eve of her wedding, an African American jazz pianist, a displaced southerner working in San Francisco, and her own version of the sorceress Circe. She had, with equal success, set stories in her native Mississippi, in New York and San Francisco, and in Ireland and Italy. Her prose style had ranged from the lyrical to the colloquial; her stories and novel had balanced the tight interplay of imagery that typifies poetry with plots that resisted closure; her concerns with love and death, with family structures, with social hierarchies, had been complexly rendered. No wonder Cambridge wanted her to be part of its summer faculty. Even before she was invited, however, Eudora felt somewhat intimidated by the prospect of lecturing there. At the end of March, she told Diarmuid, that she would "have to make up my mind whether or not to say I could—if asked from those being considered—go to England and be on a program at Cambridge." She feared that agreeing to be on the program would put her "in anguish from now till July." Still, she told him, she would love to "stop in Ireland, as Elizabeth [Bowen] has been asking me, and I might never get back any other way." Russell was clear in his advice: "What fun if you get asked to England—and of course you'd go."[23] And, of course, she was asked, and as Russell predicted, she agreed to go.

In May Eudora made her usual trip to New York. She saw Audrey Hepburn and Mel Ferrer in *Ondine* and was enchanted by Hepburn's performance. Producer Herman Levin urged Eudora to turn *The Ponder Heart* into a play. And at a lively party given by playwright Abe Burrows, she met a lady who "turned out to have played straight opposite Bea Lillie for years." To Hubert, Eudora reported, "It was a gay evening—Abe B. (a darling man) played

& sang—somebody played the squeeze-box (accordion to some) & there were lots of jokes I didn't get & never will. Home 3:30."[24] From the high life, Eudora moved to high culture, hearing Lehman Engel's opera *Malady of Love,* and then moved to the high jump, watching her godson Will Russell participate in field-day events. Then it was time to go home and finish preparing for the lectures she would give in England.

Just in advance of setting sail, Eudora traveled to Madison, Wisconsin. Her alma mater had awarded her an honorary degree, the first of many she would receive. Dolly Wells, herself on an extended European tour, wrote from Italy to congratulate Eudora on this degree, to ask if they might meet in England, and to report on seeing John Robinson. "Just before we left Rome, John turned up in his car and took us on a little 4 day trip to the hill towns (Perugia & Assisi et al.) The countryside was beautiful and we had a lot of fun. Also John drove us out to Hadrian's Villa, one of the most impressive & exciting sights I've seen on the whole trip. Of course J. asked all about you. I feel sorry for him now because I don't think he is a bit happy; but then his situation is one that only a good psychiatrist can figure out—not me. (I never thought I'd come to a statement like this but the whole thing defeats me.) Anyway, he seemed reasonably well and perhaps if he could get transferred to Italy from Heidelberg (which he doesn't like) he might be better off. He is trying to get USIS job in Naples."[25] John had found work in Germany as a United States Department of Army Civilian, supervising an education center in Heidelberg and, later, Nuremberg, where he coordinated programs to help Army personnel complete high school degrees and coordinated correspondence programs through the University of Maryland so that they might receive college credit. He longed to be based in Italy, not merely to vacation there. That would eventually happen, but not for six years or so.

Dolly's letter may have prompted concern for John, but such worries no longer consumed Eudora. She left for England with eager anticipation of new experiences, undisturbed by the knowledge she would not meet him during her travels. Her first days abroad were spent in London, where she saw Elizabeth Spencer, Eva Boros, Elizabeth Bowen, and Hamish Hamilton, the English publisher of *The Ponder Heart*, where she met W. H. Auden at a cocktail party, and where she loved seeing *The Boy Friend*, a musical comedy set in a 1920s girls' school on the French Riviera. Then it was on to Cambridge, where she was thrilled to be the first woman in six hundred years to dine at Peterhouse Hall. Even more thrilling was her lunch with E. M. Forster in his rooms at King's College. In a letter to Frank Lyell she described that auspicious occasion.

> I had lunch with Forster. He wrote me a note saying he had learned from David Daiches I was in Cambridge, was just about to set off for the Continent, and could I have lunch with him in his rooms at King's, the last day, which was also the next day I think. I of course had overwhelming feelings of joy—had meant to write and ask if I might "wait on him," but had not yet done it. He had all his own things in his rooms, bookcases 2 rows deep. The electric heater was on—for my benefit, I'm sure, because later on I heard him agreeing with the gyp that it was quite hot todday [*sic*]—sherry waiting, and the lunch brought in and served on his own little table—hors d'oeuvres and chops and vegetables and fresh raspberries and cream, white wine, and then coffee by the fire. He talked about his family portraits hanging round the room, and some letters and papers he'd just come into possession of—and when I asked if he might be going to write something about them, he said a sketch was rather in his mind. He asked if the college people attending the Conference knew anything about books—"They generally don't"—and was very kind about what I was up to. He said he hardly saw how he would ever get back to America, be-

cause of the need, if he came, to lecture, and to be put on show, and said the same thing was true of India—that he would very much like to go, but just didn't feel he wanted to undergo any more of that. Isn't it sad? . . . After lunch he put on a jaunty fat tweed cap with a button on top and took me for a walk. We cut across the grass (!), and went down into the Backs and along the river, then back and into the Chapel. He showed me over it, and then at the last took me up the winding stair into the organ loft, where a man was playing Handel (I think, but I was having such a lovely time I can't remember exactly), and we looked down into that lovely place from above. He was absolutely darling. As we parted in front of King's he said, "I shouldn't worry for a moment about what to tell them about writing—just tell them to stop it!"

And then, that night, at something called "General Discussion—Literature," Arthur Mizener oratorically said, "Now you can't go saying *Passage to India* is a great novel, come come! It's simply a novel of manners that's gone wrong. When you finish it, you're left with nothing but a vacuum!" I was put in the ridiculous position of having to defend *A Passage to India*. You *know* what I think of him [i.e., Mizener]. He regards the conference as a show, that's obvious, and doesn't really care what he's saying, so long as people gasp, laugh, defend themselves, get mad, and the rest—all of which I do, to my fury. I was so upset after General Discussion: Literature that as I was coming home I literally kicked myself and got in with my foot all covered with blood.[26]

Mizener's attack on *A Passage to India* was unbearable for Eudora, who treasured all of Forster's novels, who had that very day been in his presence, and who was herself fascinated by India. In 1933 Eudora had loved performances by the Indian dancer Shan-Kar, who, according to dance critic John Martin, provided "a genuine and trustworthy, if not an intellectual or rational, experience of Hindu culture." Similarly, reading Forster's novel focused on Indian life and thought (and the British failure to understand it) had been an intense experience for her. It may also have been an experience that influenced her development as a writer. Her depiction of the cultural collisions she had witnessed in Mississippi and during her European travels, her contrasting portraits of conventionality and daring, her descriptions of characters whose motto might be "only connect," and her use of frontiers, swamps, rivers, and amphibious landscapes to embody the same kind of mystery Forster located in the Malabar caves—all evoke *A Passage to India*.[27] This book, which she valued so highly and which had such powerful connections to her own fiction, Mizener had branded "nothing but a vacuum," thereby winning Eudora's anger and distaste.

Many others in Cambridge won her favor. She enjoyed the company of noted literary critic David Daiches and of noted theater director George Rylands; Rylands, Eudora told Frank Lyell, "is the Dadie in Virginia Woolf's diary. Quite a boy."[28] Eudora also liked Mr. and Mrs. Edward Malins; Malins was a master at Christ's Hospital in Sussex, and he and his wife had ventured to Cambridge for the American Studies Conference. Eudora's own performance at the conference for secondary and college English teachers went well; as she took the podium for the first of three general lectures, some Scottish participants assured her, "Ye'll do just grand!" They were right. The lecture "Place in Fiction" particularly entranced the Welsh and Scots in attendance, and it attracted the attention of Jack Fischer of *Harper's Magazine*, who wanted to publish it.

The topic of place seems a particularly appropriate one for Eudora to have chosen, for place in her own fiction had become increasingly important over the course of her career. The rather limited descriptions of setting in *A Curtain of Green* had given way to more expansive and emblematic accounts of the Natchez Trace when she wrote *The Robber Bridegroom* and *The Wide Net*. In *Delta Wedding*, Eudora created a fictional world, a world of plantation houses and the cabins inhabited by field hands and servants, of cotton fields and a cypress swamp, of the small town of Fairchilds with its cemetery and railroad station. In *The Golden Apples*, Eudora went one step further. She depicted a town called Morgana, Mississippi, as it evolved over a forty-year period: the Feed and Seed Store, Morgana's public park, the MacLain and Stark and Morrison houses, the Big Black River, where Virgie Rainey takes her late-night swims, Morgan's woods on the outskirts of town, the local cemetery, are all subject to time and change. Homes fall into decay or are converted to boardinghouses, woods are depleted by loggers, the cemetery acquires more and more headstones, and the passage of time brings to characters like Virgie Rainey and Loch Morrison a sense of vulnerability and urgency.

Place was central to Eudora's achievement as a writer, but in her lecture, she attempted to explain why place, one of fiction's "lesser angels," was so important to many other writers, to Flaubert and Forster, Faulkner and Joyce, Katherine Mansfield and Emily Brontë, Ernest Hemingway and Laurence Sterne. Place, she argued in a published version of the lecture, provides the novelist with his raw material and helps him to make the world of his novel credible; place grounds him, provides him with roots and perspective and with a point of view. Beyond this, she contended, place is the locus of feeling in the novel. The writer may find his settings at home, Eudora asserted, "without necessarily moving an inch from any present address," but she added that "there may come to be new places in our lives that are second spiritual homes—closer to us in some ways, perhaps, than our original homes." Place, she felt, could not be prescribed for a novelist. Neither could novels be dismissed on account of their place. "'Regional,'" she observed, "... is a careless term, as well as a condescending one, because what it does is fail to differentiate between the localized raw material of life and its outcome as art. 'Regional' is an outsider's term; it has no meaning for the insider who is doing the writing, because as far as he knows he is simply writing about life. Jane Austen, Emily Brontë, Thomas Hardy, Cervantes, Turgenev, the authors of the books of the Old Testament, all confined themselves to regions, great or small—but are they regional? Then who from the start of time has not been so?"[29]

In another of her lectures, subsequently published in part as an unsigned essay in the *Times Literary Supplement*, Eudora argued that writing from the American South transcended the regional, and then she sought to account for the "generous flow of writing" that had come from the South. "It is nothing new or startling," she asserted,

> that Southerners do write—probably they *must* write. It is the way they are: born readers and reciters, great document holders, diary keepers, letter exchangers and savers, history tracers—and, outstaying the rest, great talkers. Emphasis in talk is on the narrative form and the verbatim conversation, for which time is needed. Children who grow up listening through rewarding stretches of unhurried time, reading in big lonely rooms, dwelling in the confidence of slow-changing places, are naturally more prone than other children to be entertained from the first by life and to feel free, encouraged, and then in no time compelled, to pass their pleasure on. They cannot help being impressed by a world around them where history has happened in the yard or come into the house, where all round the countryside big things happened and monuments stand to the memory of fiery deeds still to be heard from the lips of grandparents, the columns in the field or the familiar cedar avenue leading uphill to nothing, where such-and-such a house once stood. At least one version of an inextinguishable history of everybody and his grandfather is a community possession, not for a mo-

ment to be forgotten—just added to, with due care, mostly.
The individual is much too cherished as such for his importance ever to grow *diminished* in a story. The rarity in a man
is what is appreciated and encouraged.

Eudora located the impetus for southern writing in the oral tradition of the South and in its reverence for the individual, a reverence that certainly animated her own writing. Then she added that
"place must have something to do with this fury of writing with
which the South is charged. If one thing stands out in these writers, all quite different from another, it is that each feels passionately about Place. And not merely in the historical and prideful
meaning of the word, but in the sensory meaning, the breathing
world of sight and smell and sound, in its earth and water and
sky, its time and its seasons. In being so moved, the Southerners—one could almost indisputably say—are unique in America
today. One would have to look to those other writers of remote
parts, to the Irish and the Welsh—to find the same thing."[30]

This lecture, like "Place in Fiction," proved a highlight of
the conference. But for her part, Eudora took more pleasure in
the informal discussion sessions she held three times a week with
young teachers who had enrolled in her class, and in the walks,
teas, and pub visits she made with that group. She was particularly impressed by a Welsh scholar named Alun Jones, and he introduced her to the fiction of a fellow Welshman named Gwyn
Jones. Eudora responded enthusiastically to the Gwyn Jones stories collected in *Flowers Beneath the Scythe* (1952) and *Shepherd's Hay
and Other Stories* (1953). To Diarmuid she wrote that she had suggested that Alun Jones edit a collection of Welsh stories, and she
wondered if Diarmuid could help both Joneses find American
publishers.[31]

When the Cambridge conference ended, Eudora took the
train to Edinburgh, where she was entertained by David Daiches's
mother and aunt, managed to tour the city, and attended the

Edinburgh Festival. "Yes I did love the look of Edinburgh—those closes, and hills, and haunts!" she wrote to Frank Lyell. "I went down the Royal Mile on foot, and went in a bus on a tour of the city twice—so as to see things more carefully and again—and of course walked miles everywhere all day! The feeling of savagery and wildness you get permeating the grand things is marvelous, isn't it? Helped I must say by the presentation of *Macbeth* in the Assembly Hall—so much space and so much darkness to act it in, on that big apron stage that held the banquet with ease, and where the fights could range all over the place." At the Festival, Eudora "saw Fonteyn do Firebird, heard Isaac Stern play (though he did play Prokofiev and I'd rather have heard another concerto), went to the Tattoo (!!—isn't it marvelous!) and visited the Diaghelev and Cezanne exhibitions several times."[32] The performance of *Macbeth* with actors carrying freshly cut boughs as they brought Birnam Wood to Dunsinane was destined to remain vivid in her memory as was the spectacular conclusion of the Edinburgh Tattoo—spotlights focused on a white steed with rider on the ramparts of the city's massive castle.

From Edinburgh, Eudora made her way through Wales. Then, on September 1, she sailed to Ireland for a two-week stay at Bowen's Court. To Lyell she reported that she was

> still going to bed with a hot water bottle here, and drawing close to the fire, but we've had lovely bright days, and wonderful rides and trips over the mountains and down to the sea. I leave here the middle of next week for London, have 10 days there, and sail on the 24th ... Very happy busy times here—we go out a lot, either riding or visiting, and have company in for dinner, etc. It's rained madly at times—and the little girl who brings in my breakfast said, "'Twas a wild night in Ireland last night!" Eddy Sackville-West is visiting here too, and he is such a sweet man. Very Edwardian—travels with a little barometer in a case, and changes

of stones for his ring. I wish for you when he gets to talking about his family. He said his grandmother, who was Irish, was a fearful old party, and when her breakfast toast was not done absolutely uniformly, she sent it back to the kitchen with *pins* stuck in to show where it was wrong. Do you know his *Record Guide?* Supposed to be *the* one. He's apparently just revised it for a new edition. He says the only publishers who can be trusted to get it right, all those numerals and things, are Collins—who print the Bible! He is supposed to inherit Knowle [*sic*] when his father dies, but does not want it, and is turning it over to his cousin Lionel, who is married and has children. He *does* want to buy a John Nash castle [i.e., one designed by Nash, an English architect of the Regency period] near here, a Gothic one standing empty in a perfectly beautiful situation—it really is marvelous, we've been to see it twice and are going back.[33]

These good times in Ireland were followed by more good times in London, where Eudora met Dolly Wells and Dolly's friend Sue Crane, who were nearing the end of their European tour. Eudora took Dolly to see *The Boy Friend,* the musical by Sandy Wilson that she had so enjoyed during the summer. In London she also entertained David Daiches and his wife, taking them to see *Salad Days*— "Julian Slade's musical for the Bristol Old Vic."[34] And she had a visit with Alun Jones, who came down from Oxford, pleased at the prospect of discussing Welsh literature with Eudora. Then she left for New York, sailing on the *Britannic* and arriving on October 2.

Eudora had been away from home for three months, but she delayed her return to Jackson for another week. In New York she visited with Mary Lou, Bill Maxwell, the Bill Smiths, and Hildy Dolson; she joined Hubert Creekmore for an evening of theater, seeing Shirley Booth in *By the Beautiful Sea.* She met with Jack Fischer to discuss *Harper's* proposed publication of "Place in

Fiction." She conferred with her Harcourt editor Robert Giroux. And she spent a good bit of time with Diarmuid, stressing her love of Gwyn Jones's stories, a love Diarmuid did not share.

Back in Jackson, Eudora's attention was focused on Broadway negotiations. *The Ponder Heart* was the object of continuing theatrical interest, and Eudora was herself interested in having Danny Kaye play the role of Uncle Daniel. She had written him from England about her hopes, and in October Diarmuid informed her that he had managed to get the letter to Kaye's West Coast agent. Kaye himself responded to the letter, expressing his appreciation for her fiction and regretting that previous commitments would prevent his participation in the play. The option with Herman Levin had also come to naught, and Lehman Engel endorsed granting an option to playwrights Jerome Chodorov and Joseph Fields. By late November Eudora had signed a contract with them. Even as she kept track of *The Ponder Heart* theatrical negotiations, Eudora managed to revise "Place in Fiction," cutting ten pages and mailing it to Russell, but *Harper's* would decide against publication, leaving Russell to try other periodicals.

In January 1955 Eudora attended a Jackson concert by the celebrated Polish pianist Witold Malcuzynski. Then, late in the month, she and Dolly traveled to New Orleans, where Eudora had lunch at Galatoire's with Frank Lyell's English friend Pamela Redmayne. In 1951 she had visited Redmayne in the English Cotswold town of Burford, and now Redmayne was on vacation, touring the United States by bus. Eudora sent word to Frank about his friend. "[Pamela] was just as we expected. Big as a house—has gained 18½ lbs! ('You Americans never let one walk or take exercise'). Looked well, and had just come from Atlanta, where she visited Warm Springs and told them how to run the March of Dimes campaign, showed them where to take the pictures they used in publicity, etc. Had been to Bellingrath ('Shocking weather!')—had been in Virginia ('I used the word 'apprehensive' and a young girl said to me, 'Oh, Miss Redmayne, please don't use any more of those 3-syllabled words, we don't understand what you mean'). Had a wonderful lunch at Gala-toires's—drink, trout amandine, green salad, creme caramel, cof-fee, and I asked her to order the wine which she did—a lovely imported Chablis and she even approved the temperature of it. I don't know if she approved the lunch, but she couldn't have helped eating it, it was just divine." During this visit, Redmayne mentioned a talented student she had met at Duke University and advised Eudora to make his acquaintance when she lectured there in February. A few days later she wrote to remind Eudora of this recommendation. "Edward Reynolds Price is the boy at Duke University—and he is, I think, exceptional."[35]

By February Eudora had completed an essay to be published both in Robert Penn Warren's *Understanding Fiction* and in the *Virginia Quarterly Review.* She worried about the essay, "Writing and Analyzing a Story," telling Frank "I hate trying to write criticism and agonize and rewrite a thousand times, then feel unhappy about it." She was also worried about the length of a new story. "Have done a draft of a 60-page story, which I hope to cut down considerably when revising. Kind of Smith County. Names: June (Junior—hero), Miss Dovie (his mother), Willowdean (his wife), Essie Dee, Empress, & Elvie (his sisters), Lady May (his baby), Aycock Odom (his friend), Mr. Seeb Matthews (a neighbor), Judge Moody (his enemy, sent him to the pen) and Mrs. Moody. Scene is combination family reunion and welcome home from the pen. He didn't do anything much, just tried to teach Old Man Mix, at the store in Toonigh, a lesson."[36] The story would not be cut down, nor would it be completed for many years. It eventu-ally grew into the novel *Losing Battles,* published in 1970.

It was perhaps worry about her work, about her mother, who was scheduled for spring cataract surgery, and about Bill Maxwell and Katherine Anne Porter, who both had pneumonia, that left

Eudora feeling rather low in early February. Or perhaps she was lonely in Jackson, far from those friends she most cherished—Diarmuid, Mary Lou, Bill and Emmy, Frank, Hubert, and Dolly. But by month's end, the gloom was lifting. Eudora traveled by train to Durham, North Carolina, where she was to read and to meet with students at Duke University and to visit nearby North Carolina State for another reading. Reynolds Price wrote in advance of her visit, volunteering to meet the train. Eudora declined the offer, but Reynolds met the train anyway. He felt that Eudora would need assistance, since she was arriving in the middle of the night in a town with few taxis available. He vowed, upon this first meeting, not to trouble her with conversation, but just to see her settled. Many conversations were to come.

In North Carolina, Eudora saw old friends as she worked at the two universities—she spent time with Frank's former colleagues in Raleigh, saw her old Jackson friend Bill Hamilton, who was now teaching history at Duke, and visited with her former Harcourt editor Lambert Davis and his wife, who were now based in nearby Chapel Hill. But the most important encounter of this trip was with Reynolds. In William Blackburn's fiction-writing class, Eudora was tremendously impressed by Price's reading of a story, and she enjoyed a more personal visit with him when he and Blackburn took her to dinner. Soon after returning home, she wrote to thank the young man for his hospitality and to encourage his writing.

> Meeting me in the dead of night, to start with—then guiding me rightly, having me to the story session, and treating me to that fine dinner at the Ranch House in Chapel Hill. I had a good time altogether, but it was more than the welcome, it was the pleasure of meeting and talking, and I'm delighted to have become acquainted with your writing too. I hope to have a chance to see more. The best of luck with your work and the next three years [as a Rhodes Scholar], and the writ-

ing especially. If there's ever anything useful I could do and you know of it, I look for you to let me know. As you may have heard, writers get along on one another's little notes and bits of information passed along, all their lives, and if you should ever want to try for a Guggenheim, for instance, I should feel very pleased to be named as a reference.[37]

Eudora also regaled Reynolds with a humorous story about the flamboyant Pamela Redmayne and recommended that he meet her friends Alun Jones at Oxford, Mr. and Mrs. Edward Malins in Sussex, and Elizabeth Bowen in London. And she promised to see if it might be possible (and it was) for Duke's student magazine *The Archive,* which Reynolds edited, to publish her essay "Place in Fiction" before it appeared in Bill Hamilton's *South Atlantic Quarterly,* the academic journal to which Diarmuid had finally given his blessing.

In March, Chestina Welty underwent cataract surgery, with its then difficult period of hospitalization and recuperation; Eudora felt that both the operation and follow-up had gone well and praised the work of her mother's doctor. Soon after Chestina came home from the hospital, Eudora met with *The Ponder Heart* dramatists Jerry Chodorov and Joe Fields, who had come to Mississippi to develop a sense of the place about which they were writing. By the end of the month Eudora had read their draft script and was unhappy with it. She wrote to express her areas of concern. She felt that Uncle Daniel's innocence needed to be "more carefully established"; that the community viewpoint also needed to be established; and that the "texture" of the play was too "thin." The play, she asserted, should focus upon "family, friends, stories, gossip, the town reaction in general—which is peculiarly southern." The play, she further noted, suffered from the loss of the novel's narrator, Edna Earle. "Uncle Daniel's world cherishes him, protects him, enjoys him, and is *responsible* for him—the attitude as embodied whole in Edna Earle."[38] After writing to Joe and Jerry, Eudora again consulted Lehman Engel, who assured her that her letter was helpful and not insulting.

In the midst of the strain of caring for her mother and worrying about the *Ponder* script, Eudora learned that she would receive the William Dean Howells Medal for Fiction from the National Institute and American Academy of Arts and Letters. The academy then contacted Bill Maxwell about the possibility of displaying *The Ponder Heart* galleys from the *New Yorker,* and he immediately wrote to congratulate Eudora on her first major award. Eudora was deeply honored by the academy's decision, and because her mother's health seemed stable, she planned to attend the ceremony, go to Ohio for an honorary degree from Western College for Women, and, after that, spend some time in New York. "I'm sure Mother is tired of having me hover over that eye like a chicken with its one egg (her words)," she told Frank Lyell.[39]

The Bride of the Innisfallen was published in early April, just in time for Eudora's forty-sixth birthday. Orville Prescott, who so long ago had resented Eudora's position on the *New York Times Book Review* staff and who had afterward negatively reviewed her fiction, continued his hostility in the pages of the daily *Times.* This time he also damned two writers whom Eudora and most critics admired greatly, Elizabeth Bowen and William Faulkner. "From Elizabeth Bowen she seems to have acquired her taste for ambiguity, her way of hinting evasively while withholding essential information, her habit of circling around the point of a story without bothering to reveal it. From William Faulkner she seems to have learned the questionable device of narrating a story from the point of view of a mentally incompetent observer and to have derived her pleasure in grotesque horrors. There are seven stories in 'The Bride of the Innisfallen.' Three of them are wanly Bowen-esque and one is gruesomely Faulknerian. That leaves three that seem to be undiluted Eudora Welty." Other reviewers offered unqualified praise. John Barkham of the *Saturday Review* syndicate wrote, "This new volume contains only seven tales, but they exhibit both her infallible ear (which Katherine Anne Porter has called 'pure as a tuning fork') and her power to register a sensitive awareness of people and places. In two of these stories she exchanges her familiar South for the European scene, with results that are just as unerring." And Frances Gaither, in the *New York Times Book Review,* joined Barkham in praising the "Bowenesque" stories that Prescott had damned. "Miss Welty's talents, invested in these foreign ventures, have, however, suffered no adverse sea-change."[40]

On May 23 Eudora left Jackson for New York and dined that evening with Mary Lou, with Dolly Wells and Ruth Forbes, Jacksonians transplanted to New York, and with Jimmie Wooldridge, who was visiting from Jackson. Then the same group accompanied her to the National Institute and American Academy, where Eudora received the Howells Medal. After spending the Memorial Day weekend at Western College for Women, Eudora was back in Manhattan. There she and Reynolds Price were reunited and went to see *Bus Stop* together. She also managed to see *Cat on a Hot Tin Roof* and *Fanny* before returning to Jackson, where a letter from Reynolds soon reached her. "It's largely because of you that I have given so much thought to writing these past months. I think we must declare our debts when we see them, and I am proud to say that it is your example, your kindness, your encouragement, above all your wonderful way of treating me like I knew so much more than I did, like I had done something worth doing and *might* do something worth even more—it is this that has determined me, for better or worse, to a life given to writing."[41]

Eudora's response to this high praise was modest. "You know all I did was say what I thought, and you don't owe me a thing for that! I wouldn't want you to feel anything but my warm appreciation and pleasure, my admiration and high expectations—practically a prophecy, I guess that amounts to. I'm the one [who] owes you thanks for the cheer and reassurance it gives me to see a young writer coming along who's so undoubtedly good. It was such a pleasure to read 'The Heart is a Chain' (still sounds a lovely title) and I look forward a great deal to seeing what you're doing with it now." She volunteered to send the story to Diarmuid or to Bill Maxwell, and then she discussed her response to *Cat on a Hot Tin Roof.* "I had to take back everything I was mad at Tennessee Williams about—for this play seemed honest, serious, *about* something (this is like the 'goal' in that Chekhov letter, a little) and a good *use* of all that material he sometimes seemed to me to just fling about like a child with a dollar's worth of fireworks." To reservations about J. D. Salinger that Reynolds had expressed, she offered a demurrer: "I feel a deep vulnerability about him in his stories—it's what makes him veer, perhaps, and put on those endings you mention. I don't believe he's ever really and positively stated his subject through his stories—he does it negatively. Things are wrong, people can't speak to each other, the innocent aren't respected, etc. I respect him for whatever way he's said this at all, for I feel he's got it to say—and perhaps he'll do it in other ways later on, better, or not better—anyway I very much hope to see what he does next." Eudora closed her letter by discussing the writing life. "What you say about the need to know what one's really worth, what the things one does are really worth—I still feel the same, and I bet that never leaves you. In fact I imagine that's part of the drive that makes you write to begin with. Each story is a new trial. But I know, until you get something done and behind you, it's the harder pressure. I think that's why first stories get written so fast (comparatively) and plentifully. They're the base to put the others on, in one sense. Not that you learn from one story to the other, about the *story*, but can count on the act of writing as the process you'll learn it from."[42] Eudora had not written such letters since the late 1940s when she wrote so often to John Robinson. In Reynolds she had found a shared passion for writing, a passion that Robinson ultimately lacked.

A month later Eudora answered another letter from Reynolds, this time to explain his need for an agent and to urge that he not doubt himself. "Don't worry about the 'professional' feeling— you may never have it, I haven't after all these years. That is, if the feeling of something new, fresh, difficult, and strange which comes to you with each story is the mark of the amateur spirit, then I still have the amateur spirit. The excitement comes from what's still to be learned at least as much as from what's been struggled with before or partway, for the time being perhaps, mastered. This does! sound a little confused, but I'm just saying it's the writing alone that's important and keeps on being important, the interior part—so it's a blessing to have someone you trust to look after all the externals." Then, in the generous fashion that was her hallmark, she asked him to let her know "if there's anything (now or ever) I could do that's useful. You'll find that there's give-and-take among writers all your life, so don't feel shy should you decide to apply for a Guggenheim, or anything like that ever, to mention it so as to give people that like your work a chance to speak up. At the time I was applying for my Guggenheim in 1950 I was also recommending someone, as it happened, so you see how it goes on."[43] Eudora offered Reynolds the very sort of encouragement and support that John Robinson, filled with self-doubt, had both sought from her and then found oppressive. Reynolds's response, however, was not ambivalent. He accepted advice and encouragement with thanksgiving, and eventually he would be able to provide Eudora with similar gifts.

At Eudora's suggestion, Diarmuid Russell had read Reynolds's work; Russell shared her high estimation of the twenty-two-year-old writer and agreed to take him on as a client. Eudora's intercession on behalf of Lehman Engel was not so successful. Diarmuid feared that Engel's autobiography would not interest a wide audience. Eudora then sought to put Mary Lou and Lehman in contact, hoping that Ballantine Books might accept the manuscript. When that prospect failed, she volunteered to send *This*

Bright Day to her own publisher, but that attempt would also result in rejection for Lehman. Whether she met with success or failure, however, Eudora repeatedly sought to provide publication assistance to her friends.

During the fall, Chestina's eyes were again troubling her. Though she had been fitted with new glasses, she continued to have what Eudora termed "flare-ups." Between September and December, Eudora needed to be at home and care for her mother. During this time she had to forgo travel, including a meeting in New York with Elizabeth Bowen, but she still was able to offer good-humored travel advice to others. In a letter wishing Reynolds well on his departure for Oxford and a Rhodes Scholarship, she counseled, "If Pamela Redmayne is standing on the docks with hypodermic needle rampant (she's so keen on medicine!) get off the Atlantic side of the boat, it will be safer, and swim for it." In a more serious vein, she added two names to a list of individuals for him to contact—the writer Pamela Travers and the young tennis star Ham Richardson, whose mother was an old Jackson friend. Then Eudora launched into a discussion of *Death in Venice.* In the novel, she asserted, "The pit is indeed the pit, but that equally important and perhaps longer sustained in the eye is that presence of illusion—that the vision of beauty still stands on the edge of the sea, beckoning through contamination and horror and all . . . I don't indeed follow Mann through his equations of love and disease and art and evil, if I understand him rightly and I may not—but I feel that in 'Death in Venice' the allusions and evocations are so far flung out, and so delicately strung one upon the other, that any fish (because I see that sounds like a net) might likely be brought up. It is a wonderful story, isn't it—terrifying, and to me it seems almost unbelievable at the same time it's seeming inevitable as it goes. He has absolutely no warmth, to me, not even one little candle's worth, and I can think of other things he hasn't got too, plenty of them, but though I don't 'take to' him, I feel an amount of power coming out of him that's almost strange for a man with such cold passion—makes you think of medieval powers and magic."[44]

Her letter to Reynolds, however, did not discuss the relationship of fiction and politics, even though this relationship was becoming troubling to her. The growing public tension over the issue of civil rights had led to demands for political correctness in phrasing, regardless of a work's thematic statement or its historic context. Eudora, who had long since denounced racist demagogues like Theodore Bilbo and John Rankin, had been confident that her belief in the common humanity of black and white and her rejection of racial oppression were evident in stories like "A Worn Path," in which a very old and courageous black woman walks miles and overcomes white hostility in an effort to obtain medicine for her grandson. But, as Eudora told Frank Lyell, textbook editors who wanted to reprint "A Worn Path" also wanted to "delete the word 'Negro' from it or else would I change the story and not call the character 'Aunt Phoenix' but 'Mrs. Jackson.'" In a telephone conversation, Eudora instructed her publisher, William Jovanovich, to say no. "I said I wouldn't," Eudora wrote in a letter to Lyell.

> Told him [Bill Jovanovich] the story was written in its own terms of time and place and vernacular, and it wasn't up to me to change those—that I had never meant disrespect in the first place, and didn't think it was up to me to prove it by making changes—that the feeling was what mattered, and if the textbook editors couldn't see the feeling plain, they didn't know what the story was saying anyway.—No, over the telephone I couldn't think at all,—as I never can and especially at such a request—I just said no, I wouldn't change it at all, and I wrote this all to him afterwards. I know it was a small matter, and these are cautious times, but I

think it's still an important point, a matter of the truth. Don't you. It really made me mad, to imply that I meant disrespect and that if I did they could so easily correct it for me by changing a few words. Ugh! How far could such 'editing' lead? Trespassing into what realms of gold? On the way to Othello they could hop on poor Robinson Crusoe for not saying "Mr. Friday" on the island.[45]

Another issue of misprision, less ominous in import, involved the Chodorov and Fields script of *The Ponder Heart*. By October, Robert Douglas had been signed to direct the play, and he spent five days in Jackson. He and Eudora discussed the revisions Joe and Jerry had incorporated after a springtime visit in Jackson, but Eudora remained skeptical about the play's success. Douglas asked her to "try to fix up what's left so it would make a plot," but Eudora told him she "wouldn't touch it with a 10-foot pole." To Diarmuid she wrote, "It makes me sick to think of the fate of my carefree little story." In November, Lehman sent encouraging words, praising the script and saying that he had been asked to compose some music for it. When Eudora expressed reservations, he sought to reassure her: "About THE PONDER HEART: What I mean about the dramatization is that I think Joe and Jerry have done a simple, theatrically valid job in *their* terms. I believe it ought to be a big hit. I don't think they understand the core of your work, but something about your book has struck a responsive chord in them and they have done their work with enthusiasm and ON THEIR TERMS I think they succeeded. The result is a bare connection with what you have written, but I think it's all right this way as regards you because everybody knows you really are not involved in it artistically at all, and I hope you will make lots and lots of money out of it."[46]

By early 1956, however, Lehman himself was skeptical. His music was rejected in favor of a song by Dorothy Fields, Joe Fields's sister, and Lehman wrote to warn Eudora that he had seen the play in Philadelphia. "I did not like it at all and I hope you will be prepared in advance so that you have great control of your most personal feelings when you go to see it. It lacks the essential quality of your book and is about as far away from genuine Southern-ness as anything could possible be."[47] Others were more positive in response. Dolly Wells and Rosie Russell managed to see the play in New Haven and sent endorsements of it. Happily, some of Lehman's music was reinserted. Eudora resolved to control her emotions, attend the play, and make her own judgment. Then arose the problem of obtaining tickets. After much struggle, she finally secured eight, but did not have enough for all the friends she wanted to invite. Bill Maxwell managed to get another four tickets, and everything was arranged.

For a time, it seemed that one of her mother's eye "flare-ups" might prevent Eudora from attending the premiere performance, but Chestina's doctor insisted that all would be well. Chessie had moved downstairs in the Pinehurst Place house and was thus in far less danger of falling. Reassured, Eudora arrived in New York the weekend before the play opened and spent that weekend with the Russells at Katonah. On February 16, she was feted at a pre-theater party given by Mary Lou. The Russells, the Maxwells, Mary Lou and her friend Agnes Sims, Dolly, Hubert, the David Rockefellers, and Charlotte Capers were all able to join her for the play. Afterward, at the Algonquin Hotel, there was a celebration lasting late into the night. Eudora had fallen in love with the theatrical experience, and the reviews of the performance were, for the most part, worth waiting up for. In the *New York Times,* Brooks Atkinson wrote, "Between the novel and the play nothing essential has been lost. 'The Ponder Heart,' which opened at the Music Box last evening, is original, charming and funny." In the *Herald Tribune,* Walter Kerr called the play "recklessly charming." Though he found it somewhat superficial, Kerr noted that "a gentle, wry, unpredictable chuckle is what the authors seem to be after, and they got an almost uninterrupted one from me." Robert

Coleman in the *Daily Mirror* was less charitable. "It is always regrettable to have to say 'almost but not quite' about a worthy try. Still, a miss is as good as a mile, even though it be a near miss, in a present-day theatre that demands nothing less than perfection." But Richard Watts in the *New York Post,* offered high praise, calling *The Ponder Heart* "one of the funniest and most engaging of the season's comedies."[48] All of Eudora's worries about the production had vanished, and the reviews suggested that a lengthy run was in store.

The next day the seasoned theater veteran Lehman gave a dinner party in Eudora's honor—his own Broadway work commitments had kept him away from opening night. A few days after that, Eudora made her second appearance at the Cosmopolitan Club, reading for a handsome stipend. Before leaving Manhattan for home, she managed to have lunch once with David Wayne, who starred in *The Ponder Heart* and whom she liked immensely, and once with Sarah Marshall, who played the role of Bonnie Dee Peacock. On Washington's Birthday she attended a matinee performance of *The Ponder Heart*—it and its cast had won her heart.

At home on the first of March, Eudora wrote to thank Diarmuid for his calming influence during all of the Broadway excitement. "It was just grand being up, and having that astonishing and lovely time. Thank goodness though for the Russell presence, or the Welty bearings might have been lost. The weekend in Katonah was just what I needed—combination of peace and fun to get ready on and gird all our selves." The only sour note of this trip sounded after it had ended. As Eudora reported to Diarmuid, "There was a ghastly 'interview' with me in the *World Telegram* which made me a little sick—made me out a complete fool, professional Southerner and an old maid, and I'm just one of those. Very humiliating, all invented. I wondered what malice made that get printed. It was odd too, because the actual interview was quite pleasant and matter of fact—I was just praising the production of the play." Though the interview was displeasing, Eudora liked the photographs of the play that ran in *Life* magazine, and she told Russell that "Faulkner has a good letter to the North in the same issue." In that letter, Faulkner reiterated the public support he had already declared for integration and racial equality, but he feared violence from southern whites if schools were forcibly integrated. He asked "all the organizations and groups which would force integration on the South by legal process" to "stop now for a moment" and give the southern segregationist time "to look about and see that . . . he himself faces an obsolescence in his own land which only he can cure; a moral condition which not only must be cured but a physical condition which has got to be cured if he, the white Southerner, is to have any peace, is not to be faced with another legal process or maneuver every year, year after year, for the rest of his life."[49] Underestimating the stubborn resistance of his own neighbors, Faulkner anticipated that the South would heal itself. Like Faulkner, it seems, Eudora hoped that southern resistance might yield to the moral and practical arguments for integration. She did not yet sense the volatility of the racial situation.

Eudora now turned her thoughts to playwriting. She had been reading George Bernard Shaw and, in light of *Ponder*'s Broadway success, had in mind two plays of her own. But more immediately pressing were negotiations involving Archibald and Bergersen's dramatization of *The Robber Bridegroom*. Russell was inclined to extend their option, but Eudora wanted to talk to Bill Archibald before any decision was made. Her agitation over *The Ponder Heart* script writing had made her wary, but her enthusiasm for David Wayne made her think of him as an ideal lead over Zachary Scott, who had expressed keen interest in the project.

Beyond her continuing focus on the theater, Eudora had been reading Eva Boros's novel *The Mermaids* and was delighted to send an expansive publicity quote for the book. "Eva Boros's first book, THE MERMAIDS, is sensitive, haunting work of a quality distinctly its own. While it probes deeply for unsparing truth, it is delicate as a flower to the senses; while it has a tragic story to tell, it carries an unimpeachable plume of gaiety, a gaiety of the spirit. Miss Boros has a sense of the wonder of things, of the soft illumination and the hard endurance of the spirit, of the bravery and comedy and despair of the hospital world she tells about; her instinct for presenting it is in the unerring terms of imagination and suggestion." Having paid tribute to her Hungarian friend from the 1949 stay in Paris, Eudora then penned a review of E. M. Forster's new book *Marianne Thornton: A Domestic Biography.* Forster had shown Eudora portraits of Thornton and other family members when she visited his rooms at King's College, and now she was entranced with the book he had produced. Calling Forster "our foremost writer of fiction," as if in answer to Arthur Mizener's criticism of him at the 1954 Cambridge American Studies Conference, Eudora closed her review with lines that anticipated *The Optimist's Daughter,* a novel she would publish sixteen years later. "Mr. Forster has employed [imaginative] powers Marianne might not knowingly have countenanced, but she has not been hurt: she has been celebrated and loved. Continuity has been taken care of; and we are the gainers."[50]

The continuity of love in Eudora's own family was strong, and in April 1956 she was concerned about the health of her brother Walter, whose arthritis had restricted the hours he was able to work and who now was afflicted by shingles, and about her mother, whose eyes were still troubling her. Nevertheless, Chestina seemed well enough to travel, and Eudora planned to take her to New York and to see *The Ponder Heart.* First, however, she traveled alone to the University of Chicago, to read and to meet with classes, returning to collect Chestina. On April 29, mother and daughter left for New York, where both enjoyed the play and cast. They also saw *The King and I* with Zachary Scott. And Eudora was pleased to have her mother finally meet the Russells and the Maxwells. Chestina charmed both couples, enjoying the gardens they had at their homes outside the city and enjoying the gardening talk that ensued. Eudora later told Diarmuid that "I thought you and Mother hit it off specially well, and so did she and Rosie, and that made me beam, like something being proved to my satisfaction, and it was all so very satisfying and nice. She talks about her trip a good deal, and that's good, because life can become sort of dull to her with not too much she can do." And Bill Maxwell wrote to Eudora, "Your mother's dear letter made us both very happy. Now that she knows the way to our house, she must not wait too long before she comes again. Just long enough for the carpenters to pick up their clutter would be ideal."[51]

Chestina returned to Jackson after a two-week sojourn at the Algonquin Hotel; Jimmie Wooldridge, who had himself been on vacation in New York, was her escort home. Eudora stayed on. While in Manhattan, she met with Bill Archibald to discuss his *Robber* script and had the good fortune to see Eva Boros along with Mary Lou Aswell; the three women dined together at the Cosmopolitan Club and had a fine evening of conversation. At some point, Eudora also met S. J. Perelman. She had admired him from her college days and had written to him periodically over the years, sending clippings that had inspired his comic pieces "Sorry—No Phone or Mail Orders" and "Well, Roll Me in a Turkish Towel." Now the two chanced to see each other, and Perelman was somewhat in awe. He wrote to Eudora immediately: "It was indeed a privilege to meet you at last, and in my usual tongue-tied way, I didn't give you one single hint of my admiration for your work. Will you take it for granted even if I don't write a carefully manicured appreciation setting it forth in detail in three thousand words?" Shortly after running into Perelman, it seems likely that Eudora saw *The Littlest Review*, which opened on May 22 and included her skit "Bye-Bye Brevoort," written for the revue she and Hildy Dolson had planned years ago. A week later Eudora took in a matinee of *The Ponder Heart*, joining the cast for the play's third act and surprising David

Wayne. When a startled Wayne, playing Uncle Daniel Ponder, saw Eudora seated in the onstage courtroom, he inquired, "Can you see all right, Miss Welty?" Early in June, Eudora went to Northampton, Massachusetts, for the Smith College graduation; she and actress Julie Harris received honorary degrees, and Eudora saw "nice Newton Arvin [a Smith professor] again."[52] Then it was back to Manhattan and meetings with Eva, the Louis Kronenbergers (he was a noted editor and drama critic), and Jean Stafford. With poet and *New Yorker* editor Howard Moss, Eudora attended *The Ponder Heart* for the last time—it was due to close on June 27. The cast gave her a copy of the play with notes from each of them, and her first Broadway adventure came to a close.

Once home in Jackson, Eudora found a letter from Forster awaiting her. He wrote to express gratitude for her review, saying, "I sit thanking you at the Battersea Rise nursery table which you yourself once honored by sitting at." After basking momentarily in the glow of Forster's letter, Eudora labored at playwriting, but within a month she was back at work on the long story that was to become *Losing Battles.* She told Diarmuid, "I'm about to type up that story I had lying around that was too long, and let it be too long. I was driven to it, because working on a play has showed me how much more I know about the short story. (Only it's too long.) What you'll do with it I don't know."[53]

A New York theatrical triumph, the admiration of E. M. Forster, and work on a new story suggested that Eudora was successfully finding a way into a more fulfilling existence, one based in both New York and Jackson. Her correspondence with Reynolds Price was another key element in this new life, though Reynolds hoped that correspondence might soon be replaced by conversation. He wrote from England to suggest a trip for the following year. "This has been in my mind for a long time and now I'll ask you: would you like to come over here and go to Greece with me next Easter Vacation for a month? We could drive down through Yugoslavia, down the Dalmatian Coast—which is surely the grandest there is—and into Greece and then we could sail the car back to Brindisi and drive up through Italy. I ask you because I can't think of a greater place to go, or anyone else I'd rather go with than you. I mean that." However pleasant that prospect, Eudora had more immediate travel plans in view. She wanted to take her nieces, now ages eight and a half, and twelve, to New York. Though they would not be able to see *The Ponder Heart*, she wanted to give Elizabeth another taste of the city and to introduce Mary Alice to its diverse cultures and rich educational opportunities. For a week in early fall, she played tour guide, though her faulty sense of direction led the girls to call her "Wrong-way Dodo." Boat rides around the island, trips to the United Nations, the zoo, the Empire State Building, Chinatown, and the Museum of Natural History, tickets to the Broadway shows *Damn Yankees* and *No Time for Sergeants*, and a stay at the Algonquin Hotel all pleased the girls. So, too, did the attentions of their uncle Hubert Creekmore, meetings with Bill Maxwell, Diarmuid Russell, David Wayne, and Lehman Engel, and stops at a Japanese restaurant, Schrafft's, and the Russian Tea Room.[54] The trip was an unmitigated success, but it would be Eudora's last carefree journey for many years.

In September, health problems began more seriously to threaten those dearest to Eudora. The eye on which her mother had had cataract surgery provided little vision, and her other eye was failing as well. Then Diarmuid was stricken with a heart attack. Eudora wrote to Eileen McGrath, a doctor and friend, about both problems. Eileen replied in a dispassionate way, hoping to be reassuring.

> Glad to get your letter. Was thinking about you & knew you'd be very upset about Diarmuid. Apparently he'd had several minor attacks, in retrospect, which went unrecognized & I do think his doctor in Katonah was very sloppy & did everything wrong. Stopped him drinking, but let him

smoke, which is upside down of course. However he seems to be doing well & is planning to come home next week, three weeks after the attack & then spend 3 weeks resting at home. No one can say how things will go. He certainly will have to cut down his strenuous outdoor activity—but he may be perfectly well for years.

Sorry to hear about your mother's eye—I would be rather inclined to think there's little use in someone else seeing it. But I know how she must feel about having surgery on the other. The only way to look at it is that the lost eye was useless to her for many years & still is—It's really nothing new—even though a terrible disappointment.

Have just talked to Rose on the phone, who says Diarmuid is really looking & seeming fine & it sounds from what she says as though this had been a very mild attack.[55]

For a time, Eileen's heartening words seemed prophetic. Diarmuid steadily improved, and Chestina seemed no worse. Eudora took pleasure in seeing Charlotte Capers and other friends stage *The Ponder Heart* at Jackson's Little Theatre. And she turned her attention to the draft of a new story by Reynolds Price, which reached her in mid-November. By December, however, new worries had arisen: Mary Lou wrote that the Soviet invasion of Hungary had brought tragedy into Eva Boros's London home. Paul Ignotus, Eva's friend and fellow Hungarian, had "managed to escape with his wife (both of them released after 7 years imprisonment in the 'thaw' before the storm). The wife seven months pregnant, suffered so much during the escape, that her baby was born dead *in Eva's apartment*." The horror of an international situation had taken on a personal dimension, perhaps making the niceties of fiction writing seem less significant to Eudora. When she sent Reynolds her reactions to his story, her tone was uncharacteristically tart. She liked the story, she wrote Price, but had "a few reservations." "I think the focus needs to be sharper—*your* focus, if not Miss Lillian Belle's. It is proper for her to be wandering and vague, but the picture we get from the story must be absolutely clear . . ." Eudora then advised against employing the same stream of consciousness for Rosacoke and the old lady, suggested that he not make the "wrenching" comparison of Miss Lillian Belle with the mother dog, and noted that "the false teeth on page one make Miss Lillian Belle a figure of ridicule before you have time to show what she really is. If it were my story I'd take out those teeth."[56]

Her duty to Reynolds fulfilled, if somewhat impatiently, Eudora celebrated Christmas with her family. But beyond Christmas 1956 loomed a season of severe trials on the home front. During the fall, three members of the Welty family had been hospitalized; "nothing drastic," Eudora told Diarmuid, "but the able-bodied, that's me, needed to be here."[57] The drastic was soon to come: Walter's arthritis would disable him and cause heart problems; Chestina would begin to have a series of strokes and would be all but blind; Edward would again be plagued by depression and would be stricken with the same arthritis that afflicted his brother. Eudora and her sisters-in-law would be called upon to become primary caregivers as they watched their deeply loved family members decline and suffer. The resilience with which Eudora had met the end of her romance with John Robinson would have to be greater still during the trials that lay ahead.

SIX

Losing Battles
1957–1966

As 1957 began, Eudora had not yet completed a long, darkly comic story begun two years earlier. Nine years later this tale of a Depression-era family reunion was still unfinished, though it had grown into a novel. Eudora eventually considered three different titles, *Slack Times, Ring Around,* and *Ignorance,* but ultimately decided to call it *Losing Battles,* a title that might well have emerged from her experiences between 1957 and 1966. During these years, she fought losing battles on the political front, in her writing life, and in her personal life. There were victories, of course, principles proclaimed, two stories and a children's book published, relationships deepened, but there were also losses, many losses. During these years, Eudora supported two successful Democratic candidates for president but was devastated by the assassination of one and came to question the policies of the other. She acted in support of racial integration but felt powerless and horrified as her own state government became more and more repressive. She struggled to write, working on *Losing Battles* and on a long story, but completed neither. And she saw the lives of deeply loved family members diminished by illness and taken by death. In *Losing Battles* the character Beulah Renfro faces equally difficult trials. Though she joins in celebrating her grandmother's ninetieth birthday and the large family reunion it occasions, she knows that stoicism must replace jubilation. When the reunion is over, Beulah wearily but resolutely tells her husband, "I've got *it* to stand and I've got to stand *it*. And you've got to stand it . . . After they've all gone home, Ralph, and the children's in bed, that's what's left. Standing it."[1] Such was Eudora's plight between 1957 and 1966.

In January 1957 Eudora was worried about personal and public matters: Her mother's deteriorating health, the conservative policies of the Eisenhower administration, and the tragic plight of Hungarians whose hopes for independence from the USSR had been crushed. Eudora told Mary Lou Aswell that her mother now led a restricted life because of difficulties with her eyes. "The heat of the stove, the light of day, the brief and sparse attempts to read with her 'good' eye; the walk in the garden, the visit to a child or a friend and the change of temperature in the other house—all, all do harm to her eye. Besides the foods that seem to harm it by way of allergy. She is so patient and good, but I feel life is so dismal for her."[2] But these worries had not yet become all-consuming. The second defeat of Adlai Stevenson and continued Republican rule seemed a larger concern. Certainly, Eudora was distressed by the Eisenhower administration's unwillingness or inability to provide effective diplomatic support to the Hungarian rebels, and she and her mother sent money to the International Rescue Committee.

Eudora continued to write, though the demands of caring for her mother limited what she was able to accomplish. During the holiday season, she dashed off a short poem and sent it to Howard Moss as a Christmas card. The poem, "A Flock of Guinea Hens Seen from a Car," impressed Moss, who in his role as poetry editor of the *New Yorker* asked permission to print it. But her long story that would become *Losing Battles* and her attempt at a play were not progressing as she had hoped. She told Diarmuid Russell,

Some days it [my story] appears all ready to shoot in the typewriter, other days it looks like just "material." What I need of course is some *consecutive* time. This would be possible at night, only I'm not a night person. Anyway, what I feel tempted to do—when you've caught up with all that was waiting on you, and things aren't too demanding—is send up one of the fragments. An opening section of a story, and if I can bring myself to it, a scene from a play. I love the play more, but (partly because) the story is so much easier. It seems stupid not to get the story behind me, but I wake up with the other people in my head. The play is hard and is teaching me things, so I won't mind so extremely much if nothing should ever come of it. One thing I am curious to know is about publication of a play and when it would come. If produced, afterwards, I assume, but what if production is a big question mark.[3]

A lifelong fascination with the theater was taking center stage in her imagination just at the moment when she was least able to build upon it. Eudora's inability to find "consecutive time" for writing forced her to abandon this attempt at a play and would continue to torment her during the coming decade. Though her friends would consistently urge her to find help with her household and familial duties, she was reluctant to relinquish her role as primary caretaker.

Diarmuid was concerned with Eudora's economic situation now that she seemed unable to complete new work, and he continued his negotiations about a dramatization of *The Robber Bridegroom.* Zachary Scott was still interested in playing the lead, and Baldwin Bergersen and William Archibald had worked on a script and music. But February saw hopes for this production plummet. When Bergersen and Archibald's London opening of *The Crystal Heart* was an unqualified flop, investors seemed unlikely to back the duo's future productions.

Through February and March, Chestina's eye troubles and Eudora's attention to them persisted, but she did manage an occasional evening out. Especially compelling was an appearance in Jackson by piano virtuoso Eugene Istomin. To Frank Lyell she wrote, describing Istomin's performance. "He was easy to imagine *somehow* (hard to believe) as both Turkish & Spanish—& it seems he's closely identified with the Cassals [*sic*] festivals, & played as encore a piece by De Falla (I thought) very stylishly— Mostly he tended to Chopin, with some showy Liszt—a Haydn no.— I can't myself judge rightly, but I could feel the exposure to brilliance, fluidity, etc.—but he had something uncommunicative in his performance, however, perfect, to me."[4] The classical artist, who in the form of a guitarist had played an important role in Eudora's story "Music from Spain," continued to fascinate her, whatever the instrument, and having cultural events come to Jackson made her long absences from New York more bearable. So, too, did the prospect of April and May engagements in Manhattan and Washington. Though Eudora contemplated cancelling them because of her mother's health problems, Chestina insisted that her daughter go, and Eudora somewhat reluctantly complied. As she told Russell, "Mother's morale will sink if I don't go, and my conscience and mind will bother me if I do. I realise I need the trip in other ways."[5] She did need a break from being a solitary caregiver, and the break would prove reinvigorating. She journeyed to New York with "a big chunk" of her reunion story, as she then called *Losing Battles*, and was delighted when both Diarmuid and Bill Maxwell found it compelling. She read "Place in Fiction" at the Poetry Center and repeated that reading in Washington at the Corcoran Gallery. Then she returned to Manhattan and joined the Russells for a trip to Smith College, where Pam Russell was now studying. Finally, she came home by way of DC in order to appear on NBC television.

Back at home Eudora took her mother to an allergist, whose dietary recommendations provided Chestina with considerable relief, and Eudora found relief herself in the form of a woman hired to do cooking and cleaning. During the summer, freed from many household demands, Eudora worked on two stories; wrote "A Sweet Devouring," an essay about her childhood reading, for *Mademoiselle* magazine; and took her nieces to New Orleans, where she and they were impressed by the new film *Around the World in Eighty Days.* At summer's end, however, the stories were still incomplete, *Mademoiselle* was dissatisfied with the essay, and Walter Welty's health was precarious. Walter, who had been seriously troubled by arthritis for the past two years, now learned that his heart had been affected and that he "must take off from work and rest several months."[6]

If concern for her brother were not upsetting enough, Eudora was also appalled by Arkansas Governor Orval Faubus's attempt to prevent the court-ordered integration of Little Rock High School and by the need for armed federal troops to enforce the integration order. To Diarmuid she wrote, "Such awful things happening, I feel like emigrating from the whole country. Bayonets!" But Eudora did not move beyond such private expressions of horror into public political declarations. As she told Diarmuid, "Along with everybody else living here who ever got printed, I've been telephoned by syndicates and networks and asked what I had to say about it, and I said that all I ever had to say about anything was expressed only in fiction, which they regarded as the run-around all Southerners know how to give, but which is as you know just a fact."[7] For Eudora, fiction was political and the means of expression in which she felt most confident, but in the 1950s this perspective was shared by few. Though Eudora herself would seem to contradict this belief in her 1965 essay "Must the Novelist Crusade?" even there she would argue that great fiction engaged crucial political issues though it avoided editorializing.

The fall 1957 Little Rock debacle had made Eudora contemplate emigration, but she remained in Mississippi for the rest of the year. Driving car pool for her nieces in an effort to give her sister-in-law the time needed to care for Walter, spending pleasant evenings with the Basic Eight, hearing the Florence Symphony perform, reading Kenneth Tynan's theater reviews and regretting his departure from the London *Observer*, revising "A Sweet Devouring," writing a review of Isak Dinesen's *Out of Africa*, going to the movies, and entertaining visitors like author David Cohn and his wife—all these activities replaced her autumn trip to New York. And during this time of racial tension, her personal relationships with African Americans in Jackson testified to her belief in equality for all, a belief that won her the enduring affection of housekeeper Eddie Mae Polk. Eudora did venture out of town on one occasion, traveling with Charlotte Capers to the Mississippi State College for Women in Columbus. There she read to the assembled students and was feted at social gatherings. At MSCW Charlotte observed the kind of reverential treatment that Eudora would increasingly receive in her home state, and Charlotte ultimately lampooned this adulation in a brief essay called "Eudora Welty To Date." "When we got to the hotel in Columbus to register," Charlotte reported, "the desk clerk was very nice to Eudora. 'Miss Welty, we have our very best suite reserved for you.' I stepped forward. 'And we have a small room in the back for Your Friend.' I stepped back. Later, at the reading, I was joining the swarm of eager ladies about the Star when someone grasped my arm and said, 'You're with Miss Welty, aren't you?' I stepped forward, 'Well, here, hold her coat,' she said. I stepped back, coat in hand. During the reading two faculty members croaked at me in hoarse whispers, 'Do you think She is cold?' For a minute I was afraid I would be commanded to rush onstage and fling the coat around her."[8] Eudora, never prone to take herself too seriously, was encouraged in this restraint by her Mississippi friends. But Charlotte, now the director of the Mississippi Department of Archives and History, nevertheless took Eudora seriously indeed, asking that she donate her correspondence and manuscripts to the state of Mississippi. In doing so, Eudora established a collection that has become one of the nation's most complete and distinguished.

For Eudora and her family, 1958 began with renewed worries for Walter, who had been hospitalized for "a spooky business of fluid around the heart, caused by arthritis."[9] In March, Walter's health was still problematic, and his wife, Mittie, drove him to New Orleans to consult specialists. While her brother and sister-in-law were away, Eudora cared for her nieces, who came to stay in the Pinehurst Street house. Though Eudora had tried to work on her long reunion story, her concern for Walter and then her duties as a substitute parent kept her from accomplishing very much. "I'm still working a little," she told Diarmuid. "I hope to gird up in that respect too, for it's stupid not to get work done and freeze in your tracks when you are worried, which helps nobody."[10] But frozen in her tracks she was. Even when the New Orleans specialists reported that Walter's prospects for treatment were good, Eudora did not turn immediately to work. Walter's situation was still unresolved and troubling, and her story, even though it dealt with the absence of a beloved son, husband, and brother from his family, was comic and seemed far from the lifeline. It could neither command her concentration nor provide a catharsis.

Certainly, religion was not a sustaining source of consolation or comfort for Eudora, though she knew it was for Flannery O'Connor, whom she had yet to meet, and for the writer Brainard Cheney and his wife, Fannie. When Fannie Cheney came through Jackson at the end of March, she brought a new report of O'Connor's devout faith. "Flannery O'Connor is on her way to Lourdes this summer," Eudora subsequently wrote to Frank. "She is suffering from lupus, [Fannie] says—sounds dreadful, and I don't know whether she's taking any other, profane treatment or not." Eudora then added, "The Cheneys were fun 15 years ago when they were rather poor, brash, gay & full of beans— Now Fannie made me sad a little, giving out incense like that."[11]

For Eudora, the only real relief from anxiety came when she was able to leave home for a two-week span, to luxuriate in the cultural riches of New York City, and to enjoy the company of friends in the literary world. From the start, the trip seemed blessed. There were glorious evenings of theater and dance— British comedienne Joyce Grenfell doing *Monologues and Songs*, Martha Graham in *Clytemnestra*, a performance by Russian folk dancers, *Look Back in Anger*. There were parties—an after-the-performance celebration of Martha Graham's opening night, at the home of playwright Sidney Kingsley and his wife, the actress Madge Evans; a small closing-night party for the Martha Graham cast, at the home of Graham's patroness, the Baroness de Rothschild; weekends in the country with the Russells and the Maxwells. And there was the added delight of unexpectedly seeing Elizabeth Bowen, who had stopped in Manhattan between engagements elsewhere in the country.

In her new role as Honorary Consultant to the Library of Congress, Eudora came home by way of Washington, DC, where she was the houseguest of John and Catherine Prince. John, who had been a college professor, run a catering business, and was now involved in real estate, had in 1949 been introduced to Eudora by his distant cousin Caroline Gordon. He and his wife, Catherine, shared Eudora's literary, political, and social interests, and the three were boon companions. During her time in Washington, Eudora also saw Cleanth and Tinkum Brooks (friends from Cleanth's days as editor of the *Southern Review*), met the poet and essayist John Crowe Ransom, went to Randall Jarrell's house for lunch, and found the scholar and poet R. P. Blackmur disagreeable indeed. "The odd person at the Library meeting," Eudora wrote to Diarmuid, "was Mr. R. P. Blackmur. You know! He looks like a dandy of uncertain age. And of pure uncertainty, I guess. Has lots of withering remarks that he delivers as if they were blooms. Robert Frost was mentioned (secret) as next poetry consultant, no business of our group, whereupon Mr. Blackmur said 'I put it that you should declare the office of poetry consultant in hiatus for the next three years. Say you have a Person in Residence, but please! don't call him a poet. That I really can't allow.'"[12]

Eudora's late-April return to Jackson was a reentry into a world of caregiving. Mittie journeyed to New Orleans to bring Walter home, and the two daughters stayed with Eudora and Chestina in their mother's absence. Though the adults tried to shelter the girls, worry about Walter was now a constant. To Mary Lou, Eudora confided, "Walter is still not truly diagnosed. They think he has some rare fungus infection affecting his heart, but just exactly what is still not determined, so he is taking a quantity of pills and shots to take care of a range of things, as far as we understand it now." Troubling as this situation was, Eudora's concern for her mother's ability to cope had eased somewhat. "Mother is taking it all fairly well and would of course take it wonderfully if she could see well enough to do things and read. She can still play bridge & does sometimes—I urge her on." For her own part, Eudora felt some financial relief when she was awarded the fall 1958 Lucy Donnelly Fellowship at Bryn Mawr. Divining that Mary Lou had nominated her, she immediately thanked her old friend. The prospect of extra funds helped to convince Eudora that she could afford to send her nieces to summer camp, "where," she told Diarmuid, "they can let off their high spirits and not have to be quiet and all."[13]

During the summer months, Eudora managed to type 108 pages of her reunion story, by now a novella. She told Frank Lyell that she had another hundred pages still to write, but she penned nothing new about the family tentatively named Bunting, only putting previously revised work into a fair copy. Concern for Walter and his family precluded writing fiction. Reviews proved another matter. Perhaps, like Virginia Woolf, Eudora found a release in writing criticism. In any case, her reviews in fall issues of the *New York Times* lauded Woolf's posthumously published *Granite and Rainbow* and S. J. Perelman's *The Most of S. J. Perelman.*

In August, Eudora spoke at Tougaloo Southern Christian College, an African American institution located just north of Jackson. During the 1950s, typically in the company of Millsaps history professor Ross Moore and his wife, Eudora had frequently attended lectures and plays there. Now Tougaloo Professor Ernst Borinski invited her to address his Social Sciences Forum. According to Millsaps College political science professor John Quincy Adams, Borinski had designed the Forum as part of an effort to provide a "model of an integrated society," and Millsaps professors of history, sociology, and political science had been frequent speakers. The invitation for Eudora to speak about her work was a very unusual one for the Social Sciences Forum— her fiction and her creative process seemingly had little to do with the social sciences—but simply by addressing the group, Eudora was issuing a call for integration. In fact, this lecture came only five months after a 1958 furor about the Millsaps College Religious Forum that had dared to invite integrationists to speak, and her lecture seems almost to have been a response to the clamor raised by local newspapers, a clamor that had prompted Millsaps to close its public events to African Americans and to discourage its professors from teaching or speaking at Tougaloo. Eudora clearly regretted that Millsaps would no longer provide a "model of an integrated society," but she participated in such a model at Tougaloo, even though speaking at Tougaloo involved some personal danger. By 1958, white visitors to Tougaloo might have expected to have their visits monitored by the State Sovereignty Commission or its informers. Eudora's friend Jane Reid Petty recalled that she and others often carpooled when going to Tougaloo, varying the car they took as often as possible so that the sheriff, whom they suspected of recording the tag numbers of white visitors to Tougaloo, would not see a pattern in their visits. Though the possibility of harassment loomed in the offing, neither Eudora nor her friends were deterred from this activity.[14]

A September trip to Yaddo promised release from such public

tensions and from personal worries, but the trip never occurred. Her mother, after a lifetime of being self-sufficient, had grown dependent and agreed to Eudora's absence only at the last minute, too late to hire a caregiver. But Eudora succeeded in convincing Chestina how important a November trip to Washington, Bryn Mawr, and New York would be for her daughter's "peace of mind." Frank encouraged Eudora not to miss this opportunity and not to worry about trouble on the home front. "I hope you get off all right," he wrote. Then he admonished her, "Stop being 'petrified'! All will be well. Grand for you to have this trip."[15] Eudora took Frank's advice, hired a local college student to stay with her mother, and on November 3 was in Washington to deliver a reading at the Library of Congress. Then she settled into the "Deanery" at Bryn Mawr as the Lucy Donnelly Fellow. Eudora was greatly pleased by her accommodations and wrote to tell Bill and Emmy Maxwell about them. "I just walked in on this bed, of Constantinople origin, metal from apex to toe, filligree [sic] birds, passion flowers, lotuses, some panels burnished bright, some dark. When it lightnings at night, just think. There is a closet big enough for you to get out the *New Yorker* in, with 52 double-headed hooks screwed into the ceiling, like a flock of bats, and rows of additional hooks at 3 levels around the sides. Also built-in cupboards with sliding doors and drawers (bin like) in all 3 walls . . . I'm most comfortable, they are good to me, even break-fast in bed. I'm not asked to do anything but be available, and I'm being that right this minute. I like the girls very much, and the two faculty members who look after me [Laurence Stapleton and Bettina Linn] are kindness itself. So I seem to be blessed." These blessings were increased when Elizabeth Bowen, "in fine form & look[ing] ever so well, as she always is & does," arrived for a visit.[16] Then it was off to New York for a round of theater-going and for reunions with Mary Mian, Bill and Barbara Smith, Eileen McGrath, the Maxwells, and the Russells.

After Thanksgiving, Eudora came home to ill tidings. Walter was back in the hospital, suddenly in critical condition, and her mother's eye troubles had not only returned but intensified. In January 1959 Walter Welty, only forty-three years old, died. Eudora wrote to reassure Frank that her family was managing to cope with this devastating loss. "This is just a short note for now, but just wanted to let you know we're all all right & getting along pretty well—Mother is really being fine. Mittie is, as all the way through, calm & wonderful. The little girls, so shocked & crushed at first, have after that first day been little towers of strength themselves—Elizabeth by her nature holds all in—& comforts Mary Alice—who of course also has all that born ebullience and is apparently fine. They've helped Mittie a lot—by just being there of course, but also practically." Help of a sort also came from the memory of Walter's courage and his support of medical research. "As for Walter, & how well *he* did—it was plain heroic. Every day that goes by, with letters that come to Mittie & us, & what people say & do, I realize more what a well-loved boy he was. The doctors—everybody—wrote to say such things— It's still incredible, all of it, & incredible that a disease like arthritis, that you hear of everywhere, that goes clear back to the Greeks, that so many people put up with in mild forms, could reach such devastating proportions, & in a young, healthy man— & could remain so mysterious— One of the research doctors said he hoped they'd learned something about it from this— which I guess is something." But hope for future arthritis cures was merely "something" and could offer only slight mitigation for a powerful sense of loss. And even a visit from Elizabeth Bowen, Eudora told Frank, was unconsoling. "Heavens, Elizabeth Bowen passed through! Seemed so unreal I was about to forget to tell you. She stayed at a hotel (she planned it all over long distance from N.Y., didn't know till she called, about our trouble) & Charlotte fed us— She & a friend were on a trip, & E. is going to do a piece about Natchez & the river country for *Holiday*."[17] Grieving for her brother rendered "unreal" what would normally have been a joyful encounter.

In the face of Walter's death, Eudora for a time found herself unable to return to fiction. As she wrote to Mary Lou, "It's funny but *words* are temporarily the very thing I can't seem to deal with." Unable to produce fiction, she was nevertheless able to comment on the creative endeavors of others and to come to the aid of her friend Frank Hains. Hains, a columnist at the *Jackson Daily News*, was also directing a Jackson Little Theatre production of *Cat on a Hot Tin Roof*. In an effort to support Hains and to help local citizens to recognize the brilliance of the play, Eudora wrote program notes, which were then reprinted in the *Daily News*. She observed that "Mr William's [*sic*] plays burst in on us with such extraordinary voltage that—just as after a crisis in real life—we find it hard to describe afterwards what hit us." She then went on to ask, "Aren't we convinced by the time the curtain falls that an even greater power lies in something within, in his driving wish to show us something about ourselves? Behind every play he's written we seem to hear crying out a belief that as human beings we don't go so far—no matter how far we do go—as to tell each other the truth." Walter's death had hit all the surviving Weltys with "an extraordinary voltage," and perhaps in her own life, as in the plays by Williams, Eudora felt "a driving wish to show us something about ourselves."[18] At some point during February or March, Eudora acted upon that driving wish and once again worked on her reunion novella. She took it with her in April when she returned to Bryn Mawr as part of her Lucy Donnelly Fellowship. During her Bryn Mawr stint, Eudora managed to see Diarmuid in New York and to show him her 141-page saga, which he pronounced "marvelous," but she was unable to see Bill Maxwell. Maxwell was saddened not only by missing Eudora but also by not getting to see her novella. "Oh those Buntings!" he wrote. "I cannot wait to renew the acquaintance."[19]

This month away from home was spiced by an exciting evening in New York. There Eudora saw the Bolshoi Ballet. "What happened," Eudora told Frank Lyell, "was Sidney & Madge Evans Kingsley asked me (by phone to Jackson) to come sit in their box—with Martha Graham, LeRoy Leatherman, Lincoln Kirstein & others— It was of course gala—and *I* was the only one in the party who had a good time! Madge E. said 'a crashing bore!' Lincoln K. went home before waiting for the finale— Martha said Ulanova was 'a great, great artist' but the ballet was nothing." Unlike the other guests, Eudora was transported. "Ulanova was magical and quite apart from anything, either on stage or on earth." The group went to a party after the play, and there Eudora was introduced to Kenneth Tynan, the theater critic whose reviews she had admired in the *Observer* and who was now at the *New Yorker.* The two planned to meet again, but suddenly Eudora was summoned home. Her mother had suffered a small stroke, had fallen, cutting herself rather badly, and was in the hospital. Eudora was distraught that the fall had occurred during her absence. As she told Frank, "Of course I was desolated because it happened while I was gone, but Gayden Ward says I could not have prevented it coming out of the blue. The maid was right beside her & she fell too quick for her. Good quick help she got—well, I am hoping that she'll gain her strength back now & can go home." But whatever reassurance Dr. Ward offered, Eudora was left feeling that she could "never go off for suppose it happened again?"[20] She immediately cancelled speaking engagements in Denver and Texas and resolved to remain close to her mother; she would not leave Jackson for the next eighteen months.

By July, Mary Lou had become concerned that Eudora was losing touch with her friends and was working too hard as a caregiver. Eudora sought to reassure her, writing Mary Lou that she had hired "Emma—a colored 'settled' woman—school teacher— who is so *kind* & who wakes up at the slightest move or sound— she sleeps on the cot instead of me 5 nights a week—a great help." But even with Emma's help, Eudora reported that she was "tired at night & can hardly read at all, just for the present" and added that she hadn't "written either, letter or story lately."[21] Luckily Frank Lyell was home for an extended visit late in the summer, and Eudora had the opportunity for long conversations and evenings out with Frank, one of the handful of friends in whom she would confide. Members of the Basic Eight—Charlotte, Jimmie Wooldridge, Ann and Bill Morrison—she loved, but the relationships among this group of friends were not of the self-revelatory sort Eudora shared with Frank and Dolly, with the Russells, the Maxwells, and Mary Lou.

In September Chestina suffered another small stroke and again had to be hospitalized. This time there was no fall—the stroke had occurred as Eudora brought her mother breakfast in bed—and there seemed to be no lingering consequences. Nevertheless, Eudora found the episode "terrifying," and she cautioned Frank Lyell not to mention the word "stroke" to her mother. The word might cause Chestina too much concern. For Eudora there would be no autumn trip to New York; caring for Chestina was her number-one priority. This was not, however, the priority Diarmuid Russell wanted his favorite client to adopt. He worried about Eudora, and he arranged for her to apply for a Ford Foundation grant in playwriting, a grant he hoped would take her away from the rigors of caring for her mother and allow her time to write.

Chestina was now almost totally blind, was "depressed about Walter all the time, of course," and seemed a likely candidate for more small strokes. The dependable Emma would for an extended time be unavailable to help with Chestina's care, but Eudora, urged on by Diarmuid, Frank, Mary Lou, and other friends, tried to hire capable replacements. Carrie, she told Frank, was very helpful to her, but "I let her off whenever she's tired as she has a sick mother she also nurses." Another substitute was wholly unsatisfactory. Given the difficulty of finding nurses who were both able and available, Eudora did not feel she could leave home. On Halloween, when her old friend Eileen McGrath was married "in that beautiful little country church in Bedford," Eudora was not in attendance.[22] Nor did she attend *Take Me Along*, starring Una Merkel, with musical direction by Lehman Engel—neither the actress who had played Edna Earle in *The Ponder Heart* nor a Jackson compatriot could entice her to leave home for Broadway.

Eudora had not yet seriously contemplated placing her mother in a nursing home. Chestina loved her house and her garden; to move her away from Pinehurst Place would seem an act of betrayal. And the varieties of institutional care for the elderly and the standards of care were not good. During the 1950s, accounts of dangerously inadequate facilities and workers had frequently been reported by the national press, and in 1959 a special Senate Subcommittee on "Problems of the Aged and Aging" reported that "few nursing homes were of high quality, and that most facilities were substandard, had poorly trained or untrained staff, and provided few services."[23] Eudora's 1941 story "A Visit of Charity" had suggested how grim nursing homes could be for aged individuals unable to reside with family members. In subsequent decades, adult children continued, understandably, to be reluctant to entrust their parents to professional facilities. Charlotte Capers had been through this torment: Her father, who died in 1952, had spent one night in a nursing home before Charlotte returned to collect him, and in 1959 Charlotte's mother continued to live at home, though she suffered from dementia. Now Eudora must have felt that she, like Charlotte, would be unable to bear the idea of Chestina's move to "an old lady's home," even if it were a more hospitable institution than the one described in "A Visit of Charity." Even with good home care, however, aging involved battles that could not be won. When Mary Lou's father unexpectedly died at Christmastime, Eudora sent her condolences and added, "It *was* merciful, though, about the lightning-like way it happened, wasn't it, as you said. Oh lord, to have age come over

you that slow terrible way, until you look & don't know it's your
daughter standing there, or that it's Christmas, or that you've had
a thing to eat, or even want that—like Charlotte's mother."[24]

In January 1960 Chestina suffered another blackout or stroke,
but did not need to be hospitalized. With help from the re-
doubtable Carrie, Eudora nursed her mother through good days
and bad, though the resignation of a night nurse posed some difficulties. Then, in February, Eudora received a Ford Foundation
playwriting grant. Diarmuid expressed his hope that nothing
would stand in her way of accepting the award, but he also urged
her to complete her reunion novella before going on to her "new
life of the stage." Eudora herself felt that she must find a way to
accept the grant. She told Frank, "I feel it would be madness to
do anything but accept—and hope that by then Mother will be
well enough to either come with me, or be able to do without me
for periods of time."[25] Almost a year after her mother's first stroke,
Eudora at last saw the prospect of consecutive time for writing.

Diarmuid was heartened by Eudora's new plans, and he
worked diligently to provide his client with the financial where-
withal to hire caregivers for her mother and salvage time for herself. He first wrote to tell Eudora that he could obtain a good
advance for her long story if she would send him "a slab of the
ms," and a month later he told Eudora that Random House had
offered a substantial advance (twelve thousand dollars) if she
would agree to move from Harcourt. Eudora was interested, but
when late in April Chestina "had another spell," Eudora asked
Diarmuid to put negotiations with Random House on hold.[26]

The remainder of the spring and summer in 1960 were especially difficult for Eudora. Her mother was discontent and demanding. She minced no words complaining about Carrie or other
caregivers Eudora hired. If a nurse or sitter mispronounced a word
when reading to her, Chestina would summarily announce that the
individual was fired. Eudora's constant attendance was seventy-
six-year-old Chessie's desire. Eudora acquiesced, telling Diarmuid

that she could not attend his daughter's wedding and informing the Ford Foundation that she would not be able to accept their grant. Then, late in August, the situation became so desperate that doctors urged Eudora to consider nursing-home care for her mother. To Mary Lou Eudora confided her deep worry.

As you can gather things just grow worse with my poor mother and she no longer trusts me or believes me. This may pass, but the doctor says it is true to form in her illness, that she feels this way toward the closest one to her. I haven't even yet talked to my brother, who feels things even more sharply than I do, because he also feels for me and my efforts to nurse—which seem to have done no good. You can see that I don't even know yet what we are going to do. I could never have dreamed that I'd let her go into a nursing home, and I think if she realized it it would be the last straw. Yet for me, or for the nurses, the ones that come to the house, she will no longer try to get up, eat, or do anything— she has also in the last few days refused to take the therapy. The doctor says it's the very people with the greatest independence in their natures and lives who react this way when they get these little strokes or seizures due to arteriosclerosis, as I think you know about too. Well, I felt comforted by your letter—which was something I felt I needed as much as if my mother had just died or something . . . I'll write as soon as anything is settled about what we are going to do. Something must be done, for you are right, I was getting so tired that I felt I was no longer a decent nurse or person, much less writer. I think mostly to keep from succumbing to self-pity I'd started working on my long story at 5:30 AM till time to fix breakfast, which was peaceful and uninterrupted, and had really got a little way—so don't be worried about that, you are the one who knows writers well enough to know you just about can't kill it.[27]

Then suddenly worries eased. Doctors discovered that a sedative being given to Chestina was the source of her suspicions and delusions, and Eudora was delighted to be free from the prospect of sending her mother to a nursing home. Though Chessie continued to verbally harass her nurse Carrie, she and Eudora were once again living harmoniously.

The experience, however, left Eudora in dire need of a break from the routines of home. When Carrie felt driven to resign her job at the Welty house, Eudora managed to hire Virgie Renfro, whose name evoked *The Golden Apples* and anticipated *Losing Battles,* as a replacement and to plan a trip to New York. Early in November that trip materialized. Eudora told Frank that "everybody was wonderful to me and couldn't seem to do enough, it was such happiness to be back." She spent a weekend with Diarmuid and Rosie at Katonah, saw old Jackson friends Dolly, Hubert, Lehman, Nash and Marjorie Burger, and Ruth Forbes, went to the theater with Hildy, and visited with Eileen and her husband. She and Howard Moss spent a late evening with Jean Stafford and her new husband, A. J. Liebling, and made what Eudora called "a good foursome."[28] She also saw the Kahn sisters, mystery-fiction editor Joan and artist Olivia. And she loved spending time with the Maxwell daughters and going with their parents to an Indian film, Satyajit Ray's *The World of Apu.* No responsibilities, no conflicts, no worrying messages from Jackson marred the trip.

Back at home, Eudora found things on an even keel. To Frank she wrote, "All went fine while I was away, as far as I can tell, and Mother was glad to see me when I got back—some of her old humor even has come back—so, even if it's not to stay, it's making things easier now." Also making things easier for Eudora were her friends. Bill Maxwell phoned Diarmuid to volunteer free secretarial help for Eudora—whether or not Eudora's reunion novella came to the *New Yorker,* Maxwell wanted to help her bring it to conclusion. Mary Lou arranged for a different sort of help.

She recommended Eudora for the Ingram Merrill Foundation Award in Literature for 1960, and on November 21 the foundation informed Eudora that she had won the five-thousand-dollar award. Eudora immediately wired her thanks to Mary Lou and then wrote at greater length to her, saying, "I am grateful—and I only wish I knew a way to do something for you that would bring as much peace and whatever reassurance you would be happy to have too as this is to me."[29]

Peace and reassurance for Eudora were soon interrupted. Early in December Chestina was once again demanding her daughter's unqualified attention, but Eudora resisted, seeking to find some time for herself and some time to spend with friends. Hubert, Frank, Dolly, and John Robinson all planned Jackson visits during the month, and Eudora told Mary Lou that spending time with these friends "*can* be done if I just have the guts." Once, when Frank called upon Eudora, Chestina had predicted her own death should Eudora go out for the evening; a tearful daughter had remained at home. But this time, Eudora asserted her will in the face of her mother's irrational demands. She took particular comfort in the arrival of John Robinson, whom she had seen only twice since their parting in 1952. During John's three-week Jackson visit, she found him "seeming like his original old self again." Any resentment about the past was now gone, and the two of them went out to dinner with British writer and biographer Angus Wilson, who was traveling by car across the United States. Eudora told Frank that the evening was "a welcome relief from the house which has been strenuous lately but I hope relaxing now. Mother is gaining strength, just mad at me."[30]

During her fall 1960 trip to New York, Eudora had rented a typewriter and completed an essay about novelist Henry Green, who, she felt, had "the most interesting and vital imagination in English fiction in our time." Diarmuid had sought to no avail to place the essay with the *Atlantic*; then Frank indicated that the *Texas Quarterly* would like to publish it. As the new year began,

Eudora worried that the essay might not be worthy of its subject, and she asked Mary Lou to read it and provide a verdict. Mary Lou praised the piece, and Eudora then sent it to Green himself for approval. On February 1, Green wrote to thank Eudora for every word of the essay. He also offered a piece of personal advice: "Don't forget about aged parents—they are FIENDS."[31] Eudora certainly did not think her mother a fiend, but she did know that age and illness had transformed Chestina in sad ways. By the beginning of 1961, however, Eudora was far better able to cope with her demands.

No longer was Eudora content to forgo her extended visits to the East Coast. Bryn Mawr had invited her to join Elizabeth Bowen for four days in late February, Vassar wanted her a month later, and Eudora wanted to "gather those NY rosebuds while I may." Her mother posed an obstruction to these plans. As Eudora told Mary Lou, "We wear out nurses fairly fast, & Mother abominates the one we have now— (She's been getting stronger physically but is on the warpath a good deal so I have to find just the right person which is a tricky business & I've made several bad guesses before now.)"[32] But Eudora would not be deterred. A nurse was in place when Eudora arrived at Bryn Mawr on February 24.

Eudora's time at Bryn Mawr was pleasant, as always, but her subsequent days in New York seemed glorious to her. There she continued to see Elizabeth Bowen on a daily basis, "the longest & best visit we've had in years, & so refreshing to me." She and Bowen shared an evening with Howard Moss, and the three gleefully speculated "what would happen if Elizabeth could do something she said she'd like to do, take over a radio station."[33] Another evening, Lehman gave a small dinner party for Eudora, and on still another, Eudora attended a party given by agent David Clay for Elizabeth Spencer. At the party she chatted with Robert Penn and Eleanor Clark Warren—the next morning the Warrens met her at the Algonquin for coffee, conversation, and laughter. A particular pleasure was a reunion with Mary Lou and meeting with James Merrill, whose foundation had so recently honored her. But as usual, perhaps her greatest pleasure was spending a weekend at the Russell's Katonah house. Eudora and Diarmuid had long been soul mates, and the opportunity to talk, survey Diarmuid's garden, perhaps watch Diarmuid paint—this sort of domestic peace must have been especially healing to Eudora, whose own home offered no peace.

Eudora concluded her month-long trip with a five-day stint at Vassar. An international conference brought notable women from around the world to discuss "world problems and their implications for education." Eudora found this heady environment exhausting and told Bill and Barbara Smith that "we meet, international, from *breakfast on till midnight every single day.*" However exhausting the conference proved to be, Jackson promised to be more so. As Eudora reported to Bill and Barbara, "Life at home is very confining & dreary but am trying to organize things better to get away more in future." Yet when she reached home, discord still reigned. By the end of April, Virgie had quit her job as Chestina's nurse, but Eudora had persuaded Carrie to return. Three weeks later Carrie quit, then a few days later seemed willing to consider returning. Eudora told Frank, "I have no pride, and besides she is so good, and so essentially sweet, and it would be foolish of me not to beg her, I think." In the midst of the household confusion, an invitation to an "Evening with Robert Frost" sponsored by President John F. Kennedy's Cabinet "under the Chairmanship of Mrs. Kennedy" arrived. "Wish I could go," Eudora told Frank.[34] Long the ardent liberal Democrat and grateful for an administration that valued literature, well might she have longed to attend. But for a few months, at least, she would travel only to Birmingham Southern College—a trip that would add needed funds to her income.

The summer brought improvement. Chessie seemed more content, and Eudora settled down to work on her novella, thankful for the typing help provided by Bill Maxwell's secretary. Hot summer days had always proved good working days, and the Bunting reunion novella claimed those days in 1961, growing into a novel— *Losing Battles*-to-be. By fall, however, Eudora was ready for another trip east. Now on the Yaddo board of directors, she headed for Saratoga and a September meeting. She found the town far less beautiful than it had been in the forties. Yaddo itself she found far more casual than before, but, she told Frank, "There are still more little signs everywhere, Do Not Put Anything on this Fragile Cabinet. Please Direct your Morning Walk in Another Direction. Please Be Careful in this Bathroom, Yaddo's Plumbing System is Old." Despite the somewhat off-putting signage, there were old friends and new to see at the artist colony: Morton Zabel from the University of Chicago, the Robert Penn Warrens, the Louis Kronenbergers, Malcolm Cowley, Robert M. Coates, and John Cheever were all in attendance. Also present were Ulysses Kay, an African American composer and board member, and his wife, one of the Freedom Riders who, in the late spring and summer of 1961, had been arrested in Jackson and given six-month sentences for disturbing the peace. Like most of her compatriots, Barbara Kay had chosen to remain in jail for forty days, "the maximum amount of time one could remain in jail before losing the right of appeal." Though Yaddo had given Eudora a break from her filial duties in Mississippi, it could not shelter her from reports of injustice in her home state.[35]

With some relief, Eudora left Yaddo for New York. There she presented Diarmuid with parts 2 and 3 of the reunion novel, and she asked that he pass the typescript on to Bill Maxwell. Most of her time in the city Eudora devoted to Alun Jones, the young Welsh scholar she had met at Cambridge University in 1954 and who was now touring the United States. Together again, she and Jones had long conversations about the southern resistance to integration—Eudora branded Jackson "benighted"— but her time with Jones did not center on political issues. She was glad to see the young man and set about showing him New

York City as she had once showed it to her nieces—the Empire State Building and a "Chinese Treasures" exhibit were part of the itinerary. She introduced Jones to Bill and Emmy Maxwell, to Nash Burger, and to Nona Balakian. And one memorable day, she took him to lunch with Diarmuid, to drinks at Hubert's, to supper at Dolly's, and then to a "dreary tasteless Beat place, Phase Two."[36] Jones saw Eudora off on a train called the Southerner when she left New York. Eudora had played a sort of parental role with him as she had with Reynolds Price, but perhaps because she was not a parent, she did so without ever seeming parental, authoritative, directive. As a result, Eudora would always have close friendships that spanned generations.

Chestina had tolerated Eudora's absence from home so well that within a month Eudora felt free to travel again. And she would be able to travel without worrying about her novel: both Diarmuid and Bill Maxwell had sent words of praise for the first sections of it. Bill registered only one complaint—he wanted to read the installments yet to come.

Well I find it very hard not knowing how they got the car down in time for the funeral. Or what part Miss Footsie Kilgore played in the operation. Don't worry about the form. It has it. And don't whatever you do cut any of the physical descriptions of the place, the night, the moon, etc. The whole going to bed passage is so beautiful that it is like reading an opera. The mind supplies the music. Harold Brodkey has a theory that most novels run out of gas, that is to say the original inspiration, after the first seventy or a hundred pages. And then the novelist gets his second wind, with a different inspiration. This doesn't run out of gas, but it takes on a certain musical solidity when they are at the table and begin to talk about Miss Florence Hand. Partly from the fact that they talk so long about her, and up until that point have refused to stick to any one subject for longer than three sentences. Anyway, it builds, all the way to the end of Part III. There are a hundred remarks that delighted me they were so much like the people I remember. And made me laugh out loud. The only book I ever read that it reminds me of is *Delta Wedding*, it is so completely just like you and nobody else. It also has the richness of being the only thing you have been working on all these years. One feels that, more and more. Now what else can I tell you?[37]

Eudora found reassurance in the high regard of an individual she regarded highly; she now felt confident that the novel, which would become *Losing Battles*, had kept its vitality during her six years of labor on it.

In late October she left for Chicago; Morton Zabel had arranged an appearance for her at the University of Chicago. Then it was on to Washington for an overnight stop and participation in a seminar at the Institute for Contemporary Art. This engagement permitted Eudora to see John and Catherine Prince, with whom she spent the night, as had become and would remain her pattern. During her day in Washington, Eudora also managed to spend some time with Katherine Anne Porter. Eudora found that Porter was in fine "fettle about the silk worms & what the dear Lord only could make," and these hours for the long-time friends felt like "old times . . . but better."[38] Porter also had news about her long-delayed novel: *Ship of Fools* would be published in 1962.

Work commitments completed, Eudora journeyed on for a week in New York. There she saw Elizabeth Bowen again, meeting for dinner parties, drinks, conversation, and a Matisse show. She found Diarmuid thriving and loved seeing the Maxwells, parents and children. On Halloween she brought friends together, taking Elizabeth, Howard Moss, the Russells, and the Maxwells to dinner at a French restaurant. An unexpected pleasure was a chance encounter with Yves Montand, the performer she had so admired during her 1949 stay in Paris. Eudora told Mary Lou that Montand "was living at the Algonquin while I was there & one day came down in elevator when I did, along with another Frenchman. They talked in French (so you know how much I got) all the way down, when M. Montand said, '*You're telling me!*'"[39]

Eudora returned to Jackson to find that her mother's health and spirits had continued to improve. Chestina's new glasses greatly helped her vision, and her hostility toward Eudora was gone. "She is not against me any longer (that's for the nurses) and is often strongly *for* me," Eudora told Mary Lou. "She really has done a wonderful job of getting back to herself—takes no medication now, is clearly herself in the mind—We go riding in the car etc."[40] Buoyed by her mother's improved condition and thinking that she might be better able to write away from Jackson, Eudora accepted an invitation to spend the spring 1962 semester at Smith College. Chestina was reluctant to see her daughter leave home again, however, and began waging war against the idea. But by the end of January, Eudora had prevailed. As she told Frank, "For a while I felt I wouldn't make it because we couldn't or didn't keep a nurse at all, lost 4 since Christmas. But now we have at last one who's congenial to Mother, a retired practical nurse, ladylike, never says she has 'a gnawing and a craving for fresh meat' or that the Lord spoke to her last night in bed about missing church."[41]

Eudora was soon ensconced in a comfortable apartment at Smith. Her downstairs neighbor was Shakespearean scholar Al Fisher, a fine cook who invited her to dinner before each of her lectures, then presented her with a flower, and escorted her to the lecture hall. Other good faculty friends in the English Department were Kenneth Connelly, who at one point in the semester met Eudora in New York City for a Martha Graham performance, and Dan Aaron, who, Eudora reported, "is exceedingly nice, warm-hearted, attractive, likes Fats Waller, has a nice wife Janet."[42]

"Words into Fiction," the speech Eudora had written specifically for Smith, was a great success there. At a key moment in the lecture, Eudora described a childhood visit to Mammoth Cave in Kentucky, where she had waited in complete darkness, apprehensive about what was to come, when suddenly "a light was struck. And we stood in a prism. The chamber was bathed in color, and there was nothing else, we and our guide alike were blotted out by radiance." This experience, she told her audience, was a metaphor for the act of writing. "Without the act of human understanding—and it is a double act through which we make sense to each other—experience is the worst kind of emptiness; it is obliteration, black or prismatic, as meaningless as was indeed that loveless cave. Before there is meaning, there has to occur some personal act of vision. And it is this that is continuously projected as the novelist writes, and again as we, each to ourselves, read." She then went on to discuss the ways that novelists through style, narrative point of view, and structure impose a "personal act of vision" upon their materials. Immediately after hearing Eudora speak, President Thomas Mendenhall of Smith wrote to thank her for the "splendid lecture" and to suggest that Smith publish the series of speeches she was to deliver.[43] Diarmuid was quick to say that two of the Smith lectures, the ones that Eudora had previously given at Seattle and Cambridge, had already been published separately in magazines. He wanted the new lecture to have its separate publication as well. He suggested allowing Smith to publish a collection of the three after that had happened.

Eudora's time at Smith brought her in close proximity to Bill Smith and Barbara Howes, who were now living in Vermont, near Bill's Williams College teaching job. Eudora visited them there, lecturing at Williams during her stay. Then, during spring break, she went home to check on her mother. Chestina had done very well in Eudora's absence, writing "sweet, long, good letters, in her own restored handwriting" and accepting both the weekday "*nice* lady companion, & the one she never would tolerate, the weekend shift."[44] During Eudora's seven days at home, the Welty women enjoyed each other's company, taking long car rides in the beautiful weather. And this time Chestina raised no opposition to Eudora's departure.

Eudora's return to Smith was a circuitous one; she went first to Spartanburg, South Carolina, in order to attend the Southern Literary Festival. There she met Flannery O'Connor and found her a very engaging individual, "with a real sharp tongue, all rightie!" But the festival was in some ways distasteful to Eudora. She objected to the "self-laudatory, self-infatuated" tone taken by a number of southern writers and also objected to the conference's focus on religion in the region's literature. Ever the individualist, she was uncomfortable with efforts to delimit southernness. Old friend Cleanth Brooks suggested that "all the Agrarians if they had it to do over would 'fall back on' not the agrarian philosophy but religion." Eudora disagreed. As she later told Frank Lyell, "Meaning nothing against anybody's church, but can't we all just try to work out things (fiction & poetry) with what's in front of us, & so on. And not be in this or anything else a Southern *clique*." Only Flannery O'Connor's lecture transcended Eudora's rejection of religious writing. "Her lecture was funny besides holy. 'People ask me why it is that Southerners write about freaks. I tell them it's because we can still recognize one.' 'They call Southern novels "grotesque" except when they *are* grotesque & and then they call them "realistic." (She said it better than that.) 'Faulkner has conditioned all of us by his mere existence. Nobody wants his wagon standing on the track when the Dixie Limited is coming roaring down.'"[45]

Having heard O'Connor speak, Eudora headed back to Smith to finish the term. Then it was on to New York, where she presented William Faulkner, the Dixie Limited himself, with the

National Institute of Arts and Letters Gold Medal for Fiction. Eudora was a bit nervous about the ceremony, worrying that she might drop the rather heavy medal. She asked Faulkner if he would like to take it in advance of the podium presentation. He replied in a courtly fashion: "If you so prefer." And so prefer she did. Though the medal had already passed from her hand to Faulkner's pocket, Eudora gave Faulkner a more significant prize at the appropriate moment: Her presentation remarks were a well-wrought paean, expressing her great admiration for Faulkner in an elegantly succinct fashion. "The most evident thing in all our minds at this moment," Eudora told Faulkner and the audience, "must be that your fictional world, with its tragedy, its beauty, its hilarity, its long passion, its generations of feeling and knowing, the whole of your extraordinary world, is alive and in the room here and with us now. We inhabit it; and so will they, each one for himself, the readers in days to come."[46] After the ceremony, Eudora went to Katonah to spend the weekend with the Russells. On Sunday afternoon, Diarmuid drove her to the Mount Kisco home of composer Samuel Barber, where Reynolds was a guest. She had a fine time there, along with the William Styrons and John Hollanders, and Reynolds privately showed her two Rembrandt etchings he had just bought in London.

Eudora spent the summer of 1962 in Jackson, working on her novel while Diarmuid in New York worked out details for the book publication of three lectures. "Words into Fiction" had not been accepted at major magazines, so Russell granted Smith College the one-time right to print it along with "Place in Fiction" and "The Short Story" under the title *Three Papers on Fiction*. New installments of Eudora's novel, however, would not reach Russell's desk. Her progress with them abruptly stopped when in August her mother fell out of bed and broke a hip. After being hospitalized for a month, Chestina was able to come home, but she was very unhappy over her new immobility and dependence upon others. The interlude of smooth sailing had ended.

Smooth sailing had also ended at the University of Mississippi, 150 miles to the north of Jackson. The courts had ordered the University of Mississippi to accept the enrollment of James Meredith, an African American, but Governor Ross Barnett demanded that admission be denied. Attorney General Robert F. Kennedy then sent federal marshals to enforce the court order, and riots broke out at Ole Miss. On the thirtieth of September, students gathered to chant support for Barnett and opposition to Kennedy. As night approached, the students turned violent, throwing rocks, bottles, and metal pipes at the marshals. Marshals responded by firing tear gas into the crowd. By this time, armed segregationists from within and outside the state had joined the students and began firing rifles at the U.S. Marshals. The next morning found 2 men dead, 160 marshals hurt or wounded, buildings damaged, cars still burning on the campus. Eudora was horrified by the violence and by the segregationist stance that Barnett and the university had taken. She told Frank Lyell, "I can't even *start* to go into the Oxford mess— The really depressing thing is that Miss. thinks Barnett is a 100% glorious *hero.* Wish I was in Timbuctu [*sic*]—or Xanadu." Still she was not ready to speak out publicly. The *New Republic* had sent a telegram requesting her reactions to the "Mississippi crisis," but Eudora did not respond. As she confided to Frank, "They also phoned & said 'Speak for the unheard voices in Miss. I said no because (a) I'm a coward—look what they've done to R. McGill (b) it wouldn't help (c) I don't madly admire the *New Rep.* though haven't seen it lately." Speaking out was indeed dangerous. When Ralph McGill's editorials in the *Atlanta Constitution* denounced the Ku Klux Klan bombing of an Atlanta synagogue, "outraged racists responded with death threats, garbage piled on McGill's lawn and abusive telephone calls. Politicians stoked the fires by calling him 'Red Ralph' or nigger-lover Ralph McCoon."[47] Yet, although Eudora feared such attacks and called herself a coward, she was not. She did not embrace editorializing, her published letters attacking Gerald L. K. Smith and supporting Adlai Stevenson not withstanding; she needed to find another way to express her political views. Within a year she would discover that lecturing at integrated events and publishing timely short stories about racial atrocities were formats that suited her talent. Using those formats, she would prove her bravery.

In the face of personal stress and public violence, Eudora did not escape to Timbuktu or Xanadu as she had wished, but she did manage to keep a speaking engagement at LaSalle College in Philadelphia. The nurses she had hired for Chestina assured her that Mrs. Welty was more tractable when Eudora was "clear away,"[48] and clear away she went. Both Katherine Anne Porter and Kay Boyle were scheduled to join Eudora on the program at LaSalle, but when Porter was unable to attend, Boyle delivered an extra lecture—an account of her expatriate days—and Eudora must have recalled her own 1949 meeting with Boyle in Paris. The pleasure of reminiscing, however, was disrupted by a national crisis. Reports of Soviet missiles in Cuba led to an international confrontation between the United States and the Soviet Union. Eudora wrote to Frank, expressing deep concern. "Isn't the Cuba thing awful? So headlong & full of danger of God only knows what." Thankfully "God only knows what" did not happen, for on October 28 Soviet Premier Nikita Khrushchev agreed to withdraw missiles from the island. The moment of national danger past, Eudora left Philadelphia for a relatively carefree week's vacation in New York. The city, as usual, was a tonic to her spirits. Twice lunching with Diarmuid, seeing the madcap British farce *Beyond the Fringe* with Hildy, and dining with Hubert all pleased Eudora. For the space of a week, she did not have to cope with the public and private pressures of home. Hubert was luckier still. He told Eudora that he wouldn't be home for Christmas because he couldn't stand having family and friends chastize him "about being a brainwashed-intellectual who doesn't love Ross Barnett."[49]

Eudora returned to domestic chaos. Chestina was distressed by her slow recovery from the broken hip, by her inability to get herself out of bed or out of chairs, by her inability to walk. She had made progress and was now able to stand unsupported, but her impatience led nurse after nurse to resign or be fired, even "dear, patient, kind Emma," who had returned to the Welty employ. Eudora's brother was not able to help. His wife, seemingly jealous of Edward's home ties, was ill at ease with Eudora and Chestina, and Edward himself was in poor health and low spirits. Eudora resumed the role of head nurse, but was scarcely more satisfactory to her mother than the professional caregivers had been. Early in 1963 Eudora wrote Mary Lou about this taxing situation. "I'm tired in body of course but what is beginning to worry me is I'm tired in mind. But if the therapist keeps coming, & mother tries (she adores him, 'my only friend') so that she can get to feeling less dependent on us, which is naturally repugnant to her spirit, maybe the atmosphere will lighten."[50] Mary Lou, now living in Santa Fe, responded immediately, urging Eudora to recuperate there once sitters could be located. But a month later, the situation had not improved. To Mary Lou, Eudora finally replied, "As you may have guessed when I didn't write right back, things have not gone too well here—*no* nurse seems to last over a few days, & now Mother is very much against me, which I hope will let up. I've been doing all the nursing & some of the time don't know *what.* But as of this AM (This is early before bkfst) I'm trying a new arrangement—2 new alternating ladies. I *have* to keep my March 21 date, & also I filled up April more or less with 4 or 5 *separated* lecture dates (for the cash) and don't intend to let them down."[51]

Like Mary Lou, Diarmuid recognized that Eudora's own health would be ruined if she continued the current domestic arrangements. In February he criticized her indecisiveness in facing these difficulties: "I get more & more worried about your situation. You can't look after your mother by yourself—buying food, cooking, washing, making beds, looking after her, answering telephone & necessary letters—and all the rest of the business of a house, laundry, cleaning & God knows what. You've got to come to some conclusion as to what to do (Nothing is ever perfect)—but you are living & must do your work. You must also look after your mother as best you can—but *as best* does *not* mean you must be sacrificed and left without work or pleasure or society. This kind of solution is nonsense, from any point of view. And still love, even if I write harshly." In March he more gently recommended a solution that his client had long been reluctant to embrace, reporting on two elderly ladies who had found residence in a sanitarium preferable to continuing at home: "There was more life going on with nurses and doctors and other patients and . . . in the end when one went to see them they were quite wrapped up in the life around them, which had a good deal more liveliness than the life at home."[52]

Eudora, so clear-sighted in her fiction, had been slow to recognize the losing battles she fought as a caregiver. She was not able to cope with the transformations that age and illness had wrought upon her mother. Though there had at times in the past been tension in her relationship with Chestina, her mother's courage, intelligence, support, and love had been constants for Eudora. She in turn loved her mother and hated to see her now in such distress. And she hated further having to reverse the roles of parent and child, making decisions for Chestina. Eudora might have continued to resist doing so, but a trusted physical therapist told her "of a new facility run by a hospital, by hospital staff, in a nice new spacious building with patio, beauty parlor, bathtubs that the hydraulic lift will let you down into, real splashing baths—all kinds of special things." The timing of this announcement seemed propitious. And, as Eudora wrote to Mary Lou, there were other advantages to the Martha Coker Nursing Home in Yazoo City. "A nurse we used to have that Mother used to like has moved to that very town and can nurse her 8 hrs a day—and the therapist goes there 3 times a week, so Mother would get his treatments just the same, and see him. He is at present the fair-haired boy with her. So, although it costs a lot, I hope to try it for a month."[53]

Of course, the psychological costs of this attempt would also be high. To Mary Lou, Eudora noted,

It nearly kills me, too. I don't know how I can stand to leave Mother down there, no matter how nice—she will be (is now, about so much) bitter toward me. And when she takes a notion to show her independence, they may not have patience. It is a nightmare any way you try to solve things. But I must have a breathing spell and I must get back to work if I can as we are much in need of some cash coming in, of course. If only I didn't have to *work* (lecture) from March 21 through most of April. I am tired but it would rest me to write some. But you can see how I cannot now afford a side trip to Santa Fe—the money, or the time, or the being away from the scene, as my brother feels unable to go down there—it's 50 miles away—much or any, he is not in good health. This is all confused, but has been a time of confusion and trying to get something settled, all the time with little or no help here so that I have to think when tired which is often no good. I went down to see the place and interview the people there, and so on. I'll write a better letter when all this is settled. I dread it. It seems so wrong. I won't think of it except as temporary, to let me earn some money to keep us going some better way.[54]

Despite the difficulties at home and her inability to complete the long novel, Eudora had been able to work on a children's book, titled *Pepe*. She sent it to Diarmuid in March, and his reaction was enthusiastic. "Came this morning. I've read this afternoon and it is totally charming—something all ages can read." Having completed this story and settled her mother in the Yazoo

City nursing facility, Eudora traveled by bus to the University of Arkansas, where she read from her fiction and met with students. Then it was back to Mississippi, where she found her mother's situation heartening. To Frank she reported, "Mother is responding well, has taken 15 steps at a time in the walker (never went over 5 here, I think, at best), is gaining weight, has good color in her face, eats well, has been on the whole cooperative—they are really all such nice people there—and has been only glad to see me, not pleading with me to take her home—which I don't know whether I could have stood."[55] Reassured and in need of funds, Eudora left again, this time speaking at Davidson and at Duke, where Reynolds Price was on the faculty. According to Reynolds, Eudora's anxiety about her mother cast a pall over the trip. Eudora wrote to Chestina each day, using a brush, India ink, and butcher paper to create letters large enough for her mother to read. Reynolds found Eudora's efforts disturbing, almost obsessive, and felt she was wholly unable to deal rationally with the situation.

When Eudora saw Chestina next, Reynolds's fears seemed justified. The devoted daughter learned that efforts at communication from afar had not improved her mother's spirts. With lectures at Yale, Vanderbilt, and the University of Texas in the offing, Eudora was distraught, overwhelmed with guilt. To Frank she wrote, "Mother is so depressed I can hardly bear it. It kills me to start off again. I don't know what to do. But I do have to do these lectures, for every reason—financial, and obligation to the schools, all. She is well looked after, but feels abandoned. All so terrible to me."[56]

Before leaving on her 1963 lecture tour, Eudora spoke at Millsaps College in Jackson. Despite her preoccupation with Chestina's situation, Eudora must have been keenly aware that her April 18, 1963, appearance at Millsaps occurred at a particularly tense moment in the history of both the state and the college.

The riot and deaths at the University of Mississippi when James Meredith had arrived in the fall of 1962 were followed in December by a black boycott of downtown Jackson stores, a boycott that would be the source of racial hostility for more than six months. Then in January 1963, twenty-eight young white Methodist ministers caused outrage in the white community when they published a *"Born of Conviction* statement . . . in which they asked for a free and open pulpit in the racial crisis and full support of the public schools instead of the private schools that were being established to maintain segregation."[57]

At Millsaps there was tension as well. Both faculty and administration overwhelmingly supported efforts for integration, but the administration, in particular, feared both violence and the loss of its financial base if the school were integrated. Nevertheless, on January 24, 1963, the Millsaps faculty voted 36-22-1 to support the twenty-eight Methodist ministers who had signed the *Born of Conviction* statement. The Millsaps resolution read, in part: "We are concerned . . . that encroachments upon the liberties of ministers to speak freely their sincere interpretations of the Christian gospel constitute but one manifestation of those evil tendencies which would deny men freedom in every sphere. Such tendencies are a constant threat, not only to a free and valid church, but also to a democratic society." Nor was this the end of consternation felt by Millsaps faculty over the racial situation in Mississippi. On April 2, 1963, a professor and several African American students from Tougaloo College were turned away from a play at Millsaps, and on April 11, the Millsaps American Association of University Professors (AAUP) chapter passed another controversial resolution, this time asking the college president to appoint a committee to study the possibility of integrating the Millsaps student body.[58] A week later it was time for the college to host the Southern Literary Festival, which was directed by Eudora's friend, Millsaps English professor George Boyd, one of the signers of the AAUP resolution. The college thus faced a dilemma—whether to abide by its policy of segregation, so recently enforced, or to allow open admission to Eudora Welty's April 18 address because it was sponsored by the Southern Literary Festival rather than Millsaps.

Early on that day, officials from Millsaps called upon Eudora to discuss the prospect of an integrated audience—they feared conflict. Eudora, nevertheless, asked that her lecture be open to all, and it was. That lecture, previously published by Smith College under the title "Words into Fiction," seems detached from any sort of political situation. In it, Eudora acknowledged that a reader may have a conception of a novel that differs from that of the writer, but she contended that this difference "is neither so strange nor so important as the vital fact that a connection has been made between them." The novel, she argued, is "made by the imagination for the imagination." After delivering this address, however, Eudora went on to show her audience the political import a work made by the imagination for the imagination could have—she read the story "Powerhouse" to the interracial audience, which included a contingent from Tougaloo Southern Christian College.[59]

Written in 1940 and inspired by a Fats Waller concert Eudora had attended, "Powerhouse" is the story of an African American pianist and his band playing at a segregated dance; it focuses on the white audience's simultaneous fascination with and repulsion by the band leader, Powerhouse, and on the band's ability to find intermission conviviality and refreshments only at a black café. In reading this story at the festival, Eudora took a considerable risk. The narrative voice located in the story's white racist audience might have offended black listeners at Millsaps even as the author's clear identification of Powerhouse as representative of artists like herself might have offended whites. But Eudora trusted in the ability of her listeners, and she might well have expected the story to bring together the two factions attending the lecture and reading.

Eudora, Edward, Chestina, and Walter Welty, circa 1917.
Courtesy Eudora Welty LLC and Mississippi Department of Archives and History

Eudora, circa 1919.
*Courtesy Eudora Welty LLC
and Mississippi Department
of Archives and History*

Eudora, late 1920s.
Courtesy Eudora Welty LLC

Christian and Chestina
Welty, 1925.
*Courtesy Eudora Welty LLC
and Mississippi Department
of Archives and History*

Hubert Creekmore in front; Eudora, Margaret Harmon, and
Nash Burger in back, Brown's Wells, mid-1930s.
Courtesy Eudora Welty LLC

"Tall Story." Photograph taken by Eudora Welty, mid-1930s.
Courtesy Eudora Welty LLC and Mississippi Department of Archives and History

"Ida M'Toy, retired midwife." Photograph taken by Eudora Welty, circa 1941. *Courtesy Eudora Welty LLC and Mississippi Department of Archives and History*

"The Rides, State Fair." Photograph taken by Eudora Welty, circa 1935.
Courtesy Eudora Welty LLC and Mississippi Department of Archives and History

John Robinson and
an unidentified friend,
Lexington, Mississippi,
late 1930s.
Courtesy Eudora Welty LLC

Frank Lyell, Katherine Anne Porter,
and John Woodburn, Yaddo, 1941.
Courtesy Eudora Welty LLC

Karnig Nalbandian and Eudora, Yaddo, 1941.
Courtesy Eudora Welty LLC

Publication party for *A Curtain of Green*, Murray Hill Hotel, New York, 1941:
John Woodburn, Eudora, Eugene Armfield of *Publishers Weekly*,
Robert Simon, president of Carnegie Hall, and Henry Volkening, seated;
Ken McCormick of Doubleday and Diarmuid Russell, standing.
Photograph first published in Publishers Weekly

Eudora, comic relief, 1942.
Courtesy Eudora Welty LLC

Eudora, perhaps at work on "The Delta Cousins," circa 1943.
Courtesy Eudora Welty LLC

Rosie, Pam, Diarmuid, and Will Russell, circa 1947.
Courtesy Eudora Welty LLC

William Jay Smith and Eudora,
in front; Dolly Wells, John
Robinson in back, Florence 1950.
*Photograph by Barbara Howes, courtesy
Gregory Smith and Eudora Welty LLC*

Ella Somerville and
Elizabeth Bowen,
Oxford, Mississippi, 1954.
Courtesy Eudora Welty LLC

Mary Lou Aswell and Frank Lyell,
wishing Eudora bon voyage as she leaves
for England in the summer of 1954.
Photograph by Louis J. Lyell

Mittie, Mary Alice, Chestina, Eudora, and Elinor Welty, in front;
Walter, Edward, and Elizabeth Welty in back, 1956.
Courtesy Eudora Welty LLC

Bill and Emmy Maxwell
with daughter Kate, 1956.
Courtesy Eudora Welty LLC

Kenneth Millar
in Hollywood, 1970s.
Courtesy Eudora Welty LLC

Diarmuid Russell and
Eudora Welty, circa 1972.
*Courtesy Timothy Seldes and
Eudora Welty LLC*

Eudora and Kenneth Millar,
mid-1970s.
Photograph by Virginia Kidd

"We Will Curl Up and
Dye for You," Oxford,
Mississippi, 1977:
Karen Gilfoy, Jane Reid Petty,
Eudora, Reynolds Price.
Photograph by Patti Carr Black

Mississippi Governor William Winter, Eudora, Leontyne Price,
Elise Winter, 1980 Governor's Inauguration.
Courtesy Eudora Welty LLC

Eudora receiving an honorary degree from Columbia University, 1982.
Courtesy Eudora Welty LLC

Jane Reid Petty, Eudora, and Patti Carr Black, boarding the *Queen Elizabeth 2*, 1984.
Courtesy Eudora Welty LLC

Eudora visiting Dorothy and Victor Pritchett, London, 1984.
Photograph by Patti Carr Black

Eudora and Jim Lehrer,
Jackson's New Stage Theatre, 1988.
Photograph by Chuck Allen, courtesy New Stage Theatre

Eudora and Reynolds Price,
Durham, North Carolina, 1988.
Photograph by Daniel Voll

Eudora and Suzanne Marrs, Mississippi University for Women,
Columbus, Mississippi, 1989.
Photograph by Nancy Ellis

Elizabeth Thompson, Eudora, Donny White, and Mary Alice White, 1992.
Gil Ford Photography

Ann Morrison and Suzanne Marrs, in front;
Patti Carr Black, Eudora, Charlotte Morrison, and Charlotte Capers, in back, 1992.
Courtesy Eudora Welty LLC

Eudora Welty, 1980.
Photograph by Robert Williams, courtesy Mississippi Department of Archives and History

In "Powerhouse," Eudora suggests that a shared act of imagination can bridge, if only momentarily, the separateness between individuals. Though both Powerhouse's white audience at the dance and his black admirers at the World Café at first feel separated from him, either by race or by fame, his performances involve them fully and variously bring them "the only time for hallucination," leave them in a "breathless ring," send them "into oblivion," and cause them to moan "with pleasure." The song that closes the story seems particularly relevant to this issue of communication and imagination. "Somebody loves me," Powerhouse sings and then concludes, "Maybe it's you!"[60] Despite the odds, maybe Powerhouse will have a deep and lasting effect on a member of his audience; the probability seems slight. Still, the story's very existence suggests that imagination can transcend the boundaries of race. The Fats Waller concert in Jackson brought forth at least one powerfully imaginative response in the form of a story from Eudora Welty.

More than twenty years after writing this story based on the Waller concert, Welty read it to proclaim the destructiveness of segregation and the emancipating effect of imagining oneself into other and different lives. Combining her story with a lecture about the power of the imagination to unite reader and writer was a political act for Eudora, an act of courage and vision, an act that built upon the integrated readings she had earlier given at Tougaloo College. And Eudora's presentation at Millsaps did unite, however briefly, black and white Mississippians. John Salter, the professor who led the Tougaloo contingent on April 18, reported that "Eudora Welty gave an excellent lecture, including a reading of one of her short stories—which we could follow as she read since we had brought along several copies of her work. When the evening was over we walked slowly outside. A group of Millsaps students came up and indicated that they were quite glad that we had attended. Other than that, no one appeared to notice us, and that, in its own small way, marked a significant breakthrough in Mississippi." Eudora's part in this breakthrough won her the enduring respect of Tougaloo Chaplain Edwin King, who attended the event along with Salter and black students from Tougaloo, and of Anne Moody, one of those black students, who in a February 1985 appearance at Millsaps recalled how important it was for her to hear Welty read.[61] In her lecture/reading Eudora proved she was far from the "coward" she had earlier labeled herself, and in performance she found her own way of taking a stance and perhaps making a difference, a difference she had previously thought it impossible to make.

Shortly after her Millsaps appearance, Eudora learned that her children's book *Pepe* was in difficulty. Diarmuid had sent the manuscript to Harcourt, Brace, Jovanovich, but its reception there was lukewarm. Editor Margaret McElderry found the book long on dialogue and short on action and thought the Dodo and the Phoenix characters would mystify children, but McElderry was hesitant to reject the book, knowing that doing so would release Eudora from any obligation to Harcourt. McElderry told Diarmuid that she'd have to speak to William Jovanovich before making any decision—a decision to publish and an advance would not come until July. Eudora was briefly annoyed and self-questioning about this reaction, but she was soon occupied with a month of travel. Leaving both the tense racial situation in Mississippi and demands from her mother temporarily behind, she read at Vanderbilt, Yale, and Vassar, saw friends and shows in New York, and took a train to Austin, Texas, where she was scheduled to speak at the University of Texas under the sponsorship of Frank Lyell. The train ride itself provided Eudora, from childhood a lover of the railroad, with "utter peace." A description she sent to Bill and Emmy Maxwell was expansive.

> When you leave the city goes away immediately and it's mountains, or valleys with beautifully ploughed fields and yellow barns till dark. There was the biggest thunderstorm I

ever rode a train through, you could even *hear* the thunder through the roof and windows, but we were all enclosed and it was quite like added scenery, the wild heavens. After you leave St. Louis, you ride another good train, following the Mississippi from 4:30 till dark, as close to the water as the train used to go along the Riviera (it may still!). There's no very frequent sign of human habitation at all, and it's the way the river must've looked in the days of the Indians, or of Audubon anyway, so you imagine. Then that night, the whole *world* was lit up with fireflies. The train must have been going through wild country, hardly any *electric* lights, all darkness, and flashing, flashing from the ground to way up in dark trees, mile after mile. Then of course wake up eventually to oil wells—but not too many, because it's fairly green and full of trees, hilly, in East Texas. Austin is green, with huge live oaks, and oleanders, magnolias, gardenias, etc. in bloom. The wildflowers along the tracks were so thick—gaillardias, cosmos, phlox, thistle, calliopsis, & of course bluebonnets. There is a wild clematis called the leather flower—dark ruby red.[62]

The peace and beauty of this train journey soon faded from Eudora's consciousness, for her late May return to Mississippi marked a return to public and personal conflict. On May 28, a faculty member and some students from Tougaloo College were beaten and one student arrested when they attempted to integrate the lunch counter at Woolworth's variety store. On June 12, Medgar Evers, field secretary of the Mississippi NAACP, was assassinated. And on June 18, John Salter and Edwin King, leaders of the Tougaloo contingent that sought to integrate Millsaps and Jackson's commercial establishments, were injured, King very seriously, in a suspicious car accident. In the wake of these events, Eudora quickly wrote "Where Is the Voice Coming From?" a devastating portrait of the racist mind-set. At the *New Yorker*, Bill

Maxwell was filled with admiration for the story, and so was his boss, William Shawn. Bill and Eudora edited the story over the phone, removing names of actual people or places that the legal department believed might cause difficulties. Then Bill returned the original manuscript to Eudora with this comment: "I thought you might want a copy of the story the way you wrote it, so here it is. Nothing but praise. Emmy shook her head in wonder at it, and Mr. Shawn stopped me in the hall to ask if I had talked to you and I said, 'Yes, four times,' and he said, 'Does she know how good it is?' I expect you do, somewhere, if not exactly on top of your mind. Being brought up the way we were, it has to be that way."[63]

All involved with the story knew that it was not only good, it was also courageous. Even before Eudora's story was in print, Diarmuid Russell expressed concern about violence in Jackson and about Eudora's safety. Eudora, on the other hand, was afraid not for herself, but for her mother. For months now she had been consumed with anxiety about her mother's health and spirits, and in late July 1963 that anxiety coupled with alarm for her mother in the local climate of hatred prevented Eudora from undertaking what would have inherently been a symbolic act in support of integration: She decided at the last minute, after much agonizing and with deep regret, to decline to be interviewed by Ralph Ellison on television. She worried that a nationally televised appearance with this friend and fellow writer would create a good deal of white hostility in Mississippi, hostility that she feared would be deflected from daughter to mother. She worried that such hostility would affect her ability to hire desperately needed caregivers for her mother, who in August would be coming home from her five-month stint in the convalescent facility, and that it might also affect the quality of care her mother received in the future. A desire to shelter her ailing mother from a volatile environment of racial tension and especially from white recrimination governed her decision, as she confided to Reynolds Price, not to be interviewed by Ellison. Instead, old friend and dramatic collaborator Hildegard Dolson conducted the interview for the CBS program *Camera Three*. Ellison for a brief time was understandably mystified by Eudora's decision. Shortly after the cancellation, Ellison told Price how open and outgoing Eudora had always been with him, and he worried that he might have in some way unwittingly offended her. Price explained Eudora's situation to him and also told Eudora of Ellison's worries. According to Price, Eudora then wrote to Ellison to explain her deep-seated apprehensions for her mother, and the Welty/Ellison friendship endured.[64]

The *Paris Review*, which had planned to publish the televised interview, was less understanding, and the incident threatened to become a cause célébrè. Hildy Dolson was offended by the *Paris Review*'s posturing and wrote to Eudora to express her support. "Diarmuid wasn't supposed to tell you that the *Paris Review* people had backed out. But he knew that was the reason I got involved, and as long as he mentioned it, I'll add now that they behaved very badly. Unlike Ralph Ellison, who understood and felt you were right, the *Paris Review* crowd were as snide as a Pink Citizens Avant-Garde Council. For them to take that attitude, on top of your powerful story in the *New Yorker*, was all the more idiotic and infuriating. When Clare Roscom [of *Camera Three*] phoned me, he said it threatened to blow up into a distorted, unpleasant news story, and for that reason he refused to try any of the writers I suggested as being more suitable [as interviewers]. He wanted a friend of yours. And that's what he got—and now enough of that."[65]

Eudora's resentment was directed not so much at the *Paris Review* as at the state of affairs in Mississippi, a state of affairs that she felt had compelled her decision. Worry about her mother compounded by worry about Mississippi politics left Eudora mentally and physically exhausted, and her doctors urged her to find a place where she could rest and be free of stress. Eudora, however, felt she could only find peace of mind when her mother was at home and she herself was writing. In mid-August, again in Mississippi after her New York television interview and a summer school stint at Columbia University, she brought her mother back to Jackson, a decision she felt would be beneficial for them both. As she explained to Mary Lou,

> When Mother went to take her therapy at the convalescent home in March, and the pressure was off, it was then, not before, that I felt as if I'd fly to pieces. And the worry I had seemed really worse, and guilt or whatever it is (though nothing wrong was happening to her, just a temporary course of treatment) drove me down there every other day anyway. But now she's coming back (tomorrow) and I've got things set up that I'm hoping will work better. I told the doctor that work (the novel) was the best way I could relax, so he said I could try doing it this way, otherwise must get away. But really I do feel it will turn out better this time, for a while at least. But you can imagine how sometimes I wish I could leave Jackson—Mississippi—the South. If Paul Johnson is elected Governor in a few weeks time I think I'll pack up mother and nursie and go to—yes, where. Coleman is having to wage a hot, awful campaign, but is really a sane man, good, and can at least sit around a table and reason with other people, whereas Johnson is a fanatic and probably crooked, and at any rate has a little tiny button size brain. I dread the outcome. Charlotte and a few others are the only people who feel as I do, that I know of.[66]

Two weeks after sending this letter, Eudora knew that Paul B. Johnson Jr. had won the Democratic primary and thus would certainly be elected; she also knew that coming home had not ended her mother's unhappiness. Once again Eudora confided her deepest worries to Frank. "Mother is very well, though not as happy about things as I'd hoped—I'm always hoping for what would mean a *difference*, and there won't be much difference. She *is* glad to be home, but the nurse problem is as much with me as ever, 3 in 9 days. But she was so homesick, and I was so homesick to have her here." Then, after reporting on Johnson's election, Eudora added, "if I had a way at all I'd pick up Mother and move away from this place for good. No hopes for us I can see with somebody even worse (because without even the cunning he's got) than Barnett. Ugh!"[67]

Though Eudora felt free to damn Mississippi in letters to Frank and Mary Lou, she was unwilling to do so publicly. Only her close friends would hear words like these; at a very profound level, Eudora loved her home state, its natural beauty, cultural riches, and eccentricities. There lived her family and friends with whom she shared her earliest memories. "The home tie is the blood tie," she had earlier written.[68] And Eudora would never break this tie, though the public events of 1963 prompted her to consider doing so.

Instead of packing up her household and taking her mother away from Mississippi, Eudora contented herself with two weeks at Yaddo. Elizabeth Ames, Yaddo's director, wrote to tell Eudora that "she had had my experience & this rest should not be put off till too late." Eudora agreed. She found new nurses for her mother and took herself to upstate New York. There she spent a productive two weeks, typing seventy pages of her novel and readying forty more for typing. Then she stopped in New York for a week, having a "splendid reunion" with Elizabeth Bowen, seeing Diarmuid, the Maxwells, Hubert, Dolly, and Mary Lou, and accidentally running into Bill Smith at the Algonquin. Then "things fell to pieces" at home, and she was summoned back.[69] During her time away, however, Eudora had gained considerable perspective upon the home situation. She did not believe that her mother intentionally caused crises, but she knew that such crises meant that professional care for Chestina would be essential.

Home troubles were soon compounded by national ones. The

assassination of President Kennedy horrified Eudora as did the callous reaction of some Mississippians. To Frank she wrote: "I can't even start on the assassination— Like you I was glued to the TV—the whole weekend. Thought of you of course, in Austin where they were due just 3 hours from the time—Sickened and really awe-struck at what is now possible to happen."[70]

In December Eudora once again took her mother to the Martha Coker Convalescent Home in Yazoo City. Chestina, who had ardently protected and cared for her young daughter, who had become the close friend of her adult daughter despite the inevitable tensions that arose from their living together, who had in the past few years become dependent, now required institutional care and would remain at the convalescent home until her death in 1966. Eudora, ever dutiful, settled into a routine of regular visits to see her mother, several times a week driving the two-lane hilly road fifty miles to Yazoo City and fifty miles back. As she drove, she jotted down notes for her novel in a stenographer's tablet—friends feared that this habit might lead to an accident, but Eudora persisted.

In February 1964 Robert Penn Warren paid a welcome visit. He was in Mississippi doing research for his book *Who Speaks for the Negro?*, and one evening Eudora invited him to join her and Charlotte Capers for dinner. The three had a wonderful time; Warren reported that he "woke up the next morning with my stomach muscles sore from laughing." Much of the laughter had been directed at former governor Ross Barnett. When not entertaining friends like Warren or on the road to Yazoo City, Eudora readied for publication her children's book, which after some delay had finally been accepted by Harcourt. *Pepe* was now entitled *The Shoe Bird*, and Eudora asked Bill and Emmy Maxwell if she might dedicate it to their daughters. Emmy replied for the family, writing, "I was—am—so happy that you wanted to dedicate the children's book to Kate and Brookie, but I didn't tell them, wanting to keep it a surprise."[71]

During the spring, Eudora finally ventured away from home. Working the college lecture circuit helped her to set aside money that might eventually be required for her mother's long-term care. And work the circuit she did. Wellesley, Elmira, Denison, Purdue, were stops on her schedule as was a writers' conference in Gatlinburg, Tennessee. Talking with students and with old friends like Robert Daniel and Caroline Gordon in the course of the tour was pleasant, but the travels proved exhausting. And wherever she went, Chestina remained Eudora's primary concern. In particular, Eudora feared that racial conflict in Mississippi might separate her from her mother, and she again briefly contemplated leaving the state and finding a convalescent home in Gatlinburg or Santa Fe. In a low moment Eudora wrote to Mary Lou about these worries. "Mother is in Yazoo City, which is a little, rich Delta town with many more blacks than whites, and is reputed to be now the headquarters of the Ku Klux Klan. Our state is now authorized to get 200 more patrol cars on the roads and arm the highway patrol—just *one* thing. I hear that this summer all hell is going to break loose. Mother and I might even find ourselves separated—oh, it's frightening, I think, really. I want to get her away from Miss., but don't even know how to start, because first I have to find a place, find a way to transport her— with some nurse along, to travel—find a way to pay, find a new doctor— The poor, frail little thing, she begs me all the time to take her out of 'that hell-hole'—and it's the nicest place, newest, best equipped, best staffed of any in the Southeast, I believe— and anywhere she'd go it would be the same story." Mary Lou acted immediately, asking Eudora to bring her mother to Santa Fe and arranging a lecture date that would pay for her trip. A decline in Chestina's health prevented Eudora from pursuing this prospect. As she told Mary Lou, "Mother has developed a hernia of the diaphragm and still I thought she could make a trip if carefully done—until I saw her get a kind of strangling the other day—just from not being propped up high enough at the head.

Even traveling with a nurse, as she'd have to, she couldn't control the motions of the plane or train."[72] Chestina's condition had greatly improved by May, but Eudora did not further pursue any Santa Fe arrangements.

In May and June 1964 Eudora was able to devote some sustained attention to the reunion story that had become first a novella and now a novel. Harcourt was eager to have the manuscript that summer, and Eudora sought to oblige. A bit uncertain about the quality of her work, she asked William Maxwell if he would again read it and comment. Maxwell replied in the affirmative, offering encouraging words about the project. "I am always utterly at your disposal, about that manuscript," he noted, "but at your disposal with a certain amount of fear and trepidation, because I know—I have read—how you feel on the subject of neatness, and *New Yorker* editing is essentially a neatening process, and after twenty-six years I cannot utterly disassociate myself from it. So this you must be on guard against. What I have found is that you can trust the opinion of people who love you until the moment comes when you can't trust it, and when that happens you know, so perhaps it is not serious, what I am saying. I am sure you haven't ruined it. It is unruinable."[73]

Eudora stopped in New York late in June after appearing at the Suffield Writer-Reader Conference Bill Smith had organized for the second straight year. She delivered a copy of her manuscript to Bill Maxwell and returned home. During the summer, she seems to have worked on a story she had begun perhaps as early as 1957. Running to more than a hundred typescript pages and called "The Last of the Figs" and then "Nicotiana" in two of its incarnations, this incomplete story deals with the failure of white and black Mississippians to see each other as individuals, to grant each other their identities. Focusing on a mother and daughter much like Eudora and Chestina and on their black servant Esther, the story in draft form is complex and compelling. Exasperation with southern racism, with northern sanctimoniousness, with the possibility of white and black violence—all are part of the story. The forty-something protagonist Sarah Ewing, who like Eudora had experienced a failed romance with a man thought to be "queer," also shares Eudora's faith in the power of art to unite individuals, to transcend racial and cultural differences. "It's delight in difference, it's respect for the sanctity of difference that every honest feeling starts with," Sarah thinks. "Love and art and learning and teaching—blindness is the enemy of all . . . It's what drawing a picture starts with, what *seeing* starts with. Difference inspired it and taught the hand to learn it. Difference, variation, branching forth, reaching out—that's what's beautiful. That's still what's beautiful. That's what means something, and what it means is difference again—*identity*. And when you see identity at last—and when identity finds you—then they'll embrace."[74] But though Eudora eventually thought of this story as part of a trilogy that would also include the Wilder/Livingstone/Longstreet/Darden story she had worked on in the early fifties and "The Demonstrators," which she would write in 1965, she never produced a polished text.

In September any hopes for promptly completing either "Nicotiana" or the reunion novel had to be abandoned; she took a job as writer-in-residence at Millsaps College. Arranged by her old friend and English Department Chairman George Boyd, the job made traveling the lecture circuit unnecessary and enabled Eudora to see more of her mother. The students were carefully selected by the college, and Eudora enjoyed meeting with them in a workshop fashion. She told Bill Smith, "My class at Millsaps college is with 18 young boys and girls, all bright and by no means all English majors—which I like—for instance, there are two French majors and both had been in Algeria, so when we came to Camus that was very informing for me too. I forgot to say that we have a book in the class and I chose Sean O'Faolain's paperback 'Short Stories' which is the greatest joy . . . The school is congenial—a number of the faculty are already friends of mine and among the liberals around."[75] However congenial this teaching situation was, she found that it did not leave her the time she wished to devote to writing. And being at home put other demands on Eudora's time. Long dissatisfied with the conventional, predictable theater offerings in Jackson, Eudora sought to help young friends who planned to establish a new community theater, to perform serious dramas, and to do so in an integrated setting. And feeling melancholy because her mother could no longer work in the garden, Eudora set about digging up the iris bed and setting out new plants.

In November, Robert Penn Warren wrote Eudora for permission to use a fictionalized account of the evening he had spent with her and Charlotte. He wanted to incorporate it in his book *Who Speaks for the Negro?* Eudora consulted Charlotte about the piece, and Charlotte was immediately opposed to its use, feeling that she would easily be recognized and that her criticism of Ross Barnett and Paul B. Johnson Jr. might result in the loss of her job as director of the Mississippi Department of Archives and History. "I think," Charlotte told Warren, "they would be reasonable in firing me when considering the use of the words: idiot, drooling, face like an old wash rag, ripped right open like hog killing, and defective child, in connection with the chief executive and chief executive-to-be. Incidentally, some of these expressions are not familiar to me." Warren promptly replied "to hell with publishing it," and the difficulty was resolved. Charlotte and Eudora's dismay at the state of Mississippi politics was not. And Eudora was further concerned with Mississippi's role in the coming presidential election. As she told Bill Smith, "There's not a Johnson sticker in Jackson. Thousands of Goldwater ones and a brand that says 'Goldwater + Wallace = States Rights' and 'Goldwater plus Walker = States Rights'—which must have come from Goldwater headquarters—they match. I have a strong feeling, though, shared by friends here, that there will be a lot of secret voting for Johnson on the day."[76]

In December Eudora delivered a large public lecture at Mill-saps as part of her contract with the college. She did not on this occasion have to request unrestricted attendance—Millsaps now welcomed all to its public events—but she once again spoke dur-ing particularly tense times. The previous summer had seen the murders of three civil rights workers in Philadelphia, Mississippi, the firebombing of forty black churches, and the white Citizens' Councils' intimidation of whites known to have "moderate" sen-sibilities, intimidation that had not ceased. In her lecture, entitled "The Southern Writer Today: An Interior Affair," Eudora deliv-ered comments that she would later publish as "Must the Novel-ist Crusade?" Here, she rejected an ostensible political purpose for fiction, arguing that "there is absolutely everything in great fiction but a clear answer," that fiction is concerned more with the complexities of human experience than with proposing solu-tions to human difficulties. But she also asserted, "What matters is that a writer is committed to his own moral principles. If he is, when we read him we cannot help but be aware of what these are. Certainly the characters of his novel and the plot they move in are their ultimate reflections. But these convictions are implicit; they are deep down; they are the rock on which the whole struc-ture of more than the novel rests." The great novel, she argued, is grounded on the bedrock of principle, the very principle for which the crusader speaks. As an example, she offered *A Passage to India*, which she had praised while at Cambridge in 1954. It is, she said, a "moral" novel, but not a crusading one: "It deals with race prejudice. Mr. Forster, not by preaching at us, while being passionately concerned, makes us know his points unforgettably as often as we read it . . . The points are good forty years after their day *because of the splendor of the novel.* What a lesser novelist's harangues would have buried by now, his imagination still reveals. Revelation of even the strongest forces is delicate work."[77] Eu-dora followed this address with a reading of "Keela, the Outcast Indian Maiden," which, appropriately, examines the complexities of human relationships. The story, written in 1938, describes a crippled black man who was once kidnapped into carnival work as a geek called Keela, the Outcast Indian Maiden, and who, notwithstanding the horror of his past, feels nostalgic about the carnival experience in which he was noticed as now within his own family he is not. The story further deals with the guilt felt by Steve, the carnival barker, and with his inability, nevertheless, to overcome the separation of race, and finally, the story depicts a bystander's courting of detachment from the horror and guilt Keela represents.

Complex though it is, however, "Keela" makes an inescapable political and moral statement—the dehumanizing nature of racism is infinitely more grotesque than a carnival sideshow. Certainly, Steve recognizes that by acquiescing to this evil, he has become part of it: "'It's all me, see,' said Steve. 'I know that. I was the one was the cause for it goin' on an' on an' not bein' found out—such an awful thing. It was me, what I said out front through the megaphone.'" On the other hand, his acquaintance Max, the owner of Max's Place, represses any guilt that might be his. "'Bud,' said Max, disengaging himself, 'I don't hear anything. I got a juke box, see, so I don't have to listen.'" Max, in his disengaged state, might be speaking for many white Mississippians in 1964—they did not want to recognize their own complicity with evil, they did not want to accept the guilt they shared with Steve. But in reading this 1940 story to her 1964 audience, Eudora called attention to that guilt. She did not ask that her audience become political activists, but she did ask, implicitly, that they refuse to be part of racist activities, that they recognize the humanity and complexity of all individuals. Within three months Millsaps College would announce that African American students were welcome to enroll.[78] In 1965 five students would become the first African Americans to do so.

Diarmuid sent Eudora's Millsaps lecture to *Harper's Magazine* associate editor Willie Morris, her fellow Mississippian. Morris accepted the piece, contingent upon Eudora making substantial cuts. Resenting the contingency, Diarmuid told Eudora she should feel free to reject the *Harper's* offer. She did, and Diarmuid promptly sent "Must the Novelist Crusade?" to the *Atlantic Monthly*. For her part, Eudora was depressed, but not about her essay's fate. The Christmas season and her mother's condition combined to make her blue. She wrote to Mary Lou, saying, "All goes just about the same with my mother—she is still in Yazoo City, still frail but well, still fiercely unhappy, and it will never heal with me that she isn't in her home and with me. The part of her that was our best and deepest relationship gets lost or nearly disappears, and then flashes of it strike up like little lights in dark caves. She is not against me now, just feels I have made some terrible mistake in putting her where she is and that she is being punished and hurt there. My brother and I had Christmas dinner there—really, they have a first-class kitchen—and I was up yesterday on a warm sunny day and we sat out by the fountain a long time." The tone of Eudora's letter worried Mary Lou, but Eudora dismissed these concerns. "I feel ashamed of having caused you alarm for me. I am really a facer of facts by now, I think, though it took me a long time—took being a writer, perhaps, and of course it took being a reader—and I have had you and Bill and Emmy and Diarmuid for friends, and, after all, I have had my mother. Please don't feel uneasy about me—it would be unjustified, and I would tell you if I felt I was slipping and all my friends could come and give me a good solid spank—that would be what's called for. So remember and don't worry." Eudora was in a retrospective mood and experienced the sort of doubling emotion that she had felt during World War II and that Virgie Rainey had experienced in *The Golden Apples*; for Eudora, at this moment in time, hope and despair were the closest blood. She felt deep regret that "Mother is mentally changed, though it doesn't often seem like a mental illness—just what happens to us all, I suppose, if we're 81."[79] But she also felt deep gratitude that her mother had been one of her closest friends, a friend numbered with Mary Lou, Bill, Emmy, and Diarmuid.

Mary Lou's alarm for Eudora did indeed prove unfounded. Eudora did not break down. Instead she returned to her teaching job at Millsaps for the spring semester of 1965 (Ellen Gilchrist, who would go on to have a distinguished writing career, was now one of her students), regularly visited her mother in Yazoo, and scheduled a number of lectures that would enlarge her income without taking her too far from home. During the spring and early summer, she visited the University of Alabama, the University of Illinois, the University of Chicago, and the University of Texas. And in April she spoke at the Southern Literary Festival in Oxford, Mississippi. There she was reunited with many old friends, Robert Penn Warren, Ruth Ford, Zachary Scott, John Robinson (visiting from Italy, where he was now settled), and the writer Donald Sutherland among them. And there she opened the festival with an address reiterating her faith in fiction's power to expose and combat racist hatred. In the midst of a wide-ranging discussion alluding to many Faulkner texts, Eudora called the audience's attention to the brutal murder of Joe Christmas, "waiting with his hands in chains, 'bright and glittering,' . . . as Percy Grimm arrives with his automatic." Later she noted that Faulkner's characters "are white, Negro, Indian, Chinese, Huguenot, Scotch, English, Spanish, French, or any combination of these, and known always or at any point of their time on earth from birth till death and in between." And she added that these characters constitute "a population that has *reality* as distinguished from *actuality*: they are our hearts made visible and audible and above all dramatic; they are ourselves translated, and, at times, transmogrified." Eudora thus suggested that race is as artificial a concept as nationality and that whatever race or nationality Faulkner's characters belong to, they represent our common humanity. After delivering this address, Eudora learned that a mob had the night before harassed an African American Tougaloo College delegation that had hoped to participate in the festival. Eudora found the mob and its views "so bad," as did Robert Penn Warren, who then issued a powerful statement for civil rights in his festival lecture that evening.[80]

When not teaching, tending to her mother, or making public appearances, Eudora was working on her novel. She didn't have it ready for Harcourt in March as they had wanted, but she did send Diarmuid a big chunk of the manuscript. He found it "enchanting" and "a wonderful piece of work," but he asked Eudora to send him a completed text, not bits and pieces.[81] Still the text was not complete when she came to New York at the end of June for a trip that she undertook more for pleasure than for business. She appeared at the Suffield Writer-Reader Conference for a third time, enjoying the company of Bill Smith and of Padraic Colum, the Irish poet who had helped to found Dublin's Abbey Theatre. Meeting and hearing Colum speak was a highlight for Eudora, as she told Bill Maxwell.

> If I had had to walk all the way from Jackson and work free all the week through, I would have gladly, because of Padraic Colum. Imagine having him in the same place as you and telling stories, reciting poems of anyone anywhere any time in the whole history, and just remarking . . . To think of his still being with us and the liveliest one for miles around— the last link with all that. Last night came his lecture in the barn, which is the Suffield Academy Theatre, and of course it was so much more than a lecture—about growing up in his grandmother's house, with the peat fire which you look *down* on, and so is so much better than other fires, and the greyhounds sleeping "in a loop" on the hearth, and the story-teller coming, taking a seat (in his grandmother's house there was always a pile of clean grass and leaves kept

ready near the hearth for any wanderer) and beginning
"Now by the power that has seized me, I will tell you:" (better than that, can't remember right now.)[82]

The excitement of seeing Colum was followed by a good visit
in New York. Eudora and Reynolds had a happy reunion there—
he took her to see the Beatles in *A Hard Day's Night*. She went to
the Russells for a party where she chatted with the Malcolm Cow-
leys and met Hildy Dolson's new husband. And visits with Hubert, with Bill and Emmy Maxwell, and with Joan and Olivia
Kahn delighted her. But the talk of Viet Nam was distressing.
Eudora felt ill-equipped to understand the issues involved. Still,
she sensed that President Lyndon Johnson's "maneuverings" were
"headlong and heedless."[83]

Not long after Eudora returned to Jackson, Diarmuid contacted her with news of a lucrative offer. Bennett Cerf, who had
tried to lure Eudora to Random House in 1960, was still eager
to add Eudora to the Random House list and offered the very
handsome sum of thirty-five thousand dollars for her new novel.[84]
Diarmuid felt that Harcourt lacked the proper enthusiasm for
Eudora's work, and he suggested that she carefully consider
Cerf's offer. Eudora, however, felt unable to produce a finished
manuscript in a timely manner and worried that the publishers
might lose money on her work. Diarmuid counseled her not to
worry about profit margins, but he also agreed that a decision to
change publishers need not be made immediately.

Late in July Mary Lou's son, Duncan, who had been working
in Memphis, decided to visit Eudora in Jackson. Eudora had earlier assured his mother that travel in Mississippi would be safe
for the young man. "Things are better in the South now," she
had written Mary Lou. "I feel the difference very much myself.
I'm sure you've read that there are responsible businessmen now
speaking in sensible words, and that the good colleges and schools
have acted responsibly and with pretty good cheer."[85] She added

that Millsaps College, where she had continued to teach, was now integrated, and she expressed the wish that African American students would join her class. But by the time Duncan's visit was imminent, Eudora was not so confident that Mississippi was really experiencing widespread, positive change. She had heard reports that civil rights lawyers were being abducted, and she urged Duncan, whose car would sport northeastern license plates, to stay on main roads if he drove down from Memphis. He did, and all was well.

In the fall, after a working trip to the University of Kentucky, Eudora settled in for a new semester at Millsaps. Her focus on the classroom, however, was hard to maintain. Her mother's health was failing sharply, and then in October her brother fell in his bathroom, breaking his neck. He managed to phone Eudora, who drove him to the hospital, but a long convalescence seemed in store. Eudora kept the news from her mother and drove from hospital to nursing home and back, trying to assist both Edward and Chestina.

In the midst of trial, miraculously, Eudora produced a new story. Frustration with the ingrained racism that dominated Mississippi, frustration with the tensions that often overwhelmed daily life in the sixties, relief that needed change was finally coming about, regret that reasoned discussion had been replaced by loud and violent confrontations—all this sparked the story. Early in November "The Demonstrators" reached Diarmuid, who found it "most moving" and sent it straightaway to Bill Maxwell at the *New Yorker*. By month's end Bill wrote to Eudora: "I've been calling you, to tell you that we *all* think the story is wonderful, but all I get is the sound of a phone ringing in an empty house: *drrrrr . . . drrrrr . . . drrrr.*" Eudora had little time to rejoice in the success of her new story. In a letter to Bill, she described her situation. "This is the first note I've written since I got yours— thank you for it, and thank you for liking the story, and for taking it. I am so glad. I'd love to have heard you on the telephone, but it's nice to have the letter to go back to. Things are getting better but we've had a family crisis with two heads—my mother had a stroke and my brother, several weeks earlier, broke his neck and is in a hospital in Jackson—so they've been bad off fifty miles apart, and of course neither knowing about the other. My mother's come through it very well. I was told by the doctor she wouldn't, and the first thing she said to me in a tiny little voice when she was able to speak was that he was a moron. So I hope he stays wrong for a good long while so she can get some strength back."[86]

For a while both Chestina and Edward did seem to improve, and Eudora worked long-distance with Maxwell on revisions to the story. But in the new year catastrophe struck. Complications from a stroke claimed Chestina's life, on January 20, 1966. She was eighty-two. Four days later, fifty-three-year-old Edward, who had developed a brain infection, died as a result. Of her immediate family, only Eudora remained. The crises that had dominated her life since 1957 had ended tragically, and she was bereft, feeling at a loss for words, though words had long been her source of strength. Eudora needed time for healing, but that healing would ultimately depend upon her ability to distill into fiction these losing battles, these years of worry, guilt, and, now, grief.

SEVEN

Defending Against Time
1966–1973

At the end of January 1966, Eudora Welty was struggling to cope with the deaths of her mother and brother and to recapture a sense of purpose and meaning. At first she thought travel might be her salvation. It seemed to offer literal and figurative respite, for Eudora had always found that travel led away from self-absorption. For the next three months, she pursued this course, but she would ultimately find that only by writing, by confronting and understanding her deepest emotions, could she achieve peace. And write she did, creating her most autobiographical work, a novella that focused on the nature of grief and loss, and completing the long comic novel begun in 1955. The profound sources of consolation these works evoked—the power of memory, the continuity of love—would be needed as the coming years brought new trials. At age fifty-six Eudora was entering the stage of life in which loss becomes more and more frequent. In 1973 she would have to face the deaths of the writer with whom she felt the most profound affinity, of her oldest and perhaps closest Jackson friend, and of the agent whom she depended upon as an advisor and loved as a friend. In the wake of these deaths, her faith in memory as "a living thing," her belief that through memory "the old and the young, the past and the present, the living and the dead" join and live, would be put to the test and would eventually be reclaimed, though not immediately.[1] But the confluence of memory was not Eudora's only defense against time during these years. She saw her nieces marry and have children. She continued to support the career of Reynolds Price, whom she viewed almost as her own child. And through a series of apparent coincidences that seemed fated, Eudora felt her life converge with that of Kenneth Millar, the author who wrote detective fiction under the pen name Ross Macdonald. Though Ken made his home in Santa Barbara, California, far from Eudora, and though the two would be in each other's presence for very limited times, their love would transcend separation and sustain both their lives.

Following the deaths of Chestina and Edward in January 1966, Eudora was the center of concern for family and friends. Her young nieces and their mother offered support to Eudora and to Elinor, Edward's wife. Friends from Jackson rallied about Eudora, and in letters, other friends sought to provide a measure of comfort. These devastating losses, nevertheless, threatened to leave Eudora bereft and, as she told Lehman Engel, without words for fiction. The death of Edward was shockingly unexpected. From the time they were children, Edward and Eudora had been kindred spirits, and they had remained close, bound by a common sense of humor and a lifetime of shared experiences. The death of Chestina had not come as a surprise; for years her health had been in decline, and the mother who had also been Eudora's champion and friend had long been ebbing away. Throughout this process there had been hope, however tentative or diminishing, for improvement. Now that hope was gone. Mary Lou Aswell perceptively recognized the nature of Eudora's despair and might well have been speaking for all of Eudora's friends when she sent condolences. "I hope you can feel," Mary Lou wrote,

> that for your poor mother death was a blessed release from suffering, but your brother—. Too young, like my brother.

If you're like me you are now the Older Generation for your family, and it's a lonely feeling ... Eudora, I'm so glad I knew your mother in good times. You know how much I enjoyed her when she visited you—I could even see some of your qualities in her, humor and acute observation and the ability to make contact. That she lost those qualities when she was so ill was the tragedy and I'm glad it is over. But I do know what you are going through, dearest E. I wonder if the small comfort I found when my mother died after a long illness would help you. I found that I could bear any suffering better than I could bear hers. I've been reading the great biography of Proust. What he said to a bereaved friend might help you too, "that when at last the wound of separation was healed his mother would return, young and happy, and live for ever." So with your father and brothers, perhaps, as with mine.[2]

For Eudora the wound of separation would heal, but the healing process would be slow. Thinking of Edward brought Eudora many regrets. Over the last fifteen years of his life, this deeply loved brother had suffered bouts of depression, been devastated by the loss of Walter, regretted that his wife Elinor felt alienated from his family, endured unhappy times in his marriage, and found himself unable to cope with his mother's declining health. Could Eudora have done more to help him during these years? Given Elinor's jealousy of her and the demands of caring for Chestina, it clearly seems not. But Eudora must have wondered.

The death of Chestina evoked an even more lingering, doubling and redoubling, response. On the one hand, her absence left a gaping hole in Eudora's life. Chestina had been a model of courage. She was the mother who as a girl of fifteen had single-handedly taken her desperately ill father from a West Virginia mountaintop to a Baltimore hospital, who as a young married woman had braved fire to save her beloved set of Dickens novels, and who had later faced cancer surgery without telling her children. Chestina had been Eudora's kindred spirit as a reader, immersing herself in books by Charles Darwin and Wilkie Collins, in guides to bridge playing and gardening. She had not allowed social convention to dominate her life or lives of her children. Her focus upon household matters had given Eudora time to write. She had tended the house and garden, forwarded mail, handled business and banking matters for Eudora whenever her daughter was away for lengthy periods of time. And Chestina's interest in politics, her hatred of war, and her devotion to family were values Eudora shared. As Eudora told Mary Lou in 1965, her mother had been one of her closest friends. She loved her mother and keenly felt her loss.

Of course, Chestina was also the mother who, in her last years, had demanded Eudora's closest attention, who wanted to remain at home yet fired home care nurse after nurse, who bitterly resented life in a professional facility and blamed Eudora for it, and who prompted Eudora to blame herself. Her mother's death freed Eudora from almost daily trips of a hundred miles to and from a nursing home, from the verbal abuse that an old and ill Chestina periodically heaped upon her, from the financial burden of her mother's care, from the mental and physical exhaustion that kept her from writing, and from the need to remain close at hand in Mississippi. Like the character Virgie after the death of her mother, Katie Rainey, in "The Wanderers," Eudora experienced the withdrawal "of some bondage that might have been dear, now dismembering and losing itself."[3] Ironically, however, being free from many constraints brought its own guilt— guilt at feeling relief or release. Moreover, Eudora continued at some level to blame herself for the unhappiness of her mother's last years. The guilt was illogical; no daughter could have been more supportive, but emotions defy logic. Only after Eudora transformed these experiences into fiction would she really be at peace with them.

In the meantime, work and travel were an anesthetic for pain. Eudora resolved to fulfill all speaking commitments she had previously made, and thankfully those commitments allowed her to visit friends whose love had long sustained her—Diarmuid Russell, Bill and Emmy Maxwell among them. From the end of February until mid-May she was on the road. First stop was Wellesley College, though on the way, Eudora paused in New York in order to see Diarmuid, who was deeply concerned about her. From Wellesley, she went to Elmira College, where she took a particular interest in Mark Twain's octagonal study, which had been moved from Quarry Farm to the campus. Back home in Jackson she briefly regrouped and then left for the University of North Carolina, at Greensboro, where her host was old friend and fiction writer Peter Taylor. Reynolds drove over from Duke and found Eudora radiant. She went home with Reynolds and one evening regaled him with hilarious passages from her reunion story. But she could not sustain the high spirits that Peter and Reynolds observed and she sought solitude in the Smoky Mountains before going on to DC. In Washington she managed more good times, escaping from thoughts of the past. She saw Bill Smith and spent an evening with Katherine Anne, who cooked a fine dinner for her. Though laryngitis forced her to cancel a speaking engagement, Eudora went to see the Mellon Collection, "one of the most beautiful I ever saw in my life—the Boudins!"[4] Then it was on to Bryn Mawr, a bout with the flu, and recuperation in New York, where Monroe Wheeler, the director of exhibitions and publications at the Museum of Modern Art, gave the Maxwells and Eudora a private tour of a Turner exhibition; where the Russells hosted her for a Saturday night dinner party; and where she and the Russells had Easter lunch at the David Rockefellers.

Still the traveling was not over. With an engagement at Brandeis and a return to Bryn Mawr lying shortly ahead, she spoke at Agnes Scott in Atlanta and appeared at the Southern Literary Festival in Tuscaloosa, Alabama. She and novelist Caroline Gordon found themselves equally and comically exasperated by "the 24-hour gabble & gush" there. As Eudora reported to Katherine Anne, "Caroline was in Tuscaloosa with me and rode back on the train as far as Princeton with me ... The first thing Caroline said to me as we gained our roomettes was: 'I hate every word you've ever written and I can't stand *you!*' And I thankfully replied 'The Same!' We had really had it. Katherine Anne, I swear it to you, which makes it count more than just swearing it out the window here, where just some doves are walking around in the grass not listening, Never Again. I'm through with lecturing. They were a blessing when I needed the quick cash, and I liked most of the people, but you know that's a killing life. So this Friday I start home, after a month & a half away, and I'm going to work on my own work."[5] On April 24, Brandeis presented her with its Creative Arts Medal for Fiction; shortly afterward Bryn Mawr gave her the M. Carey Thomas Award. Then it was home to Jackson.

Home alone, with no demands upon her time, Eudora sought to bring order to the novel on which she had worked for more than a decade. But near the end of May, tragedy struck again. Hubert Creekmore suffered a heart attack and died in a New York taxicab on his way to catch a plane for Europe. In the 1930s Hubert had advised Eudora about submitting her fiction for publication, and his sister had married Eudora's brother Walter. He and Eudora had remained close friends over the years. In June, when Mary Lou Aswell learned of Hubert's death, she wrote to Eudora. "How could *so much* calamity happen to the person who least deserves it? I don't see how you've survived this year. The only way this horrible year can be redeemed for you and for the world is if your novel gets finished, and the war in Vietnam. I add a wish for your state—may the civil rights disturbances be settled peacefully."[6] Mary Lou linked her condolences about Hubert's death to concerns about the war in Viet Nam and about the shooting of James Meredith during his march from Memphis to Jackson. It would not be long before Eudora's expressions of grief regained a strong public dimension, but for the moment she was focused on the personal toll 1966 had taken.

Despite this new loss, Eudora continued to work on the novel. In July Diarmuid expressed pleasure with the section she had mailed him and with the steady progress she seemed to be making. Eudora remained unsure that she was whipping her unwieldy saga into shape, and in August she asked Mary Lou to read the novel and provide an opinion. Mary Lou's response was qualified but encouraging.

> I will tell you, since you ask, that without the introduction, it's confusing at first, you have to get into the swing. And I'll remind you of something I'm sure you know that you've rearranged so often (I remember that MS of yours I saw pinned together like a quilt) you've got the sequence of events out of order occasionally, so that a few references (I've pencilled some ?s) aren't clear. You've changed some names too, haven't you? Those details will be ironed out in the final version. What I feel from reading just these two chapters I may revise when I see the whole, but I'd better tell you that Chapter 2, being all reminiscence, seems not interminable . . . , but long. Chapter 3, when the present action begins goes like a blaze. I can't imagine what you'd sacrifice from the "tell," each voice is so individual and delicious, but I think the reader's attention may lag unless that's just my natural (probably unnatural) impatience one of my bad faults. For your public the book will be a Gift because it's so entirely of you . . . *Yes it comes through.*[7]

Eudora took the spirit of Mary Lou's comments, not her reservations, to heart, and at the end of October told her friend that "the *good* feeling about my work that you helped restore to me is still with me."[8] So much more confident did Eudora feel, that she also began to contemplate a book of stories and a play.

Though "good feeling" about her work was being restored,

her grief at the loss of family and friends began more fully to encompass a public grief. When, at Thanksgiving, she appeared in Houston before the National Council of Teachers of English, Eudora read "The Demonstrators." This story, accepted a year earlier by the *New Yorker*, just now being published, and destined for an O. Henry first prize, suggested much about Eudora's contemporary mood. It depicted white racists unable to see beyond the negative stereotypes they impose upon African Americans, a young civil rights worker who engages in his own form of stereotyping, and a white doctor, who thinks himself free of such deceptions but who fails to recognize his own African American maid as he treats her for a stab wound. This story struck a resonant note for many readers. Jesse Jackson wrote the *New Yorker* to say the story was "so true and powerful" that it made him "weep for my people," and Brendan Gill found it to be "a whole novel." To Frank Lyell, Eudora said, "I did want it to show (demonstrate, I guess) the break-down of so many ties and of lines of understanding and communication, wanted it to be sad, but not nauseating. It's just a picture of the way I feel things have got to. I had a number of other communiques about it."[9] Eudora had seen conflict over civil rights cause tensions among family members, friends of long standing, and paternalists and reformers—this high cost, she knew, would have to be paid if necessary change were to occur. In her story and her public reading of it, Eudora grieved for the cost even as she endorsed the change.

The Viet Nam War was another source of grief. When Mary Lou wrote from Santa Fe about her despair at seeing young Mexican Americans drafted into military service and her dismay that a local write-in Peace candidate had not been elected to the House of Representatives, Eudora ardently responded, "I too feel the hideousness of the Viet Nam war in many personal ways—sons of friends and bridegrooms of young friends and maid's son . . . It's so baffling to me, knowing nothing of military or diplomatic affairs, *how* to get out of there—without letting the Communists start it up again somewhere just the same. I desperately feel we should never, never have gone in there. And it seems that life has taught us nothing if we do not make a way to negotiate. But how. Of course I never trusted [President Lyndon] Johnson, did you? Your feelings as a Quaker must be lacerated every day in more ways than horror and distrust and confusion, and I'm sorry about your candidate."[10] War and violence dominated the American political scene, and for Eudora personal and national sources of despair seemed to converge.

Bill Maxwell was troubled by Eudora's dark mood and sought to assuage apprehensions she had expressed in their recent phone conversation. "What I am trying to say," he wrote, "is there is no pattern in years, no constancy of good or bad luck. Who knows what the day after tomorrow will bring—the very thing we most wanted and haven't allowed our hearts to hope. If what I heard in your voice persists, will you drop everything and come to New York and settle down in the back room and let us hang garlands of love around your neck, day after day, until you are feeling yourself again?"[11] Eudora did not hie herself to New York and the loving Maxwell household, but she did begin to move beyond the despair Bill had sensed in her voice on the phone. And the source of resolution came when she turned away from her long comic novel and began to write autobiographically, to deal with the personal experience of loss and to set it in a public context.

By mid-February Eudora reported to Frank Lyell that she was less depressed and was "writing on a long story— It may be grim but can't help it." Grim though this story was, it proved therapeutic for Eudora and consumed her attention. She did take time away from this work to speak at St. Andrew's Cathedral in downtown Jackson: Members of the congregation had organized a series of readings, lectures, concerts, and plays, which were open to all Jacksonians, and they hoped African Americans would attend. Eudora was the first speaker in the series, but as it turned out she read to an all-white audience.[12] She also took time away from writing in order to make a quick trip to Hollins College, where she received a medal. Soon, however, she was devoting each morning to her new story. She had always loved the intense experience of writing—the actual time at the typewriter, the preoccupation with a story even when engaged in other activities, the emergence of material from the subconscious. Now she was back in flow.

The shadows darkening her life seem to lift in other ways as well. She heard poet Dick Eberhart read at Belhaven and then attended a party for him. John Robinson came to town, and the two old friends met for drinks and dinners. And in mid-March Eudora attended a recital given by the young African American soprano, a fellow Mississippian, Leontyne Price, and the racial conflicts in Mississippi seemed for the magical hours of the recital to evaporate. As Eudora told Bill Maxwell, "Yesterday afternoon Leontyne Price gave a concert in Jackson and I heard her sing the Dove Son[o] from Marriage of Figaro, along with a big work-out of a program—she was all radiance and glory, simply beautiful. The only other time she'd appeared in Jackson was when she was a young girl just starting to the Juilliard, and it was private and invitational because it was in a downtown hotel and at that time you could only integrate privately and by invitation— she sang like an angel and was so astonishing that she was asked to please just sing it over, she repeated the whole program because we just couldn't believe it . . . She wore a beautiful Mediterranean blue chiffon gown with green and white shaded feathers around the top and green lining to a panel, and when she existed [*sic*] what a gay fling of that panel—she was so gay and loved singing, so visibly loved every minute."[13]

By May, Eudora had finished her story now titled "Poor Eyes" but a month later to be called "The Optimist's Daughter." In its pages, Laurel Hand, whose mother has long since died, must confront the haunting memory of her mother's loss, face the death of her father, and deal with his surviving second wife, the wholly self-centered Fay. Eudora mailed the story to Diarmuid, who deemed it a masterpiece, and in turn sent it to the *New Yorker.* There Bill Maxwell added his praise and Emmy's. In a letter to Eudora, he wrote, "I thought you wouldn't mind my showing the story to Emmy, who felt the same way I did about it. 'What I liked best,' she said, 'was Mr. Allday [the handyman] going through the whole house like hope and leaving everything worse than before.' And today at lunch Diarmuid said he thought it was your best work, which is what I think. He also said that you thought it should not be published [in book form] all by itself. My own instinctive feeling was that it should be. Don't make up your mind on this point in a hurry." Back from six weeks on the road—a trip to Washington, DC, a meeting of the Katherine Anne Porter Foundation, a visit with her old friends John and Catherine Prince, stops at the University of Virginia and Denison University, and a visit with her West Virginia relatives—Eudora was in good spirits. Those spirits lifted even higher when Diarmuid reported that the *New Yorker* would take "The Optimist's Daughter." It would be two more years before Maxwell secured enough space for this long story to be included in a single issue, but the completed manuscript, published or unpublished, was reward enough for Eudora. After Lehman Engel saw her in Jackson late in June, he wrote to exult that "you have become your own self wholly again."[14]

In her story, Eudora confronted the long years of her mother's illness and the emptiness left by her death. Chestina Welty had been self-reliant for most of her life, and she hated finding herself old and weak and blind. In "The Optimist's Daughter," Chessie becomes Becky, blind, "tied down," ill and nearing death. When her husband, Clinton McKelva, cannot understand her resultant despair, Becky feels forsaken. "He loved his wife," daughter Laurel recalls. "Whatever she did that she couldn't help doing was all right. Whatever she was driven to say was all right. But it was *not* all right! Her trouble was that very desperation. And no one had the power to cause that except the

one she desperately loved, who refused to consider it. It was betrayal on betrayal."[15] This particular betrayal did not happen to
Chestina—Christian Webb Welty had died thirty-five years before his wife. But a sense of betrayal deepened Eudora's investigation of love and separateness, an investigation that went beyond
the bounds of individual experience but that also drew upon the
helplessness Eudora herself felt when, despite the ability to recognize and consider her mother's desperation, she was unable to
assuage it. To speak her feelings of guilt, to recognize the impos-
sibility of countering her mother's despair, to forgive herself for
embracing the freedom that resulted from Chestina's death—all
made "The Optimist's Daughter" a source of release and renewal
for Eudora and helped her again to live fully in the present.

For Eudora, living fully in the present had always involved
placing private experiences in their social context. In "The Optimist's Daughter," Mississippi's continuing racism enters the novel
in the form of "white caps" or Klansmen whom, his friends say,
Clint McKelva once prevented from lynching a black man. Laurel
is not so sure that her father would have taken such a risk or behaved so heroically—such memories provided false comfort to a
white public unwilling to confront its collective guilt. The presence of this community recollection is thus tied to the story's
wide-ranging investigation of memory and understanding. Four
years later, when Eudora began to revise her story, and later still,
when she completed it as a novella, public and private became
even more closely tied, and the power of memory—its vulnerability to the present moment and its ability to sustain and restore
the bereaved—became more fully rendered.

Both Diarmuid and Bill Maxwell were firmly convinced that
"The Optimist's Daughter" should receive separate book publication after its appearance in the *New Yorker.* Eudora was less sure;
she resisted the generic expectations that the term *novel* or *novella*
might create for readers, and she feared that separate publication would fuel scholars' quests for biographical interpretations.

Diarmuid was more pragmatic; he wanted to follow the most beneficial financial course for his client. But he assured Eudora that this decision would be hers alone.

As if to celebrate her restored joy in living, Eudora planned a vacation to Santa Fe, where she could explore new country, enjoy the companionship of Mary Lou, and see Agnes Sims again. No lecturing, no readings, and no meetings with students would interrupt this journey. And she was delighted when Charlotte Capers, who was scheduled to attend a fortuitously timed and situated convention of archivists, accepted her invitation to join forces in Santa Fe. There Eudora and Charlotte shared in dinner parties, "picnics & mountain rides & all day excursions" with Mary Lou, Agi, and their friends. During a wonderful trip to Taos, they visited eighty-four-year-old Lady Dorothy Brett, the artist and friend of D. H. Lawrence. Brett was, Eudora recalled in a thank-you note to Sims, "sitting in her room with the visionary Ring pictures of the Indians all around, and right on the same sofa with us that dog grinding up his bone, and her gay, brave talk about 'No needles! No operations!'—and that amazing Autobiography of hers in the Review she sold us—autographed did you notice." To commemorate her time in New Mexico, Eudora bought one of Agi's paintings, *Rome,* and arranged for it to be shipped to Jackson. When the painting arrived in November, Eudora told Agi that she and Charlotte had offered toasts to it. Then she added, "It's very much the color and feel and grandness and sweep and density of Rome, but for me it carries some of the same qualities as part of all I saw in the world around Santa Fe."[16] Eudora hung the painting in her living room, in a place of honor above the mantel. It would remain there for the rest of her life, a symbol of Rome, of Santa Fe, and of her own renewed equanimity.

The year ended on a sad note. Chestina's brother Carl died in December, and Eudora traveled to Charleston, West Virginia, for the funeral and to provide comfort to her one remaining uncle. Carl was buried upriver in the mountains near, but not at, the

Andrews' home place Eudora had incorporated into "The Optimist's Daughter," the burial site that she "would have wished for all of them." Perhaps the trip "up home," to use Chessie's words, sent Eudora back to her long comic novel with greater resolve than she had earlier been able to muster. Certainly, as scholar Thomas McHaney has noted, the novel's Banner, Mississippi, setting seems very similar to Clay County, West Virginia. And after her West Virginia trip, Eudora set out to organize the boxes of manuscript pages she had written about Banner and its citizens. Early in February 1968, she told Frank Lyell that she had "worked with long daily concentration trying to get the boxes of novel pages down to the best number—I xerox them as I go, without bothering about carbons, so the typing goes faster & freer—I still enjoy it—maybe I'm a nut."[17]

As she worked on the long novel, Eudora relaxed by reading totally unrelated materials. She began Tom Stoppard's *Rosencrantz and Guildenstern Are Dead*, left it to reread Shakespeare's *Hamlet*, and then returned with more informed interest to Stoppard's play. And she took great pleasure when the Maxwells sent her *The Sweet Flypaper of Life*, a book of Ray DaCarava's photographs with text by Langston Hughes, who had died the previous spring. Eudora told Bill that Hughes "was an early discovery of mine in the local library, then I lost track of him, and now he is gone, and I was feeling I'd lost him. It's odd, but in 1936 I too made a book of pictures and captions almost the same thing, only of course not urban, and I was able in those days to get pictures that were unposed or even unaware. It was one way I tried (unsuccessfully) to get something published in the hope of getting someone interested in my stories."[18]

Though her work and reading were sources of pleasure for Eudora, a bit of unpleasant tension temporarily distracted her. Lehman Engel had devoted much time to composing a score for a ballet presentation of Eudora's children's story *The Shoe Bird*. Now the Jackson Ballet Guild found itself in financial straits and proposed to decrease the size of the orchestra and to limit paid rehearsal time. Lehman was furious, and Eudora to some extent caught in the middle. Diarmuid attempted to mediate the disagreement. The experienced agent was very sympathetic with Lehman's "point that he doesn't wish to lend his efforts to something which would be reviewed by New York papers and if done in a half-hearted way might not only tarnish his reputation but perhaps put the kiss of failure on the ballet itself for future use. So I think it's right that he insist that as far as possible an attempt must be made for a good production—on the other hand if this is made possible then I think I must try to see that Lehman will reconsider his present stand that he wouldn't go down to Jackson under any circumstances—and I must try to change his mind on this provided his legitimate demands are met. So if you can be good enough to let me know what goes on then I can see what may be done."[19] But not even Diarmuid Russell's skills could resolve this dispute, and Engel did not conduct the orchestra for the one performance permitted the Ballet Guild. Eudora's diplomatic skills, on the other hand, were more effective—she maintained close ties to Ballet Guild chairman Herman Hines, and her friendship with Lehman was as strong as ever.

Family life was free from such difficulties. In December her niece Mary Alice had made her Jackson debut. Though Eudora was uninterested in this social ritual, she was interested in her niece. She told Bill Maxwell that in 1956 Mary Alice was "the one you gave your fortune to out of the fortune cookie—well, here it is. She is both beautiful and good."[20] And for niece Elizabeth, there was the college graduation gift of a new car, the popular Mustang, a present that pleased aunt as much as it did niece. Not so pleasing was Allen Tate's first directive as President of the National Institute of Arts and Letters; his request that all members wear the rosette of the institute struck Eudora as perfectly ridiculous.

April and June 1968 were months of national tragedy, but

strangely there seem to be no extant letters in which Eudora discussed the April assassination of Martin Luther King, the riots that racked the country afterward, or the June assassination of Robert F. Kennedy. Eudora's response to the murders of Medgar Evers and of John F. Kennedy, her hatred of violence, her distress over the war in Viet Nam, and her actions in support of civil rights all indicate the horror that she must have felt in the face of twin assassinations. And her novel in progress was affected by these events. There Uncle Nathan confesses that years earlier he had killed Herman Dearman and allowed a "sawmill nigger" to be convicted and executed in his place. As an act of atonement, Nathan has cut off his hand. Eudora had not specified the source of Nathan's guilt in the early versions of the novel; she did in the draft upon which she was working in 1968. Nathan's sense of guilt and need for atonement reflect the guilt Eudora saw plaguing the nation and the heartfelt repentance she felt was needed. In a 1972 interview, she called this brief episode "a very telling and essential incident in *Losing Battles*."[21]

In May, Eudora took a break from her work on the novel and enjoyed a stint at Vassar, a weekend with the Russells in Katonah, the National Institute meeting (presumably sans rosette), and reunions with many old friends. In Manhattan she was impressed by Zoe Caldwell's performance in *The Prime of Miss Jean Brodie* and relished a rock musical version of *Twelfth Night*. At Vassar she was pleased to receive in the mail an inscribed copy of Reynolds Price's new novel, *Love and Work*. And on her way home, she stopped in Washington to attend Katherine Anne Porter's seventy-eighth birthday party. But by month's end, Eudora was back at her typewriter.

At the end of July the novel seemed to be nearing completion. Eudora, ever in ardent quest of character names, wrote to ask Reynolds, "Is it still all right if I use Ears for a name? I remember you said I could, but it's been so long I thought maybe that sweet permission had run out." Reynolds responded promptly, "Yes, Ears is yours, by all means—take it away, Ears Broadwee! The news that you're hard at work, with an end in sight, is more than adequate recompense." As September drew to a close, the end seemed a sort of mirage, temptingly in view but elusive. On her way to a meeting at Yaddo, Eudora wrote Bill and Emmy Maxwell, "I am within sight of end of novel at last—dog tired, so that I was writing it in my sleep as well as while at type-writer, & when I had to buy a new refrigerator the other day I wrote that into the novel that night in my dreams—I'm sure you know the non-stop feeling." But at the end of November, Eudora was still not finished. She had decided on a title—*Losing Battles*—and had sent the manuscript to a typist, but more revisions lay ahead. As she told Mary Lou, "Sometimes I wonder if it is taking me so long and making me so reluctant to finish because it's the very last thing that ties me to the old days—my family were all alive when I began it."[22] Though Eudora planned to deliver the manuscript to Diarmuid before year's end, she did not. Impatient for a Welty novel, Harcourt's chief executive, William Jovanovich, encouraged Eudora to allow publication of *The Optimist's Daughter* as a book before the house brought out *Losing Battles*. Eudora demurred, leaving the matter in Diarmuid's hands. Diarmuid felt that Jovanovich, in attempting to bypass him, had placed the financial concerns of Harcourt before the welfare of his author, and as a result both author and agent surely returned to thoughts of changing publishers.

Early in 1969 Eudora began to receive increased critical attention. Two book-length studies of her fiction had been published (one in 1962, another in 1965), and scholarly articles that dealt with her work had appeared in disparate journals. But in 1969 *Shenandoah* planned an entire issue devoted to Eudora Welty. Diarmuid set out to write a requested piece about Eudora's early struggle for publication. "I've been digging into old records and old letters," he told her, "—dear me what a long association it has been. It was May 31, 1940 when you first wrote saying 'be

[my] agent' and what a long happy time it has been for me and I look with amazement at the old cards and how many people and places turned your work down—and what they said. You remark that at Breadloaf the opinion was unanimous that nobody would want POWERHOUSE and that STORY was always writing 'This is almost it, but not quite.'" By 1969 such rejection notices were a thing of the past for Eudora, thanks in good part to Diarmuid's efforts. But with his typical modesty, Diarmuid refused to make himself central to the shift in Eudora's fortunes. "I am not going to say anything about myself—I don't think agents are important, just convenient, and no more than that," he wrote her.[23]

In addition to requesting Diarmuid's essay, *Shenandoah* also asked that Nash Burger write a personal reminiscence about Eudora's Jackson background and that Reynolds submit something of his choosing. After obtaining the *New Yorker* galleys of "The Optimist's Daughter"—it was finally on schedule for publication—Reynolds decided to focus on this story. He wrote to Eudora, telling her of the story's powerful effect upon him, "I read it all in a stretch, yesterday afternoon," he reported, "with a kind of sustained, rising excitement that I've never felt before. It feels at once the strongest, richest thing you've ever done—the strangest, most painful and (strangest of all) most comic. That— at first reading—is what awed me most: that you've welded the parallel visions and pitches of your earlier work into this single unassailable voice, stating *facts* (one fact—'it is all like this'). I can guess what it cost you. But you've made this grand thing, and it stands already with nothing but the Russians. I couldn't be prouder!"[24] For Reynolds, Eudora's achievement equaled that of Turgenev, Chekhov, and Tolstoy.

Reynolds's response to "The Optimist's Daughter" was tremendously exciting for Eudora; and equally exciting was finally completing *Losing Battles.* The mirage had become an oasis. Using participants in a Depression-era family reunion as her narrators, Eudora had managed to tell the story of Jack Jordan Renfro, who escapes from prison one day before his scheduled release so that he may be present for a family reunion and who, without any plan to do so, also returns in time for the funeral of Miss Julia Mortimer, the elderly school teacher with whom generations of local students have been at war. The anticipation of his homecoming prompts Jack's family members to relate the hilarious circumstances leading to his incarceration, and the death of Miss Julia prompts them to tell stories of her "losing battles" against ignorance. The many episodes, which Eudora had written over the past fifteen years, she had now stitched together into a cohesive whole. On May 14, in New York, Eudora wrote to Mary Lou, "I've turned it in! This sounds as if I had had my novel apprehended and put behind bars, but I finished it and brought it up, Diarmuid has just read it and likes it, warm words—and I just had to tell you, because you know how this makes me feel. In a way I'm like Bert Lahr in the opening line of Foxy, after they get the bear trap off his foot—he howls and says—'I miss it!'—I'll get used to doing without it, I guess—and I do so much want you to read it & hear what you say— It's a very old-fashioned piece of work in some ways—subject, form, organization, and 'message'—I hope it's more down to the basic, although I can imagine how some critics would ignore it or scorn it—I'm not 'with it.'"[25]

These apprehensions proved somewhat prophetic; a Harcourt Brace editor was less than enthusiastic about the book so long in progress, calling for extensive cuts and substantial editing. As Eudora later reported to Mary Lou, "'To start with,' said the editor to whom I first talked, 'we would eliminate the cast of characters at the beginning—so many characters would put most readers off—and eliminate the dating of it in the thirties, just leave it unspecified, along with the setting.' 'Since it is too long, of course, we suggest that you go page by page and cut out many of the images. We find that you sometimes use as many as five on a page. And there are ways to combine several characters into one.'

This stunned me, for though I was prepared for them not to like it and would have accepted exactly that, I wasn't prepared for them to instruct me how to get it down to their requirements—it was so much worse than disliking it or hating it would have been."[26] Eudora and Diarmuid discussed the Harcourt response, and then in a letter to William Jovanovich, Diarmuid informed Harcourt that Eudora would seek another publisher:

> I had lunch with Eudora to-day to talk over your letter and for her to tell me about her lunch with Dan Wickenden. I'm afraid we both came to the conclusion there is no enthusiasm shown by Harcourt for the new novel, nothing save demands for changes, and that the only thing to do is have the ms. returned to me.
>
> I am sorry about this, as is Eudora, for we are both reluctant about change. Still it is manifest this new work leads to no liking on the part of Harcourt and Eudora would not wish to be published, or to deal with, people whose attitude is unsympathetic.
>
> I wish I did not have to write this parting letter but it's probably better so. It's clear the novel has no great appeal for your firm and it should be obvious that Eudora, a greatly distinguished writer, is not going to have her work edited in the manner you describe. It has to be her work, liked or disliked as may happen, but run as written.

Jovanovich sought to save the situation, writing directly to Eudora and enclosing a copy of Diarmuid's letter to him. Eudora's response was terse and to the point. "I don't see how you could really disbelieve," she wrote, "that I didn't want to 'collaborate' with anybody in cutting or changing my novel, and didn't want my new long story 'The Optimist's Daughter' given its book publication as one of a collection of old stories." And she took particular offense in Jovanovich's suggestion that Diarmuid had acted without her knowledge. "Diarmuid Russell does not need my testimonial to his integrity, and I did not need the xerox of his letter to you. He and I had talked over your letter to him, and I read him my letter to you and he then wrote and showed me his letter to you before either was sent you. Both were direct expressions of what I thought about your suggestions."[27] A Harcourt author since 1943, Eudora would be one no longer. Her passion for her work, her love and trust of Diarmuid—these were the overwhelming forces for change.

Eudora and Diarmuid now discussed the future and the process by which they would select a new publishing house. They wanted, as Eudora told Elizabeth Spencer, "a smaller, more discerning house where there was an editor I knew, liked, & respected, and Diarmuid & I together had selected 3 to read the novel & make an offer." Editors at Random House, Atheneum, and Farrar, Straus each read *Losing Battles,* and all were enthusiastic about it—two of them told Diarmuid that "the novel is a masterpiece and one of the great novels written in this country." The choice between them was then Eudora's: "I decided (it was hard when all were so nice, yet I think he's who I'd most wanted all the time) on Albert Erskine at Random—whom I'd of course known since *Southern Review* days. I was not 'up for grabs,' though when word got out I was leaving H-B I was approached as if I were, here & there." By the end of July the new contract was being prepared. According to Michael Kreyling, "the advance, royalties over the advance, the author's share of paperback rights, and a belated sale to the Book-of-the-Month Club" brought Eudora the very handsome sum of almost a hundred thousand dollars.[28]

Early in October Eudora returned to New York so that she and Albert Erskine could edit *Losing Battles.* She spent a week in residence with the Erskines, and the two old friends examined the 750-page manuscript line by line. To Mary Lou, another valued editor, Eudora described the process. "Albert and I worked 6 days, morning till evening, getting all the little facts consistent—geographical, chronological, spelling and type-face and page numbers and map (I enclose one I did, xerox)—he is easy and careful to work with, and it's awfully nice that he likes the book in the first place—we could both get hilarious at times on the job." Off the job, Eudora also enjoyed being with the Erskines. Marisa Erskine prepared sumptuous meals, the couple took Eudora to meet their distinguished neighbors (including composer Richard Rodgers), and one evening the Erskines hosted an "old *Southern Review* reunion—Warrens, Brookses, & John Palmer . . . I had a lovely time."[29] Participating in an informal *Southern Review* reunion, hearing or perhaps telling stories surrounding that journal, was especially appropriate as Eudora completed her work on *Losing Battles,* for it is a book about a reunion and about the power of storytelling. In an essay closely based on the unsigned one that she had published in the *Times Literary Supplement* in 1954 and that would itself be published in the November/December issue of the *Delta Review,* Eudora identified reunion stories as central to southern life and to any individual's battle against time. In the South, she wrote,

> stories could be watched in the happening—lifelong and generation-long stories watched and participated in, first by one member of the family and then without a break by another, allowing the continuous and never-ending recital to be passed along in full course and to grow. The event and the memory and the comprehension of it and taking a role in it were scarcely marked off from the other in the glow of hearing it again, telling it anew, anticipating, knowing the whole thing by heart—and all right here where it happened. A family story is a family possession, not for a moment to be forgotten, not a bit to be dropped or left out—just added to. No good story ever became *diminished.*[30]

Eudora's more than thirty-year-old personal and professional ties to Erskine, Brooks, and Warren were powerful sources of continuity in her life. Even more so were her family stories, stories she had heard her mother tell, stories she had in turn told to her nieces and was now sharing with readers at large: Episodes from the life of her mother and grandparents are translated into the "continuous and never-ending recital" of the Beecham/Renfro clan in *Losing Battles*. And the memory of Eudora's brothers, too, lives on in the novel—it is dedicated to Edward Jefferson Welty and Walter Andrews Welty. The confluence of "the old and the young, the past and the present, the living and the dead" was embodied by *Losing Battles*.

In Jackson exciting news awaited Eudora. Her niece Elizabeth was engaged to be married in January. The doting aunt was pleased for Liz, though the prospect of change prompted a slight sense of apprehension. As Eudora told William Maxwell, "She's 26, has known plenty of boys and has her own apartment (with some other girls) and a job, so I think she knows what she is doing, I trust her judgment—but it's that anxious feeling, of course, that I have. Fred has a small printing business here—prints county newspapers from all over, etc. and I think that's a good sort of thing." Eudora had long loved to read news of rural Mississippi; now she was to have a nephew-in-law whose occupation was to make that possible. Moreover, the ongoing, growing, developing nature of family life symbolized by the coming marriage of her niece was one of the defenses against time that Eudora had made so central to *Losing Battles*. Eudora herself had no children, the members of her immediate family had all died, but through her nieces she knew the family would continue. She shared the faith in love and renewal that Jack Renfro voices at the end of the novel. As Jack looks at the grave of his grandparents, he tells his wife, Gloria, "There's Mama and all of 'em's mother and dad going by . . . Yet when you think back on the reunion and count how many him and her managed to leave behind! Like something had whispered to 'em 'Quick!' and they were smart enough to take heed."[31]

In November Eudora read from her work to members of the

National Institute and American Academy. To Bill Maxwell, now president of the organization, she wrote to say how meaningful the experience had been for her. "Seeing so many old friends and old acquaintances, and having the feeling of reading to many people of understanding and sympathy was its own reward and it was the first chance I'd ever had, I believe, to do something for the Institute, on my own." The institute itself provided a wider sort of family to Eudora. The community of writers, the connection of one writing generation to the next, was itself a defense against time. Shortly after this meeting, Eudora arranged a more private celebration of the writing family to which she belonged. She invited Elizabeth Bowen and Reynolds Price to join her for a New Year's Eve celebration with her Jackson friends. Elizabeth, now seventy years old and spending a year at Princeton, was ten years Eudora's senior, a sort of older sister to admire and emulate. Reynolds was twenty-four years her junior, a sort of son who had excelled in the very career Eudora had earlier chosen. Now she brought her writing family together with her old Jackson friends. Afterward she wrote to thank Price. "It was the first New Year's Eve party I'd had in years, and it was great joy. I was specially pleased you were there at the same time Elizabeth was— it was a wonderful event for me altogether." Elizabeth and Reynolds were similarly moved by the gathering. Elizabeth wrote, "Oh your house: I do miss it, and see everything in it so distinctly. I loved my room that you gave me, and hated leaving it in a mess. But most of all, I miss you. One consolation will be reading your novel when you can send it. Eudora, I *know* it is going to break most effulgently on the world, in April. I can't help hoping you'll come to Europe . . . All my love, & my most loving *Thank-you*." Reynolds echoed these sentiments: "You were valiant, in everything, *through* everything (from crab to roast-beef); and I really can't think of a better time I've had. Driving to the airport in the sun, we mentioned voyages with the wrong sort; and I thought, somewhere over Alabama, that our three days had been like a voyage—the three of us confined there on Pinehurst by the weather and waited on, as Elizabeth said, by eagles (not really; by *you*). But definitely a voyage with the *right* sort. Again, warmest thanks for thinking of it and *doing* it all. I especially enjoyed our talks in the kitchen, me sitting and you washing-up or making pecan-paste in the blender; and I'll hope for more of those in February."[32]

In January Elizabeth Welty married Frederick Thompson, with Eudora in proud attendance. Then Eudora was off for a brief visit to New York for a meeting of the Grants Committee of the National Institute and American Academy. She spent two nights with Dolly, one with the Russells, and dined once at the Maxwells, where English writer Elizabeth Taylor was also a guest. Eudora had met Taylor in 1951 in England and was pleased by this reunion. Shortly thereafter, Eudora was back in Jackson to greet a steady parade of welcome visitors. Reynolds arrived in mid-February for a speaking engagement at Belhaven College. Again he stayed with Eudora. One day Charlotte and Eudora drove him to Vicksburg, where they toured the Civil War military park, stood on the bluffs above the Mississippi River, and had a "hilarious" time doing so. Not long after Reynolds's visit, Elizabeth Spencer was in town and spent a good bit of time with Eudora. Then Robert Penn Warren came to participate in the Belhaven College lecture series. He and Eudora had drinks and dinner both nights of his stay in Jackson, and Eudora found his reading from and discussion of the long poem "Audubon" to be "beautiful." Years later Warren would write to thank Eudora for "A Still Moment," her story about the great nineteenth-century ornithologist and artist. Warren admired the story itself and acknowledged that it had prompted his study of Audubon and subsequently his poem.[33]

A month before publication day for *Losing Battles*, Walter Clemons of the *New York Times Book Review* arrived in Jackson to interview Eudora. The interview would share front page with

James Boatright's review of the novel on April 12. Nash Burger of the *Book Review* had vouched for Clemons with Eudora and for Eudora with Clemons, and the two immediately hit it off. In his article, Clemons reported that Eudora had collected him at the airport, prepared lunch for him, and described another luncheon meeting, one in 1954 with E. M. Forster. "The luckiest thing happened," the Mississippi writer told her interviewer. "Our waiter was drunk, he came lurching on like a Shakespearean clown, and that put us both at ease and made our meeting so easy." Clemons's meeting with Eudora was also easy. "How," concluded Clemons, "could a meeting with Eudora Welty be difficult?"[34]

This happy interview notwithstanding, Eudora was apprehensive about reviews of *Losing Battles*, fearing that the novel would be damned as apolitical and old-fashioned given the intemperate political climate of the present. That climate certainly disturbed Eudora. Duncan Aswell, his mother suspected, had been denied tenure at Wellesley for his outspoken opposition to the Viet Nam War. Eudora was outraged, but she was equally outraged by the refusal of war protestors to accept the possibility of views contrary to their own. To Mary Lou, she had described "the self-righteous, platitudinous, ignorant, loud, loud mouths" she had encountered late in 1969 in New York. Then she added, "I felt when I was up last month that I was in a nation of Holy Rollers, all foaming at the mouth and shouting 'Are You Saved?' And everybody wants a victim—as a Southerner I should know—and now Duncan's been made into some kind of victim, and it makes me sick." *Losing Battles*, set in 1930s Mississippi, did not deal with the politics of 1970, nor did it denigrate either the traditional rural life or the progressive liberalism that it showed in conflict. No reviewers found *Losing Battles* to be political in any sense, but the novel was far from damned. It was embraced. Reynolds had already alerted Eudora to James Boatright's admiration of the novel, and his review for the *New York Times* lauded *Losing Battles*, as did reviews in *Life* and *Newsweek*. The *Atlantic* and the *Saturday Review of Books* printed positive, if more reserved, assessments. Eudora was particularly pleased that Jonathan Yardley in the *New Republic* separated her "from the Southern Lady Shangri-La deda." Reynolds himself was overwhelmed by the book, and before he reviewed it for the *Washington Post*, he wrote to tell Eudora of his first reaction:

I finished *Losing Battles* late last night, after five days underground in it. I'd normally want to sit back now for a while and test what I felt, feel; but I want now to say what I feel (sure as I've ever been that the feeling cannot diminish, can only grow)—that it's a very great book, that increasingly I read it with a kind of panic of suffocation in its beauty, richness, strangeness (but suffocated in pleasure, excitement, gratitude—a response to plenitude of a sort I've previously only felt in reply to music). The surest test of that, for me (of its bigness, durability), is that all through I kept asking, "What's it about? What's it about?" (wanting of course some simple take-home gift to hold in the hand, portable, clean, harmless). But then as the day ends (the reunion day) and Jack and Gloria embrace and Vaughn wanders alone and then is invited into bed by Granny and Lady May speaks, my neat hopes surrendered: it's about life, merely—all imaginable life—in the way that very little else in fiction is—the Russians again. You may remember my saying that *The Optimist's Daughter* called to mind Turgenev's *First Love*, Tolstoy's *The Cossacks*, Chekhov's *The Steppe* (though more piercing, more diving than they). *Losing Battles* clearly stands with bigger things—late Shakespeare, *War and Peace*—not in some silly writer's all-time sweepstakes, couturier's hyperbole, but in the impression it leaves of fullness, comprehension, of all things seen (laughed and raged upon, but finally *held*).

Not only seen but *shown*. You could stop now and know
you'd done the biggest thing yet (that's no news; you know
it) but don't. Sail on—as Gloria told the children, her first
day of school.[35]

Friends in Jackson had supported Eudora through all stages
of the novel's composition. Jane Petty and Patti Black had worried about Eudora's habit of jotting down notes as she made the
long drive back and forth to see her mother in Yazoo City. Charlotte, Ann and Bill Morrison, and Eudora had speculated about
names for characters as they had drinks in the afternoon. And
now on publication day, also Eudora's birthday, these friends
threw a party, which Eudora described to Mary Lou. "One friend
had made herself a dress out of Robin Hood flour sacks (reasonably exact facsimile, done in paints on a sheet), we had fried
chicken, corn on the cob, etc., home-made cake & home-made ice
cream turned in the freezer, and the centerpiece on the table was
made of azalea blooms and *fresh watermelon slices*— There was a
birthday cake with candles, & presents of preserves, jelly, etc.,
plus a beautiful gold pin with my initials, the date, & 'Losing
Battles' on it—wasn't that grand? I didn't mean to leave out the
bourbon, there was lots of that too."[36] Yes, many glasses of bourbon were lifted in honor of *Losing Battles,* and well they should
have been. It was not only the Welty work longest in the making,
but was also her most sustained performance and her most ambitious undertaking. She had written, to use Reynolds's words,
about "all imaginable life."

Her birthday and publication party passed, Eudora prepared
for her annual May visit to New York, but without her usual ea-
gerness. The violent war protests and the violent war, including
the bombing of Cambodia, Eudora found profoundly unsettling.
As she told Mary Lou, "Both extremes of this mess seem . . . as
faithless & opportunistic and dangerous as McCarthy (the old
one), it seems many times to me—and use his tactics with a cer-

tain *glorification* in doing so— The idea that the end justifies the means is contemptible no matter how noble the ideals."[37] To Eudora, New York seemed the center of conflict on the home front. There radical war protestors had accidentally caused one explosion and had purposely bombed another building; the fact that these two incidents had by chance or mischance occurred near Dolly Wells's apartment and office made the city a rather frightening destination.

A week later, however, violence struck not in New York, but in Jackson. Jackson State College students opposed to the war in Viet Nam, horrified by the killings in Ohio of Kent State University protesters, angry about racial discrimination in Jackson, took to the streets. Highway patrol and city police responded, and their gunfire took two lives on campus. A tense situation ensued. New Stage Theatre, an integrated organization from its start, was then preparing for a performance of *The Ponder Heart* with an integrated cast, and many feared that this performance might provoke further white violence. A black Jackson State student who was a cast member of *The Ponder Heart* nevertheless resolved to continue in her role, living with a white cast member for the run of the show. Frank Hains, the director of the play, devoted a regular *Jackson Daily News* column to his deep sorrow about the recent loss of life, to his admiration of Jackson State student Florence Roach for continuing in her role, and to his faith in the play's relevance to this Jackson crisis. *The Ponder Heart*, he wrote, though it seems far removed from questions of "race relations or problems of the day," actually has "everything to do with them." This play, he continued, is "all about love and Uncle Daniel's unbounded love for all the world—and it's a reflection of the great love of humanity which lifts its author, Eudora Welty, into a state of grace few achieve on this earth." Though the saintly image Hains invoked must have seemed strange to her, Eudora appreciated both Hains's call for understanding and his own understanding of her work. She later sent Reynolds a copy of

Hains's column, suggesting that New Stage's defiance of the current climate of distrust and violence was "an expression of what so very many people in the South feel and no one ever knows it elsewhere, the knowledge and intimacy and understanding between the races that is still, amazingly still, undestroyed."[38] Eudora was perhaps feeling a bit defensive about negative portraits of her home state, but certainly the New Stage commitment to integrated casts and audiences combined with a black cast member's commitment to the theater bore testimony to the existence of multicultural enclaves in the South, enclaves which, however isolated, represented a hope for broader interracial understanding.

Late in May, Eudora went to New York for the National Institute Ceremonial and to visit friends. She had a far better time in the city than she had expected. Her stay in New York coincided with Charlotte Capers's attendance at a national archives meeting, and the two Jacksonians had a good time together in Manhattan. Eudora spent one weekend with the Russells at Katonah and another with the Erskines in Westport. Lehman took her to see the hit play *The Effect of Gamma Rays on Man-in-the-Moon Marigolds*, which she found somewhat disappointing despite its many awards. And she managed to do an interview with Linda Kuehl for the *Paris Review.* The ceremonial at the institute was a memorable one—José de Creeft, Martha Graham, Georgia O'Keeffe, and Muriel Spark were all honored. Eudora had known and admired de Creeft from the time she met him in Yaddo in 1941; she had seen Martha Graham's troupe in Jackson in the late 1940s and had since become a friend of hers; she had revered O'Keeffe's paintings from the time in 1944 when she saw her paintings hanging in Stieglitz's studio; and she held Spark's fiction in high regard.

Eudora spent the summer of 1970 at home, reading, relaxing, having dinner and drinks with friends, free from the pressures of uncompleted work. *Losing Battles* was selling well—forty-five thousand copies by early July, Diarmuid reported, enough to put it on

the bestseller list. And Eudora had won the Edward MacDowell
Medal. On August 23 she was in Peterborough, New Hampshire,
for the presentation of this annual award given "to an American
creative artist whose body of work has made an outstanding contribution to the national culture." In attendance was Mississippi
writer Cid Ricketts Sumner, known to Eudora as Bertha. She
journeyed over from Duxbury, Massachusetts, where she was now
living. Before the year's end, Bertha would be murdered and her
grandson charged with the crime. Eudora would speculate that
the young man had been robbing his grandmother's house, been
surprised by her, and "panicked." He "certainly didn't come there
to kill her, he loved her," Eudora told Frank Lyell.[39] And when
Bertha's granddaughter enrolled at Millsaps College, Eudora
reached out to her. But these events lay in the future and did not
darken the happy day of the MacDowell presentation.

From New Hampshire, Eudora traveled on to Portland,
Maine, where her godson, Will Russell, collected her and drove
her to Seal Harbor. There the Russells spent their vacations, and
there the David Rockefellers had a magnificent summer home.
Eudora's time in Maine proved enchanting, as she reported to
Frank Lyell. "Cadillac Mountain, the Rockefeller Gardens, the
lobster picnic in front of the house by the water—there was Diarmuid, Rosie, Pammy, Willy, his wife Maudie, his 2 little children Daisy and Liam, & me in the house. David & Peggy's house
next door, and the marvelous garden on up behind—at its height,
& made (by the old lady, Abby) especially to be a setting for her
collection of Chinese & other oriental sculpture—really a place
to meditate—utterly peaceful, quiet, fragrant, filled with color &
then with big trees & shade." The Rockefellers' thirtieth anniversary party was the highlight of this visit. The party took place
on an island

about 4½ hours out by sailboat, a small piece of pure
wilderness they hacked a clearing in & built a sort of lodge.

Then planted tuberous begonias & all around, & Peggy herself made the lawn furniture—simple & good. No sign of man anywhere else in sight, just water & other islands. The party was of course outside— Everyone came in their own sailboat, I learned—about 60 people—& the boats were rafted together out in a cove & a dinghy brought them in to the party & took them back later to sleep aboard. Of course we had no sailboat but were taken out, D., Rosie, & I, in a motor launch & slept aboard that. Fires burned on the shore, fish stew & cornbread were cooking, & we had some luscious dessert I remember—& of course drink—and David had a guitarist & folk singer flown in from the Bohemian Club in San Francisco to entertain, but I thought he was a little corny, and the music I really did enjoy was the intermission when Dickie Rockefeller, their 21 year old & a boy & girl he brought with him, played & sang *their* songs. Freezing cold by midnight, but worth it. And riding on the boat away out of sight of the fires & lights, when it was nothing but wild, Maine night—the stars! Just *blazing*, & thousands of them, in that pure clear air.[40]

September in Jackson was less exciting and more taxing. Educational Television of Mississippi was filming a New Stage production called "A Season of Dreams," a tribute to Eudora that consisted of scenes from a number of her stories. Eudora served as a consultant for the entire filming process, a process she found a drain on her time and energy, however complimentary it was. She did, nevertheless, manage to finish reading *Permanent Errors*, the story collection Reynolds had dedicated to her. On publication day, she wired Reynolds: "PERMANENT ERRORS MY PERMANENT JOY. I COULD HARDLY BE LESS PROUD AND HAPPY THAN YOU ON PUBLICATION DAY. CONGRATULATIONS AND LOVE AND GRATITUDE." He received the telegram moments before teaching his first class of the year at Duke, and the following day wrote to tell

Eudora that "the only thing in the book immune to error is the dedication."[41]

Eudora's next book project was photographic in nature. She turned her attention to the photographs she had taken in the thirties and early forties, selecting images she felt were the most powerful or representative, pondering ways of organizing them for book publication. In December she took the photographs with her to New York. Work, however, was not her first priority there. In the days after arriving, Eudora managed to see Ralph Richardson in *Home*, to spend an evening with the Maxwells, and to attend the National Institute meeting, including the evening of tributes to members who had died in the past year. Due to a taxi strike, she and Allen Tate shared a limousine for the trip from midtown Manhattan to the West 139th Street institution; the strike delayed the arrival of W. H. Auden, who was to deliver the tribute to Louise Bogan—Auden arrived on foot, having walked through the snowstorm in house shoes. The next day, Eudora was with the Erskines in Westport, where she and Albert worked on the photograph book. That task completed, she relaxed with the Russells in Katonah, then left for Christmas at home.

In Jackson an important piece of mail awaited Eudora, one that would change the course of her life. Kenneth Millar, whose pen name was Ross Macdonald, had responded to a fan letter in which Eudora praised his fiction. For Eudora, Millar had selected a card bearing the "Prayer, Mountaintop Way":

> Restore all for me in beauty,
> Make beautiful all that is before me,
> Make beautiful all that is behind me,
> Make beautiful my words.
> It is done in beauty.
> It is done in beauty.
> It is done in beauty.
> It is done in beauty.

Beside this prayer, Millar wrote: "Dear Miss Welty, I haven't been able to answer your beautiful letter, which filled me with joy and made me cry, but will let the quotation opposite allude to it." Then he added, "You didn't know my daughter Linda but you have suffered grievous losses in recent years and would perhaps wish to be told that Linda died last month, very suddenly, aged 31, of a stroke in her sleep. She left her husband Joe and their son James, seven, who have become central in our lives. But I am willing now to grow old and die, after a while. Our very best wishes, seasonal and personal." Eudora immediately responded, linking the "Prayer, Mountaintop Way" to Millar's words in a way he might not have consciously intended: "Do you remember what Forster said in *The Longest Journey*—'They'll come saying "Bear up—trust to time." No, no, they're wrong. Mind it. In God's name, mind such a thing!' It's good that the little boy is seven—that gives him a good strong memory, and the memory will be the right one, unharmed— It will be like the Prayer, Mountaintop Way somehow, maybe— You saw this— I hope it will be for you." For Eudora, memory had become the "treasure most dearly regarded."[42] Her understanding of the past and her living, evolving memory of it were powerful sources of consolation. She sensed and hoped that memory would also be restorative for Ken Millar. In this epistolary exchange of intimacies between strangers, to paraphrase Henry Green, an evolving relationship began. Though they had not yet met, Millar and Eudora had moved beyond admiration and gratitude to reveal heartfelt emotions to each other. Given such an exchange, they could not remain strangers; through sustained correspondence and periodic encounters they would establish a close and confiding bond that enriched both their lives.

In the meantime the *New York Times Book Review* wanted Eudora to review Millar's new novel, *The Underground Man*, and she was delighted to do so. In January 1971, when the review was complete, she sent it to Millar, asking if he objected to any of

her observations. He immediately wired his response: "MY DEEP-
EST THANKS FOR YOUR MAGNIFICENT REVIEW BLUSHING I FIND NOTH-
ING I WISH CHANGED." That very day, Millar posted a more
expansive reaction to the review: "As you know a writer and his
work don't really exist until they've been read. You have given me
the fullest and most explicit reading I've ever had, or that I ever
expected. I exist as a writer more completely thanks to you."[43] He
was also moved by Eudora's comments about the young boy in
his novel and told her the boy was closely based on his grandson.

To Eudora's concern for Millar and his grandson, who had
lost daughter and mother respectively, was soon added her concern for Mary Lou. In great distress, Mary Lou informed Eudora that her son, Duncan, who in September had begun a
teaching job at Haverford, had suffered a nervous breakdown during the Christmas vacation and now had disappeared. Mary Lou
speculated that Duncan might have taken a freighter to Europe,
but she was tormented by uncertainty. Eudora sought to comfort
her friend. "He can't let you stand it any longer than he can
help—and the freighter does sound plausible—I'm feeling
for you & with you whatever it is, as you know. Call me up
anytime."[44]

On March 10, having given her next week's itinerary to Mary
Lou, Eudora left for Washington, DC, where she spent a night
with John and Catherine Prince before busing to Norfolk and a
speaking engagement. As she told Mary Lou, "dear cousins" of
Chestina's had invited her to read for the Virginia Poetry Society.
"Since I don't ever do readings any more I accepted on the condition they didn't publicise [sic] it and didn't pay me—but I couldn't
say no, with my cousins there." Reynolds Price had agreed to
meet Eudora in Norfolk and to drive her back to Jackson, and
they spent a pleasant first leg on the road to Asheville. Then it
was on across Georgia and half of Alabama, but as Reynolds recalled, "Our planned second night in Birmingham proved problematic—all motels were filled. Forcing our exhausted selves on

to the next opportunity, Tuscaloosa, we found a similar dire situation—no rooms." Reynolds set about phoning every source of housing he could discover in the yellow pages and at last learned that there was a three-bedroom trailer for rent adjacent to a motel called the Bel Air. Could you sleep in a trailer, Reynolds asked Eudora. "I could sleep in a gunny sack in the back of a pick-up truck," Eudora replied. So the Bel Air it was. In an address to the American Academy, Reynolds recalled the evening there: "Late in the night . . . and in vast relief to have found a harbor, I poured us stiff drinks of bourbon and offered a toast to our entirely plastic surroundings—plastic beds, plastic walls and floor, plastic furniture. Eudora was seated on the long plastic couch. As she raised her plastic glass to join me in the toast, she said in her usual dead-level quiet voice, 'If this sofa could talk, we'd have to *burn* it.'"[45]

Reynolds spent a week in Jackson with Eudora, and there she introduced him to a Ross Macdonald novel and asked him to read her foreword for the forthcoming photograph book. Reynolds enjoyed both activities and later wrote Eudora about them.

One of the greatest pleasures for me was to sit there quietly reading *The Chill* while you put together the photographs in the next room; I only hope I didn't slow or clog the process. I wanted to talk with you some more about my reactions to your foreword—not that they were crucial or involved any real changes. But maybe I did say, after all, what I meant— that what was already on paper was superb but that I wanted a little more: a little more sense of the girl you were when you began to take them and a little more explicit pointing- up of some of the *news* which the photographs bring (of the *fullness* of the life they show, the brave happiness in the face of trouble, the getting-on-with-life). Maybe all that is only to ask you to be someone other than yourself, to over-

state. But then a book of pictures isn't a story; and I wonder
if these pictures—in the world now—wouldn't make their
statement to more (and more needful) people with the help
of a few more words from you? That's all.

Eudora took Reynolds's reservations to heart; by the end of the
month she had mailed him a revised foreword to which he offered this response: "I think you've strengthened the foreword
beautifully, entirely in your own way. I've read it through three
times since it arrived on Saturday, and I really do think it's one of
your very best essays—statements—so true as to be unanswer-
able, *unquestionable.* And with the photographs, it drives a hard
wedge into a lot of careless and criminal nonsense. Not that the
nonsense will know the wedge is there, but you've done it and it
won't ever need doing again in this way (no one else that I know
of could have done it). Thank you for letting me see the revision." The way Eudora had conveyed "a Deep South racial complexity" and had declared her desire "to part a curtain, that
invisible shadow that falls between people, the veil of indiffer-
ence to each other's presence, each other's wonder, each other's
human plight" won Reynolds's enduring admiration.[46]

In April, Eudora accepted another *New York Times Book Review*
assignment: Arthur Mizener's biography of Ford Madox Ford.
When she had met Mizener in England in 1954, she had found
him arrogant and his views of literature alien. His new book also
failed to satisfy her. To Ken Millar she wrote of her dislike, and
Millar immediately responded. His old friend Richard Lid had
written a scholarly study of Ford, and Millar recommended the
book to Eudora. The book reinforced her high opinion of Ford
and buttressed her objections to Mizener. She told Millar, "The
more I read of Mizener the more insensitive and wrong-headed
he appeared to me." She then went on to note that "there was a
personal complication. Ford, who helped all those other young
writers, helped me too—he tried to interest a publisher in my

stories. He couldn't—it must have been one of the last things he
busied himself on, it was the last year of his life—but I have
about four little notes he sent to me, out of the clear sky, in that
handwriting Mizener found so hard to read." For Millar, this
story of Ford confirmed a bond he had sensed between Eudora
and himself: "When I got your letter today, something went
through me like a vibration of light, as if I had had a responsive
echo from a distant star. As if a half-imagined relationship to the
great past had come real in my life before my life ended. It came
down to me through you, through your defense of the tradition
of humane letters, but I think above all through the fact that Ford
had done you a service, or tried to, and you had done me one—
that *personal* connection with history is what tripped the gong—
and I had done Ford a service, though not a personal one, by
helping Dick [Lid] with his book. I sometimes think, don't
you, that these musical and moral recurrences are almost the
whole meaning of life and art, or at least the grounds of their
meaning."[47]

This sense of a shared and personal connection to literary
history also struck Eudora forcefully. "I feel glad that I ever happened along when I did and the way I did, to be part of it—glad
for my own sake, my own beliefs too—I believe it was bound to
happen for you somehow— But thank you for telling me this,
which has made me a part of some perfect occurrence— Nothing ever gave me that feeling before, and I doubt if anything ever
will again. And it takes recognizing all around— The perfection
of such a thing, itself, I believe in, just as if it were familiar, not
rare, and the extraordinary is really the least surprising by the nature of it— I believe in it, and I trust it too and treasure it above
everything, the personal, the personal, the personal! I put my faith
in it not only as the source, the ground of meaning in art, in life,
but as the meaning itself."[48] Following this exchange, the two
writers knew that they were friends as well as colleagues, and in
their next letters they would address each other by first names

and abandon the formal "Mr." and "Miss" that had previously characterized their correspondence.

In April, Eudora's niece Elizabeth gave birth to a baby girl, Leslie Allison Thompson. Eudora wrote to tell friends around the country about her first great-niece, and to Bill Maxwell she reported that "Gruss an Aachen opened its first flower on the morning that my niece Elizabeth had her first baby— I took her the flower, and she told me she pressed it and put it in a book. I thought you'd like to know it was a real and wonderful as well as lovely Gruss."[49] A rosebush Bill had given to Eudora provided Eudora's first gift in honor of Liz's daughter, a symbol of the connections between her family and friends. Eudora felt similarly linked to the families of her friends. Before leaving for an extended trip to New York, Denison, and Sewanee, Eudora apprized Mary Lou of the coming travel schedule and volunteered to help pay for private investigators who might be able to locate Duncan. Mary Lou responded with thanks but was aghast at the prospect of taxing Eudora's resources. Mary Lou assured Eudora that James Merrill had already offered funds and noted that Merrill was far more able to part with them.

On May 15, Eudora checked into the Algonquin Hotel. A day later, unbeknownst to either of them, Ken Millar checked in as well. Fortunately, common friends told Ken that Eudora was also at the Algonquin, and on May 17 he waited in the hotel lobby, hoping to catch sight of her. In an interview with Millar's biographer, Tom Nolan, Eudora recalled the meeting. "As I came into the lobby and got my key and went for the elevator . . . a man came across the lobby and said, 'Miss Welty? Kenneth Millar.' I just couldn't believe it! . . . Isn't this just like a Ken story? You know how he used to say, there's no such thing as coincidence? So I just saddown [*sic*] in the lobby and threw my coat down and we started talking, and we just didn't stop for I don't know how long." After talking into the evening, they discovered that their rooms were adjacent—perhaps another non-coincidence. The next day Ken took Eudora to a cocktail party given by Alfred and Helen Knopf and then out to dinner. Afterward they walked about Manhattan and into the theater district. Eudora was Ken's guide. "I took him down Broadway, . . . and he just came to life. He said 'Now *this* is where it *is*.' The side streets had been sort of genteel, but here everything was going on. There was a cop chasing a man, shooting; the fire department was whizzing by. In fact I was kind of scared, with people running through the streets. But Ken just said, 'Oh, my.' He knew what all that was about. I said, 'I've never seen a man chase another man in public with a gun before.' He said that was an old story to him. And all this time he was so calm, and rather formal and everything; but he was all eyes and ears." Sometime after midnight, they returned to the Algonquin, and the next day Ken departed New York for his native Canada. He, however, left a note for Eudora. "Dear Eudora: I never thought I'd hate to leave New York, but I do. I feel an unaccustomed sorrow not to be able to continue our friendship *vive voce* and in the flesh, but these are the chances of life. But there is a deeper and happier chance which will keep us friends till death, don't you believe? And we'll walk and talk again. Till then, Ken. Meanwhile there are letters." Before the week was out, Ken had sent a postcard to Eudora at the Algonquin; the card featured a picture of the Kissing Bridge in West Montrose, Ontario, and on it Ken wrote that he was "treasuring fond memories of New York and you."[50]

Eudora doubtless regretted that her time with Ken had been so short, but her days in New York continued to be filled with propitious events. She was delighted to find Irish writer Mary Lavin in residence at the Algonquin, though it took a week before the two old friends discovered each other. And a particular pleasure for Eudora was seeing Reynolds receive an award from the National Institute and then introducing him to the Maxwells. To Bill and Emmy she later wrote, "Thank you for coming out with me so Reynolds could get to meet you and you could see him—he's almost like my child in a way. It meant a lot to him."[51]

Weighing heavily on Eudora's mind throughout her New York stay were the danger faced by Duncan Aswell and the torment endured by Mary Lou. Even her meetings with Ken had been punctuated by descriptions of Mary Lou's unhappy situation. Eudora would also discuss it with the Maxwells, the Russells, and Reynolds. At the institute's ceremonial, Eudora was seated next to Truman Capote, who had already sought to help Mary Lou by providing FBI contacts and who told Eudora of his continuing concern.

On May 29, Reynolds put Eudora on a bus for Denison University—she still hated to fly, and this bus was touted as especially luxurious. It proved to be amusingly so—red carpets whenever passengers stepped on or off the bus, a stewardess, reserved seats, and refreshments. From Denison, with one honorary degree, Eudora took a more conventional bus ride to Sewanee for a second. The degree-granting itself proved lavish. Eudora was happy to see Allen Tate, but was nonplussed when she "had to kneel and put my hands in the taffeta lap of a bishop, and he and the vice-chancellor spoke over my head in Latin—I asked Charlotte if they'd made me a nun and she said she thought they'd made me a saint. My real worry was that I couldn't get up afterwards, but I made it." When Eudora recounted her Sewanee experience in a letter to Ken Millar, he wryly responded that "a tendency to saintliness is your only fault." In his next letter, Millar worried that this comment might have offended Eudora, and he assured her that "I adore your virtue."[52] Given Ken's code of fidelity to his wife, it seems unlikely that in New York six weeks ago he had asked Eudora to be less than saintly. And given Eudora's open, honest, and cautious nature, it seems equally unlikely that she would have precipitously begun a secret liaison. It seems quite likely, however, that Eudora and Ken's relationship had taken on a romantic, though not a sexual, dimension.

Back at home, Eudora soon received good news from Mary

Lou. Duncan had phoned a friend and asked that friend to phone his mother. He was not ready for direct contact but wanted to relieve her mind and promised eventually to be in touch. Mary Lou expressed gratitude to Eudora for support during the four-month ordeal. "What a resource, what a comfort you have been and are to me. I can never thank you, but I bless you and love you always." Eudora's response was immediate: "Oh the blessed news! I'm so glad, so thankful and what a wonderful *kind* of news, so significant of hope and a future. You were wonderful to let me know— so like you to think of your friends at once, and to write the *good* to us at once, after keeping the bad for so long to yourself."[53]

During the summer Eudora turned back to "The Optimist's Daughter." Diarmuid and Bill Maxwell had urged her to publish it as a book, and she now hoped to improve upon the original story. As she told Mary Lou, "I see things it needs, if I can just fix them right." Her musings upon the power of memory, the sort of musing she had sent to Ken in December, were closely related to what she wanted to fix. And Ken's thoughts about one of Eudora's early stories pointed to another key concept. He had found himself mesmerized by "A Still Moment," Eudora's account of an imagined meeting between John James Audubon, Lorenzo Dow, and John Murrell, of their awe when a snowy heron lands in front of them and seems to hold time suspended, and of their dispersal when Audubon shoots the bird, but Ken wanted Eudora to develop more fully the import of the characters' shared experience. "Your 'convergence' story," he wrote, "keeps haunting me. It baffles me, as I said, perhaps because though the three men are influenced and go their ways, essentially the death of the heron leads only out of this world, in two senses. I don't believe the story of the herein convergence that you wrote to me about has been written yet. Could you write it from now about this? Or are the involutions of your thought beyond the reach of such a simple suggestion?"[54] Convergence in the here and now, the convergence of lives through marriage, the convergence of times through memory, these are the concepts that Eudora would ultimately work into the plot of "The Optimist's Daughter," but not until the suggestion of Ken's letter had worked upon her imagination for some months.

Eudora wrote throughout the summer, expanding "The Optimist's Daughter" into a novella, establishing more fully the character of Laurel's husband, who had been almost absent in the story. The summer of work was punctuated by happy interruptions—dinners with friends, hopeful letters about Duncan from Mary Lou, the continuing exchange of letters with Ken, the Apollo 15 landing of Americans on the moon and the opportunity to see the landing on television. To Ken, Eudora wrote ecstatically of this stunning scientific accomplishment. "Did you hear them just say on the Moon: 'Boy, that view is unearthly!'? Isn't that wonderful? After all these centuries, the word turns into the plain literal."[55]

In mid-August, Eudora informed Reynolds about her work on "The Optimist's Daughter." She had not completed the revisions but hoped that she might send them to him for a response once she had. The process of revision, she told Reynolds, had become quite far-reaching. "I'd started reading it over for the first time since it came out in the magazine, and before I knew it I was taking it to pieces and putting it back together again, much like Jack Renfro with an old car. I hope it's simply more what it was meant to be." Reynolds looked forward to seeing these transformations, and he also asked for Eudora's advice on the Hemingway article he was writing. Eudora, typically generous in her comments about writers, was not so sympathetic in her remarks about Hemingway. She told Reynolds, "I don't respond to him as you do—I'm not against, I'm rather for, but it is the 'for' of respect and admiration for the marvelous technique rather than the emotional 'for'—there's no warmth there for me, and nothing at all personal. So far as my feeling for the man himself goes, he has consistently put me off (as in 'A Moveable Feast') by his coarseness of treatment of his friends and lovers and those who were good to him—a shabby sort of friend, he seemed to me, and not minding it, using people. I suppose I may let this color my feeling about his so steady use of 'real' and 'true' in his work." For Eudora, Hemingway's betrayal of friendship was a powerful barrier; the honoring of friendship was for her a moral absolute. When Ken Millar had written to apologize for devoting so many of his letters to descriptions of friends, Eudora's reply had been quick and sure. "I do like reading what you tell me about your friends, and do get a feeling of what they have meant and do mean. My own play the same large part in my life. I take it as a compliment when you write of them to me. I love and need and learn from my friends, they are the continuity of my life."[56]

On October 5, Mary Lou arrived in Jackson for a visit. She was on her way to see Duncan in Atlanta and was nervous about the coming reunion. Eudora embraced the opportunity to support her old friend, and Mary Lou was grateful. After four days in Jackson, then a good meeting with her son, Mary Lou sent thanks to Eudora. "It did me *worlds* of good," Mary Lou wrote, "to see you, to be with you. Did the visit exhaust you? When I think of the preparations you made (that refrigerator stocked to bursting!), the trays you carried, the meals you prepared—and then that heavenly long ride through your beautiful countryside. I know you strained your precious strength to the limit. But you made me feel you wanted to, the essence of friendship." While in Jackson, Mary Lou had read the revised "Optimist's Daughter" and learned that Eudora had also put a copy in the mail to Albert Erskine at Random House. By October 10, Eudora had Erskine's evaluation, which tallied with Mary Lou's. "Albert called me Sat. night and said he thought the story had lost in concentration but gained in fullness & depth (I *think* in those words) and that he thought the gain was unquestionably greater than the loss. He also said what you said—he wished he hadn't already read the earlier version. May make some small changes when I've thought things over. You were so generous and it meant such a lot to me when you read it—I'm grateful."[57]

The manuscript passed from Erskine to Reynolds Price, who gave it a detailed reading and worried that it was not as powerful as the original story. He wrote Eudora a long letter expressing his reservations. Confessing that his love for the first version might have made him reluctant to accept the changes, still he felt Eudora had weakened her text in two important ways: "What the additions make me see now is a gentler story, one in which the movement from almost intolerable pain into fierce joy becomes, now, a movement from pain into a more familiar kind of consolation. And that change is worked in two ways, I think—through the greater hardening and coarsening of Fay in this version, and the addition of most of the material on Laurel's marriage."[58]

For her part, Eudora was reluctant to accept Reynolds's evaluation, and the tone of her October 27 reply to Reynolds betrayed exasperation. "Many thanks for your quick & long & (I'm sure) careful response about the ms—but as yet I'm not going to read it through because I'm in the midst of reading the story through for the first time ever, since I finished it—I want to have the mind as objective & clear as possible. I'm making notes, cuts, etc. and am now only on p. 101. Made the deadline of turning it in to Albert only by a hair, & he said I might correct even on galleys. It was too close to me till day before yesterday to attempt it. I did gather quickly from your beginning you didn't like the new version, but you really are mistaken in saying they are two different stories. But I'll reply to your letter properly when work's over & I've read the letter."[59]

Over the next two weeks, Eudora revised again. Whether prompted by Reynolds or by her own rereading, she ultimately did change the sections Reynolds had found most problematic. On November 6, Eudora wrote to Mary Lou, saying she had "cut 144 lines out of the version you read. Mostly the part about the husband that seemed now too thin, keeping just the pertinent parts. Trouble was, I'd written that part both fuller and down to very little at all, and I think I'd hurt the story by some attempt to have it both ways."[60] The novella that would win the Pulitzer Prize had reached its final form.

Of course, the novella was not the sole focus of Eudora's life during October and November 1971. She was pleased by the marriage of her niece Mary Alice to Donald White, she was planning her fall trip to New York, she was sending copies of her recently published and well-reviewed photograph book, *One Time, One Place*, to friends around the country, and she was consulting a doctor about arthritis in her hands. The arthritis had begun to trouble her in April and had bothered her throughout the early fall. As she told Bill Maxwell, "My right hand has played a trick on me—the bone dr. said it's worn out, isn't that the craziest thing? Two bones scrape together and make my hand feel broken. However, it's not as bad as I first thought—shots of cortisone help, and I've got onto typing with part hunt-and-peck. Meantime, whether I could do it or not, I did revise *The Optimist's Daughter* and get it in on time for spring book."[61]

In New York, the hand seemed better, and Eudora had many good times and saw friends at an almost frantic pace. Frank Hains was in New York sending theater stories back to the *Jackson Daily News*, and he took Eudora to see *Follies.* At the National Institute dinner, Eudora had the good fortune to see Janet Flanner, alias "Genet" of the *New Yorker*, who "looked much the same to me," Eudora told Mary Lou, "as she did at Mary's and Aristide's Reveillon in Meudon 20+ years ago."[62] Eudora spent November 18 in Katonah for Diarmuid's birthday party, dined with Reynolds the next day, devoted the weekend to work on *The Optimist's Daughter* with Albert at the Erskines', and dined with Bill and Emmy the following Monday. In the course of these engagements, she also managed to see Jean Stafford, Peter Taylor, Nash Burger, Nona Balakian, Walter Clemons, Lehman Engel, Joan and Olivia Kahn, Cleanth and Tinkum Brooks, Howard Moss, and Eileen McGrath. Then it was on to Washington, DC, where she joined John and Catherine Prince for Thanksgiving dinner, before heading home.

In Jackson, Eudora began to catch up on her correspondence. Perhaps forgetting that she had already thanked Margaret Millar, Ken's wife, for sending *The Birds and the Beasts Were There*, she wrote to thank her again. Margaret Millar was herself an award-winning mystery writer, but this work of nonfiction was Ken's favorite of her books. Both Margaret and Ken were avid bird-watchers, and *The Birds and the Beasts Were There* described their avocation. Eudora's second note of thanks to Margaret included a special gift—a story about a bird lover from Mississippi, Miss Fannye Cook, who had been head of the state wildlife museum and who had roomed with the Weltys. Miss Cook's surroundings, Eudora told Margaret,

> were *nothing* to her except for bird connotations. One Sunday morning she invited me to go with her to see some birds, and we went "across the river"—the bootleg part of Jackson, (Miss. being dry)—then a nice, tree-hung river, now a drainage ditch, the Pearl—and pulled up in the yard of a night-spot called, appropriately, First Place, and parked. Miss Cook said we were likely to see both red-eyed and white-eyed vireos. Well, sitting on the bench outside First Place were what I would call red-eyed and white-eyed vireos, left-overs from Saturday night, but Miss Cook didn't waste any time noticing them. She was stopped once by a road-block on the Natchez Trace where they were chasing an outlaw in the swamps, just where she was headed, and she told the fellows she had no intention of interfering with either them or the outlaws, and she would thank them not to interfere with her, she was looking for some birds, and she went right on. (She called all men "fellows.") I used to find baby hawks in the bathtub and once an owl in the

refrigerator. I helped her hunt for a baby bat in the window
curtains, and found it. She asked for a little warm milk, fed
the baby bat from a medicine dropper, and then I saw a baby
bat belch.

Whether Margaret Millar was amused by Eudora's letter we can
only surmise. She never replied to it and may well have resented
it. Surely she was jealous of her husband's devotion to Eudora
and the regular, lengthy letters they exchanged. Ken was evidently
embarrassed by his wife's failure to answer Eudora's letter, and he
answered for her. He explained that Margaret would write eventually, but that she was "a much worse correspondent" than he;
then for the first and only time in a letter, he suggested to Eudora
some dissatisfaction with his marriage. Margaret's book, he explained, described their best years together, and though the present was fine, he felt that they had "lost a good deal of our
unconscious glee."[63]
    When Eudora next wrote to Ken, she made no mention of
this revelation. Instead, she simply asked him to assure Margaret
that no reply was expected and then changed the subject. The fiction of Flannery O'Connor impressed her, and she wondered
what Ken thought. "We must talk about Flannery O'Connor
some time. Isn't she wonderful? She can strike like a bolt of lightning. Thunder? I would settle for 'Revelation' too, I think, though
there are those rivals—for the boldness and power and hair-raising wonder of the revelation itself that she makes happen before
our eyes. I loved it on another count for the way she made Mrs.
Turpin not only outraged that this assault . . . had been made
upon her, but disappointed and hurt that it *hadn't* been made on
those others, the white-trash, right there and ready-made for it,
deserving it." Eudora ultimately returned to a personal note,
comparing Ken to her brother Walter and adding that Walter's
wife and two daughters were now her family, "the little girls now
grown, one just had her first baby this year, the other just got

married last month. I know I am blessed, Ken. We'll all have Christmas dinner together—and I hope you will have a lovely one too—your little grandson must be a wonderful age for Christmas. And I hope never the crutches again. Fine swims in the ocean every day instead, and a new bird every day—or an old bird friend."[64] At age sixty-two, Eudora clearly recognized that home ties—the demands of family, the need for family, the bonds of family—precluded a romance for her and for Ken, but implicit in her words was a message of love nevertheless. She and Ken had, over the course of their twice-monthly letters to each other and their single meeting, established a powerful relationship. Ken had written or told Eudora about his Canadian background, about his friends Herb Harker and Bob Ford, about his love of bird-watching and fears for the California coastal environment, about his passion for the fiction of F. Scott Fitzgerald and Ford Madox Ford. Eudora had written to Ken about her Mississippi setting, about the death of her brother Walter, about the poetry of William Jay Smith, about her fears for Duncan and Mary Lou Aswell, about her love for the work of Henry Green and Ford Madox Ford. The close ties between Ken and Eudora were and would remain personal, literary, philosophical, and loving, a blessing to each of them even though they were separated by half a continent.

For Eudora, Christmas 1971 included other blessings. John Robinson and his companion, Enzo Rocchigiani, were in Jackson, and Eudora, long since reconciled to the relationship, could enjoy the visit. After years of loss, her family now included two nephews-in-law and a great-niece. In the presence of friends and family, Eudora sensed a continuity with the past that she had earlier felt endangered. A mark of this renewed faith, gained perhaps as she revised *The Optimist's Daughter*, was evident in the Christmas gift she sent some of her closest friends—reproductions of a photograph showing a two- or three-year-old Eudora in the arms of her maternal grandmother. To Mary Lou she explained the gift, sending similar explanations to Bill and Emmy Maxwell, Reynolds, and others: "An itinerant came through long years back & told Mother he could 'permanently preserve' any photograph and she let him carry off this one, the one she most wanted kept & he finally sent it back, after she had despaired of ever seeing it again, stuck forever between 2 sheets of glass—I wanted you to have it because of the story & because of her & me & everything."[65]

For Reynolds, Eudora's Christmas gift had special meaning because it evoked scenes from *The Optimist's Daughter.* His early review of that story had been passionate, and his comments on Eudora's first expansion of the story into a novella had likely helped her shape the finished manuscript. Now he wrote to thank Eudora for the photo and to comment on the texts, old and new. "You know that it's still, for me, so nearly unbearable each time I read it—like a nearly fatal visitation which finally, beautifully, deigns not only to spare but heal. And I think the present version, as it stands on the galleys, is what you knew it was—the strongest yet." So strong did he find the revisions that Reynolds planned to update his essay "The Onlooker Smiling: An Early Reading of 'The Optimist's Daughter,'" and he enlisted Eudora's help: "I haven't yet written my little postscript on the changes—I still have a couple of weeks and would like to phone you during Christmas and discuss one or two questions I have, if you wouldn't mind. Not to ask you to write my essay for me—but out of curiosity about one or two of the new emphases: Fay's new (and beautifully enriching) denial of the existence of her family, for instance. Nobody, I'm sure, is going to doubt that this is the great masterpiece of your shorter work till now—though some readers will be threatened and a little panicked by it (as they should, they should)."[66]

The new year began with word from Ken Millar, telling Eudora how much she had helped him cope with the death of his daughter. On New Year's Day, he wrote, "May I say that your

friendship and understanding both spoken and unspoken lightened the year as nothing else did." Eudora was touched and responded, "I value so much what you told me—if my friendship
helped, I am glad. You were speaking out of the deep kindness
and perception of your own when you told me. 1972 will be a
good year, I hope—everything in it, and evenly so, all the way
through." Beyond responding to Ken's declaration of gratitude,
Eudora told him about *The Optimist's Daughter* and thanked him
for providing a key concept for the novel. The novel, she told
him, "is so close to me that I have held onto it for two years, uncertain about publishing it alone as a book. It's about sad
things—about a few of those things we can't ever change but
must try through fiction to make something with— The question is, did I make it? And without doing hurt to lives I cared
about? I worked & hoped— There is one paragraph in it, Ken,
that never existed in the first version at all, and it wouldn't be
there now if it hadn't been for our writing each other some letters. You will know. It came nearly at the end, where and when it
came to me—came back to me." Ken's discussion of convergence
had found its way into Eudora's novel. Protagonist Laurel Hand
recalls a train journey she and her fiancé had shared; from a high
railroad bridge they had looked down upon the confluence of the
Mississippi and Ohio Rivers and had seen the sun reflected in
the water while above them they had observed birds flying in a V
formation. As she remembers this event, Laurel realizes that the
confluence of the rivers, of sky and water, of the birds' flight
represents the confluence that love brings to individual lives, a
confluence that continues after death. The paragraph might also
have applied to Ken and Eudora's sense that their lives were con-
verging, that their interests, their friends, their pasts, and their
futures were linked. That recognition came to embrace their common regard for Reynolds Price. Ken had written to say he admired Reynolds's book *Permanent Errors* and to ask if Reynolds
were not part of "the Algonquin magic" that had marked their

May 1971 surprise meeting in the famous New York hotel. Eudora replied, "Yes, he *was* part of it—he called up & was reading [your novel] 'The Far Side of the Dollar,' open beside him. I'd timed my trip so as to see him get a prize. And all the time you were headed there to get a prize, and that's how I was there to meet you."[67]

The pattern of confluence in her relationship with Ken was soon matched by others. As president of the National Institute and American Academy, Bill Maxwell wrote to say that Eudora would receive the National Institute's Gold Medal for Fiction. Eudora found "joy and pride" in receiving this award and in hearing the news from Bill, an editor who had meant so much to her career and a friend who had so enriched her life. "*You* know," Eudora told Bill, "this is the most wonderful thing that could happen, just as well as if I were the one that was president . . . and you were the one that was being given the Gold Medal, come next May 17th."[68]

In February Eudora traveled to San Antonio where an exhibition of Agnes Sims's paintings had been mounted. Eudora enjoyed seeing Mary Lou and Agi again, she took in an Edward Lear show, she visited the Alamo, where she found "the sense of history and real human beings . . . very strong," and she dined at a house with Monets in the dining room and "a little line of beautiful Mary Cassatts going up the staircase wall, that you couldn't really look at, for being too close and for having to go on upstairs—the only way you could have seen them any less well would be by sliding down the bannisters."[69] A successful February journey over, Eudora traveled to New York and Washington, DC, in March. Ostensibly in New York for a committee meeting at the National Institute, Eudora stayed several extra days, seeing the Rodin drawings at the Guggenheim, attending the Picasso and Matisse shows at the Museum of Modern Art, visiting with friends, and being bothered by arthritis in her hands. Then she left for DC and a happy reunion with Katherine Anne Porter, who two months later would actually present Eudora with the Gold Medal for Fiction. Eudora wrote Bill and Emmy a description of her evening with Katherine Anne.

> Katherine Anne was in exuberant spirits, never stopped talking for 6 hours (there are some fairy tales going at the age of 84, too) and we sat in her dining room on gold chairs and ate catfish with gold knives and forks and drank champagne and we also had fresh asparagus which we ate in our fingers, holding them dripping in melted butter (like grapes in orgies), then we moved back to her study, with the gold mirror—she's goldleafing everything, at the present—and with all her books and pictures, and talked some more. Her bed also is golden. She's happy carrying out wishes—who could wish anybody anything more?—and very gallant about her life which actually is that of an old lady with a broken hip behind her and cataract operations, and whatever heart condition necessitates digitalis every day . . . She already has the outfit ready to give me the gold medal in—white Italian silk pants suit. Oh, I hope she makes it. She talked a good deal about death and dying, and is changing her will at the moment—I wonder how many times.[70]

From the gold-leafed home of Katherine Anne, Eudora headed back to Jackson and soon was involved in jury duty. Having fulfilled this civic responsibility, she was then free to enjoy spring in Mississippi and even see her home state in a new way. As she reported to Ken Millar, "Yesterday my young niece & her new husband took me up the river (the Pearl) in their boat. This inland town now has a reservoir & you can get away up the feeding river, where you could never go before— It's all serpentine & brown—Big cypresses & forest oaks—untracked sandbars—red-winged blackbirds, woodpeckers, & an owl & probably countless other birds you or Margaret would have seen but I didn't— I love the sign that I guess is in all marinas? 'Leave No Wake'—you can't imagine how odd a boat is in Jackson."[71] The Pearl River, so often a setting in Eudora's fiction, was more accessible than it had ever been. So, too, was the Mississippi River country. While Martha Duffy of *Time* magazine was in Mississippi to interview Eudora, the two women traveled to Port Gibson and then to another spot Eudora had long ago photographed and made part of her story "At the Landing." To Frank Lyell, Eudora wrote that she and Duffy had driven "to Grand Gulf & out a gravel road to a clearing on the bank of the Mississippi that looks like the very spot where we found that fisherman's camp so long ago—and what did we see but the *Delta Queen*, the steamboat—it happened at that very time to go by! headed north up river. It was galvanizing."[72]

Though Eudora felt that she needed to work on "a story that had me licked for a while" (perhaps "Nicotiana"), she never brought it to completion. A limited edition of *The Optimist's Daughter* was, however, complete and in print on March 23. Eudora mailed inscribed copies of the novella to her close friends, and they responded ecstatically. Ken found the novella "a marvellous piece of writing, with so much in so little space—whole families of characters, whole ranges of experience. It seemed to me that towards the end particularly, you got into quite new territory, even for you. The whole business of the mother and the 'other place,' under the threat of that trapped bird, and then the *confluence* opening out, filled me with joy. I felt as though I had been allowed somehow to leave a fingerprint in your enduring clay. That's too static an image. To see you flying like an untrapped bird through a town of symbols and a community of voices. You really do fly in this one." Mary Lou agreed, and she found a world of meaning in the novella's dedication. "I think I know why it's For C.A.W. For her daughter, too, and her mother. For all of us who have to learn how to live."[73] To Mary Lou, the pattern of Chestina Andrews Welty's life and death had found a worthy tribute and become powerfully symbolic.

In May Eudora was again in New York—this time to see Bill
Smith receive the Loines Poetry Award from the National Institute, to see Walker Percy inducted into membership there, and to
herself be elevated into the American Academy and receive the
Gold Medal for Fiction. Iris Murdoch delivered the annual address, and Katherine Anne, duly dressed in the white silk pant-
suit, presented Eudora with the Gold Medal. In the audience were
Reynolds, Bill and Emmy, Walter Clemons, Howard Moss, and
Lehman Engel. Eudora's acceptance remarks were gracious and
heartfelt. "Not many symbols are given us into our hands in real
life. If they come, we feel their weight. This medal carries the
weight of the Institute, of the art of fiction, of the benevolence
of those here today whom I love and revere, and who have taught
me. Katherine Anne, it's symbolic too that yours is the hand from
which this medal comes. You are its right and proper bestower, as
all the world knows. And you are at the same time my dear & generous friend of almost 40 years. I treasure this medal for every
good reason, symbolic and human, and for always."[74]

Reynolds had been worried about Eudora's increasing problems with arthritis in her hand and had convinced her to come
home with him. He thought perhaps specialists at the Duke University Hospital could help with the arthritis. From Durham,
Reynolds then drove Eudora "'through the country' & through
the cicadas, to Washington & Lee," where James Boatright, the
editor of *Shenandoah*, which had devoted an issue to Eudora, was their
host and where Eudora received an honorary doctorate.[75] Then
Eudora and Reynolds went on to Charlottesville and a party given
by Peter and Eleanor Taylor.

Having enjoyed her time with Reynolds and other friends,
Eudora now had the leisure to enjoy reading reviews of *The Opti-
mist's Daughter*. They had begun to appear in May, would continue
to appear into the summer, and were filled with praise. Alan
Pryce-Jones, writing for the *Times Literary Supplement*, found
Eudora's work as compelling as that of Proust while Walter

Clemons found her "merciless tenderness toward her people" to be Chekhovian. Paul Theroux called the novel "a superb affirmation of life and of healing." Howard Moss labeled it "the best book Eudora Welty has ever written," and Jonathan Yardley asserted that the novel brought readers "a richer understanding of life."[76]

During the summer of 1972, Diarmuid wrote to tell Eudora of changes at Russell and Volkening: Henry was now retiring, his health and interest in work on the wane; Timothy Seldes, a young man experienced in the publishing business, was joining the firm. Diarmuid was pleased that *The Optimist's Daughter* was selling well, but he himself seemed to be thinking ahead to retirement. Eudora herself had no such intentions, but she did not complete any new fiction during the summer or fall. The bulk of her writing may well have taken the form of letters. Certainly, her correspondence with Ken Millar continued to flourish. Letters from Ken reported on his reading of her early stories and his fascination with the novels of Henry Green. Green, Eudora then told Ken, shared a faith in mysterious connections that predestined friends to be friends. "Back in the 50's in London, I met him at a party—well, it was a party for his book that was out that day— *Nothing*—so that would be the year. Then I saw him after that a little and liked him so much— I'm telling you so I can explain how I know one more thing connects up: he loved more than anything, he told me at length, coming upon the person, the family conversation, the story, that is a link—that fills in the long connection with the past that's missing (personal past always, I believe I'm right). He wanted really to touch the person who'd touched the person who'd touched—who'd spoken & listened & knew. 'The only thing is,' he said, 'when you *find* that person, they don't remember the right thing, do they ever? The very thing you've waited panting to ask.'"[77] By contrast, Eudora, it seemed to Ken, had always remembered the right thing, and now Ken hoped that his new book *Sleeping Beauty* would pay tribute to the confluence of their lives. "I'd like to dedicate the book to you," he wrote her. "Would you object? We haven't known each other terribly long, but we know each other well, do we not, and if I have to wait to a later book my writing may fall off in the meantime. I hope it hasn't already. Being in touch with you this past year or so has been an inspiration to me. I hope you will take the risk of letting me put your name on the dedication page." When this request arrived in Jackson, Eudora was away. She had been appointed to the National Council on the Arts and had gone to Washington for a meeting and then to New York to see friends. As soon as she returned and found Ken's letter, she wired her happy acceptance and followed the wire with a letter of her own. "I wish I could tell you how much I value and cherish the dedication of your novel— You would have to already know, and I trust my feeling that you do. And I am so anxious to get a look at the book."[78]

The delight Ken's proposed dedication brought Eudora was countered in early October by dark, dark news. Diarmuid was to undergo an operation for lung cancer; Henry Volkening's wife had already died of this disease, Henry was near death from it, and now Diarmuid had been added to the list of sufferers. When Mary Lou learned of Diarmuid's situation, she immediately wrote Eudora. "Rosie [Diarmuid's wife] wouldn't understand this, but my first thought was of you. No one ever *appreciated* Diarmuid in every sense of the word, as much as you. No one appreciated you more than Diarmuid. I know what your long association has meant to you both, and I know it can never be replaced. Of course I do feel for Rosie and the children and for Diarmuid's many other friends and clients, but my heart aches for you. Would it be possible for you to see him, or would it be too hard on you both? One doesn't *know.* Your comfort must be the knowledge that your work was the crown of his career, just as it was the crown of mine. We both lived, in a way, through our writers, through the privilege of presenting them to their public.

I know how Diarmuid felt about that because we discussed it. You made me happy and proud and fulfilled." Mary Lou's letter provided great comfort to Eudora. As she told Mary Lou, "Nobody here even *knows* Diarmuid, except for Dolly, a little. I carry the letter in my purse as I roam around in my car escaping the painters in my house."[79]

Within a month, Eudora's mind was somewhat eased. Diarmuid wrote to say he had come through the surgery, would have cobalt treatments, and expected to be back at work in January. Eudora was now able to respond fully to the manuscript Ken had sent her. She wrote to praise *Sleeping Beauty*.

> As I've thought about your book, it's seemed to me that the whole of it might rest on the one image—Archer's wish that he could throw the gun and send it cartwheeling over all their heads and over the edge of the world (forgive me if I don't say it right). And just as surely as the oil surges in on the tide and up onto the beaches, and just as surely as all the fires in the story are brought into relationship, the filth and the fires of all war are implied and say Vietnam, though you leave it unspoken. The intensity of the scenes has a moral source, and a moral strength. (This was what made me think of Goya.) I think all this time you've been taking a popular form and making it something entirely of your own, and in *Sleeping Beauty* to the highest degree yet. It's not new country for you because it's been there all the time (or so it seems to me) but is more openly revealed around us— and explored for us as Archer detects. I may be speaking clumsily of something that's been so delicately achieved. "The dangerous lair of the past" is there, as in the other novels, but this time the danger shows itself in its high blaze and its long shadows as never before, and you've given it its full implications. The title as looked back on after the story ends is responsive to all that too, and I think from the first

we know it to be as you meant it, an abstract noun. —I was delighted to be told that one of the threads of your book led back to Henry Green—there are many threads in it leading back to things I cherish but most of all I cherish the book itself. My gratitude and pride in the dedication are things I think of every day.[80]

In December, Eudora made a memorable television appearance. William F. Buckley Jr. wanted Eudora and Walker Percy to appear on his Public Broadcasting Service program *Firing Line.* Jeanne Luckett, a producer at Mississippi Educational Television, had contacted Eudora with the invitation. Eudora was reluctant to accept; she didn't feel confident in discussing politics. After checking with the Buckley producers, Luckett assured Eudora that the program would deal with southern literature, not southern demagogues. Eudora then agreed to be interviewed, as did Percy, and the program was taped on December 12. The very sort of discussion Eudora had not wanted soon transpired. Buckley broke his producers' word to Luckett and turned the program to political issues. "What one wonders, and what a lot of people have asked themselves, is how in the atmosphere, let's say, of the First World War or of the twenties, could a sensitive Southern writer have lived here?" Buckley asked. Percy rejected the concept that moral disapproval of southern racism involved leaving one's southern home and suggested that writing could be enriched by one's staying at home. "Faulkner was always dealing with the complexities of human relations between white people and black people and between black people and black people. So he could create a character like Dilsey, in my mind one of the great characters of American literature, in spite of the fact that there was a great deal of social injustice in Mississippi at the time." For himself, Percy stated, "the best thing to do is stay where you are," not leave the South in protest. Eudora agreed. "I was here all that time and I felt the unreality of late-night telephone calls from strangers asking me, 'How can you stay in that place? Why don't you use all of your novelistic powers and so on and write some things against this?' And really, I assumed that my whole life I had been writing about injustice, if I wanted to, and love and hate and so on. They are human characteristics which I had certainly been able to see long before it was pointed out to me by what happened in those years. I was always against it, but what I was writing about was human beings. I put it in the form of fiction; that is, in dramatic form. I was writing about it from the inside, not from the outside, and when it was stated from the outside it seemed to me so thin and artificial." Later in the program, Gordon Weaver, one of the panelists who joined Buckley in the interview, asked if writers felt they had to steer away from political controversy in order to remain in the South and avoid ostracism. Eudora's answer was clear. "I didn't feel any avoidance in anything I was doing and I might get just as mad as I could be about things at home and then I would go up to New York and the things that people would say there made me madder and I would feel defensive because there was a great void of ignorance between the two parts of the country. I think a writer, all his life, is aware of all sorts of threatening and menacing things going on. This time was very open and dramatized and the whole world knew about it, but there are always the human threats of people, of injustice and all these other things that go on through your whole life, and you can't run away from that. That's the life of which you are writing . . ." For Eudora and Walker, home was a powerful force and staying home a powerful statement; at home, they were what David Chappell has called "inside agitators," seeking to eliminate racial prejudice by refusing to countenance it in their private lives and by exposing it in their fiction.[81] And for Eudora, the sense of continuity with her past, the garden her mother had created, the house her father had built, friendships that had begun in childhood, friends who had established New Stage Theatre and refused to capitulate to racist threats—these were as much a part of the Mississippi landscape as the Jim Crow social order. Though she had indeed briefly contemplated moving away during the sixties, she had not. The home tie was far too strong, and through her fiction and through her moral example, she had helped to improve the racial climate of her home state.

After the program, Eudora felt dissatisfied with her responses; Walker, she believed, had been more articulate. But there was nothing to be done now. Christmas lay just ahead; shopping for friends far and near and preparing for seasonal festivities occupied her attention. Then suddenly both family celebrations and William F. Buckley Jr. seemed insignificant in light of the United States' massive Christmas bombing of Hanoi. Ken Millar wrote to Eudora on Christmas Day, "I believe the country has gone through a moral crisis and failed to recognize it. We proceed cheerfully on our desperate way like a man with a bad doctor and a fatal illness." But then he added, "I believe we'll turn back from our own violence, and see what we have done is something that we can never do again. What other meaning could this present violence have?" On January 12, Eudora replied that she had "the same feeling about the awful things we were perpetrating upon that midnight clear. I hope and hope, while knowing there's damage that can never be undone and something lost we can never get back. Just hope for the end of the killing—I think it has to come soon, don't you? And I believe it will happen as you said in your letter, that we will see what we have done as something we can never do again." Two weeks later, the war came to an end. Eudora rejoiced in the fact, though she saw a tragic irony in the procedures for stopping hostilities. To Mary Lou, she wrote, "The signing's signed—however little it does for the past and however much it can do for the future—but the killing will stop in exactly eight hours and fifteen minutes—is there any answer as to why that couldn't have stopped with the moment of the agreement?"[82]

Eudora's own writing of fiction seemed at this time to be on hold. Instead of producing new material, she contemplated collecting her previously published essays and reviews into a book. Ken had suggested this idea to her, and she wrote to him about the hazards of such a project.

> It was sympathetic of you to say not long ago that you thought a book of my essays might be a good thing. It is a problem to me to know just what to do. The pieces were all written as needed for the lecturing and so on I was doing, '50's & 60's, and were the best I could do, and I think are respectable pieces of work—but what puzzles me is whether or not they will mean anything to readers now. To the young, what meaning would a paper on "Place in Fiction" have? That was the subject of the one I worked on the hardest. Nobody really cares about many of the things I feel most passionately about—and I am not for a minute saying that I consider the beliefs dated or the subjects, rather, dated or unimportant. They matter more than ever—to me. Another consideration that stops me is that a book of these pieces might seem to be saying I thought of myself as a critic, with some systematic theory about literature—of course none of that is so. I love books—that's about it. All the pieces were written about what I like, more than a little for my own pleasure. This would probably be my criterion when I chose what to include. Somehow I can't start in—I would risk my neck on a story without this kind of hesitation. I can be professional about stories, that's the reason, I suppose, and as any sort of essay writer I'm an amateur, and feel vulnerable altogether. So I mull it over.

Ken dismissed Eudora's insecurities. He had read "Place in Fiction," "The Reading and Writing of Short Stories," and "Words into Fiction" and felt these pieces deserved a wider audience than they had yet reached.

I think they are beautiful, wonderfully posed on the knife-edge of pure truth. Perhaps what makes you uncertain about them is precisely their most valuable quality: they were written by an artist in your own figurative language, cut from the same piece of imaginative cloth as your stories. They are not written in the language of the schools, into which even most artists tend to shift when they write criticism. And partly for that reason they manage to get and stay closer to the meanings and workings of fiction than almost anything I can remember. You yourself are there in the prose, close up to and involved with the things you love, and I think it would be a mistake to hold these papers back from further publication. They are beautifully clear, succinct and to the point, done with great art; and I loved all your examples. What you do with Faulkner, for instance, is astonishing and will send me back to him now for the dozenth time.

Not having read the bulk of Eudora's nonfiction, Ken conceded that her other essays might be uneven in quality, but he added, "I honestly can't conceive of your ever having written anything in this line that shouldn't be retained for the use of future readers. So though you haven't really asked my overall opinion, sight unseen, I'll give it anyway. I think you should collect your pieces fugitive and otherwise ('I was a fugitive from Eudora Welty') with a foreword saying what you choose about their origins, and turn the book loose into the stream of history."[83] This book would not be published for six more years, but when *The Eye of the Story* was published, Eudora dedicated it to Kenneth Millar.

In February 1973, Eudora attended another National Council on the Arts meeting in Washington and then hurried on to New York. She was anxious to learn firsthand how well Diarmuid was recuperating. The old friends were glad to see each other at long last and had much to discuss. Diarmuid now knew that he was not physically able to continue his career, and he reassured Eudora that Tim Seldes, who was taking over at Russell and Volkening, would be a fine agent for her. Eudora, on the other hand, was not concerned about herself but about Diarmuid's well-being. As she wrote to Mary Lou, "He is as thin as can be, and more frail than I'd been prepared for somehow, but of total matter-of-factness & good spirits, and the same vital spark in the eye—undiminished in every way but this way he can't help." Eudora and Diarmuid talked about her friendship with Ken, and Eudora wrote to tell Ken how highly Diarmuid regarded the work of Ross Macdonald. "He is one of your long time readers, and he is the first person I'm going to make a present of the new book to— He was so delighted to know about the dedication— He asked me about you, saying 'Obviously he knows Yeats and so on' which interested him in you long ago (he is AE's son), and so by now I know a little I could tell him—and none of it surprised him. As a little boy in Dublin it used to be his duty to bring his father a new detective story every day—begged, borrowed, or somehow, and of course D. read them for himself— I think he began with [Scottish mystery writer John] Buchan—your man. He put me onto him too, in time."[84]

Though Eudora had been racked by worries about Diarmuid, she did not know that Elizabeth Bowen was seriously ill. Shortly after returning to Jackson, Eudora learned that Elizabeth had died. Though she and Elizabeth had met repeatedly over the years, they had not maintained their correspondence. Now she was stunned by the bad news. To Ken she confided her grief, and she also told him how much Elizabeth had loved his mysteries.

I have just lost a good friend in the death of Elizabeth Bowen—I loved her, and such was her vitality and zest and tireless absorption in life—*care* for life, hers & others, deeply both—it never occurred to me that I might not be going to see her again—

She was one of your most devoted readers, and I remember years ago, when she first came to my house, her telling me that wherever she went in the U.S. (She was on a long lecture tour) kind hosts put out some cosy English murder in a vicarage for her "when of course what I wanted was Ross Macdonald"—I'm not sure she didn't say "beloved Ross Macdonald"—(Henry Green was always "beloved" to her too.) In the last few years Elizabeth had got to be very good friends with Agatha Christie, by the way, in London, and told me how she'd come to revere her as "an older friend"—which sounded right because you didn't think of Elizabeth as being in any way old too,—though she thought of herself right along, accurately, as being "as old as the century"—we took lots of little excursions in each other's company, in her car in Ireland and in my car in Mississippi . . . I'd been waiting to see her again to tell her that I had come to know you—I wish *she* had! Yet she knew so many things intuitively about writers. I wish she could have read *Sleeping Beauty*.[85]

Clearly, Eudora, in anxiety or in grief, sought solace in communicating with Ken and in establishing connections between Ken and her old friends. And Ken's replies to her comments about Diarmuid and Elizabeth did provide comfort. He recounted his youthful passion for A.E., Diarmuid's father, a writer Eudora herself had discovered as a college student. A.E., Ken told her, had had a powerful influence in Canada and upon him, "perhaps because he was the most assimilable by a provincial society which loved its poets to be bards (though its leading writer was Stephen Leacock), and I started out being a bard myself, a beardless bard." Of Elizabeth Bowen, Ken wrote: "I'm so sorry you lost your friend Elizabeth Bowen. No wonder we grow more thoughtful as we grow older. I loved some of her stories—do you remember her wartime stories? was the title *Ivy Gripped the Steps?*—and think it remarkable that she enjoyed mine. These connections made through you however distantly are important to me. I've spent my life living by and for such connections, tuning in on relayed signals from the far side of the world, a prover of the McLuhan village in a way, but the connections are personal."[86] These personal and ongoing connections, both Eudora and Ken felt, were a stay against time and an unbreakable bond between them.

At the end of February, Reynolds arrived in Jackson. He was on his way to a speaking engagement in Mobile and had arranged to take Eudora with him for the event and then for a leisurely drive along the Gulf Coast before returning to Jackson. With Reynolds's visit completed, Eudora turned her attention to the 1973 Mississippi Arts Festival. Scheduled for the beginning of May, the festival's first two days were devoted to Eudora's work, and the state of Mississippi had declared May 2 Eudora Welty Day. Organizers asked Eudora for a list of out-of-town guests she would like to invite, and invitations for an all-expense-paid visit were mailed coast-to-coast. Eudora took it upon herself to write each of her friends, telling them how much she hoped they could come, but assuring them that they should feel no obligation to do so. Acceptances began to pour in. Reynolds, William Jay and Sonja Smith, Katherine Anne Porter, John and Catherine Prince, Joan and Olivia Kahn, Nona Balakian, Mary Lou Aswell, and Agnes Sims all planned to attend. So, too, did Ken and Margaret Millar. And best of all, so did Diarmuid and Rosie Russell. Eudora wrote to tell Ken her excitement at this news: "Such a wonderful thing also happened in that Diarmuid Russell, who is ailing and frail, has decided *he* is going to come. He and his wife Rose, for all the times I've visited them, have never been here to see me. I'm terribly moved. They will of course be staying with me, and this means I am not asking other guests to stay at the house too—so although I did want you and Margaret to stay here if you could and would, I feel it's better all around just to have it this way, don't you?"[87]

Late in April, Ken wrote to say that Margaret would not be making the trip after all. Her blood pressure had been high, he said, and travel seemed unwise. Whether Margaret's blood pressure or her resentment of Ken's friendship with Eudora prevented the trip is unclear, but Ken came alone. Katherine Anne Porter also found herself at the last minute unable to travel—the news came as a relief to Eudora, who had feared conflict between Katherine Anne and some of the other guests. The guests who did come from afar found themselves embraced by Eudora's Jackson friends, and they enjoyed parties, a production of *The Ponder Heart*, and a reading by Eudora in the course of the week. Reynolds and Ken, who had written to each other during the past two years, were pleased to meet and spent a good bit of time in each other's company. One evening after returning to their motel, they sat together and talked about Eudora and their love of her. "You love Eudora as a friend," Ken told Reynolds. "I love her as a woman."[88] The love implicit in the letters Ken and Eudora had exchanged was for this moment out in the open, but it soon would be subterranean again.

From California, Ken wrote to thank Eudora for his time in Jackson and to praise the reading she had given. The passages she had selected to read on this occasion might well have been chosen with Ken in mind. Though they came from *Losing Battles*, they focused not on loss but on love, particularly the love of Jack Renfro and his wife Gloria, who for two years have been separated because of Jack's prison sentence, who spend the day of Jack's return with his family, and who late at night are at last alone on the pallet that will be their bed. The reading included this memorable description of the young couple by themselves in the dark. "[Gloria] put her mouth quickly on [Jack's], and then she slid in her hand and seized hold of him right at the root. And so she convinced him that there is only one way of depriving the ones you love—taking your living presence away from theirs; that no one alive has ever deserved such punishment, although maybe the dead do; and that no one alive can ever in honor forgive that wrong, which outshines shame, and is not to be forgiven until it has been righted." Eudora might have been telling Ken how much she missed his "living presence." Whatever her intent, he responded ardently to the entire reading and especially to the novel's erotic moment. "I never saw such a completely and spontaneously happy group of people as those (including me)," Ken wrote, "who came to hear you read in the Old State Capitol. Even the governor was happy. I was particularly happy about *what* you read, celebrating dawn and the triumph of old age, mortal love (that was a bold and excellent celebration), and intellect and character." To his friend Julian Symons, Ken had been more direct in discussing the reading. "Eudora boldly read aloud, in that same chamber where secession was first declared, and in the presence of the current governor, a passage from *Losing Battles* celebrating the sexual life." With Eudora, however, Ken was discreet, and he stopped short of proclaiming his love to her. He simply said, "It made me sad to leave you. I hope I'll see you again before too long."[89]

Before she had received this letter, Eudora was on her way to New York via rail, though scheduling difficulties in the coming years would increasingly force her to travel by air. From the train, she wrote to thank Ken for attending the festival. "Before I leave Mississippi, which I am rapidly doing (for a train traveler) I want to tell you how much it meant and means to me that you were here— It was wholly generous and good and kind of you to make the long trip— I was glad to think you knew the happiness your being here would give to me. And you must have seen how much pleasure it was for so many others to get to meet you. Diarmuid in particular. He said to me he took most to you of anybody—'a man with a great deal of tenderness in him, it seems to me.' And Reynolds got to talk to you surely—that was in the cards. And all my friends, and it was nice for me to know of my town that it is thoroughly packed with your admirers, with the ones who'd wanted to speak to you most the most tongue-tied, they've told me. But to me—it was so lovely to have you in my house. I went to your party in New York when we first met and now you've come to my party— Naturally, but like a dream too." Later in the letter, Eudora expressed her hope to meet Margaret and thanked Ken for wiring congratulations when the Pulitzer Prize for Fiction was awarded to *The Optimist's Daughter.* "The Pulitzer news," she told Ken, "was out of the blue and wonderful. Nothing was as meaningful though as the presence of my friends here a few days before— That was the real prize and the real treasure."[90]

A week later a reviewer for the *New York Times* panned Ken's *Sleeping Beauty.* "This detective story," Crawford Woods wrote, "carries a dedication to Eudora Welty—a gracious and appropriate gesture, but one that suggests, as the book suggests, that the author has fallen prey to the exuberance of his critics and is now writing in the shadow of a self-regard that tends to play his talent false." Eudora immediately expressed her outrage to Ken, calling the review "a shameful piece of work" and offering a story of consolation. "If it is any comfort to you in companionship," she wrote him, "I have had the exact same charge made against me, of trying to do something out of my bent, because of a dedication, which was to Elizabeth Bowen— It was a book of stories laid in Ireland, Italy, etc., and I was advised to keep to something I know and not try to be so pretentious as [to] write about anything outside Miss., and Elizabeth's name was used against me, just as mine was against you, and just as without reason."[91]

In New York, Eudora and Diarmuid were able to spend more time together, and the agent asked his client what he should do with all the letters she had written during the thirty-two years he had been her agent. Eudora was unsure how to respond, wondering whether or not the letters should be preserved and made public. She described her dilemma to Ken.

I might have said on first impulse (in my sorrow for him now) to just get rid of them, but the thing is, I have all the other half of that correspondence, and it is really the whole factual story of my working life, and so to me it would matter to have it— I just never would have thought of it objectively that way. I don't suppose there's a word in any of the letters from either of us that isn't just exactly how it was.— But would other people care, or should they care, that's something else and something I shy off from too much to think about. Of course the letters are also the letters of close friendship. I can tell you the exact truth, if it had not been for Diarmuid I doubt if any of my work would ever have reached any general publication. From the start, when he and Henry began the agency, they never took on a client whose work they did not like and believe in—regardless of how well or how little they might be known. I was the prime example, completely unknown, and the first client. Diarmuid spent two thankless years trying to get me into the *Atlantic Monthly*, and I remember his writing me once "If Ted Weeks doesn't take this one, he ought to be horse-whipped." Enough to make me write another story overnight! He has guided me toward, and protected me from, more than I knew, and never once pressed me. All the years I didn't publish anything, before I got *Losing Battles* done, he never once was anything but compassionate. He never had to say much about a story I'd send, he never did say many words, but "It's good" would be pure gold to me. He *knew*—he told me that a story I sent in was really chapter two of a novel. It was, too (*Delta Wedding*, my first novel). It is sweet of you to be interested in the letters and what happens to them. It's just a jump-shift in my thinking to imagine any eyes reading them but those they were meant for, and the understanding they were meant for. I rely so heavily on the other end.

Unlike Eudora, Ken felt sure that other eyes should see the letters. "In the light of what you say about that career-long relationship I can't help foreseeing a time when the letters that record it will be of the very first literary and historical importance, more valuable I should think than the Fitzgerald-Ober correspondence which my friend Matt Bruccoli did recently. It's an important book, basic in its new field, but the Fitz-Ober relationship wasn't really imaginative or creative."[92] Eudora ultimately decided to accept the letters, but it would be many years before she allowed them to be seen by anyone other than herself.

In July Eudora was again confronted by the death of a close friend—Dolly Wells, who had left New York and moved back to Jackson. Eudora immediately wrote to Reynolds, Mary Lou, and Ken about the death, but she kept this news from Diarmuid, himself gravely ill. In her letter to Reynolds, just home from a stay on Long Island, Eudora expressed the depth of her grief. "I'd have written you to the Long Island spot but have been in a state of shock & grief here because my old friend Dolly Wells died suddenly. She was found dead by one of her sisters, late Saturday night when she hadn't answered her phone all day. Sitting in her chair with her supper untasted on a tray before her, a martini poured, the TV & lights on, her little dog at her feet— She may have been there since Thursday. It must have been sudden and soon over, whether heart attack or what—they never were sure— You know how bereft I feel—my old friend of over 40 years, in Jackson, New York, and back in Jackson again. I'd been over for a drink on Tuesday."[93]

In September, Eudora traveled to Washington for a National Council on the Arts meeting, and the entire council was welcomed by President Nixon in the Oval Office. For the past few months, Eudora had been fascinated by the U.S. Senate's investigation of the break-in at the Watergate offices of the Democratic National Committee and by attempts to force the president to surrender tapes of conversations held in his office. Now she came face-to-face with the man for whom she felt intense disdain. To Ken, she sent a description.

> Oh, God! I had to meet Pres. Nixon! We (the Council on the Arts) were all taken over to the Oval Office (in the rain) & made to go in a line to shake hands with him. I felt a bad hypocrite to touch him. (I who had never missed a session of Watergate.) He had a soft handshake & very feverish looking brown eyes. Make-up, I thought (& we all had to be photographed with him, our hands being clasped, 'a copy will be sent to your hometown paper'). He seemed unreal as a man and poor as an actor—very jerky-jovial. All the same, while I resented being asked to look on this man as a fellow human being, who must in fact be suffering, we don't know how much, this *was* the case—I hated the whole thing. We were given souvenirs from trays as we went out—pens, Nixon's signature on same, & a pin with presidential seal on it, & cuff-links, with seal. They've been loading down my suitcase. In the Oval Office there was a perfectly smooth bare desk, and on a little table beside it a tape recorder. Yes there was! Nobody was offered *that* souvenir.[94]

From Washington, Eudora went to New York and a weekend visit with Diarmuid. To Ken, she reported that Diarmuid was "unalterable in mind and spirit, but so frail and very tired now. I'm glad he felt like having me come. I took greetings to him from friends—and yours brought him a smile of pleasure. I'm glad that you and Diarmuid got to meet each other, at no matter what point."[95] An affinity between Diarmuid and Ken meant the world to Eudora, who was devoted to both and who saw so many similarities between them. For his part, Diarmuid must have been pleased and relieved to know that after his death, which loomed so near, Eudora would have a formidable champion.

In October, Mary Lou came through Jackson on her way to

visit Duncan in Atlanta and her daughter Mary in upstate New York. During that same month, Ken and Eudora continued their regular correspondence, conferring about writers to be included in a mystery anthology Ken was editing. As the month drew to an end, Eudora celebrated the arrival of Mary Alice's first child, Donald Alexander White Jr. and began to prepare for two trips. During the summer and fall, she had written two new lectures, one for the October 25–28 Willa Cather Conference in Nebraska and one about her photographs for the Museum of Modern Art in New York City. The time in Nebraska proved pleasant indeed. As Eudora told Frank Lyell, "Nebraska was at its best, I imagine, because it was all golden everywhere, still fall—completely flat, but high—and the plains really did have that feeling of reaching, which WC described—and you see with full clarity 360 degrees of horizon, and not a single human being on it—utterly open and empty and somehow evocative—of what, you don't quite know or care to say—you think of prehistoric times and of Indians and of the pioneers, who couldn't ever have seen a soul except their own little party. This was on the all-day trip to Red Cloud." As for the conference itself, Eudora particularly enjoyed spending time with Alfred and Helen Knopf and hearing Alfred give a thirty-to-forty-minute extemporaneous talk about his "publishing life with Willa Cather."[96]

The time in New York was not this pleasant. Workers at the Museum of Modern Art were on strike and hoped Eudora would refuse to cross their picket lines. She decided, however, to honor her commitment. The results were predictable. "Picketers were yelling 'Eudora Welty is a liar!' and 'Eudora Welty, we read your book, and you have betrayed us.'" Eudora told Ken that "they had threatened over the phone that they would do this unless I withdrew my lecture from the Museum and delivered it to the strikers in another place. I was not informed on the issues, and thought it was only right to keep to my engagement, made months ago. It gave me a trip up here so I can go out to see

Diarmuid, as I'll be doing tomorrow, if he feels like it."[97] This visit with Diarmuid, prefaced by such an ominous occurrence, would be her last.

On December 16, 1973, Diarmuid Russell died. Bad weather and difficulties scheduling transportation kept Eudora from the memorial service and the comfort of being with Diarmuid's family and friends. From Ken and Mary Lou, however, came powerful letters of consolation. Ken wrote, "I don't know of anyone who has given more than you have to other people, or has more love resurging back to her. Such considerations are not terribly comforting, I know, when you have been bereaved. But that long friendship and creative partnership with Diarmuid is the living truth of the matter, and won't die. While I don't believe in the immortality of the soul—neither, I doubt, does my friend Bishop Corrigan (*Right*-Way Corrigan)—there are certain souls that live on intensely in their work and in the minds of people who knew them. Diarmuid's certainly one of them. And he will live on, as he would have wished, in the work of you and other writers which he helped to bring to birth. There is a great deal, too, to be said for an end to suffering. I hope your own suffering won't be too hard to bear. You've had a difficult season. But you've had long joyful seasons—you've left a full record of them; you're the most irrepressibly joyous person I know—and you'll have other good seasons and know what to do with them, too." Mary Lou's message was similar.

> Ah E, this can't be a joyous Christmas for you, and for all Diarmuid's friends today is a day of mourning—and re-membrance. Like you I wish I could be at the memorial service simply to pay tribute . . . How he'll be missed. How wonderful that you could be with him so often during his illness, proof of devotion such as few—any?—agents have had from clients, and proof that your devotion was so much more than that. I believe you were his best friend, as he was

yours. Of course your work *crowned* his professional life, and my hunch is that your lasting contribution to literature made his life worthwhile to him, because he'd helped. He did help, especially in the early days of your career. When he sent your stories to the *Bazaar*, it was made quite clear that we were *privileged* to see them. As we were! He could be quite fierce, you know, in defense of work he believed in. Take comfort from his pride in you. You never once let him down. Wasn't it splendid that he could be with you on Eudora Welty Day! I can see him in that beautiful room where his presence blessed you as no Governor's could, however complimentary— And I can see him on the porch of your house, where I sat with him for a few minutes before others came up to thank him for what he'd done for them. Of all the many times I've been with him I'm most grateful for that last time, I suppose because he was a living example as you said, of Valiance. In these times, how *admirable* the great virtues are when they're embodied before our eyes. No longer only legends.[98]

EIGHT

"The Strong Present Tense"
On and Off the Road 1974–1980

The death of Diarmuid Russell in December 1973 left Eudora in agony. Her immediate family members were all gone; Hubert Creekmore, Dolly Wells, and Elizabeth Bowen had died as well; and now Diarmuid, her closest friend and most trusted advisor, had succumbed to lung cancer. There was a huge gap in Eudora's life. Between 1974 and 1980 she sought to deal with Diarmuid's loss, with the deaths that followed his, with love and separateness, as she had with earlier trials: She went on the road. She traveled to give readings, receive honorary degrees, encounter new landscapes and cityscapes, revisit old haunts, meet with old friends. In particular, she sought to see as much as possible of the far-flung friends in whom she felt most free to confide: Ken Millar, Bill and Emmy Maxwell, Mary Lou Aswell, and Reynolds Price. At home, Eudora became an even more active supporter of New Stage Theatre, providing advice, reading at fund-raising events, and she accepted more and more invitations from friends, for dinners, concerts, and other gatherings. She lived, as Emerson phrased it, in "the strong present tense," recognizing the principle that Emerson set forth after the death of his young son: "To fill the hour,—that is happiness; to fill the hour and leave no crevice for a repentance or an approval. We live amid surfaces, and the true art of life is to skate well on them." Such skating, however, took its toll upon her energy and creativity. When, at intervals, she ceased skating and sought to write, it was to no avail. Between 1974 and 1980, she wrote scene after scene for a long story about an interracial rape in the contemporary South and worked on other shorter pieces. None did she complete. Fiction, her greatest passion, had become a great frustration. Life and the writing life during these years continued to bring her joy, but along with joy she felt the dark apprehension that her career might be drawing to an end and that the same might be true of Ken Millar's. Then, after a 1976 trip to visit Ken in Santa Barbara, the second of three trips she would make there in successive years, Eudora's concerns for him grew more serious. Not merely was his career in jeopardy. His identity was as well. His lapses of memory would become progressively worse. Doctors had not yet made the diagnosis of Alzheimer's disease, but by the end of 1979, one truth was clear. He was losing his past, and Eudora was losing him. In Ken's plight, Eudora would recognize what she had long ago learned: Life's "present tense" can only be strong when it is informed by memory.[1]

Eudora spent January 1974 in Jackson, grieving for Diarmuid, but telling Mary Lou, "for Diarmuid I can only be glad it's over. This is what I concentrate on."[2] She also began to concentrate on a summer trip to Italy and France in the company of John and Catherine Prince, friends of many years who lived in Washington, DC. This trip promised to be a distraction from grief; at home distractions were few. Instead, a New Stage Theatre production of *A Long's Day's Journey Into Night* must have intensified thoughts of loss and of her own writer's block. In this play, Eudora saw Eugene O'Neill's despair transformed and transmuted, and she admired the performance that Broadway actress Geraldine Fitzgerald brought to the Jackson production: "She is a

wonderful, powerful presence—and a generous person, with
much help for the local cast supporting her."³ For Eudora, however, anguish could not, at least yet, be transformed into art.

In February, Eudora made her first trip of the year. She spent
four days in Washington, DC, at a meeting of the National Council on the Arts, went next to Bryn Mawr to see her old friend
Laurence Stapleton and to give a reading for the freshman class,
and then traveled back to DC for a night with the Princes before
going by bus to Hollins College. At Hollins, Bill Smith and other
members of the English Department had arranged a celebration
for Eudora Welty. Over a two-day period Reynolds Price, a number of scholars, and Bill himself paid homage to Eudora's work,
and the celebration concluded with Eudora reading from *Losing
Battles* and receiving a standing ovation as a result.⁴ From Hollins,
Eudora left for a week in New York and reunions with old and
dear friends, but not, for the first time in thirty-four years, for a
reunion with Diarmuid. She saw the Maxwells for three consecutive nights—with Bill and Emmy she could share the kind of intimacy that Reynolds and Bill Smith had offered at Hollins. And
there were other friends to visit as well—Lehman, Walter
Clemons, Joan Kahn, and Nona Balakian among them. Unhap-
pily, she did not manage to see Rosie Russell. Eudora told Mary
Lou, "We talked on the telephone, though, and I felt very sorry
for her—she feels lost still, she says, & bewildered."⁵ While in
New York, Eudora undertook one piece of work: She labored on
a review of Annie Dillard's *Pilgrim at Tinker Creek*; though she felt
serious reservations about the book, she did not want to be critical of a young writer making her first appearance. Nor did she
want to prejudice other readers—she did not, for *Pilgrim at Tinker
Creek* went on to win a Pulitzer Prize for nonfiction.

At home in Jackson by early March, Eudora was weary. At age
sixty-five, she now found travel exhausting. Similarly, she was frustrated by her role at the National Council on the Arts, an advi-

sory board to the chairman of the National Endowment for the Arts (NEA). She liked Chairman Nancy Hanks and was particularly fond of fellow council members Maurice Abravanel (formerly a conductor at the Metropolitan Opera and now director of the Utah Symphony) and Billy Taylor (a jazz pianist, composer, and band leader). The council's business, however, seemed alien to her. Its members were expected to vote on grant proposals recommended by NEA committees, to provide budgetary oversight for the agency, to identify initiatives to be undertaken in conjunction with related government agencies, and to recommend policy directions involving Congress. As Eudora told Ken Millar, "They do many good things, and I am for them, but I belong in another part of the program—a reader of candidates' books and projects, not a voter on the money (can't even spell it, much less vote it by the millions). I'm waiting now to be replaced."[6] Her wait to be replaced lasted, nevertheless, almost until the end of her six-year term, perhaps because journeys undertaken for council business repeatedly helped enable her to see far-flung friends. She planned, for instance, to visit Mary Lou in Santa Fe in April 1974 on her roundabout way to meet Frank Lyell in San Antonio, where she would be attending a Council on the Arts meeting. In the course of this trip, she also hoped to see Ken, and she asked if he and Margaret might stop by Santa Fe on their way to New York. Ken responded with regret, saying that difficulty with his blood pressure left him with little stamina for extended travel. This was the first of Eudora's reasons to worry about Ken's health, but she hoped that the problem would soon be under control and that they might find another and more convenient time to meet. Before March was out, she suggested such a time: "Today Reynolds phoned me about something and said he was getting ready to invite you to Duke to some kind of seminar thing, and would invite me to it also—he talked to me about this a good while back and probably to you too. So that might be a nice time (it's oft in the Fall) to all three meet and be (perhaps) easy. Wait and see."[7]

On April 27, Eudora arrived in Santa Fe, where she enjoyed the company of Mary Lou, Agi Sims, Mary and Aristide Mian, and their numerous Santa Fe friends. Then it was on to San Antonio for the National Council on the Arts meeting, hosted by the distinguished Texas architect O'Neil Ford. Highlights were visits with Frank, Maggie Cousins (once managing editor at *Good Housekeeping,* later the senior editor at Doubleday Publishing Company), and Lady Bird Johnson, the widow of former president Lyndon Johnson. Cousins, who had edited the first lady's *White House Diary,* liked her tremendously, and so did Eudora. Eudora reported that Lady Bird had asked her "to go to a quiet little end of one room" for a talk and that the talk had been fine.[8]

Eudora was home only a month before embarking on her next journey; on June 5, she sailed aboard the *Raffaello* for Italy. On the last day of her crossing, she wrote to Ken, "The Raffaello itself—herself, I guess—is the most casual & confused ship in the running— For example, I had to change my cabin 3 times the first night out—getting thrown out of one & guided to another one, no reason known— This is tourist class, but some acquaintances upstairs tell me it was the same there— Slightly comic opera, but I just go on reading Lord Byron's Letters and the autobiography of the Emperor of China, and on— An old friend from home who now lives in Italy is meeting the boat in Genoa & I'll go home with him & friend for the weekend, near Pisa— Then John & Catherine Prince & I will connect—they're heading toward Italy from Greece— It ought to be the nicest, easiest trip—back roads & good food—they've already cased the way— Will postcard you." The "old friend from home," John Robinson, did indeed meet Eudora's ship, and she enjoyed a weekend on his farm "up in the mts. above the sea (you can see Elba, 70 miles away)." The house "on top of the world" proved idyllic, with cherry and peach trees around it, and as John had earlier written, nearby was "the beach and a fisherman [with] a shack of a restaurant there. We eat whatever he catches that day made usually into a *zuppa di pesce* (the particular Livornese one is called '*cac-cinco*')." John had become a country gentleman, not of the Mississippi Delta, but of the Tuscan coast, and Eudora sensed that he was truly at home.[9]

The Princes, in a time that to Eudora must have seemed all too soon, collected her in Pisa, and the three friends drove into France, having a wonderful meal at Chagny and admiring in Autun the cathedral's twelfth-century stone capitals sculpted by master craftsman Gislebertus. In Paris they stayed at the Hotel des Saints Pères, just as Eudora had in 1949, and Eudora relished her return to the city. The Cluny Museum, the Louvre, the Place des Vosges, the Luxembourg Gardens all captivated her again, and she found that the trip had "had some recuperative powers for me and I hadn't realized quite how much I needed them." Perhaps a letter from Mary Lou had another recuperative power for Eudora. When Eudora opened this letter in Paris, she discovered a message about Diarmuid: "Isn't it significant that, much as we miss his presence, his essence is with us forever. Terribly alive he is—not in the sense of fear, but in the O.E.D. definition 'exciting some feeling akin to awe.'"[10]

In mid-July, Eudora sailed home on the SS *France*, the last ship built as a transatlantic liner for the French line and due now to be retired from service because of the oil crisis. Both Eudora and Jacksonian Stuart Irby, a fellow passenger on this crossing, were smitten by the *France*, and both vowed to protest its retirement. On arrival in New York, Eudora paused briefly to see friends, and Walter Clemons took her to a literary cocktail party in honor of young British novelist Margaret Drabble. Then it was back home, where she doubtless was pleased by the resignation of President Nixon and where she regrouped and planned to welcome Mary Lou Aswell as a week-long houseguest. The two women were to be joined by Nash Burger and Reynolds Price in constituting the jury for the Eudora Welty Americana Awards, given by Mississippi Educational Television to outstanding public television programs. In September, Eudora's time was further occupied by a visit from Nancy Hanks and by members of the National Council on the Arts.

In October and early November, Eudora remained in Jackson, seeing friends for drinks and dinner, watching the Lord Peter Wimsey mysteries on public television, tending to her house and garden, going to the New Stage opening of *The Night Thoreau Spent in Jail* and the cast party that followed, attending the Americana Awards ceremony, and presumably trying to write. Ken Millar applauded this respite from travel and urged Eudora to be more protective of her time in the future. "You are a writer, and too many duties and occasions have been getting in the way of your writing. I wish you some clear space to work in, and a renewal of the selfish dedication that used to be our armor. I include myself, because I've been suffering from the same dissipation of my energies. We are not lotus eaters, but we are duty eaters, and we must return to what my friends in college used to call *the higher selfishness.* I am willing to cooperate to the extent of sacrificing one of my greatest pleasures and suggesting that you not answer this letter at all."[11]

Eudora, frustrated by her inability to write fiction, recognized the wisdom of Ken's advice, but she would not stop traveling. Grief at Diarmuid's loss had been an important prompt to her spring and summer journeys, and she found them therapeutic. But grief alone cannot explain the arduous, nomadic routine that would characterize her life in the coming years. Perhaps, one might speculate, her oft-stated desire to produce new work was counterbalanced by a sense that she could not write without Diarmuid. He had been not only her agent and devoted friend, but also her most trusted reader. Beginning in 1940, his short, suggestive responses to her work had served as her primary guides for revision. After his death, she could continue to rely on Bill Maxwell, Reynolds, and Mary Lou for advice, but Diarmuid was the reader with whom she felt most in tune; writing without his participation must have seemed both difficult and melancholy.

Memory of past collaborations was inevitably sparked by new writing efforts, and perhaps those memories were not as healing as those that resulted in *The Optimist's Daughter*. Traveling across the country and across the ocean freed her from work that evoked the past and forced her to live in "the strong present tense."

In addition, the death of Diarmuid, following upon the deaths of her brothers and mother, of Hubert Creekmore, Elizabeth Bowen, and Dolly Wells, certainly made Eudora powerfully aware that in human transience lay "the one irreducible urgency telling us to do, to understand, to love."[12] She must have regretted missed opportunities to enjoy the living presence of those now gone, and her letters between 1974 and 1980 repeatedly stress her desire to seize the day. Writing was not now Eudora's number-one priority. Human contact was. Ironically, however, the person she most wanted to see was the very one she could not. Ken Millar's marriage and his wife's antipathy for any visitors, much less a woman whom her husband loved, limited Ken and Eudora to a total of only six weeks or so in each other's company. Eudora must have been frustrated that the warmth of her correspondence with Ken could not be matched by the warmth of actual conversations and shared experiences. Love and separateness seemed inextricably tied; circumstances denied Eudora a stable, fulfilling relationship. She may have turned to travel as a way of diverting her attention from that profound frustration.

Whatever the reason, Eudora remained on the move in late 1974. On November 15, she was in Sewanee for Allen Tate's seventy-fifth birthday celebration; on November 19, she arrived in New York for an Academy meeting about the Howells Medal; and she delayed her return home by stopping in Washington, DC, for a weeklong Arts Council meeting. Once back in Jackson, she learned she had missed seeing Ken in New York. Unbeknownst to each other, they had been at the Algonquin Hotel simultaneously, but this time there had been no fortuitous encounter. "Accidents balance out in life," Ken wrote to Eudora, "and probably this is the price I have had to pay for the most happy accident of meeting you, for the first time, in the Algonquin lobby."[13]

At some point, either before or during her November travels, Eudora managed to review three books of photographs for the *New York Times Book Review*, paying particular attention to Leni Riefenstahl's *The Last of the Nuba*. Riefenstahl, whose pre-World War II film *The Triumph of the Will* had recorded triumphant appearances by Adolf Hitler, eventually undertook a far different project. She traveled to Africa in 1962 and spent ten years documenting the lives of the Mesakin Nuba, a "tribe of perfect human beings still living in innocence and harmony." Eudora was impressed by the physical beauty of the people photographed, by the account of their work and their ceremonies and their ethical standards, and by the fact that each individual Nuba owned a lyre and composed his own music for it. Riefenstahl's photographs, Eudora concluded, "give us fresh comprehension of man in, as might be, his original majesty and acceptance of life, in his vanity and courage, his beauty, vulnerability, pride."[14] One wonders what reaction Eudora's celebration of an African society prompted in Jackson, a city troubled by white flight from and racial tensions in its now integrated school system, but probably the review received little attention or seemed removed from local concerns.

As December began, Eudora arrived at home to face further distractions from writing: Her furnace had broken down in her absence. Now she faced the expense of a new one and the presence of workmen in her house. Despite the success of *Losing Battles* and *The Optimist's Daughter*, Eudora was apprehensive about her finances. A writer's income was typically irregular and uncertain, and as a self-employed person, Eudora had to provide her own medical insurance and save for her eventual retirement. Nevertheless, during the 1970s, except for two lean years, she would earn substantially more than the median income for a man, much less a woman, in addition to holding a modest portfolio of well-chosen stocks and owning her home outright. Her financial worries were probably unfounded; still, given her generally cautious nature and her experience of the Great Depression, she worried. But for the moment, the Christmas season at home proved pleasing. She and Charlotte visited Frank's mother, Clarena, now old and infirm but still as clear of mind as when she had been their bridge partner or a star in Little Theatre productions. Family gatherings were also heartening; Liz and Mary Alice were both happily married, and their children were the center of family attention. Eudora did accomplish one bit of writing during December; she reviewed Elizabeth Bowen's *Pictures and Conversations.* This autobiographical work, incomplete at her death, had been published at Elizabeth's request by Spencer Curtis Brown, her agent and friend. The book brought Elizabeth's presence back to Eudora. "Fragment that it is," Eudora noted, "it is whole in its essence, which survives interruption to the page. That relationship between her life and her art—and here I use, for her, the word she forbore to use for herself—she *has* divined in its spontaneous and still-mysterious source, and has traced it part way at least toward its broadening stream. What is here holds a particular blessing for those who loved Elizabeth, for they will not be able to read any sentence of it without being brought the cadence of her voice and the glow of her company."[15]

In January 1975, Eudora turned again to reviewing. This time her subject was a collection of stories by the Australian writer Patrick White. For Eudora, one story in *The Cockatoos* was particularly haunting, and it may have affected her own return to fiction some months later. "In 'The Night the Prowler,'" Eudora wrote,

> we are plunged into the world of a seventeen-year-old girl whose state of being has everything to do with today. When Felicity was raped, she hadn't been afraid; she'd even hoped something real and revealing might be going to occur, but the rapist is a failure and pathetic. She sees that her conventional parents, in the shock of what's happened, think

mostly of themselves and that the conventional boy she'd been about to marry is relieved to get his ring back, and she enters into a secret life of her own. Beginning by breaking in and wreaking havoc on a house near hers and like hers, she goes on the loose into the city night with its derelicts, drunks and hoods. She remains alone, roaming the park, kicking at lovers, accusing and punishing all the world, shouting up at God "for holding out on me," calling out only to others like herself for guidance, so they can give each other "the strength to face ugliness in any form," which might offer some kind of revelation. She herself becomes the night the prowler. As we see her "whirling in the air above her head a bicycle chain she had won from a mob of leather-jackets," she is like some saint-to-be of the Troubled Young. This story with all the rawness of today in it is not without its old progenitors. Felicity's progress through the scarifying world of Sydney nightlife is also a path of self-mortification. She is divested of that pride too; when she comes in the final scene to an abandoned house and finds there a naked, diseased, dirty, solitary old man lying on a mattress at the point of death, she has her revelation. It is a stunning story.[16]

Patrick White in some ways reminded Eudora of Ken Millar, and she wrote to Ken about *The Cockatoos.* These stories, she told him, are "potent and heavy & throbbing stuff, like hunks of fallen meteors or something cast upon us from another orbit." White's stories about "the predicaments of growing old" might also have seemed particularly poignant to Eudora as she reviewed the book. Having watched the ravages of time visited upon her own mother and now reading about them in White's book, she feared for Clarena Lyell, who had developed a deep and persistent cough. She wrote to alert Frank to this situation and to chide him a bit. "She feels discouraged & worried when she doesn't hear from you," Eudora noted. "I told her that I believed a letter must have got lost in the mail—maybe one did—so anyway, do write a good one now."[17]

Eudora was back on the road in February, but this time only briefly. She spent four days in Washington at a Council on the Arts meeting, never a favorite activity, but was rewarded with an after-hours visit to the National Gallery of Art and its Exhibition of Archaeological Finds of the People's Republic of China. Eudora was entranced and went back again by herself. She continued to have, as V. S. Pritchett would later say, a quality of "passionate astonishment" in her reaction to the world, and that quality is clearly evident in the description she sent Ken of the Chinese exhibit. "Nothing they used, not any pot or cooking pan, or lamp, or anything in all those centuries, was not beautiful. I liked the little domestic things—two bronze leopards inlaid with gold—both would have fitted into the palm of the hand—curled up with the most catlike spines, and jeweled eyes in their masks—these were made as weights to hold down the silk sleeves."[18]

Eudora and Ken were eager to see each other again—they had not met since Eudora Welty Day in 1973, so Eudora accepted an invitation to appear at the Santa Barbara Writers Conference in June. Ken was a fixture at the conference, and it provided an occasion for the two to meet on his home grounds. That prospect brightened the spirits of both. In the meantime, Eudora reported on Ken's appearances in her dreams. A day after writing him about her Washington adventure, she dreamed she was in Venice, California, next to Ring Lardner, who told a shoe clerk that he was there to see Ken and "was on his way to keep the appointment very shortly—end of dream." Ken responded with enthusiasm, "I don't know what your dream means, either, but it was a lovely dream and it makes me happy. What more could a storyteller ask than to be associated with Ring Lardner, in your mind!"[19]

What more could a storyteller ask? Perhaps for popular dramatizations of his or her stories. Movies and a television series about his protagonist Lew Archer had proven disappointments to

Ken, but Eudora had had better luck with the legitimate theater. In the fall of 1974, *The Robber Bridegroom* had been presented as a musical by the Musical Theatre Workshop at St. Clement's Church in New York. The script by Alfred Uhry and music by Robert Waldman had attracted the attention of John Houseman, who now planned to stage it on Broadway.

In March, *The Robber Bridegroom* continued to occupy Eudora's retrospective attention. At the invitation of Charlotte Capers, she delivered a lecture about her 1942 novella to the Mississippi Historical Society, and the society soon decided to publish "A Fairy Tale of the Natchez Trace." Though discussing the origins of her novel was a small autobiographical venture that she enjoyed, Eudora was somewhat troubled at the prospect of a television biography. She approved of the support the National Council on the Arts had offered Richard O. Moore to produce programs about noted American writers, but she worried about becoming the subject of one. Those worries proved needless. Reynolds came to Jackson to offer his moral support, and Moore and his crew charmed Eudora when they arrived in April. She thoroughly enjoyed their filming at various Mississippi locations, and they enjoyed her tales about the various locales.

After the crew had departed, Eudora turned her attention to the galleys of Reynolds's new novel, *The Surface of Earth*, and she was dubious about its merits. To Reynolds, she wrote in perhaps too frank a fashion. She praised the brilliance of the writing and said she planned to read the novel again, but she rejected what seemed to her the novel's vision of human nature: "I am not persuaded—not made able—to see along with you human relationships as time after time and in all the variations they're shown, demonstrated, dwelt upon, dreamed about, as essentially bloodsucking; voracious self-satisfactions." Then Eudora tried to retreat from this criticism: "When I read it another time, I'll see if I might have fallen back on some sort of unconscious resistance to that 'devouringness' of human relationship; certainly I don't

see it as you do, but this isn't necessary—I just need to understand and follow your dramatic use of it. All you are asking of
your readers is belief in what you show us, not agreement with it.
And whatever I feel next time, I am committed fully already to
admiration for the novel's huge challenge you put to yourself and
met with such sureness and power, for the huge accomplishment.
You did exactly what you set out to. Not many can claim the
same."[20] Saddened by the loss of those whose living presence had
so enriched her life, Eudora seems to have resisted a portrait of
possessive and manipulative relationships even as she admired
Reynolds's craftsmanship.

For a time there was no response from Reynolds, and Eudora
was busy with other matters. She flew to Seattle for an Arts
Council meeting and returned to Jackson to plan for the fiftieth
reunion of her high school class. As the program chairman for
this gathering, she arranged to have old friend, classmate, and
Episcopal priest George Stephenson speak, along with Mary
Larche and Willanna Buck Mallett. Then it was off to Tulane
for an honorary degree on May 16, to Dallas for another on May
18, and to Yale University for a third on May 19. Finally, she enjoyed a week in New York before coming home to repack and regroup for a trip to Santa Barbara.

At home a letter from Reynolds awaited her. He had been
surprised and unhappy with Eudora's response to his novel and
thought his explanation of it might help to change her opinion.

I'm sorry that the book didn't make its full effect for you;
I'd hoped and trusted that it would.

I can understand your instinct to turn away from what's
violent and baffling in the lives of the characters. What puz-
zles me is that you seem not to have responded to the fact
that the clamor of famished selves in Book One (and the
bafflements you mention all center there) is slowly stilled
and eventually comprehended and controlled—or begins to

be controlled—in Book Three . . . Something has been *worked out* in this family, with the terrible tragic slowness of whole lives and years—the way things *do* get worked out in the world, in my experience at least (the only way). And what is worked out is to a large extent mysterious, as it always is in life and in comparable works of fiction—a "curse," and a family curse; the apparently senseless violence, greed, and pride of ancestors . . . Inexplicable but credible human acts which can only be lived through and down. That movement in human life—the hope of that movement, the fact of it in many lives—is the chief thing I think I know, having had my own family, my own life; and it's what I labored to show. I think it's there.[21]

Eudora had little time to reread the novel and respond. She was celebrating the arrival of Liz and Fred's second child, a boy named Zachary Welty Thompson, and getting ready for her California trip, but before the month was out she would send a generous, supportive reply that began to mend matters.

The weeklong reunion with Ken in Santa Barbara proved exhilarating, and even Margaret was warm and welcoming. Margaret had published no fiction since the death of her daughter, in 1970, but meeting Eudora made her feel ready to write again. "Your visit had a peculiar effect on me," Margaret later wrote. "I want to start writing again after a long layoff in which I told everyone I'd retired. But I guess the record shows *very* few completely retired writers. (How many times did Somerset Maugham retire? Twice a month, I think.) Anyway, for better or worse, I'm going to start a book soon. Thanks. *Really thanks.*"[22] The good feeling between herself and "Maggie" pleased Eudora, but more pleasing were her long conversations and long drives along the coastline with Ken. She discussed Reynolds's book with Ken, and Ken turned to it shortly after Eudora had gone. His analysis of and praise for the book would help to overcome Eudora's resistance to it.

From Santa Barbara, Eudora flew to San Francisco for a brief stay—Richard Moore needed her help in editing his film about her. They worked on it, and then Moore showed her a program about Janet Flanner that he had completed for a series to be titled *The Originals: The Writer in America.* Eudora loved the Flanner interview and told Mary Lou that it reminded her of meeting Flanner in Paris in 1949 "when she was so full of everything." In sponsoring films like the one on Flanner, Eudora was finally convinced, the Arts Council could "protect literature."[23]

Eudora returned to Jackson in time for the birth of Andrews Welty White, Mary Alice and Donny's second child, pleased that the Welty name would continue in both Mary Alice's and Liz's families. Not so pleasing was the review Reynolds had received in the *New York Times Book Review.* The North Carolina writer, who seemed almost like her own child, had been ravaged by Richard Gilman. A noted drama critic and a Yale University professor, Gilman asserted that a traditional southern novel like Reynolds's was no longer viable: "Who could have imagined that any novelist presumably sensitive to the prevailing winds of consciousness—Price's previous fiction has moved between competent conventional story-telling and a mild and somewhat brittle thrust into fantasy—could have written a relentless family saga at a time when most of us feel self-generated, inheritors of obliterated pasts?" *The Surface of Earth,* in Gilman's condescending view, was "a great lumbering archaic beast, taking its place among our literary fauna with the stiff queer presence of the representative of a species thought to be extinct. A mastodon sprung to life from beneath an ice-field, it smells at first of time stopped, evolution arrested."[24] Eudora was appalled. She responded with the anger of a mother whose child had been scorned, but she also responded as a novelist whose imagination could not brook the review's proscriptive concept of fiction. Although she had been compelled to reread Reynolds's novel in order to overcome her own reservations about it, Gilman had not addressed the reservations she had earlier felt; instead he had attacked on generic and cultural grounds, and this Eudora found wholly unacceptable. A week before reporting to jury duty at the Jackson courthouse, she wrote to the *New York Times Book Review* to express her dismay and to offer a literary verdict. "I don't, myself, see *how* any novelist, applying himself to any subject at all—and I thought choice of subject, like choice of home address, was free—could benefit by cutting off any source of wisdom that he was heir to, or that he knew of at all—or *why* he should. Yet his reviewer, proclaiming himself thus crippled in feeling and cut off from some primary sources of understanding, is here swearing it's better that way. So did the Fox Without a Tail offer his suggestion to improve the rest of his tribe."[25]

Eudora sent Reynolds a copy of her letter as soon as she had written it, and Reynolds promptly wrote to express his gratitude for this defense: "It was grand to talk this noon, as it had been— a little earlier—to get a copy of your letter to *The Times,* taking on Richard Gilman. As I told you, it was more or less precisely what I would have said—the parts about his ignorance and self-proclaimed incompetence for the job—and it has taken some jaw-clenching in the past week to *keep* from saying it; but I've never answered a reviewer before and had decided that I wouldn't start now. Well, it's *done*; and whether Mr G will ever get all his bones back in joint again, I wouldn't want to guess. It's one of the kindest things you've done for me, in a list now more than twenty years long."[26] On July 20, the *Times* published Eudora's response to Gilman along with his response to her. Gilman, who had clearly savored his opportunity to turn a devastating metaphor upon Reynolds, was not happy that Eudora had turned her (considerably greater) talent for metaphor against him. He sought to deny the implications of his review and lashed out at Eudora for identifying them, asserting that Eudora's "rhetoric of praise" for

The Surface of Earth was "more pompous, more flaccid and emptier than the worst moments of the book itself." By this time, however, Gilman's judgment had also been called into question by the *New York Times*'s own staff reviewer, Christopher Lehmann-Haupt. Despite reservations about the novel's length and about the "unbelievability of [its] resolution," Lehmann-Haupt asserted that *The Surface of Earth*'s composite portrait of characters was "monumental and tragically heroic, and it inhabits not only the details of Mr. Price's story, but also his very conception of the 20th-century South."[27]

In Jackson, tragic events, not a reviewer's pettiness nor his comeuppance, concerned Eudora. Frank Hains, the director of New Stage Theatre's *Ponder Heart,* had been murdered, and a young, gay, transient, African American man was suspected. Hains's violent death haunted Eudora. To Mary Lou, she wrote, "There's a terrible thing that's happened here— It was to Frank Hains, my good friend, on the newspaper and at New Stage— He was found murdered. At his house, a few blocks from me. Tied up & struck over the head—completely senseless act. It happened last Sunday a week ago, and has cast a pall over this town— I can't tell you, and don't need to, how much shock and grief I've been feeling myself. A good friend for 20 years—all besides the things you know about that I have him to thank for— ... How it happened to Frank I don't suppose anybody will ever know— that utterly gentle, kind, helpful person— But I do know he never locked his door—and he would have said 'Come in' to someone who knocked—" The murder, Eudora told Ken Millar, was "completely random and senseless and ... the poor soul plainly needed helping a long time ago—and the strongest & saddest thing is that Frank (who never locked his door) was a person who would have tried to give help if he could, & especially to a black person in trouble. For instance, he ran a summer workshop for young people in the theatre in the poor part of town, to keep them off the streets—very successful."[28]

In the midst of dealing with Hains's loss, Eudora had to finish an autobiographical essay for *Esquire.* Her recent reading had focused upon biography and autobiography: Joseph Blotner's biography of Faulkner, the letters of Lord Byron, the autobiography of the last emperor of China, Elizabeth Bowen's *Pictures and Conversations,* V. S. Pritchett's *Midnight Oil.* Now she added a short piece to this genre. Titled "The Corner Store," and later reprinted as "The Little Store," the essay described the attractions and mysteries of a small grocery store, where the owner and his family lived upstairs. As a child Eudora had regularly run to the store to pick up small items for her mother and to select a piece of candy or a cold drink. Then one day the affable storekeeper and his family had simply disappeared. "There was some act of violence," Eudora wrote. "The shock to the neighborhood traveled to the children, of course; but I couldn't find out from my parents what had happened. They held it back from me, as they'd already held back many things, 'until the time comes for you to know.'"[29] The account of the little store had become an account of Eudora's own sheltered childhood, which had itself vanished.

Once this essay was completed, Eudora began work on a new story, to be titled "The Shadow Club." Whether Frank Hains's murder prompted Eudora's return to fiction is uncertain, but there are parallels, and by September she had a rough draft pinned and taped together. In this story, a young, simpleminded, forlorn black man rapes a middle-aged white schoolteacher. The rapist is not the sex-crazed brute of white southern myth, but a displaced and disturbed individual, longing for the secure home he had once known with his auntee. He seems, like Hains's murderer, to be a "poor soul" who "plainly needed helping a long time ago." Eudora at one point set the rapist's character in contrast to that of a kind and articulate African American college president, who describes his father's days in slavery and his own discovery of literature as a student at the University of Chicago. But she must have realized that this character's narrative recollection, one drawn from actuality, was not organic to her story, for she decided to eliminate it.

In fact, the story is less about a rapist than it is about his schoolteacher victim. The concept of this female protagonist and her situation came directly from an actual event. Some years earlier an elderly Jackson high school teacher had surprised a burglar in her home and had struggled with him, breaking her arm in the process. Whether she had been raped or not, she was surely the prompt for Eudora's character. The novel's schoolteacher, however, in being forced to deal with sexual assault, finds herself confronted with terrifying childhood memories she has repressed, memories of her mother's infidelity, of her father's murder of her mother, and of his subsequent suicide. In creating this plot, Eudora seemed still under the influence of Patrick White's "The Night the Prowler," for the story's teacher finds, as does White's protagonist, that those closest to her respond with thoughts of themselves rather than empathy for her. Or perhaps Eudora was recalling the rape of Rosamond in *The Robber Bridegroom*; in late August she had seen a touring musical version of her novella performed at Ravinia in suburban Chicago. For Eudora, rape was a terrible violation of an individual's sanctity, but she also saw it as representative of a panoply of dangers. In *The Golden Apples*, interracial-rape victim Miss Eckhart "considered one thing not so much more terrifying than another," and her opinion was Eudora's. Though fear of rape had a strong resonance in the white South, where southern ladies remained on the pedestal of white male consciousness, Eudora had sought in her stories, and now sought again, to show that fears could not be so sharply focused and circumscribed.

In September worry about Ken Millar began in earnest and would continue until his death in 1983. Ken, whose letters had come once or twice a month since he and Eudora began to correspond, had not written since July. Eudora inquired about his well-being, and he immediately responded that hard work on a new book had "completely absorbed" his attention. Then he added,

"You know, Eudora, if I were *really* in trouble, I'd get in touch with you right away. But my life seems very lucky at the moment. I hope yours is the same, and the work goes well."[30] Despite this reassurance, Ken was probably beginning a pattern of forgetfulness that would become increasingly serious during the next eight years and that would eventually and prematurely put an end first to his fiction writing and then to his letter writing.

Though Eudora had worked hard on her new story for two months, she went on to deny herself any consecutive time for it. In late September 1975, she was back in Washington for a National Council on the Arts meeting and, on a free evening, managed to see the Princes. Then she headed to New York. There she dined with Lehman, the Maxwells, and Walter Clemons on successive days. She saw Geraldine Fitzgerald in *Ah, Wilderness* and had a backstage visit with her. And she took in a show of Elie Nadelman sculptures at the Whitney. But the highlight of her time in New York was seeing the Acting Company, which had taken *The Robber Bridegroom* on tour, bring her story to Broadway's Harkness Theatre for a limited run. Kevin Kline and Patti Lu Pone had the leads, and Eudora enjoyed their performances. To Mary Lou, she wrote that "The young performers of Mr. Houseman's Acting Company are superb—bright, dynamic, full of life and verve." Though she thought the show was "pretty much Ozarked up," she also felt that "it entered on a life of its own."[31] After the show, Eudora, her agent Tim Seldes, Walter Clemons, and *Washington Post* book reviewer Jonathan Yardley went to the cast party, where Eudora was happy to meet Marian Seldes, Tim's sister, who came to the party after performing her role in the Broadway hit *Equus.*

Eudora returned to Jackson after the Broadway excitement, but within a month she was on the road again. This time she went to Mount Holyoke for an honorary degree and stopped again in Washington, where she saw Reynolds. Finally back at home, there were other distractions from work on her new story. She spent a good bit of time with John Robinson, who was in town for an extended visit. She began reading novel after novel in her role as a judge for the Pulitzer Prize in Fiction. And a "high school oral interpretation contest held at Jackson State College from over the state (nearly 100% black)" occupied her "for 2 whole days 9–6:00, but I thought it was deserving as a project."[32]

By the end of January 1976, four months had passed since Eudora had spent any sustained time on her rape story. She had seen the New Year in with friends, and then during January she had screened films for Mississippi Educational Television, continued reading Pulitzer Prize nominations, entertained Frank Lyell and Shelby Foote, attended New Stage board meetings and productions, read *Middlemarch* for the first time and with great delight, and lunched at the Governor's Mansion. She had not, however, managed to write. Still she was hopeful about the story. "After the Pulitzer reading was done with," she told Mary Lou, "I did feel the removal of a great reef of imprisoning material." Writing about rape in the 1970s, however, posed difficulties that it would not have earlier in her career. Feminist books on the subject were now being published, and an emblematic use of rape would not satisfy those who defined it, in Susan Brownmiller's terms, as "a conscious process of intimidation by which all men keep all women in a state of fear." For her part, Eudora wanted to remain clear of feminist theory. Though Jean Stafford had reviewed Brownmiller's *Against Our Will: Men, Women, and Rape*, Eudora did not see the review and told Stafford that she hadn't "read the book (on purpose besides every other reason, as I'm trying to write a story with rape in it of one kind or another)."[33]

In February Eudora was again in Washington for a National Council on the Arts meeting, but she then settled down to hard work on her story. Though she continued to be active at New Stage, attended family parties, dined with E. L. Doctorow and Robert Penn Warren, and saw friends regularly for drinks and dinner, she traveled only to Oxford, Mississippi, where she visited with her old friend Vassar Bishop and met Vassar's three dashing nephews. Her active social life notwithstanding, Eudora wrote steadily, but by mid-April she despaired of her story. To Ken Millar, she confided her frustration. "I've been working too hard, I think, and fighting off distractions too hard, because I'm tired and realize the work is showing it. I began dreaming in manuscript form, revising and writing in the margins as I went—ruining (ruining!) the dream. Yesterday I took off and went to hear some music—the Mozart Requiem being sung in a church— wanting not only the music but the washing away of words, but they handed out the texts to us and I couldn't take my eyes off it—in Latin, so I had to work on it besides. The marvelous hour and a half of the music won over everything though, of course."[34]

Eudora's uneasiness about her story perhaps led in turn to uneasiness about the loss of Bill Maxwell as her *New Yorker* editor. Maxwell was retiring from the magazine, and she expressed at least a note of opposition before retracting her words. Maxwell assured her that no retraction was necessary:

In the first place you can say *anything,* and I would always know, we both would always know that it comes from love. As for my leaving the *New Yorker,* I didn't just turn my back on that job which I had loved passionately for forty years, I got ready to leave it by degrees, and not by letting go of my writers but by training those two gifted young men in so close and open and (so far as my feelings were concerned) exposed a fashion that I hoped whatever virtues I had accumulated as an editor would simply pass into them. More than seems reasonable, this is what actually happened. I rejoice, from 544 E. 86th Street, that you have finished a story, and I know that when it arrives at the *New Yorker* office there will be a similar rejoicing. Updike said, speaking of my leaving, it doesn't matter who I have for my new editor because any strictures they have about my work will be nowhere like as severe as my own are. The same thing is true of you. Will you bring a copy of the story for us to read when you come?

Eudora, however, would not bring a story to the Maxwells. Not even a new typewriter could keep her on task. Instead she decided to put the story aside for a couple of weeks. At the end of April, she told Mary Lou, "I've been working so hard I couldn't think, and what I really needed of course was a new brain instead of a new typewriter, but did know to stop what I was writing before I ruined it. Just a story, but it was trying to grow too much, so I put it away till now."[35]

Though Eudora briefly returned to her story, she did not do so for long. The literary panel of the National Council on the Arts came to Jackson early in May, and Eudora played hostess. Then she and Reynolds, who had come for the event, journeyed to North Carolina, where Eudora received an honorary degree from the University of North Carolina at Chapel Hill. This trip also enabled Eudora to visit, as she reported to Ken, "an old Virginia cousin* of my mother's now in her 80's, & her journalist daughter—darling people, and it's keeping in touch as my mother would & always did—her family's way and I feel it's mine. (*She is also Bob Woodward's aunt!)"[36] From Norfolk, she traveled on to New York for meetings with Bill Maxwell and with Albert Erskine, who, like Maxwell, was retiring. In New York Eudora saw Walter Clemons and Lehman Engel, had drinks at Joan Kahn's along with a favorite mystery writer, Dick Francis, and had a good visit with Rosie Russell, Diarmuid's widow. Then it was home for a month before an eagerly anticipated trip to Santa Barbara.

Ken was delighted to host Eudora again, even abandoning his insistence that the local writers' lunch group be an all-male preserve and even inviting Eudora to his home, although Margaret preferred not to have guests. For Eudora, however, the time in Santa Barbara proved disturbing. Ken was not himself. He seemed

anxious and forgetful, and Margaret was impatient with him. As
Eudora told Ken's biographer, "when she got mad, there wasn't
anywhere to *go*. It could be pretty explosive; it could be anything.
I used to get very upset inside, nothing I could do about it, when
she would have a temper tantrum without any cause and just blast
Ken to the devil, right in public. And slam doors, she was good
at that. Everybody knew it, because she did it in public all the
time. But Ken would say, 'Well, in a house with any two people,
any two people, it can be like this.'"[37]

From Santa Barbara, Eudora flew to Santa Fe and a peaceful
visit with Mary Lou, Agi, and the Mians. Then as June drew to a
close, Eudora arrived at home and took up her story again. A
month later she was still dissatisfied with it. To Ken she wrote, "I
tried writing some things I'd been feeling for the last year into a
new scene that I introduced into it but hard as I'd worked I knew
it honestly didn't belong and so I've just taken it out. It's hard to
keep things hewing to the line in a short story—or it proves so
for me." For his part, Ken was similarly concerned about his inability to write effectively, but for him this inability seemed more
ominous. He told Eudora, "My life is going through a change
which I am slow and unwilling to define because definition would
tend to determine it. I am more at peace with the world but less
with myself. I'd like to take a further step but perhaps have taken
not enough previous ones. I am woefully ignorant but not suffi-
ciently concerned about it to educate myself. Still I love to work
and am waiting to be able to, in my fashion."[38]

Eudora regretted that she and Ken had not discussed these concerns when she was in Santa Barbara, and she now sought to explain her reticence and to lift his spirits. "In some ways I am a very
shy person—and I revere the privacies— But reading your letter, so
sweet and kind as ever, I feel the uneasiness still and I hope whatever you do think now of doing, taking a fresh turn, will be good
and restoring and so positively to make things the way they ought

to be for you." Concerned that he had burdened Eudora with his worries, Ken responded to her letter. "I was rather depressed when I last wrote you, and indeed for some weeks before that, but now that I feel some relief I hasten to assure you that all is comparatively well here. I was suffering from a failure of memory function which is probably within the normal limits at my age but which, because I had usually had a nearly perfect memory, scared and depressed me. I got a psychologist to give me a series of tests, got through with colors if not flying ones . . . The sharing of the pressure with a professional really helped, and so did my return to work, if you can call revising a screenplay work."[39]

Far less disturbing than Ken's plight, but worrisome nonetheless to Eudora, were major household expenses. The large Pinehurst Street house that had been her home since 1925 needed a new roof, and Eudora told Ken that in order to pay for it, she was accepting speaking engagements at Denison University in the fall and at Agnes Scott and Cornell in the spring. Thus began a pattern of what would come to seem almost incessant trips to colleges and universities. Her earnings from these appearances would send her income, which for the past year had substantially declined, soaring above the national median. But the urge simply to travel may have been more compelling than any financial strait. Travel may have been one way Eudora avoided focusing upon her inability to help Ken or upon the import of her writing difficulties. She was on the road long before her October 26 date at Denison. Early in October, she gave a reading at Smith, then went to New York in order to see *The Robber Bridegroom*, with a new cast, begin an open-ended run on Broadway. She told Mary Lou that she "liked the show for its youth & high spirits & inventiveness— the cast was fine, the hero especially, Barry Bostwick, who went on with his broken elbow in a big leather sling—and was so compelling a performer that you forgot it (except in the love scenes)."[40] Rosie Russell, Bill and Sonja Smith, and her sister-in-law Mittie

joined Eudora for the premiere and for a postshow party at
Sardi's. Then it was on to Bryn Mawr for another reading—
"Powerhouse," as requested by Laurence Stapleton. Afterward
Eudora was home for two weeks before venturing to Denison,
but scarcely had she returned and cast her presidential ballot for
Jimmy Carter before it was time to go to Washington for yet an-
other meeting of the National Council on the Arts. There she
saw Reynolds, and they both enjoyed dinner with John and
Catherine Prince. There also she was thrilled with a private show-
ing of the treasures from the Egyptian tomb of Tutankhamun.
Not until Thanksgiving was drawing nigh did Eudora settle back
into her Jackson routines.

During the intervals between trips, Eudora found time to
write a review of Virginia Woolf's letters and to work on her
new story. From Washington, she wrote to tell Ken of progress
being made. "I've been working hard myself. A long story that's
tantalized me is slowly finding its shape, I believe—and my hope
is that when I get back home (Sunday night) I can bring it off,
then. It's a hard one, but the hard parts were all new, so I very
much want to solve them as well as I'm allowed."[41] But the story
remained incomplete as the year drew to a close.

Her own inability to complete a story did not disconcert Eudora so much as did Ken's growing despair over his writing difficulties. The tone of his letters in late 1976 was decidedly
melancholy, and Eudora sought to provide aid from afar as best
she could. She wrote,

> When your letter came today I wanted to ask you *now* if
> there is any way you know of that I could be any help? Of
> course you have written around and about it—your father's
> (I know no word—his doing)—and into it and out of it,
> while you yourself have made a whole life that is good, and
> truly good, aware and *un*hurting and understanding of oth-
> ers, a shining way to have dealt with what was done to

you— But it hasn't seemed to have been enough for *you*, to bring you real peace of mind. Would it be any use to you to write about this to me? Trying a new way if it came to you? You have written about it to me in letters, you know. The time I first thought of asking you this was when I read your letter about walking in Kitchener—that you wrote when you came back from your trip to London. The old stone rooming house where there was a happy week or so in your seventh year, with your father—I know you've thought and thought, so much and so long, about putting it down—and have worked it out in many circuitous ways. Maybe there are endless circuitous ways. I know I may be out of my depth— You will understand, though, what makes me try— I would try to be a reader of understanding and imagination and safety.

Eudora concluded her letter by reminding Ken of the powerful bonds between them. "When we were little we were so very far away, but now we are growing old (not in feeling, I hope) we are close—perhaps both are reasons, when taken together, why you might some day try this, if the spirit moves you. It would help that we share a sense of continuity in life, and that there's a continuity that we have between us of caring and concern." Ken promptly sought to reassure Eudora about his mental state. "I've been reading over your recent letters and really should regret the tremor I caused in your strings, except that the sound it made was so beautiful. I am grateful for your love and caring. I wasn't in such bad shape as I may have seemed to be, and certainly am not now, with memory improving and urge to work returning."[42] But such letters of reassurance offered false hope.

Early in December, Eudora wrote to Frank Lyell, sending him news of his mother, who had just had a stroke, and expressing the wish that his Christmas visit to Jackson would be a long one. During the past two years, the two old friends had grown apart, and Frank told Reynolds that he was mystified by the coolness he sensed in Eudora. The correspondence between them had not been as active as it had been in earlier years, but Eudora was writing fewer letters across the board. And her arthritis could make it physically painful for her to write or even to type. When Eudora did write, she wrote to Frank as often as she wrote to Reynolds or to Bill Maxwell. Still, both Charlotte Capers and Reynolds believed Eudora was distancing herself from Frank. Eudora had in two or three letters seemed critical of Frank for not promptly visiting or writing when his mother was distressed or ailing. And perhaps Frank had made some slighting remark about Eudora's relationship with Ken Millar. In the summer of 1976, he had ironically written to Reynolds suggesting that an infatuated Eudora equated Ken with his detective-protagonist Lew Archer. A similar, even if more veiled, comment to Eudora, especially given the depth of her love and worry for Ken, would have been ill advised. Now, however, time seemed too short for alienation between friends. When Clarena Lyell, age ninety-one, died in January, Eudora and Frank drew back together in their common grief.

For Eudora, 1977 was a year of troubles and tributes. The year began with letters from Ken, letters that expressed his deep affection for Eudora and his gratitude for her concern. "Sometimes your insight is so dazzling that I have to shut my eyes. But you must not feel that it has ever hurt me to be touched by it. Your rays are wholly benign and leave no mark. The fact is—if I may step to one side and comment simply as an innocent bystander—the power of your empathy is so great that it fills me with glee on behalf of the whole human race. I'm sure you understand me, you always do. Too well, indeed, except that your perceptions are *always* benign and never harmful. And if there is some unease in my letters from time to time, you are never the source of it, merely a witness. And always, dear Eudora, a witness for the defense."[43] Ken rejected, however, Eudora's suggestion that he turn to autobiographical writing. His memory problems would ultimately preclude any kind of writing, but Eudora would herself eventually take the advice she had given to Ken.

For the moment, however, Eudora followed advice Ken had long since given her: She selected previously published pieces of nonfiction for book publication. She also continued to write non-fiction. Her review of the *Selected Letters of William Faulkner* appeared in the February 6 issue of the *New York Times Book Review*, and she began a long essay. In the midst of such work, she returned inter-mittently to her rape story. As she told Ken, "Doing a piece on Chekhov, which is absorbing as well as hard—but yesterday, the story I've been writing but had to interrupt for this, made an ap-pearance again in my mind like a fish leaping in the river when I thought it was quiet and I wrote on it again for about an hour. Anyway I took it as a sign the thing was still alive. And I hope yours is the same." The story was alive, but it failed to command an intense enough focus and commitment. Instead Eudora lived by a principle she enunciated in a letter to Mary Lou. "More and more I prize the present, and if you look at the strange device on the banner *I'm* carrying 'mid snow and ice, it's CARPE DIEM."[44]

In March, Eudora's resolve to seize the day led her to under-take an ambitious travel schedule. Of course, a desire to supple-ment her income to some extent continued to prompt her trips to colleges and universities. In 1976 she had earned a third less than she had the previous year, and now unexpected household expenses and an audit by the Internal Revenue Service worried her. In 1970 she had donated the many, many typescripts of *Los-ing Battles* to the Mississippi Department of Archives and His-tory, typescripts that an appraiser believed would fetch a healthy sum on the open market, but the IRS had disallowed that deduc-tion. Might the IRS be about to pose some additional hardships? Eudora was apprehensive, and friends were concerned for her. Bill Maxwell wrote to inquire about her finances, noting, "It is presumptuous of me to ask, but how *can* you be 'broke' with that musical running on Broadway? Every time I see the ad I think cheerfully Money in Eudora's pocket, and now it seems I am mistaken. Hasn't that incompetent young man ever got that contract straightened out? I start to get wild and then I think if what I think is true is true then Lehman Engel is already wilder than I could possibly get, being in the trade. Do send me a postcard saying— well I guess there is no good in your saying what I would like to hear if it isn't true, but saying something. Otherwise I will lie awake at night grinding my teeth." When Eudora failed to reassure him about her Broadway income, Bill wrote again: "And before I forget it, if you ever should find yourself up against the wall, as in financially, that is, more going out than is coming in, or less coming in than is supposed to go out, will you kindly remember that, thanks to Emmy's father, we have more money than we quite need, and helping you would be a piece of great good fortune."[45]

Eudora, of course, had no intention of accepting money from her friends, though the offer marked the depth of affection between them. Instead she set out on a round of moneymaking readings and lectures. First, she made a trip to Duke to read, see Reynolds, and meet with her Virginia relatives who had moved to Raleigh. While she was with Reynolds, she learned that Margaret Millar had undergone surgery for lung cancer, and she immediately wrote Ken to express her concern. He soon replied that all had gone well and the cancer had been wholly excised. In April she appeared at Agnes Scott College, and in May at Cornell University. Cornell had invited her to discuss Chekhov, and Eudora found the prospect of rereading one of her favorite authors intriguing and was interested in writing about him. The work seemed even more worthwhile when Eudora came to the Cornell campus and was reintroduced to her sponsor, Professor James McConkey, himself a writer and a student of Chekhov. After Cornell, Eudora spent three days in New York, read at Berry College in Georgia, went to Washington for a National Council meeting, regrouped for four days at home, traveled to receive two honorary degrees—from Washington University and Kent State

University—paused for two weeks at home (attending family parties and New Stage meetings), then went to Harvard for another honorary degree before flying directly to Santa Barbara.

This was Eudora's third trip to the Santa Barbara Writers Conference, but it was not a happy one. Margaret Millar, who had recovered from her surgery, was rather hostile to Eudora. The previous fall Ken had been away from home for an extended period, and Margaret told Eudora, "When Ken is away, of course, I open your letters to him, but only to see if there's anything in them he needs to be informed about."[46] Margaret's jealousy was now out in the open. Eudora may also have found herself somewhat dissatisfied with the conference itself, feeling that it put too much emphasis upon established writers and did too little to encourage young writers. For whatever reason, she would come to Santa Barbara and endure Margaret's enmity only once more—when Ken had almost totally lost his memory.

From Santa Barbara, Eudora continued her travels. She went to Santa Fe for a relaxed and enjoyable visit with Mary Lou, the Mians, and their Santa Fe friends. Then finally she returned to Jackson for a lengthy three-month stay, broken only by a short trip to Washington for the National Council on the Arts. She now finished all work on her book of nonfiction and dedicated it to Ken. He was overwhelmed and told Eudora,

> The gift you propose to offer me is the kind of thing that might happen once in a life-time if a man is lucky—like being knighted by a queen, not with a sword though, with a human hand—and cause him every time he thinks of it, to laugh with pleasure. Love and friendship are surely the best things in life and may, it seems to me now, persist beyond life, as we wish them to, like the light from a star so immeasurably distant that it can't be dated and questions of past and future are irrelevant. The source of the starlight might as well be thought to be inside us, and we take credit for the

forces that sustain us, as being loved makes us feel loveable. If I may compound my image, staying within the elastic bounds of astronomy, or astrology, it's as if you had stopped time and handed me a glass which admits the future to our present vision, and the past too, joining present and future times, as if we had lived beyond life, as indeed we are going to do now to some extent, together. You make me very happy. You often have. And I await your book with gratitude and anticipation. I expect I'll never have awaited a book so intensely as I will this one.[47]

In mid-July Frank Lyell arrived home in Jackson from an extended European vacation. He got off the plane a sick man. On July 19, Eudora wrote to tell Mary Lou of Frank's death: "I hate to tell you that our poor Frank got home from Europe very ill with congestive heart failure, and died in the hospital this morning. I went to see him when he felt like it, & he would talk lovingly about his trip— But I'm afraid that's exactly what he shouldn't have undertaken—driving all those places, eating all that German food. He would have had to have drastic surgery to survive, and then would have been a very weak invalid, the doctor said—they were preparing to operate when he died, and he might have definitely preferred it the way it happened. I'm glad he did get to see that baroque, though—for him it was the dream trip. And I'm glad he made it home." Eudora's grief at Frank's death was intense, and she described it to Ken. "I know I'm at an age when the loss of friends is not considered surprising, and I have lost my three dearest in Jackson (I was counting Diarmuid, though he wasn't exactly of Jackson). But I am not going to learn to *accept* it for being not surprising, I'm going to hate it & protest it straight ahead—I'm indignant for their sakes—up to my last breath. I testify to their absence."[48]

Eudora's resolve to protest the loss of Dolly, Diarmuid, and Frank was matched by a renewed commitment to live fully in the present. She met old friends and new for dinner, she attended family gatherings, she helped with fund-raising and scheduling for New Stage Theatre, and she saw numerous films, *Dinner at Eight, Singing in the Rain, Tomorrow, Streetcar Named Desire,* and Ingmar Bergman's *Smiles of a Summer Night* among them. Her only late summer writing venture was to review *The Never-Ending Wrong,* Katherine Anne Porter's recollection of the 1927 Sacco and Vanzetti trial and execution. Eudora found Katherine Anne's account of governmental injustice and of manipulative, self-interested protest leaders to be powerful and timely.

At the end of August, Reynolds arrived in Jackson to help select the winners of the Eudora Welty Americana Awards and to be Eudora's houseguest. Laughter and recollections of the past were the order of the day, or rather days. After Reynolds's departure, Eudora wrote still another *New York Times* book review, this time turning her attention to the *Essays of E. B. White.* Her comments about White seemed to reflect her current mood. "What joins all these essays together," she wrote, "is the love held by the author for what is transitory in life. The transitory more and more becomes one with the beautiful. It is a love so deep that it includes, may well account for, the humor and the poetry and the melancholy *and* the dead accuracy filling the essays to the brim, the last respects and the celebrations together."[49]

Though for the last three months her life at home had been active, Eudora was loath to remain settled, and in October she began to travel again. She read at Yale University, saw the Paul Mellon Collection of English Art there, and then spent a night with the Robert Penn Warrens. She continued on to Manhattan, took the train out to Katonah for a visit with Rosie Russell, returned to the city, met with a copy editor about *The Eye of the Story* (the title selected for her nonfiction book), visited with the Maxwells, Lehman, and Walter Clemons, and enjoyed a Cezanne exhibit. Her final stop on this junket was at Bryn Mawr. Two weeks later she was back on the road for two more university readings.

A few days after this, the University of Mississippi held a three-day symposium in her honor—Cleanth Brooks, Bill Smith, Charlotte Capers, and Reynolds Price delivered papers about her, and Eudora read excerpts from *Losing Battles* to a large banquet audience in Oxford. Still her travels for the year had not ended. In December, Eudora went to the University of Michigan for her seventeenth honorary degree and a good visit with the Faulkner biographer Joseph Blotner. This continuing effusion of academic recognition must have pleased Eudora, whose work had been slow to attract such adulation. Though she found working the academic circuit taxing, she must have known that the academy could prove crucial in bringing her fiction to generations of new readers. But perhaps academic recognition was also helping to create a "petrified" image of Eudora. Over the course of her career, she would receive at least thirty-nine honorary degrees and would come to seem a sort of institution herself.

Despite her many awards, Eudora's spirits were rather low as 1977 drew to a close. She continued to be apprehensive about Ken. Though he had begun seeing a psychiatrist for help with his memory and reported that he was making real improvement, his letters also betrayed considerable doubt. He had written to Eudora about the possibility of writing a story that moved "in and out of the mind, through fiction and dreams and back into solid reality; which is not solid, which is not reality. Reality is in the relationship between the tenses. You know so well what I mean, you are a master of those who find meaning everywhere, which is one among several reasons I am so grateful for your letters." After Eudora wrote to encourage this concept, Ken expressed hope that a story moving between fiction, dream, and reality might prove therapeutic for him: "I am grateful for your thoughts, the more so that they seem to chime with mine. I mean our joint idea that I might use my kind of structure to mix approaches to reality—approaches ranging from external through psychological realism into the more dreaming part of our experience, and out again.

Certainly the best thing for a writer to do with a trouble of any kind is to find a personal narrative or artistic use for it. I'd been making a few more notes along those lines, and your letter parallels and strengthens them."[50]

During the autumn, in the midst of her worry about Ken, Eudora had anticipated a lonely holiday season. In October she told Mary Lou that the "old friends' reunion," a Christmas tradition, was no longer possible—"no Frank, in addition to no Dolly and no Hubert." Then on Thanksgiving Day Eudora faced the death of still another friend. Bill Morrison, one of the Basic Eight who had dined and partied together for twenty-five years, succumbed to cancer at age fifty-two, the age at which Eudora's father had died, and Eudora was deeply concerned for Bill's wife and children. In the face of grief, Eudora also felt an intense urgency to see friends, both at home and around the country. She planned another trip to Santa Fe, for, as she had told Mary Lou, "I do believe in seizing the day at all good chances, don't you?"[51]

The need to see Ken again was also great, but the prospect of encountering Margaret probably kept Eudora from accepting a fourth invitation from the Santa Barbara Writers Conference. Instead she invited Ken to join her and Reynolds in Jackson for the February publication date of *The Eye of the Story*. Ken demurred, telling Eudora that Margaret still feared the return of her lung cancer: "She is still sitting in the shadow of the big scene, and I suppose I am, too. Clearly it would cause her pain for me to be gone for even a few days. So I will stay here instead, and hope that your invitation will be a re-open-able one. You know how I'd love to come, and celebrate with you and Reynolds the publication of a book which is so important in my life; and will be in the lives of many people."[52] Both Eudora and Ken must have sensed, but declined to say, that Margaret's jealousy was now a powerful barrier between them.

Eudora's life in Jackson remained active. As always, she cherished her family and took pleasure in her great-niece and -nephews.

Bob Padgett, Paul Hardin, and George Boyd, all members of the Millsaps College English Department, were friends with whom she socialized, as was psychiatrist Thomasina Blissard, who had written a Vanderbilt master's thesis on William Faulkner before she became a doctor. Jack Wiseman, a Mississippian who had long worked in New York, was now living in Jackson, and the two women regularly watched the evening news and talked politics. Bethany Swearingen, a Millsaps librarian, and her sister Crawford were friends to whom Eudora was devoted. Patti Carr Black, one of the founders of New Stage Theatre, and Jane Reid Petty, another founder and the theater's managing director, became regular dinner companions and the closest of friends. They relished talking about the New York season, about state and national issues, and about the Jackson scene. And the surviving members of the Basic Eight—Eudora, Charlotte Capers, Ann Morrison, and Jimmie Wooldridge—continued to enjoy one another's company and to laugh heartily at tales told by Eudora and Charlotte. In addition, a steady stream of scholars began to make their way to 1119 Pinehurst Place, Jackson, Mississippi. Danièle Pitavy from France, Jan Gretlund from Denmark, and Michael Kreyling from Tulane University all visited Eudora during 1978, and all would eventually publish books about Eudora's work.

At the beginning of the year, Eudora was firm in her resolve not to travel to colleges and universities; those trips left her exhausted. She stayed at home, reading murder mysteries and writing the afterword to E. P. O'Donnell's *The Great Big Doorstep,* which Ken's friend Matthew Bruccoli was publishing. In Jackson she and Reynolds celebrated the publication of *The Eye of the Story,* and she mailed old friends offprints of her 1930s, previously unpublished story, "Acrobats in a Park," which had now appeared in the French magazine *Delta.* In March, however, she commenced a relentless travel schedule. She spent five days at a University of North Dakota writers' conference, where her former Millsaps student John Little was a faculty member and where feminist writer Tillie Olsen, also participating in the conference, proved an alien spirit. Though Eudora found Olsen's discussion of women's hardships "touching," she also found Olsen to be closed-minded. "She will brook no disagreement," Eudora observed.[53]

Eudora was home for the March 28 birth of Elizabeth Eudora White, Donny and Mary Alice's third child, but in April she was on the road again, giving three readings at universities. As May began, she took a break from the academic circuit and spent several days at Santa Rosa Island, off the west coast of Florida, where she and Jackson friends Jane Petty, Patti Black, Charlotte Capers, Ann Morrison, and Karen Gilfoy were joined by Reynolds. Eudora wrote to tell Ken about her good time at the beach. "Last night we ate fine fresh fish—and while we were sitting around the driftwood fire in our house the most astonishing wind came up—very loud & strong without a break, tremendous, & yet the sky was perfectly clear overhead, brilliant with stars— The wind went on all night— I thought of that ghost story, do you know it—by M. R. James—'Oh Whistle and I'll Come to You, My Love'—the ancient Saxon ring that when turned on the finger (I think) called up the wind."[54] Ann Morrison found one subsequent moment at Santa Rosa less enchanted. The vacationing friends had spotted a large wounded bird, down the beach, mired in the sand, oil on its wings, flailing, screaming in fear and pain. Eudora knew that Ken, the ardent bird-watcher and conservationist, would have immediately recognized the bird and handled the situation, and she must have recalled *Sleeping Beauty*, the novel, dedicated to her, in which Ken had so movingly presented the plight of wildlife in the midst of an oil spill. Feeling helpless to act, distressed by the bird's suffering, Eudora also wanted to know the bird's species, perhaps so that she might tell Ken. Ann, the group's contrarian, thought that issue irrelevant, and said so. Eudora turned remote and unusually quiet, clearly miffed. In this situation, which surely evoked thoughts of Ken, had Eudora become not only concerned for the wounded bird, but also, at some level, impatient about her separation from Ken, worried about his memory problems, resentful of his wife? Had she become frosty at someone near to hand in frustration at her powerlessness to change the situation either in Santa Rosa or in Santa Barbara? Was her behavior part of a pattern of displacement that recurred during the years between the publication of *The Optimist's Daughter* in 1972 and *One Writer's Beginnings* in 1984, between her meeting Ken in 1971 and his death in 1983? Might Eudora two or three years earlier have been cool to Frank not for anything he had done but as a result of frustration with her own inability to write or to cope with separation from Ken? Certainly, she would subtly spar with Charlotte about Episcopal rituals or social life at the University of Mississippi. And eventually Eudora, the most equable and even-tempered of individuals, would flare up at Reynolds with slight pretext. These oh-so-human moments of annoyance were mild, infrequent, and typically short-lived, but they may well have been significant. With those she held dear, perhaps, Eudora turned her frustrations outward rather than inward, and those who loved her discounted these moments and even laughed with her about them.

From Florida Eudora returned to Jackson for a few days and then set out again on a round of engagements. Her last stop was New York, where she attended the annual meeting of the National Institute and American Academy, saw Nona Balakian and Joan and Olivia Kahn, took in a Monet show, and went to two plays—*Death Trap* and *Ain't Misbehavin'*. She particularly enjoyed the latter because it focused upon old-favorite Fats Waller, the musician who had inspired her story "Powerhouse." To Ken she wrote that it was "a wonderful show—a new young company of black entertainers who'd come to Fats's music as whole-heartedly and rapturously as if they'd grown up with it." Unbeknownst to her, Eudora may have influenced the shape of this production. Murray Horwitz, along with Richard Maltby Jr. had put the show together. Ten years later, when the show was revived in New

York, Horwitz recalled having met Eudora at the home of Kenyon College professor Robert Daniel and having discussed Fats Waller with her. "The line from Fats through 'Powerhouse' through Bob through Kenyon to the show now on Broadway is, to me," Horwitz wrote, "a strong and beautiful one."[55]

From New York, Eudora went to Rutgers to accept an honorary degree and stopped at Bryn Mawr to visit Laurence Stapleton. Then at the end of May, she went home and began work on a review of V. S. Pritchett's *Collected Stories.* Pritchett had long been one of her favorite writers, and she wanted to do justice to him, although an accelerated deadline left her unsatisfied with the product. Pritchett, nevertheless, was thrilled by the review and wrote to tell Eudora so. "Your words," he told Eudora, "add that something extra which comes as a revelation; one that enlarges oneself and gives a new stimulus to gathering together what havens one is trying to do something with."[56]

The review completed, Eudora at long last could return to her lengthy story "The Shadow Club." The four-month stretch from July through October was free from commitments. Now, however, the physical demands of writing proved a problem. Arthritis in her hands had become increasingly painful, and as a consequence, she began to use an electric typewriter, "which *waits* on you—as if drumming its fingers while you think. But it's a help in not being (manually) such heavy work." Writing fiction remained, however, heavy intellectual work. At the end of July, she sent Ken a progress report. "Here, I've been working steadily, on a story that I'm enjoying the problems of but trying not to let it get out of the shape of a story—it threatens to. I work most of the day but do most of the typing while it's early and not so hot."[57] The story of a school teacher's rape was on the road to becoming a multigenerational saga of neighborhood friends.

Throughout the summer, Eudora continued to be distressed about Ken's plight. He had indicated that the physical care of

Margaret was an all-consuming task, and he had expressed concern about his memory loss. Ken depended upon Eudora's sympathetic ear. "I am sorry to have given you reason for concern," he wrote her, "and yet I did so knowingly because it is in the nature of our loving friendship to record the dark as well as the sunny hours. Not that my life is dark now, or ever was. But there are a few clouds across the sun, gradually lifting and dispersing as I go. The worst of them, an almost literal cloud, was the shadow on my memory and therefore on my mind. But it was never dark enough to cut me off from hope or even from pleasure in the use of my mind. The only limitation, really, was in the kind of work I could do, and its extent." Having received this letter, Eudora ventured to offer some carefully phrased advice drawn from her own experience caring for Chestina. "From time to time I can't help thinking that strong as you are and being such a source of strength to all those you care for (all that 'strength' implies) you must some time need a little time or a way to restore some for your own— Forgive me if I need forgiving for saying that, and poorly as I put it in words too. I guess I felt I could say it because you've been a source of strength to me and because I had to learn for myself about that kind of tiredness." To Eudora, and to many of Ken's friends, it seemed that Margaret was too demanding of his time and energy and was often cruel in her treatment of him. Though Eudora had feared her frankness might bother Ken, it did not. In September he wrote to Eudora, "You did spell out one danger in my life, I hope not in yours, that one can be used up in the services of pain and trouble not one's own. Well, I'm not used up. I hope I was able to lean on your strength without abating it, and on your knowledge of trouble and its meanings without deepening your own troubles. The best thing that can happen to a man is to be known, and by a woman of your great kindness and light and depth. I think you read the situation and showed me a step towards change." Ken's ardent praise of Eudora was soon matched by hers of him. "We do want to be known truly, and I want to know truly. I'm glad that you feel you can lean on me—it's part of trusting—you mustn't worry or imagine that anything but good could happen to me from our knowing each other—truly—the dark times as well as the bright—for you know as I do there is nothing destructive in it, only everything that moves the other way— Depressed or happy and serene, our spirits have traveled very near to each other and I believe sustained each other— This will go on, dear Ken— Our friendship blesses my life and I wish life could be longer for it."[58]

September and October were busy months for Eudora in Jackson. Her days were primarily devoted to writing, her evenings to dinners with friends. She continued to offer support to New Stage Theatre, which was now buying another building for its productions, and on September 24 she gave a benefit reading to help in the cause. Early in October, Eudora welcomed Irish writer Mary Lavin and her husband, Michael Scott, to Jackson, and Mary found that seeing Eudora for the first time on her native turf was revitalizing. Her husband later told Eudora that Mary "had to a certain extent lost her 'sense of place'—the quality in you (both of you) which had drawn you together in the first place. But meeting you again in your place—talking to you again and seeing for the first time your beloved Mississippi—and then later, seeing Faulkner's house in Oxford—and re-reading you both—all this has given her back her own sense of place—and with it a new contentment."[59]

Mary may have returned contentedly to her Irish home, but Eudora had scheduled another extensive time on the road at the end of October. She and poet William Meredith shared the podium at Connecticut College; an overnight stay with the Robert Penn Warrens and five days in New York were advantages of the trip. Then she flew to Boston and drove with Elizabeth Spencer to the University of Southern Maine, where a southern writers' festival was underway. An outing with scholar Louis Rubin to the L. L. Bean store in Freeport delighted Eudora, who had long shopped via the Bean catalogs, and seeing Rubin selecting nightgowns for his wife by measuring them on himself ("We're the same size," he told Eudora) sent Eudora into gales of laughter. A week after she returned to Jackson, Eudora left again for Agnes Scott College, and at the end of November she went to New York for a MacDowell Colony gala, to spend some time with Rosie Russell in Katonah, and to record two stories for Caedmon Records. She spent most of December at home, but at the end of the month was in New York again for the Modern Language Association meeting. She came home on December 30, met Mary Lou at the Jackson airport on January 2, and three days later flew with Mary Lou to Santa Fe, where she spent five days. The resolve to limit travel had again fallen by the wayside.

Reynolds Price, for one, was worried by Eudora's peripatetic existence. He felt that the key to her happiness lay in writing fiction, not in traveling hither and yon. "My own sense," he later recalled, "was that what she needed to do was get-to-work on the main thing she could do so supremely well . . . and I said as much to her on so many occasions that I ultimately annoyed her, I know (though she never said a single cross word to me in private, only in the company of others)." Certainly, Eudora was most happy when she was gripped by a story in progress, but all her life she had loved travel as well. Trips to New York, Europe, and Santa Fe had allowed her to see cherished old friends, satisfied her continuing desire for a richer cultural life than her home state could offer, brought her joy. They consumed time that could have been devoted to writing, but for Eudora the price was well paid. Other trips, those to National Council meetings or to colleges and universities, seem not so much to have prevented her from writing as to have been undertaken because she found herself unable to write. After years of recognizing compelling subjects for her stories and bringing them into focus, she was having serious trouble doing so. She was not able to find, as Elizabeth Bowen once put it, a subject "that *would have* you at work writing on it."[60]

Once she had returned from Santa Fe in January 1979, Eudora did for a time heed Reynolds's advice and "get-to-work on the main thing she could do so supremely well." She remained primarily in Jackson for several months. Her stint on the National Council on the Arts had ended, and she was free from the travel that position entailed. Moreover, from January to March she had no college engagements. How much she accomplished on "The Shadow Club" is impossible to ascertain, but she worked at fiction during this time. At some point in the composition of what was now an incipient novel, Eudora's relationship with Ken began to inform her development of characters. The Welty/Millar correspondence had by now become less frequent and less expansive. Ken's failing memory and consequent depression limited his ability or willingness to write. So Eudora turned to fiction as a way of comprehending and accepting this situation. Her schoolteacher protagonist recalls an abortive romance with a man named Henry: "Justine had told him her whole life, she had told him her worst, her deepest secrets. He had kissed her for letting him hear all she wanted to tell him. Henry had listened and fallen asleep with his trusting head in her lap. Yes, they had loved each other, and they loved each other now." The love, however, is doomed by Justine's (or Carrie's, as she is also called) caution. "My chance to get away from myself is gone. My chance to move into arms that reached for me I gave back to the giver. I ran away home. And home is where I found what's been waiting for me. But what's been waiting for me is what *I* am, too."[61] This event seems to be fictional, but it conveys both the love and the trust Ken and Eudora felt for each other and the mutual restraint that had characterized their relationship.

Such heartfelt autobiographical writing must have been very difficult to sustain, and during the first part of 1979, there were other trials to endure. Understandably, Eudora sought distance from her story and from the ongoing pattern of loss that it confronted. She filled her days with everything but concentrated efforts at writing fiction. She continued to serve as a trustee of Millsaps College and to lunch regularly with her high school class. She was a fiction judge for the University of Michigan's Hopwood Awards in Creative Writing. She went to the movies and particularly liked Woody Allen in *Manhattan*. She gave a reading in Jackson and participated in a two-day writers' seminar in Greenwood, Mississippi. Then, in April, she attended an American Academy meeting, visited with friends, saw *Sweeney Todd* with Walter Clemons, and taped a Public Television interview with Dick Cavett.

On her birthday, April 13, there was a major flood in Jackson. Eudora told Ken that "It was almost unbelievable—it trespassed on all likelihood—a lake appearing in front of you on your neighboring street where no water had ever been near before—not a rampaging flood, a quiet creeping up— And in the calm clear Easter moonlight, no sound in the city, except trucks carrying dirt & sand for the levees & helicopters flying over to spot what was happening. The rebuilding is going on now. I must say people everywhere behaved well— They helped each other with might & main, and nobody looted. It was scary about the snakes. Of course they were displaced too— People getting back in their houses found them high & low. The YMCA, when it was able to be entered, had 5 cotton-mouthed moccasins in the gym, one wound around the clock." To Elizabeth Spencer, Eudora reported on speculations about the prospect of the Pearl River Dam giving way and about the long-term effects of the flood: "'Will the reservoir dam hold?' is the local question— A taxi driver told Reynolds Price a year ago that 'that dam is eat up by crawfish,' and 'if we ever have high water, Lord help Jackson.' The new Woman's Hospital was evacuated of mothers and 35 new babies, all, m. or f., sure to be named Pearl."[62]

Near the end of April, Eudora joined Jacksonians Jane Petty, Patti Black, Charlotte Capers, and Ann Morrison in a second trip to Santa Rosa Island. Then on May 1, she set out on a round of academic and professional engagements. She read at Harvard and journeyed on to Montreal for a Forster Conference. Elizabeth Spencer, who now lived in Montreal, was Eudora's guide to the city, and to Elizabeth, she sent special thanks for her visit. "What a fine and lovely time you gave me in Montreal! The glow of it stays with me. So many thanks to you for so much—the early morning meeting at the Airport—the installation in my charming room in Chateau Versailles—the good times at your apartment, the party, the rides everywhere, the wonderful night on the town—seeing me off again— Well, you were my steady welcome, and I loved every minute of seeing you again. And what a good thing that we got in that nice leisurely delicious lunch at home, Elizabeth, to catch up on talk—and another one after the Conference to get *that* talked over. It made me feel so happy to see where you live and how much it agrees with both of you and what a variety of interesting & stimulating people you move about with... It was all marvelous for me— And didn't we laugh a lot, we might as well have been in Mississippi, for laughing."[63]

Later in the month, Eudora went to Urbana, Illinois, for an honorary degree and for the opportunity to honor Charles Shattuck, who was retiring from the faculty. Long ago Shattuck had published "Ida M'Toy," and now Eudora signed a new limited edition of the essay published with photographs. Then it was on to New York, where she spent a welcome evening with the Maxwells and attended a meeting of the American Academy and Institute of Arts and Letters, as it was now named. One more stop remained on this tour: Eudora delivered the commencement address at Brandeis (actually she read the introduction to *One Time, One Place*) and received yet another honorary degree. Afterward she relaxed with Dan and Janet Aaron, friends since she had taught at Smith in 1962. She told Mary Lou that she "lay in their Pawley's Island hammock, & had drinks, and the radio played wonderful jazz & we danced & cavorted, and ate spaghetti, which made up for the rest, beautifully."[64]

Eudora returned to Jackson in good spirits but soon discovered that her house had developed serious foundation problems. The workmen had to drill down past the Yazoo clay of the surface to a blue clay that lay beneath. As Eudora told Ken, "It was rather wonderful to learn what blue clay looks like—it's the solid stuff that doesn't move around (in Mississippi) (different from the way it moves around in California) like the clay on top—and it has small, whole seashells all through it. I knew the Gulf had once covered us here, or more than once, and that whales swam in it— their bones have been unearthed—but these were just lovely little undisturbed seashells—I've been sleeping over them 35 feet down under me all these years."[65] But marvelous as the sight of the blue clay was, repairing the foundation was expensive. Despite the arthritis in her hands, Eudora agreed to sign a limited edition of *The Optimist's Daughter* in order to pay the bill. The Franklin Mint, a corporation manufacturing all sorts of collectibles, from plates and medallions to figurines and model cars, would now list a Welty title among its leather-bound books.

In July Eudora left home again, this time for an extended trip to England. Bob Padgett and Paul Hardin, faculty friends at Mill-saps College, had invited Eudora to join them and their students on a summer program at University College in Oxford. Eudora served as a faculty member but also designated herself as a student. To Ken she described the summer's activities: "The summer in Oxford was wonderfully interesting but too much for me in numbers of people always, a little class on Tues. & Thurs. afternoons, and so alluring to see & hear and go back to, the whole world of the University—and yet all that medieval got me down in a way— Every morning, before the ringing of the bell and breakfast in Hall, I'd walk out the gate and see the whizzing buses & bicycles & taxis go by in the High Street—present life! Then to a lecture by some Oxford eminence—I went to 2 a day mostly & never came out of the Renaissance till time for a beer in the garden before lunch—the heavenly gardens—I walked a lot, of course, so much to see and go back to see again— My own part would come late in the afternoon, well, it was called 'Tea with Miss Welty,' when I'd talk back & forth with students, 20 at a blow. I liked the students. They made me one of them, which I guess may be the reason I'm so tired!"[66] Here Eudora sounded the major patterns that now constituted her life: a need to seize the day and live in the present, and a weariness that came as a result of doing so.

Beyond her academic life, Eudora enjoyed visiting old friends around the English countryside and meeting new friends in London. As she told Ken,

> On weekends I went to the country several times, to visit friends of the last time I was in England, about 20 years ago, who were so dear as to remember me and give me a wonderful welcome. And in London I met Mr. Pritchett, as I told you. He had written to me several notes & letters over the years, which I saw to be like him—he spontaneously enjoys getting in touch with other writers, especially the short story lovers—and had asked me to let him know if I were ever in England, so I did—how could I have forgiven myself if I had been too shy to? He and his wife Dorothy asked me to lunch at their house and had just ourselves so we could talk, and we sat talking away the whole afternoon— They're both the liveliest, kindest, most open-hearted, open-minded people—you know from his writing just what he is, he's so generous there too— I loved every minute, shall never forget this. He *rejoiced* me. He is the brightest-eyed 79-year-old you could ever hope to see. After lunch he walked me through his neighborhood to where I could catch a bus—I elected to ride home that way so as to see more—and stood and waved me out of sight. That was the best of my summer, my year.

The summer in England was generally a happy one, but there was one melancholy aspect to the trip. "I've had a difficult time in one respect," she confided to Ken. "My closest friends of the 50's visit here, Elizabeth Bowen most of all, are now gone, and I miss them so sharply—London didn't seem the same place at all."[67]

From mid-August through the first week in October, Eudora remained at home. She worked on an essay about her first story, "Death of a Traveling Salesman," to be published in the *Georgia Review* along with the story. She also worked on a review of Elizabeth Bowen's *Collected Stories.* Worry about Ken continued to nag at her; Ken had expressed concern about his grandson leaving school at age sixteen. Eudora responded, in hopes of reassuring him. "Since reaching home & reading your letter I'd been so concerned to know about Jim and his leaving school, to think of its troubling effect on you & Margaret—as well as its meaning for Jim of course— I think of how you are the best understander of the young I know of, and their champion, but also their protector from threats of harm which you understand better than they do, and this is not just the young, but Jim. Yet, Ken, *he* knows this too and knows you and Margaret are *there.* He's got that trust, and going with him it is its own kind of protection, don't you think?"[68]

Two weeks later Eudora wrote to tell Ken that she was leaving for New York and to volunteer to run errands for him there. She concluded her letter by mentioning a dream she had recently had: "By the way I had a dream in your handwriting. (My dreams sometimes come in words.) It was a little less than a page long, written in very dark ink or with a soft black pencil, on lined paper—You wrote my dream!—Or I dreamed you wrote my dream. Where do these things come from, then? If only I could remember after waking what it said.—But you see it's left traces." Ken had once told Eudora, "Your spirit lives in my mind, and watches my life, as I watch yours."[69] Her account of this dream delivered a similar message.

After a four-day trip to Manhattan for an American Academy and Institute meeting and for reunions with friends, Eudora returned home for two weeks. John Robinson arrived for a visit, and the two old friends went on the sort of picnic they had enjoyed forty years earlier, "down by an arm of the river, where the flood had come in so high— It was lovely—(we took another picnic)—the sweet-gums were starting to turn scarlet, the oak-leaves were falling & covered the ground where the Pearl River has clawed and peeled it clean, and the water itself was just *full* of fish!—leaping up & popping up & splashing all over— Birds singing—the flood had obviously been enjoyed by all that called the place home."[70] The romance between Eudora and John may have long since passed, but their interests continued to be similar and their friendship endured.

Eudora's fall travels were not over. She made three trips to universities, finishing her academic obligations on November 8. Ken's book reviews had by this time been collected and published by Lord John Press, and Eudora was pleased to receive the book. Reading the book, she told Ken, allowed her "to be in your company past and present—and in the present seeing back into the past, as in the Foreword—the most touching of autobiographical writing I've seen of yours—and there was the pleasure of receiving all those flashes your reading brought forth from your mind, so many books and writers I've never had the chance before to know your thinking or feeling about." In the future, only in reading Ken's autobiographical fiction, his reviews, and his novels, or during one last trip to Santa Barbara, would Eudora be in his company. In the two months after Eudora responded to *The Collected Reviews*, Ken wrote to her four times, but then he wrote no more. His loss of memory, she would eventually learn, made composing even a letter impossible for him. In his last letter, save one, he told Eudora, "There seem to be times when one doesn't want to talk much, simply rest in the quiet security of love and friendship."[71] For Eudora, not simply a *quiet* but a *silent* security of Ken's love and friendship would have to be enough.

NINE

"Ceaselessly Into the Past"
Self-Portraits 1980–1984

For eight years Eudora had been unable to complete any work of fiction. She had continued to write, but by taking repeatedly to the road, she had denied herself the consecutive time required to bring any project to fruition. During those same peripatetic eight years, however, Eudora's focus had begun to move away from fiction and toward autobiography. Her essays "The Corner Store," "Fairy Tale of the Natchez Trace," and "Looking Back on the First Story" were autobiographical in nature. Her reviews had focused not upon novels or short-story volumes, but upon self-reflective works or collections of letters: Elizabeth Bowen's *Pictures and Conversations,* Katherine Anne Porter's *Never-Ending Wrong,* and the letters of William Faulkner and Virginia Woolf. Her correspondence with Ken Millar often involved the relationship between autobiography and fiction. Eudora had urged Ken to write about his life. Now Eudora was beginning to look at her past work in relation to her own life, and ultimately she would deliver three long, autobiographical lectures and turn them into *One Writer's Beginnings.* A writer's autobiography is most likely to be written near the close of a career, when intimations of mortality prompt the revaluation of experience. Such was the case with Eudora; her desire to seize the day did not wane, but her attention upon the past grew, and her focus on writing was renewed.

As 1980 began, Bill Maxwell sounded a familiar note in a letter to Eudora. Like Reynolds, Bill believed the key to Eudora's happiness lay in her work, and in a lighthearted way, he urged her to avoid commitments that interfered with that work. "I will undertake to keep my study in better order (not to mention my life)," he promised her, "if you will undertake to say no oftener, to people who only want your life's blood . . . yesterday I said no, to a nice man whom we often meet jogging in the sandy roads of Cape Cod, a psychoanalyst, who wanted me to read a thirty-three-page story, by his thirteen-year-old son, and evaluate it, and help him find a publisher. Politely. But I SAID it. And what I can do you can do. Better. If it is a matter of money, just tell me and I will dig around in the back yard in Yorktown Heights until I find you some."[1] Eudora failed at first to take this advice. She had been thrilled with the November election of William Winter as governor of Mississippi, and she now played a part in his inauguration, participating (along with Leontyne Price) in a symposium titled "Mississippi and the Nation, 1980." She told Ken, to whom at intervals she continued to write, that Winter was a "good, first-rate, vigorously thoughtful and firmly spoken man. I wouldn't be surprised if he didn't prove himself to be one of the best governors in the nation. His third try— This time he beat the disgraceful redneck scoundrel who beat him before, & who has outraged everybody so, that our man won this time by a landslide."[2]

Immediately after the January 21 inauguration, Eudora left for New York and a meeting of the American Academy and Institute, but at the end of the month she settled into her Jackson routines and would remain at home for the next six weeks. New Stage Theatre, high school class luncheons, family gatherings, dinners with friends, occupied her attention, and she was pleased by *Eudora Welty's Achievement of Order*, which had been written by

Tulane University professor Michael Kreyling and which she found "a book of seriousness and deep perception, valuable to me."[3] Eudora was beginning to think about the shape of her career, and the coming publication of her *Collected Stories* would prompt further thought along these lines. In January 1979, at the request of editor John Ferrone of Harcourt Brace Jovanovich, she had agreed to such a volume, but permission difficulties had caused delay. Random House, where Eudora was now under contract, was slow to relinquish its rights to previously uncollected stories. In March 1980, however, Ferrone informed Eudora that the book would go into production.

In mid-March, Eudora returned to the sort of travel schedule that had typified the past few years. She went to Bryn Mawr, came home for three days, and left again for Randolph-Macon Woman's College, where she spent several days as artist-in-residence. Then in April, strange though it seemed to Eudora at the time, she visited the Citadel. She had jokingly told Mary Lou, "I'm considering giving my reading in Confederate dress with sword gestures." There she watched the cadet corps on parade, feeling at first repelled and at last emotional. "A dreaded thing, the cannons were fired in a 19-gun salute," she wrote to Ken. "I'd never been close to any fire-arms. Not only deafening but the earth under your feet seemed to rock, and the shocks went right up you. Terrible. Then there was a lot of marching and wonderful music, and bagpipes & Scots in their plaids—we got up time after time (like in the Episcopal church) & laid our hands over our hearts at the playing of various tunes, as they marched, ending of course with *Dixie*, which whenever I hear it makes the tears jump out of my eyes."[4] The Citadel itself seemed wholly alien, and Eudora mocked an atmosphere of worship in the parade audience. Still, the South, despite everything, was home, and a song evoking her southern roots was moving, even if she found it vaingloriously placed on the program. Though family obligations no longer bound her to Jackson, Eudora had chosen to remain.

At the Citadel, Eudora shared the platform with Cleanth Brooks, Andrew Lytle, and Sally Fitzgerald, the editor of Flannery O'Connor's collected letters and collected essays. This was Eudora's first meeting with Fitzgerald, and the two had a good talk there and on the plane when they left. Eudora was headed not home, but to the University of Chicago, where she stayed in a dormitory, met with resident students, and gave a dormitory reading. After her work was completed, Eudora managed to attend a performance of the Chicago Symphony conducted by Sir Georg Solti. She drew a picture of Solti, which she sent to Bill and Emmy Maxwell along with a description of him, a description that evokes her character Powerhouse. "He has so much drive & energy he looks like a wizard in mid-spell, moves so instantaneously & absolutely so fast that you see him first in one position, then in another, but your eyes can't catch up with him, can't see the motion. So demon-like, crouching and pointing and fixing a player— He has Dracula ears (seen from behind—bald head, but you've most probably seen him in London or somewhere). A young man from Tupelo, Miss., was the Seigfried [sic]—Couldn't hear too well how he sang, because of Solti— Thundering—Leaving, we ran into [the Tupelo man's] wife in the lobby—she recognized me because she used to work in a bookstore in Jackson. (It never fails—Mississippians turn up everywhere. I didn't know about Dennis Bailey or have any idea he was from home.) It was a strange juxtaposition—Solti & Tupelo!"[5]

From Chicago Eudora returned home but made two trips to New York in May—one for work on her *Collected Stories*, the other for an American Academy and Institute meeting. Between those two trips, she managed to complete an introduction for a Lord John Press limited edition of her 1934 story "Acrobats in a Park." In this brief essay, Eudora recalled the early childhood "experience of coming under the spell of travelling performers who appeared from time to time in my town—then a small town—of Jackson, Mississippi. It would be the event of the year to be taken by my parents to our Century Theatre, the Chautauqua, the Ringling Brothers Circus. I was exposed to the trusting wonder of seeing and hearing the visiting artists perform, the agonizing knowledge that they were not with us to stay. Galli-Curci, Blackstone the Magician, troupes of acrobats and clowns, were all as fleeting as dreams. How much more vivid were their appearances to me than those of visiting aunts and uncles, and how much more poignant. Aunts and uncles returned, but hardly, it seemed to a child, the troupe of Living Butterflies, wings unfurled, slowly ascending by their teeth while the band played them to the top of the tent." Eudora went on to describe the discovery that her family and the performers were not really so alien. In her imagination as a story writer, the pyramid formed by an itinerant acrobatic troupe came to represent her true subject in fiction and the center of her inner life: "the solid unity of the family thinking itself unassailable."[6]

Her brief essay completed, Eudora again traveled to New York. The American Academy had chosen William Maxwell to receive the Howells Medal for Fiction for his novel *So Long, See You Tomorrow*, and Eudora was delighted to present it to her good friend, offering high praise as she did. "In the writing, the novel's tension is finely strung and unremitting. Its quiet carries its own reverberations, so accurate and true that in the end they shatter the crystal: We are face to face with other people's mystery and with our own. There is nothing between us and the realization that without love and without death we should never have come into the presence of human mystery at all." Maxwell responded with these remarks: "Miss Welty has just slipped me an empty box. The catch is broken and she was afraid the medal would fall out. When *she* got the Howells Medal a stranger came up to her afterwards and asked to see it. Miss Welty obliged, and the stranger dropped the gold medal and, since it really *is* a gold medal, it cost fifty dollars to have the scratch removed. My medal has been in my pocket since ten minutes after three." For Emmy

Maxwell, the occasion was particularly moving, and when Eudora sent the comments she had handwritten for the occasion, Emmy responded: "Thank you for sending us your presentation speech so quickly! It's very beautiful, because your words are so carefully chosen, and your voice is in them. It brings back for me that moment of complete happiness—undiluted. I see you & Bill seated side by side on the stage, both looking so radiant."[7]

From New York, Eudora went first to the University of Tennessee, then to Kenyon College for her twenty-third honorary degree and a reunion with old friend Robert Daniel. After a brief stop at home, she headed to Memphis for her twenty-fourth honorary degree, this one from Southwestern College, and then to Washington, where President Carter presented her with a Medal of Freedom. Receiving this medal from a rather liberal Democrat and a southerner was especially gratifying to Eudora, and she invited Reynolds, Rosie Russell, Charlotte Capers, Bill and Sonja Smith, John and Catherine Prince, and Walter Clemons to join her for the occasion. "It was a bright, absolutely cloudless, refreshingly cool day in Washington," Eudora later wrote to Mary Lou, "and the medal giving was outdoors, in the back part of the lawn, down those circular steps at the back of the White House that you see in newsreels. The Marine Band played, our guests were seated on chairs in the shade facing a little low platform, and we came toward it in alphabetical order (you know where I was—between Robert Penn Warren and in front of Tennessee Williams (the end)—each of us escorted by a young Marine aide that wasn't going to let us fall down. Then (we were all announced as we approached) just at the last minute, another W was inserted between Red and me—turned out to be Mrs. John Wayne, a little late getting there from Calif., but the only lady with a hat—all in white, her hat was a cartwheel, and she was very dark, Spanish." The president himself made a wonderful impression upon Eudora. "The interesting part to you I think (as it was to me) was the way the President himself came through as a man—he seemed to me a very genuine and aware person, and he conducted the little ceremony—it was short, right on time, and all to the point—with a sure, natural graciousness . . . Mrs. Carter told me that the selections were personal with Jimmy and that he had made it his business to do his homework on us all (she didn't put it like that) but I think this is not surprising in him." In his citation for Eudora, President Carter said, "Eudora Welty's fiction, with its strong sense of place and triumphant comic spirit, illuminates the human condition. Her photographs of the South during the Depression reveal a rare artistic sensibility. Her critical essays explore mind and heart, literary and oral tradition, language and life with unsurpassed beauty. Through photography, essays and fiction, Eudora Welty has enriched our lives and shown us the wonder of human experience." As moving as the citation was, Eudora felt that the best moment of the ceremony came after the president had presented her medal and shaken her hand. "He kissed me too, and what he said to me was 'God bless you, Eudora.' I was very much stirred, I can tell you. (I forgot to say, Beverly Sills was another medalist, and *she* kissed the President.)"[8]

Eudora returned home on June 10, and the page proof of her *Collected Stories* awaited her. She immediately began proofreading in an effort to meet her June 19 deadline. She had earlier decided not to revise the stories. She told Mary Lou, "'I could do it,' as Nixon said, 'but it would be wrong.'" She did, however, ask permission to make some changes in terminology. Editor John Ferrone recalled her request. "Eudora wrote to correct a typo in the story 'Powerhouse' and another in 'Ladies in Spring.' Then she said there was a third change, not due to a typesetter's error but a 'way of speech forty years ago.' She wanted the word 'nigger' to be deleted from 'Why I Live at the P.O.' In a later letter, she asked to have it deleted wherever it appeared, explaining that while it cropped up naturally in conversation in the older stories, 1980s readers might find it 'throbbing with associations not then part of it.' She decided instead to review the offensive word case by case, because in the end it was dealt with in several ways."[9] In Eudora's stories, narrative voice was seldom unitary, and in the 1930s and 1940s, it at times shifted into the voices of white characters for whom *nigger* was a culturally inherited concept and who unselfconsciously and obtusely used the term without thought of or care for its effect. Given the political climate of 1980, however, Eudora feared that such characters might seem more bullying than benighted and that her stories might be misconstrued.

Beyond enabling her to correct typos and forcing her to reflect upon racially charged language, rereading all of her stories revealed many connections between life and art to Eudora. She realized that though the stories were "not in any literal way autobiographical . . . they showed me my life—I guess they *are* my life." Yet, though her thoughts were turning more and more toward autobiography, she continued to work on her long story called "The Shadow Club." She wrote to Bill Maxwell about her hopes for the story. "I look forward to trying to straighten some mistakes out in a story too long & hopeless to mention, but I do to you—I'm really filled with delight at the chance to start in on it—hoping to dig out the weeds and find & separate the true things I could swear I planted: That's to make sure about." Bill was thrilled to learn of Eudora's summer plans and again urged her to use her time wisely. "I am so happy to learn that there is a story that has some mistakes that need straightening out and that is too long, which could mean, of course, that it is not long enough. If I had my way, I would disconnect your telephone and discontinue the mail service and make the people that want you to come and address them or read to them walk to Jackson to ask you to do it. And when they did I would fix it so you weren't home that afternoon."[10]

Three months later, having made a brief visit to Utah and Brigham Young University, Eudora had still not finished the story. Then on September 30, novelist Anne Tyler arrived in Jackson to

interview Eudora for a *New York Times Book Review* article. The two
writers already felt acquainted; Reynolds had told Anne, his
former student, and Eudora about each other. Now Anne's questioning of Eudora evoked many reminiscences that would become part of her Harvard lectures in 1983 and of *One Writer's
Beginnings* in 1984. And when the article ran on November 2, in
conjunction with the publication of Eudora's *Collected Stories*,
Tyler's description of Eudora proved particularly incisive and
sympathetic. She contrasted Marcella Comes's portrait of a
youthful Eudora with the appearance of the seventy-one-year-old
woman she had just interviewed. Then Tyler discussed qualities
that had not aged: "Her hair is white now, and she walks with
some care and wears an Ace bandage around her wrist to ease a
touch of arthritis. But the eyes are still as luminous as ever, radi-
ating kindness and . . . attention, you would have to call it; but attention of a special quality, with some gentle amusement
accompanying it. When she laughs, you can see how she must
have looked as a girl—shy and delighted. She will often pause in
the middle of a sentence to say, 'Oh, I'm just enjoying this so
much!' and she does seem to be that rare kind of person who
takes an active joy in small, present moments. In particular, she is
pleased by *words*, by ways of saying things, snatches of dialogue
overheard, objects' names discovered and properly applied." Although Eudora had suffered one grievous loss after another in
the last fifteen years, although she must now have been concerned
about Ken Millar's decision not to correspond with his friends,
although she was surely frustrated by her own inability to complete "The Shadow Club," she revealed no dejection, no worry,
and no frustration to Tyler. Of course, as a very private person,
Eudora would have been unlikely to reveal the dark side of her
emotional life to a *New York Times* audience, but in showing bright
spirits to Tyler, Eudora was not dissembling. In fact, as Tyler
noted, Eudora was one of those persons able "to take active joy
in small, present moments." That ability had sustained her just as

it had the people she photographed during the Great Depression. "Trouble, even to the point of disaster," Eudora had long ago realized, "has its pale, and these defiant things of the spirit repeatedly go beyond it, joy the same as courage." In Herman Melville's terms, she possessed the "wisdom that is woe" but never experienced the "woe that is madness."[11]

Two weeks following Tyler's visit, Eudora went to New York to promote her new book and promptly came home for a Millsaps College board meeting. Then she made an overnight trip to Baltimore. Katherine Anne Porter had died and Eudora attended the memorial service for her old friend. Robert Penn Warren was too ill to be present, but his daughter and wife were there, as was Peter Taylor. After the service, Eudora spoke with the Warren women and Taylor. "I brought along a little extra money. Why don't we go somewhere and eat some crabs. I think that is what Katherine Anne would want us to do." And so they did, sharing dinner and private remembrances. When Eudora returned to Jackson, she at last received word from Ken, though indirectly. Santa Barbara book dealer Ralph Sipper, concerned that Ken was going through a particularly bad time, proposed to publish a collection of his autobiographical pieces. Ken, Sipper reported, wanted Eudora to write an introduction to the volume, but preferred that Sipper make the request. Eudora, however, preferred to respond to Ken directly. She did not yet realize that memory loss had made correspondence impossible for him. "Today a letter came from Ralph Sipper about a proposed book of yours," she thus wrote to Ken, "but before I answer it I wanted to write and say I was glad of it as a sort of communication from you to me, that you thought his idea of my doing a bit at the beginning was a good one. I know you said the last time you wrote that sometimes things go better without letters, and I wanted to follow your wish with this but it has been such a long time."[12] Eudora went on to say that writing the introduction would be helpful to her, and indeed it proved so in more ways than one. It not only helped her to feel close to Ken, but it also pushed her to think yet further about autobiography as a genre, the genre that she would ultimately use so effectively.

At the end of October, Eudora went to New York for the publication of her *Collected Stories*. According to Harcourt's John Ferrone, "We invited Eudora to come to New York . . . to help give the book a send off. She and I were meeting for the first time. Well, not really. I had met her twenty-five years before at a small party given by the *New Yorker*'s poetry editor; I had even seen her jitterbugging—to Fats Waller—but I was too shy to speak to her. I doubted she would remember. I took her to lunch at The Four Seasons, the place to be seen by the publishing world—a mistake, I thought afterwards. We had a happy time, but Eudora might have felt more comfortable at some cozier place . . . The next evening we gave her a gala reception at the St. Regis Hotel with one hundred guests."[13] Eudora enjoyed the hoopla and found Ferrone as agreeable in person as he had been on the phone; a new friendship was cemented. Old friends also shared in her pleasure about the new book: She saw Bill and Emmy, Tim Seldes, the Kahn sisters, and Walter Clemons during her week in Manhattan. And reviewers were unanimous in praising the *Collected Stories*. Writing in the *Saturday Review*, Mary Lee Settle observed, "The short story may be an American invention, but the tale is worldwide, as ancient as myth told by the fire at night; quiet, seductive, portentous, amoral. It is in this classic company that Eudora Welty takes her rightful place, with the ironic tenderness of Chekhov, the almost feral edge of Maupassant, the ominousness of Poe and Bierce, the lacy strength of Henry Green. She is probably the finest Mozartian stylist writing in the English language in this century." Hortense Calisher concluded her *Washington Post* review by noting that in Welty's "gallery, so moving, so tumbling with the hundreds of precise human gestures and enchanting images calling to be collected and cited aloud, so entertaining in the deepest sense, one hears that pure voice vocalizing behind the events. May readers swarm." And in the *New York Times Book Review*, Maureen Howard asserted, "Her work is filled with characters who do not hear, literally or figuratively, with people who talk and do not listen. Their stories bear the sadness and the folly inherent in ignorance and self-absorption. Eudora Welty's writing is an act of generosity—for the partial and incomplete vision of her characters is pieced out and made whole for us: In such completeness there is care and intimacy, something like mature love. The richness of such talent resists a summing up. We can place her with her models, Chekhov and Katherine Anne Porter: She is always honest, always just. And she is vastly entertaining. The stories are magnificent."[14]

Eudora arrived home to find another letter from Ralph Sipper awaiting her. He was delighted that she had agreed to write an introduction to Ken's book, but he also delivered some disturbing news. "I will say that although Ken recognizes the need for a preface of his own, the possibility exists that he will not write it. I say this because he has not, to the best of my knowledge, written much if at all within the last year. Not only has he been distracted as I wrote to you, but he seems not able to remember or focus on those little mundane details necessary for communication with friends and acquaintances. Perhaps he's just going through a bad period. I fervently hope so, but we are not banking on anything more than a short note from him at this time. Therefore, feel free to write as extensively as you like." The reason Ken had ceased writing to his friends and had resolved to "rest in the quiet security of love and friendship" was becoming clearer.[15] The memory problems he had experienced during the past few years were now incapacitating. Eudora surely had sensed this much earlier, but she had continued to hope that Ken's memory would return. Sipper's letter called that hope into question.

On November 9 and 10 Eudora was in Dallas to give a reading and participate in a panel discussion at Southern Methodist University, and there she met Herb Yellin, whose Lord John Press had just published the collector's edition of *Acrobats in a Park*. Yellin had also published Ken's *Collected Reviews*—and he promised to send Eudora word of their common friend. Four days after leaving Dallas, Eudora gave a reading at Agnes Scott. This was Eudora's last college appearance of the year, and she was now free to enjoy some time in Santa Fe with Mary Lou and her friends.

She returned from Santa Fe a day before Thanksgiving so that she might celebrate the holiday with her nieces and their families. She enjoyed Thanksgiving dinner at Mary Alice's and then came home to find that her house had been burgled. To Mary Lou, Eudora reported that the thief took her typewriter, instruction manual, seat cushion, and gold membership pin from the Institute. "He's sitting at my typewriter now, on my cushion, writing, and wearing my pin," she joked. But the robbery was no joking matter. It seems likely that Eudora interrupted the thief, for obvious valuables—the silver serving pieces on her dining room sideboard, for instance—were untouched. More upsetting than the robbery was a waiting letter from Herb Yellin, reporting that Ken might have had a small stroke. Eudora certainly knew the effects of such strokes—her mother had suffered from a number of them—and her worry about Ken must have intensified. There was a sense of urgency in Eudora's brief Christmas message to Ken: "You're dear in every way to me and I think of you in such concern and love." A subsequent letter from Ralph Sipper did little to ease Eudora's mind. Though Sipper reported that Ken seemed better than he had a month or so earlier, he added that "Ken's devoted attention" to his now nearly blind wife had "so totally superseded his own life that his writing has come to a standstill." In the midst of cheerful Christmas parties with friends and family, Eudora must have felt a wrenching anxiety— for Eudora, as for her character Virgie Rainey, "all the opposites on earth were close together."[16]

During the first two months of 1981, Eudora remained at home. Her positions on the New Stage and Millsaps College boards, visits with friends, appointments with scholars, attempts at fiction, and the foreword to Ken's book occupied her attention. Ralph Sipper was delighted with Eudora's piece about Ken and asked her advice about a title for the volume. Sipper himself, however, made the ultimate choice—*Self-Portrait: Ceaselessly into the Past*, incorporating one of Ken's favorite F. Scott Fitzgerald lines.

Shortly after completing her work for Sipper, Eudora began a rigorous travel schedule. During the next ten months, she would make eleven different trips around the country. She would speak at colleges and universities, ranging from Vassar to the University of Alabama at Huntsville, from the Mississippi State College for Women to the University of West Florida. She would receive her twenty-sixth honorary degree from Randolph-Macon Woman's College, which had long before refused to accept her transfer credits. And she would enjoy a trip on the trans-Canadian railroad and meetings with friends in New York. As a consequence, at least partially, she would not complete any stories, and she would write relatively few letters. Eudora's correspondence, voluminous for so long, was becoming more and more limited.

Early in March, however, she engaged in a sharp exchange of letters with Reynolds about his review of short-story collections by Mark Helprin and Elizabeth Spencer. In this piece for the *New York Times Book Review*, Reynolds had discussed the American short story as a genre and had raised a number of questions.

> Have older writers concluded what most of the young have not? That the form itself is tired? If the form in question is the realistic story, then it would be hard to deny that many locales, ethnic pools, modes of thought and speech have been handled (and brilliantly handled) to the point of obliteration. Are there, for instance, new ledges from which to observe urban Jewish life or Southern small towns or Northeastern WASP nests or that country of the mind which is the locus of so many stories by younger writers—

the Land of the Impossible Marriage? Is realistic short fiction doomed, like Egyptian sculpture, to the endless manu-
facture of nearly interchangeable hawks and sphinxes? Does
the short story now provide an alarmingly exact parallel to
the decapitated snapping turtle whose heart may beat on
for days? In the face of cries of Yes from many quarters,
here are two claims of No: a slim second volume of stories
from Mark Helprin and a collection of nearly 35 years'
work from Elizabeth Spencer.

To Eudora, these comments seemed to denigrate the genre she
most valued and must have also recalled Richard Gilman charac-
terizing *The Surface of Earth* as a mastodon. She fired off a response
to Reynolds: "I was sorry to read your attack on the short story
in the review of Elizabeth Spencer and Mr. Helprin. There's a
lot of evidence around to correct a belief that the form must be
pronounced extinct—who else says so? You had some sympathetic things to say of the books in question in the space remaining, but in the light of your lengthy dismissal of the form itself
the effect of any good word was soured." Eudora then added, "I
feel you make a serious mistake in writing off the short story—
after all, it began far earlier than the novel (the Bible is full of
short stories) and will carry its vitality I daresay for far longer
than anybody would be safe to predict at our particular moment.
(Who *wants* to?) I'll be up to see our best short story writer alive
in a few weeks—V. S. Pritchett, at Vanderbilt this semester. He's
writing new ones right now, God bless him." Reynolds was
stunned by this letter and promptly answered it. He felt that Eudora had misread his essay, and he noted that he "certainly would
not have spent a week in writing the review or years in translating
and expounding the stories in *A Palpable God*—or weeks in affirm-
ing the endless vigor of your own *Collected Stories*—nor would I be
spending the greater part of my own life in writing stories—if I
did not believe passionately in the durability of the form in able

hands." Eudora remained unconvinced and wrote to say so: "No, no trouble in understanding what you said—I just disagreed with your pronouncements on the short story. For another view on the health of the short story, you might read V. S. Pritchett's essay which has just come out in *Vogue*—Nona [Balakian] put me onto it— Published along with it is his fine review of Elizabeth Bowen's collection."[17] For Eudora, the zest and metaphoric efful-gence with which Reynolds had posed questions about the short story overwhelmed his answers to them, answers which declared the genre's vitality. But perhaps Reynolds's questions also struck a personal nerve. Perhaps Eudora feared that her own short-story writing was now extinct. Whatever the case, this rift between friends would be short-lived; the continuity of love would not be broken.

A week after her dismissive letter to Reynolds, Eudora went to Vanderbilt, where Pritchett was teaching for the semester. The opportunity to see Victor and Dorothy was irresistible to Eu-dora, and Eudora's reading of "The Wide Net" was irresistible to her Vanderbilt audience. Pritchett was impressed that a gather-ing of professional academics and graduate students could re-spond so wholeheartedly. "The peculiar thing about universities is that they are so alien to the kind of life we writers lead. The academic voice is so distant and, often, so self-interested. Whereas we writers, at any rate, live in the congenial vulgar world at large. Yet the academic world *does* respond to what most members of it cannot achieve, the reckless creative impulse in its visitors. I shall never forget the standing ovation you got when you came here to read your story, how they sat on the stairs—defying Fire Regula-tions—and others had to hear you (which they did) in the over-flow rooms. You stirred up the deep regard for the imagination which does, thank heavens, lie in the public; in your case, the recognition that you have made 'your truth' out of what, almost unknown to them, was *theirs*."[18]

The Pritchetts and Eudora basked in one another's company,

and, as Eudora told Mary Lou, "had good plans made, so that we could meet alone, without the Vanderbilt people (he was writer in residence for the spring semester and I was asked up to take part in a seminar) and it was pure plain pleasure, every minute of it. I love Victor and Dorothy both—a marvelous pair. I'll never forget their conversations. Victor is a wonderful mimic, too—and can leap up and jig to show you an old Irish lady coming out in the rain under her umbrella, on their shopping street in London."[19]

Though this visit was "pure plain pleasure," the two writers seemed to sense that their literary powers might be waning. In a letter to Eudora, Dorothy Pritchett certainly indicated that this was the case with her husband. "There is a state of anxiety in him about his work at the moment and I deplore it. I think he feels he has to get such a lot *done* and the more he feels that and worries, the less good. But I don't need to tell *you* this. We will get through it and he will be comfortable again: He got reminded too much—every hour on the hour for weeks—about being eighty last December and it was not a good idea. I have not discussed this with him, hoping to rise above it, and I don't tell it [to] you as any secret exactly but please do not refer to it when you write because your letters would, of course, be shared. It isn't told to burden you but to deepen your acceptance of what your visit meant to us. We'd looked forward to it so eagerly, dreaded that we wouldn't be allowed to keep you to ourselves, and everything was so much better than we'd dared hope."[20]

Eudora's own anxiety about her work was great, but late in March her anxiety about Ken's well-being became even greater. Herb Yellin wrote to tell her that Ken was very unhappy. Yellin and John Gardner had visited with Ken and Maggie and were profoundly disturbed by the visit.

We met at the Coral Casino [Beach Club] and Margaret swept by me without a word. It appears that their electricity had gone out that morning and Margaret was furious because Ken couldn't fix it. Once inside the club she began berating Ken and literally screaming at him. He just stood there and took it. Then Margaret turns to us, all smiles, and asks us to take him off somewhere to lunch. She storms off. Ken apologizes for Margaret's behavior, stating she is quite ill.

At lunch he is even more quiet than usual but explains that he has had a stroke but he is not sure what kind of stroke it is. Ken thinks it may be a psychological stroke involved primarily with writing. He said that he can't even write a letter. He asked me to explain that to you and for you to be patient with him. The only time he lit up at lunch is when your name was mentioned. He wanted to know all about Dallas and how you were. He showed me his hand and said, "I can't write a letter!" When I was alone with him, he said that he was very grateful for the books and to be sure and express his love for you.

We asked him what he does with his time and he declared that he mostly sits around and thinks, trying to figure things out . . . The electricity at the house was bothering him so we offered to go to the house and take a look (neither one of them knew to throw the circuit-breaker) but first we had to locate Margaret. Another shouting match (all on her side, ensued). Margaret did not want us around but Ken held on to us, literally holding my hand at one point, and asked us to stay. He said she would not confront us. It was almost a warning to her. She disdained any offers of our help, saying it was useless and that she was legally blind. She finally contacted an electrician on the phone and they left together to go back to the house. He asked me to come up soon again.

The whole two hours was painful, depressing and sad. I think she is killing him. She is mean-spirited and vicious.

And I think that he tunes out . . . just to preserve his sanity. Whenever I have seen him before he is often witty and frequently smiling. But there was no wit or smiles on this day.

And the crazy thing is that he worries about her and is constantly explaining why she does things like this.

It must be like living in a lunatic asylum. Margaret talked pleasantly enough to people working at the Coral Casino but even though we were within earshot she referred to us as his stupid friends and wished we would go away.

I can't find any sympathy within me for her, no matter how sick she is. She is despicable. I wish there were some way to remove him from her presence but he would not hear of it.[21]

Eudora was worried. What could she do? Ken had asked that they suspend their correspondence, and in the past fifteen months, only rarely had she gone against his wishes and written him. For a brief time, in the wake of Yellin's revelation, she made no overtures to Ken. She appeared on the program for Founder's Day at the Mississippi State College for Women, dined at the Mississippi Governor's Mansion along with Leontyne Price, attended a New Stage production and party, and on April 7, left for a week in New York at the Algonquin. But by April 13 she felt she must contact Ken. "This is my birthday," she wrote him, "and I wanted to send you my love on it, and from here. Of course I send it on the other days and from wherever I am." Then, after telling him of her visits with Rosie Russell and Joan Kahn, she volunteered to help him in any way she could: "Ken, if at any point you needed me or if I could just come a day to see you, you could say so to Ralph Sipper and he would give me the message, I know. In the deepest sense we could never be out of touch— In the daily, enduring way, I think of this too. It does me good. Please dear take care of yourself."[22] There was no response.

Eudora continued upon her scheduled rounds, traveling to Chattanooga, Huntsville, and Atlanta, and she took time to write a foreword for a new edition of Virginia Woolf's *To the Lighthouse.* Her foreword began in a personal vein. "As it happened, I came to discover *To the Lighthouse* for myself. If it seems unbelievable today, this was possible to do in 1930 in Mississippi, when I was young, reading at my own will and as pleasure led me. I might have missed it if it hadn't been for the strong signal in the title. Blessed with luck and innocence, I fell upon the novel that once and forever opened the door of imaginative fiction for me, and read it cold, in all its wonder and magnitude."[23] Having recalled her discovery of this novel, Eudora then went on to discuss the autobiographical basis of the novel itself and the way that basis was transformed and transfigured by Woolf's imagination.

Despite occupying herself with travel, writing, community activities, Eudora had not ceased to worry about Ken. On May 18, Ralph Sipper wrote to tell her about some surgery Ken had just undergone, the insertion of a brain shunt designed to improve his memory by relieving the pressure caused by fluids inside his skull. A month later, Sipper reported that the surgery had not helped Ken, and he described the situation to Eudora at some length.

It looks as if the original diagnosis [made in March or April] was correct—Alzheimer's disease. It was a shock to Carol and me, as it must be for you. And so unfairly inappropriate for our dear friend's fine mind to be subjected to such a dismal final path.

I visited Ken the day before yesterday. We walked through Hope Ranch. The day was beautiful and I know he liked having me with him, his dogs trailing us as we chatted. When we got back to the house I helped him sort his mail, discovering in the process four royalty checks from foreign publishers which had been lying on his desk for weeks

(totaling almost $2,000). It is quite obvious that someone
(I) must act as his amanuensis. Maggie seems not terribly
interested in the mail. She did hire a young woman to be
with Ken during the weekdays.

You see, Ken has moments when he cannot remember
simple but fundamental things. On our walk he seemed lost
for the moment at a cross street. He will forget the name
for a household object like a pen. And, he may be experiencing moments when he has difficulty reading.

It is hard for me to write this letter and I am truly sorry
to hurt you with its sad information, but I know that you
want to and must know what is happening to Ken. We have
talked about you and it is clear that you are very dear to him.

It occurs to me that you might want to think about visiting him. I mention this possibility even though travelling
is not something you look forward to, I am sure . . .

Or, you might consider the merits of a telephone conversation with Ken. Perhaps, I could arrange to bring him
here to the office, where the two of you could talk without
the kind of interruptions that might come from his home.
Please know that I am offering these ideas only because I
know that you and Ken are unhappy over the breakdown in
communication between you. Again, my apologies for in-
flicting such bad news on you.

Immediately, Eudora decided to write Ken, proposing that she
come to Santa Barbara: "I've been feeling for some time that I'd
give anything to see you. Now some time has opened up for me—
I'd be free to come out, if you found it a good time for you too.
Would the last week in June be too near—I could come later, in
July or August, if that's easier. Just to walk or sit or ride by the
sea and talk again. I would dearly love to see you." Then, after
saying that Ralph Sipper had been good enough to let her know
how he was doing, Eudora spoke obliquely about Margaret and

about Ken's medical care: "It's so rotten, the time they've been giving you—I hate it for you—I pray for it to change."[24] She placed this letter in an envelope marked only "Ken" and evidently mailed it care of Ralph Sipper. Again there seems to have been no reply from Ken, but Sipper would continue to keep Eudora informed about the situation.

It seems quite likely that, in addition to her heavy travel schedule and troubles with arthritis, deep-seated anxiety about Ken now kept Eudora from writing to friends around the country. She was also beginning to be overwhelmed with mail from admirers and students—to respond to everyone was impossible. To Mary Lou, she attempted to explain the situation by way of apology. And in a rare 1981 letter to Bill Maxwell, she further berated herself for failing to work on "The Shadow Club" or to answer letters. "I'm ashamed to say I haven't cleared the decks so as to get down to work as I'd vowed to myself I'd do— By decks I mean the dining room table, in addition to my desk and all— covered with undone tasks, unanswered mail and the rest. When I ask company to dinner, I have to carry the old mail off the dining room table and hide it on my bed. Isn't that one of the cardinal sins? Sloth, I mean. I *suffer* from it."[25]

For three weeks in July Eudora had enjoyed the companionship of John Robinson, home from Italy for a family visit. The two met often to share good food and good conversations. Eudora, along with Charlotte Capers, Jane Petty, Patti Black, and New Stage supporter Tom Spengler, heard Alice Parker single-handedly perform a witty operatic version of *The Ponder Heart*. The group seemed convinced that a full-scale production was in order. And Elizabeth Spencer's August visit was still another pleasure. The national political scene, however, distressed Eudora. She told Mary Lou that President Reagan had "made the country a different, uglier, more shifting, more dangerous, more corrupt and far less hopeful place, in just this little time. He's consistent—everything he announces is some new proof of what he doesn't mind doing to our lives. And all in aid of *weapons*—for us & the rest of the world."[26]

On September 12, Eudora began a journey she hoped would help her work, not hinder it. She met John and Catherine Prince in Montreal, where they were welcomed and entertained by Elizabeth Spencer and her husband, John Rusher. Then Eudora and the Princes boarded the trans-Canadian railroad for a journey west. Inevitably the journey reminded her of stories Ken had told about his youth in Canada, stories that disease had largely erased from his memory. But these days were nevertheless filled with beauty and pleasure. In Calgary, Eudora left the train for a week alone in Banff, where she hoped "to try to sort out a story." That hope proved delusory, and at week's end she left Canada for New York with nothing sorted out.

During her ten days in New York, Eudora wanted to see Rosie Russell and had agreed to speak at the Katonah Gallery, where a traveling exhibit of her photographs (paired with quotes from her stories) had just opened. Rosie had arranged for the exhibit in order to honor Eudora. The two were now quite close friends, bound by their love of Diarmuid. In the past, Rosie had at moments been jealous of Diarmuid's devotion to Eudora, but any resentment had disappeared. They had the kind of friendship that Eudora shared with Emmy Maxwell and with Dorothy Pritchett but that she would never share with Margaret Millar.

When Eudora returned to Jackson on October 5, a letter from Ralph Sipper awaited her. Ralph had sent "a progress report that speaks not of progress but of a status quo condition as far as Ken is concerned. Carol [Ralph's wife] and I visited him last week and he remains cheerful and alert if one confines himself to conversation dealing with the present. While we were there Maggie said that she had been meaning to telephone you because she had 'seen' the review of *Self-Portrait*, and your wonderful introduction came to mind. I told Maggie that I would relay her message to you, one of thanks and good wishes. They are getting on alone despite their handicaps, with the exception of the driver who takes them to the Coral Casino [Beach Club] at late morning and brings them back late afternoon."[27] Maggie's word of thanks about Ken's autobiographical book of essays came to Eudora only through an intermediary.

At the end of 1981, Eudora made still another trip to New York, this time for an Academy meeting. There she saw the Maxwells and Bill Smith before returning home for the holiday season and for work on a story about Ken's vicissitudes. New word of Ken finally arrived in mid-December. Ralph Sipper sent a relatively encouraging message. "He has his alert moments, which are heartwarming to witness, and he has times where he just seems not in touch with anyone or anything except his own fantasy world. Last week Margaret called me and asked me to join Ken at one of the regular 'writers' lunches.' He seemed to enjoy himself there, in the company of friends and acquaintances, and I met the young Chilean man who chauffeurs Ken around. Jorge is a sensitive and intelligent photography student with whom Ken feels comfortable, it seems to me."[28]

As 1982 began Eudora had resolved to limit her travels and to be a better correspondent with old friends. She wrote to Mary Lou, expressing concern about a mysterious skin ailment that had left Mary Lou constantly uncomfortable, shedding much skin, and unable to travel, and also wrote about her own inability to help Ken. "From so far away it is just a matter of thinking about him every day and sending love—through *my* mind, *my* memory. I still hope, too, because let nobody forget, Ken has a very remarkable mind, and no one can say his memory just might not resurrect itself." At last Eudora felt able to mention Ken's Alzheimer's to her close friends. Margaret Millar, however, was not content with telling only close friends; when a *Los Angeles Times* reporter interviewed her, she informed him of Ken's memory loss and provided specific examples of its effect. Both Ken's agent, Dorothy Olding, and Ralph Sipper sent Eudora copies of the article; Olding deplored the revelation, Sipper was more ambivalent. "I believe that the pressures of coping with it all by herself got to her," Ralph told Eudora, "and I am not certain whether she did right in telling all as per the enclosed interview. I know that reading it will make you sad. The day after the interview was published Maggie telephoned me and broke down over the phone, but I know she thinks she did the right thing. Ken *does* seem cheerful, is cheerful. He couldn't fake that in my opinion. So time moves on and eventually he will have to be institutionalized. Maggie has begun some inquiries about quality rest homes where Ken would be given the best attention. I will keep you posted." Then, after saying that he would gladly relay messages from Eudora to Ken, he added, "or you might like to write directly to Maggie, who might appreciate hearing from you." In March, Eudora took the first option, sending Ken a letter via Sipper. Knowing of Ken's great love of the natural world and particularly of the sea, Eudora wrote, "I think of you every time I see the wonderful 'Life on Earth' program on public television— Tonight we heard the singing of the whales, deep down in the sea. All the whales sing the same song, and the song is a new song every year. There are so many wonders." Then she closed her letter with a declaration of enduring love. "Dear Ken, I have all your letters to keep me company. Every day of my life I think of you with love."[29]

In Jackson, Eudora continued to work ardently on behalf of New Stage Theatre and to serve on the Millsaps College Board of Trustees. At the end of January, Charles Kuralt of CBS News arrived to videotape an interview with her about Franklin Delano Roosevelt and the most famous of his Depression-era relief programs, the Works Progress Administration, and in early March, Alice Parker returned to Jackson to begin preparations for staging her opera version of *The Ponder Heart.* But Eudora's schedule was relatively clear. She could not, however, overcome the "persisting block" that was so frustrating to her. She had finally saved time for writing but still found herself unable to complete a story. Worry about Ken was surely a contributing factor. Eudora confided as much to Reynolds. "I want to . . . try to *finish a story* no matter what. I wonder if you know how ailing poor Ken is. A fearsome disease of the brain, Alzheimer's Disease, is the diagnosis. It destroys the memory, & progresses. It is on my mind all the time. He doesn't write or read—really unbearable."[30] To Reynolds, Eudora felt free to confide her distress. His published comments about the short story had for a time alienated Eudora, but the friendship was far stronger than any literary disagreement.

On March 15 Eudora took great pride and pleasure in hearing Walker Percy inaugurate Millsaps College's Eudora Welty Chair in Southern Studies. Walker's brother LeRoy had been the driving force behind the chair's establishment, and now Walker delivered an address titled "Novel Writing in an Apocalyptic Time." The apocalyptic nature of contemporary America may have been a factor in Eudora's "persisting block." She was finding it difficult to bring the world of the late 1970s and early 1980s under imaginative control, and her first trip of the year sent her thoughts back to the past. On April 1 she went to Converse College in Spartanburg, South Carolina, where in 1962 she had joined Cleanth Brooks and Flannery O'Connor at a conference. The 1982 conference was a reunion of the earlier one, marred only by the absence of Flannery, who had died in 1964.

After the 1962 Converse College gathering, Eudora had traveled from Spartanburg to Smith College and then to New York, where she saw Reynolds, who was himself visiting in the area. Now another spring meeting with Reynolds was in store. NBC's *Today Show* wanted to interview the two writers from the World's Fair in Knoxville, and they seized the chance for a few days together. In Knoxville, the interview itself proved superficial and became a bit ridiculous when they were asked to comment on the fiction of "Percy Walker." How should one correct an interviewer on live television? As tactfully as possible. However unprepared the *Today*

Show staff and cast had been was really irrelevant to Eudora and Reynolds. This trip provided an important opportunity for long conversations. Eudora told Reynolds how much she wanted to see Ken and asked if he thought she should go to Santa Barbara. She found it difficult to believe that Ken's memory could not be restored, and she wanted not only to be supportive of him, but also to learn firsthand about his plight. Reynolds told Eudora that she should make the trip; he felt she could be at peace only after doing so, and he volunteered to accompany her if she wished. Eudora did indeed want Reynolds to come with her, but for the time being she resolved to wait.

In mid-May Eudora made her annual spring trip to New York. She attended a party with Pulitzer-Prize–winning journalist Lucinda Franks; dined with the Kahn sisters; saw her Random House editor, Albert Erskine; and spent the weekend at the Pennsylvania farm of her Harcourt editor, John Ferrone. She also attended two formal engagements: She received an honorary degree from Columbia University, where she had studied in 1930–1931 (the distinguished scholar Carolyn Heilbrun, the scholar who would later be sharply critical of *One Writer's Beginnings*, wrote the university's citation); and she participated in a Morgan Library celebration for the Library of America, the publishing venture undertaken to guarantee that great American writers would always be in print. This celebration was chaired by Daniel Aaron, general editor of the Library of America, Harvard professor, and Eudora's longtime friend. Eudora contributed to the program by reading Hawthorne's "The Birthmark," but Aaron's contribution to Eudora was greater. He asked her to deliver the William E. Massey Sr. Lectures in the History of American Civilization at Harvard. What would I talk about, Eudora inquired. Your beginnings as a writer, Aaron responded. Bill Smith had already published a memoir about his literary origins, and to Eudora, this book suggested that Aaron's idea could work for her.

As June began, Eudora received encouraging news about Ken.

Ralph Sipper wrote, "Good news! When I telephoned the Millars this morning, Ken sounded particularly alert. I remarked on this to Maggie after she came on the phone and she told me that Ken had had a very good two weeks, the best she could remember in recent months. She conjectured that perhaps Ken did not have Alzheimer's after all (you will remember that the disease is diagnosed by a process of elimination) and that the doctors could be wrong."[31]

The end of June brought another very pleasant distraction from worry. The International Ballet Competition, an annual event rotating among four cities, had chosen Jackson as its only site in the United States. Eudora attended each stage of the competition. She spent eight evenings at the ballet, especially enjoying a Gala Performance by the winners and a party for them. Then, the ballet competition having ended, she began to look forward to Alice Parker's opera version of *The Ponder Heart*. Parker spent August in Jackson, working with cast and orchestra, and Eudora attended rehearsals.

On August 26 Margaret and Ken Millar phoned Eudora. What prompted the call is uncertain, but its effect on Eudora was electric. After the call, she immediately wrote to Ken. "I was so grateful for the call—Thank you and Margaret—I hold those moments dear when we were hearing each other's voices— It was like a wonderful and unexpected present, one I would rather have had than any other I can think of." Eudora clearly appreciated this act of generosity on Margaret's part, but Ken was at the center of her thoughts. She closed her letter by telling him, "Dear Ken, I think of you every day, but today was when I heard your voice on the telephone." The joy of hearing Ken's voice was replaced three days later by the sadness of learning that Lehman Engel had died unexpectedly in New York. Eudora attended the services and burial in Jackson and accepted an invitation to speak at a New York memorial service for Engel. Shortly afterward, a letter from Margaret Millar arrived. She sent a photograph of Eudora with Ken and his friend Don Freeman and then added some discouraging news: The previous night Ken had wandered away from home and been found by the police; when they brought him back, Margaret wrote, "He asked me if I had a room for him, he didn't know who I was or my name. He had never done such a thing before, and of course has no memory of it. I wish I could forget as easily." She signed the letter: "Much love & admiration—Margaret."[32]

During the second week of September, a number of Eudora's friends arrived in Jackson for the operatic premiere of *The Ponder Heart*, Joan and Olivia Kahn, Reynolds, and agent Tim Seldes among them. The event attracted a good bit of media attention, and Diane Sawyer interviewed Eudora for CBS television. A black-tie reception at the Governor's Mansion preceded the Friday-night opening, and after the performance there was an elegant dinner party. The proceeds from the opening went to New Stage Theatre, which used the money to establish the Eudora Welty New Playwrights Series. But Eudora could not bask in the glow of this success; two days later she was on a plane, headed for Lehman's memorial service. When Frank Lyell had died, she had resolved to "hate and protest" the death of friends up to her "last breath." She would not miss this opportunity to testify to Lehman's absence. She delivered a tribute from the stage of the Shubert Theater. Editor Ellis Amburn cherished Eudora's remarks and wrote to thank her. "The moments you were on the stage at the Shubert yesterday for my friend Lehman Engel will haunt and comfort me forever. While others—though I appreciate their tribute—too often seemed self-aggrandizing, or preoccupied with pointless assessments of Lehman's worth and place in history—as if it mattered in the democracy of dust to which we are all heir—you took my hand and placed it on Lehman's heart."[33]

In October, Eudora decided that she definitely must visit Ken and wrote to ask Margaret if she might. Then, as Eudora told Reynolds, "Ralph Sipper called up, saying Margaret asked him to do so for her. It would be OK there 'if I was up to it' she said, I 'didn't need to get permission from her,' and that the sooner the better because of the weather, which will be the rainy season before long. She also said she had a car if I wanted to use it. (But I can't drive in S.B.—the Freeway!) Ralph is going to be out of town at the beginning of November for about a week, and what I think is that I'll go out on Nov. 11 and stay till the 20th—I very much would like any element of rush or strain to be out of it so Ken would feel it was an easy time, & we could meet without anything pressing. If Ralph is in town (I pray I'm right on his dates—I'll check to be sure) he will help make things easy."[34] Eudora hoped that Reynolds might join her on this trip and volunteered to pay his expenses. Reynolds, tied up with teaching his classes at Duke and grading student papers, was not free until semester's end. Eudora could not wait that long. On November 15 she flew to Santa Barbara.

Ralph Sipper and his wife, Carol, met Eudora at the airport, made Ralph's office available for her afternoon meetings with Ken, and gave her dinner at night during her eight-day stay. The Sippers were for the first time aware that behind Eudora's reserved demeanor lay a deep attachment to Ken, an attachment that matched Ken's for her. Eudora's discoveries, however, focused solely on Ken. His physical condition was fine, but his mental state sad to observe. As Eudora told Ken's biographer, "He could still swim. He remembered how to swim, and he had someone to go swimming with him every day . . . He swam well, and it did him good. When he got out of the pool, he seemed so much more alert, you know; he would say, 'When did you come?' to somebody, or 'I'm glad to see you. I'm gonna eat lunch,' or somethin' definite. Then it would sort of trail off. He took care always to have a good physical condition, and he had a wonderful swimmer's body; in his bathing suit, he just looked wonderful, right at the last. All of that, it did him no good."[35]

Margaret's sister, a nurse, was helping care for Ken, and Eudora thought highly of her efforts, but she found Margaret's

behavior appalling. Despite the detente in recent communica-
tions, Margaret now seemed vituperative. Ralph Sipper felt that
her harshness was uncalculated. Unlike most people, who pause
and censor themselves before speaking, Sipper believed, she simply said whatever she thought. But to Eudora, Margaret seemed
deliberately cruel. She, for instance, made a point of saying that
Ken, when asked if he remembered Eudora, had replied, "Sure,
he's a fellow I used to do business with." And Margaret was even
more cruel to Ken himself. During an interview with Ken's biographer, Tom Nolan, Eudora recalled a day when she, Margaret,
and Ken were having lunch at the Coral Casino.

> Margaret said, "Well, of course I had to poison the dogs."
> They had three dogs when I was there earlier; two German
> shepherds and one little mongrel that Ken found on the
> beach and brought home, a real sweet little kind of female
> terrier. "I didn't have any time left to attend to those dogs,"
> she says, "so they're all gone now." She tells this to Ken. You
> know: the loves of his heart . . . It doesn't matter whether it
> was true or not, it was just—telling him that: that she had
> to poison 'em. I don't understand that, I mean she just—
> *Punishing* him all the time. *She* loved those dogs too. It was
> terribly difficult, the whole situation, of course, just terri-
> ble. No telling what she did go through. She was probably
> at her wit's end about everything and just flew out with that,
> I don't know why. I couldn't see into her mind, at all.[36]

Eudora's time with Ken and *without* Margaret went smoothly.
As she told Mary Lou, "he did know me, smiled that same big
smile, and put his arms around me and kissed me, as indeed he
did every time he saw me. We spoke back and forth in perfectly
clear conversation, only there was a lot of silence too, but it was
Ken. At one point somebody said it was nice I'd come so far to
see him, and when I said that he'd come just that far to see me, he
looked delighted and *recognizing* of that. I never did feel sure the

diagnosis was right . . . He was as always gentle and courteous and sweet. The loss of abstract thought and all the wonderful workings of his mind was terrible, but even the non sequitur of his thinking didn't keep his character from its firmness and kindheartedness." Ralph Sipper's assessment of Eudora's visit tallied with her own. Sipper believed that Ken was more frequently lucid when Eudora was with him. "She could reach him," Sipper said.[37]

One way Eudora reached Ken was by talking of her 1981 trip across Canada, calling forth his memories of his boyhood there. "I told him that at one part of the trip they stopped the train because of an earth slide in front of us, and its sister train that starts at the Vancouver end had to stop for the same reason. So what they did was take everybody off each train and switch 'em, and the trains just went back where they'd come from! This kind of appealed to him, I think. And I said, 'So that was the best part of the trip, 'cause we went on a bus into Medicine Hat.' And he knew the name of the bus: he said, 'Moose Mountain bus.' Yes! It's what it was. And I said, 'We saw elks running along,' and he, he could just see, he could just *see* that road! And he was just so alive to it all, and he remembered. So I remembered as much as I could, because everything I could tell him was something that rang a bell. It was amazing. But I was thrilled, because it turned out that we could really talk . . . You know it both broke your heart, and—you realized how much would go through his mind, even fleetingly, and clue him in on something, and he *knew* it. And I know so much of his boyhood was with him all the time, and he could call on it if he needed to."[38]

Eudora returned to Jackson, happy that she had made this journey to see Ken. It would be her last sight of him. Now she gathered herself for a trip to Duke University. Reynolds had arranged to have Eudora and Anne Tyler meet with Duke students. The visiting writers would participate in a panel discussion, talk separately with small groups of students, and each give a reading. The event was a spectacular success, as Reynolds subsequently told Eudora. "The rafters have gone on ringing round here, with praise for and delight in your and Anne's visit. Really, nothing in all these years I've been here has come anywhere near approaching it for richness and pleasure. I've never felt better rewarded ... thanks again."[39] The praise for her public appearances notwithstanding, Eudora valued this trip for the private meetings with Reynolds. They gave her the opportunity to tell him about her time in Santa Barbara and about the horror that Margaret Millar evoked in her.

Eudora's burdens were somewhat lightened at the beginning of 1983. Work was suddenly going well. As she wrote the series of lectures for Harvard, she remembered more and more about people who had influenced her and about events that had led to her writing career. Some memories were cheering—those of school days, family car trips, sights and sounds that had prompted stories— but not all. Recalling conflicts with her mother and the deaths of family members must have been disturbing. Still, a moment of great tragedy, witnessing the death of her father, had compelled the youthful Eudora to transfuse heartfelt experiences into fiction. She must have felt a similar impetus in composing what would become a memoir. Eudora knew, as she had long ago told John Robinson, that writing "purifies experience, in a way, ... you can't let anything false go from you, it has to be true from a certain moment. Then you know the lovely ease this makes happen." The "lovely ease" that had been absent from her life for more than ten years was returning. And the catharsis achieved in the act of writing her autobiographical lectures seemed again in the offing for Eudora the fiction writer, who sought to imagine herself into other lives and to explore "emotions, in which all of us are alike involved."[40] A story kept drawing her attention and seemed promising. That story may well have been one she eventually destroyed, the story of an architect who has the *Ideal City* of Piero della Francesca thumbtacked to his wall. Or it may have been one titled "Henry" and clearly based on Ken's battle with Alzheimer's disease.

Not only work was going well. Friends long absent from the South had come to Jackson for the spring semester at Millsaps College. Cleanth Brooks was the college's first Eudora Welty Chair of Southern Studies. Cleanth and his wife, Tinkum, must have filled an important gap in Eudora's Jackson social life; many of her old Jackson friends were gone, but Eudora and the Brookses could draw on common memories dating back to the 1930s. They saw each other regularly for dinners, and Eudora occasionally attended the class Cleanth was teaching.

Though her writing and her social life in Jackson were both fulfilling, Eudora was worried about Mary Lou, who had written that she was afflicted by "a form of mild leukemia." Then at the end of January, Ralph Sipper wrote with bad news about Ken. Ken had been having periods of total memory loss, was unable to dress or shave himself, could not recognize friends or his dogs (still alive despite Margaret's report to the contrary), and had been falling. His doctor had recommended that he move to a convalescent home, and he was now ensconced there, "serenely" according to Sipper.

A long-anticipated early March reunion with Victor and Dorothy Pritchett must have seemed a particular blessing in light of Sipper's news. The Pritchetts were again in residence at Vanderbilt, and Eudora had invited them to see Savannah, Georgia, at her expense. They agreed that she might pay for their lodging, but insisted that food and drink be their responsibility. A bargain had been struck. The four days in Savannah turned out perfectly for all three. The name "Savannah" had made the city one of the "Sirens of geography" for Victor, and it lived up to its name. He would turn his observations into a *New York Times* article. But he found his greatest pleasure in "writerly talks" with Eudora, and told her, "It's extraordinary how intimate working chats with

writers one so greatly admires are." Dorothy was even more effusive in a letter to Eudora. "I am glad, I shall always be glad, of
that magic time in Savannah which we snatched from a grudging
world. It has taught me that I must try to make the time for pleasure that I would so urgently and willingly make for *work!*" Then
she added, "I lie when people here ask how long Victor and I
have known you! It's such a deep intense loving that to measure it
by three or four years doesn't give it the importance it has in both
our lives, separately and together. I ought to be ashamed of telling
you this but I'm not."[41]

For a month after returning from Savannah, Eudora worked
long hours on her three Harvard lectures, though she still managed to see friends for dinner, attend family parties, and hear the
distinguished poet Richard Wilbur read at Belhaven College. On
April 12 she at last gave herself a true break from work. She
wrote to Mary Lou, explaining the need for this vacation: "At the
moment I have Harvard ahead of me and have been working
against the clock with the three lectures still to finish. Haven't
done anything but work, and have been having dreams you'd appreciate: they're in words, and I am editing them and *proofreading*
them as I dream them. Lordy! Jane Petty (you may remember her,
New Stage) and 3 or 4 other young friends, have invited me to
Santa Rosa Island off Pensacola for my birthday this month and
I ought not to take the time off but it will be so refreshing to the
gaga brain that I think I just must." Three days later, back in
Jackson, she further revised the lectures and did so until the very
eve of her trip to Cambridge. On April 23 Eudora wrote to Bill
Maxwell, "I couldn't write back because I was (still am, franti-
cally) working against time to get my 3 Harvard lectures done. I
go up at 7:30 AM tomorrow to Cambridge. Pray for me."[42]

No prayers were necessary. Eudora inaugurated the William
E. Massey Sr. Lectures in the History of American Civilization
to rave reviews. Held on the campus of one of America's premiere academic institutions, before an audience of students and

faculty one might have expected to be blasé, the lecture series evoked an outpouring of veneration. As Bill Maxwell noted in an article for the *New Yorker*, "The audience was, for the most part, Harvard and Radcliffe undergraduates, many more than the hall could accommodate, with the overflow in other rooms that were wired with speakers. After the last lecture, bringing flowers, they waited in long lines for the privilege of speaking to her. Not bunches of flowers. Just one flower."[43] One of the Harvard graduate students who longed to speak with Eudora was Carol Ann Johnston. Johnston, who has since become a well-published Welty scholar, recalls almost stalking Eudora at Harvard, hoping for an extended conversation, all to no avail. Her ardor was not unusual; it possessed the campus. What had prepared the way for such a response? Certainly, the Pulitzer Prize of 1973 and the publication of Eudora's *Collected Stories*, in 1980, had attracted readers to her work, and the work was masterful. The topic of the lectures, moreover, promised the sort of self-revelation that Eudora had evaded. But a cult of personality also seemed to be in play. Eudora had been seen by television viewers of *Firing Line* (1973), the *Dick Cavett Show* (1979), *Today* (1982), *Sunday Morning* with Charles Kuralt (1982), and *CBS Morning News* with Diane Sawyer (1982). Richard O. Moore's film biography of her had appeared on PBS in 1978. Reynolds Price and Anne Tyler had published *New York Times Book Review* interviews with Eudora, in 1978 and 1980 respectively, and Scott Haller's interview had appeared in a 1981 issue of the *Saturday Review*. Eudora's wry wit, her engaging sense of humor, her deft use of language, her penetrating observations, her love of home and family, her sanity and stability, had won her "friends" as well as readers. The response at Harvard partook of passion for her work and for the lectures she read, but also for herself. At a time when French philosophers Jacques Derrida and Michel Foucault were generating wildly enthusiastic responses from college audiences interested in literary theory, Eudora represented the antithesis of theory. Yet this was truly her moment. Her reception outstripped theirs. And at a university where outstanding writers regularly lectured or were faculty members, Eudora claimed the sort of adulation that no other writer had. In her unassuming way, Eudora was charismatic. She represented high literature but in a down-to-earth, unpretentious, real, nonacademic manner. Harvard embraced her, and readers at large would soon participate in that response. Harvard University Press was ready to publish the lectures. That prospect pleased Eudora, though she wanted to revise once more for book publication.

From Harvard, Eudora set off for three weeks of seeing friends. First stop was Bar Harbor, Maine, where she spent a few days with Rosie Russell. Then it was on to New York for two weeks, broken by a weekend excursion to John Ferrone's farm in Pennsylvania. Finally, Eudora visited Laurence Stapleton at Bryn Mawr and then went to Washington, where in front of a Smithsonian audience she delivered a fifteen-minute address on the assigned topic "A Southerner Looks at Hawthorne." After discussing the spell that Hawthorne's New England setting was wont to cast upon his readers, she concluded, "When I read Hawthorne no boundary runs between that spell and my eyes, certainly not the Mason-Dixon line."[44] Having proclaimed her admiration for a literary forebear and her belief that art both emerges from and transcends region, Eudora finally returned home on May 18 and set about preparing the Harvard lectures for book publication, mailing the manuscript to Cambridge five weeks later.

In mid-June Ken Millar had suffered a "cerebrovascular accident" and been hospitalized. Now his condition deteriorated, and on July 11, he died. As soon as she heard the news, Mary Lou phoned Eudora to express her condolences. A month later, Eudora wrote to express her gratitude for the call: "I felt so warmed to hear your voice—I knew your thoughts would be with me when Ken died. They did me so much good and still do. The utter sadness of such a large part of his life and his bearing with it in patience and kindness and sometimes perplexity—I'm glad it is over for him, and what I've come to feel is that he is FREE. In particular of Margaret Millar, whose screaming abuse of him (it was in public) never did cease, when all he could do was stand there and take it. After he was dead, when she was talking to her agent Dorothy Olding (also Ken's agent) in New York, when Dorothy asked if Ken had yet been cremated, she said, 'Well, I really don't know—he may have been. At some point a charter plane scatters the ashes over the Santa Barbara Channel, it's a service—I have nothing to do with it, and I'm working.' She was home working the night Ken died, and I don't know whether or not anybody was with him."[45]

Having come to Jackson because his brother Will was dying from viral hepatitis, John Robinson had been with Eudora when she learned of Ken's death. Now John and Eudora sustained each other, perhaps in a more balanced fashion than at any other time in their relationship. Nearly every day for a month they met for conversation and comfort. John himself seemed rather frail, however, and Eudora must have worried about him.

Throughout the summer and early fall, Eudora continued her regular social rounds in Jackson, meeting with scholars who came through town, celebrating friends' birthdays, working for New Stage, and concealing her deep sorrow from all but a few. Bill and Sonja Smith were among those few, and with them Eudora felt free to invoke the love she and Ken had shared. "I've been grieving," she wrote the Smiths, "about Ken Millar who died of Alzheimer's Disease, or so it was diagnosed. I went out to see him in December and we had a good visit—talked together and got to be together every day for a while for about a week—As you know, we loved each other, and what happened to him was so abominable—He hadn't been able to write for two years but a mutual friend in Santa Barbara had kept me in touch. He remained himself—gentle and enduring."[46]

At the end of September, knowing that Mary Lou's health was in a serious decline, Eudora went to Santa Fe. Tired and bereaved, Eudora still found her New Mexico visit a good one. She admired the way Mary Lou's son Duncan helped his mother, she and Mary Lou had the opportunity for long talks, and she enjoyed seeing "the balloons in Albuquerque—Internat'l Contest—they rose every morning at dawn in 'mass ascension.'"[47]

By the end of October, both Bill Maxwell and Reynolds had read *One Writer's Beginnings* in manuscript, and both found it to be a masterpiece. Reynolds wrote, "What struck me mostly deeply, of course, were the pictures of your parents and grandparents—some of the stories you'd told me before and some that came as wonderful news. And the glimpses of yourself that, without 'explanation,' finally add up to a coherent and (to my mind) entirely truthful map. The haunting picture of the young soldier, leaving the train without warning and heading off into the green valley, becomes finally the metaphor of the book's whole meaning—for me, at least. So—thanks, deep thanks, one more time." Then he added a note about Ken. "I too find myself thinking about Ken, every day. Just those few days I saw him in Jackson, left a deep print. What I think we can trust is, it was a painless ending—the only gift of that dreadful illness. And how much he *did,* in the time he had; how it still stands there for all to see."[48] The juxtaposition of praise and consolation in Reynolds's letter was appropriate. For Eudora the triumph of her Harvard lectures and the tragedy of Ken's death were closely linked, and perhaps witnessing Ken's loss of memory over the years had pushed Eudora to plumb her own subconscious and to put her past on paper. She knew firsthand how important memory was to identity and survival. As she wrote at the close of *One Writer's Beginnings*: "The greatest confluence of all is that which makes up the human memory—the individual human memory. My own is the treasure most dearly regarded by me, in my life and in my work as a writer. Here time, also, is subject to confluence. The memory is a living thing—it too is in transit. But during its moment, all that is remembered joins, and lives—the old and the young, the past and the present, the living and the dead."[49]

As 1983 drew to a close, Eudora checked the page proof of her self-portrait and then made another round of academic appearances: At Radcliffe she received an award and delivered three lectures; at Stanford she met with students and gave a reading for an overflow crowd—an outdoor telecast of the reading was quickly arranged. Then Eudora settled down in Jackson, content to remain for the next six months. Those months included many days of happiness. In February 1984 Harvard University Press published *One Writer's Beginnings* to outstanding reviews. Old friends Bill Maxwell and Walter Clemons sang the book's praises in the *New Yorker* and *Newsweek* respectively. And reviewers across the country, from the *New York Times* to the *L.A. Times* to the *Jackson Clarion-Ledger*, joined in the accolades. The book hit the *New York Times* bestseller list and remained there for forty-six weeks. In the midst of the publication hoopla, from April 12 to 14, Jackson, Millsaps College, and the Southern Literary Festival celebrated Eudora's newest achievement with a literary conference—scholars from around the country and from England and from France were present to analyze Eudora's fiction, and Reynolds, Elizabeth Spencer, James Whitehead, and Margaret Walker Alexander also made addresses. On April 13 conference participants and Welty admirers gathered for an elegant buffet supper; a smaller and more informal party, complete with belly dancer, followed at a local Greek restaurant with the unlikely name of Bill's Burger House. It was a fine seventy-fifth birthday celebration. Eudora's gift in return was first a public reading and then a donation to the Mississippi Department of Archives and History. An autobiographical story about Courtney, which she had written as a teenager, and five hundred Welty family photographs became part of the department's Eudora Welty Collection. So, too, did the typescripts of her Harvard lectures and the subsequent revisions of them. Self-portraits and portraits, fiction, autobiography, and photographs would now be available for students of her fiction. Eudora's journey to *One Writer's Beginnings* had borne her into the past; now her archival collection would bear scholars "ceaselessly into the past" and transcend the temporal nature of unrecorded memory.

TEN

"The Lonesomeness and Hilarity of Survival"
1984–1991

By 1984 Eudora had lost many confidantes. She would soon lose two more and see one in serious jeopardy. In 1984 Reynolds Price underwent surgery to remove a cancerous tumor that was wound about his spinal cord, and Mary Lou Aswell battled, then succumbed to, a form of leukemia called Sezary Syndrome. In 1989 John Robinson died in Italy from a heart attack. Throughout this time and afterward, Eudora felt the inevitable guilt of the healthy survivor, and she sought to testify to the absence of those who had died and to support those in dire straits. At the same time, her writing remained a source of concern. During the years in which her mother and brothers suffered ill health, Eudora had struggled to complete new fiction. She did eventually finish *Losing Battles*, but a novella-length work, titled "Nicotiana" or "The Last of the Figs," was still in disarray. In the seventies, she wrote away at "The Shadow Club" but never put it into polished form. *One Writer's Beginnings* might have, but ultimately did not, herald the production of new fiction. Until 1988 Eudora worked hard at a number of stories, but she prepared no fair copies. Certainly, increasingly painful arthritis in her right hand made the physical act of writing very difficult, but surely much more was at stake. Though Eudora seems not to have discussed the situation with anyone, a number of possibilities suggest themselves. Perhaps she lacked the drive she had possessed as a younger woman. Perhaps her writing powers had waned, even though her intellectual acumen remained sharp. Perhaps she felt that her new work did not meet the high standard she expected of herself. Perhaps, though she desperately tried to write about Ken Millar, she found that reliving his final years in memory was simply too nightmarish to be borne. Whatever the reasons, Eudora did not complete any stories to her satisfaction.

By 1988, having relinquished almost all hope for producing new fiction, Eudora directed her creative energies into other channels. She permitted the University Press of Mississippi to publish a large collection of her Depression-era snapshots, assisting in the process. She turned her hand to editing: As she and Kenyon College professor Ron Sharp selected the entries for the *Norton Book of Friendship*, Eudora delighted in wide-ranging reading and in discussing that reading with Sharp. She participated in projects that allowed her to pay tribute to the people who had been so important to her literary career. And she herself became the subject of film interviews as well as an hour-long BBC film biography. In her seventies and eighties, Eudora remained open to new experiences, and by doing so, retained her vigor.

Just as she coped with changes in her professional life, Eudora also came to terms with and often transcended loneliness. Though the special intimacy she had with Diarmuid, Ken, Mary Lou, and John could not be replaced, many old and dear friends remained: Bill and Emmy Maxwell were close friends; Reynolds would manage to overcome his cancer, though he had still to cope with paraplegia; Bill Smith, Elizabeth Spencer, Victor and Dorothy Pritchett, saw Eudora periodically as did Charlotte Capers and Ann Morrison of the Basic Eight in Jackson; her nieces were also close at hand, and Seta Sancton lived in nearby New Orleans. And to this inner circle of friends, Eudora would add others. Jim Lehrer and Roger Mudd, two journalists she greatly admired, also admired her, and they became, through an initial chance meeting, important to her. Jane Petty and Patti Black, longtime friends at New Stage, late in 1983 consciously decided to meet on a weekly basis with Eudora for drinks or dinner, hoping that they might provide the kind of intellectual stimulation they felt she missed. And in the summer of 1983 I arrived in Jackson, a young scholar who had begun to write about and teach her work. She took me under her wing, included me in gatherings of her friends, and talked with me about her past, a past which came alive for both of us as we talked. It would be fifteen years before I asked permission to write her biography and before she warned me that the project might place me in areas of "deeper water" than I imagined. She was right, and one of those areas involved writing about the years in which she and I were friends. Should I maintain the biographer's distance and speak of myself in the third person or allow a personal element to enter the biography? I have chosen the latter.

In the spring of 1984, having published a bestselling memoir and having been celebrated at an international literary festival in her hometown, Eudora surely felt a sense of accomplishment, even triumph, but beneath it ran a strong current of grief. Ken Millar's struggle against Alzheimer's disease still haunted Eudora. Like Ken, she believed that "the best thing for a writer to do with a trouble of any kind is to find a personal narrative or artistic use for it." She possessed a wealth of letters from Ken, and hers to Ken had now been returned by Ralph Sipper. Ralph urged Eudora to consider eventually publishing both sides of the correspondence: "I don't mean baring every last detail and certainly this is not the time to contemplate a book in which you and Ken share thoughts on literature, life, and love. But someday the confluence (it *is* a wonderful word) of your lives should, in my view, be a matter of human record. What you and Ken exchanged was a pureness that need not be buried. And I would welcome the opportunity, with your guidance, to make a book of it for all seasons."[1] Eudora, however, resisted this suggestion. She had openly discussed her past in *One Writer's Beginnings*, but that past was for the most part a rather remote one. And Eudora had refused to cross a tenuously defined boundary between public and private. She wrote about her parents' devotion to each other, for example, but did not quote from their presumably ardent letters of courtship. She told of the Mississippi environment that sparked her imagination, but not of her passion for John Robinson, a passion that informed so many of her stories. Just as she had been protective of privacy in these instances, she would be much more so in the future. Though in her 1986 will she provided for the preservation and archival availability of her correspondence, in her lifetime she was unwilling to publish the Welty/Millar letters or even a memoir about the relationship. Instead she sought to transform life into fiction. Writing *The Optimist's Daughter* in the late sixties had helped her cope with the loss of her mother and brothers. In the spring of 1984, she turned again to this strategy: Drawing upon memories of her relationship with Ken and accounts of his suffering, she resumed work on a story she had since 1981 variously titled "Henry," "Affinities," and "The City of Light." She could not and would not complete it. So painful was the story to write, that it exists in a most fragmented state, almost an enactment of Alzheimer's itself, with some scenes written by hand on envelopes and a page torn from the *Saturday Review*, with bits of dialogue or description on partial pages of paper.

In what remains of this story, the central characters are most often Henry, a college linguistics professor, whose life is devastated by Alzheimer's; his wife, Donna, driven to her wit's end by this illness; and Rachel, a middle-aged, unmarried woman, who typically has been Henry's graduate student in a summer-session class and who a year or so later returns to visit him. In writing about this trio of characters, Eudora confronted the horror of Ken's memory loss, drew upon Margaret Millar's fury, frustration, and self-concern in the face of that loss, and revealed her own love of Ken. In one key scene, Donna tells Rachel that any sense of the past or of self have abandoned Henry:

> "He used to get so upset. In the beginning," said Donna. "He didn't know what things there in front of him were *for.* He didn't understand, oh, the return-address labels he found on his desk. He just sat at this desk looking at them. *My husband didn't understand what those little stickers were for with his name and address on them.* That was the first time he blacked out. Down on the floor breaking his glasses. I just threw the labels away. All I could do when Henry was upset was put things out of his sight. He sits in here content, like you see him now. I don't think he'd even ask if he saw them today what the labels said. He's more contented now than he ever was in his life." She looked at me. "You understand he's lost his memory."
>
> "Now he doesn't worry any longer that he's lost something he knows he once had without knowing what it is. He doesn't try to understand what's happening to his mind. Well, that's a good thing."

Such had been Ken's plight, and his plight left Margaret Millar feeling as desolated and helpless and self-absorbed as Donna: "'Henry doesn't feel things. Henry's content with things now, whatever way they are . . . It's *me!*' she screamed. 'What am I going to do? What am I going to do with *him*?'"[2]

In another scene, Eudora's alter-ego narrator tries to establish contact with the memory-bereft Henry, going to his bedside and taking his hand. "I went forward to my knees, put my head down on his pillow, touching his. I was face down no longer seeing. I was as still as he, as if some safety might be discovered to run back and forth between our heads, like words, more urgent than words between our skulls. As if we could tender our foreheads from bud and budded, to each other, like deers unseen. This was my own momentary dream." This gentle, silent meeting stands in contrast to a noisy one between the story's female protagonists. When Henry's wife sees the narrator with him, she explodes in anger. "'What are *you* doing still here after all this time? I daresay spreading your legs for my husband.' She slammed the door after her." The narrator herself in one fragment wonders whether she and Henry should have become lovers. "Henry in being so preeminently a married man was that much the dearer to me, for of course I knew it was this that made him need me. What you could call my bringing-up can't be blamed for what I did . . . I think that I was simply afraid of great joy. It had never come so close to me before. And I didn't know what to do. Any more than Donna, with Henry disappearing in front of her eyes, knew what to do now. Does anyone know how to love?"[3] Whether Margaret Millar gave voice to suspicions of infidelity cannot be determined, but the scene dramatizes her very real jealousy of Eudora, and like the story's narrator, Eudora must have felt regret that she and Ken had not known a physical as well as a romantic and intellectual intimacy. The details of the story, with more sexually explicit dialogue than Eudora had yet attempted, may well vary from actuality; the emotions do not.

When the story's narrator returns home after spending several days with Henry, she literally cannot find her bearings. In a passage that she stuggled to revise, Eudora moved from third- to first-person narration and powerfully related what must have been her own experience driving home from the Jackson airport after a last visit to Ken in Santa Barbara:

This was the town where I was born but the past had left few signs (the years had it seemed, without warning, changed it). He could no longer read, or write a word, even his own name. Driving over the streets of my home town where he had never been except for once, finding myself nowhere that looked familiar, finding wherever I turned, and then reversed myself and turned again, that I was lost, I thought now that all this while I had been very close to him. It had brought [us] together when [I] needed it most, this aimless and timeless ride through the gray rain of a city thus easily slipped from memory, as if we had clasped each other one last time. I felt a surging comfort of not knowing where I lived, the loss of any certainty—almost blindness itself—this was all nearness to him. As if it were a confidence or a promise, I treasured that hour and forty minutes just given to [me]. Anything, anything can affirm love. And I am seizing it.[4]

Clearly, the triumph of *One Writer's Beginnings* had not been absolute. Eudora remained rueful and troubled, attempting to translate her experience into fiction and frustrated in the attempt. Jane Petty and Patti Black, who sensed her melancholy bent, more and more encouraged her to discuss the past and anticipate the future. At one point they began to ask about Eudora's 1949, 1951, and 1954 trips across the Atlantic by ship. As Eudora described the pleasures of sailing, the three agreed that a trip to England on the *Queen Elizabeth 2* would be a happy prospect. For her part, Eudora was eager to see Victor and Dorothy Pritchett again, so the three Jacksonians booked a September passage. When she learned of the coming visit, Dorothy Pritchett was elated. She worried about Victor's writer's block and thought a visit from Eudora might help: Victor, she wrote Eudora, "has found it hard to write his own work and has to write too many critical pieces to earn his living. He thinks he's lost his imaginative powers—I don't—but a talk with a *practicante* would be so much to his need so may I make a plea that you will keep all the space you can for us—and separately for him when you come?"[5] Little did Dorothy know that Eudora had problems very akin to Victor's.

On May 17 John Robinson arrived in Jackson to tend to business matters and see doctors, and Eudora met his plane. This reunion must have seemed a poignant reminder and a special blessing. John had been with her a year earlier when Ken had died, and now the two old friends surely discussed the magnitude Ken's loss held for Eudora. Before her romance with John had ended, the two had spoken with each other in the most open way, and their friendship endured on a similar basis. To have John nearby for the next month or so must have offered tremendous solace, and the two planned to meet again in Italy in the fall.

In the midst of John's Jackson visit, Eudora made a long-scheduled trip to New York. There she saw Joan and Olivia Kahn, Bill and Emmy Maxwell, Tim Seldes, and Walter Clemons. She spent the weekend with John Ferrone and Johan Theron at their Pennsylvania farm. Then, back in New York, she was introduced to Jim and Kate Lehrer. She admired the *MacNeil/Lehrer Newshour* and was delighted to meet one of the journalists who provided in-depth television coverage of the news. The Lehrers, themselves both fiction writers, were equally delighted to meet Eudora. They promised to introduce her to Roger Mudd, their close friend and another of Eudora's favorite journalists. This first encounter would lead to a round of visits between Washington, the Lehrers' home base, and Jackson, and would enrich Eudora's life in the coming decade.

One disappointment in New York was a call from Reynolds Price, who had planned to meet Eudora at the Algonquin Hotel but now found himself unable to come. A troubling weakness in his legs necessitated medical tests. Then, on June 5, disappointment became heartfelt anxiety. Reynolds's niece phoned Eudora to say that Reynolds had undergone surgery for a tumor on his spine. Eudora immediately wrote to express her concern and support. "You know you have all my love and strongest wishes and hopes and prayers. Your sweet and clear-spoken niece gave me all the information she could, this morning after, and I'll keep in touch—I'm thinking of you—With love always."[6]

On June 13 Eudora returned to Jackson but did not hear from Reynolds until July 9. His phone call brought both relief and worry—relief that Reynolds had survived his surgery, but intense worry about his long-term prospects. Eudora had never acknowledged taking comfort in the thought of an afterlife, but as she faced Reynolds's desperate situation, she did. To Reynolds she wrote, "I hope you don't think this is a strange remark, but I feel that Ken has knowledge of what you've been going through and is sending love and encouragement—the things he always sent you. I've never ceased to feel close to him in matters close to me. I can say this just to you." Then she offered her own more mundane sort of help, telling Reynolds that she had made "an unexpected lot of money with the recent book [*One Writer's Beginnings*], which is here for you to make use of any time you might find it handy. I trust you not to hesitate to let me know."[7]

Eudora spent the remainder of the summer at home in Jackson, seeing friends and family. She reviewed the *Oxford Companion to Children's Literature* for the *New York Times Book Review*. And she followed Democratic politics, as she long had. Walter Mondale was running for president against Ronald Reagan and would name Geraldine Ferraro as his running mate. When Texas Senator Lloyd Bentsen came through Jackson campaigning for the Democratic ticket, Eudora was in attendance, and later she welcomed a visit from Joan Mondale, the presidential candidate's wife. I was in Jackson that summer, doing research at the Mississippi Department of Archives and History and teaching at Millsaps College for the June and July terms. Eudora and I had lunch or dinner at various points and talked politics; she strongly supported the Democratic slate. We also talked about Eudora's coming trip to England and about our respective experiences there. Before I left that summer, we had become friends. Late in the summer, another scholar claimed Eudora's attention. Michael Kreyling, whose critical study of her work Eudora admired, wrote to propose a new and different sort of book. He wished to write about Diarmuid Russell as a literary agent who was also "a cooperating artist."[8] Such a project was one dear to Eudora's heart.

She had from the first found Diarmuid's advice crucial to her own achievement, and she embraced Kreyling's project. It would begin in earnest the following spring.

In September Reynolds phoned with encouraging news about his progress, and Eudora then sent him the itinerary of her trip to England and Italy, which she could now make with a lightened heart. On September 13, Eudora, Jane, and Patti left for New York, where they would board the *Queen Elizabeth 2* two days later. In the city they saw Joan and Olivia Kahn, whom they would meet in London; dined with writer Ellen Gilchrist, a Jackson native; attended *Sunday in the Park with George,* Eudora for the second enchanted time; and were treated to a gala farewell lunch by two Mississippians who happened also to be staying at the Algonquin—political activist Patt Derian, a former student of Eudora's, and her husband, Hodding Carter Jr., the former State Department spokesman for the Carter Administration and son of the legendary Mississippi newspaper editor. Then it was off to the ship, where Eudora's celebrity won the Jackson contingent invitations to the captain's exclusive cocktail party—other celebrities on board included Catholic priest Andrew Greeley, the prolific author of romance novels combining religion and sex. No shipboard friendship ensued.[9]

In London Eudora was busy and held worry at a distance. She managed to have tea, lunch, and dinner with the Pritchetts on various days; she met with interviewers and with representatives of her English publisher Virago; at a dinner gathering they hosted, Joan and Olivia Kahn introduced Eudora to a galaxy of British mystery writers, Ruth Rendell among them; Paul Binding (who had delivered a paper at the Millsaps College celebration of Eudora's seventy-fifth birthday) threw a party in honor of Eudora, Jane, and Patti; an English friend took the three Americans to Hampton Court, Windsor, and Eton; eighty-year-old Molly Keane, a writer Eudora admired for her continuing productivity, joined her for tea; and Stephen Spender entertained Eudora at a dinner party. Sometime during her two and a half weeks in London, Eudora went to the theater, seeing *The Boy Friend*, an old favorite, and taking in *Wild Honey* at the National Theatre. Then she flew to Italy, where John met her plane. To Mary Lou, Eudora reported that she and John, both now seventy-five years old, "tottered a bit but went to Florence, Siena, and to his house near Pisa, while we talked."[10]

After this flurry of activity, Eudora returned to London to regroup and repack before boarding the *QE2* for the voyage home. In London she received a letter from Reynolds, who reported on his difficulties and his hopes.

> I'm still . . . with my cousin Marcia Bennett, in her comfortable home, and have been for nearly a month. But I'm due back in Durham on about 8 October. A young friend Daniel Voll will be staying with me there.
>
> From midway through radiation—late July—my strength has steadily weakened. I now walk only with a walker, & the doctors aren't saying whether that's a temporary result of radiation (a real possibility) or new pressure from the tumor or permanent radiation damage. They only say "Be patient for a few more months." (It's four months tomorrow since the surgery.) My own undiminished faith is that I'm to survive this thing, so patience is what I'm after. And I'm not doing all that badly at it, if I do say so.
>
> I draw a lot, & reading has become possible again (for weeks I lacked the attention-span), & I listen to hours & hours of music on a little Sony Walkman that Stephen S. sent me. I've written a few poems, but extended prose still seems a ways off.

Then Reynolds wrote movingly of Eudora's importance to him: "I miss you & think of you so often—all our laughter. You've been, and are, one of the really big lights for me." Eudora immediately responded, describing her trip, relaying the concern

Spender and Binding had expressed for Reynolds, and thanking him for the letter. But above all, Eudora expressed her admiration. "The one thing I was certain of, and knew wasn't going to change, is your determination and faith and valor."[11]

After these days of intense activity, Eudora returned home on October 25. Five days later she checked in at the Algonquin Hotel and the next day received the Modern Language Association Commonwealth Award with its substantial cash stipend. In her acceptance speech, Eudora thanked her parents, Diarmuid, John Woodburn, Red Warren, Bill Maxwell, and Mary Lou Aswell. Not long afterward, back in Jackson, she learned that Mary Lou's health had declined and that her situation was critical. Eudora wrote to suggest that her newly received cash might offset Mary Lou's medical bills and to say she hoped to schedule a visit at a time convenient for Mary Lou and Agi. Before such a visit could be arranged, Eudora again headed to Manhattan to receive, along with Harold Pinter, James Merrill, and Malcolm Cowley, a Bobst Award from New York University. Being honored along with such distinguished company may well have prompted Eudora to bemoan the twelve years that had passed since she had published her last piece of fiction. Certainly Mary Lou's plight cast a pall over this trip. Eudora was depressed. Once she completed her obligation to NYU, she lay alone in her room at the Algonquin, unable to stir herself or to phone her closest friends. To Bill Maxwell, she later wrote, "I was in NYC and didn't call you—I began to feel sinking-low, it was all in my spirits, and you'd know this on sight of me, so I waited—and *was* all right next morning but had to make my plane— It was a quick trip, to be given an award by NYU, and you know I've just had too much awarded me— I can't bear not seeing you, and getting to do that might have been my cure, but I just stayed on the bed (though dressed) reading your Christmas present, which I brought with me & was going to tote to you, as you see— I won't do this way any more." This letter disturbed Bill and Emmy, and

Bill wrote to Eudora, urging her to turn to them when her spirits were low.

> If I were to say what I was prompted to say when I read your letter, you would think, quite reasonably, that I hadn't understood a word of it. I do understand. Who hasn't, at our age, at some time, turned his face to the wall. We both worry about you—about the never quite going away tiredness. And about the way you are plucked at by people all over the country wanting something. Wanting *you*. Wanting you to do something for them. They don't mean to be heartless, and, of course, don't know or can't imagine about the others, but the effect is the same as if they were. I was even struck, at the library that day, by the fact that a purpose not entirely honoring (meaning PR) is sometimes served by the giving of awards. Dr. Gelbenkian or however it is spelled, had read the book. With the others it was doubtful. There is also the matter of living alone. If you live with somebody you are saved (often by petty irritation) from having to confront despair. But anyway, you did it, and got through it, and got home safely. Which is the main thing . . . What I was going to say, and felt it made no sense to say, at the beginning of this letter, is that there is this room with the four-poster bed, very comfortable, Kate's room no longer occupied by her, and it would have made us so happy if you had rung the bell and said I am at the end of my rope, will you take care of me till I get over it? We would have put you to bed in that bed, and driven that despair right out of the apartment. Remember that this is possible, won't you?

Bill felt that Eudora needed someone to share her life and her home and her sorrows. That sort of relationship, he believed, was the antidote to despair.[12] No such antidote, however, lay in Eudora's future. She would continue to face her trials as a single, separate person.

On Christmas Eve 1984, Mary Lou Aswell died. Unable to attend the services, Eudora wrote to Mary Lou's children. Deeply moved, Duncan Aswell responded, "Your letter about Mother has comforted me more than anything I've seen or read since her death. You're right, of course, about her presence and influence lasting and enriching all of us." To Reynolds, Eudora also expressed her sense of loss. "She had suffered much with heart trouble and other troubles—had lost her sight nearly altogether—But *herself* at all times—you know she was a part of so much of my life— She was of many lives. A giving spirit & heart. She was always so eager to hear what you were doing. (I didn't let her know what you've been going through with.)"[13]

Despite Mary Lou's death, Eudora honored her long-standing commitment to appear at the Modern Language Association's annual meeting at the end of December in Washington, DC. Old friend Daniel Aaron introduced her to a large and appreciative audience, and she read her first published story, "Death of a Traveling Salesman." But the most restorative aspect of the trip had nothing to do with the academic meeting that had brought her to the nation's capital. As she told Reynolds, "In Washington after MLA was through, I had a fine evening with the Jim Lehrers—they had a small dinner party to which they invited me (I'd met them in N.Y.) and the Roger Mudds—it was very special— And I think there was as much laughing as when you and I get going."[14]

For almost three months after her MLA appearance, Eudora remained in Jackson. An ice storm disrupted power in the city and caused some inconvenience, but life generally continued apace. Reynolds's play *Private Contentment* inaugurated the Eudora Welty New Playwrights Series at New Stage Theatre, and Eudora was pleased by this local tribute to Reynolds, even though he was still too ill to attend. She was also pleased that E. J. and Roger Mudd, en route to Natchez, Mississippi, were able to join her and Charlotte Capers for a pretheater dinner and the performance. The dinner, however, proved ill-fated. While her guests chatted in the living room, Eudora retreated to the kitchen to check on the crab casserole she was preparing. Suddenly there was a crash; she had dropped the casserole onto the floor. Later Eudora sent E. J. and Roger the recipe for the crab dish they had missed. "Combine ingredients," she wrote. "Place in buttered Pyrex dish. Top with cracker crumbs and paprika. Bake at 350 for about 30 minutes. Remove from oven. Immediately invert and allow dish to reach the kitchen floor. Test thoroughly to see if shattered. If Roger Mudd is dinner guest he will kindly appear and take care of everything. Serves zero."[15]

Other events were more routine. Jane, Patti, and Eudora continued to meet regularly for drinks and dinner, and Eudora was part of family gatherings for birthdays. At the end of March, however, the peaceful lifestyle came to an end, and intensive travel began anew. On March 21, Eudora visited Bryn Mawr and was excited to hear Seamus Heaney's poetry reading. From Philadelphia, Eudora stopped briefly in Manhattan and managed to visit the Kahn sisters; then it was on to Cornell for a week as the A. D. White Professor-at-Large. There she delivered a public reading of "The Wide Net," discussed *The Optimist's Daughter* with James McConkey's writing class, and held office hours; Eudora was charmed when the granddaughter of her old Columbia chum Nettie St. Helens Norris stopped by to visit.

After her stint at Cornell, Eudora returned home for two weeks. Awaiting her was a letter from Bill Smith, full of gratitude. In mid-March Eudora had written him, expressing concern about his heart condition and offering to help with the medical bills. Bill responded that the bills had "turned out to be less than I had anticipated and manageable." He also told Eudora that her "letter was so wonderful and such a testimonial to our long and beautiful friendship that I have been carrying it about with me ever since—as if, like the king's letter in Isak Dinesen's tale 'Barua a soldani,' you remember—it had a magic quality that would cure whatever ailed me. And cured me it has."[16] To this happy news

was added a visit from Pam and John Jessup, who were in Jackson
on April 13 for Eudora's birthday. Eudora introduced Diarmuid's
daughter and her husband to Charlotte, Jane, and Patti. She also
suggested that during their time in the South, the Jessups meet
with Michael Kreyling, who was teaching at Tulane University in
New Orleans—they did and were helpful in guiding Kreyling's
forthcoming research for the book about Diarmuid.

On April 16 Eudora made a quick trip to Memphis so that
she and historian Joel Williamson might present a program to-
gether at Rhodes College. Two days later she set out for New
York. There she read at the Ninety-second Street Y, home of the
Poetry Center, and visited with friends. She broke her stay in
New York briefly, so that as Princeton University's first Chauncey
Belknap Distinguished Visitor in the Humanities she might read
for a large audience and meet informally with creative-writing
students; the invitation from Princeton had been extended by a
Mississippi artist and faculty member, James Seawright, and
surely that connection appealed to Eudora. Then, on April 29,
she flew south for an engagement at Agnes Scott College; her old
friend Jane Pepperdene was retiring, and Eudora joined in the
tribute. On April 30 Eudora was back at home but stayed only
two days before she again set out for New York. There at a party
she heard Bill Smith and Ruth Ford perform, and at the Morgan
Library she herself spoke, with Katharine Hepburn in attendance. An added bonus was the opportunity to dine with Ralph
and Carol Sipper, Ken's good friends who had been so helpful to
her in Santa Barbara. The Sippers took Eudora and Larry
Moskowitz, a rare-book dealer, to dinner at an Italian restaurant
in the Village, which, according to scuttlebutt, was owned by Village mafiosi who needed it as a cover and ran the restaurant at a
loss. Eudora loved that story, one of many recounted during a
delicious, three-hour dinner prepared by an elderly Italian
woman, who was the restaurant's longtime cook. Eudora saw the
Sippers again at the Ellery Queen Mystery Writers of America

Awards Dinner. In the course of that evening, she received the 1985 Raven Award as Reader of the Year, and Ralph's *Inward Journey*, a collection of essays by and about Ken Millar, one of which Eudora had contributed, was honored as a nominee for an Edgar Award in the critical/biographical category. So the Welty/Sipper reunion must have seemed a reunion with Ken.

Eudora came home by way of Williamsburg, Virginia, where she received her thirty-second honorary degree, this one from William and Mary University. On May 13 she was at last in Jackson. The year was almost half over, and she had not yet given herself a stretch of uninterrupted time to write. But on June 1 a postcard from Bill and Emmy Maxwell, who were in Italy, seemed a good omen for the career of the now seventy-six-year-old writer. Eudora wrote to thank her good friends for the reproduction of Piero's Urbino (the *Ideal City*) and to say that the card "let loose feelings of mine about a story I've been working on off & on for 2 years, or 3, going back to, despairing over, and earlier this year tearing up probably 100 pages of—a story in which that very painting has a central part, thumbtacked to an architect's drafting room wall—And here Urbino came back to me, recalling its own wonder, its persistence in the mind & heart, through everything, and I felt that coming from you it was a sign."[17] Perhaps in writing about an architect, Eudora had in fact been trying to write about Ken, trying to move away from the clear autobiographical parallels in the "Henry" manuscript. Unfortunately, the content of the "Urbino story" seems destined to remain a mystery. Though Eudora hoped that she might return to it, she did not, and there is no extant copy.

On June 6 Eudora went to Manhattan yet again. Walker Percy was scheduled to receive the Compostela Award from St. James Cathedral in Brooklyn, and Eudora was to be in proud attendance, though a hair-raising cab ride to the event left her, along with Walker and his wife, Bunt, amazed and dismayed. Then on June 9 Dorothy and Victor Pritchett joined her at the Algonquin Hotel for a reunion. Eudora greeted them with "glorious paeonies," and the threesome saw each other repeatedly during the six days of the Pritchetts' stay.[18] Eudora took the Pritchetts and the Maxwells to dinner, and the Pritchetts entertained Eudora and the Kahn sisters another evening. From New York, Eudora journeyed on to New Orleans at the behest of Harvard University Press. There she read from *One Writer's Beginnings* at a banquet sponsored by the American Association of University Publishers.

The rest of the summer Eudora spent mostly at home, seeing friends, entertaining visitors, and talking with filmmakers who wanted to dramatize a story or produce a documentary about her life. She also met regularly with me. In my new capacity as scholar-in-residence at the Mississippi Department of Archives and History, a post I would hold for the next eighteen months, I had begun to reorganize the manuscripts, photographs, and correspondence Eudora had donated to the department. Now Eudora and I looked at each of her almost fifteen hundred photographs at the archives, and she attempted to tell me where and when a picture had been taken. She also helped me to identify individuals and events mentioned in her correspondence. During this process, we spent a good bit of time telling stories and getting to know each other better. I think Eudora relished the opportunity to talk expansively about her past to someone who was vitally interested in it and whom she intuitively trusted. Her accounts of New York and Paris, of Madison and small-town Jackson, of Florence and San Francisco, were vivid and engaging, and her old friends seemed to become my own. We eventually talked about them on a first-name basis.

By August 1985 Eudora was anxious about a lapse in her communication with Reynolds. He had been undergoing physical therapy, and Eudora was eager to know how helpful it had been. She also wanted to reassure Reynolds of her ongoing concern. "You know I think of you every day that comes. It isn't you alone

I've not written to, though I've hated the most not writing to *you*, even a decent short note. I can't really understand the way my handiest tool has let me down. But I expect to get over it yet. Fatigue, simply physical fatigue, may be the trouble and I haven't really got rested since the spring trip. Nothing for anybody to worry about, I am going to lick it—I just wanted to *remind* you of my care, concern, love and hopes, which go on just the same." In the letter, Eudora enclosed a favorite poem by Seamus Heaney, "Changes," and asked Reynolds, "Have you read much of him? To me he is away up there with the likes of Yeats. I thought this one especially would be for your eyes." To Reynolds, ever the close observer of the natural world, Eudora sent Heaney's description of an old pump, which had once been the center of a vital community and which has become home to a nesting bird. By the time the poem's narrator brings a young companion to the pump, however, the bird has flown, leaving an unhatched egg and its tail feathers behind. But all is not lost; the speaker has recovered a sense of community and of possible renewal in the face of urban anonymity and blight. This character concludes the poem by saying to his friend and to himself, "'Remember this. / It will be good for you to retrace this path / when you have grown away and stand at last / at the very center of the empty city.'"[19] For Reynolds, now at the center of a devastating physical change, Eudora sent a tough-minded message of hope for nature's renewal and for memory's power. She might have been sending the same message to herself.

Though her writer's block prevented sustaining such correspondence even with a close friend like Reynolds and though arthritis now made the physical effort of writing difficult for her, Eudora remained an active reader and appreciator of writing new and old. She had not long before met Mississippi novelist Richard Ford, and she admired his writing. A letter from Ford revealed what a powerful influence she had had on his work.

In an essay I wrote three years ago, in ESQUIRE, I said, in describing my ignorance about writers and literature, that I used to see you when I was a young boy, in Jackson. More to the point, though, my mother used to walk me over to Jitney 14, and we'd stand in the crowd at the steam table. Maybe this was 1953. And she would now and then say to me, "There's Eudora Welty." I don't know how she knew exactly, but I know now that she had read THE WIDE NET and A CURTAIN OF GREEN, and that you meant something special to her that the notions of acclaim or celebrity have nothing to do with. You did something she admired, and I honestly believe that her admiration for you was unalloyed. She and I never really talked about you; we didn't have conversations about books at my house, though it was a wonderful house to live in anyway. I didn't read a word you'd written until much later, ten years, probably, when I began to read voluntarily. But I think my mother's admiration for you, for your work and for what she could see and suppose of your life—and then later my own independent regard for your writing—are probably two of the strongest if not the strongest corroborative impulses I had when the moment came in my life when everything else I was doing wasn't working out, and writing a story seemed like not just a good idea but the only one I had. I'm sure that in your life and for a long time now, you've gotten the thanks from writers for one generosity or another. Mine is like theirs. But mine is also to express my mother's appreciation, words she never spoke herself, but, I'm sure, would've liked to. In whatever way she wanted to imbue me with something good, she did it in what was so clearly her esteem for you. It's complicated business, as you can see. But I'm like she was and could never have gotten around to saying these few things out loud to you. And so, I trust them to this letter, thinking that they'll mean something to you that is kin to what they mean to me.[20]

Unable to lick her own writer's block, Eudora must have been pleased to learn that she had inspired the work of a writer like Ford. He would become her friend, and she would take pride in his steady production of stories and novels.

Eudora devoted the autumn of 1985 to literary gatherings. She spent ten days in New York, during which time she read at a PEN International fund-raiser "in front of the backdrop of 'Sunday in the Park with George'—the grand jette." Unfortunately, despite suggesting the plan to Reynolds, she did not appear "holding a parasol over my head and leading a monkey." Not long afterward, Eudora traveled to Baton Rouge for a celebration of the *Southern Review* and for a reunion with Robert Penn Warren and Cleanth Brooks. Late in October she heard the Millsaps Singers and the Mississippi Symphony perform Samuel Jones's "Trumpet of the Swan," which took its text from her story "The Wanderers." Then in November she went to Washington, DC, where she gave a reading to benefit PEN/Faulkner and was the guest of honor at a fund-raising dinner for the same organization. Her greatest pleasure was the opportunity to stay with the Roger Mudds, who hosted the dinner, but the dinner itself must have been particularly lively. In attendance were novelists Susan Shreve, Peter Taylor, and Anne Tyler; Hodding Carter; Jim and Kate Lehrer; Nick Kotz, a Pulitzer Prize–winning reporter; Senator David Pryor; Congressman Sonny Montgomery; Richard Berendzen, the president of American University; Robert Squier, the producer of a television biography of Faulkner; and John Deardourff, a political consultant for television. At some point during Eudora's stay with the Mudds, Roger interviewed her for his new NBC program *American Almanac.* He had promised "not to ask you about your Gothic tales or why you didn't write racial polemics during the 60s," and he was true to his word.[21]

Eudora was back in Jackson in time to make arrangements for the year's most notable event—Reynolds felt well enough to travel and was coming for Thanksgiving. Eudora booked a caterer and invited Jackson friends to a Thanksgiving celebration in honor of Reynolds and his friend Daniel Voll. Reynolds and Dan arrived on November 27, spending some private time with Eudora before the next day's festive meal, and staying through the weekend. This reunion was soul-lifting for both Eudora and Reynolds, and he later wrote to express that very sentiment: "You know how much it meant to me—and it *did*. (It had a fine meaning for Dan too, but he'll tell you about that.) Your strongly broadcast help has been a permanent *dependable* through all these strange months, and it was all the better to celebrate the present state of calm with you."[22] The celebration continued for the remainder of the year. Christmas parties abounded in Jackson, and on New Year's Eve, Eudora joined Charlotte, Ann Morrison and her children, Patti Black, and me in toasting both absent friends and a new year.

Six days into 1986 Michael Kreyling was in Jackson and eager to talk with Eudora about Diarmuid Russell. Eudora herself was ready for Kreyling's visit, and to his surprise she lent him both sides of her lengthy correspondence with Diarmuid, so many letters that he had to purchase a large suitcase for transporting them back to Nashville, where he was now teaching. Kreyling's project was now assured of success. Shortly after meeting with Michael, Eudora received a manuscript from Mary Doll, who had written a memoir about her mother, Mary Lou Aswell. Mary Doll had been my colleague at Oswego State, and so Eudora discussed the manuscript with me. She was disturbed by Doll's assertion that Mary Lou had "never shown interest in [her daughter's] work, . . . never asked about [her] life, . . . forgot [her] successes," and by what seemed a dismissive reference to her mother's friends. Eudora wrote to offer a very different portrait of Mary Lou's character and relationships, to oppose publication, and to express concern for Doll.

I have been reading until I couldn't read any more without writing to you. What a bad, awful time you have been going

through. And still are, of course. The ms. is full of hurt
and gives out hurt. I felt it for Mary Lou, and for you, who
must have suffered a great deal to have let it culminate in
this book. Your mother's portrait in it is unrecognizable to
me, and I would not have recognized you, either, in the
woman who wrote this. I'm writing to you as the way I think
of you. Of course I can't claim to really know you, though I
first saw you when you were 3 or so, with your parents and
Duncan at home in Chappaqua—and last in that meeting
we had in bitter winter in New York, when that was so
lovely, the three of us having the chance to talk—do you remember—? And of course I had heard, and read in her letters, for all those decades, about you, and spontaneously
bursting out with pride and love—well, I felt we were
friends, or had the basis of friendship. All that terrible time
of Duncan's disappearance you were her standby. He came
back—thank God for that and his sweetness to her in the
dreadful time to come—but now it seems that *you* had disappeared in your own way, somewhere where you still are
and wrote this book from.

I would like to help you—out of love for your mother
but also for you, but what your letter asks me to do is not
the help that I can give or that—as it strikes me—you need.
You say what you want is to publish this book, and to get
something "pocketable" out of it, but that distances you
even further from what I thought I knew of you: I could be
mistaken of course. I did know Mary Lou. We were dear
and close friends for 40 years. I loved her deeply and still
do. I'm one of many friends—you refer to her friends in
one single way, "Mother's lesbian friends," and I am not lesbian, but reminding you how many and how different her
close friends were, men, women, young, old, friends that she
loved present and absent, in their whole lifetimes and after,
lifetime friends like me. She never forgot anybody she cared

for. She was extraordinarily giving and deeply remembering. Also forgiving. You announce in the beginning of this book that your authorities are the Catholic Church, the feminist movement, and later on say you are a Jungian. But whatever they have done for you, they have not kept you from the suffering, from what seems to my troubled mind some passionately willful misunderstanding—of your mother, of yourself, of the relationship in its own right. Until you can express physical disgust at the symptoms of your mother's growing illness and pain. Hurt has made hurt, and it seems to me the publication of this book would make it worse. Attacking the memory of those now dead is a sad form of dealing them (and ourselves) punishment.

Your letter (as opposed to your book) is somehow hopeful to me, where you say in the beauty of the West you feel closer now to your mother. It could be the beginning of healing, don't you believe? . . . But what you've written about her [in the manuscript]—and about yourself—is icy cold. So cold that it calls up what might be the urgent need for the opposite. I thought your sending me this might possibly be a *cri de coeur*—I'm taking the risk of treating it something like that, almost as if Mary Lou, who could spot a *cri de coeur* when she heard one (though you don't think so now) had put the idea into my head herself, might be helping me answer it, helping us both. It would be so essential to her if she somehow knew.

. . . Mary, I care a lot how you are, and I hope if in trying to express it I've failed, or gone too far, you will still be able to take it in the way it was meant, in love and hope. I can't do anything about your book, but I send my love and hope for your life—that's a hell of a lot more.

In this letter so full of desire for personal truth and integrity, Eudora sent words of dismay and of sympathy. She sought to testify to Mary Lou's greatness of spirit, to help a daughter recognize the beauty of her mother's life and accept its complexities, and to demonstrate that love and friendship transcend the boundaries of gender, age, and sexual orientation. Eudora stated that she was not herself a lesbian, but also asserted that she held Mary Lou, whatever her sexuality, in the highest regard. Her fervent wish was for Doll to do so as well. Doll immediately responded to this letter, explaining that her memoir moved from resentment to acceptance and that she had hoped the piece would be seen as a tribute to Mary Lou. She thanked Eudora for the letter, which had expressed such genuine concern for her, and she regretted that her manuscript had failed to convey the love she felt for her mother.[23]

Though in the first two months of 1986 Eudora had spent time with Doll's manuscript and had provided assistance to Michael Kreyling, her own writing continued to languish. She remained at home until March 6, attempting to write during the morning hours, but finding many distractions from work. She regularly dined with Jane and Patti, with Charlotte, Ann Morrison and me, and with other friends; she joined in family celebrations, met occasionally with Paul Binding, the English writer and critic who held the Eudora Welty Chair of Southern Studies at Millsaps during the spring 1986 semester, and gave readings at New Stage and at Galloway Methodist Church; and she welcomed far-flung friends like Mary Mian and Seta Sancton to the gala opening of Jackson's new public library building—from henceforth it was to be known as the Eudora Welty Library.

Early in March Eudora made a quick trip to Birmingham, Alabama, for the Birmingham Southern College Writers Conference. Once home she talked with two groups of filmmakers. One group approached Eudora about a television documentary designed to introduce viewers to her work and her creative process, and they sought her blessing before seeking a National Endowment for the Humanities grant. A second group also hoped for

an NEH grant, one supporting a televised version of "The Wide
Net." Neither would receive NEH funding. The first group did
gain Eudora's trust, but the second group alienated her. As a
potential consultant, I had been given a copy of "The Wide
Net" proposal and I showed it to Eudora. She had received two
drafts of the script but not, she told me, this. She immediately
wrote to her agent, Tim Seldes, informing him about its misleading statements:

> I thought you ought to see what is being submitted to the
> Endowment—unless I can first get it across to them that I
> can't allow them to make the claims they do. That the story
> was adapted "with the support, advice and supervision of
> Eudora Welty," that they were continuing to revise the
> screenplay "in collaboration with Eudora Welty," that
> screenplay rewrites "will continue with the guidance of Eu-
> dora Welty," and in their budget itemization I am listed as
> a member of the personnel—title "writer"—in the Salaries
> and Wages category. And that "Eudora Welty will continue
> to be consulted throughout the course of production re-
> garding all major artistic considerations." They clearly didn't
> show the application to me for their own good reasons,
> since none of these things is true. . . . They also imply that
> it was I who chose the story and expressed the wish to see it
> made into a film. I know they've worked hard, but they've
> also lied hard, and all the way through. I do have to stick up
> for myself, though. They have ignored everything except the
> use of my name, and don't hesitate to use it in these ways
> we see in the applications, and expect to get what they want
> by the exploitation.[24]

Despite the exasperating nuisance of "The Wide Net" project, there were many cheering events in the works. New Stage
Theatre planned to produce two short plays by Jim Lehrer in a
workshop version, and Jim was eager to be in Jackson and to work

with the cast and director. His exuberance was evident in a letter to Eudora: "I am so excited about coming to Jackson! I will be there most of the week. Would you save me an evening so I could take you to dinner? Kate will be there for the weekend. So will EJ & Roger. A good time will be had by all. Thank you so much for 'connecting me up' with Jane Petty & the theater."[25] Anticipation of spending an extended period with Jim, of watching theater-in-the-making, and of being reunited with Kate, E.J., and Roger pleased Eudora and cast a glow over the spring.

Lehrer arrived on April 14, and work on his plays *Cedar Chest* and *Silversides Thruliner* began in earnest. Then at week's end, Kate and the Mudds arrived, bringing a film crew with them. Roger was still working on his *American Almanac* segment about Eudora. He wanted footage of Eudora's Jackson and the surrounding countryside. Mudd's filming was successfully accomplished during the week, and on Friday night Lehrer's plays opened to an enthusiastic reception. After the play, Jim and the cast answered questions from the audience, and in the midst of the excitement Kate fainted. A doctor in the audience quickly saw to her, all was well, and the discussion adjourned. A cast party followed, and Mudd and Lehrer talked with various Jacksonians about Eudora's need for secretarial help. They hoped to find time for her to write. Someone suggested that Mary Brister, a retired bank secretary might be glad to assist Eudora with the great bulk of mail she was now receiving, and soon Mary agreed to the plan. To Eudora, however, the arrangement proved unsatisfactory. She felt compelled to indicate lines of response for Mary to take and was unable to let go of the task. Eudora must have sensed that her failure to answer letters was part and parcel of an all-encompassing writer's block. In the past, voluminous letter writing had complemented her writing of fiction. No more. Secretarial assistance could not solve her problem.

On Sunday, April 20, Eudora left Jackson for a second term as Cornell's A. D. White Professor-at-Large. This year she discussed

The Golden Apples with an advanced seminar, *One Writer's Beginnings* with another class, participated in a book signing, and spent a good bit of time with Jim McConkey. Upon her return to Jackson, Eudora met with Mildred Wolfe, a local artist whom she had asked to paint individual portraits of her parents and to do a third portrait of them together. Having been persuaded by Patti Black to donate her Pinehurst Street house to the Mississippi Department of Archives and History and anticipating that the house would then become a museum, Eudora wanted the three paintings to be part of her bequest and to honor her parents. The first of the three was hanging when a BBC film crew arrived in mid-May and was featured in a fine British documentary about Eudora.

Patchy Wheatley, the BBC documentary producer, proved a very congenial spirit, and Eudora actively participated in the entire two-week venture. She gamely climbed a metal staircase at the top of the ten-story Lamar Life Insurance Building so that the BBC could film her outside her old WJDX radio station office. As cameras whirred, she had lunch at a small-town restaurant where locals shared large round tables and served themselves with typical southern fare placed in abundance on lazy Susans. She met with old friends for drinks and conversation and allowed the meeting to be filmed. And on a key day of production, she missed the annual meeting of the American Academy. To Bill Maxwell she wrote in explanation, "I was wandering around the weedy ghost town of Rodney, Miss., sitting on the steps of the Presbyterian church there, while the BBC was taping me reading a bit of *The Robber Bridegroom*—isn't that the unlikeliest reason you ever heard for not being with *you*?" Unlikely, yes. Unpleasant, no. Eudora found the whole enterprise engaging, and her spirits were high. Good omens seemed to abound, as she also noted to Maxwell, "The other night I came into the dark kitchen for a glass of milk and saw the flashing of a lightning bug moving in the dark, from refrigerator to cabinet and soaring over the sink.

I caught it lightly in a Kleenex and carried it through the house to the front door, flashing all the way, and let it out again. 'You may have 3 wishes,' it might have said, without seeming any stranger."[26]

Early in June, Eudora, with Jane Petty as her companion, flew to Los Angeles and was ensconced in luxury at the Beverly Hills Hotel, the guest of former Miss Mississippi and Miss America Mary Ann Mobley and her husband, Gary Collins. They had invited Eudora to speak at their daughter's high school graduation, and Eudora had accepted. Then at month's end Eudora went to New York. Random House wanted to prepare a book-on-tape edition of *The Optimist's Daughter,* and Eudora had decided to be the reader.

June 1986 had been a month of diverting travels, but July brought tremendous news, one of the three wishes the lightning bug might have promised. Reynolds had successfully undergone a new surgical process, and his prospects seemed far brighter. Eudora wrote to express her relief and joy. "I'm glad you put it in a letter. It seems likely I couldn't have stood it for you, the fact of what you'd been through (*again*) without your words to tell me the way. Thank God too for the doctor's belief in his new instrument and his resulting good positive hopes from now on." Eudora further rejoiced that in the midst of illness Reynolds had managed to complete his novel *Kate Vaiden.* Two years earlier, at Millsaps College, before his struggle with cancer had begun, Reynolds had read from a draft of this novel; now Eudora was reading an advance copy of its page proof and remembering, as she told Reynolds, "that unforgettable morning when you read it for us at Millsaps— The quickness of life, the spring and vigor, the mysteriousness & certainty."[27] *Kate Vaiden,* she assured him, would be her reading material when she went to Washington to receive the National Medal of the Arts from President Reagan.

Escorted by John Ferrone, she received that medal on July 14. Ever the ardent Democrat, Eudora found this ceremony far less moving than the one conducted by President Carter in 1980. To Roger Mudd she wrote:

> I found it amazing, being in the White House at this occasion and seeing everything (and everybody) up closer but no realer, somehow. At the luncheon I had the feeling, I don't know why, that it was unlikely that anything was going to work with any of their plans. For instance, just beforehand, the medalists were told they were to walk onto the platform while Mrs. Reagan read out their citation, cross it in time to stand on a little piece of paper lying on the floor that said "Recipient," next to the President, and not to say anything. (Or fall down when the medal had been received. It turned out to weigh 8½ lbs.) How did we ever come out of it bemedalled? This is not to say I don't value the Endowment's choosing me for one of their medals and in very good company. I do of course, but the staging— Even more Alice-in-Wonderland-like was the presenting of the medalists at the [State Department] reception. Did you happen to hear Ambassador [Daniel J.] Terra (but not Firma) introducing us but not knowing who any of us were and calling the stand-ins by the names of those they represented . . . I thought maybe it was because he was such a recent bridegroom, he told us he was, but Alan Lomax said he'd been in the same confusion last year . . . What is a Cultural Ambassador?[28]

At home Eudora fell into the routine of reading fiction and poetry in the mornings, of perusing the *New York Times* at some point in the afternoon, of watching the *MacNeil/Lehrer News Hour*, of having drinks and dinner with friends, and of attending to household matters along the way. She attempted to write but could not bring anything into a final, polished form. In September she spent three days at Wellesley and in October she spent a few days in New York. The New York visit, as usual, was a great pleasure. Bill Smith, now poet-in-residence at the Cathedral of

St. John the Divine, had asked Eudora to give a reading of Hawthorne's story "The Birthmark" at the opening of the cathedral's Poet's Corner, and she happily obliged. This story, which Eudora had read some years earlier at the Morgan Library, depicts a scientist named Aylmer, who in seeking to remove his beautiful wife's single "flaw," a mysterious birthmark on her cheek, kills her. The "tyrannizing influence acquired by one idea over his mind" and his inability to accept mystery as an inherent and indestructible part of human existence—these qualities were ones that had also destroyed the happiness of characters in Eudora's own stories "A Still Moment" and "The Demonstrators." Small wonder that she had twice read "The Birthmark"; she was paying homage to Hawthorne and to nineteenth-century American literature, as well as acknowledging insights that had proved central to her own fiction.

A letter from Reynolds awaited Eudora after this last trip. "I've been hard at work every day on a new novel," he reported, "and now have about two-thirds of a whole. I'm not sure I like it—really, for the first time ever, I feel unsure about something that's almost done—and I may well finish it and then store it away for a while. But in this new life of mine, I have to keep working steadily or go mad. So it's been daily work, thank God. When I realize how much *writing* energy I wasted all those years— in busyness and dispensable chores—I could kick myself. Well, I know I learned a lot. But I could have sat still more often and to a damned-sight better effect. At least I'm getting a second chance." Then Reynolds told Eudora that he was to have a new surgery in November, and he asked her to "keep me right there near the center of your thoughts. Your granite strength behind and around me has been among the most important certainties for me, in all this mystery." Eudora promptly responded, reiterating her admiration for his strength and her hopes for the future. "This is just to send you all my love and wishes and hopes for you, as ever but calling on that extra strength and *willing* that seems to so consciously *be* there when times need it most. Well, you'll take this for granted, as I do, and you have all the rest of us too, your friends all around with you in their hearts and minds. Most of all, best of all, you've got *you*, and all you've learned and proved and plumbed for yourself and have won those two major battles with [cancer] already. I was grateful for your letter, the facts on just what is planned and what it can accomplish, and the good expectation that the marvelous new ultrasonic scalpel will make this final surgery easier on you in every way."[29]

On the home front, Eudora worked with a lawyer to revise her will, leaving her house and library to the Mississippi Department of Archives and History subject to a life estate during which she would continue to bear the expenses for upkeep and taxes. Having long been reluctant to make private correspondence available to scholars, Eudora had decided that her letters would be available after her death. Like Ralph Sipper, Patti Black had campaigned for such a decision, and Eudora had decided to follow her advice. Eudora shaped the provisions of her will in November and December, traveling to a meeting of the National Institute and American Academy and to an awards ceremony given by the National Institute of Social Sciences during the same period. Finally, on December 27, she, her lawyer, former Archives director Charlotte Capers, and Archives Board of Trustees Chairman William Winter met to finalize the agreement. On January 8, 1987, Winter sent Eudora the formal acknowledgment of her generous gift.

Near the end of January, Eudora traveled to Washington to celebrate the engagement and upcoming wedding of her agent, Tim Seldes, to the novelist Susan Shreve, and in DC she enjoyed being the houseguest of Jim and Kate Lehrer. Except for this trip, however, she spent January, February, and March in Jackson. Late in February, Patchy Wheatley of the BBC returned to do additional work on a Welty documentary. She, Eudora, and a film crew went to Davis Elementary School, where Eudora met with students and strolled through the halls. On this site Eudora had begun her education, and she noted how progressive the school's curriculum had become and how poor the students' spelling. She was particularly struck by the positive changes that integration had wrought. Now six-year-old African American students, enrolled in a school originally named for Jefferson Davis, envisioned an America free from oppression and full of opportunity. Such optimism was cheering and boded well for the future, but it could produce a misleading portrait of the past (and present), as Eudora implied in a letter to fellow Davis alum Nash Burger. "I was at the Alternative School (née Davis) on George Washington's Birthday and the first-grade posters were up. One showed George chopping down the cherry. His papa was watching him do it out of a second-story window; a balloon coming out of his mouth said 'George don't you chop down that tree.' Both were black as coal."[30]

In March an occasion both heartening and disturbing occurred. Reynolds had come through his two 1986 surgeries and felt well enough to travel to Jackson. Confined to a wheelchair, he managed to find accessible hotel accommodations and to see Eudora for extended periods over several days. One evening Eudora's friend Ann Morrison hosted a party for Reynolds, and in the midst of dinner he unexpectedly had to leave the table in intense pain. Seeing him suffer was difficult for all there and especially so for Eudora. For Eudora's sake, Reynolds later downplayed the physical agony he was enduring, but all recognized how extreme it was and how courageously he faced it. Eventually, he would learn to manage pain through self-hypnosis, but for now debilitating drugs provided the only relief.

Shortly after this visit to Jackson, Reynolds wrote Eudora to thank her for her hospitality and to urge that she write. "You well know that for, going on forty years, your work has meant an enormous amount to me—literally to my life. You and the example of your work were one of the few absolutely steady pole-lights that got me through the black months at the beginning of my ordeal. And the hope of new work from you—the certainty that new work is there, waiting to happen—means just as much right now. In fact it means far more than ever before, now that I myself understand so urgently the life-or-death deep-down soul-feeding necessity of work for a mind like yours or mine which (unlike those of some of our married, childbearing colleagues) has always had work as one of its two or three absolutely central supports."[31]

In addition to seeing Reynolds during the spring season, Eudora met with Michael Kreyling. Kreyling wished to discuss his ongoing research into Diarmuid's career. Eudora, eager for Diarmuid to receive the literary recognition he deserved, was happy to present Kreyling with newly found letters that she and Diarmuid had exchanged. She herself did not feel able to write biography, and so she entrusted this second batch of letters to a man she believed could do the project justice. But Eudora still wanted to write fiction, and in April she was at work on a story. Perhaps Reynolds's plea that she do so, this plea from a writer who seemed almost like her own child, from a writer who managed to produce fiction in the face of tremendous obstacles, inspired her to again put pen to paper. Whatever the case, Eudora now struggled with a darkly comic short story called "The Alterations." This account of a seamstress, who repeatedly stabs her husband with a pair of scissors and who, by the time the police arrive, has put Band-Aids on all thirty-eight of the wounds she had inflicted upon the now dead man, was based upon a long-past Jackson murder and may also have had contemporary relevance: Eudora certainly felt that Margaret Millar had metaphorically stabbed Ken. Yet the husband in "The Alterations" bore no resemblance to Ken, and the story did not move beyond irony. It failed to address the tragedy of Ken's situation. It was too distant from, not too close to, the lifeline. Eudora would never complete it.

In the midst of work on her story, Eudora took to the lecture circuit again. To Bill and Emmy Maxwell, Eudora described her five days at Bryn Mawr. "I'm here all week to meet with students and read, on a cause of friendship— There's been a gift to the college in the name of Bettina Linn, a teacher, who first invited me to Bryn Mawr on the first Lucy M. Donnelly scholarship back in the fifties, and I was invited to be on the program in honor of the one for her. What a sentence, when she was a scholar. Her friends are my old friends now, as is her sister who came. Elizabeth Bowen used to come at that time too, and once we coincided in the Deanery and had a fine rowdy time—what a shame they tore the Deanery down anyway, it had seen Henry James and W. B. Yeats and the whole flow of the grand."[32] Laurence Stapleton, poet, scholar, and Eudora's best friend at Bryn Mawr, had not managed to save the Deanery but was passionately involved in an attempt to save the editorial correspondence, manuscripts, and other papers associated with *The Dial* (1916–1929), the very distinguished art and literary magazine, which had been edited by poet Marianne Moore and literary critic Kenneth Burke, among others, and which had published the work of T. S. Eliot, Ezra Pound, and William Carlos Williams. Yale University had decided to sell this archival collection through Sotheby's, and Eudora became very engaged by Laurence's efforts to keep the collection in the public domain.

From Bryn Mawr, Eudora made the short journey to New York, where she saw Bill and Emmy and spent a weekend at the Ferrone-Theron farm before flying back to Jackson. Ten days later she was off to Charleston, West Virginia, to receive an honorary degree and the Appalachian Gold Medallion Award from the University of Charleston and the State of West Virginia. Eudora was touched by these awards because of her mother's West Virginia roots. An added bonus, as she told Bill and Emmy Maxwell, was the fact that "all my first and second cousins for miles around came and clapped for me, and then gave me a party themselves—about 40 of them! My mother's brothers were all prolific. Nearly all the kin I ever knew are gone now, but the young ones are rousing. One of my cousins, at whose home I stayed, has her father's banjo which I heard him play hung up on the wall above the smart-looking bar. It was very stirring for me."[33]

During the summer, Eudora stayed in Jackson, seeing friends like Jane and Patti, Charlotte, Ann Morrison, Tommie Blissard, and Bethany Swearingen on a regular basis. She also saw a good bit of me; in January I had returned to my upstate New York teaching position, but I summered in Jackson, working on a book about Eudora, interviewing her occasionally, and dining with her each week. On July 1, I joined Eudora and a number of other friends for a showing of Patchy Wheatley's BBC program about Eudora. We were all impressed, particularly with the scene in which Eudora, Patti, Ann, and Charlotte exchanged funny stories about Jackson's past. Another sort of television program, however, repeatedly occupied Eudora during the summer. The Iran/ Contra hearings disturbed and intrigued her. Just as she had watched the Watergate hearings some years earlier, now she watched a new cast of characters. To Bill Maxwell Eudora confided, "I am hypnotized by these days of testimony—every face, every intonement of voice, every damning word. (I decided I'd choose Maine to move to if I could pick the senator and congressman to represent me—Cohen and Mitchell. The response of the national TV audience is also something we'd better know, just as unbelievable as what's on the screen. A report from Dallas (for example) after the first couple of days of Col. North said that he was the most wonderful man! who reminded them of 'So-and-So' on the soaps—of no real people but the heroes of the serials they daily watched—fantasy characters."[34]

Summer 1987 also involved Eudora in providing for her own literary legacy. She and Charlotte strolled through the Pinehurst Street house with a tape recorder, Charlotte asking questions about the house and Eudora answering them. They were establishing a preliminary inventory of contents that would pass to the state of Mississippi upon Eudora's death. Doing so must have turned Eudora's thoughts to the way she would be posthumously honored, and she may have been apprehensive. Certainly, as she wrote Bill Maxwell, she felt that Faulkner was receiving the sort of recognition that in life he would have rued. "Do you want a William Faulkner stamp?" she asked.

> The U.S.P.O. is getting ready to issue one. A ceremony in Oxford, Miss. where Faulkner early on had a job working at the University Post Office on the campus. They invited me (through mysterious reasoning) to pas [*sic*] a few remarks at the scene (and have also asked me to read (so I read in the paper) "Why I Live at the P.O." the night before. It's all madness. The postmaster in Washington wrote to me saying he'd understood I intended to make a few remarks at the ceremony, but he wanted to tell me that *he* was to make the main address.) It will really be funny, because it's during the Faulkner Conference with scholars from everywhere, and everybody there but the postmaster general, or whoever he is, will know the tale about Faulkner and the job at the post office. He quit, saying he was not going to be at the beck and call of every son-of-a-bitch who had the price of a two-cent stamp.[35]

During the fall of 1987, Eudora was on the road a good bit. On October 7, she went to Mississippi State University, where she joined Michael Kreyling, Jane Pepperdene, and me for a three-day Welty symposium and where she and Kreyling were able to talk about his work on Diarmuid. She came home long enough to receive the Chevalier de l'Ordre des Arts et des Lettres from the French government, then was off to the Mississippi Gulf Coast, where she and Richard Ford were honored by the Mississippi Library Association. Finally, at month's end, she left for New York, where she spoke at the Whitney Writers Awards Ceremony held at the Morgan Library. In her public appearances, Eudora typically read from her fiction, but for this occasion she had composed an address on the pleasures of reading and writing. "Pleasure in literature," she told her audience, "takes many a different form, but we're not here speaking of pleasure in the personal sense, that is, of the sentimental kind. Rather we're concerned with the pleasure Henry Green unforgettably described in his autobiography *Pack My Bag*, which can leave you wordless with happiness, but not easy with yourself."[36] Such was the pleasure Chekhov and Green himself had brought Eudora; such was the pleasure Eudora's work had brought her readers; and such was the double-edged pleasure she could no longer find as a fiction writer. She could not transform pain into the beautiful order of literature; they would henceforth remain separate in her life.

Eudora spent the following weekend at the Ferrone-Theron farm in the Pennsylvania countryside and the next week seeing friends in Manhattan. Then she headed north to Mount Holyoke to receive its Sesquicentennial Medal. On November 11 she at last flew home, arriving in time to join in a party celebrating a new edition of *The Robber Bridegroom*, one illustrated by Barry Moser's haunting woodcuts.

On November 30 Jim Lehrer was back in Jackson. New Stage Theatre had decided to produce his full-length play *Church Key Charlie Blue*. Jane Petty, the director, and Lehrer had agreed to spend a week workshopping the play in advance of the rehearsals scheduled to begin at the end of December. Eudora attended workshop sessions and dined regularly with Lehrer. For his part, Lehrer was entranced. "I had a wonderful time with you in Jackson," he wrote Eudora. "It was a special time. I will remember & cherish it forever."[37]

Not long after Lehrer left Jackson, I arrived yet again, this time to interview for a professorship at Millsaps College and to devote a few weeks to studying Eudora's manuscripts at the Department of Archives and History. The interview went well, and the job offer was forthcoming two or three months later. But for the immediate future, Eudora, Charlotte, Patti Black, Ann Morrison and her children, and I would happily see in a promising new year. Bill Maxwell's wishes for Eudora were my own. "My wish for you for 1988 is that there will not be a single envelope containing somebody's manuscript he hopes you will read and criticise. My wish for Emmy is that she will feel that she owes it to herself to paint more than she owes anything else to anybody. And for myself that I will wake up every morning full of energy and rush to my dear typewriter. While I'm at it, I might as well wish that (SINCE IT DOESN'T COST ANY MORE) for you too."[38]

The new year did prove to be a rather happy one, though not one in which Eudora rushed to her typewriter. Activities other than writing claimed her attention. For the first eight months of the year, she kept to a hectic schedule, effectively denying herself time for fiction but enjoying friendships new and old. On January 16 Jim Lehrer arrived for his play *Church Key Charlie Blue*, and Eudora observed the final week of rehearsals. The night before the play opened, Kate Lehrer and Roger and E. J. Mudd joined Lehrer and Eudora for a reception at the Governor's Mansion, and the next day, John Ferrone joined the group in attending both the performance itself and a cast party following the play. Three days later, Robert and Donna MacNeil flew into Jackson to see the play. The only disappointment of the two-week run was a lukewarm review in the local paper. But, as Lehrer afterward told Eudora, his high spirits were scarcely affected. "I've only been back for two days but I already miss Jackson—the theater, the warmth, the actors, Jane, and, mostly, you. Thank you for making it possible—and 'starring' in—two of the most wonderful weeks of my life." Robert MacNeil was grateful that his *News Hour* colleague had had such an exhilarating experience, but above all, he was filled with admiration for Eudora herself: The opportunity to know her, he wrote, had further convinced him that "truly talented people, people of great accomplishment, have a core of modesty that is like being in the eye of the storm—a wonderful respite from the general gale of self-congratulation today."[39]

In February another prominent newsman made his way to Jackson. Charles Kuralt, whose CBS *On the Road* features were so popular with television audiences, appeared at a fund-raiser held by the Friends of the (Eudora Welty) Library, paying a visit to Eudora in advance of his speaking engagement and being introduced by her at the festivities. Kuralt had once interviewed Eudora for a piece about Franklin Delano Roosevelt and the Works Progress Administration and in 1989 would focus an interview on Eudora herself. He would also narrate the American broadcast of Patchy Wheatley's documentary about Mississippi's literary first lady. He was a journalist with whom Eudora felt particularly simpatico and who found her company a delight. The Friends of the Library had been wise in choosing this speaker.

Eudora's first trip of the year came at the end of March, a three-day jaunt to Washington, DC, where she was the houseguest of Roger and E. J. Mudd, attended a dinner party given by Hodding Carter and Patt Derian, and heard Richard Ford read for PEN/Faulkner at the Folger Shakespeare Library. After briefly regrouping at home, Eudora next went to Randolph-Macon Woman's College for an engagement and to Charlottesville, Virginia, where on April 12, the eve of her birthday and Thomas Jefferson's, she and Charlotte Capers dined with the trustees of the Thomas Jefferson Memorial Foundation in the parlor and dining room of Jefferson's Monticello. The next day the two Mississippi women attended a memorial service at Jefferson's grave site and later had a private tour of his estate. Eudora had long admired Jefferson, and she appreciated this intimate encounter with his home and garden. Two weeks later she was on the road again, this time to a visit with Reynolds at his Durham, North Carolina, home and to a speaking engagement in nearby Greensboro, where, for a rapt audience, she read the text to Samuel Jones's "Trumpet of the Swan" and then herself became an audience member, hearing a performance of this fantasia for orchestra and chorus.

In May, John Robinson made his annual visit to Jackson, having medical checkups, seeing his family, and spending time with Eudora, and Eudora relaxed at the prospect of a month free of travel. It was not free of honors, however; they kept arriving at a rapid pace. This time the Mississippi Institute of Arts and Letters gave Eudora its Lifetime Achievement Award. Walker Percy was also present for the ceremony, receiving an award for his novel *The Thanatos Syndrome.* The two writers, in a predinner conversation, discovered that they both loved the British television program *Dr. Who,* a witty sci-fi series.

Early summer found Eudora in the northeast. She went to Bryn Mawr, where she and Laurence Stapleton had good conversations. She received an honorary degree at Princeton; saw Bill and Sonja Smith, Bill and Emmy Maxwell, and John Ferrone in New York; and then appeared at Smith College with Jim Lehrer. All of this was great fun, but a writing project was soon due. Eudora returned to Jackson and prepared an introduction for *The Democratic Forest,* a book of Mississippian William Eggleston's photographs.

Another more ambitious publishing prospect lay ahead. In August Ron Sharp of Kenyon College arrived to discuss a jointly edited anthology on the theme of friendship. He had written to Eudora about the book early in the year, but she had not replied. Six weeks later, undeterred, Sharp had phoned Eudora. As they talked about the prospects for this book, Eudora had become engaged by the idea and agreed to the proposal. Eudora then took on the preliminary responsibility of selecting fiction, Sharp of deciding about essays and poetry, with each providing suggestions to the other. Now it was time to begin collaborating in person. Ron had been a longtime colleague of Robert Daniel, the man with whom in the 1930s Eudora and Frank Lyell had coauthored "Lilies That Fester," a never-published anthology of parodies. Sharp thought that the friendships both he and Eudora had shared with Daniel constituted a bond that would well serve the proposed book. More basically, friendships were at the center of Eudora's life; she treasured her friends, was absolutely loyal to and supportive of them, and found her own life enriched by these relationships. A book on this topic sparked her interest, and she was eager to work with Sharp. Eudora had found a project into which she could channel her creative energies, but which would not entail the physical and emotional demands of fiction writing. In so doing, she may have begun to recognize that her own fictional canon was complete. The time for writing fiction, she told interviewer Dannye Romine Powell, "may be forever away."[40]

Shortly before Sharp's visit, Eudora had been delighted to find in the *New Yorker* a story by one of her closest friends, and she had written Victor Pritchett in praise of "Cocky Olly." Dorothy Pritchett immediately responded, saying how much Eudora's letter had meant to her husband. "Victor got your letter yesterday and has been moving two feet above the ground ever since. You said all the perfect things and he will be writing to you himself when he comes down those two feet. It was a *marathon* writing that story—he is supposed to be writing a *nouvella* but you will understand more than I that after all these years of cutting, cutting, cutting and weeding out all extraneous matter stretching to a nouvella is unnatural to him—it smacks more of writing a short *novel* and he has never seen himself as a novelist. At one moment he was going to see if this Cocky Olly material would stretch to nouvella length but I used all my powers to persuade him to confine it to what it is . . ." Victor himself saw a link between this new story and Eudora's work: "I who have learned so much from your writing and who will never forget your reading of that rich story of yours—the one that you gave at Vanderbilt—am deeply stirred by your praise of *Cocky Olly.* It had been simmering in my mind for years. It is strange that so much of my own boyhood flows into scenes of my own and other people's later lives and turns into something new. And, unerringly you have spotted those scenes and asides that fly, as it were, by accident, into the story. Your own art is full of these divine, illuminating 'accidents' of the imagination."[41]

Eudora's generosity had from the start been central to her character, and it continued to be. In September, at my request, for instance, she agreed to read from *One Writer's Beginnings* for the incoming freshman class at Millsaps College, and she then answered questions posed by the students. In October she traveled to Chapel Hill, North Carolina, to honor Louis Rubin, an early champion of her work, a prolific scholar, and an accomplished novelist. She had met Rubin when he invited her to speak at Hollins College in the 1960s, had found his articles about her work illuminating, had enjoyed a shopping trip to L. L. Bean with him when they were both at a conference in Maine, and had seen him periodically through the years. Now she joined with Elizabeth Spencer, Kaye Gibbons, Clyde Edgerton, and others in paying tribute to his distinguished career. Two weeks later she flew to Baltimore at the request of Anne Tyler. Tyler's husband, a child psychiatrist named Taghi Modarressi, wanted Eudora to discuss her work at a conference of his colleagues. Eudora, like Elizabeth Bowen and Reynolds Price, believed that childhood memories were key to any writer's achievement, and she and the psychiatrists found much common ground for discussion.

Eudora, however, was no longer drawing upon memories of childhood or upon any other memories to produce works of fiction, and Reynolds was distressed by her lack of productivity. Shortly after she returned from Baltimore, Eudora received a letter from him urging her to write. "The thought of your working there, right while I was working here, has been a powerful warmth in my head for more than half my life. Don't hate me for saying it; don't feel that I'm trying some sort of cop at the crossroads, trying to flag you out of traffic. But it's something I feel, and hope to keep feeling."[42] Eudora took Reynolds's plea to heart; several times she asked me if she might find office space in my house, a place where no one could reach her or interrupt her work. I, of course, was thrilled at the prospect and offered her a writing room. But nothing ever came from our discussions.

In October and November, politics occupied much of Eudora's attention. The presidential campaign pitted Governor Michael Dukakis against Vice-President George H. W. Bush, and the Republicans and many southern Democrats castigated Dukakis for his "liberal" leanings. Not Eudora. A Dukakis sticker adorned the bumper of her car. And before the election, she offered support for the Dukakis philosophy in a more public way. Noted historian C. Vann Woodward phoned Eudora to say that many intellectuals were dismayed by the pejorative connotations being attached to the word *liberal,* and he asked if Eudora would be willing to sign a letter in defense of the word. She was delighted to do so, and the letter signed by many distinguished Americans appeared in the *New York Times* shortly before the election.

However displeasing she found the nation's political climate, Eudora found her personal life moving in a positive direction. Her worries about Reynolds had eased, and time had begun to heal the grief she felt at the loss of Ken and Mary Lou. The Christmas season of 1988 was filled with happy gatherings—dinners with Charlotte, Ann, and me, with Patti and Jane, with Mike and Chris Kreyling; a party at the home of the architect Tom Biggs and his wife, Louise, old friends of her brother Edward; and, of course, a family celebration on Christmas Day.

In 1989 Eudora encountered new opportunities and pleasures. William Winter, the former governor of Mississippi, had been named Eudora Welty Chair of Southern Studies at Millsaps College, and Eudora resolved to become one of his students. A gentleman of the highest integrity and of true liberal credentials, Winter had long claimed Eudora's admiration, respect, and affection. The chance to hear him discuss the course of twentieth-century Mississippi politics delighted her. The new year also brought Ron Sharp repeatedly to Jackson, and he and Eudora worked diligently to select entries for their book on friendship and to organize those entries. And Eudora contributed to still another project—she had given the University Press of Mississippi permission to bring out a substantial book of her photographs. It was to include many of the photographs she had already donated to the Mississippi Department of Archives and History and photographs of friends that Eudora had kept for herself. Eudora further agreed to an interview, to be conducted by the book's editors and to be published along with the photographs.

All of these activities and her typical social gatherings with Jackson friends kept her busy. Eudora may have worked intermittently at fiction, but she produced nothing she wanted to show to her agent or colleagues. Celebrations of her past accomplishments were instead the order of the day. On April 2, in honor of her eightieth birthday, the city of Jackson and the Jackson Symphony Orchestra paid tribute to her. Roger Mudd was the master of ceremonies at the afternoon festivities, and later that night Eudora took Mudd, his wife E. J., John Ferrone, and other close friends to her favorite Greek restaurant.

On April 7 Reynolds arrived to join in another eightieth-birthday celebration. The next evening, Ann Morrison invited Eudora's close friends to dinner, and all were delighted to see how much better Reynolds seemed to feel; that was itself cause for celebration, as was the public reading Reynolds delivered at Millsaps on April 9. On April 10 and 11, Richard Ford and Barbara Ascher joined the parade of visitors paying homage to Eudora. By her actual birthday, April 13, Eudora might well have wished to retreat into solitude, but instead she came to a small party at my house, where Ann, Charlotte, Patti, Jane, and I toasted her and where we all watched a repeat of Patchy Wheatley's film about her.

Late in April Eudora left Jackson for a week in New York. There, on April 23, the birthday of William Shakespeare, she, Helen Hayes, Toni Morrison, Leontyne Price, and twenty-six other notables, primarily actresses, became the first women members of the famous Players Club. According to Eudora, "That was the least" that the formerly all-male club "could do for Shakespeare." But all joking aside, Eudora was pleased. "I'm

stage-struck," Eudora told the *New York Times.* "I'm absolutely
thrilled to be in the Players."[43] The next night, Eudora dined with
Robert and Donna MacNeil and loved the panoramic view of
New York from their apartment. She spent the rest of this New
York week with the Maxwells, the Kahn sisters, and Walter
Clemons. Then, after a two-week respite at home, she came back
to the city for the American Academy Ceremonial and for a me-
morial tribute to Malcolm Cowley, taking a trip to the Ferrone-
Theron farm on the weekend between these events.

Soon after her late May return to Jackson, Reynolds phoned
to discuss the introduction he was writing for Eudora's photograph book and to offer congratulations on a lucrative award Eudora had received from the National Endowment for the Arts.
The conversation cheered him; in the midst of all his medical trials, Reynolds had been worried about Eudora. Now he sensed
that she was happier than she had been in many years. He wrote
to express his delight. "You sounded so good on the phone just
now—I feel like running down and helpin' you spend that
lagniappe! We could head back down through Sullivan's Hollow
to the coast and eat oysters, check on those ladies at the Jeff
Davis home; it was just about this time of year we saw them last."
What had brought about the change in spirits? Or had they really
changed? In retrospect, Reynolds felt they had not. After reading
an early draft of this book, he wrote to me on just this topic.

> What I believe (from my own experience, informed now by
> your narrative) is that, from at least her early fifties onward,
> Eudora had a life that was—emotionally and physically—
> gravely deprived and that her inability to write more fiction
> in the last thirty years of her life (a fact that I still find hard
> to comprehend, especially since I haven't seen those later
> unfinished stories) may have derived from an otherwise great
> writer's unwillingness or refusal or inability to confront cer-
> tain personal deprivations head-on . . . After her first pub-

lished short story—"The Death of a Traveling Salesman"—
she never wrote about the potentially killing weight of sheer
loneliness, the lack of something as simple as a loving mate
or another enduring friend with whom she had shared a sexual intimacy. As Bowman, her salesman, realizes "anyone
could have had that." But E. didn't. In the case of Katherine
Anne Porter, whom I met only once, numerous—but ultimately loveless—marriages seem to have produced an unen-
viable meanness in KAP, a meanness that sank her long
project (*Ship of Fools*). In the case of E, it seems to me that
the life-long absence of an intimate love silenced her before
she was ready for silence. And it left her somehow deeply
puzzled for the last decades of her life.[44]

As powerful as Reynolds's words are, my own experience with
Eudora suggests a somewhat different interpretation. Eudora, I
do agree, was well acquainted with the oppressive nature of loneliness. From the 1930s until the 1980s, she repeatedly wrote (in
"Clytie," "Livvie," "The Whole World Knows," "No Place for
You, My Love," "Circe," "Kin," *Losing Battles, The Optimist's Daughter,* "Nicotiana," and "The Shadow Club," for example) about its
heft, more than once, it seems to me, depicting the weight of
loneliness as "potentially killing." And clearly, as Reynolds observed, Eudora had longed to know first John and later Ken as "a
loving mate . . . with whom she [could share] a sexual intimacy."
But loving relationships with John and Ken, whether or not they
were consummated, had enriched, not merely complicated, Eudora's life, and she had known many profound and sustaining
friendships. "Besides the physical," as Eudora herself once noted,
"there are other orders of intimacy, other ways to keep life from
splitting asunder." Those other orders of intimacy, it is true, were
never as deep after Diarmuid, Frank, Dolly, Mary Lou, and Ken
died, and their absence seems to me to be the source of Eudora's
melancholy. Perhaps such intimacies were possible only with those

who had shared her long journey through the discoveries and frustrations of love, the rewards and demands of a writing career, the deaths of friends and family members. Perhaps, as a result, she did not confide the depths of her emotional life to Patti, Jane, or me, the three friends to whom she was probably closest in her last decades. Certainly she was separated by an ocean and by Enzo Rocchigiani from John. And certainly she restrained herself in conversations with Reynolds, feeling that her difficulties were insignificant in view of his own physical and emotional struggles. Her reluctance to confide in any of us was, moreover, matched both by an unwillingness to lay bare in autobiography the details of her adult life and by an inability to complete and publish a story drawing upon Ken's ordeal as a victim of Alzheimer's disease—she would not establish these connections with her readers. Her writing silence seems not to have been caused by but to have constituted a sort of loneliness. Nevertheless, from the time in late 1988 that I began to see Eudora on an increasingly frequent basis, eventually almost daily, I felt more joy than sadness in her. She was not despondent or withdrawn. She took a keen interest in the lives of her friends; she often asked, for instance, about my career, the texts I was teaching (whether by Chaucer or Shakespeare, Faulkner or Warren), my family members, my travels. She took a keen interest in the physical world around her, in the camellia blossoms she cut for her living room, in the squirrels dashing up and down the oak tree in her front yard, in the nighttime sky over Jackson. She took a keen interest in the *New York Times*, reading reports of scientific discoveries and political intrigue with equal zest. And she kept her sense of humor; conversations with Eudora were always lively and amusing. So, I think Reynolds's 1989 sense that Eudora "sounded so good" may be just as accurate as his sense, informed by subsequent visits, of her "deprivation" and may signal that she had once again come to terms with loss. Eudora's comments on Depression-era Mississippians seem to describe her situation in the later 1980s:

"Whatever you might think of those lives as symbols of a bad time, the human beings who were living them thought a good deal more of them than that. If I took picture after picture out of simple high spirits and the joy of being alive, the way I began, I can add that in my subjects I met often with the same high spirits, the same joy. Trouble, even to the point of disaster, has its pale, and these defiant things of the spirit repeatedly go beyond it, joy the same as courage."[45]

What were the sources of joy for Eudora as she entered her eighties? Her work on the *Norton Book of Friendship* and the photograph book must have been one. Reynolds's victory over cancer certainly was another. Relationships with scholars like Michael Kreyling, Ron Sharp, and myself, scholars who were fascinated by her past and who longed to discuss it with her, must have helped to keep that past vivid and alive. The news that Kreyling's book about Diarmuid would be published by Farrar, Straus, and Giroux ensured that Diarmuid would receive his due recognition. And her developing friendships with Roger Mudd, Jim Lehrer, Robert MacNeil, and Richard Ford must also have been important; throughout her life Eudora had relished the companionship of *men* who shared her passion for language. Diarmuid and Ken could not be replaced, but these younger men enriched her life.

During the summer and early fall of 1989, Eudora remained at home, seeing friends, reading, watching television coverage of the Voyager exploration of outer space, and working on the Norton book. In early October she attended a fund-raising event for Dick Molpus, a Democratic candidate for governor; support of Molpus may have been the ostensible reason, but the appearance of Georgia's Democratic Senator Sam Nunn, whom she had greatly admired in his television interviews, was the more compelling factor. Then in mid-October she began to travel again: to Columbus, Mississippi, to read at the Mississippi University for Women's annual Welty weekend and to participate in the inauguration of its new president; to the University of Chicago to deliver the Moody lecture; and to Washington for a PEN/Faulkner gala fund-raiser, where she and twenty-one other writers, Larry Mc-Murtry, Annie Dillard, Amiri Baraka, and Reynolds Price among them, discussed their beginnings. While staying with the Mudds, as was now usual, Eudora taped an interview with Roger that would be broadcast on the *MacNeil/Lehrer NewsHour* and would focus upon her photographs. From Washington, Eudora returned home to repack and journey to San Diego, where her publisher Harcourt was now based and where she would speak at the University of California's local campus.

The rest of 1989 she would spend in Jackson. Dianne Donovan of the *Chicago Tribune* arrived to interview Eudora about her photographs. Calvin Skaggs of Lumiere Productions came to film a conversation with Eudora, one focusing on her photographs as well as her fiction. The *New York Times Book Review* ran a front-page interview that Hunter Cole and Seetha Srinivasan had conducted with Eudora on behalf of the University Press of Mississippi. And on November 26 Robert MacNeil spoke at the Old Capitol Museum about the new University Press book *Photographs.* Shortly thereafter, Roger's taped interview appeared on PBS. Bill Maxwell was captivated by the sight of Eudora on the television screen and immediately wrote to say so. "It was a three-cornered love affair involving Roger Mudd, you, and the camera man. He caught you so beautifully, and especially your eyes, that several times I wanted to reach out and touch you, the way I am sure cats and dogs want to do when they watch TV. I have a fondness for Roger Mudd, which is not based on an acquaintance but solely on his appearance and personality. He reminds me of the men of my childhood. There is an easiness about him which is not often found any more."[46]

Eudora could not, however, bask in the happy memory of MacNeil's visit and Mudd's program. On November 25 John Robinson died at his home in Italy, and word of the death reached Eudora a few days later. Her love of John, the transformation of that love into an enduring friendship, the comforting communication only possible in long-term relationships must all have been in Eudora's thoughts. She wrote to Nash Burger, "I thought you might want to be told that John Fraiser Robinson died in Florence, Italy, of a heart attack about a week ago. We had always been in touch—I had heard from him not very long ago when he was taking a trip on the Black Sea—having a fine time by himself. He had wanted to come to Jackson again but he had qualms about his heart on such a hard plane trip. I learned today that he was buried in Florence— He had taken much care of the old family burial place in Sidon, Miss.—but I guess it is all the same to him now, and he loved Italy, too."[47] At age eighty, Eudora knew well the experience of loss, and the melancholy experience was with her again.

As Christmas approached, Eudora welcomed Charles Kuralt and his CBS film crew into her home. This interview concluded the public attention she received in 1989. But a private and very meaningful letter of praise arrived as the year ended. Victor Pritchett wrote to thank Eudora for sending him *Photographs* and to say, "I can't resist reading some of your fine marvellous stories into them. —I keep a copy of these stories of yours beside my bed and am always gripped by your clarity and subtlety. You really are at the top of your genius. We wish you would come over again . . . Still, *do* come and we'll talk!"[48] In 1990 Eudora would respond to Pritchett's invitation and travel, at age eighty-one, by herself to London once more. John Robinson's death had made all too clear the urgency of seeing one's elderly friends.

For Eudora 1990 began at home with local compatriots and with family. Then on January 22 Vann Woodward arrived to spend a week at Millsaps College under the auspices of the Eudora Welty Chair of Southern Studies. The two dined together twice, and Eudora heard Woodward's public lecture at Millsaps. Their common friend Robert Penn Warren might well have been on their minds; Warren had died the previous October, and

Eudora attended a memorial service for him at New York's Century Club on March 8. In mid-March Ron Sharp visited Jackson for another week of work on the friendship book; at the same time, friendship, her own friendship with Katherine Anne Porter, was also the subject of an essay Eudora was preparing for the *Georgia Review*. Once her week with Sharp was complete and her essay was safely in the mail, Eudora left for New York City. There she would speak to Columbia graduate writing students and give a benefit-reading for their magazine.

On April 12 Reynolds arrived in Jackson to celebrate Eudora's birthday and to oversee the production of his play *Full Moon*, which would premiere five days later at New Stage Theatre as part of the Eudora Welty New Playwrights Series. His health and spirits vastly improved, Reynolds brought great happiness to Eudora, and more happiness was in store. The day after Reynolds's play opened, Eudora boarded a plane for London, where, as mentioned, she would spend three weeks visiting the Pritchetts, seeing plays, and touring the countryside. Patchy Wheatley had arranged housing for Eudora, a hotel where there would be few steps for her to climb. Paul Binding took her to Jane Austen's house at Chawton in Hampshire, and she was delighted to see the home of this writer whom she so revered. But for Eudora, surely the house was less moving than Austen's fiction. In "The Radiance of Jane Austen," Eudora had written, "The brightness of [her] eye simply does not grow dim, as have grown the outlines and colors of the scene she saw herself while she wrote—its actualities, like its customs and clothes, have receded from us forever. But she wrote, and her page is dazzlingly alive." Literary pilgrimages aside, there were other auspicious occasions. One occurred when Patchy invited Eudora to meet the poet and critic Ian Hamilton and asked the Pritchetts to join them as well. But private meetings with Victor and Dorothy were the highlight of Eudora's trip. Before she left London, the Pritchetts wrote to tell Eudora how important the visit had been to them. "It has been difficult to tell you how deeply touched we are that you'd make this giant leap across the ocean to let us have another time with you. When, to us, it hadn't seemed possible—It's been like 'family' it's made us so close." Eudora felt the same, as she told Richard Ford in a letter that prompted this reply: "I read a sentence out of your letter, yesterday, to a friend of mine who was asking the inevitable '. . . and how is Miss Welty?' question. Your sentence was that you'd had one of the best times of your life visiting the Pritchetts. I said that if you were eighty-whatever, and having the best time of your life, you must be okay."[49]

Eudora's return to the United States found her in great demand. On May 31, at the annual dinner of the Mississippi Institute of Arts and Letters, she paid tribute to Walker Percy, who three weeks earlier had died. In early June she traveled to Natchez to deliver a reading and participate in the Natchez Literary Celebration. At month's end she gave a reading at the Governor's Mansion in Jackson. Then in July she joined Reynolds for two days at the Writers Workshop in Asheville, North Carolina, where both would receive Distinguished Author Awards and where they would each meet with readers and writers and each deliver a public reading. Four days after her return to Jackson, Ron Sharp arrived, and the two collaborators discussed their *Norton Book of Friendship*. Earlier in the summer Sharp had sent Eudora a large number of manuscripts to consider for inclusion, and Eudora had expressed serious reservations about adding material at this point. "We'd worked so hard," she wrote Sharp, "to the point of exhaustion, choosing, comparing, proportioning, and honing our final choices, working toward a whole that had in itself in the final analysis something to say—or so we prided ourselves in thinking, or had allowed ourselves to hope, do you remember? We toasted that, didn't we? Do you think that it's now worth tearing into that achievement, necessarily ripping out a lot of those hard-come-by choices to accommodate new ones—just because other fine choices exist? We'd have to consider both additions and eliminations in relation to one another and to a significant whole—which I think the book has now." From July 26 to August 2, Eudora and Ron addressed these questions face-to-face. They rented a hotel conference room, asked the management to furnish it with long tables, laid their possible selections out, moved them about, seeking the best order possible, and finally compiled a manuscript for their publisher. Organized in an innovative fashion along chronological, generic, and thematic lines at various points, the manuscript surveyed works from ancient to contemporary times and included 139 authors from more than twenty countries. Eudora and Ron had selected poems, invitations, letters, and essays for inclusion, but no excerpts from novels or plays, with the exception of Shakespeare's. And scattered throughout the manuscript were works by writers who had directly influenced Eudora's career or who, quite appropriately, were her good friends: Elizabeth Bowen, Anton Chekhov, Guy Davenport, William Faulkner, Janet Flanner, Ford Madox Ford, E. M. Forster, Seamus Heaney, Edward Lear, William Maxwell, Reynolds Price, V. S. Pritchett, Peter Taylor, Robert Penn Warren, W. B. Yeats, among them. Not included was nihilist Friedrich Nietzsche; Ron wanted to use a series of aphorisms from his work, but Eudora grew passionately angry at the thought: "The very idea in a book on friendship!"[50]

Although the selection process was complete except for a few last-minute changes to come, the summer continued to be a busy one for Eudora. Scholars from Russia were in Jackson to visit Welty sites and to discuss her work. Then Tom Nolan, Ken Millar's biographer, interviewed Eudora on three successive days. Finally, there was a respite, and Eudora settled into her regular Jackson social routines, dining with friends, celebrating the birthdays of her niece Mary Alice and of Basic Eight member Ann Morrison, and attending lectures at Millsaps College. She was in good spirits and displayed them when in September my parents came for one of their regular visits. I vividly remember listening to my father and Eudora exchange after-dinner stories about the past. Dad, born in 1910, recalled seeing the evangelist Aimee Semple McPherson ("she looked like an angel"), and Eudora recounted a visit to the Jackson branch of McPherson's Foursquare Gospel Church, where women dressed in clinging white gowns combined sexual allure with spiritual appeals. Somehow the conversation moved on to baseball, and Eudora told us of hearing Babe Ruth speak at Jackson High School. "Boys," she remembered him saying, "don't drink, smoke, or chase skirts." Such evenings and such recollections were vintage Eudora, and laughter was abundant.

During September, Eudora also signed copies of her *Georgia Review* essay "My Introduction to Katherine Anne Porter" and mailed them to friends about the country. Emmy Maxwell was delighted by the piece. "It is the tenderest possible evocation of a deep friendship," she wrote Eudora. "It's magical, as the friendship was, and I knew from this piece how nothing could alter your affection for each other." Perhaps inspired by Emmy's language, Eudora began to think about her introduction to the *Norton Book of Friendship*. In it she would eventually write, "Lately, in my old age, it has seemed to me, when friends meet to hold a public service to pay tribute to one of their number who has died, that without words to that effect ever being said, they are drawing a circle around that friend. Speaking in turn one after the other, joining themselves together anew, they keep what they know of him intact. As if by words expressed they might turn friendship into magic, the magic that now, so clearly, it had been."[51]

In October, Eudora took to the road. Her first stop was Washington, DC, where she again attended the PEN/Faulkner Gala and was a houseguest of the Mudds. At the gala itself, Eudora was the first of sixteen writers to discuss their sense of place, but she was the last of the sixteen to prepare the requested three minutes of remarks. She began working on them around four in the afternoon, completed them not five minutes before the 7:30

curtain time, and received a standing ovation for her beautifully phrased, incisive comments. Ten days later she made the short journey to Columbus, Mississippi, where she again saw the Mudds, this time at the Mississippi University for Women's Welty Weekend, where she was a reader and Roger the master of ceremonies.

November and December were calmer months, but one striking musical experience and one bit of exceptionally welcome news remained for 1990. The poet John Stone and the composer Samuel Jones, both Millsaps graduates, had collaborated on a piece titled "Canticles of Time" which the Millsaps College Singers and the Mississippi Symphony Orchestra presented on November 30. Stone had written a libretto dealing with the joy that can endure time's power, and Jones had provided a challenging and powerful score. The gala performance proved a stirring one for the large audience at Jackson's Municipal Auditorium and for Eudora herself. Equally stirring for Eudora was the news that the publication date for Michael Kreyling's *Author and Agent* would come early in the new year. Eudora had read the copyedited text and had told her niece Mary Alice, "This is the way it really was." Now others would learn what she had long known about Diarmuid's work on her behalf. In his book *Creating Minds,* Howard Gardner, the distinguished Harvard University Professor of Cognition and Education, found that the creators he studied (Freud, Einstein, Picasso, Stravinsky, Eliot, Graham, and Gandhi) "needed, and benefited from, a special relation to one or more supportive individuals." Diarmuid had been that special individual for Eudora, but unlike Gardner's representative creators, who had dropped their supportive peers when "usefulness was judged to be at an end," Eudora cherished and praised Diarmuid throughout not only his life but also her own.[52]

In early 1991 Eudora stayed close to home and worked on her introduction for the *Norton Book of Friendship.* Working on such an essay seemed strange in the light of international events. The United States had begun air and missile strikes against Iraqi forces, and a ground war in the Persian Gulf seemed imminent. Still Eudora wrote away, and on Valentine's Day she sent her introduction to Ron Sharp. "The war is so ghastly," she told Sharp, "that nobody can feel very balanced about much, but it's a good thing, ain't it, that we have got Friendship."[53] By April the Gulf War had ended, but friendship endured. And it was friendship that sent Eudora to Chattanooga, Tennessee, in April, for the annual meeting of the Fellowship of Southern Writers. Travel now was very daunting for her. She was suffering from severe back pain, climbing stairs was impossible, and walking could prove difficult as well. Still she made the journey. She checked into the hotel and got into an elevator with numerous other conference participants, including writers Lee Smith and Richard Bausch. As the elevator started upward, one rider regretted that he had failed to collect his conference badge. When Eudora said that she, too, had left her badge behind, the crowd in the elevator burst into laughter. The meeting proved as congenial as this beginning. One morning Eudora and Alfred Uhry arranged to have breakfast together, taking me along since I was Eudora's traveling companion; a passing Peter Taylor then joined us, and a few minutes later Shelby Foote did as well. It is hard to imagine a more engaging conversation than the one the four writers had that morning; I was delighted merely to be present. The departure from Chattanooga, however, was not pleasant for Eudora. There was no jetway access for the plane, only a stairway. Eudora could not climb the stairs and was very reluctant to be taken up them on a sort of litter. She finally acquiesced and was carried to her seat, but not without expending a good bit of nervous energy.

Back in Jackson, Eudora continued to have back pain, but she kept to a normal routine of social engagements and actively participated in the life of the community. For many years, the once all-white Davis School located across the street from Eudora's childhood home had been thriving as a fully integrated magnet school. Former students, along with current teachers, wanted to celebrate their school's longevity, vitality, and diversity, and they had arranged a reunion. Richard Ford and Eudora both attended, as did one of Eudora's former teachers, Louella Varnado. For Davis School, Eudora could overcome her pain. So, too, could she overcome it for an old friend. Jane Pepperdene, who had retired at Agnes Scott College, was now teaching at the Paideia School in Atlanta. Eudora flew to Atlanta, spoke at Pepperdene's new school, and returned to Jackson. In mid-May five Russian scholars arrived in Jackson to participate in a Eudora Welty Symposium along with five American counterparts, and Eudora was gracious in receiving them.

At month's end, Eudora undertook another trip in honor of old friends. Bobby Davis of Shreveport, a childhood friend of her brothers, had invited Eudora to speak there. The Davises collected her in Jackson and drove her to Shreveport and back. A few days later she was in agonizing pain, unable to rise from a chair even with assistance. Her niece Elizabeth found her in this plight and phoned Eudora's doctor; he in turned ordered an ambulance, and Eudora was taken to a hospital. There examinations revealed that she was suffering from compression fractures and would have to undergo therapy and to have sitters once she returned home; the risk of a fall made staying alone too dangerous. The good health that Eudora had so long enjoyed was in peril as were her independence and freedom to travel. Reynolds, however, felt that Eudora's forced inactivity might prove to be "what my mother used to call a B.I.D.—Blessing in Disguise. Maybe for once it will teach people to leave you the hell alone for a while, to let you rest and have your own thoughts, your own time and peace. I want that for you as much as anything, knowing how good it was for me to get in a position where every person with two legs didn't feel justified in hunting me down and draining off a pint of blood just because they felt like it."[54] Reynolds's hopes would not come to pass. A sea change was imminent in Eudora's life.

ELEVEN

"Old Age Hath Yet Her Honor and Her Toil"
1991–2001

In September 1991, after an early July stay in the hospital and weeks of recuperation at home, Eudora was finally able to go out with friends and maintain an almost normal social schedule. But physical limitation had begun to affect her in what would become a more and more constricting fashion. For the very first time in her life, Eudora had been hospitalized, and the experience left her with a sense of vulnerability. She had long suffered from osteoporosis; the woman, who had towered over the five-feet-six William Faulkner in 1962 when she presented him with the Gold Medal for Fiction, had over the subsequent thirty years become bent, as a dowager's hump gradually formed. From five feet ten or so, she was no longer even five feet four. Her arthritis had also intensified, leaving her unable to type, able to write only in the most cramped longhand, and unwilling or unable to shift to dictation as a method of composition. The compression fractures, which had sent her to the hospital, presented an even more difficult physical challenge. They would mend, but their effects would linger. Eudora would ever after be considerably slowed. Even in the fall of 1991, she continued to experience pain when she had to rise from chairs or climb even the shortest stairways. Travel, for so long a cherished activity, would never again be a prominent part of her life. Neither could she, who loved driving her four-on-the-floor Olds Cutlass, ever drive again. Her life became quite literally circumscribed, her freedom of movement, of body and hands, radically limited. At the insistence of her doctor, Eudora agreed that she must hire someone to help her during the days: to make her breakfast and lunch, to drive her to appointments, to assist her in bathing and dressing. Fortunately, Eudora's assistant was Daryl Howard, a keenly intelligent woman with whom Eudora could converse and upon whom she would rely for the rest of her life.

During the fall of 1991, Eudora led a rather active life in Jackson, but at first was hesitant to venture further. She saw her friends one or two nights a week, having drinks and going out for dinner, walking cautiously into and out of restaurants, using a cane and relying on the strong arm of a friend. She entertained John Ferrone, who had come from New York for a three-day visit. Later she welcomed the actresses Sarah Marshall and Jeanne Shelley, who had played Bonnie Dee and Johnnie Ree Peacock in the 1956 Broadway version of *The Ponder Heart.* And at the end of October, she was glad to see Louis Rubin, in town from his University of North Carolina base to deliver a lecture at a local college. During the fall, she sent friends autographed copies of the newly published *Norton Book of Friendship,* she granted interviews to the *Houston Post,* to *Publishers Weekly,* and to National Public Radio; she composed an introduction for Bill Ferris's book *"You Live and Learn. Then You Die and Forget it All." Ray Lum's Tales of Horses, Mules and Men,* and she prepared the tribute to Walker Percy that she would deliver at the November meeting of the American Academy of Arts and Letters. The Ferris and Percy pieces she painstakingly did in longhand; I prepared typescripts for her.

Eudora had planned to attend the Mississippi University for Women's annual Welty weekend in October, but back pain prevented her from doing so. It did not prevent her from taking two trips to New York City in November. She attended the American

Academy meeting on November 5 and stayed an extra day in order to dine with the Maxwells and Walter Clemons. Then on November 20 she returned to Manhattan and attended the National Book Awards, where she received the National Book Foundation Medal for Distinguished Contribution to American Letters. In accepting the award, Eudora noted that "there are more stories to write, always more. This award can encourage an 82-year-old to keep on writing."[1] Reynolds must have hoped these words would be prophetic, and perhaps he sounded this note when the two old friends met privately the next night. But these journeys did not lead to new work; instead they took a toll on Eudora. By the time she and I left Jackson for Tulsa, Oklahoma, on December 6, Eudora was in considerable pain. The Tulsa Public Library was awarding Eudora its Peggy V. Helmerich Distinguished Author Award, which carried a $25,000 stipend, and she had been invited to bring a companion to the ceremony. Because I was a native Oklahoman and my family still lived in the state, Eudora chose me. This trip made me very aware of the difficulty she must have encountered in New York, for fulfilling her commitments to the Tulsa library proved very challenging. Negotiating airports and airport transfers required wheelchairs and porters. In Tulsa, at a rehearsal for a public reading, Eudora discovered that she was expected to climb several steps to an elevated stage; that was impossible for her, and arrangements were made for a ramp and a wheelchair. An elegant black-tie dinner commenced the weekend of festivities, and Republican Senator Don Nickels came to call for Eudora and me; little did he know that an ardent Democrat would occupy each arm, and that those two women would have to stifle their political opinions for the night. Politics aside, Eudora charmed the evening's audience and the next day gave an excellent reading for a most receptive crowd.

Upon returning from Tulsa, Eudora settled back into her Jackson routines and would not leave Jackson for almost a year.

She saw Michael Kreyling on a regular basis, for he held the Eudora Welty Chair of Southern Studies at Millsaps College during the spring semester. She was busy signing each of the eighteen images in a limited-edition portfolio of her photographs. And she was enthusiastic about the Eudora Welty New Play Series (as the Playwrights Series had been retitled)—this year's winner was a clever, witty, musical version of *Paradise Lost*, with book by local lawyer Frank Wood and music by local composer and musician David Womack. Nevertheless, when Princeton professor Clarence Brown visited Eudora in March 1992, she was feeling a bit trapped. Brown arrived from the airport by taxi, and Eudora met him on her front porch, with an ironic but plaintive comment. "I'd have come to get you, but I don't drive anymore. I don't do anything anymore."[2] Since Eudora did not get around much anymore, Reynolds resolved to come to her. Confined to a wheelchair, Reynolds faced more serious obstacles to travel than did Eudora, but he was twenty-four years younger than she, had learned to cope with pain through self-hypnosis, and was determined not to become housebound. Eudora could hope her back pain would eventually subside and permit travel; Reynolds knew that his paralysis was irreversible and that he must seize the day. So he came. His late summer visit pleased Eudora greatly, and she sent him home with the handsome portfolio of her photographs.

During the fall, Eudora and I attended the wedding of Daryl Howard's daughter and took great delight in seeing bride and groom jump over a broom at the end of the service—African American traditions were alive and well in Jackson, Mississippi. Then, as September progressed, Eudora found herself increasingly engaged by yet another political campaign. She stuck a Clinton/Gore bumper sticker on her front door, attended a garden-party rally at which Hillary Clinton spoke, and enlisted me to take her to the polls on November 7. When I arrived, she was wearing the Millsaps College Young Democrats T-shirt I had given her—hardly the attire for a Jackson matron—and when we reached the polling place we learned she would not be permitted to enter in partisan dress. I drove back to her house and picked up a sweater to cover the political advertisement. Eudora was amused but unrepentant.

Though her arthritis had left her as physically unable to write as to drive, Eudora continued to accumulate awards for her lifetime achievement. On her 1992 birthday, Eudora had learned that she had received the Rea Award for the Short Story from New York's Dungannon Foundation. In October, New Stage Theatre honored her by presenting Jane Petty's one-woman show titled *Edna Earle,* a version of *The Ponder Heart.* Then, in November and December, Eudora took to the road three times, traveling to Washington, DC, to receive awards: the Charles Frankel Prize from the National Endowment for the Humanities, the Distinguished Alumni Award from the American Association of State Colleges and Universities, and the PEN/Malamud Award for the Short Story. Clyda Rent, president of the Mississippi University for Women, had nominated Eudora for the Distinguished Alumni Award and had invited Patti Black and me to join Eudora for the presentation. We did; I was impressed by Eudora's ability to manage the airport, hotel, and taxis we faced during the trip. I was also impressed to see Eudora and General Colin Powell together as recipients. A week later, she felt well enough to return to DC, and to read "The Wide Net" and receive the PEN/Malamud Award. The reading and award presentation were originally scheduled at the Folger Shakespeare Library's rather small theater, but the demand for tickets prompted a move to a nearby church, which would seat six hundred people. There Eudora read to a sold-out audience.

In 1993 Eudora was busy and happy, though she seldom traveled; walking any distance was a time-consuming ordeal, and she stayed close to home, avoiding dependence on wheelchairs. She continued to scour the *New York Times* each day, to watch the *Mac-Neil/Lehrer News Hour* on television, and to read widely, keeping to her practice of having a different book going in the bedroom, breakfast room, and living room. Throughout the year, she dined almost once a week with Jane and Patti and once a week with Charlotte, Ann, and me. She and I had drinks and watched the television news on other evenings. Eudora saw friends beyond this core group less frequently, but regularly nevertheless. And she celebrated birthdays and holidays with her family members, seeing them informally as well. Friends and family alike found Eudora's storytelling prowess, her interest in current events, her wry sense of humor, undiminished.

In addition, Eudora received a steady stream of visits from far-flung friends, interviewers, and scholars. Her days were filled with activity but no longer with efforts to write. In January, Eudora taped an interview for Mississippi Public Television; the network was preparing a program about Jackson architects Noah Webster Overstreet and his son Robert. Edward Welty had once worked for the elder Overstreet, and Eudora was pleased to comment on that association. A month later Eudora welcomed Ron and Inese Sharp to Jackson; Eudora had enjoyed her collaboration with Sharp on the *Norton Book of Friendship*, and Sharp was devoted to Eudora. Her "brilliant" comments, often made in passing, her unexpected and striking use of words, it seemed to Sharp, had made their every conversation a memorable one.[3] In March the actor Michael Jeter paid a call on Eudora and asked if he might write television scripts based on some of her short stories. Witty, articulate, and knowledgeable, Jeter convinced her that his adaptations would be effective ones. Later in the month, John and Catherine Prince arrived from Washington, DC, and Eudora took the couple to dinners with her family and with Jackson friends. No longer able to join the Princes for trips through France or across Canada, she did join them for a drive to Vicksburg, so that they might see the historic city and gaze across the Mississippi River. March concluded with a four-day visit from Pearl McHaney, who was editing a collection of Eudora's book reviews. The two women looked at photocopies of each review. McHaney made an audiotape of Eudora's comments about them. Eudora's memory was sharp and her remarks incisive, a great aid to McHaney's work. In April Eudora was on camera again; her friend David Crews, on behalf of the North Carolina Center for the Advancement of Teaching, filmed two or three days of interviews about her career. Not long afterward Richard Ford interviewed her for a French production directed by Catherine Berge. During this conversation, Eudora gave a hilarious imitation of Bea Lillie singing "I Love Paree."

By May the frantic pace of visits slowed, and Eudora resumed her Jackson routines in good spirits. She did undertake one brief but difficult journey. When she learned that Albert Erskine had died, she wanted to honor her Random House editor and old friend from the *Southern Review*. She traveled to New York, then joined the Ralph Ellisons in attending Erskine's Westport, Connecticut, memorial service, at which she read a tribute.

During the summer, Eudora met with Sally Wolff of Emory University and again saw Pearl McHaney about the collected reviews, but mostly she spent time with family and local compatriots. In the fall, however, a new round of welcome visits began. Dianne Donovan, book-review editor of the *Chicago Tribune*, had become a friend who came to Jackson on a yearly basis; William Styron was not a regular caller, but he and Willie Morris took Eudora to dinner late in October; and on October 27 Michael Jeter hand-delivered a television script of "Petrified Man." Early in November, Danièle Pitavy of the University of Burgundy in Dijon, France, brought Eudora an honorary degree. And later in the month, Elizabeth Spencer spent three days in Jackson and saw Eudora twice. Thanksgiving and Christmas were reserved for family. Then Eudora saw in the New Year at a festive party given by Tom and Louise Biggs; Tom had practiced architecture with Edward, and Louise and Edward had played many duets together on the piano. Now Eudora, Charlotte, and many friends gathered around a piano played only by Louise, but played by ear with great flair. The evening boded well for happy days ahead.

Nineteen ninety-four was a rather happy year, but it was perhaps the first year in her adult life that included no long journeys. Travel was no longer possible. She and the dearly loved but equally elderly Maxwells and Pritchetts would therefore not meet again, though they would correspond. At eighty-five Eudora was physically frail and low on energy, and at long last she began to protect her time and to allow friends and family to do the same for her. In Jackson, Eudora saw friends, granted interviews, attended large local gatherings, but on a greatly reduced scale. She knew it was time to take in sail. And she recognized, more fully and more consciously than ever before, that the emotional and physical demands of writing were too much for her and had been for some years.

In January, Eudora made one of her few public appearances for the year. The Mississippi Museum of Art had mounted a show of paintings by Mildred Wolfe, and Eudora agreed to speak at a luncheon honoring the artist. One of the three portraits Eudora had commissioned Mildred to paint of her parents was in the current show. Mildred's portrait of Miss Fannye Cook, former Welty tenant and former director of the Mississippi Wildlife Museum, was also hanging at the museum. Eudora had known, liked, and admired Mildred for more than forty years; she welcomed the opportunity to praise Mildred publicly.

In February, Eudora granted an interview to journalist Joseph Dumas. She had met Dumas a year earlier and found him a very engaging young man. Now she agreed to a conversation that would be published by the *Oxford American,* and that conversation between an elderly white southern woman and a young black man proved particularly personal and revealing. Neither race, nor gender, nor age was a barrier between them; there was a sort of intimacy in their interaction. To Dumas she joked about the beginning of memory loss. "I can barely remember what I had for dinner." She discussed a longing for the days when she was writing, a longing for the intense involvement she no longer had the stamina for. "I think what I miss when I am not working is that I haven't got this thing to grip me; this piece of work that I want to lose myself in." She commented on her sense of life's transient nature. "It's a strange feeling. It's something that old people like myself feel often because you think back to the days when your familiar friends were around you and with whom you could talk and whom you counted and could discuss the nature of things; then you realize it isn't anymore." And she discussed the aging process. "I have an old friend who wrote me not long ago and something sticks in my mind. She said, 'I'm 90 years old now, and I feel like there's somebody else living inside my skin and not a friend.' I loved that! Isn't that wonderful? I know what she means. I understand. I guess she feels her body is not obeying her. She didn't mean an enemy but not a friend."[4]

Another interview followed shortly. Hollywood director Bruce Schwartz had begun filming "A Worn Path" on location in Canton, Mississippi. He felt that a production of the oft-taught story would have great appeal in high schools, colleges, and universities, especially if it were paired with an interview in which Eudora discussed the story. Eudora had confidence in Schwartz and agreed to be questioned by playwright Beth Henley, herself a Mississippi native. Eudora and Beth clearly were at ease in each other's company, and Eudora's commentary on the story offered new insights and answered, once again, the question so often posed about the story's protagonist: "Is Phoenix Jackson's grandson really dead?" No.

Eudora's flourishing national and international reputation had meanwhile captured the attention of Jacksonians Jo Barksdale and David Morris. Barksdale hoped to transform Eudora's birthplace, which now housed Morris's consulting business, into a Mississippi Writer's Center and a tourist mecca. Eudora, having already given her Pinehurst Street home to the Mississippi

Department of Archives and History, did not want to lend her name to this new project but in attempting politely to withhold such support, she failed to say no in a convincing fashion. Conversations about the possibility would continue for the next two years or so.

In April, Eudora celebrated her eighty-fifth birthday at least four times. Danièle Pitavy had come from France to toast the actual date, and she joined Eudora's close friends for an April 13 dinner party at an upscale Jackson restaurant. The next day was reserved for a family gathering. Then, on April 17, Eudora joined a large crowd at Lemuria Book Store for a tribute to her and to her collected book reviews, which had just been published under the title *A Writer's Eye.* Friends from far and near had composed poems for the event or sent greetings, President Clinton, Jim Lehrer and Roger Mudd, Bill Smith and Bill Maxwell among them. Finally, a week later, Eudora joined one of my Millsaps classes for a cookout in the countryside where she had located her fictional town of Morgana. One more celebration lay ahead in 1994, though it was not a birthday party. At the end of May, the Natchez Literary Celebration had hoped to present her with its first Richard Wright Award, but Eudora's back was causing problems once again. Since she was unable to make the ninety-mile journey to Natchez, the Celebration came to her and captured her acceptance speech on videotape.

In June, Reynolds spent three days with Eudora in Jackson, and the days were filled with laughter and reminiscences and with Reynolds's report of Margaret Millar's death. "Thank you for that information" was Eudora's only reply.[5] After Reynolds's visit, Eudora settled into a leisurely summer; she relished the time spent reading, and she saw friends several evenings each week. Before the summer ended, however, a new interest captured her imagination. Her problems with arthritis and osteoporosis had long prevented her from working in the garden, an activity she had loved. Now the Mississippi Department of Archives and History pro-

posed to restore the garden under the direction of Susan Hal-
tom, a local historic-garden conservationist. Eudora was pleased,
and over the course of the next seven years, she would provide
Susan with a colorful drawing of Chestina's garden plan and with
an essay her mother had written. In giving the Department of
Archives and History her house and garden, Eudora had hoped
to honor her parents. Here was a concrete step in that direction.

Sad news, however, did arrive during the summer. Walter
Clemons, age sixty-four, unexpectedly died. Eudora liked Walter
tremendously, respected his skills as a critic, and admired his
book of short stories entitled *The Poison Tree.* Learning of his
death, which had been caused by complications from diabetes,
saddened her. She placed a snapshot of him on her mantel, and
with friends, she reminisced about the happy times she and Walter had shared. Walter's death also posed a practical problem for
Eudora. She had asked him to be her literary executor and now
he was gone. She wanted a younger person who intimately knew
the world of publishing to help with her literary estate, and she
began to wonder if Richard Ford might be willing to accept this
responsibility. Eventually, urged on by Jane Petty who felt that
for peace of mind Eudora needed to resolve the issue, Eudora
spoke with Richard. He agreed and promised that when the time
came, he would be pleased to advise her nieces, who, according to
the terms of Eudora's will, would become her only executors.

In the fall of 1994, Eudora continued at home, seeing friends
and attending New Stage Theatre productions as she had done
for many years. The William Faulkner Foundation at Rennes II
University of Haut-Bretagne in France had hoped she might be
present at a conference featuring discussions of her fiction, but
such a journey was now out of the question. When the enterpris-
ing French, however, arranged for a video-telephone interview,
Eudora and I made our way to the local telephone headquarters,
dressed in pastels, as requested. Our images soon crossed the Atlantic, and the conference participants saw us quite clearly on a

large screen; we, on the other hand, had to rely on a small moni-
tor. Eudora found her hearing particularly problematic when she
could not see her questioners, so I repeated the inquiries that
came over the telephone lines. She then responded in her typically articulate, understated fashion, and international understanding of her work was enhanced.

The year came to an uneventful close. Because of her increasingly severe arthritis, Eudora found it more and more difficult to
cope with being an automobile passenger or a restaurant customer,
and as a consequence, she met with fewer and fewer people. There
were pleasant gatherings of friends and family, visits from
Michael Kreyling and Richard Ford, and a small dinner party or
two in honor of historian Wayne Flynt, who was the Welty Chair
of Southern Studies during the fall 1994 semester at Millsaps.
But that was all.

At home Eudora had long since moved downstairs, leaving her
large bedroom/writing room with regret, and had resolved to live
on one level. Donny White, her nephew-in-law, had provided her
with a lift chair, so that getting up and down would not be a
problem. Beyond her front door, however, she was likely to encounter problems. Eudora continued to come to my house once
or twice a week for dinner. I had placed a large pillow in the front
seat of my car, so that she might more easily get in and out, and I
had arranged to use my neighbor's driveway so that Eudora would
not have to mount steep steps from the street to my front yard.
Patti had resolved to purchase a small pickup truck, knowing that
the height of its seats would prove easier for Eudora. Jane arranged for Eudora to enter her town house through the garage,
thereby avoiding unnecessary steps. Gatherings of relatives were
scheduled for Mary Alice's home, the most handicapped-accessible
family dwelling. Bill's Burger House, too, continued to be a friendly
place for Eudora, with parking just in front of its door and with
an armchair that Judy Matheos, Bill's wife, arranged to have

brought from their home. Still, these measures could not overcome Eudora's problems with mobility. One afternoon I arrived at her house, letting myself in with a key Eudora had provided me, and found that she had fallen and been unable to rise. Eudora insisted that I call Daryl, who promptly came to help her up. Another evening I phoned to check on Eudora but received no answer. I drove to her house, quietly let myself in the door, and nervously peeked into her new bedroom. She was sleeping peacefully, and I silently retreated, never to mention the incident to her. I had feared another fall and perhaps disastrous consequences. Happily that was not the case. In addition to experiencing physical difficulties, Eudora was increasingly bothered by memory lapses. Always meticulous in matters of business and household accounts, she began to let matters slide. Alarmed, her nieces conferred with her, and she agreed to turn financial management over to Donny White. The independence she had valued from childhood was slipping away from her, a fact she rued. She continued to be an engaging conversationalist, recounting past events in a vivid narrative style, but she began to repeat stories, not realizing that she was doing so. As she approached her eighty-sixth birthday, Eudora was more dramatically showing the effects of old age.

Nineteen ninety-five brought a string of visitors whom Eudora was eager to entertain and for whom she defied her arthritis. Michael Kreyling and his wife Chris, Dianne Donovan and her sons, were March visitors; in April Brookie Maxwell, the daughter of Bill and Emmy, came through Jackson with her husband and joined Eudora for dinner. Eudora's birthday this year was not the moveable feast of 1994, but her friends and family feted her on both April 13 and April 14. In late May, Sally Wolff of Emory University brought Jimmy Faulkner to meet Eudora. Faulkner's nephew bore an uncanny resemblance to his uncle, and seeing him with Eudora catapulted my imagination back in time to the 1948 meeting between Mississippi's most famous writers.

I don't think it had the same effect on Eudora. She had been more moved by attending, with Jane Petty's assistance, the May 20 wedding of Eleni Matheos, the daughter of restauranteur Bill. And she was thrilled when, on June 9, Kate and Jim Lehrer, along with John Ferrone, arrived for a visit. Jim brought Eudora an Atlanta Olympics baseball cap, which she promptly donned. Always unathletic and now physically infirm, Eudora was amused by her new headgear. John snapped her picture in it before the four friends went to Bill's for dinner. The next afternoon Eudora planned a party for John and the Lehrers, inviting her family and Jackson friends. Her niece Mary Alice and I set about providing ice (always in short supply at Eudora's), hors d'oeuvres, and whiskey for a group of about twenty. A fine time ensued, but everyone was *hot*; Eudora had steadfastly refused to air-condition the house, and the June temperatures were high. As the cocktail hour drew to a close, Jim invited everyone to dinner in a cooler environment; a reservation was quickly secured at Nick's Restaurant, a favorite of Eudora's, and the party reconvened there.

One more guest from afar came to Jackson during the summer of 1995, but his meeting with Eudora was a private one. Nicholas Dawidoff of the *New York Times* arrived on July 11 to interview Eudora. He found her full of good anecdotes about Faulkner, about Diarmuid Russell, about the spark for her story "Powerhouse," about that 1941 visit from Henry Miller. In fact, Dawidoff wrote, "Everything, it seems, reminds her of a good story. Sometimes one word is sufficient tinder. When she hears 'antipathy' in a conversation, she beams and says, 'I love that word,' and tells of Mark Twain's 'invincible antipathy for the name of Samuel.'"[6]

The pleasures of the summer came to an abrupt end early in September. Compression fractures returned to plague Eudora; so severe was the pain that she could neither rise from a chair nor walk. She had to be hospitalized. Jane and I were regular visitors at the hospital, sneaking small bottles of bourbon into Eudora's hospital room at the cocktail hour. A drink with friends may or may not have sped her recovery; it did make incarceration seem more bearable. Still Eudora was insistent about her desire to come home, and the doctors finally agreed she might if there were a hospital bed for her there and if there were round-the-clock care. Her nieces, with the assistance of Eudora's caregiver Daryl Howard, made the arrangements, and her nephews-in-law moved the furniture. Back at home in late September, Eudora now faced a season of decline.

From 1996 until July 2001, I continued to see Eudora on a regular basis, stopping by her house almost daily. In 1996 and 1997 I often brought her home with me for dinner, but she gradually became less and less able to venture out. She might consent to go driving with me or Willie Morris or Mack Cole, to have dinner at Mary Alice's house with Liz and other family members, to join Tommie Blissard, Jo Haxton, and Elizabeth Spencer for lunch, but such events were unusual. And for the last three years of her life (1998–2001), Eudora remained primarily at home and saw friends and family there. During these last three years, memory problems also intensified. Some days she was sharp of mind, engaged by the world around her, initiating conversations. Other days she seemed distant, her memory hazy. A change of medication for a time alleviated this difficulty, but by January of 2001, the bad days tended to outnumber the good ones. The recognition that her memory, her "treasure most dearly regarded," was failing must have been far more devastating than her immobility. The memories that had fed her fiction writing and that had provided a sense of continuity with the past were becoming less consistently accessible. For a time Eudora's memory was sound enough for her to recognize loss, and she must have been terrified to suspect in herself what she had seen happen to Ken Millar. She attempted to cope and to cover, often asking me to be present when out-of-town visitors stopped by, but those attempts became less and less successful. Throughout her final years, however, Eudora faced her situation with dignity. Seldom was she impatient with friends, family, or caregivers; never did she rail about her declining powers of mind and body. She did not recapitulate the pattern of her mother's life; she did not feel exiled or betrayed. Never did she seem to fear death.

On January 25, 1996, Eudora was awarded the French Légion d'Honneur. Eudora's nieces and I, using her old address books and the 1973 Eudora Welty Day records, had prepared a list of people to be invited to the ceremony at Mississippi's Old Capitol Museum, but we, along with other family and friends, were worried about Eudora's ability to cope with this event. The seating in the House Chamber of the Old Capitol would pose difficulties for her as would getting in and out of the museum. We were also concerned that she might not be able to deliver an extemporaneous speech with the verve that had previously been hers. Charlotte Capers, Ann Morrison, and I discussed the prospects and asked Ann's daughter Charlotte Morrison, a physical therapist, to be available for Eudora, even though Richard Ford was her official escort. Still we could do nothing to help with the acceptance speech. We need not have worried. Just before the ceremony, Jane Petty, Richard Ford, and I waited in an anteroom with Eudora. The conversation was lively, and Eudora seemed delighted about the ceremony to follow. And at the ceremony itself, she rose grandly to the occasion, accepting a kiss on each cheek from French Consul General Gerard Blanchot, and eloquently thanking the French government for the honor and her friends for sharing the moment with her. Eudora would not make another such public appearance.

After this stirring event, Eudora experienced a number of rather contented, if uneventful, months. She was able to visit Jackson pals in their homes, to eat at favorite restaurants, to entertain visitors, to attend her great-niece Leslie Thompson's wedding, and to talk with far-flung friends on the phone. She found

Daryl Howard, Lottie Anderson, Linda Cheaton, and Nora Kern, the women who provided her with round-the-clock care, efficient and agreeable, and she continued to depend on Eddie Mae Polk, who was much more than a housekeeper. Conversations with these individuals might focus upon their children or travels, upon their sense, as African Americans, of the Jackson political scene, upon Eudora's political views, her travels, her friends, and her encounters with black artists ranging from Fats Waller to Leontyne Price. Not surprisingly, her household staff cherished Eudora and told me so. All was going as well as possible. Then, just before Christmas, Charlotte Capers unexpectedly died. Long one of Eudora's closest friends, the woman who had convinced her to donate her papers to the state of Mississippi, a raconteur whose stories had brought forth gales of laughter from one of the nation's most accomplished comic writers, Charlotte would be sorely missed. Her death must have strengthened Eudora's resolve to spend more time with those she held close and less time in meeting with academics and admirers.

In April 1997, when I codirected a Welty conference in Jackson, I assured Eudora that she need neither attend nor speak. All of those attending the conference, entitled "Mississippi Home Ties," greatly admired Eudora's work, and they were eager to see the city and the surrounding countryside that had so often supplied settings for her. But most were disappointed not to meet the writer herself. Eudora did welcome a few scholars for private visits in her home, scholars she had long known and liked— Danièle Pitavy, Michael Kreyling, and Sally Wolff among them—but only those few. After the conference had ended, Eudora continued to limit the number of people she would see. That summer, when Jill Krementz appeared in Jackson along with Joseph Dumas, Eudora chose to see only Dumas. Krementz, who had taken so many fine photographs of her, had done so by being irrepressible with her camera. Eudora was not willing to risk that happening now, and Krementz left Jackson deeply offended. Daryl

Howard, Eudora's chief caregiver, had played and would continue to play the role of gatekeeper, though almost always in consultation with Mary Alice. When friends or interviewers or scholars phoned, asking to meet with Eudora, Daryl would inform them that Eudora's health and energy could not be predicted very far in advance and would have to be confirmed on the day of the visit. Eudora, who had always had a difficult time saying no, was now often relieved to delegate that responsibility.

Eudora spent the remainder of 1997 and the beginning of 1998 at home, seeing relatively few people—primarily her family members, Jane and Patti, Mack Cole, Tommie Blissard, Willie and Joanne Morris, Tom Spengler (her old friend from New Stage), Ann Morrison, and me. Jane's visits, however, became fewer in number as her health declined, and not being able to see Eudora regularly troubled Jane. One afternoon as Jane and I slowly made our way up the sidewalk to Eudora's house, Jane stopped and told me she did not expect to live much longer. "Take care of Eudora," she implored. I promised that I would. Not long afterward, when Patti, Tom, Ann, and I gathered at Eudora's for her eighty-ninth birthday, Jane's daughter appeared on the doorstep, delivering her mother's deviled eggs and saying her mother was too unwell to attend the party. Four days later Jane died. With Daryl's help, Eudora attended the funeral, bidding farewell to yet another devoted and supportive friend.

In July the first annual Mayor's Arts Achievement Awards were scheduled, with awards going to Thalia Mara, founder of the Jackson Ballet; to Margaret Walker Alexander, novelist, poet, biographer; and to Eudora. Eudora was not well enough to attend. And by the fall of 1998, Eudora's most treasured possession, her memory, was failing her on an intermittent basis. Now not only writing, but also reading anything longer than a *New York Times* article posed problems. In one sense this was a blessing, for Eudora never read Ann Waldron's unauthorized biography of her. Some years earlier, Waldron had asked permission to write this book, and Eudora had denied the request. Waldron proceeded nevertheless, arguing that biography did not constitute "an invasion of privacy, especially when it is a biography of a woman who has been on innumerable television talk shows and given countless print interviews to newspapers all over the country."[7] Those innumerable and countless sources were destined to prove thin. Waldron had no way of knowing about the richly informative manuscripts and correspondence (most crucially, the letters exchanged with John Robinson and Kenneth Millar) that Eudora and her nieces would later make available to me, and she managed to interview only an unsuspecting few of Eudora's friends. Typically those whom Waldron contacted for interviews in turn phoned Eudora, who repeated her opposition to the project. The eighty-something writer did not want to spend time with a biographer, nor did she want her friends to be imposed upon, and she certainly did not want the private lives of friends to become part of a public record if they or their surviving families might find that record invasive or hurtful. Nevertheless, in 1998 *Eudora, A Writer's Life* was published by Doubleday, the first full-length Welty biography.

The book's interpretation of Eudora's life, based on limited resources, inevitably had gaps—Eudora's loving relationship with Ken Millar was not discussed—and proved at times to be misleading. For example, Waldron acknowledged Chestina Welty's devotion to her daughter and her role in supporting Eudora's career, but in Waldron's eyes, Chestina was ultimately a "powerful, terrifying woman." Certainly when she was old and ill, Chestina had been very needy and demanding, but this was not the pattern of her life. Eudora's unpublished story entitled "Nicotiana" suggests, moreover, an absence of any kind of terror in the Welty home. In this story, upon which Eudora worked in the early 1960s, the relationship of Sarah Ewing and her mother seems clearly to emerge from the lives of the Welty women a decade earlier. Mrs. Ewing, a widow who is now almost blind, is assertive, but also supportive, outspoken, but also quite rational. When her artist daughter shows her a new drawing, Mrs. Ewing is filled with a tender pride: "It was Sarah's charmed face, not the drawing, Mrs. Ewing was looking at—looking at plainly, for this was one of those flashes of close vision that sometimes opened to her, like a window in a wall. In a voice like that of gratitude, she felt compelled to say it again: 'Your father always expected you to give your mind to something entirely different from drawing pictures, honey.'" Clearly, Mrs. Ewing is pleased that Sarah has found an untraditional career and prospered in it. Mrs. Ewing is not pleased, however, to feel dependent on her daughter. Her displeasure emerges after a maid fails to appear for duty and leaves the Ewing women to fend for themselves. Sarah suddenly realizes she must carry out the garbage:

> "It's garbage day!" cried Sarah, jumping up from the breakfast table as if delivered from danger.
> "Well, its not Doomsday," argued her mother. "Wait. I'm going to carry the other handle." She was following her out to the back. "That always hurts your bad knee."
> "Mama, go back this minute!" cried Sarah.
> So now this had started again—the dismay of two women helping and being helped.

Issues of dependence and independence take another form when Sarah gives a party. Mrs. Ewing is happy that Sarah is again entertaining friends. She makes her good yeast rolls for Sarah's guests, joins the gathering long enough to speak politely, but then declines to join them for dinner:

> "But you've got to be at the table! Everybody expects you," said Sarah as her mother turned and started away.
> "I think I'll go to bed. I have no intention of sitting down just for the amazement of your company," said Mrs. Ewing. "And I'm in the mood to just go to my own room,

and listen to what the radio has to say, . . . though it's all bad. You can bring me a tray in there, if you like. I can eat it in the dark and enjoy my own fan."

"But that's what you do every night."

. . . "All I ask," she suddenly called back, "is that you serve them some of my tiny hot rolls with your dessert. That's what will make those figs *taste* good. You keep some back, buttered and hot. It just happens to be a whim of mine," said Mrs. Ewing as if Sarah had never heard before of her harboring such a thing.

"I promise," said Sarah.[8]

Both love and guilt, possessiveness and the shared recognition that mother and daughter belong in separate social spheres, are held in tension during this scene. Issues of power are involved, but neither mother nor daughter is all powerful, and certainly the mother is not terrifying, as Waldron believed Chestina was. Waldron's portrait of the domineering mother strikes a false note.

So, too, does Waldron's decidedly antifeminist focus on Eudora's appearance, on remarks stressing her homeliness as it was offset by her winning personality. Waldron asserts that in 1984, when she was named one of "Ten Great Faces" by *People* magazine, Eudora had at last triumphed over the conventional belles of her youth. My own sure sense is that Eudora measured triumph in far different terms, and that Waldron had access to few pictures of Eudora, many of which reveal both her physical and intellectual attractiveness over the years, her truly beautiful eyes alight with interest in the world. Depending on her pose, of course, Eudora in photographs could seem either statuesque or awkwardly tall; somber, handsome, and dignified or smiling a bit too broadly; well-coifed or disheveled. But she was not interested in striking poses, in spending hours in a beauty shop, in applying makeup, in amassing a vast wardrobe. It is true that Eudora was occasionally self-denigrating when discussing her appearance. To a visiting Reynolds, who was eager to set out for dinner and urged her to stop primping in front of a mirror, the sixty-something writer lamented, "You haven't had to live behind this face all these years." A decade or so later, I suggested that Eudora resembled her mother, only to be contradicted: "No. My mother was a beautiful woman." Then early in the 1990s, I was surprised to hear Eudora and Charlotte Capers agree that their mothers had always wanted them to be prettier, and I was taken aback when Eudora told us of a comment Katherine Anne Porter had made to her: "You will never know what it means to be a beautiful woman." Probably Eudora agreed, failing to see the beauty that Reynolds, John Robinson, Ken Millar, and a host of others saw in her, but she was not tormented by the issue. Her comments about beauty were always matter-of-fact, and she had long been dismissive of the American obsession with cosmetic enhancements. In the thirties, friends had photographed Eudora in a mock Helena Rubinstein/Elizabeth Arden pose. A decade later Eudora's story "Hello and Good-Bye" satirically depicted two rather shallow-minded beauty contestants participating in a photo shoot. Lacking beauty-pageant perfection was even a source of camaraderie between Eudora and Charlotte and between Eudora and Dolly Wells. When the very presentable Dolly, professionally known as Rosa, had worked for Jack Fischer at Harper & Brothers, Fischer bragged on her to his wife and children, creating some jealousy on their parts. Dolly recalled that when she finally came to dinner at the Fischer home, she heard the children yelling to their mother, "Rosa's here and she's not at all pretty." Eudora and Dolly often laughed about this story, focusing on the comedy of the scene and on the children's expectation of a veritable siren, not on any wounding impact. Such a response belies Waldron's suggestion that an unhappy Eudora sought to overcome the liability of her appearance by being a dutiful daughter and a generous friend; she was a dutiful daughter and a generous friend, but not by way of compensation.

Shortly after Waldron's book was published, Claudia Roth Pierpont proceeded to write a lengthy *New Yorker* article about Eudora. Accepting fully Waldron's discussion of beauty, she moved beyond Waldron in discussing politics. She concluded that Eudora was "a born outsider in a stifling, hypocritical, yet tantalizingly charming society" but that she wrote "her way into acceptance." According to Pierpont, the youthful Eudora had been "an intrepid explorer," but as she grew older she became "a perfect lady—a nearly Petrified Woman—with eyes averted and mouth set in a smile."[9] How palpably unjust those charges seem in the light of biographical information even then available and certainly in light of new information. Eudora was far, far from a petrified woman holding to the mores of the southern past; she was a woman who sought to understand the meaning of her experience and whose life was a record of growth and development.

The literary world in 1998, Waldron and Pierpont not withstanding, never saw Eudora as petrified, and continued to extol her achievements. On October 8, 1998, New York's Ninety-second Street Y, home to the distinguished Unterberg Poetry Center, presented "A Tribute to Eudora Welty." Prompted by the publication of the two-volume Library of America collection of Eudora's work, the Y invited Michael Kreyling, Ann Beattie, Richard Ford, Randall Kenan, William Maxwell, Joyce Carol Oates, Reynolds Price, and Elizabeth Spencer to speak. Reynolds was unable to travel, and Maxwell unfortunately was at the last minute too ill to appear. There would be no substitute for Reynolds, but poet Karl Kirchwey, director of the Poetry Center, ably spoke in Maxwell's stead.

Kreyling opened the evening, presenting an overview of Welty's career and accomplishments. He was then followed on-stage by the other participants, each of whom commented on and read excerpts from their favorite Welty story. Ann Beattie began by reading from "Old Mr. Marblehall" and by providing a compelling interpretation of the story. Richard Ford presented selections from "No Place for You, My Love," a story that he had long admired. Randall Kenan followed with a reading from "Powerhouse." Before reading, Kenan explained that as an African American, he had found his first encounter with "Powerhouse" somewhat off-putting, but that as he had reread and reread the story, he had come to recognize its brilliance and its powerful portrait of a narrator who intuitively longs to break free from the racism that is part of his or her makeup. Following Kenan's presentation, Karl Kirchwey quoted from a letter William Maxwell had sent: In the letter Maxwell explained that "The Bride of the Innisfallen" was the first Welty story he, as a fiction editor of the *New Yorker*, had convinced the magazine to accept. Kirchwey then drew upon a very convincing Irish accent in reading "The Bride of the Innisfallen" as excerpted by Maxwell. Joyce Carol Oates came next; she discussed her admiration for "Where Is the Voice Coming From," commented on her experiences teaching the story, and read from the story. The evening's final story was "Moon Lake," read by Elizabeth Spencer with her delightfully appropriate Mississippi accent and comic timing. Richard Ford then returned to the stage to describe his own efforts to write, for Eudora's signature, a letter of appreciation to the Ninety-second Street Y and the October 8 audience. He read briefly from his witty and Welty-like letter, but then reported that Eudora had been loath to sign a letter she had not herself written. She had instead, Ford told the audience, simply asked that he convey her unwritten gratitude. With that, the evening came to a close. The speakers and readers had been outstanding, the overflow crowd had been entranced, and the variety and virtuosity of Eudora's work had been affirmed—both as part of America's literary canon and in the hearts and minds of working writers.

I attended this event and celebrated the Library of America edition as enthusiastically as everyone else. Then, back at home, I celebrated Reynolds's late October visit to Jackson. During that visit, Reynolds and I discussed the possibility of my writing Eudora's biography. He encouraged me to do so. I subsequently asked Patti Black if she thought I should try to provide a more informed biographical record than now existed. "Yes, but don't tell Eudora you want to write a biography for her sake," Patti cautioned me. "Tell her this is a project that would mean a lot to you." And so it would and so I asked.

Six months later Eudora celebrated her ninetieth birthday. Mary Alice, Ann and Charlotte Morrison, Patti Black, and I planned a party for her. My friend and colleague Harriet Pollack was visiting me and joined us for the celebration at 1119 Pinehurst. I asked Harriet, who had heard rumors about Eudora's failing powers, for her reaction. Having seen Eudora occasionally over the years, she noticed a change from those earlier meetings. Eudora was repeating anecdotes and seemed very tired. But Harriet was surprised and pleased to find Eudora engaged by conversation and initiating stories, still very much herself. I was glad to see Eudora welcome the gathering; the previous October only Reynolds's coaxing had brought her into her own living room for a small party with old friends at which she had been somewhat irritable and distant. The cycle of bad days and good days had continued. This was a good day. Harriet was fortunate in timing her visit. Mack Cole was also fortunate that, at age ninety, Eudora was interested in a new publishing venture. The University Press of Mississippi, with Mack as editor, wanted to bring out a book of photographs Eudora had taken in Mississippi cemeteries, and she approved, even granting Mack a February 2000 interview for publication in the book titled *Country Churchyards.*

A year later Eudora's health and memory were precipitously failing. I continued to visit almost every day, but I found it harder and harder to engage Eudora in conversation, to interest her in the world of politics or theater or literature. She knew me, as she knew her family members and other Jackson friends, but some days she did not know that she was at home. The house she had inhabited for seventy-six years seemed unfamiliar to her. When Michael and Chris Kreyling visited that spring, they were not sure that Eudora recognized them. She was slipping gradually away. In July, Eudora had difficulty breathing and swallowing; an ambulance took her to the hospital, where she seemed to revive and where she responded well to her doctors. Family and friends, myself included, heaved a sigh of relief, and Eudora returned home. A day or two later, breathing problems recurred, and she was rushed back to the hospital. There, surrounded by family members, she died of cardiopulmonary failure, on July 23, 2001.

On July 25, Eudora lay in state in the rotunda of the Old Capitol Museum, as friends and admirers filed past her closed casket and paid their respects to her nieces and their husbands, to her sister-in-law Mittie, and to her great-nieces and -nephews. The next day an estimated six hundred people attended the funeral at Galloway United Methodist Church. Though never a regular churchgoer, Eudora had been a member of Galloway since childhood, and now Methodist bishop Clay Lee paid tribute to her. In the congregation were Jackson friends Patti Black, Ann Morrison, and Tommie Blissard, writers William Jay Smith, Elizabeth Spencer, Ellen Douglas, Ann Patchett, and Kaye Gibbons, Eudora's editor John Ferrone, Walker Percy's widow Bunt, Roger Mudd and wife E. J., Mississippi governor Ronnie Musgrove, and Jackson mayor Harvey Johnson. Timothy Seldes and Mississippi's former governor William Winter delivered the eulogies. Tim read from letters about Eudora that he had just received from Pamela Russell Jessup, Diarmuid's daughter, and from Reynolds. The letters reminded all present of Eudora's keen sense of humor, and laughter filled the sanctuary. Governor Winter asked the congregation to "celebrate the enchanted memories of her time with us," and everyone present did, filling Galloway with the strains of "Joyful, Joyful We Adore Thee" set to the music of Beethoven and proclaiming "the triumph song of life."[10] Burial took place at Jackson's Greenwood Cemetery, beneath a beautiful magnolia tree, next to the brother who had died before Eudora's birth, and within sight of the house where she had been born. Richard Ford, Mack Cole, John Evans, her great-nieces Elizabeth Eudora White and Leslie Thompson Jacobs, and her great-nephews Donald Alexander White Jr., Andrews Welty White, and Zachary Welty Thompson served as pallbearers.[11]

> There was a ringing for each car as it struck its wheels on the cattleguard and rode up into the cemetery. The procession passed between ironwork gates whose kneeling angels and looping vines shone black as licorice. The top of the hill ahead was crowded with winged angels and life-sized effigies of bygone citizens in old-fashioned dress, standing as if by count among the columns and shafts and conifers like a familiar set of passengers collected on deck of a ship, on which they all knew each other—bona-fide members of a small local excursion, embarked on a voyage that is always returning in dreams. (*The Optimist's Daughter*)[12]

This was the very cemetery that Eudora had seen from the sleeping porch of her childhood home, that she had so often photographed during the 1930s, and that she had described in one of her first stories and in her last. She had returned to the neighborhood where she began.

ACKNOWLEDGMENTS
. . . .

In many ways, a biography is a collaborative effort, and I am thankful to the many individuals who have shared their time and expertise with me. Elizabeth Welty Thompson and Mary Alice Welty White, Eudora's nieces and heirs, supported this biography and assisted me in all ways possible. Reynolds Price granted me long interviews on three separate occasions, read the manuscript of this biography, and provided a wonderful "term paper" of comments and suggestions. William Jay Smith and his wife, Sonja, welcomed me to Cummington, Massachusetts, and entertained me royally. Bill's memories of Eudora were crucial to the development of chapter 4 and inform many chapters in this book. In 1985 and 1986 when I was Welty Scholar at the Mississippi Department of Archives and History, I was privileged to interview Richard Ford, Barry Hannah, and Toni Morrison. More recently, Lois Cleland, Daryl Howard, Pamela Russell Jessup, Edward King, Jeanne Luckett, Willanna Mallet, Eddie Mae Polk, Jane Reid Petty, Michael Robinson, Louis Rubin, Seta Sancton, Ron Sharp, Ralph Sipper, Elizabeth Spencer, Elinor Saul Welty, and Mittie Creekmore Welty also granted me engaging and informative interviews.

Many of Eudora's Jackson friends were also friends of mine, and each of them has helped this biography immeasurably. My debt to Ann Morrison and Patti Carr Black is long-term and ongoing;

both are fonts of information, and Patti generously read, commented on, and helped to correct my manuscript. I am also particularly grateful to Charlotte Capers, the incomparable raconteur and archivist, who died in 1996, for teaching me much about Eudora. In addition I have been fortunate to have three wonderful research assistants: Alison Beard, Michael Pickard, and Lekesha Perry. Special thanks to Alison, who has worked with me for the past year, becoming familiar with most of the Welty correspondence at the Mississippi Department of Archives and History, reading my manuscript, providing perceptive comments, and serving as an eagle-eyed proofreader.

Senior Vice-President Richard Smith and my colleagues at Millsaps College have given me their wholehearted backing, and the College provided released time for this project. My far-flung colleagues Pearl Amelia McHaney and Harriet Pollack generously shared their knowledge with me, and Harriet offered valuable editorial advice as well. Forrest Galey and Amy Steadman assisted me in working with photographs of and by Eudora Welty. My cousin Sherryl Sanders-feld read an early manuscript and improved it with her comments, and my sister, LuAnn Marrs, discussed many of the book's key issues with me. I also thank Scott Naugle of Pass Christian Books and the fine staffs at the Mississippi Department of Archives and History, the Harry Ransom Humanities Research Center, the National Library of Canada, the New York Public Library, and the libraries of Duke University, the University of Sussex, Cambridge University, the University of Illinois, the University of Colorado, Washington University, Millsaps College, the University of Maryland, the University of the South, the University of Virginia, and the University of Mississippi for so efficiently helping me locate manuscripts and correspondence.

I am deeply in debt to two Tims—Timothy Seldes and Timothy Bent—and to one Sara. Tim Seldes, who was Eudora Welty's agent and generously agreed to become mine, ably guided me in business and textual matters. Tim Bent was a model editor, helping me to shape and develop the book and to improve my prose style.

And Sara Branch, Harcourt managing editorial assistant, deftly piloted the biography through production channels.

My fiancé, Rowan Taylor, deserves much of the credit for this book. He has encouraged me at each step of the process, read the manuscript repeatedly, talked with me about it in what must have seemed an incessant fashion, and never complained if I seem distracted or preoccupied. I could not have written the biography without his love and support.

Of course, above all, I am grateful to Eudora Welty, who was a devoted friend, who trusted me to write her life, and whose genius endures in her work.

EUDORA WELTY CHRONOLOGY

1879—Father Christian Webb Welty born.

1883—Mother Chestina Andrews born.

1904—Christian Webb Welty and Chestina Andrews marry.

1907—The Weltys' son Christian Welty dies at age fifteen months.

April 13, 1909—Eudora born in Jackson, Mississippi, at 741 N. Congress Street.

1912—Brother Edward Welty born.

1915—Brother Walter Welty born.

1924—A sister is stillborn.

1925—Graduates from Jackson High School.

1925–27—Attends Mississippi State College for Women, Columbus, Mississippi.

1927–29—Attends and graduates from the University of Wisconsin, Madison, Wisconsin.

1930–31—Attends Columbia University School of Business.

1931—Christian Webb Welty, Eudora's father, dies.

1931–34—Eudora works in Jackson at WJDX radio station.

1933–35—Eudora writes Jackson society columns for the Memphis *Commercial-Appeal*.

1936—Eudora publishes her first stories, "Death of a Traveling Salesman" and "Magic," in *Manuscript* magazine, and she works for the Works Progress Administration.

1937–39—Eudora publishes ten stories in *Southern Review, Prairie Schooner, River.*

1939—Eudora works for the Mississippi Advertising Commission.

1940—Diarmuid Russell becomes Eudora's agent.

1941—Eudora publishes stories in the *Atlantic Monthly* and *Harper's Bazaar.* Her first book of stories, *A Curtain of Green,* is published.

1942—*The Robber Bridegroom*

1943—*The Wide Net*

1944—Eudora works for several months as a copyeditor and staff reviewer for the *New York Times Book Review.*

1946—*Delta Wedding*

1946–47—Eudora has two extended stays in San Francisco.

1949—*The Golden Apples*

1949–50—Eudora travels through Europe on a Guggenheim Fellowship.

1951—Eudora spends a few months in England and Ireland.

1952—Elected to the National Institute of Arts and Letters.

1954—Eudora lectures at Cambridge University in England and publishes *The Ponder Heart.*

1955—*The Bride of the Innisfallen*; Eudora receives Howells Medal from American Academy of Arts and Letters.

1956—Jerome Chodorov's and Joseph Fields's dramatization of *The Ponder Heart* runs on Broadway.

1959—Eudora's brother Walter dies.

1963—Eudora publishes "Where is the Voice Coming From?" in the *New Yorker.*

1966—Eudora's mother Chestina and her brother Edward die.

1966—"The Demonstrators" appears in the *New Yorker.*

1969—"The Optimist's Daughter" appears in the *New Yorker.*

1970—Eudora publishes *Losing Battles,* a novel begun in 1955.

1971—Eudora's book of photographs, *One Time, One Place,* is published.

1972—*The Optimist's Daughter* in revised and expanded form is published, and Eudora receives the Gold Medal for Fiction from the National Institute of Arts and Letters and is elected to the American Academy.

1973—*The Optimist's Daughter* receives a Pulitzer Prize.

1974—Eudora travels through Italy and France.

1976—Alfred Uhry's dramatization of *The Robber Bridegroom* runs on Broadway.

1978—*The Eye of the Story*

1979—Artist-in-residence, British Studies Program, Associated Colleges of the South, held at Oxford University

1980—*The Collected Stories of Eudora Welty;* Eudora receives Presidential Medal of Freedom

1983—Eudora delivers the William E. Massey Sr. Lectures in the History of American Civilization at Harvard University.

1984—*One Writer's Beginnings;* Eudora travels to England and Italy.

1986—Eudora receives National Medal of the Arts.

1989—*Photographs*

1990—Travels to London

1991—*Norton Book of Friendship,* coedited with Ronald A. Sharp

1996—Receives French Legion of Honor in ceremony held at the Old Capitol Museum in Jackson.

1998—The Library of America publishes two volumes of Eudora's fiction and nonfiction, making her the only living writer whose works had become part of this distinguished series.

2001—Eudora Welty dies on July 23.

EUDORA WELTY HONORARY DEGREES

1954	University of Wisconsin
1955	Western College for Women (Ohio)
1956	Smith College
1969	Millsaps College
1971	Denison University
1971	University of the South
1972	Washington and Lee University
1973	Queens College, N.C.
1975	Tulane University
1975	Southern Methodist University
1975	Yale University
1975	Mount Holyoke College
1976	University of North Carolina, Chapel Hill
1977	Washington University
1977	Kent State University
1977	Harvard University
1977	University of Michigan
1978	Rutgers University
1979	University of Illinois
1979	Brandeis University
1980	Drew University

1980	Belhaven College
1980	Kenyon College
1980	Southwestern College
1980	Brigham Young University
1981	Randolph-Macon Woman's College
1981	William Carey College
1981	University of West Florida
1982	Columbia University
1982	Emory University
1984	Wake Forest University
1985	William and Mary University
1986	Queens College, N.Y.
1987	University of Charleston, W. Va.
1988	Princeton University
1989	Chesnut Hill College
1991	Centenary College
1993	University of Burgundy
1998	Mississippi University for Women

Between 1998 and 2005, thanks to Eudora Welty and later to her nieces, I had access to many manuscripts and letters, which in 2005, with the settlement of the Welty estate, passed into the able care of the Mississippi Department of Archives and History. They are scheduled to be open for research in 2008.

INTRODUCTION

1. Eudora Welty, "Why I Live at the P.O.," "Circe," "The Wide Net," "The Wanderers" (1941, 1955, 1943, 1949), revised and reprinted in *The Collected Stories of Eudora Welty* (New York: Harcourt, Brace, Jovanovich, 1980), 46, 531, 171, 460; Eudora Welty, *The Optimist's Daughter* (New York: Random House, 1972), 160; Welty, "First Love," (1943), revised and reprinted in *The Collected Stories of Eudora Welty*, 153, 382.

2. Eudora Welty, "The Radiance of Jane Austen," review of *Granite and Rainbow*, by Virginia Woolf (1958), "Reality in Chekhov's Stories," review of *The Cockatoos*, by Patrick White (1975), in *The Eye of the Story* (New York: Random House, 1978), 3, 191, 81, 264.

3. Eudora Welty to William Maxwell [December 1984], William Maxwell Collection, University of Illinois Library, Champaign-Urbana, Illinois.

4. Eudora Welty, "Must the Novelist Crusade?" *Atlantic*, October

1965, reprinted in *The Eye of the Story*, 153. Most essays and all reviews collected in *The Eye of the Story* were previously published in periodicals, and the essays were revised, typically very lightly, for the collection. Cited quotations from this collection are, with the exception of two minor stylistic revisions to be subsequently noted, identical to passages in the original periodical publications.

5. Eudora Welty, interview by John Little and Tom Royals, in *Conversations with Eudora Welty*, ed. Peggy Whitman Prenshaw (Jackson: University Press of Mississippi, 1984), 252–253.

6. Jonathan Yardley, "Welty's World," *Washington Post Book World*, 4 April 1984, sec. B; C. Vann Woodward, "Southerner with Her Own Accent," *New York Times Book Review*, 19 February 1984, 7; Edmund Fuller, "The Author as Reader," *Wall Street Journal*, 6 March 1984; James O. Freedman, 1990 convocation address, Dartmouth College, Eudora Welty Collection, Mississippi Department of Archives and History, Jackson, Mississippi.

7. Reynolds Price to Suzanne Marrs, 22 July 2004, private collection of Suzanne Marrs.

8. Carolyn Heilbrun, *Writing a Woman's Life* (New York: W. W. Norton, 1988), 14, 15, 118–119.

9. Claudia Roth Pierpont, "A Perfect Lady," *New Yorker*, 5 October 1998, 104.

10. John Briggs, *Fire in the Crucible* (New York: St. Martin's Press, 1988), 93; Hermione Lee, *Virginia Woolf* (London: Chatto and Windus, 1996), 3; Eudora Welty, "Henry Green: Novelist of the Imagination," in *The Eye of the Story*, 15. Originally published as "Henry Green: A Novelist of the Imagination," *Texas Quarterly* 4 (Autumn 1961).

ONE: Shelter and Beyond

1. This family photo album is part of the Eudora Welty Collection, Mississippi Department of Archives and History, Jackson, Mississippi, hereafter referred to as Welty Collection.

2. Eudora Welty, *One Writer's Beginnings* (Cambridge, Mass.: Harvard University Press, 1984), 5.

3. Family photo album, Welty Collection; Welty, *One Writer's Beginnings*,

34–35; "Partial List of Babies Seen in Last Week's Baby Parade," *Jackson Daily News*, 15 March 1916.

4. Welty, *One Writer's Beginnings*, xi, 21.

5. Eudora Welty, carbon of TS of pages omitted from William E. Massey Sr. Lectures in the History of American Civilization, Harvard University, [1982], Welty Collection.

6. Eudora Welty, Courtney story, untitled and partially unpaginated draft (1926), Welty Collection; Eudora Welty to Diarmuid Russell, 15 March 1941, Welty Collection.

7. Welty, *One Writer's Beginnings*, 13–14; Welty, "The Little Store," in *The Eye of the Story* 326–327, Originally published as "The Corner Store," *Esquire*, December 1975.

8. Welty, Courtney story, Welty Collection.

9. Ibid.; Willanna Buck Mallett, personal interview by author, 3 October 2002, Jackson, Mississippi.

10. Mackie Pine Oil Company to Eudora Welty, 29 August 1921, Welty Collection; Eudora Welty, "The Glorious Apology," Welty Collection [1921]. "The Glorious Apology" includes a reference to the song "Ain't We Got Fun," popular in 1921; thus the year seems a likely date for the story.

11. Jackson High School was also known as Central High School, which would by the 1926–27 academic year become its only name; Welty, Courtney story, Welty Collection.

12. Eudora Welty, "The Conference Condemns Caroline," in *Quadruplane* (Jackson High School), 1924.

13. Eudora Welty, "In the Twilight," *St. Nicholas*, January 1925, 328.

14. Welty, spiral notebook of notes for the William E. Massey Sr. Lectures [1982], n. p., Welty Collection.

15. Ibid., 20.

16. Chestina Welty, travel log, 19 July to 17 August 1925, Welty Collection.

17. Eudora Welty to Dorothy Simmons, n.d., private collection of Fred Smith, Choctaw Books, Jackson, Mississippi. Eudora Welty, "The Gnat," *The Spectator*, 6 November 1926; "The Great Pinnington Solves the Mystery," *The Spectator*, 14 November 1925; "'I' for Iris—Irma, Imogene," *The Spectator*, 27 November 1926; "Autumn's Here," *The Spectator*, 28 November 1925.

18. Eudora Welty, "Society," *The Spectator*, 1 April 1927; "Prophecy," *The Spectator*, 3 May 1927.

19. Chestina Welty, travel log, 7 September to 13 September 1926; Nash K. Burger to Eudora Welty [25 October 1927], Welty Collection.

20. Ricardo Quintana, open letter of recommendation, 3 September 1929, Welty Collection. Official transcript of Eudora Alice Welty, University of Wisconsin, 1929. Eudora Welty to Laura Frances Collins, n.d.; Burger to Welty [23 May 1929], Welty Collection.

21. Welty to Russell, 30 September 1941, Welty Collection.

22. Eudora Welty, "Post Offices Shifted Many Times in City," *Jackson Daily News*, 27 April 1930; "Weekly Baby Clinic Is Becoming Popular," *Jackson Daily News*, 25 May 1930; "Vacations Lure Jacksonians; Large One Underway Soon; Papa Hardest Hit," *Jackson Daily News*, 15 June 1930.

23. Record in the School of Business, Columbia University of New York City.

24. Eudora Welty, lecture notes, included in a letter from Frank Lyell to his family, 24 September 1930, Photocopy, Welty Collection.

25. Wallace Thurman, *Negro Life in New York's Harlem* (Girard, KS: Haldeman-Julius Publications, 1928), 25; Mervyn Cooke, *The Chronicle of Jazz* (New York, London, Paris: Abbeville Press, 1998), 62–63.

26. Langston Hughes, *The Big Sea: An Autobiography* (New York: Alfred A. Knopf, 1940), 228; Frank Lyell to the Lyell family, Thanksgiving Day 1930, Photocopy, Welty Collection.

27. Frank Lyell to the Lyell family, 9 October 1930, Photocopy, Welty Collection; Buckminster Fuller Institute, Gallery One, http://www.bfi.org/gallery_one.htm.

28. The married names of Nettie St. Helens, Wilma Gallagher, and Felicia White were to be Norris, Segrest, and Gossman, respectively; Eudora Welty, interview by Patchy Wheatley, in *More Conversations with Eudora Welty*, ed. Peggy Whitman Prenshaw (Jackson: University Press of Mississippi, 1996), 124. In this 1986 interview, Eudora recalled this bit of "skullduggery" as occurring in the fall of 1931 just before she learned that her father had leukemia, but her memory seems to have been a bit faulty. She had

learned of her father's illness the previous spring and I have found no evidence that she returned to Columbia University or New York City that fall.

29. Welty, "Pages omitted from *A Writer's Beginnings* notes and try-outs," Welty Collection.

30. Welty, Courtney story, Welty Collection; Welty, *One Writer's Beginnings*, 17–18.

31. Evelyn C. Johnson, "Child Life in Many Lands," *Every Child's Story Book*, vol. 5 of *Our Wonder World* (Chicago and Boston: George L. Shuman and Co., 1914), 385; Chestina Welty, travel log, 31 July 1925, Welty Collection.

32. Toni Morrison, interview by Mel Watkins, *New York Times Book Review*, 11 September 1977, 50.

33. "Miss Eudora Welty Honored at Beautiful Bridge Party of Eight Congenial Tables," *Jackson Daily Clarion-Ledger*, 22 June 1930; Welty, Courtney story, Welty Collection.

TWO: Self-Discovery

1. Welty, *One Writer's Beginnings*, 92–93.

2. Eudora Welty, "Some Notes on Time in Fiction," *Mississippi Quarterly* 26 (Fall 1973), reprinted in *The Eye of the Story*, 168. Eudora Welty, "Looking Back at the First Story," *Georgia Review* 33 (1979): 755.

3. Eudora Welty to Virginia Woolf, 23 November 1931, Monks House Papers, University of Sussex Library Special Collections, Brighton, England. Thanks to Beth Rigel Daugherty of Otterbein College for locating this letter.

4. Eudora Welty to the *New Yorker*, 15 March 1933, *New Yorker* Archive, New York Public Library.

5. John Martin, "The Dance: Hindu Art for the Western World," *New York Times*, 1 January 1933, sec. 9, p. 2; Eudora Welty to Frank Lyell, n.d., Welty Collection.

6. John J. McCusker, "Comparing the Purchasing Power of Money in the United States (or Colonies) from 1665 to Any Other Year Including the Present," Economic History Services, 2004, http://

www.eh.net/hmit/ppowerusd/; Eudora Welty to Berenice Abbott, 9 August 1934, photocopy in private collection of Suzanne Marrs; Eudora Welty, *One Time, One Place* (New York: Random House, 1971), 4–5, 5; Eudora Welty to Frank Lyell, [16 February 1935], Welty Collection; Eudora Welty to Robert Daniel, 29 July 1935, Robert Daniel Papers, Jessie Ball duPont Library, University of the South, Sewanee, Tennessee.

7. Eudora Welty, *Acrobats in a Park* (Northridge, CA: Lord John Press, 1980), n.p. Eudora Welty dated a manuscript of this story as "1934 (?)" (Welty Collection), but in its book publication said the story was "written in, or about, the year 1935."

8. Lehman Engel, *This Bright Day* (New York: Macmillan, 1974), 40; Eudora Welty, "The Wanderers," in *The Golden Apples* (New York: Harcourt, 1949), 235; Eudora Welty to Lehman Engel, 3 August 1956 and 5 August 1970, Engel Papers, Millsaps College, Jackson, Mississippi.

9. This discussion of the Night-Blooming Cereus Club appears in part in my book *One Writer's Imagination* (Baton Rouge: Louisiana State University Press, 2002), 9–10. Eudora Welty to Robert Daniel, 29 July 1935, Robert Daniel Papers, Jessie Ball duPont Library, University of the South; Robert Daniel to Eudora Welty [22 February 1934], [18 November 1935], Welty Collection.

10. Eudora Welty, "Place in Fiction." *The Archive* (Duke University), April 1955, reprinted in *The Eye of the Story*, 125.

11. Eudora Welty to Frank Lyell [16 February 1935], Welty Collection.

12. Ibid., [16 February 1935], [16 June 1935].

13. John Rood to Eudora Welty, 19 March 1936, Welty Collection; Eudora Welty, interview by Jane Reid Petty, in *Conversations with Eudora Welty*, ed. Prenshaw 208; Eudora Welty, "Death of a Traveling Salesman," in *A Curtain of Green* (New York: Doubleday, Doran and Company, 1941), 244, 248; Eudora Welty to Frank Lyell, [19 May 1936], Welty Collection; Robert Daniel to Eudora Welty, 18 July [1936], Welty Collection; Lehman Engel to Eudora Welty, 31 May 1936, Welty Collection.

14. Samuel Robbins to Eudora Welty, 21 November 1936, Welty Collection.

15. Welty, interview by Bill Ferris, in *Conversations with Eudora Welty*, ed. Prenshaw, 155.

16. Eudora Welty to Frank Lyell, 15 July [1936], 11 August 1936, Welty Collection; Welty, *One Time, One Place*, 6.

17. Frank Hall Fraysur to Eudora Welty, 29 January 1937, Welty Collection; Eudora Welty, "A Piece of News," in *A Curtain of Green*, 23, 24, 25.

18. Eudora Welty to John F. Robinson, [29 November 1946], Welty Collection; 1930s letters between Robinson and Welty do not seem to be extant; Welty to Robinson, 7 July 1943, Welty Collection; Welty to Daniel, n.d., Robert Daniel Collection, Jessie Ball duPont Library, University of the South.

19. The novella titled "The Cheated" in Linscott's 17 September 1938 letter to Welty is now part of the Welty Collection at the Mississippi Department of Archives and History, though this version is called "The Night of the Little House."

20. Chestina Welty, "The Perfect Garden," photocopy, personal collection of Suzanne Marrs, 2–3,1.

21. Eudora Welty, "A Curtain of Green," in *A Curtain of Green*, 208–209, 212, 214; this analysis of "A Curtain of Green" appeared in a different context in my book *One Writer's Imagination*, 5–7.

22. Reynolds Price, review of *The Collected Stories of Eudora Welty*, in *Eudora Welty, A Study of Her Short Fiction*, by Carol Ann Johnston (New York: Twayne Publishers, 1997), 178; Eudora Welty, "The Whistle," in *A Curtain of Green*, 114; Eudora Welty to John F. Robinson, 17 August [1946], Welty Collection.

23. Katherine Anne Porter to Eudora Welty, 25 October 1938, Welty Collection.

24. Eudora Welty, "The Hitch-Hikers," in *A Curtain of Green*, 137.

25. Eudora Welty to Katherine Anne Porter, n.d., Papers of Katherine Anne Porter, Special Collections, University of Maryland Libraries, College Park, Maryland, hereafter referred to as Porter Papers.

26. Diarmuid Russell to Eudora Welty 28 May [1940]; Eudora Welty to Diarmuid Russell, 31 May 1940; Russell to Welty, 3 June [1940], Welty Collection. The unfinished story set in Rodney's Landing dealt with "bandits and romantic love," and much of it is

"the old man's story, if I can keep the quotation marks straight, then he dies, and the girl falls into the mercy of the natural called Maurice, after Maurice Ravel"; Welty to Russell, n.d. [June 1940], Welty Collection.

27. Welty to Lyell, [17 August 1940], Welty Collection; Eudora Welty, William E. Massey Lecture III, p. 6, Welty Collection; Eudora Welty, "Powerhouse," in *A Curtain of Green*, 257; Welty, *One Writer's Beginnings*, 101; Eudora Welty to Herschel Brickell, [4 October 1940], Brickell Papers, Special Collections, University of Mississippi Library.

28. Welty to Russell, n.d.; Russell to Welty [8 October 1940]; Welty to Russell [18 November 1940]; John Woodburn to Eudora Welty, 26 November 1940, Welty Collection. This paragraph appears in a slightly different form in my book *One Writer's Imagination*, 48.

29. Welty to Russell, 5 November 1940; Russell to Welty, 27 January 1941, Welty Collection.

30. Eudora Welty, "Why I Live at the P.O.," in *A Curtain of Green*, 89, 87.

31. Welty to Russell, n.d. [late 1940]; Russell to Welty, 15 January 1941; Welty to Russell, 18 January 1941, Welty Collection.

32. Eudora Welty, "A Pageant of Birds," *New Republic*, 25 October 1943, reprinted in *The Eye of the Story*, 319.

33. Russell to Welty, 21 April 1941, Welty Collection.

34. Welty to Robinson [27 June 1941], Welty Collection; Welty to Russell, 26 June 1941, Welty Collection; Porter to Welty, 17 August 1941, Welty Collection; Welty to Porter, [29/30 August 1941], Porter Papers.

35. Welty to Russell, [26 June 1941], Welty Collection.

36. This analysis of "First Love" appeared in another context in my book *One Writer's Imagination*, 54.

37. Russell to Welty, 22 July 1941; Welty to Russell, 23 July 1941, Welty Collection.

38. Welty to Russell, 28 August 1941, 20 September 1941, Welty Collection.

39. Welty to Lyell [15 September 1941], Welty Collection.

40. Ibid., [9 December 1941].

41. Kay Boyle, "Full-Length Portrait," *New Republic*, 24 November

1941, 707; Louise Bogan, "The Gothic South," *Nation,* 6 December 1941, 572; Chestina Welty, *"A Curtain of Green* Scrapbook," Welty Collection.

42. Welty to Russell, 24 November [1941], Welty Collection.

THREE: "Being Apart from What Matters"

1. Eudora Welty, "The Wanderers," in *The Golden Apples,* 234.

2. Eudora Welty to Katherine Anne Porter [29 or 30 August 1941], Porter Papers.

3. Diarmuid Russell to Eudora Welty, 26 December 1941; Welty to Russell, n.d. [late December 1941], Welty Collection; Eudora Welty, "A Still Moment," in *The Wide Net and Other Stories* (New York: Harcourt, Brace and Company, 1943), 87.

4. Eudora Welty to Frank Lyell [21 August 1942]; Welty to Russell, n.d. [late August 1942] Welty Collection.

5. Eudora Welty to Kenneth Millar, 29 November 1976, Welty Collection.

6. Welty to Lyell, [21 August 1942]; Eudora Welty, "Music from Spain," in *The Golden Apples,* 173–174; Welty to Russell, n.d. [late August 1942], Welty Collection.

7. Eudora Welty to John F. Robinson, n.d. [1942]; Welty to Robinson, 12 September 1942, Welty Collection.

8. Welty to Russell, 24 November [1941], Welty Collection; Morison, interview by Watkins, 50; Welty to Robinson, [8 November 1946], [29 June 1947], [19 November 1947], [1 December 1948], [22 October 1949], [September 1950]; Welty Collection; William Jay Smith, interview by author, 2 June 2002; Reynolds Price, personal conversation with author, 25 October 1998.

9. Welty to Russell [31 October 1942], Welty Collection.

10. Nathan L. Rothman, "The Lost Realm," review of *The Robber Bridegroom,* by Eudora Welty, in *Saturday Review of Literature,* 14 November 1942, 16.

11. Welty to Porter, 11 November [1942], Porter Papers; Welty to Robinson, n.d. [1942], Welty Collection.

12. Welty to Porter [January 1943], Porter Papers; S. J. Perelman to

Eudora Welty, 12 February [1943]; William Faulkner to Eudora Welty, 27 April [1943], Welty Collection.

13. Welty to Robinson [11 May 1943], Welty Collection. Contacts with these Dutch fliers ultimately proved heartbreaking, as Eudora and her friends learned that three of the men died in combat. But good news about the fourth provided some consolation. Eudora wrote to Russell, "I must tell you though that one Dutch flier, out of the ones we knew in Jackson, did get home and find his family—all the others have been killed, but he got there—his house had been bombed but he found a little note on the door saying if anyone wanted to find So and So, go to a certain street and house, and he walked in," 25 May [1945], Welty Collection.

14. Welty to Porter [late May or early June 1943], Porter Papers.

15. Welty to Robinson, 8 August [1943]; Robinson to Welty, 8 August [1943]; Welty to Robinson, 26 August [1943], 24 September 1943, Welty Collection.

16. John F. Robinson, composition book, Welty Collection.

17. Welty to Russell, 27 September [1943], Welty Collection; "Sense and Sensibility," review of *The Wide Net*, by Eudora Welty, *Time*, 27 September 1943, 101; Diana Trilling, "Fiction in Review," review of *The Wide Net*, by Eudora Welty, *Nation*, 2 October 1943, 386.

18. Russell to Welty, 10 November 1943, Welty Collection.

19. Eudora Welty, "What Stevenson Started," *New Republic*, 5 January 1953, 8.

20. Welty to Robinson, [26 November 1943], 5 December [1943], 15 December [1943], Welty Collection.

21. Ibid., 15 November [1943].

22. Welty to Robinson, 8 February [1944], 10 February [1944], n.d. [April 1944], Welty Collection.

23. Welty to Robinson, 3 March [1944], 13 March [1944], 17 April [1944], Welty Collection.

24. Ibid., 1 June 1944, 5 June [1944].

25. Ibid., [19 June 1944].

26. Ibid., 31 May [1944], [19 June 1944], 13 July [1944].

27. Ibid., n.d. [Summer 1944], 10 July [1944], 11 July [1944]; Eudora Welty, "Tatters and Fragments of War," review of *Artist at War*, by George Biddle, *New York Times Book Review*, 16 July 1944,

as reprinted in *A Writer's Eye: Collected Book Reviews,* ed. Pearl A. McHaney (Jackson: University Press of Mississippi, 1994), 35.

28. Eudora Welty, *One Writer's Beginnings,* 101; Welty to Robinson, 22 June [1944], [23 June 1944], Welty Collection.

29. Welty to Robinson, n.d. [Labor Day 1944], 27 September [1944], Welty Collection.

30. Ibid., [13 July 1944]. The attitude Eudora encountered in New Yorkers she also encountered in her fellow southerner and friend Tom Sancton, and she had on 13 January 1944 written to Russell, objecting when she thought Sancton's essay in *Harper's* reiterated northern stereotypes of white southerners. See "Race Clash," *Harper's Magazine,* January 1944, 135–140.

31. Welty to Robinson [10 July 1944], Welty Collection.

32. Ibid., [19 June 1944]; Welty to Lyell [4 August 1944], Welty Collection.

33. Pamela Russell Jessup, telephone interview by author, 3 November 2004; Welty to Robinson, 10 October [1944], Welty Collection.

34. Welty to Robinson, 13 August [1944], 10 October [1944], Welty Collection.

35. Ibid., 10 October [1944]; Diarmuid Russell to Welty, 19 October 1944, Welty Collection.

36. Welty to Robinson, [20 October 1944], 25 October [1944], 9 November [1944], Welty Collection.

37. Ibid., 16 November [1944], 21 December [1944].

38. Russell to Welty, 22 December 1944; Welty to Robinson, 17 January [1945], Welty Collection.

39. Eudora Welty, "A Little Triumph," 6, Welty Collection.

40. Ibid., 10.

41. Welty to Robinson, 25 December [1944], Welty Collection.

42. John F. Robinson, to William Hamilton, 28 January [1945], Hamilton Papers, Duke University. The letter is misdated 28 January 1944, for Robinson refers to his night-fighter duty, which did not begin until many months later. Clipping enclosed in letter from Welty to Robinson, 15 January [1945]; Welty to Robinson, 7 February [1945], 9 February 1945, Welty Collection.

43. Welty to Robinson, 8 January [1945], 15 January [1945], Welty Collection.

44. Ibid., 13 February [1945].

45. Nancy McDougall Robinson, diary from 1832, Mississippi Department of Archives and History, Jackson, Mississippi.

46. The material in this paragraph appeared in my book *One Writer's Imagination*, 91–92.

47. Welty to Robinson [14 April 1945], [8 May 1945], Welty Collection.

48. Ibid., 14 May [1945].

49. Ibid., [13 July 1944], 10 October [1944], [2 February 1945], 1 May [1945].

50. Welty to Russell, 25 May [1945], Welty Collection.

51. Welty to Robinson, 8 January [1945], 12 June [1945]; Welty to Russell, 13 August [1945], Welty Collection.

52. Welty to Lyell [19 August 1945], Welty Collection.

53. According to historian Leonard Dinnerstein, "Theodore Bilbo of Mississippi liked the nice Jews of his state but railed against the 'kike Jews' of New York" ("Antisemitism in American Politics," Tom Paine.commons sense, www.tompaine.com/feature2.cfm/ID/3475/html (accessed 22 February 2004). In his book *Take Your Choice: Separation or Mongrelization* (Poplarville, MS: Dream House Publishing, 1947), Bilbo associated Jews, particularly ethnologist Franz Boas, with civil rights agitation, writing that "for some reason which has never been publicized, this German Jew [Boas], a newly arrived immigrant, wanted to destroy the racial stock which had carved this mighty nation out of a wilderness," 160. Welty to Robinson, 23 August [1945]; Welty, to Russell, 24 August [1945], Welty Collection.

54. Eudora Welty, interviewed by Charles Ruas, in *More Conversations with Eudora Welty*, ed. Prenshaw, 66.

FOUR: "Love First and then Separateness"

1. Eudora Welty to Frank Lyell, 11 November [1945], Welty Collection.

2. Twenty-three of Robinson's letters written and sent to Eudora prior to 1980 survive, perhaps because she had neglected to file them with those she destroyed. John's long letter written immediately

after the Battle of Sicily may survive because she cherished it too much to part with it.

3. "Bilbo and Rankin Get Blessings of Former Huey Long Chieftain," *Jackson Clarion-Ledger*, 20 December 1945; Walter Goodman, *The Committee* (New York: Farrar, Straus, and Giroux, 1968), 181; Eudora Welty, "Voice of the People," *Jackson Clarion-Ledger*, 28 December 1945.

4. This analysis appeared in a slightly different form in my book *One Writer's Imagination*, 100–101.

5. Eudora Welty to Diarmuid Russell, n.d. (late December 1945); Diarmuid Russell to Eudora Welty, 2 January 1946; Welty to Russell, n.d. [January 1946], 3 January [1946]; Welty, to Lyell, 10 March [1946], [29 April 1946], Welty Collection.

6. Orville Prescott, "Books of the Times," *New York Times*, 17 April 1946, 23; "Cloud-Cuckoo Symphony," *Time*, 22 April 1946, 104; Hamilton Basso, "Look Away, Look Away, Look Away," *New Yorker*, 11 May 1946, 89; Welty to Lyell [15 May 1946], Welty Collection; Welty to Russell, n.d. [April 1946], Welty Collection; Harnett Kane, "Eudora Welty's Authentic and Vital Talent," *New York Herald Tribune Weekly Book Review*, 14 April 1946, 3; Elizabeth Bowen, "Book Shelf," *The Tatler and Bystander*, 6 August 1947, 183.

7. Eudora Welty to John F. Robinson [21 May 1946], Welty Collection.

8. Marcella Comes to Anne Winslow, 2 July 1946; Welty to Robinson, 2 July 1946, Welty Collection.

9. Welty to Robinson [19 July 1946], [2 August 1946], Welty Collection.

10. Ibid., 17 August [1946].

11. Russell to Welty, 5 September 1946, Welty Collection.

12. Welty to Robinson, [21 September 1946], [28 September 1946], [18 October 1946], Welty Collection.

13. Ibid., [18 October 1946], [23 October 1946].

14. Welty to Russell, 28 October 1946, Welty Collection.

15. Welty to Robinson, [27 November 1946], Welty Collection.

16. Welty to Diarmuid and Rose Russell, 25 December 1946, Welty Collection.

17. Welty to Diarmuid Russell, 2 January 1947, Welty Collection.

18. Harriet Pollack, "Reading John Robinson," *Mississippi Quarterly*, 56.2 (Spring 2003), 181; John F. Robinson, ". . . All This Juice and All This Joy," *Horizon* November 1948, 347.

19. Welty to Russell, 4 January 1947, Welty Collection.

20. Ibid., 9 February [1947]; Welty to Lyell, 14 February [1947], Welty Collection.

21. Welty to Russell, n.d. [February 1947], Welty Collection.

22. Ibid., 9 February [1947].

23. Ibid., 13 March [1947], 11 March [1947], 27 March 1947.

24. Welty to Robinson, 10 May [1947], Welty Collection.

25. E. M. Forster to Eudora Welty, as quoted in a letter to Russell, 15 May [1947].

26. Welty to Robinson, 12 September 1947, n.d., John F. Robinson Collection, Mississippi Department of Archives and History.

27. Welty to Lyell, [15 October 1947]; Welty to Robinson, [28 September 1946], Welty Collection.

28. Welty to Robinson, [17 November 1947]; Welty to Russell, 12 November 1947; Welty to Robinson [13 November 1947], Welty Collection.

29. Welty to Robinson, [1 December 1947], Welty Collection.

30. Ibid., [17 February 1948], [9 March 1948].

31. Ibid., [30 March 1948], [22 April 1948].

32. Welty to Lyell, [10 May 1948], Welty Collection.

33. Welty to Robinson, [2 September 1948], Welty Collection; Eudora Welty, "The Wanderers," in *The Golden Apples*, 243; Welty to Robinson, [23 September 1948], Welty Collection.

34. "Department of Amplification," *New Yorker*, 1 January 1949, reprinted in *Eudora Welty On William Faulkner* (Jackson: University Press of Mississippi, 2003), 30; Welty to Robinson, [21 December 1948], Welty Collection.

35. Lehman Engel to Eudora Welty, 8 January [1949], Welty Collection.

36. Welty to Robinson [4 March 1949], Welty Collection.

37. John F. Robinson to Nancy and Alice Farley, 29 January [1949], Farley Papers, University of Virginia Library, Charlottesville, Virginia; Welty to Robinson [19 May 1949], Welty Collection.

38. Welty to Robinson [4 June 1949], [15 June 1949], [24 June 1949], n.d. [summer 1949], Welty Collection.

39. William Maxwell to Eudora Welty [24 August 1949], Welty Collection.

40. Welty to Stafford, 2 September [1949], Jean Stafford Collection, University of Colorado Libraries, Boulder, Colorado.

41. Welty to Robinson, [22 October 1949]; Welty, to Russell [31 October 1949]; Welty to Robinson [28 October 1949], Welty Collection.

42. Welty to Robinson, 28 October [1949], 4 November [1949], Welty Collection.

43. Ibid., 2 December [1949].

44. Janet Flanner, *Paris Journal* (1965; reprint, New York: Harcourt Brace Jovanovich, 1977), 112–113.

45. Welty to Robinson, 19 November [1949]; Eudora Welty to Mary Lou Aswell, 5 May [1980]; Welty to Lyell, 16 January [1950], Welty Collection.

46. Welty to Aswell, n.d. [February 1950]; Welty to Lyell, 13 [February 1950]; Welty to Aswell, n.d. [February 1950], Welty Collection.

47. Welty to Russell, 3 March [1950]; Welty to Aswell, n.d. [March 1950], Welty Collection. Sylvia Sprigge, *Berenson: A Biography* (Boston: Houghton Mifflin, 1960), 267. Welty to Aswell, n.d. [March 1950]; Bernard Berenson to Eudora Welty, 14 January 1951, Welty Collection.

48. William Jay Smith, personal interview by author, 1 and 2 June 2002 Cummington, Massachusetts.

49. Welty to Lyell, [26 April 1950], Welty Collection.

50. John Lehmann, as cited by Jeremy Treglown, *Romancing, The Life and Work of Henry Green* (New York: Random House, 2000), 202; Eudora Welty, as cited by Treglown, 203.

51. Welty to Robinson [22 September 1950], [23 October 1950], Welty Collection.

52. Eudora Welty, interview by Albert J. Devlin and Peggy Whitman Prenshaw, in *More Conversations with Eudora Welty*, ed. Prenshaw, 109.

53. Welty to Russell [February 1951], Welty Collection.

54. Welty to Robinson, 22 March [1951], private collection of Michael Robinson.

55. Ibid., 2 April [1951].

56. Ibid., 11 April [1951].

57. Maxwell to Welty, 6 June [1951], Welty Collection.

58. Welty to Lyell, [10 March 1957], Welty Collection; Welty to Robinson, 14 June [1951], private collection of Michael Robinson.

59. Interestingly enough, in the fall of 1950 Eudora wrote to ask if Bowen knew Katherine Anne Porter and proposed that they meet at Porter's New York apartment "to have a good glass of Bourbon in Katherine Anne's kitchen too— (It's just that that's the place)," 11 October [1950], Porter Papers. Eudora clearly wanted to introduce Porter and Bowen, two women who were her models for the writing life.

60. Eudora Welty to Elizabeth Bowen, n.d., Elizabeth Bowen Collection, Harry Ransom Humanities Research Center, University of Texas, Austin; Victoria Glendinning, *Elizabeth Bowen* (New York: Alfred A. Knopf, 1978), 112; Elizabeth Bowen, *Bowen's Court* (New York: Alfred A. Knopf, 1942), 451; Eudora Welty, "Some Notes on River Country," *Harper's Bazaar,* February 1944, reprinted in *The Eye of the Story* 299.

61. Devlin and Prenshaw, *More Conversations with Eudora Welty* 108.

62. Welty to Bowen, n.d., Bowen Collection.

63. Glendinning, *Elizabeth Bowen,* 262–263, 240.

64. Welty to Robinson, n.d. [July 1951], private collection of Michael Robinson; Welty to Robinson, 26 May [1951], Welty Collection.

65. Welty to Aswell, n.d. [1950]; Welty to Robinson, 26 May [1951], Welty Collection.

66. Welty to Robinson [29 August 1951], private collection of Michael Robinson; Eudora Welty, "Writing and Analyzing a Story," reprinted in *The Eye of the Story,* 111. The cited passage varies slightly from one in the original version of the essay ("How I Write," *Virginia Quarterly Review* 31 [Spring 1955]). Eudora Welty to Elizabeth Bowen, 17 August [1951], Bowen Collection.

67. Welty to Robinson, 9 October [1951], private collection of Michael Robinson.

68. Dolly Wells to Eudora Welty, [5 October 1951], Welty Collection; Welty to Robinson, 17 October [1951], n.d. [late November or early December 1951], Welty Collection.

69. Welty to Robinson [13 July 1944], Welty Collection. Years after

Eudora faced and accepted John Robinson's homosexuality, she learned that Mary Lou Aswell had established a lesbian relationship with Agnes Sims. Eudora was similarly accepting of this relationship. See page 511.

70. Eudora Welty, "Going to Naples," in *The Bride of the Innisfallen and Other Stories* (New York: Harcourt Brace and Company, 1955), 186; Ibid., "The Bride of the Innisfallen," 83.

FIVE: "Finding a Way Out"

1. Elizabeth Bowen to Eudora Welty, 18 November 1951, Welty Collection; Elizabeth Spencer, *Landscapes of the Heart* (New York: Random House, 1998), 237–238.

2. Bowen to Welty, 15 December [1951], Welty Collection.

3. Word games, Welty Collection.

4. Eudora Welty to Diarmuid Russell, 25 February 1952, Robert Penn Warren to Eudora Welty, 24 February 1952, Welty Collection.

5. Eudora Welty to John F. Robinson [13 March 1952], private collection of Michael Robinson; John F. Robinson, "Coming of Spring," n.p., Robinson (John F.) Papers, Mississippi Department of Archives and History.

6. John F. Robinson, untitled story, Robinson Papers.

7. Eudora Welty, "No Place for You, My Love," in *The Bride of the Innisfallen*, 3–4, 22. Part of this paragraph appears in my book *One Writer's Imagination;* Welty to Robinson, 17 August [1946], Welty Collection.

8. Eudora Welty to Frank Lyell, [19 August 1952], Welty Collection.

9. Eudora Welty to Jean Stafford [September 1952], Stafford Collection; Nona Balakian to Eudora Welty, 9 December 1952, Welty Collection.

10. Welty to Lyell [3 November 1952], Welty Collection.

11. Welty to Stafford [November 1952], Stafford Collection.

12. Welty to Lyell [3 November 1952], Welty Collection; Eudora Welty, "What Stevenson Started," *New Republic,* 5 January 1953, 8.

13. Welty to Lyell, [3 November 1952], Welty Collection.

14. Welty to Stafford [December 1952], Stafford Collection.

15. Welty to Lyell, 28 January 1953, 9 March 1953, Welty Collection.

16. William Maxwell to Michael Kreyling, 16 November 1988, as cited in Michael Kreyling, *Author and Agent* (New York: Farrar, Straus and Giroux, 1991), 163–164 .

17. Russell to Welty, 30 April 1953, 4 May [1953], Welty Collection.

18. Welty to Russell, 20 July 1953, Welty Collection.

19. Welty to Lyell, 21 November [1953]; Mary Lou Aswell to Eudora Welty, 3 November [1953]; William Maxwell to Eudora Welty, 4 November [1953], Estate of William and Emily Maxwell.

20. Welty to Aswell, 1 January 1954, Welty Collection; Charles Poore, "Books of the Times," *New York Times,* 7 January 1954; William Peden, "A Trial with No Verdict," *Saturday Review,* 16 January 1954, 14; Maxwell to Welty [11 January 1954], Estate of William and Emily Maxwell; V. S. Pritchett, "Bossy Edna Earle Had a Word for Everything," *New York Times Book Review,* 10 January 1954.

21. Maxwell to Welty, 25 February [1954], Estate of William and Emily Maxwell.

22. Welty to Aswell, n.d. [spring 1954], Welty Collection.

23. Welty to Russell, 29 March [1954]; Russell to Welty, 30 March [1954], Welty Collection.

24. Eudora Welty to Hubert Creekmore and Frank Lyell, [11 May 1954], Welty Collection. Elsewhere in this letter Abe Burrows's name is misspelled "Burroughs," but the context indicates that "Burrows" is correct.

25. Dolly Wells to Eudora Welty, 8 June [1954], Welty Collection.

26. Welty to Lyell, 3 August 1954, Welty Collection.

27. John Martin, "The Dance: Hindu Art for the Western World," sec. 9, p. 2; E. M. Forster, *Howard's End* (1910; reprint, New York: Vintage Books, 1960), epigraph.

28. Welty to Lyell, 3 August 1954, Welty Collection.

29. Eudora Welty, "Place in Fiction," 130, 131–132.

30. Eudora Welty, "Place and Time: The Southern Writer's Inheritance," *Times Literary Supplement,* 17 September 1954, reprinted in *Mississippi Quarterly* 50.4 (Fall 1997): 546–548.

31. Welty to Lyell, 3 August 1954; Welty to Russell, 22 August 1954, Welty Collection.

32. Welty to Lyell, 10 September 1954, Welty Collection.

33. Ibid.

34. Ibid.

35. Welty to Lyell, 3 February [1955], Welty Collection; Pamela Redmayne to Eudora Welty, 1 February 1955, Reynolds Price Papers, Duke University Rare Book, Manuscript, and Special Collections Library, Durham, North Carolina.

36. Welty to Lyell, 3 February [1955], Welty Collection.

37. Eudora Welty to Reynolds Price, 7 March 1955, Reynolds Price Papers.

38. Eudora Welty to Jerome Chodorov and Joseph Fields, 28 March 1955, Welty Collection.

39. Welty to Lyell [12 May 1955], Welty Collection.

40. Orville Prescott, "Books of the Times," *New York Times*, 8 April 1955; John Barkham, "Prismatic Observations," *Saturday Review* Syndicate, Spring 1955; Frances Gaither, "Of the South and Beyond," *New York Times Book Review*, 10 April 1955.

41. Reynolds Price to Eudora Welty, 18 June 1955, Reynolds Price Papers.

42. Welty to Price [13 July 1955], Reynolds Price Papers.

43. Ibid., [6 August 1955].

44. Ibid., 16 September 1955.

45. Welty to Lyell [10 October 1955], Welty Collection.

46. Welty to Russell, 22 October [1955]; Lehman Engel to Eudora Welty, 3 December 1955, Welty Collection.

47. Engel to Welty, 13 January 1956, Welty Collection.

48. Brooks Atkinson, "Theatre: Comedy of Rural Manners," *New York Times*, 17 February 1956; Walter F. Kerr, "'The Ponder Heart,'" *New York Herald Tribune*, 17 February 1956; Robert Coleman, "'The Ponder Heart' Needs a Stimulant," *Daily Mirror*, 17 February 1956; Richard Watts, "Courtroom Play with a Difference," *New York Post*, 17 February 1956.

49. Welty to Russell, 1 March 1956, Welty Collection; William Faulkner, "A Letter to the North," *Life*, 5 March 1956, 52.

50. Eva Boros, *The Mermaids* (New York: Farrar, Straus and Cudahy, 1956); Eudora Welty, "The Thorntons Sit for a Family Portrait," review of *Marianne Thornton: A Domestic Biography*, by E. M. Forster, *New York Times Book Review*, 27 May 1956, 5, reprinted in *The Eye of the Story*, 226.

51. Welty to Russell, 20 June 1956, Welty Collection; Maxwell to Welty [June 1956], Estate of William and Emily Maxwell.

52. S. J. Perelman to Eudora Welty, 22 May [1956], Welty Collection; three months later, Perelman thanked Eudora for providing the material that led to "Cuckoos Nesting." "Personalities in the News Today," *New Orleans Item,* 1 June 1956; Eudora Welty to Mary Lou Aswell, 6 July [1956], Welty Collection.

53. E. M. Forster to Eudora Welty, 4 June 1956; Welty to Russell, [August 1956], Welty Collection.

54. Price to Welty, 8 July 1956, Welty Collection; Mary Alice Welty White, diary of 1956 trip to New York City, private collection of Mary Alice Welty White.

55. Eileen McGrath to Eudora Welty [4 October 1956], Welty Collection.

56. Mary Lou Aswell to Eudora Welty, 11 December [1956], Welty Collection; Welty to Price, 16 December 1956, Reynolds Price Papers.

57. Welty to Russell, 12 December 1956, Welty Collection.

six : Losing Battles

1. Eudora Welty, *Losing Battles* (New York: Random House, 1970), 360. Italics mine.

2. Eudora Welty to Mary Lou Aswell, n.d. [January 1957], Welty Collection.

3. Eudora Welty to Diarmuid Russell, n.d. [January 1957], Welty Collection.

4. Eudora Welty to Frank Lyell [20 February 1957], Welty Collection.

5. Welty to Russell, 12 March 1957, Welty Collection.

6. Ibid., n.d. [27 September 1957].

7. Ibid., 25 September [1957], n.d. [October 1957].

8. Charlotte Capers, "Eudora Welty To Date," *The Tattler,* September 1966, reprinted in *The Tattler,* Special Issue 2002, 11.

9. Welty to Lyell, [23 January 1958], Welty Collection.

10. Welty to Russell, 17 March 1958, Welty Collection.

11. Welty to Lyell, [28 March 1958], Welty Collection.

12. Welty to Russell, 13 May [1958], Welty Collection.

13. Welty to Aswell, n.d. [May 1958]; Welty to Russell, 16 July [1958], Welty Collection.

14. Social Sciences Forum Announcements, Tougaloo College Archives, Tougaloo, Mississippi; John Quincy Adams, Papers and Audio Tapes, Faculty Papers, Series F, Millsaps College Archives, Jackson, Mississippi; Laura G. McKinley, "Millsaps College and the Mississippi Civil Rights Movement" (honors thesis, Millsaps College, 1989), 5–6; "Millsaps President and Wright Protest," *Jackson Clarion-Ledger* 9 March 1958; Jane Reid Petty and Patti Carr Black, Personal conversations with the author, March 1997.

15. Lyell to Welty, 28 October 1958, Welty Collection.

16. Eudora Welty to William and Emily Maxwell, n.d. [November 1958], William Maxwell Collection, University of Illinois Libraries, Champagne-Urbana; Welty to Lyell, 18 November 1958, Welty Collection.

17. Welty to Lyell, n.d. [January 1959], Welty Collection.

18. Welty to Aswell, n.d., Welty Collection; Eudora Welty, "Eye of a Poet: 'Cat' Comments," *Jackson Daily News,* 5 February 1959, 10.

19. Maxwell to Welty, n.d. [May 1959], Estate of William and Emily Maxwell.

20. Welty to Lyell [30 April 1959], Welty Collection.

21. Welty to Aswell, n.d. [July 1959], [17 July 1959], Welty Collection.

22. Welty to Lyell, [22 October 1959], Welty Collection.

23. ElderWeb, "LTC History: 1950–1959," http://www.elderweb.com/history/default.php?PageID=2846.

24. Welty to Aswell [4 January 1960], Welty Collection.

25. Russell to Welty, 29 February 1960; Welty to Lyell [28 February 1960], Welty Collection.

26. Russell to Welty, 21 March 1960, Welty Collection; twelve thousand dollars in 1960 is the equivalent of about seventy-five thousand dollars by contemporary standards, according to John J. McCusker, "Comparing the Purchasing Power of Money"; Welty to Lyell [23 April 1960], Welty Collection.

27. Welty to Aswell, [27 August 1960], Welty Collection.

28. Welty to Lyell, [14 November 1960], Welty Collection; Eudora Welty to Jean Stafford, 14 November [1960], Stafford Collection.

29. Welty to Lyell [14 November 1960]; Welty to Aswell [November 1960], Welty Collection.

30. Welty to Aswell, 10 January [1961], Welty Collection; Reynolds Price, personal interview by author, 13 February 2002, Durham, North Carolina; Welty to Aswell, 10 January [1961]; Welty to Lyell, 8 December 1960, Welty Collection.

31. Eudora Welty, "Henry Green: Novelist of the Imagination," 14; Henry Green to Eudora Welty, 1 February 1961, Welty Collection.

32. Welty to Aswell, n.d. [January 1961], Welty Collection.

33. Welty to Lyell [30 March 1961], Welty Collection.

34. "Vassar History 1961," http://vassun.vassar.edu/~daniels/1961.html; Eudora Welty to William Jay Smith [March 1961], William Jay Smith Papers, Washington University Special Collections, St. Louis, Missouri; Welty to Lyell [19 May 1961], [24 April 1961], Welty Collection.

35. Welty to Lyell, 3 October 1961, Welty Collection; David Lisker, "A Brief History of the Freedom Riders," http://www.freedom ridersfoundation.org/brief.history.html.

36. Alun Jones to Suzanne Marrs, e-mail, 18 March 2003; Welty to Lyell, 3 October 1961, Welty Collection.

37. Maxwell to Welty [4 October 1961], Estate of William and Emily Maxwell.

38. Welty to Porter, 19 December 1961, Porter Papers.

39. Welty to Aswell, n.d. [November or December 1961], Welty Collection.

40. Ibid.

41. Welty to Lyell [25 January 1962], Welty Collection.

42. Ibid., [2 April 1962].

43. Eudora Welty, "Words into Fiction," in *Three Papers on Fiction* (Northampton, Mass., Smith College, 1962), reprinted in *The Eye of the Story*, 136–137; Tom Mendenhall to Eudora Welty [10 February 1962], Diarmuid Russell papers, Welty Collection.

44. Welty to Aswell, 19 March 1962, Welty Collection.

45. Welty to Lyell [23 April 1962], Welty Collection.

46. Eudora Welty, "Presentation Speech: The Gold Medal for Fiction," in *Eudora Welty on William Faulkner* (Jackson: University Press of Mississippi, 2003), 40–41.

47. Welty to Lyell [17 October 1962], Welty Collection; Jack Nelson, "Ralph Emerson McGill: Voice of the Southern Conscience," review of *A True Legend in American Journalism, American Journalism Review* by Leonard Ray Teel, 24.6 (July/August 2002): 54.

48. Welty to Lyell, [17 October 1962], Welty Collection.

49. Ibid., [27 October 1962], [2 November 1962], Welty Collection.

50. Ibid., [11 January 1963]; Welty to Aswell, 8 January 1963, Welty Collection.

51. Welty to Aswell, 12 February 1963, Welty Collection.

52. Russell to Welty, 18 February 1963, 5 March 1963, Welty Collection.

53. Welty to Aswell [9 March 1963], Welty Collection.

54. Ibid.

55. Russell to Welty, 18 March 1963; Welty to Lyell, 30 March 1963, Welty Collection.

56. Welty to Lyell [16 April 1963], Welty Collection.

57. W. J. Cunningham, *Agony at Galloway* (Jackson: University Press of Mississippi, 1980), 8.

58. Minutes of Millsaps Faculty Meeting, 24 January 1963, Series B; H. E. Finger Jr., Papers, Administrative Papers, Series A1; John Quincy Adams Papers and Audio Tapes, Millsaps College Archives, Jackson, Mississippi.

59. Eudora Welty, personal conversation with the author, and R. Edwin King, personal conversations with the author, 20 March 1997, 7 April 1997, 19 June 1997, Jackson, Mississippi; Eudora Welty, "Words into Fiction," 144–145.

60. Welty, "Powerhouse," *A Curtain of Green*, 254, 265, 269.

61. John R. Salter, *Jackson, Mississippi* (Hicksville, NY: Exposition Press, 1979), 102; Edwin King arranged for Moody to speak at Millsaps, attended the lecture with her, and told me of her comments about Welty's importance to the Tougaloo contingent (19 June 1997). This discussion of Eudora's 1963 experience at Millsaps College appeared in my book *One Writer's Imagination*, 172–174.

62. Welty to William and Emily Maxwell, n.d. [May 1963], William Maxwell Collection.

63. William Maxwell to Welty, n.d. [June 1963], Estate of William and Emily Maxwell.

64. Russell to Welty, 17 June 1963, Welty Collection; Welty's 1963 correspondence with Russell and with Mary Lou Aswell suggests a July decision by Welty; Reynolds Price, personal conversation with author, 25 October 1998. The interview with Hildegard Dolson aired on Sunday, 18 August 1963.

65. Hildegard Dolson to Eudora Welty, 23 August [1963], Welty Collection.

66. Welty to Aswell [14 August 1963], Welty Collection.

67. Welty to Lyell [30 August 1963], Welty Collection.

68. Eudora Welty, "Place in Fiction," 131.

69. Welty to Lyell, 30 September [1963], 12 November [1963], Welty Collection.

70. Welty to Lyell, 10 December [1963], Welty Collection.

71. Robert Penn Warren to Eudora Welty, 8 November 1964, Capers (Charlotte) Collection, Mississippi Department of Archives and History; Emily Maxwell to Eudora Welty [30 April 1964], Estate of William and Emily Maxwell.

72. Welty to Aswell [25 March 1964], n.d. [April 1964], Welty Collection.

73. Maxwell to Welty, 10 June [1964], Welty Collection.

74. Eudora Welty, "The Last of the Figs," Part 3, n.p., Welty Collection.

75. Welty to Smith, n.d., William Jay Smith papers.

76. Charlotte Capers to Robert Penn Warren, 16 November 1964, Capers Collection; Capers anticipated that Barnett would win a second term, succeeding Johnson. Robert Penn Warren to Charlotte Capers, 19 November 1964, Capers Collection. Welty to Smith, n.d., William Jay Smith papers.

77. H. E. Finger Jr., Papers, 9 August 1963. Sara Ann Weir covered this lecture for the Millsaps College paper; see "Miss Welty Tells Position of Southern Writers Today," *Purple and White*, 8 December 1964; Eudora Welty, "Must the Novelist Crusade?" (1965), reprinted in *The Eye of the Story*, 149, 152–154.

78. Eudora Welty, "Keela, The Outcast Indian Maiden," in *A Curtain of Green*, 77. Most of this discussion of Eudora's Millsaps lecture previously appeared in my book *One Writer's Imagination*, 176–178.

79. Welty to Aswell [1 January 1965], 8 January 1965, Welty Collection.

80. Eudora Welty, untitled speech for the Southern Literary Festival, 23 April 1965, p. 7, Welty Collection; Welty to Lyell [24 April 1965], Welty Collection. Robert W. Hamblin, "Robert Penn Warren at the 1965 Southern Literary Festival: A Personal Recollection," *Southern Literary Journal* 22 (Spring 1990): 53–62. My discussion of these events appeared in a somewhat different form in *One Writer's Imagination*, 179–180.

81. Russell to Welty, 15 April 1965, Welty Collection.

82. Welty to Maxwell, n.d. [June 1965], William Maxwell Collection.

83. Welty to Aswell, 8 June 1965, Welty Collection.

84. According to McCusker, thirty-five thousand dollars in 1965 would be the equivalent of more than two-hundred thousand dollars in 2005, http://www.eh.net/hmit/ppowerusd/.

85. Welty to Aswell, 8 June 1965, Welty Collection.

86. Maxwell to Welty [22 November 1965], Estate of William and Emily Maxwell; Welty to Maxwell [late November 1965], William Maxwell Collection.

SEVEN: Defending Against Time

1. Eudora Welty, *One Writer's Beginnings*, 104.

2. Mary Lou Aswell to Eudora Welty, 7 February [1966], Welty Collection.

3. Eudora Welty, "The Wanderers," 219.

4. Eudora Welty to Frank Lyell, 18 April [1966], Welty Collection.

5. Eudora Welty to Katherine Anne Porter, n.d., Porter Papers.

6. Aswell to Welty, 17 June [1966], Welty Collection.

7. Ibid., 12 September [1966].

8. Eudora Welty to Mary Lou Aswell, 25 October [1966], Welty Collection.

9. Jesse Jackson to Editor, *New Yorker*, 27 November [1966], photocopy enclosed in 8 December 1966 letter to Aswell, Welty Collection; Gill, as quoted by William Maxwell to Eudora Welty, 30 November [1966], Estate of William and Emily Maxwell; Welty to Lyell, 9 December [1966], Welty Collection.

10. Welty to Aswell, 8 December 1966, Welty Collection.

11. Maxwell to Welty, 24 January [1967], Estate of William and Emily Maxwell.

12. Welty to Lyell [18 February 1967], Welty Collection; Ann Morrison, chair of the 1967 Wednesdays at St. Andrew's programs, personal conversation with the author, September 1999.

13. Eudora Welty to William Maxwell, 13 March 1967, William Maxwell Collection.

14. Maxwell to Welty [16 May 1967], Estate of William and Emily Maxwell; Lehman Engel, to Eudora Welty, 8 July 1967, Welty Collection.

15. Eudora Welty, "The Optimist's Daughter," *New Yorker*, 15 March 1969, 117.

16. Eudora Welty to Agnes Sims, 31 October 1967, 13 November 1967, Welty Collection.

17. Welty to Aswell, 16 December 1967; Welty to Lyell [7 February 1968], Welty Collection.

18. Welty to Maxwell, 5 January 1968, William Maxwell Collection.

19. Diarmuid Russell to Eudora Welty, 23 February 1968, Welty Collection

20. Welty to Maxwell, 5 January 1968, William Maxwell Collection.

21. Eudora Welty, interview by Charles T. Bunting, in *Conversations with Eudora Welty*, ed. Prenshaw, 48.

22. Eudora Welty to Reynolds Price, 25 July 1968, Reynolds Price Papers; Reynolds Price to Eudora Welty, 27 July 1968, Welty Collection; Welty to William and Emily Maxwell, n.d., William Maxwell Collection; Welty to Aswell [20 November 1968], Welty Collection.

23. Russell to Welty, 9 January 1969, 15 January 1969, Welty Collection.

24. Price to Welty, 28 February 1969, Welty Collection.

25. Welty to Aswell, 14 May 1969, Welty Collection.

26. Ibid., 12 August 1969.

27. Diarmuid Russell to William Jovanovich, 23 May 1969, Welty Collection; Eudora Welty to William Jovanovich, 3 June 1969, Welty Collection.

28. Eudora Welty to Elizabeth Spencer, 7 October 1969, Elizabeth Spencer Collection, National Library of Canada, Ottawa; Russell to Welty, 18 June 1969, Welty Collection; Welty to Spencer,

7 October 1969, Spencer Collection; Kreyling, *Author and Agent*, 208; a hundred thousand dollars in 1969 is the equivalent of more than five hundred thousand dollars in 2005, (John J. McCusker, "Comparing the Purchasing Power of Money.")

29. Welty to Aswell [25 October 1969]; Welty to Lyell, 30 October 1969, Welty Collection.

30. Eudora Welty, "From Where I Live," *Delta Review* 6 (1969): 69.

31. Welty to Maxwell, 9 December 1969, William Maxwell Collection; Eudora Welty, *Losing Battles* (New York: Random House 1970), 426.

32. Welty to Maxwell, [9 December 1969], William Maxwell Collection; Welty to Price, 29 January 1970, Reynolds Price Papers; Elizabeth Bowen to Eudora Welty, 6 January 1970, Welty Collection; Price to Welty, 4 January 1970, Welty Collection.

33. Welty to Lyell, 7 March 1970; Robert Penn Warren to Eudora Welty [23 November 1985], Welty Collection.

34. Walter Clemons, "Meeting Miss Welty," in *Conversations with Eudora Welty*, ed. Prenshaw, 34.

35. Welty to Aswell [8 January 1970]; Welty to Lyell, 24 May 1970; Price to Welty, 2 April 1970, Welty Collection.

36. Welty to Aswell, n.d. [April 1970], Welty Collection.

37. Ibid., 10 May [1970].

38. Frank Hains, "On Stage—Eudora Welty's 'Ponder Heart': A Message of Love Needed Now," *Jackson Daily News*, 17 May 1970, C4; Welty to Price, 12 June 1970, Reynolds Price Papers.

39. "The MacDowell Colony," http://www.macdowellcolony.cor/ faqstext.htm; Welty to Lyell [31 October 1970], Welty Collection.

40. Welty to Lyell, 8 October [1970], Welty Collection.

41. Welty to Price, 22 September 1970, Reynolds Price Papers; Price to Welty [23 September 1970], Welty Collection.

42. Kenneth Millar to Eudora Welty, 14 December 1970; Eudora Welty to Kenneth Millar, 19 December 1970, Welty Collection; Eudora Welty, *One Writer's Beginnings*, 104.

43. Millar to Welty, 19 January 1971, Welty Collection.

44. Welty to Aswell [24 February 1971], Welty Collection.

45. Reynolds Price, "Eudora Welty," *Proceedings of the American Academy*

of Arts and Letters, Second Series, no. 53 (2002):88; Reynolds Price, interview by author, 24 July 2003.

46. Price to Welty, 28 March 1971, 6 April 1971, Welty Collection. Price, "Eudora Welty," 90; Welty, *One Time, One Place,* 8.

47. Welty to Millar, 18 April 1971; Millar to Welty, 20 April 1971, Welty Collection.

48. Welty to Millar, 23 April 1971, Welty Collection.

49. Welty to Maxwell, 8 May 1971, Maxwell Collection.

50. Tom Nolan, *Ross Macdonald: A Biography* (New York: Scribner, 1999), 310, 311; Millar to Welty, n.d., 23 May 1971, Welty Collection.

51. Welty to William and Emily Maxwell, 12 June [1971], William Maxwell Collection.

52. Welty to Aswell [11 June 1971]; Millar to Welty, 22 June 1971, 2 July 1971, Welty Collection.

53. Aswell to Welty, 9 June [1971]; Welty to Aswell, 11 June 1971, Welty Collection.

54. Welty to Aswell, 18 July 1971; Millar to Welty, 2 July 1971, Welty Collection.

55. Welty to Millar, 1 August 1971, Welty Collection.

56. Welty to Price, 15 August 1971, [6 September 1971], Reynolds Price Papers; Welty to Millar, 1 September 1971, Welty Collection.

57. Aswell to Welty, 12 October [1971]; Welty to Aswell, [12 October 1971], Welty Collection.

58. Price to Welty, 22 October 1971, Welty Collection.

59. Welty to Price, 27 October 1971, Reynolds Price Papers.

60. Welty to Aswell, 6 November 1971, Welty Collection.

61. Welty to Maxwell, 10 November 1971, William Maxwell Collection.

62. Welty to Aswell [19 November 1971], Welty Collection.

63. Eudora Welty to Margaret Millar, 5 December 1971; Kenneth Millar to Welty, 6 December 1971, Welty Collection.

64. Welty to Millar, 17 December 1971, Welty Collection.

65. Welty to Aswell, 16 December 1971, Welty Collection.

66. Price to Welty, 21 December 1971, Welty Collection.

67. Millar to Welty, 1 January 1972; Welty to Millar, 14 January 1972, Welty Collection.

68. Welty to Maxwell, 24 January 1972, William Maxwell Collection.

69. Welty to Millar, 26 February 1972, Welty Collection.

70. Welty to William and Emily Maxwell, 17 March 1972, William Maxwell Collection.

71. Welty to Millar, 17 April 1972, Welty Collection.

72. Welty to Lyell, 29 April 1972, Welty Collection.

73. Welty to Millar, 17 April 1972; Millar to Welty, 24 April 1972; Aswell to Welty [22 April 1972], Welty Collection.

74. Welty to Price [21 June 1972], Reynolds Price Papers. Eudora enclosed a copy of her acceptance remarks in this letter.

75. Ibid., 6 June 1972.

76. Alan Pryce-Jones, "Viewpoint," *Times Literary Supplement,* 14 July 1972, 800; Walter Clemons, "Chorale of Blunderers," *Newsweek,* 2 May 1972, 101; Paul Theroux, "The Details of Death," *Washington Post,* 14 May 1972; Howard Moss, "The Optimist's Daughter," *New York Times Book Review,* 21 May 1972, 1, 18; Jonathan Yardley, "About Books," *Greensboro Daily News,* 21 May 1972, sec. E, p. 3.

77. Welty to Millar, 6 August 1972, Welty Collection.

78. Millar to Welty, 18 September 1972; Welty to Millar, 2 October 1972, Welty Collection.

79. Aswell to Welty, 20 October [1972]; Welty to Aswell, 24 October 1972, Welty Collection.

80. Welty to Millar, 19 November 1972, Welty Collection.

81. Jeanne Luckett, telephone conversation with the author, fall 2003; William F. Buckley, "'The Southern Imagination': An Interview with Eudora Welty and Walker Percy," in *Conversations with Eudora Welty,* ed. Prenshaw, 99, 100, 108–109; David L. Chappell, *Inside Agitators: White Southerners in the Civil Rights Movement* (Baltimore: Johns Hopkins University Press, 1994).

82. Millar to Welty, 25 December 1972; Welty to Millar, 12 January 1973; Welty to Aswell, 27 January 1973, Welty Collection.

83. Welty to Millar, 12 January 1973; Millar to Welty, 31 January 1973, Welty Collection.

84. Welty to Millar, 24 February 1973, Welty Collection.

85. Ibid.

86. Millar to Welty, 26 February 1973, Welty Collection.

87. Welty to Millar, 30 March 1973, Welty Collection.

88. Reynolds Price interview by the author, 13 February 2002, Durham, North Carolina.

89. Eudora Welty, *Losing Battles*, 362; Millar to Welty, 8 May 1973, Welty Collection; Millar to Julian Symons, as quoted by Nolan, *Ross MacDonald: A Biography*, 339.

90. Welty to Millar [12 May 1973], Welty Collection.

91. Crawford Woods, "The Sleeping Beauty," *New York Times Book Review*, 20 May 1973; Welty to Millar, 18 May 1973, Welty Collection.

92. Ibid., 22 June 1973; Millar to Welty, 28 June 1973, Welty Collection.

93. Welty to Price, 19 July 1973, Reynolds Price Papers.

94. Welty to Millar, 25 September 1973, Welty Collection.

95. Ibid.

96. Welty to Lyell, 6 November 1973; Welty to Millar, 17 November 1973, Welty Collection.

97. Welty to Millar, 17 November 1973, Welty Collection.

98. Millar to Welty, 20 December 1973; Aswell to Welty, 20 December [1973], Welty Collection.

EIGHT: "The Strong Present Tense"

1. Ralph Waldo Emerson, "Experience" (1844), reprinted in *The Portable Emerson* (New York: Viking Penguin, 1981), 278, 275. In Eudora's story "First Love," the character Joel Mayes is trapped in the prison of the present moment, unwilling to recall the past, until his meeting with Aaron Burr frees him to remember (in *The Wide Net and Other Stories* [New York: Harcourt, Brace and Company, 1943]).

2. Eudora Welty to Mary Lou Aswell [8 January 1974], Welty Collection.

3. Eudora Welty to Kenneth Millar, 27 January 1974, Welty Collection.

4. William Jay Smith, "Celebration for Eudora Welty," *Hollins*, 24.6 (May 1974):7–10.

5. Welty to Aswell, 7 March 1974, Welty Collection.

6. Welty to Millar, 28 March 1974, Welty Collection.

7. Ibid.

8. Welty to Aswell [8 May 1974], Welty Collection.

9. Welty to Millar, 14 June 1974; Welty to Aswell, 23 June [1974]; John F. Robinson to Eudora Welty, 25 June 1968, Welty Collection.

10. Welty to Aswell, 22 July 1974; Aswell to Welty, 19 June 1974, Welty Collection.

11. Kenneth Millar to Eudora Welty, 10 October 1974, Welty Collection.

12. Eudora Welty, "Some Notes on Time in Fiction," 168.

13. Millar to Welty, 3 December 1974, Welty Collection.

14. Eudora Welty, "Africa and Paris and Russia," review of *The Last of the Nuba*, by Leni Riefenstahl, *J'Aime Paris: Photographs Since the Twenties*, by Andre Kertesz, and *About Russia*, by Henri Cartier-Bresson, *New York Times Book Review*, 1 December 1974, 5, 22, 28, reprinted in *A Writer's Eye: Collected Book Reviews*, ed. Pearl Amelia McHaney (Jackson: University Press of Mississippi, 1994), 185, 187.

15. Eudora Welty, "As If She Had Been Invited into the World," review of *Pictures and Conversations*, by Elizabeth Bowen, *New York Times Book Review*, 5 January 1975, 4, 20; reprinted in *The Eye of the Story*, 273.

16. Eudora Welty, "Life's Possibilities Are Those Very Things Once Felt as Dangers," review of *The Cockatoos*, by Patrick White, *New York Times Book Review*, 19 January 1975, 4, 37; reprinted in *The Eye of the Story*, 266–267.

17. Welty to Millar, 25 January 1975; Welty to Lyell [21 January 1975], Welty Collection.

18. Welty to Millar, 19 February 1975, Welty Collection.

19. Ibid., 20 February 1975; Millar to Welty, 5 March 1975, Welty Collection.

20. Eudora Welty to Reynolds Price, 20 April 1975, Reynolds Price Papers.

21. Reynolds Price to Eudora Welty, 15 May 1975, Welty Collection.

22. Margaret Millar to Eudora Welty, 30 June 1975, Welty Collection.

23. Welty to Aswell, 8 July 1975; Welty to Price, 11 February 1975, Welty Collection.

24. Richard Gilman, review of *The Surface of Earth*, by Reynolds Price, *New York Times Book Review*, 29 June 1975, I.

25. Eudora Welty, letter to the editor, *New York Times Book Review*, 20 July 1975.

26. Price to Welty, I July 1975, Welty Collection.

27. Richard Gilman, reply to Eudora Welty, *New York Times Book Review*, 20 July 1975; Christopher Lehmann-Haupt, "A History of the South," *New York Times*, 18 July 1975.

28. Welty to Aswell [July 1975]; Welty to Millar, 10 August 1975, Welty Collection.

29. Eudora Welty, "The Corner Store," reprinted with very slight stylistic changes as "The Little Store," in *The Eye of the Story*, 334.

30. Millar to Welty, 12 September 1975, Welty Collection.

31. Welty to Aswell, 8 November 1975, Welty Collection.

32. Welty to Price, 17 December 1975, Reynolds Price Papers.

33. Susan Brownmiller, "Against Our Will: Men, Women, and Rape," http://www.susanbrownmiller.com/html/against_our_will.html; Eudora Welty to Jean Stafford, 10 February 1976, Stafford Collection.

34. Welty to Millar, [15 April 1976], Welty Collection.

35. Maxwell to Welty [23 April 1976] Estate of William and Emily Maxwell; Welty to Aswell, 28 April 1976, Welty Collection.

36. Welty to Millar, 5 May 1976, Welty Collection.

37. Eudora Welty as quoted by Tom Nolan, *Ross Macdonald: A Biography*, 369.

38. Welty to Millar, 28 July 1976; Millar to Welty, I August 1976, Welty Collection.

39. Welty to Millar, 14 August 1976; Millar to Welty, 15 August 1976, Welty Collection.

40. Welty to Aswell, [13 October 1976], Welty Collection.

41. Welty to Millar, 18 November [1976], Welty Collection.

42. Ibid., 29 November 1976; Millar to Welty, 20 December 1976, Welty Collection.

43. Millar to Welty, 7 January 1977, Welty Collection.

44. Welty to Millar, [31 January 1977]; Welty to Aswell, [20 January 1977], Welty Collection.

45. Maxwell to Welty, 20 February [1977], 3 March [1977], Estate

of William and Emily Maxwell. Maxwell did not realize that *The Robber Bridegroom* had closed on February 13, 1977.

46. Margaret Millar as quoted by Welty in Nolan, *Ross Macdonald: A Biography*, 370.

47. Millar to Welty, 10 July 1977, Welty Collection.

48. Welty to Aswell, 19 July 1977; Welty to Millar, [6 August 1977], Welty Collection.

49. Eudora Welty, "Dateless Virtues," review of *Essays of E. B. White*, *New York Times Book Review*, 25 September 1977, 43; reprinted in *A Writer's Eye*, ed. P. A. McHaney, 223.

50. Millar to Welty, 1 November 1977, 12 November 1977, Welty Collection.

51. Welty to Aswell, 21 October 1977, Welty Collection.

52. Millar to Welty, 28 January 1978, Welty Collection.

53. Eudora Welty, interview by Martha van Noppen, in *Conversations with Eudora Welty*, ed. Prenshaw, 249.

54. Welty to Millar, 1 May 1978, Welty Collection. In her letter, Eudora misnamed the story. Its actual title is "Oh Whistle and I'll Come to You, My Lad"; the change of "My Lad" to "My Love" seems almost symbolic.

55. Welty to Millar, 29 May 1978; Murray Horwitz to Eudora Welty, 22 October 1988, Welty Collection.

56. V. S. Pritchett to Eudora Welty, 11 July 1978, Welty Collection.

57. Welty to Millar, [26 July 1978], Welty Collection.

58. Millar to Welty, 22 August 1978; Welty to Millar, 29 August 1978; Millar to Welty, 18 September 1978; Welty to Millar, 23 September 1978, Welty Collection.

59. Michael Scott to Eudora Welty, 11 December 1978, Welty Collection.

60. Reynolds Price to Suzanne Marrs, 12 August 2003, private collection of Marrs; Welty to Robinson, 11 April [1951], private collection of Michael Robinson.

61. Eudora Welty, "The Shadow Club," "Draft 1. Observatory Street," "Blocking of scenes," Welty Collection.

62. Welty to Millar [24 May 1979]; Eudora Welty to Elizabeth Spencer, n.d., Spencer Collection.

63. Welty to Spencer [May 1979], Spencer Collection.

64. Welty to Aswell, 1 June [1979], Welty Collection.

65. Welty to Millar [26 June 1979], Welty Collection.

66. Ibid., [8 September 1979].

67. Ibid., [8 September 1979], 5 August 1979.

68. Ibid., [8 September 1979].

69. Ibid., 20 September 1979; Millar to Welty, 2 April 1978, Welty Collection.

70. Welty to Millar [22 October 1979], Welty Collection.

71. Ibid., [8 November 1979]; Millar to Welty, 8 January 1980, Welty Collection.

NINE: "Ceaselessly Into the Past"

1. William Maxwell to Eudora Welty, 5 January 1980, Estate of William and Emily Maxwell.

2. Eudora Welty to Kenneth Millar, n.d. [late January or early February 1980], Welty Collection.

3. Eudora Welty to Mary Lou Aswell, 7 March 1980, Welty Collection.

4. Ibid., 8 April 1980; Welty to Millar, 14 April 1980, Welty Collection.

5. Welty to Maxwell [April 1980], William Maxwell Collection.

6. Eudora Welty, "Introduction," in *Acrobats in a Park* (Northridge, CA: Lord John Press, 1980), n.p.

7. Eudora Welty, presentation of the American Academy of Arts and Letters' William Dean Howells Medal for Fiction, 1980, William Maxwell Collection; William Maxwell Acceptance of Howells Medal; Emmy Maxwell to Eudora Welty [3 June 1980], Estate of William and Emily Maxwell.

8. Welty to Aswell, 8 July 1980, Welty Collection; Jimmy Carter, Public Papers of the Presidents of the United States: Jimmy Carter, 1980–1981, vol. 1 (Washington, DC: Government Printing Office), paper 1061, as cited by John Bayne, "Welty and Jimmy Carter," *Eudora Welty Newsletter* 27.2 (2003): 17.

9. John Ferrone, "Collecting the Stories of Eudora Welty," *Eudora Welty Newsletter* 25.2 (Summer 2001: 20–21.

10. Welty, to Millar, 11 July 1980, Welty Collection; Welty to Maxwell, 13 June 1980, William Maxwell Collection; Maxwell to Welty, 29 July 1980, Estate of William and Emily Maxwell.

11. Anne Tyler, "A Visit with Eudora Welty," in *More Conversations with Eudora Welty*, ed. Prenshaw 70; Eudora Welty, *One Time, One Place*, 6; Herman Melville, *Moby-Dick*, (1851) in *Herman Melville: Redburn, White-Jacket, Moby-Dick* (New York: Library of America, 1983), 1248.

12. Eudora Welty, as quoted by Hubert H. McAlexander, *Peter Taylor, A Writer's Life* (Baton Rouge: Louisiana State University Press, 2001), 242; Welty to Millar, 20 October 1980, Welty Collection.

13. Ferrone, 21–22.

14. Mary Lee Settle, "Welty's Splendors," *Saturday Review*, October 1980, 84; Hortense Calisher, "Eudora Welty: A Life's Work," *Washington Post Book World*, 26 October 1980, 15; Maureen Howard, "A Collection of Discoveries," *New York Times Book Review*, 2 November 1980, 31.

15. Ralph Sipper to Eudora Welty, 28 October 1980, Welty Collection; Millar to Welty, 8 January 1980, Welty Collection.

16. Welty to Aswell [December 1980]; Welty to Millar, 13 December 1980; Sipper to Welty, 18 December 1980, Welty Collection; Eudora Welty, "The Wanderers," in *The Golden Apples*, 234.

17. Reynolds Price, "The Art of American Short Stories," *New York Times Book Review*, 1 March 1981, 1; Eudora Welty to Reynolds Price [3 March 1981]; Reynolds Price to Eudora Welty, draft of a letter, n.d. [6 March 1981]; Welty to Price, 11 March 1981, Reynolds Price Papers.

18. V. S. Pritchett to Eudora Welty, 9 April 1981, Welty Collection.

19. Welty to Aswell [12 August 1981], Welty Collection.

20. Dorothy Pritchett to Eudora Welty, 26 March 1981, Welty Collection.

21. Herb Yellin to Eudora Welty, 17 March 1981, Welty Collection.

22. Welty to Millar, 13 April [1981], Welty Collection.

23. Eudora Welty, "Foreword," in *To the Lighthouse*, by Virginia Woolf (New York: Harcourt, Brace, Jovanovich, 1981), vii.

24. Sipper to Welty, 10 June 1981; Welty to Millar, 15 June 1981, Welty Collection.

25. Welty to Maxwell, 20 August 1981, Estate of William and Emily Maxwell.

26. Welty to Aswell, 12 August 1981, Welty Collection.

27. Sipper to Welty, 15 September 1981, Welty Collection.

28. Sipper to Welty, 14 December 1981, Welty Collection.

29. Welty to Aswell [25 January 1982]; Sipper to Welty, 25 February 1981; Welty to Millar, 16 March 1982, Welty Collection.

30. Welty to Price, 23 March 1982, Reynolds Price Papers.

31. Sipper to Welty, 1 June 1982, Welty Collection.

32. Welty to Millar, 26 August 1982; Margaret Millar to Welty, 5 September 1982, Welty Collection.

33. Ellis Amburn to Welty, 15 September 1982, Welty Collection.

34. Welty to Price, 26 October [1982], Reynolds Price Papers.

35. Eudora Welty, as cited by Tom Nolan, *Ross Macdonald: A Biography*, 406.

36. Reynolds Price, personal interview by the author, 24 July 2003, Durham, North Carolina; Eudora Welty, as cited by Nolan, *Ross Macdonald: A Biography*, 406.

37. Welty to Aswell, 4 August 1983, Welty Collection; Ralph Sipper, as cited by Nolan, *Ross Macdonald: A Biography*, 407.

38. Nolan, *Ross Macdonald: A Biography*, 408.

39. Price to Welty, 10 December 1982, Welty Collection.

40. Welty to Robinson, 17 August [1946], Welty Collection; Welty, "Looking Back at the First Story," 755.

41. V. S. Pritchett, "Dreaming of Savannah," *New York Times*, 16 October 1983; V. S. Pritchett to Welty, 13 March 1983; Dorothy Pritchett to Welty, 4 April [1983], Welty Collection.

42. Welty to Aswell [9 April 1983], Welty Collection; Welty to Maxwell, 23 April 1983, William Maxwell Collection.

43. William Maxwell, "The Charged Imagination," *New Yorker*, 20 February 1984, 135.

44. Eudora Welty, "A Southerner Looks at Hawthorne," Welty Collection.

45. Welty to Aswell, 4 August 1983, Welty Collection.

46. Welty to William Jay and Sonja Smith, 19 September 1983, William Jay Smith Papers.

47. Welty to Price, 15 October 1983, Reynolds Price Papers.

48. Price to Welty, 25 October 1983, Welty Collection.
49. Eudora Welty, *One Writer's Beginnings*, 104.

TEN: "The Lonesomeness and Hilarity of Survival"

1. Kenneth Millar to Eudora Welty, 12 November 1977, Welty Collection; Ralph Sipper to Eudora Welty, 12 March 1984, Welty Collection.
2. Eudora Welty, "Part 1 Affinities," Welty Collection. In a conversation with Patti Black and Jane Petty, Eudora reported that Margaret Millar actually said, "It's me! What am I going to do?"
3. Eudora Welty, "Henry Spring 84," "The City of Light," "Part 2 Affinities Henry," Welty Collection.
4. Eudora Welty, "Part 1 Affinities," Welty Collection.
5. Dorothy Pritchett to Eudora Welty, 24 May 1984, Welty Collection.
6. Eudora Welty to Reynolds Price, 5 [June] 1984, Reynolds Price Papers.
7. Ibid., 9 July 1984.
8. Michael Kreyling to Eudora Welty, 3 August 1984, Welty Collection.
9. I am indebted to Patti Carr Black for sharing her travel journal with me.
10. Eudora Welty to Mary Lou Aswell, 9 November 1984, Welty Collection.
11. Reynolds Price to Eudora Welty, 3 October 1984, Welty Collection; Welty to Price, 16 October 1984, Reynolds Price Papers.
12. Eudora Welty to William Maxwell [December 1984], Welty Collection; Maxwell to Welty, 2 January 1985, Estate of William and Emily Maxwell. Years later, looking back on Eudora's life, Reynolds Price agreed with Maxwell. In his November 2002 tribute to Eudora at the American Academy of Arts and Letters, Reynolds suggested that Eudora's final years might have been more productive ones if such had been the case. If, instead of turning to travel as an anesthetic for loss and grief, she had found comfort in a

stable relationship, she might have remained at home, where her writing was most likely to flourish.

13. Duncan Aswell to Eudora Welty, 6 March 1985, Welty Collection; Welty to Price, 24 January [1985], Reynolds Price Papers.

14. Welty to Price, 24 January [1985], Reynolds Price Papers.

15. Roger Mudd, in "Stories about Eudora Welty," in *Writers,* DVD, Mississippi Public Broadcasting, 2004.

16. William Jay Smith to Eudora Welty, 27 March 1985, Welty Collection.

17. Eudora Welty to William and Emily Maxwell, 1 June 1985, William Maxwell Collection.

18. Dorothy Pritchett to Welty, 26 June 1985, Welty Collection.

19. Welty to Price, 15 August 1985, Reynolds Price Papers; Seamus Heaney, "Changes," in *Station Island* (New York: Farrar, Straus, and Giroux, 1985), 37.

20. Richard Ford to Eudora Welty, 8 September 1985, Welty Collection.

21. Welty to Price, 16 August 1985, Reynolds Price Papers; Roger Mudd to Eudora Welty, 20 October 1985, Welty Collection.

22. Price to Welty, 3 December 1985, Welty Collection.

23. Mary Aswell Doll, *To the Lighthouse and Back,* vol. 19 of *Studies in the Postmodern Theory of Education* (New York: Peter Lang, 1995), 19; Eudora Welty to Mary Aswell Doll, carbon ts letter, n.d., Welty Collection.

24. Eudora Welty to Timothy Seldes, 31 March 1986, Welty Collection.

25. Jim Lehrer to Eudora Welty [24 March 1986], Welty Collection.

26. Welty to Maxwell, 27 May 1986, William Maxwell Collection.

27. Welty to Price, 12 July 1986, Reynolds Price Papers.

28. Welty to Mudd, as quoted in Roger Mudd, "Miss Welty Comes to Town," *Oxford American,* March/April 1963, 66.

29. Price to Welty, 19 October 1986, Welty Collection; Welty to Price, 29 October 1986, Reynolds Price Papers.

30. Eudora Welty to Nash Burger, n.d. [spring 1987], Welty Collection.

31. Price to Welty, 16 March 1987, Welty Collection.

32. Welty to William and Emily Maxwell, 6 April 1987, William Maxwell Collection.

33. Welty to William and Emily Maxwell, 26 July 1987, William Maxwell Collection.

34. Ibid.

35. Ibid.

36. Eudora Welty, remarks for 1987 Whitney Writers Awards Ceremony at the Morgan Library, Welty Collection.

37. Lehrer to Welty [10 December 1987], Welty Collection.

38. William Maxwell to Welty, 31 December [1987], Estate of William and Emily Maxwell.

39. Lehrer to Welty [2 February 1988]; Robert MacNeil to Welty, 5 February 1988, Welty Collection.

40. Eudora Welty, interview by Dannye Romine Powell, in *More Conversations with Eudora Welty*, ed. Prenshaw, 179.

41. Dorothy Pritchett to Welty, 9 August 1988; V. S. Pritchett to Welty, 9 August 1988, Welty Collection.

42. Price to Welty, 17 October 1988, Welty Collection.

43. Glenn Collins, "A Male Bastion Bows, In Gracious Greeting," *New York Times*, 22 April 1989.

44. Price to Welty, 26 May 1989, Welty Collection; Price to Marrs, 22 July 2004, private collection of Marrs.

45. Eudora Welty, review of *The Letters of Virginia Woolf*, vol. 2, ed. Nigel Nicolson and Joann Trautmann, *New York Times Book Review*, 14 November 1976, reprinted in *The Eye of the Story*, 197; Eudora Welty, *One Time, One Place*, 6.

46. William Maxwell to Welty, 5 December 1989, Estate of William and Emily Maxwell.

47. Welty to Burger, 30 November 1989, Welty Collection.

48. V. S. Pritchett to Welty, [26 December] 1989, Welty Collection.

49. Eudora Welty, "The Radiance of Jane Austen," 12; V. S. and Dorothy Pritchett to Welty, 5 May [1990]; Ford to Welty, 25 May 1990, Welty Collection.

50. Eudora Welty to Ronald Sharp, 7 July 1990, Welty Collection; Ronald A. Sharp, telephone interview by the author, 28 September 2004.

51. Emily Maxwell to Welty, 23 September [1990], Estate of Wil-

liam and Emily Maxwell; Eudora Welty, "Introduction," in *Norton Book of Friendship* (New York: W. W. Norton and Company 1991), 40.

52. Howard Gardner, *Creating Minds* (New York: Basic Books, 1993), 369.
53. Welty to Sharp, 14 February 1991, private collection of Ronald A. Sharp.
54. Price to Welty, 30 June 1991, Welty Collection.

ELEVEN: "Old Age Hath Yet Her Honor and Her Toil"

1. Madalynne Reuter and John F. Baker, "41st National Book Awards: Poetry Returns, Knopf Triumphs, Welty Shines," *Publishers Weekly*, 6 December 1991, 12.
2. Eudora Welty, interview by Clarence Brown, in *More Conversations with Eudora Welty*, ed. Prenshaw, 224.
3. Ronald A. Sharp, telephone interview by author, 28 September 2004.
4. Eudora Welty, interviewed by Joseph Dumas, in *More Conversations with Eudora Welty*, ed. Prenshaw, 282, 285, 284.
5. Reynolds Price, personal interview by the author, 24 July 2003.
6. Nicholas Dawidoff, "Only the Typewriter is Silent," *New York Times*, 10 August 1995, sec. C, p. 10.
7. Ann Waldron, *Eudora, A Writer's Life* (New York: Doubleday, 1998), 4.
8. Eudora Welty, "Nicotiana" (1964), n.p., Welty Collection.
9. Claudia Roth Pierpont, "A Perfect Lady," *New Yorker*, 5 October 1998, 104.
10. Billy Watkins, "Scores from all walks of life bid final farewells to Welty," *Jackson Clarion-Ledger*, 27 July 2001; "The Cyber Hymnal," www.cyberhymnal.org/html/j/o/joyful.htm.
11. John Evans is the owner of Lemuria Book Store, a Jackson establishment that Eudora had patronized for more than twenty years.
12. Eudora Welty, *The Optimist's Daughter* (New York: Random House, 1972), 89.

BIBLIOGRAPHY

• • • • • • • • • • •

WORKS BY EUDORA WELTY

Acrobats in a Park. Northridge, CA: Lord John Press, 1980. Originally published in *Delta* 5 (November 1977).

"Africa and Paris and Russia." Review of *The Last of the Nuba*, by Leni Riefenstahl, *J'Aime Paris: Photographs Since the Twenties*, by Andre Kertesz, and *About Russia*, by Henri Cartier-Bresson, *New York Times Book Review*, 1 December 1974. Reprinted in *A Writer's Eye: Collected Book Reviews*, ed. Pearl Amelia McHaney. Jackson: University Press of Mississippi, 1994. 185–190.

"As If She Had Been Invited into the World." Review of *Pictures and Conversations*, by Elizabeth Bowen. *New York Times Book Review*, 5 January 1975. Reprinted in *The Eye of the Story*. New York: Random House, 1978: 269–276.

"Autumn's Here." *The Spectator* (Mississippi State College for Women), 28 November 1925.

The Bride of the Innisfallen and Other Stories. New York: Harcourt, Brace and Company, 1955.

The Collected Stories of Eudora Welty. New York: Harcourt Brace Jovanovich, 1980.

"The Conference Condemns Caroline." In *Quadruplane*. Jackson High School, 1924. 63–64.

A Curtain of Green. New York: Doubleday, Doran and Company, 1941.

"Dateless Virtues." Review of *Essays of E. B. White. New York Times Book Review,* 25 September 1977. Reprinted in *A Writer's Eye: Collected Book Reviews,* ed. Pearl Amelia McHaney. Jackson: University Press of Mississippi, 1994. 219–224.

"Department of Amplification." *New Yorker,* 1 January 1949. Reprinted in *Eudora Welty On William Faulkner.* Jackson: University Press of Mississippi, 2003. 30.

Delta Wedding. New York: Harcourt, Brace and Company, 1946.

"Eye of a Poet: 'Cat Comments.'" *Jackson Daily News,* 5 February 1959.

The Eye of the Story: Selected Essays and Reviews. New York: Random House, 1978.

"Foreword." *To the Lighthouse,* by Virginia Woolf. New York: Harcourt Brace Jovanovich, 1981.

"From Where I Live." *Delta Review* 6 (1969): 69.

"The Gnat." *The Spectator* (Mississippi State College for Women), 6 November 1926.

The Golden Apples. New York: Harcourt, Brace and Company, 1949.

"The Great Pinnington Solves the Mystery." *The Spectator* (Mississippi State College for Women), 14 November 1925.

"Hello and Good-Bye." *Atlantic Monthly,* July 1947, 37–40.

"Henry Green: Novelist of the Imagination." Originally published as "Henry Green: A Novelist of the Imagination," *Texas Quarterly* 4 (Autumn 1961). Reprinted in *The Eye of the Story.* New York: Random House, 1978. 14-29.

"'I' for Iris—Irma, Imogene." *The Spectator* (Mississippi State College for Women), 27 November 1926.

"In the Twilight." *St. Nicholas,* January 1925, 328.

Letter to the editor. *New York Times Book Review,* 20 July 1975.

"The Little Store." Originally published as "The Corner Store," *Esquire,* December 1975. Reprinted in *The Eye of the Story.* New York: Random House, 1978. 326-35.

Losing Battles. New York: Random House, 1970.

"Must the Novelist Crusade?" *Atlantic,* October 1965. Reprinted in *The Eye of the Story.* New York: Random House, 1978. 146–58.

Norton Book of Friendship. Ed. Eudora Welty and Ronald A. Sharp. New York: W. W. Norton and Company, 1991.

One Time, One Place. New York: Random House, 1971.

One Writer's Beginnings. Cambridge, MA: Harvard University Press, 1984.

"The Optimist's Daughter." *New Yorker,* 15 March 1969, 37–46, 48, 50, 53–54, 56, 61–62, 64, 67–68, 70, 75–76, 81–82, 84, 86, 88, 93–95, 98, 100, 103–106, 111–114, 117–120, 125–128.

The Optimist's Daughter. New York; Random House, 1972.

"A Pageant of Birds." *New Republic,* 25 October 1943. Reprinted in *The Eye of the Story.* New York: Random House, 1978. 315–320.

Photographs. Jackson: University Press of Mississippi, 1989.

"Place and Time: The Southern Writer's Inheritance." *Times Literary Supplement* 17 September 1954. Reprinted in *Mississippi Quarterly* 50.4 (Fall 1997): 545–551.

"Place in Fiction." *The Archive* (Duke University) 67 (April 1955). Reprinted in *The Eye of the Story.* New York: Random House, 1978. 116–133.

"Post Offices Shifted Many Times in City." *Jackson Daily News,* 27 April 1930.

"Presentation Speech: The Gold Medal for Fiction." In *Eudora Welty on William Faulkner.* Jackson: University Press of Mississippi, 2003. 40–41.

"Prophecy." *The Spectator* (Mississippi State College for Women), 3 May 1927.

"The Radiance of Jane Austen." In *The Eye of the Story.* New York: Random House, 1978. 3–13.

"Reality in Chekhov's Stories." In *The Eye of the Story.* New York: Random House, 1978. 61–81.

Review of *The Cockatoos* by Patrick White. *New York Times Book Review* 19 January 1975. Reprinted in *The Eye of the Story.* New York: Random House, 1978. 264–268.

Review of *Granite and Rainbow* by Virginia Woolf. *New York Times Book Review* 14 November 1976. Reprinted in *The Eye of the Story.* New York: Random House, 1978. 190–192.

Review of *The Letters of Virginia Woolf,* vol. 2, ed. Nigel Nicolson and Joann Trautmann. *New York Times Book Review,* 14 November 1976. Reprinted in *The Eye of the Story.* New York: Random House, 1978. 193–202.

The Robber Bridegroom. New York: Doubleday, Doran and Company, 1942.

"Shadows." *Wisconsin Literary Magazine,* April 1928: 34, http://digital
.library.wisc.edu/1711.dl/Literature.v27i04.

"Society." *The Spectator* (Mississippi State College for Women), 1 April
1927.

"Some Notes on River Country." *Harper's Bazaar,* February 1944.
Reprinted in *The Eye of the Story.* New York: Random House, 1978.
286–299.

"Some Notes on Time in Fiction." *Mississippi Quarterly* 26 (Fall 1973).
Reprinted in *The Eye of the Story.* New York: Random House, 1978.
163–173.

"Tatters and Fragments of War." Review of *Artist at War,* by George
Biddle. *New York Times Book Review,* 16 July 1944. Reprinted in *A
Writer's Eye: Collected Book Reviews,* ed. Pearl A. McHaney. Jackson:
University Press of Mississippi, 1994. 33–36.

"The Thorntons Sit for a Family Portrait." Review of *Marianne Thornton: A Domestic Biography,* by E. M. Forster. *New York Times Book Review,*
27 May 1956. Reprinted in *The Eye of the Story.* New York: Random House, 1978. 221–226.

"Vacations Lure Jacksonians; Large One Underway Soon; Papa Hardest Hit." *Jackson Daily News,* 15 June 1930.

"Voice of the People." *Jackson Clarion-Ledger,* 28 December 1945.

"Weekly Baby Clinic Is Becoming Popular." *Jackson Daily News,* 25 May
1930.

"What Stevenson Started." *New Republic,* 5 January 1953, 8.

The Wide Net and Other Stories. New York: Harcourt, Brace and Company,
1943.

"Words into Fiction." In *Three Papers on Fiction.* Northampton, MA.:
Smith College, 1962. Reprinted in *The Eye of the Story.* New York:
Random House, 1978. 134–145.

"Writing and Analyzing a Story." Originally published as "How I
Write," *Virginia Quarterly Review* 31 (Spring 1955). Revised and
reprinted in *The Eye of the Story.* New York: Random House, 1978.
107–115.

UNPUBLISHED CORRESPONDENCE, MANUSCRIPTS,
AND OTHER ARCHIVAL MATERIALS

(The letters and manuscripts, which in 2005 with the settlement of the Welty estate passed into the able care of the Mississippi Department of Archives and History, will be open for research in 2008.)

Letters to Eudora Welty held by the Mississippi Department of Archives and History, Welty (Eudora Alice) Collection:

Amburn, Ellis
Aswell, Duncan
Aswell, Mary Louise
Balakian, Nona
Berenson, Bernard
Bowen, Elizabeth
Burger, Nash K.
Daniel, Robert
Dolson, Hildegard
Engel, Lehman
Faulkner, William
Ford, Richard
Forster, E. M.
Fraysur, Frank Hall

Green, Henry
Horwitz, Murray
Lehrer, Jim
Lyell, Frank
McGrath, Eileen
MacNeil, Robert
Millar, Kenneth
Millar, Margaret
Mudd, Roger
Perelman, S. J.
Porter, Katherine
    Anne
Price, Reynolds
Pritchett, Dorothy

Pritchett, V. S.
Quintana, Ricardo
Robbins, Samuel
Rood, John
Robinson, John F.
Russell, Diarmuid
Scott, Michael
Sipper, Ralph
Smith, William Jay
Warren, Robert Penn
Wells, Rosa Farrar
Woodburn, John
Yellin, Herb

Letters to Eudora Welty held by the Estate of
William and Emily Maxwell:

Maxwell, Emily   Maxwell, William

Letters from Eudora Welty to:

Abbott, Berenice. Photocopy. Private collection of Suzanne Marrs.
Aswell, Mary Lou. Welty (Eudora Alice) Collection. Mississippi Department of Archives and History, Jackson, Mississippi.
Bowen, Elizabeth. Elizabeth Bowen Collection. Harry Ransom Humanities Research Center, University of Texas, Austin.

Brickell, Herschel. Special Collections. University of Mississippi Library, University, Mississippi.

Burger, Nash K. Welty (Eudora Alice) Collection. Mississippi Department of Archives and History, Jackson, Mississippi.

Daniel, Robert. Robert Daniel Papers. Jessie Ball duPont Library, University of the South, Sewanee, Tennessee.

Doll, Mary Aswell. Carbon typescript. Welty (Eudora Alice) Collection. Mississippi Department of Archives and History, Jackson, Mississippi.

Engel, Lehman. Engel Papers. Millsaps-Wilson Library, Millsaps College, Jackson, Mississippi.

Lyell, Frank. Welty (Eudora Alice) Collection. Mississippi Department of Archives and History, Jackson, Mississippi.

Maxwell, William and Emily. William Maxwell Collection. University of Illinois Library, Champaign-Urbana, Illinois.

Marrs, Suzanne. Private collection of Suzanne Marrs.

Millar, Kenneth and Margaret. Welty (Eudora Alice) Collection. Mississippi Department of Archives and History, Jackson, Mississippi.

The *New Yorker. New Yorker* Archive. New York Public Library, New York.

Porter, Katherine Anne. Papers of Katherine Anne Porter. Special Collections. University of Maryland Libraries, College Park, Maryland.

Price, Reynolds. Reynolds Price Papers. Rare Book, Manuscript, and Special Collections Library. Duke University, Durham, North Carolina.

Robinson, John F. Private collection of Michael Robinson. And Welty (Eudora Alice) Collection. Mississippi Department of Archives and History, Jackson, Mississippi.

Russell, Diarmuid. Welty (Eudora Alice) Collection. Mississippi Department of Archives and History, Jackson, Mississippi.

Simmons, Dorothy. Private collection of Fred Smith. Choctaw Books, Jackson, Mississippi.

Smith, William Jay. William Jay Smith Papers. Washington University Special Collections, St. Louis, Missouri.

Spencer, Elizabeth. Elizabeth Spencer Collection. National Library of Canada, Ottawa, Canada.

Stafford, Jean. Jean Stafford Collection. University of Colorado Libraries. Boulder, Colorado.

Volkening, Henry. Special Collections. University of Mississippi Library, University, Mississippi.

Woolf, Virginia. Monks House Papers. University of Sussex Library, Brighton, England.

Other Correspondence:

Capers, Charlotte. Letter to Robert Penn Warren. Capers (Charlotte) Collection. Mississippi Department of Archives and History, Jackson, Mississippi.

Comes, Marcella. Letter to Anne Winslow. Welty (Eudora Alice) Collection, Mississippi Department of Archives and History, Jackson, Mississippi.

Jackson, Jesse. Letter to the editor, *New Yorker.* Welty (Eudora Alice) Collection. Mississippi Department of Archives and History, Jackson, Mississippi. Photocopy enclosed in an 8 December 1966 letter to Mary Lou Aswell.

Lyell, Frank. Letters to Reynolds Price. Reynolds Price Collection. Duke University Library. Durham, North Carolina.

Price, Reynolds. Letters to Suzanne Marrs. Private collection of Suzanne Marrs.

Robinson, John F. Letters to Nancy and Alice Farley. Farley Papers. University of Virginia Library. Charlottesville, Virginia.

Robinson, John F. Letters to William Hamilton. William Hamilton Papers. Rare Book, Manuscript, and Special Collections Library. Duke University, Durham, North Carolina.

Warren, Robert Penn. Letter to Charlotte Capers. Capers (Charlotte) Collection. Mississippi Department of Archives and History.

Manuscripts in the Welty (Eudora Alice) Collection at the Mississippi Department of Archives and History, Jackson, Mississippi:

"The Alterations," [1987]
Courtney story, untitled and partially unpaginated draft (1926)
["The Cheated"], "The Night of the Little House" [1938]

"The Delta Cousins," 1943

"The Glorious Apology," [1921]

"Henry Spring 84," "Part 1 and Part 2 Affinities," "The City of Light," [1980s]

"The Last of the Figs" or "Nicotiana," [1960s]

"A Little Triumph," [1944]

"The Optimist's Daughter," 1967

"The Shadow Club," "Draft 1. Observatory Street," "Blocking of scenes," [1970s]

Untitled speech delivered at the Southern Literary Festival, 23 April 1965

William E. Massey Sr. lectures in the History of American Civilization, Harvard University (1983), including pages omitted from, carbon of TS of pages omitted from, spiral notebook of notes to be considered for the Massey lectures, and "Pages omitted from *A Writer's Beginnings* notes and try-outs" [1982]. These lectures were revised and published as *One Writer's Beginnings.*

Other Archival Materials:

Black, Patti Carr. Travel journal, fall 1984. Black's personal collection.

Datebooks and financial records kept by Eudora Welty. Personal collection of Mary Alice Welty White and Elizabeth Welty Thompson.

Diary, Nancy McDougal Robinson. Mississippi Department of Archives and History, Jackson, Mississippi.

Freedman, James O. 1990 Convocation Address. Dartmouth College. Welty (Eudora Alice) Collection, Mississippi Department of Archives and History, Jackson, Mississippi.

Minutes of Millsaps College Faculty Meeting, 24 January 1963, Series B; H. E. Finger Jr., Papers, Administrative Papers, Series A1; John Quincy Adams, Papers and Audio Tapes. Millsaps College Archives, Jackson, Mississippi.

Official transcripts. University of Wisconsin, Columbia University.

Robinson (John F.) Papers. Mississippi Department of Archives and History, Jackson, Mississippi.

Social Sciences Forum Announcements. Tougaloo College Archives, Tougaloo, Mississippi.

Welty, Chestina. "The Perfect Garden." Photocopy. Personal collection of Suzanne Marrs.

Welty family photographs, Welty family photo album, Chestina Welty's travel log. Welty (Eudora Alice) Collection, Mississippi Department of Archives and History, Jackson, Mississippi.

Welty Family Photographs. Personal collection of Mary Alice Welty White and Elizabeth Welty Thompson.

Word games. Welty (Eudora Alice) Collection, Mississippi Department of Archives and History, Jackson, Mississippi.

BOOKS, ARTICLES, WEB SITES

Atkinson, Brooks. "Theatre: Comedy of Rural Manners." *New York Times,* 17 February 1956.

Barkham, John. "Prismatic Observations." *Saturday Review* Syndicate, Spring 1955.

Basso, Hamilton. "Look Away, Look Away, Look Away." *New Yorker,* 11 May 1946, 86, 88–89.

Bayne, John. "Welty and Jimmy Carter." *Eudora Welty Newsletter* 27.2 (2003): 15–18.

"Bilbo and Rankin Get Blessings of Former Huey Long Chieftain." *Jackson Clarion-Ledger,* 20 December 1945.

Bilbo, Theodore. *Take Your Choice: Segregation or Mongrelization.* Poplarville, Mississippi: Dream House Publishing, 1947.

Bogan, Louise. "The Gothic South." *Nation* 6 December 1941, 572.

Boros, Eva. *The Mermaids.* New York: Farrar, Straus and Cudahy, 1956.

Bowen, Elizabeth. "Book Shelf." *The Tatler and Bystander,* 6 August 1947, 183.

———. *Bowen's Court.* New York: Alfred A. Knopf, 1942.

Boyle, Kay. "Full-Length Portrait." *New Republic,* 24 November 1941, 707-08.

Briggs, John. *Fire in the Crucible: The Alchemy of Creative Genius.* New York: St. Martin's Press, 1988.

Brownmiller, Susan. "Against Our Will: Men, Women, and Rape," http://www.susanbrownmiller.com/html/against_our_will.html.

Calisher, Hortense. "Eudora Welty: A Life's Work." *Washington Post Book World,* 26 October 1980.

Capers, Charlotte. "Eudora Welty to Date." *The Tattler,* September 1966; reprinted in *The Tattler,* Special Issue 2002, 11.

Chappell, David. *Inside Agitators: White Southerners in the Civil Rights Movement.* Baltimore: Johns Hopkins University Press, 1994.

Clemons, Walter. "Chorale of Blunderers." *Newsweek,* 2 May 1972, 10–101.

"Cloud-Cuckoo Symphony." *Time,* 22 April 1946, 104.

Coleman, Robert. "'The Ponder Heart' Needs a Stimulant." *Daily Mirror,* 17 February 1956.

Collins, Glenn. "A Male Bastion Bows, In Gracious Greeting." *New York Times,* 22 April 1989.

Cooke, Mervyn. *The Chronicle of Jazz.* New York, London, Paris: Abbeville Press, 1998.

Cunningham, W. J. *Agony at Galloway.* Jackson: University Press of Mississippi, 1980.

Dinnerstein, Leonard. "Antisemitism in American Politics." Tom Paine.common sense. http://www.tompaine.com/feature2.cfm/ID/3475.html.

Doll, Mary Aswell. *To the Lighthouse and Back.* Vol. 19 of *Studies in the Postmodern Theory of Education.* New York: Peter Lang, 1995.

ElderWeb "LTC History: 1950–1959." http://www.elderweb.com/history/default.php?PageID=2846.

Emerson, Ralph Waldo. "Experience." 1844; reprinted in *The Portable Emerson.* New York: Viking Penguin, 1981. 266-90.

Engel, Lehman. *This Bright Day.* New York: Macmillan, 1974.

Faulkner, William. "A Letter to the North." *Life,* 5 March 1956, 51–52.

Ferrone, John. "Collecting the Stories of Eudora Welty." *Eudora Welty Newsletter* 25.2 (Summer 2001): 19-22.

Flanner, Janet. *Paris Journal.* 1965; reprint, New York: Harcourt Brace Jovanovich, 1977.

Forster, E. M. *Howard's End.* 1910; reprint, New York: Vintage Books, 1960.

Fuller, Edmund. "The Author as Reader." *Wall Street Journal,* 6 March 1984.

Gaither, Frances. "Of the South and Beyond." *New York Times Book Review*, 10 April 1955.

Gardner, Howard. *Creating Minds.* New York: Basic Books, 1993.

Glendinning, Victoria. *Elizabeth Bowen.* New York: Alfred A. Knopf, 1978.

Gilman, Richard. Reply to Eudora Welty. *New York Times Book Review,* 20 July 1975.

————. Review of *The Surface of Earth,* by Reynolds Price. *New York Times Book Review,* 29 June 1975.

Goodman, Walter. *The Committee.* New York: Farrar, Straus, and Giroux, 1968.

Hains, Frank. "On Stage—Eudora Welty's 'Ponder Heart': A Message of Love Needed Now." *Jackson Daily News,* 17 May 1970.

Hamblin, Robert W. "Robert Penn Warren at the 1965 Southern Literary Festival: A Personal Recollection." *Southern Literary Journal* 22 (Spring 1990), 53-62.

Hawthorne, Nathaniel. "The Birthmark." 1844; reprinted in *Nathaniel Hawthorne's Tales.* Ed. James McIntosh. W. W. Norton and Co., 1987. 118-31.

Heilbrun, Carolyn. *Writing a Woman's Life.* New York: W. W. Norton, 1988.

Howard, Maureen. "A Collection of Discoveries." *New York Times Book Review,* 2 November 1980.

Hughes, Langston. *The Big Sea: An Autobiography.* New York: Alfred A. Knopf, 1940.

Johnson, Evelyn C. "Child Life in Many Lands." In *Every Child's Story Book.* Vol. 5 of *Our Wonder World.* Chicago and Boston: George L. Shuman and Co., 1914. 307-98.

Kane, Harnett. "Eudora Welty's Authentic and Vital Talent." *New York Herald Tribune Weekly Book Review,* 14 April 1946.

Kennedy, David M. *Freedom from Fear: The American People in Depression and War, 1929–1945.* New York and Oxford: Oxford University Press, 1999.

Kerr, Walter F. "'The Ponder Heart.'" *New York Herald Tribune,* 17 February 1956.

Kreyling, Michael. *Author and Agent.* New York: Farrar, Straus and Giroux, 1991.

———. *Eudora Welty's Achievement of Order.* Baton Rouge: Louisiana State University Press, 1980.

Lee, Hermione. *Virginia Woolf.* London: Chatto and Windus, 1996.

Lehmann–Haupt, Christopher. "A History of the South." *New York Times,* 18 July 1975.

Lisker, David. "A Brief History of the Freedom Riders." http://www.freedomridersfoundation.org/brief.history.html.

Marrs, Suzanne. *One Writer's Imagination, The Fiction of Eudora Welty.* Baton Rouge: Louisiana State University Press, 2002.

———. *The Welty Collection.* Jackson: University Press of Mississippi, 1988.

Martin, John. "The Dance: Hindu Art for the Western World." *New York Times,* 1 January 1933.

Maxwell, William. "The Charged Imagination." *New Yorker,* 20 February 1984, 133–135.

McAlexander, Hubert H. *Peter Taylor, A Writer's Life.* Baton Rouge: Louisiana State University Press, 2001.

McCusker, John J. "Comparing the Purchasing Power of Money in the United States (or Colonies) from 1665 to Any Other Year Including the Present." Economic History Services, 2004. http://www.eh.net/hmit/ppowerusd/.

"The MacDowell Colony." http://www.macdowellcolony.cor/faqstext.htm.

McHaney, Thomas. "The Tishomingo of Welty's Imagination." Unpublished MS. Private collection of Thomas McHaney.

McKinley, Laura. "Millsaps College and The Mississippi Civil Rights Movement." Honors Thesis, Millsaps College, 1989.

Melville, Herman. *Moby-Dick.* 1851; reprinted in *Herman Melville: Redburn, White-Jacket, Moby-Dick.* New York: Library of America, 1983.

"Millsaps President and Wright Protest." *Jackson Clarion-Ledger,* 9 March 1958.

"Miss Eudora Welty Honored at Beautiful Bridge Party of Eight Congenial Tables." *Jackson Daily Clarion-Ledger,* 22 June 1930.

Moss, Howard. "The Optimist's Daughter." *New York Times Book Review,* 21 May 1972.

Mudd, Roger. "Miss Welty Comes to Town." *Oxford American,* March/April 1963, 64, 66-68.

Nelson, Jack. "Ralph Emerson McGill: Voice of the Southern Conscience." Review of *A True Legend in American Journalism* by Leonard Ray Teel. *American Journalism Review* 24.6 (July/August 2002): 54–55.

Nolan, Tom. *Ross Macdonald: A Biography.* New York: Scribner, 1999.

"Partial List of Babies Seen in Last Week's Baby Parade." *Jackson Daily News,* 15 March 1916.

Peden, William. "A Trial with No Verdict." *Saturday Review,* 16 January 1954, 14.

"Personalities in the News Today." *New Orleans Item,* 1 June 1956.

Pierpont, Claudia Roth. "A Perfect Lady." *New Yorker,* 5 October 1998, 94-104.

Polk, Noel. *Eudora Welty, A Bibliography of Her Work.* Jackson: University Press of Mississippi, 1994.

Pollack, Harriet. "Reading John Robinson." *Mississippi Quarterly* 56.2 (Spring 2003): 175-208.

Poore, Charles. "Books of the Times." *New York Times,* 7 January 1954.

Prenshaw, Peggy Whitman. Ed. *Conversations with Eudora Welty.* Jackson: University Press of Mississippi, 1984.

———. *More Conversations with Eudora Welty.* Jackson: University Press of Mississippi, 1996.

Prescott, Orville. "Books of the Times." *New York Times,* 17 April 1946.

———. "Books of the Times." *New York Times,* 8 April 1955.

Price, Reynolds. "The Art of American Short Stories." *New York Times Book Review,* 1 March 1981.

———. "Eudora Welty." *Proceedings of the American Academy of Arts and Letters,* Second Series, number 53 (2002), 87–90.

———. Review of *The Collected Stories of Eudora Welty.* In *Eudora Welty, A Study of Her Short Fiction,* by Carol Ann Johnston. New York: Twayne Publishers, 1997. 173–178.

Pritchett, V. S. "Bossy Edna Earle Had a Word for Everything." *New York Times Book Review,* 10 January 1954.

———. "Dreaming of Savannah." *New York Times,* 16 October 1983.

Pryce-Jones, Alan. "Viewpoint." *Times Literary Supplement,* 14 July 1972, 800.

Reuter, Madalynne, and John F. Baker. "41st National Book Awards: Poetry Returns, Knopf Triumphs, Welty Shines." *Publishers Weekly,* 6 December 1991, 12.

Robinson, John. ". . . All This Juice and All This Joy." *Horizon* 18 (November 1948): 341–347.

Rothman, Nathan L. "The Lost Realm." Review of *The Robber Bridegroom*. *Saturday Review of Literature*, 14 November 1942, 16.

Salter, John R. *Jackson, Mississippi*. Hicksville, N.Y.: Exposition Press, 1979.

Sancton, Thomas. "Race Clash." *Harper's Magazine*, January 1944, 135–140.

"Sense and Sensibility." Review of *The Wide Net*. *Time*, 27 September 1943, 100.

Settle, Mary Lee. "Welty's Splendors." *Saturday Review*, October 1980, 84.

Smith, William Jay. "Celebration for Eudora Welty." *Hollins*, 24.6 (May 1974): 7–10.

Spencer, Elizabeth. *Landscapes of the Heart*. New York: Random House, 1998.

Sprigge, Sylvia. *Berenson: A Biography*. Boston: Houghton Mifflin, 1960.

"Stories about Eudora Welty." *Writers*. DVD. Mississippi Public Broadcasting, 2004.

Theroux, Paul. "The Details of Death." *Washington Post*, 14 May 1972.

Treglown, Jeremy. *Romancing, The Life and Work of Henry Green*. New York: Random House, 2000.

Trilling, Diana. "Fiction in Review." Review of *The Wide Net*. *Nation*, 2 October 1943, 386–387.

Thurman, Wallace. *Negro Life in New York's Harlem*. Girard, KS: Haldeman-Julius Publications, 1928.

"Vassar History 1961." http://vassun.vassar.edu/~daniels/1961.html.

Waldron, Ann. *Eudora: A Writer's Life*. New York: Doubleday, 1998.

Watts, Richard. "Courtroom with a Difference." *New York Post*, 17 February 1956.

Weir, Sara Ann. "Miss Welty Tells Position of Southern Writers Today." (Millsaps College paper) *Purple and White*, 8 December 1964.

Woods, Crawford. "The Sleeping Beauty." *New York Times Book Review*, 20 May 1973.

Woodward, C. Vann. "Southerner with Her Own Accent." *New York Times Book Review*, 19 February 1984.

Yardley, Jonathan. "About Books." *Greensboro Daily News*, 21 May 1972.

———. "Welty's World." *Washington Post Book World*, 4 April 1984.

PERMISSIONS ACKNOWLEDGMENTS

• • • • • • • • • • •

Amburn, Ellis, excerpts from a letter are reprinted by permission of Ellis Amburn and the Eudora Welty Collection–Mississippi Department of Archives and History;

Aswell, Mary Louise and Duncan Aswell, excerpts from the letters are reprinted by permission of Mary Aswell Doll and the Eudora Welty Collection–Mississippi Department of Archives and History;

Berenson, Bernard, excerpt from a letter is reprinted by permission of Villa I Tatti, Harvard University Center for Italian Renaissance Studies and of the Eudora Welty Collection–Mississippi Department of Archives and History;

Bowen, Elizabeth, excerpts from the letters are reprinted by permission of Curtis Brown Group Ltd. and the Eudora Welty Collection–Mississippi Department of Archives and History, copyright © Elizabeth Bowen;

Burger, Nash K., Jr., excerpts from the letters are reprinted by permission of Nash K. Burger III and the Eudora Welty Collection–Mississippi Department of Archives and History;

Engel, Lehman, excerpts from the letters are reprinted by permission of Beatrice Gotthelf and the Eudora Welty Collection–Mississippi Department of Archives and History;

Faulkner, William, excerpts from a letter are reprinted by permission of Jill Faulkner Summers and the Eudora Welty Collection–Mississippi Department of Archives and History;

Ferrone, John, excerpts from "Collecting the Stories of Eudora Welty" are reprinted by permission of John Ferrone;

Ford, Richard, excerpts from the letters are reprinted by permission of Richard Ford and the Eudora Welty Collection–Mississippi Department of Archives and History;

Forster, E. M., excerpts from the letters are reprinted by permission of The Society of Authors as agent for the Provost and Scholars of King's College Cambridge and the Eudora Welty Collection–Mississippi Department of Archives and History;

Horwitz, Murray, excerpts from a letter are reprinted by permission of Murray Horwitz, playwright and lyricist, and the Eudora Welty Collection–Mississippi Department of Archives and History;

Lehrer, Jim, excerpts from letters are reprinted by permission of Jim Lehrer and the Eudora Welty Collection–Mississippi Department of Archives and History;

MacNeil, Robert, excerpts from a letter are reprinted by permission of Robert MacNeil and the Eudora Welty Collection–Mississippi Department of Archives and History;

Maxwell, William and Emily, excerpts from the letters are copyright © by William and Emily Maxwell and reprinted with the permission of The Wylie Agency, Inc.

Millar, Kenneth (Ross Macdonald) and Margaret, excerpts from the letters are reprinted courtesy of the Margaret Millar Charitable Trust, Norman J. Calavincenzo, Trustee, and the Eudora Welty Collection–Mississippi Department of Archives and History;

Mudd, Roger, excerpts from the letters are reprinted by permission of Roger Mudd and the Eudora Welty Collection–Mississippi Department of Archives and History;

Perelman, S. J., excerpts from the letters are reprinted by permission of Harold Ober Associates, Inc. and the Eudora Welty Collection–Mississippi Department of Archives and History;

Porter, Katherine Anne, excerpts from the letters are reprinted by permission of the Trust for the Literary Estate of Katherine Anne Porter and the Eudora Welty Collection–Mississippi Department of Archives and History;

Price, Reynolds, excerpts from the letters are reprinted by permission of Reynolds Price and the Eudora Welty Collection–Mississippi Department of Archives and History;

Pritchett, V. S. and Dorothy, extracts from the letters are reproduced by permission of PFD (www.pfd.co.uk) on behalf of the Estate of Dorothy Rudge Pritchett, and by permission of the Eudora Welty Collection–Mississippi Department of Archives and History;

Robinson, John F., excerpts from the letters and manuscripts are reprinted by permission of Michael D. Robinson and the Eudora Welty Collection–Mississippi Department of Archives and History;

Russell, Diarmuid, excerpts from the letters are reprinted by permission of Pamela Russell Jessup and the Eudora Welty Collection–Mississippi Department of Archives and History;

Sipper, Ralph, excerpts from the letters are reprinted by permission of Ralph Sipper and the Eudora Welty Collection–Mississippi Department of Archives and History;

Smith, William Jay, excerpts from the letters are reprinted by permission of William Jay Smith and the Eudora Welty Collection–Mississippi Department of Archives and History;

Warren, Robert Penn, excerpts from the letters are reprinted by permission of the estate of Robert Penn Warren and the Eudora Welty Collection–Mississippi Department of Archives and History;

Wells, Rosa Farrar, excerpts from the letters are reprinted by permission of Erskine W. Wells and the Eudora Welty Collection–Mississippi Department of Archives and History;

Yellin, Herb, excerpts from a letter are reprinted by permission of Herb Yellin and the Eudora Welty Collection–Mississippi Department of Archives and History.

Excerpts from Eudora Welty's unpublished manuscripts are reprinted by permission of the Eudora Welty Collection–Mississippi Department of Archives and History and of Russell and Volkening, Inc., copyright © 1921, 1926, 1944, 1964, 1978–80, 1982, 1983, 1984, 1987;

Excerpts from Eudora Welty's letter to Berenice Abbott are reprinted

INDEX

· · · · · · · · · · · ·